D1716221

D1523514

Supply Chain Management

The McGraw-Hill Education Series in Operations and Decision Sciences

SUPPLY CHAIN MANAGEMENT

Benton
Purchasing and Supply Chain Management
Third Edition

Bowersox, Closs, Cooper, and Bowersox
Supply Chain Logistics Management
Fifth Edition

Burt, Petcavage, and Pinkerton
Supply Management
Eighth Edition

Johnson
Purchasing and Supply Management
Sixteenth Edition

Simchi-Levi, Kaminsky, and Simchi-Levi
Designing and Managing the Supply Chain: Concepts, Strategies, Case Studies
Third Edition

Stock and Manrodt
Supply Chain Management

PROJECT MANAGEMENT

Brown and Hyer
Managing Projects: A Team-Based Approach

Larson and Gray
Project Management: The Managerial Process
Seventh Edition

SERVICE OPERATIONS MANAGEMENT

Bordoloi, Fitzsimmons, and Fitzsimmons
Service Management: Operations, Strategy, Information Technology
Ninth Edition

MANAGEMENT SCIENCE

Hillier and Hillier
Introduction to Management Science: A Modeling and Case Studies Approach with Spreadsheets
Sixth Edition

BUSINESS RESEARCH METHODS

Schindler
Business Research Methods
Thirteenth Edition

BUSINESS FORECASTING

Keating and Wilson
Forecasting and Predictive Analytics
Seventh Edition

LINEAR STATISTICS AND REGRESSION

Kutner, Nachtsheim, and Neter
Applied Linear Regression Models
Fourth Edition

BUSINESS SYSTEMS DYNAMICS

Sterman
Business Dynamics: Systems Thinking and Modeling for a Complex World

OPERATIONS MANAGEMENT

Cachon and Terwiesch
Operations Management
Second Edition

Cachon and Terwiesch
Matching Supply with Demand: An Introduction to Operations Management
Fourth Edition

Jacobs and Chase
Operations and Supply Chain Management
Fifteenth Edition

Jacobs and Chase
Operations and Supply Chain Management: The Core
Fifth Edition

Schroeder and Goldstein
Operations Management in the Supply Chain: Decisions and Cases
Seventh Edition

Stevenson
Operations Management
Thirteenth Edition

Swink, Melnyk, and Hartley
Managing Operations Across the Supply Chain
Fourth Edition

BUSINESS MATH

Slater and Wittry
Practical Business Math Procedures
Thirteenth Edition

Slater and Wittry
Math for Business and Finance: An Algebraic Approach
Second Edition

BUSINESS STATISTICS

Bowerman, O'Connell, Drougas, Duckworth, and Froelich
Business Statistics in Practice
Ninth Edition

Doane and Seward
Applied Statistics in Business and Economics
Sixth Edition

Doane and Seward
Essential Statistics in Business and Economics
Third Edition

Lind, Marchal, and Wathen
Basic Statistics for Business and Economics
Ninth Edition

Lind, Marchal, and Wathen
Statistical Techniques in Business and Economics
Seventeenth Edition

Jaggia and Kelly
Business Statistics: Communicating with Numbers
Third Edition

Jaggia and Kelly
Essentials of Business Statistics: Communicating with Numbers
Second Edition

McGuckian
Connect Master: Business Statistics

Supply Chain Management

James R. Stock
University of South Florida

Karl B. Manrodt
Georgia College & State University

Mc
Graw
Hill
Education

SUPPLY CHAIN MANAGEMENT

1 2 3 4 5 6 7 8 9 LWI 21 20 19

ISBN 978-1-260-39559-4
MHID 1-260-39559-6

Portfolio Manager: *Noelle Bathurst*
Product Developer: *Tobi Philips*
Marketing Manager: *Harper Christopher*
Content Project Managers: *Fran Simon/Brian Nacik*
Buyer: *Sandy Ludovissy*
Design: *Debra Kubiak*
Content Licensing Specialist: *Jacob Sullivan*
Cover Image: *©Shutterstock/Dustit*
Compositor: *MPS Limited*
All credits appearing on page or at the end of the book are considered to be an extension of the copyright page.

Library of Congress Cataloging-in-Publication Data

Stock, James R., author. | Manrodt, Karl B., 1957- author.
 Supply chain management / James R. Stock, University of South Florida,
 Karl B. Manrodt, Georgia College & State University.
 1 Edition. | Dubuque : McGraw-Hill Education, [2020]
 LCCN 2019004322 | ISBN 9781260395594 (alk. paper)
 LCSH: Business logistics.
 LCC HD38.5 .S756 2019 | DDC 658.5–dc23
 LC record available at https://lccn.loc.gov/2019004322

mheducation.com/highered

Dedicated to our wives,
Katheryn Stock and Susan Manrodt

About the Authors

James R. Stock is the USF Distinguished University Professor and Frank Harvey Endowed Professor of Marketing at the University of South Florida. He was elected as an AAAS Fellow of the American Association for the Advancement of Science in 2017. Professor Stock was also the Fulbright-Hanken Distinguished Chair of Business & Economics at the Hanken School of Economics in Helsinki, Finland, on a flex Fulbright Award in 2016 and 2017. He has been an invited speaker on programs in more than 45 countries. He is the author or co-author of over 150 publications including books, monographs, and articles. Professor Stock has co-authored several textbooks on logistics management and reverse logistics. He received the CSCMP Distinguished Service Award in 2011, Armitage Medal (1988) and the Eccles Medal (2003) from SOLE–The International Society of Logistics, and Lifetime Achievement Awards from the Reverse Logistics Association (2016) and Yasar University/IX International Logistics and Supply Chain Congress in Turkey (2011). His research interests include reverse logistics/product returns, supply chain sustainability, and customer satisfaction. His background includes faculty positions at the University of Notre Dame, University of Oklahoma, Air Force Institute of Technology, and Michigan State University. He received B.A. and M.B.A. degrees from the University of Miami (FL) and his Ph.D. from The Ohio State University.

Karl B. Manrodt is Professor of Logistics in the Department of Management, Marketing, and Logistics at Georgia College & State University. He is a prolific researcher, having authored seven books and over 50 scholarly articles in leading journals. His degrees include a B.A. in Philosophy and Psychology from Wartburg College, M.S. in Logistics from Wright State University, and Ph.D. from the University of Tennessee. Dr. Manrodt was recognized as a "Rainmaker" by *DC Velocity Magazine* and was awarded the Eugene Bishop Award for Sustained Academic Excellence by the College of Business at GSU. He has served on the board of directors for the Council of Supply Chain Management Professionals as well as in other leadership roles with the Warehouse Education Research Council. Dr. Manrodt has over 25 years of experience in logistics, transportation, and supply chain research. His research projects have been funded by a wide range of participants in the supply chain: consulting firms, associations, carriers, software providers, and shippers. Some of his clients include Oracle, the State of Georgia, FedEx, CSCMP, WERC, Ernst & Young, and the U.S. Department of State.

Preface

Since the start of the new millennium, significant changes and developments have impacted organizations of all types. Omnichannel marketing, the "cloud" for data storage and software applications, smartphone technology, robotics and artificial intelligence, autonomous vehicles used in transport, and many other developments have resulted in significant improvements in business productivity, efficiency, and effectiveness. On the negative side, terrorism, economic uncertainty, global trade wars, recessions, increasing instances of spyware and malware, and political unrest have complicated the picture. At the forefront in the new millennium, supply chain management has become a mainstream strategy in organizations of all shapes, sizes, and types.

A large percentage of the GDP of industrialized and developing nations is impacted by supply chain management activities. As a concept and approach to business, supply chain management has developed into a "C-suite" activity in major corporations, and it has done so in less than four decades since its inception as a business process and strategic orientation. It was only in the mid-1980s that supply chain management began to be recognized as an approach that could benefit customers, companies, and society at large. Many firms, including Amazon, Apple, Bristol-Meyers Squibb, C. H. Robinson, Ford, Google, Walmart, and Whirlpool, to name only a few, have become major players in this new era of supply chain management.

The marketplace has become a 24/7/365 environment given global commerce and customers and suppliers located anywhere in the world. Managing supply chains has become one of the most complex processes that organizations have to implement and maintain. That is why we wrote this book. *Supply Chain Management* approaches the topic from a managerial perspective, utilizing logistics, marketing, and operations management concepts, principles, and strategies to explain and illustrate supply chain management in a global context. In each chapter, basic supply chain concepts are operationalized in a readable format that is immediately useful and practical for decision making. Discussions on customer satisfaction, logistics management, global commerce, software and hardware technologies, and marketing and operations management are the focal points of every chapter. Given the significant international experience of the authors, many of these illustrations are from a diverse group of organizations located throughout the world.

The pragmatic, applied nature of the text; its managerial orientation; and its global perspective emphasizing customer satisfaction and corporate financial well-being make *Supply Chain Management* a must-have reference book for present and future supply chain professionals.

Plan of the Book

We have attempted to provide you, the reader, with the latest and most important issues and topics facing supply chain executives, as well as the basic tools, techniques, and concepts from logistics, marketing, operations management, and supply chain management. We illustrate the discussion with many examples from leading-edge organizations. Additionally, several best-practice case examples of supply chain innovations are presented at the end of the book. These examples come from organizations that were finalists in the annual Supply Chain Innovation Award™ competition for most innovative supply chain strategies and tactics jointly sponsored by the Council of Supply Chain Management Professionals (CSCMP) and *SupplyChainBrain* magazine.

This book begins in Chapter 1 with an overview of supply chain management (SCM) and both societal and business issues that impact supply chains. Various modes of SCM are presented, although the SCOR Model will be the focus of this book. We address customer service and satisfaction, the cornerstone of successful supply chain management, next in Chapter 2. Without excellent customer service that satisfies customers, all supply chain activities are in vain. Customer satisfaction and customer service are linked to the marketing concept and logistics. Various measures and metrics of customer service and satisfaction are presented, with a discussion of how customer satisfaction strategies are developed and implemented by SCM professionals.

In Chapter 3, we examine the important role of information in supply chains, including its uses and how various technologies aid in the collection, dissemination, and distribution of information within supply chains. Related to the importance of information, sales forecasting and inventory management are the subject of Chapter 4, where we discuss some of the basics of inventory management, along with the role of sales forecasting in determining optimal levels of inventory that an organization should hold.

Chapters 5, 6, and 7 feature the fundamental elements of logistics management, often ignored or given little discussion in supply chain texts. Chapter 5 provides a general overview of transportation and transport modes, transportation infrastructure, and transportation management strategies. The importance of transportation measures and metrics shows that you cannot manage what you don't measure. Chapter 6 examines warehousing management; warehousing strategies, measures, and metrics; and external dimensions of warehousing, including international and financial dimensions. Chapter 7 examines in specific detail the equipment and systems that manage inventory within warehouses and some of the latest technologies being used to handle, store, and manage inventory. Packaging is integral in materials management, and the discussion in Chapter 7 includes the environmental and sustainability aspects of packaging.

Chapter 8 identifies the importance of good sourcing and procurement in the supply chain and examines issues of human resources, global networks, and environmental/sustainability issues. Today, much of sourcing occurs electronically, that is, by e-sourcing. Supplier relationship management is a core element of sourcing. As in most chapters of this book, measures and metrics related to sourcing and procurement are discussed.

Because supply chain management includes many functions and processes of business, Chapter 9 examines the roles of manufacturing, marketing, and finance in supply chains. Important topics such as omnichannel distribution, data analytics, supply chain financing, product stock-outs, and reverse logistics are explored in this chapter.

Chapter 10 looks at managing different types of relationships in supply chains, especially the crucial relationships with customers and suppliers. Collaboration and coordination between supply chain partners are increasingly important in the global environment of the new millennium. The chapter describes the key elements of successful supply chain relationships.

Chapter 11 is an all-important chapter that presents various approaches to integrating the many processes and components of supply chains. Chapter 11 includes more in-depth discussion of the SCOR Model. Another approach used by many organizations is the APQC Process Classification Framework.

Chapters 12 and 13 explore global aspects of supply chain management, and the inclusion of this global material represents one of the strengths of this book. Many of the basics of international supply chain management are presented in Chapter 12, including some of the controllable and uncontrollable aspects of global supply chains. Chapter 13, based on the material in Chapter 12, discusses the best approaches to managing supply chains in global markets. Topics include the business environment, logistics infrastructure, and supply chain practices.

Chapter 14 examines network design, including an overview of designing a supply chain network, synthesizing a network, and optimizing a network once it's established. Chapter 15 follows up this discussion with an examination of important issues within supply chain networks, specifically, human resource, organizational, and strategy issues, including current topics such as cloud technology, social networks, and others.

Finally, while measures and metrics have been discussed throughout the book, Chapter 16 offers more in-depth supply chain performance measurement and metrics, including the use of key performance indicators.

In sum, we have attempted to provide readers of *Supply Chain Management* with a combination of the basics and the complex aspects of supply chain management. It is our expectation that when you have completed your reading and study of this material, you will understand the important roles that supply chain management performs in organizations and society.

Acknowledgments

Any work of this magnitude is seldom the exclusive work of the authors. Many individuals assisted in the completion of this project. First, I thank God that He gave me the talents and skills to do what I do well and to achieve a modicum of success. He has been my guide and encourager throughout my many years of teaching and research. Second, I want to thank my Ph.D. dissertation chair and long-time mentor, Bernard J. La Londe. Although now deceased, he continues to be an inspiration to me. His model of hard work, caring about others, and being an all-around nice guy has served me well throughout my career. Next, at the University of South Florida, thanks go to Dean Moez Limayem for creating an atmosphere conducive to research and scholarship in the Muma College of Business. For moral support and encouragement, colleagues in the Department of Marketing's supply chain program deserve recognition, including Donna Davis (Marketing Department chair), Robert Hooker, Jeannette Mena Mercado, Richard Plank, and Kerry Walsh. Other colleagues have also been influential in the writing and structure of this book, including Walter Zinn, Kate Vitasek, and the late Tom Speh. Of course, thanks also go to our many supply chain management students in whose classes we tested out many of the concepts incorporated in this book. Gratitude also goes to the many firms who support our teaching and research efforts, especially the Founder Members of our Center for Supply Chain Management & Sustainability in the Muma College of Business at USF—MercuryGate and Bristol-Myers Squibb—and the other firms who have supported our efforts financially and through internships and full-time positions for our graduates. Monica Wooden and John Tuttle have been especially supportive. Special thanks go to Wendy Jennings (office manager) and Megan Barrios (secretary) for making the department a nice place to work. Also, thanks go to various organizations that provided many of the materials used in the book, including the Council of Supply Chain Management Professionals (CSCMP) and Warehousing Education & Research Council (WERC). Of course, many people at McGraw-Hill have been instrumental in bringing this textbook to completion. Special acknowledgment goes to Noelle Bathurst, Tobi Philips, and Fran Simon for their continued assistance and support throughout the publication process.

Finally, I wish to acknowledge the support of my family, especially my wife of 46 years, Kathy, and my two children, Beth and Matt, who have grown up to be great adults. They have always been my main focus throughout my career, and I am thankful for their continuing love, encouragement, and support.

James R. Stock

As Jim has so eloquently noted, to God goes the glory, as we are thankful for the talents He has provided us. We hope that we use them wisely in all that we do, both professionally and personally. To that end, I want to thank the many students who have encouraged me and supported my career. It is a rare privilege to be at the starting point as students consider and begin their professional careers. It is rewarding to hear of your successes and how you persevered in times of trial. It is amazing to see you grow, to meet your spouse, and be introduced to your children. I would like to thank Kate Vitasek, Joe Tillman, and Walter Zinn for their support and encouragement during our many endeavors and especially help with this book. Mary Holcomb, Donnie Williams, Rod Thomas, Stephanie Thomas, Sara Lia-Troth, Pete Moore, and Jerry Ledlow have all been understanding when deadlines have been revised. Mitch MacDonald (*DC Velocity*) and Mike Levans (*Logistics Management*) as well as Michael Mikitka (WERC) have provided me opportunities to serve the profession, for which I'm thankful. Finally, thanks to the wonderful people at Georgia College who continually model professionalism under pressure: Lynn Hanson, Rachel Noles, Renee Mosley, and Paula Jefferson.

I would like to thank Susan, my wife, for over 37 years of support and encouragement. She has made much possible. And special thanks to our children, Ben, Sarah, and Kate, and to Kate's husband Corey. Thank you for your understanding and support; we are proud of you!

Karl B. Manrodt

We would also like to thank the following instructors for their thoughtful reviews of the text throughout the development process:

- **Suryanarayanan Gurumurthi,** *Hong Kong University of Science & Technology*
- **Marcia McLure Hardy,** *Northwestern State University of Louisiana*
- **Nathan A. Heller,** *Tarleton State University*
- **Kazimierz Kleindienst,** *California State University Fullerton*
- **David L. Levy,** *Bellevue University*
- **Kathryn Marley,** *Duquesne University*
- **Seong-Hyun Nam,** *University of North Dakota*
- **Abirami Radhakrishnan,** *Morgan State University*
- **Dr. Jason M. Riley,** *Sam Houston State University*
- **Frank Reeder Scheer,** *University of Maryland University College*
- **Robert G. Stoll,** *Ashland University*
- **Richard C. Yokeley,** *Forsyth Technical Community College*
- **George A. Zsidisin,** *Virginia Commonwealth University*

Supplements

McGraw-Hill Connect® Learn Without Limits!

Connect is a teaching and learning platform that is proven to deliver better results for students and instructors. Connect empowers students by continually adapting to deliver precisely what they need, when they need it, and how they need it, so your class time is more engaging and effective.

Connect includes multiple-choice questions for each chapter to be used as practice or homework for students, SmartBook®, instructor resources, and student resources. For access, visit **connect.mheducation.com** or contact your McGraw-Hill sales representative.

Instructor Library

A wealth of information is available online through McGraw-Hill's Connect. In the Connect Instructor Library, you will have access to supplementary materials specifically created for this text, such as solutions files, sample tests, and data sets for cases.

Students have access to course materials and study tools directly within their Connect course.

SmartBook®

Proven to help students improve grades and study more efficiently, SmartBook contains the same content within the print book, but actively tailors that content to the needs of the individual. SmartBook's adaptive technology provides precise, personalized instruction on what the student should do next, guiding the student to master and remember key concepts, targeting gaps in knowledge and offering customized feedback, and driving the student toward comprehension and retention of the subject matter. Available on desktops and tablets, SmartBook puts learning at the student's fingertips—anywhere, anytime.

Assurance of Learning

Many educational institutions today are focused on the notion of assurance of learning, an important element of some accreditation standards. *Supply Chain Management* is designed specifically to support your assurance of learning initiatives with a simple, yet powerful, solution.

Each test bank and end-of-chapter question for *Supply Chain Management* maps to a specific chapter learning goal listed in the text. You can use the test bank software to easily query for learning goals that directly relate to the learning objectives for your course. You then can use the reporting features of the software to aggregate student results in similar fashion, making the collection and presentation of assurance of learning data simple and easy.

McGraw-Hill Customer Care Contact Information

At McGraw-Hill, we understand that getting the most from new technology can be challenging. That's why our services don't stop after you purchase our products. You can e-mail our Product Specialists 24 hours a day to get product training online. Or you can search our knowledge bank of Frequently Asked Questions on our support website.

For Customer Support, call **800-331-5094** or visit www.mhhe.com/support. One of our Technical Support Analysts will be able to assist you in a timely fashion.

Connect®

Students—study more efficiently, retain more and achieve better outcomes. Instructors—focus on what you love—teaching.

SUCCESSFUL SEMESTERS INCLUDE CONNECT

FOR INSTRUCTORS

You're in the driver's seat.

Want to build your own course? No problem. Prefer to use our turnkey, prebuilt course? Easy. Want to make changes throughout the semester? Sure. And you'll save time with Connect's auto-grading too.

65%
Less Time Grading

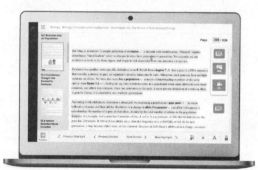

They'll thank you for it.

Adaptive study resources like SmartBook® help your students be better prepared in less time. You can transform your class time from dull definitions to dynamic debates. Hear from your peers about the benefits of Connect at **www.mheducation.com/highered/connect**

Make it simple, make it affordable.

Connect makes it easy with seamless integration using any of the major Learning Management Systems—Blackboard®, Canvas, and D2L, among others—to let you organize your course in one convenient location. Give your students access to digital materials at a discount with our inclusive access program. Ask your McGraw-Hill representative for more information.

Solutions for your challenges.

A product isn't a solution. Real solutions are affordable, reliable, and come with training and ongoing support when you need it and how you want it. Our Customer Experience Group can also help you troubleshoot tech problems—although Connect's 99% uptime means you might not need to call them. See for yourself at **status.mheducation.com**

FOR STUDENTS

Effective, efficient studying.

Connect helps you be more productive with your study time and get better grades using tools like SmartBook, which highlights key concepts and creates a personalized study plan. Connect sets you up for success, so you walk into class with confidence and walk out with better grades.

©Shutterstock/wavebreakmedia

> "I really liked this app—it made it easy to study when you don't have your textbook in front of you."

— Jordan Cunningham,
Eastern Washington University

Study anytime, anywhere.

Download the free ReadAnywhere app and access your online eBook when it's convenient, even if you're offline. And since the app automatically syncs with your eBook in Connect, all of your notes are available every time you open it. Find out more at **www.mheducation.com/readanywhere**

No surprises.

The Connect Calendar and Reports tools keep you on track with the work you need to get done and your assignment scores. Life gets busy; Connect tools help you keep learning through it all.

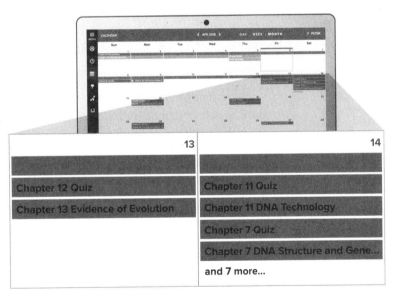

13	14
Chapter 12 Quiz	Chapter 11 Quiz
Chapter 13 Evidence of Evolution	Chapter 11 DNA Technology
	Chapter 7 Quiz
	Chapter 7 DNA Structure and Gene...
	and 7 more...

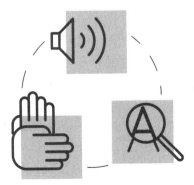

Learning for everyone.

McGraw-Hill works directly with Accessibility Services Departments and faculty to meet the learning needs of all students. Please contact your Accessibility Services office and ask them to email accessibility@mheducation.com, or visit **www.mheducation.com/about/accessibility.html** for more information.

Brief Contents

Table of Contents

Chapter 1

Supply Chain Management: Operations and Integration

Objectives of This Chapter

LO 1-1 To define supply chain management (SCM) and identify its relationships with other areas of business activity.

LO 1-2 To overview the historical development of supply chain management.

LO 1-3 To briefly examine the major approaches to modeling supply chain management, including the SCOR Model and the Forum Model.

LO 1-4 To identify how various societal issues impact supply chains and supply chain management.

LO 1-5 To identify how various business-related issues impact supply chains and supply chain management.

Introduction

SCM Has Many Implications for Consumers

Supply chain management (SCM) affects almost every sphere of human activity, directly or indirectly. Few areas of business have as significant an impact on a society's standard of living as does SCM. As customers, we tend to notice SCM only when there is a problem. For example, the following problems or difficulties tend to highlight and illustrate the importance of SCM:

- A first-run movie is a week late in appearing on the retailer's shelf after it is officially released, even though it is well known that almost half of all sales of a given movie occur within the first week to 10 days of release.[1]
- A consumer utilizes Internet shopping to purchase a birthday gift for a family member and the item does not arrive in time, even though delivery was promised before the event.
- A product that was advertised in a weekend newspaper insert supplement is not available when the customer attempts to purchase it at her local retail store.

[1] Interview with Doug Reinart of Technicolor appearing in Executive Briefings, "Supply Chain Execution Is Critical in the Entertainment Business," *SupplyChainBrain*, Vol. 15, No. 2 (March/April 2011), p. 24.

- Thousands of medical and food shipments intended for distribution to victims of a natural disaster in a foreign country cannot be delivered to the affected area because transport equipment and storage facilities are not available or are inadequate.

- An automobile plant is shut down when a trucker's strike halts needed supplies of parts and equipment essential to operate a just-in-time manufacturing system.

- A package is delivered to the wrong customer and it takes several days for the mistake to be corrected; in the meantime, a substitute shipment must be sent by air express, resulting in additional costs to the seller.

- The latest version of a high-tech gaming device popular with children is in very short supply in the marketplace because the manufacturer failed to get sufficient parts and components from its suppliers, resulting in fewer gaming devices being produced.

- A customer who purchased a product online wants to return it to a brick-and-mortar store of the seller, but the only options available are to send it back to the seller via USPS, FedEx, DHL, or UPS.

SCM attempts to minimize costs and optimize customer satisfaction. Having efficient and effective supply chains can lower operating costs; provide faster, more accurate, and more personalized product fulfillment; create profitable sales growth; and optimize fulfillment in an omnichannel environment.[2]

We often don't think of the role that SCM has in our lives until something goes wrong, but fortunately, these occurrences "are the exception, rather than the rule." More often than not, everything works well and we get the things we want, when and where we want them, and at prices that are affordable. Consider one of the most watched sporting events in the world, the Super Bowl: "According to the American Institute of Food Distribution, Super Bowl Sunday is the second highest event in America for most food consumption—following Thanksgiving."[3] Think about the supply chains involved in bringing all that food to all of those viewers: 1.25 billion chicken wings, 120 million pounds of avocados, 4 million pizzas, 11.2 million pounds of chips, and 50 million cases of beer. That translates into an average fan eating 2,400 calories during game time.

Because of the significant impact that SCM has on society, industries, organizations, and individuals, a macro approach is taken in this initial chapter. Specifically, the chapter will focus on the following: gaining a basic understanding of SCM processes; exploring how SCM has developed over time; exploring the role of SCM in the global economy and in various types of enterprises; summarizing the importance of integrated SCM; and examining the key trends and current issues impacting SCM.

Throughout this text, we will emphasize the need for organizations and supply chain executives to plan, implement, and control the most efficient and effective supply chains possible. There are considerable challenges facing organizations as they try to do this, including the ability to control costs, maintaining visibility[4] and transparency within the supply chain, management of risk, increasing customer demands, omnichannel marketing issues, rapid technology advances, and globalization. However, if organizations are

---

[2] For a discussion of omnichannel retailing, see Rafay Ishfaq, Brian J. Gibson, and C. Clifford Defee, "How Retailers Are Getting Ready for an Omnichannel World," *CSCMP's Supply Chain Quarterly*, Vol. 10, No. 2 (2016).

[3] Yohana Desta, "How Much Food Americans Gorge on Super Bowl Sunday," January 28, 2015, http://www.popist.com/s/39e3a64/; and "7 Shocking Food Stats for Super Bowl Sunday," *Food & Wine*, November 11, 2017, http://www.foodandwine.com/fwx/food/7-shocking-food-stats-super-bowl-sunday.

[4] The GEODIS 2017 Supply Chain Worldwide Survey found that only 6% of firms said that they had achieved supply chain visibility. See https://www.geodis.com/geodis-unveils-its-2017-supply-chain-worldwide-sur-@/en/view-2189-communique.html/1961.

Exhibit: Listen for the Clatter of 105,000 Semi-tractor Trailers on Your Rooftop This Christmas Eve

Each Christmas Eve, Santa Claus faces the greatest logistics challenge on the planet. How great? That's what experts from the Council of Supply Chain Management Professionals (CSCMP) set out to determine.

By their calculations, the Jolly Old Elf will need to pack, ship, and deliver over 1.5 billion gifts to U.S. households this Christmas. That's quite a job and a very special sleigh.

To put it in perspective, CSCMP says that Santa needs the hauling capacity of 105,000 semi-tractor trailers to move that many gifts this Christmas Eve. Lined bumper-to-bumper, they would represent a truck convoy stretching 1,298 miles, the highway distance from New York City to Miami, or New York City to Omaha. Imagine trying to pass that line of trucks on the interstate!

Not practical you say. What if Santa ships by rail?

Santa's helpers at CSCMP calculate that delivering that volume of gifts by rail will require 70,222 railcars.

That would result in a train measuring 665 miles long, not including the locomotives to pull it. It would stretch from New York City past Detroit, and at 40 miles an hour, you would have to wait nearly 17 hours for the crossing gates to lift in front of you.

So how big is Santa's sleigh? "Big enough to carry 316 million cubic feet of gifts," said Rick Blasgen, president and CEO of CSCMP. "That's enough to fill the Sears Tower six times or the NASA Vehicle Assembly Plant at Kennedy Space Center more than twice. And that doesn't include the bows," Blasgen said.

One final thought: If stacked under the Christmas tree, the gifts would be equal in cubic volume to three and one-half of the Great Pyramids at Cheops, Egypt. Go Santa!

Source: Council of Supply Chain Management Professionals (2013).

able to successfully overcome the challenges, the benefits to customers and stakeholders can be significant, including improved customer satisfaction and organization revenues and profits.

Conversely, when the supply chain is not operating efficiently and effectively, the downside risk can be significant, as evidenced in the supply chain "disasters" illustrated in Table 1.1. The table overviews some of the more significant supply chain disasters that have

TABLE 1.1
Supply Chain Disasters over the Years

Source: Adapted from *Supply Chain Digest*, "The Greatest Supply Chain Disasters of All Time," 2009, *White Paper*, available at http://www.scdigest.com; "3 True Stories of Supply Chain Management Disasters (And How to Avoid Them)," MaxQ Technologies, available at http://www.maxqtech.com/3-true-stories-of-supply-chain-management-disasters-and-how-to-avoid-them/; and "Samsung's Total Recall," *DC Velocity*, Vol. 14, No. 12 (December 2016), p. 40.

Company	Year(s)	Issue/Problems	Impact/Result
Foxmeyer Drug	1996	New order management and distribution systems don't work, and fulfillment cost targets built into contracts are unattainable.	Huge sales losses; Foxmeyer files for bankruptcy, and is eventually bought by McKesson.
Boeing	2007/2008	New outsourced supply chain can't deliver components for new Dreamliner 787 aircraft.	Two-year delay in product launch, more than $2 billion in charges to support/expedite component supplies.
GM	1980s	CEO Robert Smith invests $billions in robot technology that mostly doesn't work.	Smith fired; low-tech Toyota uses lean manufacturing to gain strong competitive advantage as GM's market share heads south.
WebVan	2001	Online grocer has many problems, including massive investment in automated warehouses that drain capital and aren't justified by demand.	Company goes from billions in market cap to bankrupt in a matter of months.
Adidas	1996	New warehouse system—actually, first one, then another—and DC automation just don't work.	Company underships by 80% in January; incurs market share losses that persist for years.

TABLE 1.1
(*Concluded*)

Company	Year(s)	Issue/Problems	Impact/Result
Denver Airport	1995	Complex, hugely expensive automated handling system never really works.	Airport opens late; huge PR fiasco; system is only minimally used from start and shuttered totally in 2005.
Mattel	2007	Infamous recall of tens of millions of toys made in China becomes poster child for concerns about quality of offshore goods.	Costs for the recall were huge, but damage to brand perhaps even more; starts big stock price slide that lingers for long time.
ToysRUs.com	1999	Can't fulfill thousands of orders for which it promised delivery by Christmas.	Famous "We're sorry" e-mails 2 days before Christmas cause fire storm of negative PR; eventually outsources fulfillment to Amazon.com.
Hershey Foods	1999	Order management and warehouse system implementation issues cause Hershey to miss critical Halloween shipments.	Company says at least $150 million in revenue lost; profit drops 19%, and stock goes from 57 to 38.
Cisco	2001	Lacking adequate demand and inventory visibility, Cisco is caught with piles of product as demand slows.	Company takes $2.2 billion inventory write-down; stock drops 50% and has stayed near that level since.
Nike	2001	Trouble with new planning system causes inventory and order woes.	Nike blames software-related issues for $100 million revenue shortfall for the quarter; stock drops 20%.
Target Canada	2015	Inventory overwhelmed Target's new distribution centers; products came into the distribution centers faster than they were going out because barcodes on many items did not match what was in the computer system.	Target Canada expanded too quickly; inventory problems resulted in empty shelves in Target stores, frustrating customers; the failure cost Target more than $2 billion.
Samsung	2016	Galaxy Note 7 smartphones were recalled after repeated incidents of the phones catching fire due to overheated batteries.	The recall covered 1.9 million phones in the U.S. and cost Samsung $5 billion, plus losses in market share and reputation.

occurred in the last few decades and illustrates the importance of being able to manage the supply chain efficiently and effectively.

To begin our discussion of supply chain management, let's define the concept of supply chain management, discuss what SCM is and is not, and examine some of the milestones in its historical development.

Supply Chain Management—An Overview

Definition of Supply Chain Management (SCM)

Supply Chain Management Defined

A first step in visualizing the importance and significance of SCM is to have a clear understanding of what the term means. SCM has been referred to by many names, including integrated logistics management, demand management, and others. The most commonly accepted term used by practicing supply chain executives is *supply chain management*.

TABLE 1.2
(*Concluded*)

Date(s)	Event	Significance
1990s	Supply chain management approach recognized as an important concept and its development and implementation initiated in many industries	The notion that multiple organizations and functional areas can integrate their efforts to optimize their individual and combined performances led to the development of a systems approach throughout the entire channel of distribution.
1990s	Market restructuring in global regions of Asia, Europe, and North America	Events such as NAFTA, Europe 1992, MERCOSUR, and the Asian financial crisis resulted in major changes in global markets and infrastructures.
1993	Michael Hammer and James Champy, *Reengineering the Corporation: A Manifesto for Business Revolution* (New York: HarperCollins)	Many organizations evaluated their business processes to determine if there was a better way of performing them, recognizing SCM is an area where reengineering efforts can result in significant improvements.
1994	Jeff Bezos began Amazon as a technology company whose business focus was to simplify online transactions for consumers, many of them Millennials	Now referred to as the "Amazon factor," Internet and omnichannel retailing developed into a billion-dollar business sector.
2000–2020	Terrorist attacks and severe weather disruptions (hurricanes, tsunamis, and earthquakes) throughout the world caused economic and political uncertainties	Terrorism, catastrophic weather events, and other significant events highlighted the need for security and contingency planning among supply chain members. As a result, global organizations realized they must work together to collaborate and coordinate their efforts.

No. 5: Ford Assembly Line—The continuous production line approach to manufacturing the Model T automobile in 1913 reduced product time significantly and began the movement toward the development of more optimal production processes throughout the manufacturing sector.

No. 4: Economic Order Quantity (EOQ)—A mathematical concept introduced in 1913 by a Westinghouse engineer determined the optimal amount of product to produce based on inventory holding costs and ordering costs.

No. 3: Ocean Shipping Container—Malcom McLean invented the first standard shipping container in 1956, which enabled global trade to greatly expand.

No. 2: P&G's Continuous Replenishment—Procter & Gamble implemented a computerized program that determined ordering patterns in the consumer goods industry based on distribution center withdrawals and sales data. System inventories were reduced and in-stock product availability was improved. This became the impetus for the Walmart and P&G continuous replenishment program established in 1988.

No. 1: Toyota Production System (TPS)—Toyota automobiles were produced using the lean manufacturing approach developed by Taichi Ohno and others in 1990. The lean concept has since permeated every aspect of supply chain management.[11]

[11] Dan Gilmore, "The Top 10 Supply Chain Innovations of All-time," *Supply Chain Digest*, December 3, 2010, http://www.scdigest.com.

Exhibit: The First Global Supply Chain

Perhaps the first global supply chain existed with the Dutch East India Company, which, for most of the 17th and 18th centuries, controlled the spice trade from Indonesia to Europe. "Here was the tenuous but well-structured supply-chain, extended all the way from Banda to Amsterdam, via numerous ports and functionaries, administered with brutal efficiency by the Dutch East India Company, perhaps the first business organization that bears resemblance to today's multinational corporations. The company raised money by issuing shares. It had the first widely recognized commercial logo. Even without today's computers, the company's officials were linked through a hierarchy of regular detailed reporting and accounting. Production was brought together in plantations and processed in 'factories.' Near-subsistence agriculture was replaced with scale and quality control. . . . Customer feedback was insistently relayed to producers: 'small nutmegs are of no value.'"

So successful was this early supply chain that 3,000 tons of nutmeg were produced and distributed annually to Europe.

Source: Stephen Grenville, "The First Global Supply Chain," November 3, 2017, https://www.lowyinstitute.org/the-interpreter /starting-point-first-global-supply-chain.

Since this "top 10" list was developed in 2010, newer innovations such as same-day delivery, use of drones to deliver small packages, the development of global companies such as Amazon and Alibaba, reverse logistics/product returns, 3-D printing,[12] and omnichannel retailing would probably make this list if it was replicated today. To illustrate, Amazon, on December 7, 2016, delivered its first order by drone in Cambridge, UK. What was delivered? An Amazon Fire TV and bag of popcorn. In total, it took only 13 minutes from the time the customer clicked on the purchase to the package delivery to the customer. The program is called "Prime Air" and promises order to delivery time of 30 minutes or less.[13] From the perspective of 3-D printing, Adidas sells shoes (sneakers) with 3-D-printed soles that are adapted to a customer's weight and movement.[14]

With a brief history of SCM as background, it will be easier to visualize how SCM should be viewed as an organizational strategy. While there are many approaches to viewing and managing SCM, two of the most widely accepted approaches will be discussed in the next section of this chapter.

A Model of Supply Chain Management

In order to successfully plan, implement, and control SCM, it is necessary to identify those elements or components that make up SCM and to identify the role of one of the most important elements of the supply chain—logistics. We must understand how all of the major components of SCM are linked and interrelated, that is, develop a model of SCM.

Elements of SCM

Supply chain management (SCM) is an integrating function with primary responsibility for *linking major business functions and business processes within and across companies* into a cohesive and high-performing business model. SCM includes all of the logistics management

---

[12] For a discussion of how 3-D printing can impact SCM, see David Swanson, Kristoffer Francisco, and Jiyun Huang, "Click 'Next' to Print Your Supply Chain," *CSCMP's Supply Chain Quarterly*, Vol. 10, No. 4 (2016), pp. 44–48.

[13] "From Click to Customer Delivery in 13 Minutes, Amazon's Prime Air Drone Trial Begins," *SupplyChain247,* December 14, 2016, http://www.supplychain247.com/article/from_click_to _delivery_in_13_minutes_amazons_prime_air_drone_trial_begins.

[14] Agence France-Presse, "Adidas Looks to 3-D Printers for New Generation Sneaker Soles," *Industry Week*, April 7, 2017, http://www.industryweek.com/technology/adidas-looks-3-d-printers-new -generation-sneaker-soles.

activities, as well as manufacturing operations, purchasing, and procurement, and it drives coordination of processes and activities with marketing, sales, product design, accounting, finance, and information technology.

Because SCM involves so many functions and processes within and between companies, executives in charge of SCM must be "boundary spanners." Often, supply chain executives have experience in managing many activities such as transportation, inventories, warehousing, order processing, and many others, and are selected to head up supply chain operations.

Based on the Council of Supply Chain Management Professionals (CSCMP) definition of SCM we presented in the previous section, and also drawing on other views of what SCM includes, the following have been identified as important components of SCM:[15]

Customer relationship management

Demand management

Finance

Forward logistics

Information technology

Life cycle support

Manufacturing operations

Marketing and sales

Order fulfillment/service delivery

Procurement

Product/service development and launch

Reverse logistics

Sourcing

Supplier relationship collaboration

As evidenced from the list, the number of activities and processes involved in SCM is significant. Essentially, anything that impacts customer satisfaction and the profits of multiple organizations in the supply chain is relevant to a discussion of SCM. However, no other component is likely more significant to the success of a supply chain than *logistics,* which includes both forward and reverse flows of products and information.

Role of Logistics in SCM

Inputs into the Logistics Process

Some of the many activities included within logistics management are illustrated in Figure 1.1. Logistics activities take place utilizing natural, human, financial, and information resources as inputs. These inputs are planned, implemented, and controlled by logistics practitioners in various forms, including raw materials (subassemblies, parts, packing materials, basic commodities), in-process inventory (products partially completed and not yet ready for sale), and finished goods (completed products ready for sale to intermediate or final customers).

Outputs of the Logistics System

The outcomes, or outputs, of the logistics system include competitive advantage for the organization resulting from a marketing orientation and operational efficiencies and effectiveness; time and place utility; efficient movement to the customer; and provision of a logistics service mix such that logistics becomes a proprietary asset of the organization.

---

[15] List compiled from CSCMP website, 2018, http://www.cscmp.org; and John Dischinger, David J. Closs, Eileen McCulloch, Cheri Speier, William Grenoble, and Donna Marshall, "The Emerging Supply Chain Management Profession," *Supply Chain Management Review*, January 1, 2006, http://www.scmr.com/index.asp?layout=articlePrint&articleID=CA6311321.

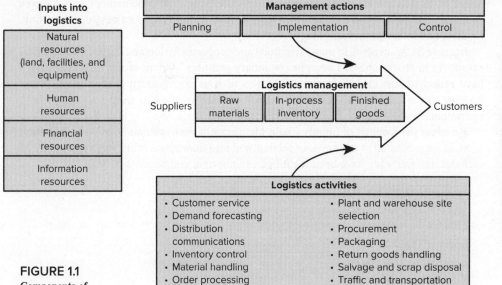

FIGURE 1.1
Components of
Logistics Management

These outputs are made possible by the effective and efficient performance of the logistics activities shown at the bottom of Figure 1.1.

When you consider that the outputs of logistics management are similar to the outputs of a supply chain, it is understandable that logistics and SCM might be viewed as the same or similar concepts. However, the major difference is that logistics attempts to optimize customer *service*, which is only one component of customer *satisfaction*; but customer satisfaction includes many other facets of the business as well. Many other functions and processes combine to provide optimal customer satisfaction, including manufacturing, marketing, finance, and information technology.

In light of the fact that logistics is a major and vital component of SCM, we present two approaches to modeling the supply chain. Each of these approaches includes logistics management as a key ingredient of the supply chain process.

Approaches to Modeling Supply Chain Management

Perhaps the most widely known model of the supply chain process is the Supply-Chain Operations Reference (SCOR®) Model, maintained by the American Production & Inventory Control Society Supply Chain Council (APICS SSC). Also well known is the Forum Model, proposed by researchers at the Global Supply Chain Forum of The Ohio State University. Interestingly, both of these models have been developed using extensive practitioner/company inputs, rather than academic research. Thus, both models are highly pragmatic and user-friendly.

The SCOR Model undergoes periodic updating and is presently in Version 12.0.[16] According to the APICS Supply Chain Council's SCOR Overview publication, the model includes the following components: Plan; Source; Make; Deliver; Return; and Enable. These components include customer interactions, all product transactions, and all market interactions. "SCOR spans all customer interactions (quote to cash), all physical material transactions (procure to payment, including equipment, supplies, spare parts, bulk product,

---

[16] For further information on the SCOR Model and the APICS Supply Chain Council, see http://www.apics.org/apics-for-business/products-and-services/apics-scc-frameworks/scor.

software, etc.) and all market interactions (manufacturing, from the understanding of aggregate demand to the fulfillment of each order)."[17]

The SCOR Model has achieved widespread acceptance among business firms because of the significant practitioner involvement in the development of the model. It is continually being updated and new refined versions of the model appear on a regular basis. Additionally, measurement metrics and standards are also being developed as they relate to each of the components of the SCOR Model.

The SCOR Model is used in conjunction with other processes, technologies, and techniques in order to achieve overall supply chain excellence. These include process reengineering, lean manufacturing, Six Sigma, ISO 9000, ISO 14000, Global Reporting Initiative (GRI), and the Balanced Scorecard. Many of these processes, technologies, and techniques will be examined in later chapters of this textbook.

The Forum Model is another SCM model that has been developed utilizing practitioner/company input. The model illustrates the structure of the supply chain, product and information flows, SCM components, and major processes occurring in the supply chain, including customer relationship management, customer service management, demand management, order fulfillment, manufacturing flow management, procurement, product development and commercialization, and product returns.[18] These flows and processes are related to, and influenced by, various management components and the structure of the supply chain itself.

With respect to the structure of the supply chain, there will likely be scores of firms involved: suppliers, vendors, manufacturers, wholesalers, distributors, retailers, raw materials producers, transportation carriers, warehouses, information providers, and others. In a conventional channel of distribution, these entities would be represented as a straight-line flow or pipeline. However, the actual relationships will much more likely be a decision tree with many branches. Of course, some branches of the supply chain decision tree will be more important or critical than others, some firms will be larger than others, and firms may be located anywhere in the world.

Every firm, process, and management component within the supply chain is impacted by various societal and business issues. The major issues in each of these two areas will be discussed in the remainder of this chapter.

Societal Issues Impacting Supply Chains

A number of factors impact SCM, the supply chain overall, and the organizations and individuals involved in SCM. While coverage of all possible societal factors that might impact SCM is not possible in this chapter, we will attempt to examine several of the most important factors in the following discussion. Specifically, the following items will be examined: gross domestic product (GDP); globalization; energy, environmental, and safety issues; infrastructure; regulatory issues; security; supply chain disruptions; and disaster preparedness and relief.

Supply Chain Management and Gross Domestic Product (GDP)

Each year the Council of Supply Chain Management Professionals (CSCMP) conducts the Annual State of Logistics research study in the U.S.[19] At present, there is no study being conducted to capture the costs associated with the broader aspect of supply chain

[17] APICS Supply Chain Council, *Quick Reference Guide: Supply Chain Operations Reference (SCOR®) Model, Version* 12.0 (2017), p. 2.

[18] Douglas M. Lambert, ed., *Supply Chain Management: Processes, Partnerships, Performance*, 4th ed. (Sarasota, FL: Supply Chain Management Institute, 2014).

[19] Mark Solomon and Toby Gooley, "Annual 'State of Logistics Report' Shows Industry Looking in Cloudy Rear-view Mirror," *DC Velocity*, Vol. 15, No. 7 (July 2017), pp. 15–16; and Mark B. Solomon and Toby Gooley, "Uncertain Times," *CSCMP's Supply Chain Quarterly*, Vol. 11 (Special Issue/2017), pp. 10–13.

management. While the report addresses logistics issues, it is representative of the magnitude of supply chain activities occurring in the economy. As one of the largest components of supply chain costs, logistics accounted for 7.5 percent of U.S. GDP in 2016, the lowest point since 2009. This translated into expenditures of $1.392 trillion and was a decrease of 1.5 percent year over year.

Given the monetary impact of logistics, it is apparent that it has an impact on interest rates, inflation, productivity, energy costs and availability, employment, and other aspects of the U.S. economy. Improvements in a nation's productivity have positive effects on the prices that consumers, businesses, and governments pay for goods and services. Productivity increases tend to hold down inflation, stabilize currency exchange rates, and improve a nation's ability to compete in global markets. Higher productivity usually means that businesses have lower costs of operation, increased availability of investment capital, economic growth, and less unemployment.

Generally, logistics costs as a percentage of U.S. GDP have declined since the early 1980s. However, because of rising energy costs and uncertainty issues relating to security and terrorism, that percentage rose during the first several years of the new millennium but decreased during the recession of 2008–2009 and thereafter. To illustrate, if logistics costs as a percentage of GDP had remained the same since 1980, the United States would be spending an additional $300 billion annually to conduct logistics. Thus, improving the efficiency of logistics operations makes an important contribution to the economy as a whole. And as one of the most significant components of SCM, it has allowed supply chains to also be more efficient.

Relative to other regions of the globe, the U.S. is more efficient at logistics and SCM. For example, in China, the ratio of logistics costs to the national GDP was 14.9 percent in 2016, down 1.1 percent from the previous year. While that percentage seems high, it had been more than 18 percent in 2005. As a result, China ranked 27th in the 2016 Logistics Performance Index published by the World Bank that covers 160 countries and regions.[20]

Globalization

Increasing numbers of organizations have become involved in some form of international marketing, manufacturing, procurement, and/or distribution. This trend will continue. With this expansion into global markets comes a need to develop worldwide supply chain networks and information systems. The supply chain executive will have to acquire additional skills and competencies in many areas (international finance, import and export documentation, political science, foreign business practices, international customs and cultures). As organizations expand internationally, integrated SCM and total cost trade-off analysis become even more complex and difficult to manage.[21]

Today, the majority of all consumer goods purchased in the United States are sourced internationally. Global trade expansion, coupled with shifts in manufacturing capacity to Asia and other sites of low-cost production, has expanded international freight movements to a level where annual growth rates of intercontinental traffic increase almost every year. As an illustration of this growth in global freight movements, the World Trade Organization estimates that the growth in world exports and imports will be 3.6 percent in 2017.[22] The largest port in the United States and 19th largest in the world, the Port of Los Angeles, imported

[20] "China Takes More Measures to Reduce Logistics Costs," *Xinhuanet*, November 18, 2017, http://news.xinhuanet,com/english/2017-07/06/c_136420503.htm.

[21] Richard R. Young, Dinesh Pai, and Girish Subramanian, "Are Supply Chains Becoming Too Complex?," *Distribution Business Management Journal*, Vol. 14 (2012), pp. 14–15.

[22] *World Merchandise Trade 2012–2017*, World Trade Organization, 2016, http://www.wto.org/english/news_e/pres16_e/pr768_e.htm; also see OECD/ITF, *ITF Transport Outlook 2017*, OECD Publishing, Paris, 2017, http://dx.doi.org/10.1787/9789282108000-en.

almost 200,000 automobiles, 500,000 TEUs (twenty-foot equivalent units) of furniture, 290,000 TEUs of apparel, and 220,000 TEUs of electronics in 2016. Exports through the Port of Los Angeles included 280,000 TEUs of paper/wastepaper, 210,000 TEUs of animal feed, and 100,000 TEUs of scrap metal, not to mention 600,000 cruise ship passengers.[23] Such statistics are always interesting, and they indicate the huge magnitude of international commerce that occurs. These trends toward globalization of the supply chain are not expected to abate anytime in the next decade.

The product expansion strategy of the more than 130-year-old UK-based grocery chain Sainsbury's provides an example of some of the supply chain issues involved in sourcing internationally. As the company attempted to expand its nonfood product lines (clothing, home electronics) in order to more effectively compete with Tesco, a major competitor, it began to source products from China, India, and elsewhere in the Far East. "Almost overnight, Sainsbury's found itself grappling with issues it hadn't faced before. The retailer quickly learned, for example, that it wasn't enough just to find low-cost suppliers with reasonable lead times; it also had to make sure those suppliers would be stable and reliable. There were new decisions to make as well. Sainsbury's had to choose whether to work with suppliers through agents or by going directly to their factories and plants. Further, the decision to do business in underdeveloped countries carried with it an ethical responsibility to investigate labor conditions in potential vendors' factories."[24]

Sainsbury's is not alone in facing these and other challenges when entering into international commerce. As companies expand their supply chain networks globally, they need to employ technology that brings visibility and transparency to the supply chain, employ partner organizations that understand the global marketplace, and develop an awareness of and expertise in the international arena that often is lacking in organizations with a traditional local, regional, or national focus. "It's often said that managing a global supply chain is a lot like running a three-ring circus. But instead of a whip, you need technology and good partners."[25]

Global Trends

In the future, several significant trends will have an impact on organizations operating globally and include the following:

- An increasing number of supply chain executives who will have international responsibility and authority.
- Reduction in the amount, and increased standardization, of international paperwork and documentation, especially the shipping bill of lading.
- Increasing number of smaller firms engaging in exporting, with larger firms utilizing licensing, joint ventures, or direct ownership.
- A growing number of third-party providers owned and operated on a global scale.[26]
- Increasing vertical integration of the supply chain, which will include firms from many countries (especially in the acquisition of raw material supply sources).
- Growth and development of global supply chains.
- Continuation of omnichannel commerce as markets expand globally.
- Development of new and expanded technologies that allow firms to link their operations globally.

[23] "The Port of Los Angeles Facts and Figures," March 13, 2017, https://www.portoflosangeles.org/about/facts.asp.
[24] Peter Bradley, "Becoming a Ringmaster," *DC Velocity*, Vol. 5, No. 4 (April 2007), p. 42.
[25] Ibid.
[26] Annually, Capgemini Consulting, Penn State University, and Penske Logistics provide an update on the third-party logistics market. See Capgemini and C. John Langley, *2017 21st Annual Third-Party Logistics Study: The State of Logistics Outsourcing*, 2017.

As organizations identify target markets in other parts of the world, they will have to establish supply chain networks and information systems that meet the needs of a variety of customers.

Sustainability in the Supply Chain

Organizations of all types have become more concerned with ensuring that their products and operations provide environmental, health, safety, and sustainable benefits to their stakeholders. Companies as diverse as Dematic, an engineering company that designs, builds, and supports logistics solutions that optimize material flow, to Nike, a global manufacturer of athletic shoes and apparel, have embraced environment, health, safety, and sustainability (EHS&S) in their supply chains. For example, Nike built a sustainable distribution center in Belgium that utilizes power from locally generated, 100 percent renewable energy sources.[27]

Other examples include UPS, which replaced outdated lighting systems with LED lights and installed energy management systems in its physical facilities.[28] A major European chemical company utilizes the waste products from other industries as raw materials into its own production. This allows the firm to acquire raw materials at low cost and it results in it having a cost advantage over its competitors. Another firm created an internal sustainability index to evaluate its product portfolio, which reduces its end-of-life concerns. The index is founded on the principle of life cycle assessment.[29]

Energy availability and prices vary over time, although long-term indicators are that fossil fuels will continue to increase in price as they become less available. Alternative energy sources will no doubt replace some utilization of traditional fossil fuels, but these sources will likely be more expensive and less widely available. In the coming decades, these changes will undoubtedly have various impacts on supply chains.

Making cost-service trade-offs is a vital part of supply chain management. Historically, companies have traded off lower inventory levels by spending more for transportation, with the result being reduced overall costs and higher customer service levels. Will the trade-off be the same if transportation costs are two or three times more expensive? Will offshore outsourcing of manufacturing or materials continue to be cheaper than domestic sourcing, especially when higher transportation costs are factored in as fuel prices increase?

Many of the overnight express companies such as UPS, FedEx, DHL, and others have introduced multi-fuel vehicles, trucks that operate on ethanol (derived from corn), and, in some instances, have gone so far as to use bicycles to deliver small packages in crowded urban locations. While energy will continue to be generally available, with spot shortages from time to time, it is important that supply chain executives develop plans for the future.

From an environmental perspective, emissions from manufacturing plants, transportation equipment, and other logistics and supply chain activities will continue to be an issue for supply chain executives. Many companies throughout Europe have adopted ISO 14000 programs, which are focused on making firms more "environmentally friendly." Other environmental efforts are under way throughout the globe. Some companies are leading by example by coupling environmental programs with sound supply chain strategies. IKEA is one such example. A global manufacturer of home furnishings with its headquarters in Sweden, IKEA is an environmental innovator. Its corporate vision statement highlights the

---

[27] Carol Miller, "Building Supply Chain Sustainability," *MHI Solutions*, Quarter 4 (2016), p. 24.
[28] Ibid., p. 26.
[29] National Association for Environmental Management, "Planning for a Sustainable Future: Ideas That Will Shape EHS&S Management in the Year to Come," *White Paper*, February 2016, p. 12.

Exhibit: The Cornerstones of IKEA's Sustainability Strategy

IKEA believes that it needs to transform its business and has outlined goals and metrics to achieve that transformation by 2020. Specifically, IKEA wants "to be able to fulfil future customer needs, promote equality, and secure sustainable access to resources, while driving down emissions and maintaining . . . low prices." IKEA believes that it "needs to do things differently. It's no longer possible to use 20th century approaches to meet 21st century demands. Simply working toward being less bad will not get us where we need to be—[IKEA] needs transformational change—which means challenging old ways and embracing the new, being bold, innovative and committed to taking action. It means taking many steps, both large and small, that, together, will have transformational impact.

"Moving forward, [IKEA] will continue to strengthen our business practices by ensuring that: There is compliance in [our] operations with our code of conduct, and compliance for all our home furnishing suppliers with the IKEA supplier code of conduct, IWAY. Sustainable financial policies are safeguarded, ensuring independence and stability as a basis for growth and responsible business, and with respect for all applicable legislation. Product quality and functionality are continually strengthened in line with our range direction. Hazardous substances are phased out in advance of legislation, and we continue to take a precautionary approach when introducing any new chemicals. The requirements of all product safety legislation and standards are met or exceeded. Wherever possible, we adopt the strongest legislation and apply it in every market. Chain-of-custody of all critical materials and processes is established. The certification schemes and standards that we are part of contribute to protecting the environment and communities where we operate, creating positive social and environmental change.

"We are a values-driven business with a culture based on strong values; togetherness and enthusiasm; desire for renewal; cost-consciousness; accepting responsibility; humbleness and willpower; simplicity; leadership by example; daring to be different; and striving to meet reality. Our culture and values shape the way we do business and create a powerful desire to do the right thing. We always do our best to maintain the highest ethical standards and to be a good partner in society."

Source: "People & Planet Positive IKEA Group Sustainability Strategy for 2020," June 2014, http://www.ikea.com/ms/en_US/pdf/reports-downloads/sustainability-strategy-people-and-planet-positive.pdf.

emphasis the company places on environmental issues by identifying three cornerstones of its strategy:

- Cost-consciousness and resource efficiency.
- The extensive use of wood in its products.
- Training co-workers and engaging them in environmental issues.

The company takes each cornerstone and explains it in detail. The Exhibit provides a description of each cornerstone. "Increasingly, global enterprises such as IKEA realize that green initiatives dovetail with supply chain management strategies, as they both strive to accomplish more with less."[30]

Complicating the practice of EHS&S management is the challenge of regulatory compliance. As more governments and industries place additional emphasis on environmental, health, and safety issues, organizations are finding that regulatory compliance can be very burdensome. "Getting a handle on product regulations is a particularly thorny risk as new regulations continue to emerge at all levels of government around the world. Even knowing what the regulations are can sometimes be a challenge. . . . An emerging issue . . . that is creeping into the scope of EHS&S responsibilities is the use of forced labor and human trafficking in the supply chain."[31] All of this increases business risk and challenges that are complex and difficult to solve. "The cost of poor compliance management or inactivity—

---

[30] "People & Planet Positive IKEA Group Sustainability Strategy for 2020," June 2014, http://www.ikea.com/ms/en_US/pdf/reports-downloads/sustainability-strategy-people-and-planet-positive.pdf.

[31] "Planning for a Sustainable Future," p. 15.

when it comes to not actively managing one's supply chain—can be high, from upfront expenses like duties and fines to goods being held, and more. A company's reputation, time-to-market and lost business opportunities are also on the line."[32]

Infrastructure

While not a part of an overall supply chain strategy of organizations, infrastructure can be a significant constraint in successfully implementing SCM. Infrastructure is most often created by governments for multiple purposes such as moving people, safeguarding or defending a country, and improving and/or expanding business commerce. Infrastructure involves roadways, rail systems, airports and ocean ports, bridges, waterways, and a myriad of other elements important to the creation of a healthy GDP for a nation and its people. However, in recent years, infrastructure has not kept pace with increasing supply chain demands. Two examples will illustrate the problem.

When the European Union was formed in 1993, with the removal of trade barriers between countries, the easing of restrictions for crossing country borders, and, eventually, the adoption of a common currency, the euro, forecasters predicted a surge in cross-border movements of freight. They were right! Freight traffic increased dramatically, but it so over-loaded the existing highway and railway systems that traffic congestion became a significant issue. In the United States, there are regular queues created from container traffic trying to be offloaded at West Coast ports, often resulting in delays of days or weeks. As a large importer of products from the Far East and elsewhere, Walmart receives more than 795,000 TEUs—or shipping containers—from abroad every year![33] Add to that number the containers being imported by other large firms such as Target, Home Depot, Ford, General Motors, Procter & Gamble, Nike, and Whirlpool, and it is not difficult to imagine the potential backlogs that could exist, especially during peak times of the year such as holidays.

In the United States, spending on transportation and water infrastructure as a percentage of gross domestic product (GDP) has declined from 3.1 percent in the 1960s to 2.5 percent in 2017.[34] The Panama Canal expansion, which was completed in 2016, doubled throughput as more and larger ships are able to pass through it. For U.S. ports to take advantage of the potential increase in shipping traffic, many eastern and southeastern seaboard ports have dredged their ports in order to accommodate the larger ships.[35] Additionally, networks of highways, warehouses, and other supply chain entities will have to be put into place. Unfortunately, all of these improvements will cost money, which the federal, state, and local governments do not have to spend.

It is a common fact that highways, ports, airports, railways, and other infrastructure do not get built and/or expanded quickly. Such expansions cost significant amounts of money. As supply efficiencies increase, customer segments expand, and transportation equipment becomes larger and capable of moving more products, the infrastructure problem will become more severe. The U.S. rail industry has spent large amounts of money on capital improvements, yet capacity constraints have not improved significantly. Airports and ocean ports have expanded, although slowly relative to the increases in cargo and passengers being transported by airplanes and ships. It seems that wherever you are on the globe, there

[32] Sri Ramadas, "Global Trace Compliance: A Cost Center or Cost Saver?," *Supply & Demand Chain Executive*, Vol. 14, Issue 5 (March 2014), p. 30.

[33] Kim Souza, "Walmart Import Exec Discusses Trade Challenges, Efforts to Boost Exports," *Talk Business & Politics*, May 2017, https://talkbusiness.net/2017/05/wal-mart-import-exec-discusses-trade-challenges-efforts-to-boost-exports.

[34] *2017 Infrastructure Report Card*, American Society of Civil Engineers, 2017, https://www.infrastructurereportcard.org/wp-content/uploads/2016/10/2017-Infrastructure-Report-Card.pdf.

[35] Robert J. Bowman, "How East Coast Ports Are Getting 'Big-Ship Ready,'" *SupplyChainBrain*, November 11, 2016, http://www.supplychainbrain.com/featured-content/single-article/article/how-east-coast-ports-are-getting-big-ship-ready.

are more trucks on the highways. And still, economies are expanding and customers are demanding more and better goods and services.

It is not within the scope of this discussion to explore the infrastructure issues facing countries, companies, and individuals. However, the solving of infrastructure problems—present and future—will require partnerships between all parties. Until those partnerships are developed and implemented, organizations will have to adapt to the infrastructure constraints imposed on their supply chains.

In much the same way, regulatory issues require partnerships between governments, organizations, and individuals.

Regulatory Issues

Many aspects of supply chain management are subject to some type of regulation—local, state, federal, and/or international. Many of these regulatory issues will be examined in the context of specific supply chain processes such as transportation, warehousing, and others, but one that deserves special mention now (and again in a later discussion of organizational issues relating to corporate governance) is the Sarbanes-Oxley Act (SOX) that was passed into law by the U.S. Congress in 2002. Because of serious ethical and legal misconduct in several major U.S. corporations (e.g., Enron, WorldCom, Arthur Andersen) during the 1990s that had significant and serious impacts on investor accounts, legislation was enacted to provide transparency in corporate financial statements. Three areas of publicly traded companies on the U.S. exchanges were regulated as a result of SOX, including

- **Internal process controls (Sections 302 and 404)**—this would include inventory and fixed-asset reconciliation and inventory write-offs; material transfers and poor inventory accuracy; segregation of duties in the procure-to-pay process; and viable SCM practices.
- **Off-balance sheet obligations (Section 401a)**—areas impacted could include vendor-managed inventories (VMI); long-term purchase agreements; lease agreements; and letters of intent.
- **Timely reporting of material changes (Section 409)**—includes issues relating to outsourcing of goods and services such as contracts with vendors, stable vendor relationships, and contingency plans for supply disruptions.

In the same way that CEOs and CFOs must certify quarterly financial statements, supply chain leaders will have to attest that their organization and processes are compliant with SOX.

Additional regulatory issues have become more important in recent years, including those related to the environment and sustainability, transportation safety, and security. These issues will be addressed in various parts of this text, but the security issue deserves some general discussion now.

Security and Risk

There are many risks facing supply chain executives in the global marketplace, with security being the most significant. However, in addition to security, there are other risks that face the supply chain executive. Generally, these can be classified into five categories: economic (oil prices/energy supplies, trade deficits, demographic shifts); environmental (natural catastrophes, climate issues); geopolitical (terrorism, weapons of mass destruction, wars, Middle East instability); societal (pandemics, infectious diseases in developing world); and technological (nanotechnology risks, breakdown of critical information infrastructure).[36] Many of these issues will be examined throughout this text within the contexts of various supply chain topics.

[36] World Economic Forum, *The World Economic Forum's Global Risks* 2007—*Part I*, April 27, 2007, http://blog.sourcinginnovation.com.

Good risk mitigation strategies are essential to the well-being of companies and the supply chains in which they operate. For example, it seems that there are reports of various cyber security breaches occurring regularly in all parts of the world. "As cyber criminals step up their game, government regulators get more involved, litigators and courts wade in deeper, and the public learns more about cyber risks, corporate leaders will have to step up accordingly."[37]

Some general caveats relating to risk mitigation include the following:

- "Monitoring risk levels in individual countries (i.e., political, economic and commercial trends) is increasingly advisable.
- Businesses have to widen responsibility for managing supply chain risks so that these risks are considered across all parts of the company (including the design, sourcing, and manufacturing functions).
- Businesses should review contingency plans for responding to short-term supply chain threats in order to manage the risks posed by complex supply chains and by overreliance on a single supplier."[38]

Because of traditional concerns about product theft and pilferage, coupled with more recent issues related to terrorism, product security has never been more important to members of supply chains. The Department of Homeland Security has implemented the Container Security Initiative (CSI) to combat terrorism's potential impact on cargo arriving in the U.S.[39] And the problem is significant in that more than 18 million containers arrive at U.S. ports every year.[40] In addition to most major ocean ports in the U.S., many of the world's largest ports such as Hong Kong, Shanghai, and Rotterdam also have implemented the CSI. The CSI involves four key elements:

- "Using intelligence and automated information to identify and target containers that pose a risk for terrorism.
- Pre-screening those containers that pose a risk at the port of departure before they arrive at U.S. ports.
- Using detection technology to quickly pre-screen containers that pose a risk.
- Using smarter, tamper-evident containers."[41]

Other measures taken to improve security in the US include the Customs-Trade Partnership Against Terrorism (CTPAT) program, which is a voluntary program where participating companies enhance their security procedures and create awareness among their supply chain partners. Several thousand companies, including importers, transportation carriers, freight forwarders, manufacturers, and port authorities, are participating in the program.[42]

---

[37] Quote of Sameer Bhalotra, Former White House Senior Director for Cybersecurity, as reported in Christopher Petersen, "The Cyber Threat Risk—Oversight Guidance for CEOs and Boards," *White Paper* (LogRhythm 2015).

[38] "Mitigating Supply Chain Risks," *D&B Special Report*, Dun & Bradstreet Limited, May 2011, p. 2.

[39] Smita Singla, "What Is Container Security Initiative (CSI) and How Does It Work?," *Marine Safety*, July 21, 2016, https://www.marineinsight.com/marine-safety/what-is-container-security-initiative-csi-and-how-does-it-work; and Mehnazd, "What Are the Benefits of Container Security Initiative (CSI), *Marine Safety*, July 21, 2016, https://www.marineinsight.com/marine-safety/what-are-the-benefits-of-container-security-initiative-csi.

[40] Julia Louppova, "US Container Imports to Grow Significantly in 2017," *Port.Today*, March 16, 2017, https://port.today/us-container-imports-to-grow-significantly-in-2017.

[41] John M. Cutler Jr., "Supply Chain Security: Legal and Regulatory Challenges," *CLM Explores*, Vol. 1 (Summer 2004), p. 4.

[42] "CTPAT: Customs-Trade Partnership against Terrorism," U.S. Customs and Border Protection, November 15, 2017, https://www.cbp.gov/border-security/ports-entry/cargo-security/ctpat.

TABLE 1.3
Cyber Supply Chain Best Practices

Source: National Institute of Standards and Technology, *Best Practices in Cyber Supply Chain Risk Management*, U.S. Department of Commerce (undated), https://csrc.nist .gov/CSRC/media/Projects /Supply-Chain-Risk -Managements/documents /briefings/Workshop-Brief -on-Cyber-Supply-Chain -Best-Practices.pdf.

"Companies have adopted a variety of practices that help them manage their cyber supply chain risks. These practices include:

1. Security requirements are included in every RFP and contract.
2. Once a vendor is accepted in the formal supply chain, a security team works with them on-site to address any vulnerabilities and security gaps.
3. 'One strike and you're out' policies with respect to vendor products that are either counterfeit or do not match specification.
4. Component purchases are tightly controlled; component purchases from approved vendors are prequalified. Parts purchased from other vendors are unpacked, inspected, and x-rayed before being accepted.
5. Secure Software Lifecycle Development Programs and training for all engineers in the life cycle are established.
6. Source code is obtained for all purchased software.
7. Software and hardware have a security handshake. Secure booting processes look for authentication codes and the system will not boot if codes are not recognized.
8. Automation of manufacturing and testing regimes reduces the risk of human intervention.
9. Track and trace programs establish provenance of all parts, components and systems.
10. Personnel in charge of supply chain cybersecurity partner with every team that touches any part of the product during its development life cycle and ensures that cyber security is part of suppliers' and developers' employee experience, processes and tools."

Security risks can take a number of different paths. To illustrate, terrorist threats can disrupt supply chain activities through suicide bomb attacks and chemical, biological, or radiological events on companies, port facilities, distribution hubs, and other infrastructure components. Cyber-attack is another area of potential supply chain vulnerability. With firms so dependent on computers and information systems, the loss of data if computer systems were compromised, or the inability to communicate with supply chain partners and customers, could be devastating. Illustrating the magnitude of risk associated with a cyber-attack on a business is a statistic published by Kaspersky Lab: "A distributed denial-of-service (DDoS) incident can cost a financial institution $1.2 million to recover on average, compared with $952,000 for businesses in other sectors."[43]

In summer 2017, the global shipping company A. P. Moller-Maersk Group had its computer systems infected by a virus. Maersk estimated that the attack impacted the company's bottom line by $200 to $300 million.[44] Such can be the costs associated with cyber risks if they occur with a large company and on a global scale.

There are numerous ways that companies can improve security measures. Table 1.3 identifies ways that organizations can become more secure within their supply chains.

A related issue to security and risk is supply chain disruptions. Such disruptions can occur due to technology failures, terrorism, severe weather, and other factors.

Supply Chain Disruptions

Managing supply chain risk has become an important aspect of supply chain management. Supply chain disruptions have become an increasing concern of organizations. As firms become leaner and technology dependent, disruptions can cause significant problems when

[43] Bob Violino, "Identifying Hazards to Better Prepare for Cyberattacks," *AkamaiVoice*, September 14, 2017, https://www.forbes.com/sites/akamai/2017/09/14/identifying-hazards-to-better-prepare-for -cyberattacks/#41e716fc2be7.
[44] Eric Johnson, "Hacked," *American Shipper*, Vol. 59, No. 9 (September 2017), p. 19.

they occur. "Over 80 percent of companies worldwide see better protection of supply chains as a priority."[45] Many factors have made supply chains more vulnerable, including longer supply lines, outsourcing from suppliers worldwide who may be "invisible" to the organization, natural disasters, labor strikes, product recalls, business failures, political unrest, and many more. To illustrate the financial implications of possible supply chain disruptions, one research study examined stock price performance of firms that had experienced significant supply chain disruptions. On average, share prices were reduced by as much as 7 percent on average.[46] Thus, there can be negative financial repercussions in firms that are not able to adequately respond to supply chain disruptions when they occur.

Two specific examples will illustrate the point that disruptions can cause negative financial impacts for an organization. In late-2000, Nike lost $100 million in sales as a result of supply chain information technology (IT) problems. Its stock price dropped 20 percent! The Swedish telecom company Ericsson lost $400 million in sales when a computer chip supplier in the U.S. had a fire that closed its facility. There was no backup supplier available in the short term and the company could not meet demand for its mobile telephones for most of the year, leading to a loss of $1.86 billion for the year.[47]

Supply chain managers must be able to develop contingency plans for potential disruptions. Because the causes of such disruptions can be varied in terms of the type of event and the duration of its impact, contingency plans must be both broad and narrow, short term and long term, and local versus regional versus global. In some instances, the duration of impact can be days (storms), weeks (major machine breakdowns), months (tsunamis), or years (terrorist attacks, trade embargoes, wars).

Periodically, there are delays at U.S. West Coast ports. These delays can be hours, days, and sometimes weeks. For a company like Limited Brands, which owns Victoria's Secret, Bath & Body Works, Limited Stores, and Henri Bendel, these delays can be deadly if they impact product sales. The company traditionally brought about 75 percent of its containerized freight into the U.S. market through West Coast ports and utilized approximately 40,000 domestic truckloads per year.[48] In order for the firm to not be adversely impacted by potential delays at the ports, Limited Brands developed contingency plans. Some of the key elements of those plans included the following:

- Notifying customers of potential delays resulting from port congestion.
- Shifting freight to Seattle and Tacoma, away from Southern California.
- Developing partnerships with carriers to handle freight movements from a variety of port locations.
- Developing intermodal options for moving freight to inland locations.[49]

As a result of its contingency planning, Limited Brands experienced delays of two days on average during the labor disputes that impacted Southern California ports in 2004, as opposed to weeks of delays experienced by many of its competitors. In terms of keeping its shelves stocked with merchandise, Limited Brands was able to minimize product shortages that plagued almost every other retailer.

In sum, there are many supply chain risk factors that can negatively impact the ability to serve customers. Throughout this text, we will examine many of these factors as they relate to the overall supply chain, individual firms, functions and processes, and customers.

---

[45] Steve Culp, "Supply Chain Disruption a Major Threat to Business," *Forbes*, February 15, 2013, https://www.forbes.com/sites/steveculp/2013/02/15/supply-chain-disruption-a-major-threat-to-business/#4e1da33273b6.

[46] Ibid.

[47] "Supply Chain Disruptions: From the Warehouse to Wall Street," *Channels*, Vol. 10, No. 1 (2005), p. 2.

[48] Paul Marshall, "It's All in the Planning," *DC Velocity*, Vol. 3, No. 10 (October 2005), p. 28.

[49] Ibid., pp. 28–29.

Disaster Preparedness and Relief

Disasters on a local, national, regional, and global scale can not only adversely impact people, but are likely to affect commerce and trade as well. Disasters can be natural disasters such as tornadoes, hurricanes, tsunamis, earthquakes, and floods, or they can be other types of events such as flu pandemics, financial market collapses, and transportation accidents (e.g., ships sinking, oil spills, train derailments).

When natural disasters strike, there are a number of supply chain issues involved. First, there is disaster relief where SCM is used to get medical and food supplies to people and areas where the need is greatest. Second, there is the ability of organizations to be able to function normally even when the supply chain is disrupted. For example, the tsunami in December 2004 that struck many areas in Southern Asia, hurricanes Harvey and Irma that devastated Puerto Rico and other Caribbean islands in 2017, and hurricane Katrina that caused devastation in the Gulf Coast region of the U.S. in 2005 seriously disrupted supply routes, storage facilities, and communications systems. The normal needs of people, organizations, and governments do not cease when disasters strike. Those ongoing needs continue, and the supply chain must be able to continue to supply the needs of its customers even in these adverse circumstances.

Individual organizations, industry groups, and consortiums of many industries must be able to respond effectively to natural or man-made disasters. One effort, American Logistics Aid Network (ALAN), was established to provide post-disaster humanitarian aid. ALAN serves as a clearinghouse for logistics-related resources. As a result of ALAN, agencies such as the Red Cross will know exactly where to turn when an emergency occurs.[50]

In attempting to "conduct business as usual" after disasters occur, the supply chain must be agile enough to be able to carry out its responsibilities in spite of infrastructure limitations, labor shortages, and/or timing problems. To illustrate, prior to the major hurricane that struck the Gulf Coast of the U.S. in 2005, one major retailer had already implemented a contingency plan. Because there is advance warning of hurricanes, although the specific location where they may make landfall is uncertain, the retailer fully stocked shelves at its retail stores and made sure that its distribution centers had all products on hand. Thus, it was prepared for the huge demand that occurred immediately after the hurricane passed. While state and federal disaster relief agencies were criticized for their slowness in responding to the disaster, the retailer was praised for its efforts.[51]

Other events are less severe than hurricanes and tsunamis, but can have significant regional impacts. Power outages and blackouts often strike industrialized areas, especially during peak demand periods. When one power outage struck one Canadian province and eight states in the U.S. in 2003, the supply chain was able to respond quickly to the emergency. The power outage caused water processing plants to go offline, interrupting water supplies to consumers. When power was restored, there were questions regarding water purity. Within hours, bottled water supplies were lining retailers' shelves, attesting to the agility of the supply chain to respond to emergencies.[52]

When a disaster of worldwide proportions occurs, such as in the event of a flu pandemic, the potential deaths and illnesses of company employees could seriously cripple supply chain efforts. Much of what gets done in the supply chain is done manually—by people—and if they are ill or deceased, the work will not get done. Unlike other disasters such as hurricanes, floods, and earthquakes, a flu pandemic would be of extended duration. Historically,

[50] For information on ALAN, see the website http://www.ALANaid.org.
[51] Michael Matacunas, "Weatherproof Your Supply Chain with Information Transparency, Responsiveness," *Global Logistics & Supply Chain Strategies*, Vol. 10, No. 7 (July 2006), pp. 88–89.
[52] Perry A. Trunick, "The Power of Logistics," *Logistics Today*, Vol. 44, No. 9 (September 2003), pp. 7–9.

the number of persons impacted by influenza pandemics has been significant. In the 1918–1919 Spanish Flu outbreaks, global mortality was estimated as high as 100 million people. The 1957–1958 Asian Flu outbreaks resulted in the deaths of 1 million people. Some have estimated that the next flu outbreak could result in as many as 360 million deaths.[53]

In sum, developing and implementing humanitarian supply chains is difficult. Perhaps the most difficult task is developing relationships between firms and various disaster relief agencies and organizations. The difficulty is increased when time is of the essence when responding to national or international catastrophes.[54]

Business-Related Issues Impacting Supply Chains

A number of business-related issues impact SCM, the supply chain, and the organizations and individuals involved in SCM. Some of the more significant issues include customer service and satisfaction; human resources; organizational issues; Internet and electronic commerce; use of information systems; and financial aspects and metrics.

Customer Service and Satisfaction

In the first scholarly book published on customer service, the authors defined it as follows: "a customer oriented philosophy that integrates and manages all elements of the customer interface within a predetermined optimum cost-service mix."[55] That definition is pretty much the same today as it was four decades ago. Customer service acts as the binding and unifying force for all of the supply chain management activities.

Good Customer Service Supports Customer Satisfaction

Customer satisfaction, of which customer service is an integral part, occurs if the organization's overall supply chain and marketing efforts are successful. Each firm in the supply chain must be focused on the customer and engaged in developing goods and services that optimize the customer's and the firm's experience. Each component of the supply chain can affect whether a customer receives the right product, at the right place, in the right condition, for the right cost, at the right time. Thus, customer service involves successful implementation of the integrated supply chain management concept in order to provide the necessary level of customer satisfaction at the lowest possible total cost.

In the 1990s, the concept of "delighting the customer" emerged. While a good concept in theory, it was difficult to implement in practice. For the most part, many organizations were not satisfying customers' basic requirements let alone going beyond those requirements to delight them. Also, the technology was not yet developed and/or implemented to allow organizations to "delight" customers. Finally, customers were not as empowered as they are

---

[53] John R. Johnson, "Inoculating the Supply Chain," *DC Velocity*, Vol. 4, No. 4 (April 2006), pp. 30–36; also see Azrah Anparasan and Miguel Lejeune, "Analyzing the Response to Epidemics: Concept of Evidence-Based Haddon Matrix," *Journal of Humanitarian Logistics and Supply Chain Management*, Vol. 7, Issue 3 (2017), pp. 266–83.

[54] For a discussion of the issues relating to developing humanitarian supply chain relationships, see Ron McLachlin and Paul D. Larsen, "Building Humanitarian Supply Chain Relationships: Lessons from Leading Practitioners," *Journal of Humanitarian Logistics and Supply Chain Management*, Vol. 1, No. 1 (2011), pp. 32–49; Peter Tatham and Luke Houghton, "The Wicked Problem of Humanitarian Logistics and Disaster Relief Aid," *Journal of Humanitarian Logistics and Supply Chain Management*, Vol. 1, No. 1 (2011), pp. 15–31; and Jose V. Gavidia, "A Model for Enterprise Resource Planning in Emergency Humanitarian Logistics," *Journal of Humanitarian Logistics and Supply Chain Management*, Vol. 7, Issue 3 (2017), pp. 246–65.

[55] Bernard J. La Londe and Paul H. Zinszer, *Customer Service: Meaning and Measurement* (Chicago: National Council of Physical Distribution Management, 1976), p. iv.

Exhibit: Even Formula One Race Cars Utilize Supply Chain Management

"Formula 1 is many things: an elaborate show, an engineering extravaganza and a logistical nightmare. There are 19 races held over eight months on six continents. The turnaround from one race to the next can be as short as one week. Each of the 11 teams will travel about 62,000 miles during the season, bringing with it two cars and roughly 50 tons of stuff. You name it and they're probably hauling it, from spare parts to the pots and pans used in the catering trailers. It's enough to fill six Boeing 747 jumbo jets, and it keeps an army of people on the road for as many as 200 days a year.

"Once the cars have been through the post-race inspection, team mechanics strip it to the last component. The engine and gearbox are removed, along with the front and rear wings, mirrors and suspension parts. Each is placed within its own foam-slotted box. The chassis is protected by its own custom-made cover, and placed within its own case.

"The cars may get the most care, but there are several dozen tons of equipment to be packed and shipped. Each team carries enough spare parts to rebuild their cars, 40 sets of tires, 2,500 liters of fuel, 200 liters of motor oil and 90 liters of coolant. And then there are the tools. And the computers. And enough food to make as many as 200 meals, plus all the stuff needed to prepare those meals. And . . . and . . . the list goes on."

Sources: The Formula One website, http://www.formula1.com/, accessed March 16, 2007; and Alex Davies, "This Is How You Ship an F1 Car across the Globe in 36 Hours," *Gear*, November 21, 2014, https://www.wired.com/2014/11/ship-f1-car-across-globe-36-hours.

today. They can now utilize social media and other Internet sources to obtain all sorts of information about firms and their products. Best-in-class firms are more than twice as likely to provide their employees with real-time access to customer data in order to service those customers on 10 or more different channels where consumers shop and seek information.[56]

Service after the Sale

One aspect of customer service that was perceived by many firms as relatively unimportant—reverse logistics—has become a vital part of any program or strategy that attempts to provide an acceptable level of customer service. In addition to the movement of raw materials, in-process inventory, and finished goods, firms must be concerned with the many activities involved in product returns and related processes such as repair, remanufacturing, refurbishing, and repackaging. A firm's responsibility does not end when the product is delivered to the customer. Service after the sale can involve providing replacement parts when products break down or malfunction.[57] Automobile dealerships, for example, must have efficient service departments that offer complete servicing and auto repair. Adequate supplies of spare and replacement parts are vital to the service and repair activity, and companies are responsible for making sure those parts are available when and where customers need them.

In the industrial marketplace, where the product may be a piece of manufacturing equipment, downtime can be extremely costly to the customer if product failure results in a production line slowdown or shutdown. The firm supplying spare or replacement parts must be able to respond quickly and decisively. Adequate parts and service support are extremely important whenever post-sale support is necessary.

Buyers may return items to the seller due to product defects, overages, incorrect items received, trade-ins, or other reasons. Return goods handling has been likened to going the wrong way on a one-way street because the great majority of product shipments flow in one direction. Most supply chains and individual firms are ill-equipped to efficiently and effectively handle product movement in a reverse channel.

[56] Omer Minkara, "CEM Executive's Agenda 2017: A Data-Driven Approach to Delight Customers," *White Paper*, Aberdeen Group, February 2017, pp. 2 and 12.

[57] For a discussion of product returns and some examples of how companies have performed with respect to returns, see David Maloney, "Many Happier Returns?," *DC Velocity*, Vol. 14, No. 12 (December 2016), pp. 39–44.

Product Returns

In many industries in which customers return products for warranty repair, replacement, remanufacturing, or recycling, reverse logistics costs are high due to the manual handling that is often required when processing returned items. The cost of moving a product back through the system from the consumer to producer may be as much as nine times the cost of moving the same product from producer to consumer. Often the returned goods cannot be transported, stored, and/or handled as easily, resulting in higher costs.

Companies are also involved in removal and disposal of waste materials from the production, distribution, or packaging processes. If waste materials cannot be used to produce other products, they must be disposed of in some manner. Whatever the by-product, firms must effectively and efficiently handle, transport, and store it. If the by-products are reusable or recyclable, the supply chain will manage the transportation to remanufacturing or reprocessing locations. Often, these activities are outsourced by one or more of the firms in the supply chain to third parties.[58]

Reverse logistics promises to become even more important as customers demand more flexible and lenient return policies and as recycling and other environmental issues become more significant.

Finally, if the firm is involved in any kind of product stewardship program, there is a responsibility to provide after-sales support of products, often for an extended time period. This will require strategies and programs that are coordinated with other reverse logistics activities.

Human Resources

It has often been said that "people make the difference." Of course, this has to be the case whenever it is people who deliver customer satisfaction. Good people can overcome a lot of poor policies and procedures, by being conscientious in the conduct of their work, quality-oriented, and empathetic toward customers, and providing outstanding customer service to those individuals or firms purchasing the company's products.

From a managerial or leadership perspective, supply chain executives are boundary-spanners within and across companies. To effectively manage the supply chain and its myriad of activities and processes, new skills are required in order to achieve optimal integration, collaboration, and coordination. Five specific tasks will be important: (1) designing supply chains for strategic advantage, where innovation is vital to competitive advantage; (2) implementing collaborative relationships, which will replace command-and-control relationships; (3) forging partnerships; (4) managing information; and (5) measuring and managing prices and costs to make money.[59]

Of these five tasks, perhaps the most important is the ability to forge or develop partnerships or relationships with individuals and organizations within the supply chain. Elijah Ray, former president of the Council of Supply Chain Management Professionals and Executive VP Customer Solutions, Sunland Logistics Solutions, identified 10 strategies that could foster and facilitate collaboration in the supply chain:

1. Leaders must have a commitment to developing positive relationships and make it part of their corporate culture.
2. Relationship management should be part of the strategic planning process of the organization.

---

[58] James R. Stock, *Development and Implementation of Reverse Logistics Programs* (Oak Brook, IL: Council of Logistics Management, 1998), pp. 87–90; and Maloney, "Many Happier Returns?"
[59] "Up Front: An Executive Summary of Industry News," *Logistics Management & Distribution Report*, Vol. 37, No. 12 (December 1998), p. 5.

Exhibit: A New Human Resources Issue: The "Millennial" Generation

Certainly, the business environment changed when commerce entered the "new millennium." Increasing globalism, threats of terrorism, technological improvements in hardware and software, and many other aspects of society have become more significant to governments, industries, companies, and individuals alike. At the same time, the workforce has also undergone significant change, and one of the sectors undergoing the most change has been the MBA market.

"Millennials" are recent MBA graduates who are entering the marketplace with different expectations and skill sets than their predecessors. According to some university and corporate recruiters, these people have different expectations and attitudes about work. They have higher expectations with respect to working environment, social responsibility of their employers, structured business environments that identify expectations and rewards, and a balance or "work-life" issues. Well-defined policies and procedures are favored by Millennials, while situations involving ambiguity are to be avoided. In today's uncertain

world that revolves around global supply chains, such perceptions may clash with real-world business environments.

On the positive side, Millennials want work to be relevant, have impact, and provide diverse experiences. Certainly, positions in SCM fulfill those expectations. Additionally, they are more interested in having international experiences, again a plus considering that most supply chains are global in scope. Another positive is that Millennials are used to working in groups in a collaborative team-oriented atmosphere, certainly a characteristic of supply chain management.

In sum, to employers operating in a supply chain environment, Millennials offer a mixed bag of benefits and challenges, making the hiring and training aspects of human resource development even more important than ever before!

Source: Adapted from Ronald Alsop, "Schools, Recruiters Try to Define Traits of Future Students," *The Wall Street Journal Online,* February 14, 2006, p. B6.

3. Establish expectations of the relationship at the beginning.
4. Develop points of communication in the organization with outside individuals and supply chain partners.
5. Periodically review the relationship to assess progress against expectations.
6. Develop joint problem resolution mechanisms for the problems that will undoubtedly occur.
7. Develop an awareness and empathy for partners' strategic goals and objectives.
8. Closely monitor continuous improvement objectives for anticipated results and make adjustments when necessary.
9. Collaborate on the selection and use of technology.
10. Conduct periodic strategic planning sessions with supply chain participants to establish clear objectives.[60]

Investing sufficient resources into these 10 strategies can mean the difference between success and failure in SCM. Obviously one of the most essential resources is people. The importance of the people component of SCM cannot be overstated. For that reason, we will devote considerable discussion to the human resource component of SCM in a later chapter of this text. In the meantime, let's briefly discuss a related topic: organizational issues as they relate to the supply chain.

Organizational Issues

SCM is multifunctional, multiprocess, and multiorganizational. Thus, it requires special leadership and organization to effectively and efficiently manage the supply chain. Much of the success of leading-edge supply chains depends on the organization having a successful leader. All firms have leaders who are one of four types. The first is a boss that makes

[60] Elijah Ray, "Relationship Management: An Enabler of Supply Chain Effectiveness," *CLM Logistics Comment,* Vol. 38 (May/June 2004), p. 8.

decisions with little to no input. Another type is the boss who makes decisions after receiving significant input from others. A further type of leader utilizes a team who make decisions with restrictions and the boss's oversight. Finally, leaders who utilize fully empowered teams work together with their people to achieve a strategic vision.[61] Which type of leader is best? Very likely, good leaders will use all four leadership styles or approaches, depending on the specific issue(s) being addressed.

At the same time that SCM is becoming more complex, customers are increasing their demand for better service. One company was organized into various groups based on product brands. The company operated a total of 54 distribution centers and was unable to significantly improve its customer service. When the company reorganized itself into one operating company with one distribution network, a total of 7 facilities were utilized and customer service levels improved.[62]

Many Firms Have Reengineered Their Supply Chain Processes

An effective and efficient supply chain organization is a vital component of overall business strategy. The problems and challenges that organizations face do not lie primarily in the area of strategic decision making, but in systems, structure, mission, people, corporate culture, and reward structure.[63] In essence, each of these is an important strategic resource and a corporate asset. The ways they fit together and interact to create a synergistic system are critical. Thus, many organizations have reengineered their processes, companies, and supply chains, essentially "re-creating" them.[64]

This effort involves the selection of the organization structure and then the design of the support, planning, and control systems that deliver the supply chain strategy via the organizational structure and its people. The challenge of developing the "right" supply chain organization can be likened to the challenge facing the military leader who has prepared a superb campaign strategy and must now create, train, and deploy the army that will execute that strategy. Without the correct assembly of different battle units and their support services, the campaign cannot proceed, let alone achieve victory.

Technology

Technological Developments

Technology has had an impact on all facets of business, but in the supply chain area the impact has truly been significant. Technology developments have resulted in supply chain innovation in informational/analytical and physical areas. In the informational/analytical area, examples include the Internet of Things (IoT),[65] big data,[66] cognitive analytics,[67] cloud

---

[61] John Dyer, "Where Is Your Organization on the Leadership Spectrum?," *Industry Week*, November 21, 2017, http://www.industryweek.com/print/414256.

[62] Paul Nazum, "How Supply Chain Leaders Are Accommodating Customers' Rising Service Requirements," *ProLogis Supply Chain Review*, March 2005, Part 4, p. 6.

[63] See Tom Peters, *Tom Peters Live* (Boulder, CO: Career Track Publications, 1991); and "The CEO Guide to Customer Experience," *McKinsey Quarterly Executive Briefing*, August 2016, https://www.mckinsey.com/business-functions/operations/our-insights/the-ceo-guide-to -customer-experience.

[64] Two of the earliest books on the topic of reengineering are Michael Hammer and James Champy, *Reengineering the Corporation: A Manifesto for Business Revolution* (New York: Harper Business, 1993); and James Champy, *Reengineering Management: The Mandate for New Leadership* (New York: Harper Business, 1995).

[65] IoT was identified as the most important upcoming technology in a survey of companies; see Eric Johnson and Zach Cole, "Analyze This: Supply Chain Analytics Benchmark Study," *American Shipper*, November 2017, p. 3.

[66] Foster Finley, James Blaeser, and Art Djavairian, "Harnessing Big Data: Building and Maintaining Capabilities That Deliver Results," *Supply Chain Management Review*, Vol. 19, No. 5 (September/October 2015), pp. 24–31.

[67] While data analytics is applicable to all facets of supply chain management, an interesting example of its application in ocean shipping can be found in Joshua Brogan, "Analytics: The Next Wave," *CSCMP's Supply Chain Quarterly*, Vol. 11 (Special Issue/2017), pp. 25–26.

storage, and supply chain digitization. In the physical area, examples include drones, wearable technology, driverless vehicles, robotics, and 3-D printing.[68]

In an omnichannel environment, many technologies are used to support initiatives that involve both physical and electronic supply chain channels. For example, in an annual study conducted by *DC Velocity* and ARC Advisory Group, technologies used by organizations to support omnichannel initiatives included warehouse management systems, demand management, total-landed-cost analytics, inventory optimization, transportation management systems, labor/workforce management systems, and many others.[69]

The Internet and electronic commerce have changed the way companies do business and the way firms relate to customers and suppliers. Computers, the Internet, and information and communication systems are being increasingly used in every SCM activity and process, including transportation, warehousing, order processing, materials management, manufacturing, and sourcing/procurement.

Traditional methods of managing the supply chain are proving inadequate in today's fast-paced economy, and executives have been forced to innovate. If firms do not respond appropriately, they may face loss of market share and create for themselves positions of competitive disadvantage. Fortunately, ample assistance is available from innovations and developments in technology.

There has been a proliferation of technological developments in areas that support logistics, including artificial intelligence (AI), blockchains, Electronic Data Interchange (EDI), bar code scanning, Internet of Things (IoT),[70] radio frequency identification (RFID), voice communication systems, local area networks (LANs), point-of-sale data, robotics, satellite data transmission, and SCM software, to name a few. As an illustration of the importance of IoT, a BI Global Intelligence survey estimated that by 2021, 22.5 billion devices would be connected to the IoT.[71] Many manufacturing and merchandising firms have employed new technologies to reap financial and customer service benefits.

An increasing amount of products are being sold to consumers and businesses via the Internet, presently $395 billion per year.[72] The significant growth in e-commerce makes supply chain efficiency and effectiveness paramount. Simply, organizations must develop optimal fulfillment infrastructures that maximize customer service and minimize costs. In such an environment, fast and accurate information systems are vital.

Many organizations extensively utilize e-commerce. The total value of transactions from U.S. consumers on Amazon.com reached $147.0 billion in 2016, which was a 31.3 percent increase compared to the previous year, according to Internet Retailer and ChannelAdvisor Corp. estimates.[73] Revenues for Internet-related businesses are expected to increase significantly during the next decade. As another, hybrid channel of distribution, organizations now often combine "brick-and-mortar" locations with Internet websites offering the same or similar products and services.

In the future, some envision a "physical Internet" that will move products in a similar manner to the way that the "digital" network moves information. To create this physical Internet, many obstacles will have to be overcome, such as product and shipping containers

---

[68] Paul Dittman, "New Supply Chain Technology Best Practices: The Application of New Technology in the Physical Supply Chain," *White Paper*, Global Supply Chain Institute, April 2017, p. 5.

[69] Ben Ames, "Multitasking DCs Deliver the Goods for Omnichannel Retailers." *CSCMP's Supply Chain Quarterly*, Vol. 10, No. 4 (2016), p. 21.

[70] For examples of how IoT can be applied in supply chain management, see James Haight and Hyoun Park, "IoT Analytics in Practice," *Analyst Insight*, Report No. A0173, September 2015 (10 pages).

[71] Merrill Douglas, "It's IoT Time," *Inbound Logistics*, Vol. 37, No. 4 (April 2017), p. 69.

[72] Stefany Zaroban, "US E-commerce Sales Grow 15.6% in 2016," *Internet Retailer*, February 17, 2017, https://www.digitalcommerce360.com/2017/02/17/us-e-commerce-sales-grow-156-2016/.

[73] Ibid.

not being standardized or modular, uncoordinated transportation equipment, inefficient use of warehousing facilities, and suboptimal delivery routing.[74]

Advances in information systems and technology have allowed organizations to better manage their supply chains and to expand their national and global market presence. In combination with an increased emphasis on customer service, growing recognition of the systems approach and total cost concept, and the realization that SCM could be used as a strategic competitive weapon, these organizations have developed fully integrated supply chains.

Communication is the vital link between members of the supply chain and between customers and the supply chain. Accurate and timely communication is the cornerstone of successful SCM. Communication systems may be as sophisticated as a computerized management information system (MIS) or as simple as word-of-mouth communication between individuals. Whatever the system, vital information must be available and communicated to individuals, firms, and customers who "need to know." Later in this text we will examine technology applications in customer service, order processing, transportation, warehousing, and other supply chain processes. Additionally, various applications of computer and hardware resources will be examined.

Financial Aspects and Metrics

"Traditionally, organizations have focused on differentiating themselves and improving operational efficiencies by owning their entire supply chain. Ownership, in fact, was the only way to achieve the seamless flow of information that would allow them to truly optimize operations. The global access provided by advances in information technology and the resulting transparency into a business's extended operations have facilitated a changing view of ownership. The Internet provides a seamless information flow at a relatively low cost. Companies no longer need to own their entire supply chain. Instead they can leverage the core competencies of their partners to create value."[75]

Intuitively, supply chains should provide higher levels of customer service at lower costs than traditional forms of distribution. Of course, the problem is measuring the combined outputs of many organizations contributing to the creation of goods and services for end customers. "Metrics can be used to evaluate how effectively the supply chain is meeting end-user requirements and each enterprise's contribution to overall performance."[76] Some organizations might have to increase their individual costs so that the entire supply chain is able to minimize costs. Calculating the financial costs and benefits associated with each supply chain member is enormously difficult. When strategies such as vendor-managed inventory, postponement, and global sourcing are factored in, such calculations are nearly impossible.

At the present time, few, if any, supply chains are able to calculate the individual financial contributions of all supply chain members. However, information and computer systems exist that theoretically can be used to assist organizations in making such calculations. To develop a successful supply chain metrics program, organizations must

- Ensure that the metrics include the key items needed to answer such questions as: "How is our supply chain performing?" and "Where do we need to improve performance?"
- Align key metrics to organizational and supply chain strategy.
- Include both financial and nonfinancial measures.
- Be process focused, not functionally focused.[77]

---

[74] Jeffrey Mervis, "The Information Highway Gets Physical," *Science*, Vol. 344, Issue 6188 (June 2014), pp. 1104–107.

[75] Roland Hartley-Urquhart, "Managing the Financial Supply Chain," *Supply Chain Management Review*, Vol. 10, No. 6 (September 2006), p. 19.

[76] Terrance L. Pohlen, "Supply Chain Metrics: Linking Performance with Shareholder Value," *CSCMP Explores*, Vol. 2 (Spring/Summer 2005), p. 1.

[77] Mike Ledyard, "Is Your Metrics Program Measuring Up?," *CLM Explores*, Vol. 1 (Spring/Summer 2004), p. 7.

A series of publications, *Supply Chain Management Process Standards,* 2nd edition, have been developed to assist organizations in developing metrics and standards for key supply chain processes. The *Standards* include six supply chain processes: Plan, Source, Make, Deliver, Return, and Enable.[78] The relationship to the SCOR Model discussed earlier in this chapter is apparent. The "Enable" item contains processes that support or enable the other five processes.

The *Standards* are meant to be general guidelines that organizations can use to develop standards for their own supply chain processes.

Summary

Supply Chain Competence cannot Be Easily Duplicated

Integrated supply chains can be a source of competitive advantage for firms just like a good product, promotion, logistics, and/or pricing strategy. However, an efficient and effective supply chain is extremely difficult to duplicate. Competitors can develop competing products in a short time. Many brands are losing their advantages over nonbranded items as more and more products become undifferentiated (generic).[79] Promotional efforts can be matched by others who have the same access to advertising agencies, mass media, and other promotional activities. Firms can provide on-time delivery consistently and be flexible in meeting customer needs. Because prices can be changed almost instantaneously, advantages arising from price reductions are very short-lived. On the other hand, however, supply chain competence cannot be duplicated easily or inexpensively by competitors in the short or medium term.

In an environment characterized by strong and sophisticated competitors, each trying to develop sustainable competitive advantage, many organizations have recognized that supply chain competency holds the key to developing and maintaining continued business success. Improving customer service through supply chain management, employee training and empowerment, computerized information systems, and other efforts can provide organizations with competitive advantage.

The power of SCM in achieving an organization's customer service goals and supporting customer satisfaction has received an increasing amount of attention.[80] Organizations that understand and utilize the potential of SCM as a competitive weapon include it as a key component of their marketing and overall business strategies.

Even though others might attempt to duplicate the efforts of the successful supply chain organization, those with the advantage will be engaged in programs of continuous improvement. While the difference between competitors may become smaller, the difference will be maintained between them as long as the leading firm is pursuing continuous improvement. In an increasingly sophisticated marketplace, customers will be able to recognize smaller differences between competitors.

Organizations that view SCM as an offensive marketing weapon, a strategy that can provide them with sustainable competitive advantage, are likely to make SCM an integral part of their organizational strategy and optimize customer satisfaction.

---

[78] Supply Chain Visions, *Supply Chain Management Process Standards,* 2nd ed. (Oak Brook, IL: CSCMP, 2009).

[79] For a discussion of how firms can protect their brands, see Gary Richards, "Protecting Brand Reputation," *Reverse Logistics Magazine,* Vol. 6, No. 2 (January 2011), pp. 36–37.

[80] See Ryan Brown, "Customer Satisfaction Begins and Ends with Your Supply Chain," *Material Handling & Logistics,* December 7, 2016, http://www.mhlnews.com/global-supply-chain/customer -satisfaction-begins-and-ends-your-supply-chain; and Jim Laverty, "Why Your Supply Chain Plays the Largest Role in Customer Satisfaction," *Blog, IRMS360,* August 6, 2014, https://www.irms360.com /blog_post/why_your_supply_chain_plays_largest_role_customer_satisfaction.

Suggested Readings

Ames, Ben, "Study: Reverse Logistics Still a Puzzle for Omnichannel Retailers," *DC Velocity*, Vol. 15, No. 11 (November 2017), pp. 32–35.

Braun, Gregory, "How Technology Is Reshaping the Modern Supply Chain," *White Paper*, C3 Solutions (undated), https://www.automation.com/pdf_articles/c3s/How-Technology-is-Reshaping-the-Modern-Supply-Chain-White-Paper_(1).pdf .

Cecere, Lora, Heather Hart, Regina Denman, and Samuel Borthwick, "2017 Supply Chains to Admire: A Seven-Year View of Progress on Supply Chain Excellence," *White Paper*, Supply Chain Insights, June 13, 2017.

Chopra, Sunil, and Manmohan S. Sodhi, "Reducing the Risk of Supply Chain Disruptions," *MIT Sloan Management Review*, Vol. 55, No. 3 (Spring 2014), pp. 73–80.

"Collaborative Outsourcing: Preparing for a Successful Logistics Outsource," *White Paper*, C. H. Robinson Worldwide, Inc., 2012, http://www.chrobinson.com.

"The Digital Global Supply Chain—Digitization Enables Real Transformation," *eBook*, Amber Road, 2017, http://www.amberroad.com.

Douglas, Merrill, "Staying Right Side Up When Your Supply Chain Turns Upside Down," *Inbound Logistics*, Vol. 37, No. 1 (January 2017), pp. 98–120.

"The Global Supply Chain," *Science*, Special Section, Vol. 344, Issue 6188 (June 2014), pp. 1100–27.

Kroll, Karen M., "Retail Logistics Bets on E-Commerce," *Inbound Logistics*, Vol. 37, No. 3 (March 2017), pp. 72–77.

Kushmaul, Chris, "8 Principles of Supply Chain Risk," *White Paper*, IDV Solutions 2015, http://idvsolutions.com/docs/8-principles-supply-chain-risk-white-paper.pdf.

Macharis, Cathy, Sandra Melo, Johan Woxenius, and Tom van Lier, eds., "The 4 A's of Sustainable Logistics," in *Sustainable Logistics (Transport and Sustainability, Volume 6)*, Emerald Group Publishing Limited, pp. xv–xxviii, December 4, 2014, http://dx.doi.org/10.1108/S2044-994120140000006018.

McCue, Dan, "Taking the Risk Out of Global Supply Chains," *World Trade 100*, Vol. 25, No. 3 (March 2012), pp. 30–35.

McLachlin, Ron, and Paul D. Larsen, "Building Humanitarian Supply Chain Relationships: Lessons from Leading Practitioners," *Journal of Humanitarian Logistics and Supply Chain Management*, Vol. 1, No. 1 (2011), pp. 32–49.

Min, Hokey, and Ilsuk Kim, "Green Supply Chain Research: Past, Present, and Future," *Logistics Research*, Vol. 4, Nos. 1–2 (March 2012), pp. 39–47.

Mortkowitz, Siegfried, Priyanka Asera, and Paddy Le Count, "Winning Omnichannel Supply Chain in Retail," *White Paper*, EFT, 2017, http://img03.en25.com/Web/FCBusinessIntelligenceLtd/%7Bf3d4dce0-a7a0-4e58-b2d8-46831479f8c8%7D_4383_D3_2017_PostConfSummary_Whitepaper.pdf.

Moser, Philipp, Olov Isaksson, and Ralf W. Seifert, "How Process Industries Can Improve Supply Chain Performance," *CSCMP's Supply Chain Quarterly*, Vol. 11, No. 3 (2017), pp. 46–52.

Newman, William, "Tips for Managing Sustainable Supply Chains," *White Paper*, TechTarget (undated).

Pascual, Al, Kyle Marchini, and Ginger Schmeltzer, "2017 Financial Impact of Fraud Study: Exploring the Impact of Fraud in a Digital World," *White Paper*, Javelin Strategy & Research and Vesta Corporation, September 2017.

Rangel, Dan, "Third Army: A World Class Logistics Company Supporting the US Army," *Reverse Logistics Magazine*, Vol. 2, No. 2 (January 2011), pp. 18–24.

"Retailers Leverage Brick-and-Mortar in an Amazon World," *Supply and Demand Chain Executive*, Vol. 19, Issue 5 (December 2018), pp. 8–14.

"Road to Growth: The Case for Investing in America's Transportation Infrastructure," *White Paper*, Business Roundtable, September 2015, https://businessroundtable.org/sites/default/files/2015.09.16%20Infrastructure%20Report%20-%20Final.pdf.

Solomon, Mark B., "Logistics Technology: Where Is It Headed?," *DC Velocity*, Vol. 14, No. 12 (December 2016), pp. 34–36.

Stangis, Dave, and Katherine Valvoda Smith, *The Executive's Guide to 21st Century Corporate Citizenship: How Your Company Can Win the Battle for Reputation and Impact* (UK: Emerald Publishing, 2017).

Stock, James R., "Supply Chain Management: A Look Back, a Look Ahead," *CSCMP's Supply Chain Quarterly*, Vol. 7, No. 2 (2013), pp. 22–26.

Trunick, Perry A., "Mitigating Supply Chain Risk," *Inbound Logistics*, Vol. 31, No. 12 (December 2011), pp. 59–63.

Questions and Problems

LO 1-1   1. How do supply chain productivity improvements affect the economy as a whole, as well as the position of individual consumers?

LO 1-2   2. Is supply chain management (SCM) the same as integrated logistics management? Indicate how they are similar and which one is more encompassing.

LO 1-3   3. Identify the major components of the Supply Chain Council SCOR Model. Briefly describe each of the six SCOR processes.

LO 1-4   4. Energy, environmental, and safety issues have become increasingly important in supply chain management. Briefly discuss why this is true and how these issues impact SCM.

LO 1-4   5. Supply chains have become more efficient and effective because of improvements in technology and management practices. In spite of these improvements, potential disruptions in the supply chain can cause severe problems for both companies and customers. Why is that the case?

LO 1-5   6. It has often been stated that good customer service supports customer satisfaction? Why is this statement true?

Chapter 2

Customer Service and Satisfaction

Objectives of This Chapter

LO 2-1   To define customer service and customer satisfaction.

LO 2-2   To examine customer service and customer satisfaction from a marketing perspective.

LO 2-3   To illustrate examples of various customer satisfaction metrics and performance measures.

LO 2-4   To define and illustrate collaborative planning, forecasting, and replenishment (CPFR).

LO 2-5   To show how to develop optimal customer service strategies utilizing a customer-product action matrix.

LO 2-6   To develop an awareness of customer relationship management (CRM) and its importance to an organization.

Introduction

Perhaps one of the most important yet misunderstood questions associated with business is "what really is customer satisfaction?" Is "customer service" the same thing as "customer satisfaction," or is the service dimension only one element of satisfaction? The terms are sometimes used interchangeably. There is agreement, however, that satisfied customers are good for business. For example, it has been demonstrated that companies with higher customer satisfaction ratings outperform the stock market as a whole.[1] Companies that have more satisfied customers typically have customers who are more loyal. A study of consumer buyers found that 45 percent of customers identified customer service as the biggest influence on remaining loyal to a company, and customer service is an important element of

[1] Colin Shaw, "Customer Satisfaction Leads to Higher Stock Prices: New Evidence," *Beyond Philosophy Blog*, July 20, 2012, https://beyondphilosophy.com/customer-satisfaction-leads-higher -stock-prices-new-evidence; and Claes Fornell, Sunil Mithas, Forest V. Morgeson III, and M. S. Krishnan, "Customer Satisfaction and Stock Prices: High Returns, Low Risk," *Journal of Marketing*, Vol. 70, No. 1 (2006), pp. 3–14.

Exhibit: What Does Customer Satisfaction Look Like?

The "marketing concept" comprises customer satisfaction, integrated programs and strategies, and long-term profitability. The marketing mix or 4 Ps—product, price, promotion, place—combine to create customer satisfaction. While the concept is decades old, many firms still are not able to fully satisfy their customers, while some firms seem to do a superb job in this regard. Amazon and L.L. Bean are two examples of companies that do a great job in providing customer satisfaction.

"Amazon.com is consistently ranked at or near the top of lists of companies with superior customer service which in turn, leads to higher customer satisfaction. One survey conducted by Prosper Insights and Analytics, reported on by *Forbes*, found Amazon was cited for its low prices, reliable and low-threshold free shipping, and quick-response customer service team. Responding customers offered the following feedback:

- *Customer service always answers with a smile. Everything is laid out plain as day. Amazon Prime is awesome with free two day shipping. And they send you a label without question for refunds.*

- *Even though the site has millions of shoppers, they are fine tuned to each individual customer.*

- *I love Amazon.com because the shipping experience is always positive, and they have competitive prices, a massive product selection, great shipping times, and free shipping on most items I buy via Amazon Prime.*

"L.L. Bean, which was founded on the principle of '100 percent satisfaction,' also scored at the top of the Prosper survey. Customer feedback about that iconic brand's service included:

- *Amazing, customer-centric policies (like lifetime exchanges).*

- *GREAT return policy and very easy to deal with across all channels. Plus their policies are largely consistent across all channels.*

- *Their policy is that the customer is always right, and first. Their return and shipping policies are very customer friendly. Employees are knowledgeable and eager to help in any way they can, and they are empowered to do whatever needs to be done to make the customer happy."*

Source: Adapted from "The High Cost of Poor Customer Service," *White Paper*, Purolator International, 2017, p. 4.

customer satisfaction.[2] Conversely, not satisfying customers is bad! Poor service costs U.S. business $41 billion annually.[3] "Ninety-six percent of unsatisfied customers won't bother to complain about poor service. Instead, most will simply stop buying from your company and will tell 9–10 others about their experience."[4]

It would seem that with a general consensus that higher customer satisfaction is optimal and beneficial, more organizations would know how to achieve it. But that doesn't appear to be the case. When noted author and speaker Tom Peters published his very popular business books in the 1980s—*In Search of Excellence* and *A Passion for Excellence*—he highlighted several organizations that were able to provide high levels of customer satisfaction. One would have thought that by the new millennium most organizations would have optimal strategies to satisfy customers.[5] However, customers see service failures, and thus are not satisfied, every day. Notable examples include the incidence of late flights and lost luggage in the airline industry, product recalls of foreign-based products such as pet foods and children's toys, and both

[2] Kathleen Peterson, "Optimizing the Customer Experience," *Multichannel Merchant*, September 27, 2007, http://www.multichannelmerchant.com; also see Murali Chandrashekaran, Kristin Rotte, Stephen S. Tax, and Rajdeep Grewal, "Satisfaction Strength and Customer Loyalty," *Journal of Marketing Research*, Vol. 44, No. 1 (February 2007), pp. 153–63; and Mohammad Majid Mehmood Bagram and Shahzad Khan, "Attaining Customer Loyalty! The Role of Consumer Attitude and Consumer Behavior," *International Review of Management and Business Research*, Vol. 1, Issue 1 (December 2012), pp. 1–8.
[3] "The High Cost of Poor Customer Service," *White Paper*, Purolator International, 2017, p. 6.
[4] Ibid.
[5] Tom Peters and Robert H. Waterman Jr., *In Search of Excellence* (New York: Random House, 1982); and Tom Peters and Nancy Austin, *A Passion for Excellence* (New York: Random House, 1985).

public and private sector social service efforts that do not provide the service levels promised when the programs were initially funded (Social Security, Medicare, education systems).

UPS Provides On-Time Guarantee to Customers

At the same time, however, there are many customer satisfaction "success stories" that can be told. For example, in the highly competitive small-package delivery business, UPS, FedEx, DHL, and the USPS compete for the same customers, often based on the service levels they can provide. Providers of these services go to great lengths to develop people, systems, and facilities that optimize customer service and satisfaction. As a result, these providers are very competitive in both rates and service levels. One such company, FedEx, with its FedEx Express Services program, is so certain of its ability to provide optimal service and satisfaction to its customers that it provides an "on-time guarantee" to its U.S. customers. If a shipment does not arrive within 60 seconds of the time it was promised, the customer can have his or her shipping costs refunded.[6]

Fundamentals of Customer Service and Satisfaction

Because the customers are the core element of successful supply chain management, in this section we will examine several basic concepts of supply chain management that relate to optimizing customer service and satisfaction. We will begin by defining customer service and customer satisfaction; relate them to the marketing concept; examine service issues occurring before, during, and after sales are made to customers; and discuss the importance of consistent customer service and satisfaction. The section will conclude with an examination of customer service and satisfaction and the SCOR Model.

Definitions of Customer Service and Customer Satisfaction

A number of definitions of customer service and customer satisfaction have been proposed. As shown in Table 2.1, there are numerous definitions of both terms, and they all sound "right"! Do they have anything in common? Is there an underlying theme to all of these many definitions? Thankfully, the answer is yes!

Definition of Customer Service

The Council of Supply Chain Management Professionals (CSCMP) defines customer *service* as "activities between the buyer and seller that enhance or facilitate the sale or use of the seller's products or services."[7] More specifically, customer service has three

TABLE 2.1
Examples of Customer Service and Customer Satisfaction Definitions from the Web

CUSTOMER SERVICE
- Activities between the buyer and seller that enhance or facilitate the sale or use of the seller's products or services [http://www.cscmp.org].
- Customer service is the act of taking care of the customer's needs by providing and delivering professional, helpful, high-quality service and assistance before, during, and after the customer's requirements are met [https://study.com/academy/lesson/what-is -customer-service-definition-types-role-in-marketing.html].

CUSTOMER SATISFACTION
- Customer satisfaction measures how well the expectations of a customer concerning a product or service provided by your company have been met [https://study.com /academy/lesson/what-is-customer-satisfaction-definition-examples-quiz.html].
- The degree of satisfaction provided by the goods or services of a company as measured by the number of repeat customers [http://www.businessdictionary.com /definition/customer-satisfaction.html].
- Customer satisfaction indicates the fulfillment that customers derive from doing business with a firm. In other words, it's how happy the customers are with their transaction and overall experience with the company [https://www.myaccountingcourse.com /accounting-dictionary/customer-satisfaction].

[6] FedEx Express Services website, 2017, http://www.fedex.com/ms/services/moneyback.html.
[7] Council of Supply Chain Management Professionals, August 2013, http://www.cscmp.org.

components: pre-transaction (before the sale); transaction (during the sale); and post-transaction (after the sale). This is where various services, including the product, are provided to customers before, during, and after the sale. From a marketing perspective, these three components fit nicely with the notion of "marketing as exchange," which is a fundamental element of the marketing concept that includes customer satisfaction as the focus of marketing efforts. This perspective will be examined in greater detail in a later section of this chapter.

An important perspective for you to have on customer service and customer satisfaction is to see their "multidimensional" natures. Delivering optimal service and achieving satisfaction involve all members of the supply chain, not just the company doing business directly with the customer. It includes the broader notion that there are many firms in a supply chain cooperating and collaborating to provide many "benefits" to customers including such things as system capabilities for handling special requests, communication of important information electronically or personally to customers, and support for a product in the event of its recall, warranty repair/replacement, or end-of-life expiration (e.g., product dating).

In a practical sense, supply chain executives view customer *satisfaction* as being all of the following:[8]

- An *activity or process* (or series of activities or processes) that must be managed, such as product delivery; reverse logistics; order processing, sourcing, and procurement; complaint handling; and production scheduling.
- *Performance measures* such as market share percentage, percentage on-time delivery, supply chain expense ratios, customer service effectiveness measures, and net profit margin.
- A *corporate philosophy* that treats customer satisfaction as an integral part of the firm's total supply chain policies, procedures, and strategies.

Of necessity, a supply chain management philosophy must permeate the entire organization. It must be managed in such a way that the goals and objectives of multiple enterprises are achieved and the needs and wants of customers fulfilled. This requires a total awareness of the roles that each individual, department, function, and process have relative to customers, employees, and owners (shareholders or patrons).

Customer Satisfaction and the Marketing Concept

"The customer is the boss!" This relatively simplistic statement highlights the overall importance of customers to individual firms and multiple firms in the supply chain. During the early 1950s, a number of large and successful companies, including Procter & Gamble (P&G), General Electric (GE), International Business Machines (IBM), and Whirlpool Corp., adopted and implemented what has become known as the marketing concept. This fundamental concept as it relates to supply chain management was relatively straightforward and comprised three basic components. A key component of marketing strategy, and, thus, supply chain management, is being able to successfully implement the marketing concept. Simply stated, the marketing concept includes three elements, all of which relate to supply chain management.

Marketing Concept

1. *Customer satisfaction:* to satisfy the needs of customers, whether they be intermediate- or end-users; those who supply firms in the supply chain with raw materials, parts, and/or subassemblies; or society as a whole.

[8] The three-component structure is based on the categorization initially developed for customer service in Bernard J. La Londe and Paul H. Zinszer, *Customer Service: Meaning and Measurement* (Oak Brook, IL: National Council of Physical Distribution Management, 1976), pp. 156–59.

Exhibit: Poor Service Can Result in Lost Customers

AT&T is one of the largest Internet and cell phone providers in the United States and has millions of customers. But even large firms can get some things wrong.

Take, for example, a person who went to an AT&T store to buy the latest version of the Apple smartphone. After purchasing the phone, the customer left the store and tried to set it up for the family member who would be using the phone. For several reasons, the customer was unable to do so and decided to return the phone to the AT&T store where it had been purchased on the same day two hours earlier.

However, prior to going back to the store, the customer remembered that the salesperson in the store had said that the phone could not be returned for any reason. That had sounded odd at the time, but the customer and his family member did not think that they would be returning it because they had previously owned Apple phones and had been generally happy with them. They telephoned Apple and asked them about the AT&T policy of not accepting returns. Apple representatives indicated that there was a 14-day return window for their products, so AT&T should take the phone back.

Armed with that information, they returned to the AT&T store with the phone in hand. At that time, a different store salesperson said that yes, they could in fact return the phone because it was within the 14-day return window. However, that's when the not-very-pleasant surprise occurred. The salesperson indicated that there would be a $45 restocking fee for the returned phone. Not surprisingly, the customers felt that such a charge was not warranted, but it was indicated to them that the restocking fee was company policy and no exceptions could be made. When the customers complained, they were told to look at their sales receipt, where, on the back of the receipt, the restocking policy and fee were stated.

No salesperson in the AT&T store had verbally told them of the restocking fee, and there was no signage in the store revealing that policy. They argued that you could not see the policy and fee until you received the receipt, which was AFTER the item was purchased—thus condemning any customers to pay the restocking fee even if they read the receipt immediately after purchase and might wish to cancel it. What a conundrum!

After failing to convince the store salesperson with that logic, they reluctantly paid the restocking fee to return the phone.

Lessons to be learned: In a supply chain, no matter the quality or reputation of the product and/or its manufacturer, customers will always hold accountable the organization with which they have directly done business. The products and services sold by those organizations also will be held accountable. While AT&T received the $45 restocking fee, the customers subsequently purchased a Samsung phone and canceled their existing service contract with AT&T, which had been their service provider for more than 20 years. When you think of the lifetime value of a customer, AT&T gained $45 but lost all income associated with the $150 per month that the consumers would have paid for future AT&T services. Doesn't seem like a good option for AT&T, but that's what happens when you don't place customers first. Interestingly, the consumers purchased their Samsung smartphone at Costco, a warehouse club, where there was no restocking fee for any product returned at any time, and switched their service provider to Verizon, which would now be getting the customer's $150 per month service fees.

Source: Personal example from the experiences of one of the co-authors of this textbook in December 2017.

2. *Integrated effort:* to coordinate and integrate the supply chain's efforts with other activities or processes (finance/accounting, manufacturing, marketing, IT/MIS, sourcing and procurement); to coordinate the supply chain's activities with suppliers and vendors; to develop synergies between activities and processes; and to integrate each of the components of the supply chain through collaboration and cooperation.

3. *Long-term profitability:* to achieve an optimal level of profitability in the long run; this may not maximize short-term profits but will enhance the supply chain's ability to maintain an adequate level of profits (given supply chain management objectives) now and in the future.

Customer satisfaction applies not only to final customers, those firms or individuals that consume the goods and services produced by firms in the supply chain, but also to suppliers and intermediate customers as well. For example, maintaining good supplier relationships is important in that delays, difficulties, and other supplier problems can have adverse repercussions on other activities or processes such as accounting, finance, human resources, logistics, marketing, procurement, and production.

Customer satisfaction must be long term. Successful supply chain management requires that many firms do a large number of things right, consistently, and over time. It takes coordination and collaboration among and between supply chain members to meet the present and future needs.

The appropriate level of customer satisfaction ultimately decided upon by members of the supply chain will be influenced by a variety of factors, including customer needs, the competition, the costs of providing that level of customer satisfaction, government regulation, and many other factors.

Integrated effort requires that the many firms operating in the supply chain treat supply chain management from a systems perspective. In other words, each activity or process of the supply chain must be viewed as being interrelated. Therefore, supply chain activities and processes must be coordinated in order to achieve synergistic results, that is, a total that is greater than the sum of its individual components. Successfully integrating these activities and processes from a financial perspective means that the firm must identify relevant costs and cost–service trade-offs within and between firms in the supply chain. Then, budgets must be developed that minimize costs and optimize customer satisfaction and supply chain profitability.

Within individual firms in the supply chain, integration must also occur between the major areas of the company such as logistics, marketing, production, and accounting/finance. Both within and between these major areas, synergies can occur as a result of integrated effort. The most successful firms are those that perform each of these activities and processes well, make certain that duplication of effort does not occur because of overlapping activities and/or responsibilities, and seek to optimize the whole rather than individual components (the systems approach).

Exhibit: The Dilemma of Harry Potter: How Do You Get 12 Million Books to Appear on Bookstore Shelves Worldwide at the Same Time?

July 21, 2007, was a magic time in the life of Harry Potter. It was on that date that 12 million copies of J. K. Rowling's *Harry Potter and the Deathly Hallows* were made available in bookstores in 30 countries around the globe. It was the largest single book distribution ever made! To be successful, it took one of the most orchestrated and coordinated supply chain efforts in the history of the book publishing industry.

The publisher, Scholastic Inc., utilized truckload (TL) and less-than-truckload (LTL) motor carriers, railroads, and air freight carriers to distribute the books to retailers. In one instance, horses and wagons were used to serve "car-free" Mackinac Island in Michigan, USA. The transportation carriers developed distribution plans in conjunction with the publisher. When books became available at the binderies, carriers moved them to distribution centers under tight security. Transport vehicles were monitored using satellite tracking systems, and when shipments arrived at intermediate staging points, transport personnel were used to provide security 24 hours a day until the books were to be delivered to bookstores. "For the

tightly controlled release, all of the books were packaged, wrapped, and labeled with security in mind. Labels, for example, did not identify the book, and opaque black shrink-wrap on skids and pallets obscured the contents and made any tampering quickly evident" (Bradley, p. 38). Interestingly, even the drivers of the vehicles were not told specifically what they were transporting.

For the international shipments, Scholastic Inc. utilized a single freight forwarder for all books being distributed to 29 non-U.S. countries. Strict security was also in place for the 17 airlines and all-cargo air carriers that transported the books. In a very unusual strategy, all delivery personnel were instructed not to make any deliveries early, thus ensuring that the books would not be available until midnight on the scheduled release date. Truly, the magic of the supply chain was at work!

Source: Peter Bradley, "Harry Potter and the Magic of Distribution," *DC Velocity*, Vol. 5, No. 9 (September 2007), pp. 34–40; and Dean Foust, "Harry Potter and the Logistical Nightmare," *BusinessWeek*, Issue 4045 (August 6, 2007), p. 9.

It should be noted that not all organizations will integrate and coordinate their supply chain in the same way. Service firms, manufacturers, governments, and global companies face different issues, constraints, market needs, goals, and objectives. While many organizations are implementing supply chain management in their daily operations, most will do so differently. Some of these differences will be highlighted throughout this textbook.

The final component of the marketing concept, *long-term profitability*, simply means that the ultimate objective of the supply chain is to earn a profit. However, it must be recognized that long-term profitability is more important than maximizing short-term profits. Also recognized is the fact that supply chain costs should not always be minimized. Rather, total costs should be minimized only at that point where an acceptable level of customer satisfaction is being provided.

Elements of Customer Service Based on the Concept of Marketing Exchanges: Before, During, and After the Sale

In a supply chain, manufacturers buy from suppliers, retailers purchase from wholesalers and distributors, and consumers buy products from retailers. People and organizations primarily exchange money for products and services throughout the supply chain, although sometimes barter and trade occur. Some type of exchange or transaction takes place between supply chain members and final customers.

As introduced earlier in the chapter, pre-transaction, transaction, and post-transaction components of the exchange process involve various elements of customer service.[9] When supply chains optimize service levels within these various components, customer satisfaction will typically be optimized as well.

Pre-transaction Elements of Customer Service

Pre-transaction Elements of Customer Service

As shown in Figure 2.1, there are many facets of customer service that need to be provided prior to any transaction taking place. In essence, customer service issues must be addressed prior to any sale being made. For example, if an organization does not have a written customer service statement, it is difficult for employees to know the service mission of the firm and how they, as employees, fit into that mission. Written statements are typically much better than verbal messages because written material is less likely to be misinterpreted or misunderstood. Management must identify those elements of service that are paramount to optimizing customer satisfaction and include those elements into a written document provided to all employees of the organization. Additionally, customers should also receive a copy of the written service statement so that they are aware of what the organization promises and can hold them accountable for carrying out their promises.

If the organization is selling a physical product, there are usually services that accompany it. For example, product installation, operating instructions, and whether the firm provides guarantees or warranties must be established prior to the sale occurring. From a marketing perspective, these services can provide selling benefits to the sales force or retail store carrying the product. Any element that must be prepared prior to the sale would be considered a pre-transaction element of customer service. Other examples include the firm having an organizational structure that allows it to provide various services, flexible systems that are responsive to customers, and the right information to answer any potential customer questions regarding the product or the transaction.

Transaction Elements of Customer Service

Transaction Elements of Customer Service

Transactions can occur directly, that is, between sellers and buyers in a "brick-and-mortar" environment, or they can occur virtually, as in Internet transactions. Irrespective of whether

[9] La Londe and Zinszer, *Customer Service*, pp. 272–82.

FIGURE 2.1
Elements of Customer Service

Source: Adapted from Bernard J. La Londe and Paul H. Zinszer, *Customer Service: Meaning and Measurement* (Chicago, IL: National Council of Physical Distribution Management, 1976), p. 281.

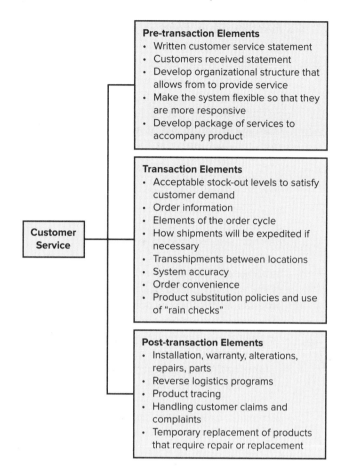

Pre-transaction Elements
- Written customer service statement
- Customers received statement
- Develop organizational structure that allows from to provide service
- Make the system flexible so that they are more responsive
- Develop package of services to accompany product

Transaction Elements
- Acceptable stock-out levels to satisfy customer demand
- Order information
- Elements of the order cycle
- How shipments will be expedited if necessary
- Transshipments between locations
- System accuracy
- Order convenience
- Product substitution policies and use of "rain checks"

Customer Service

Post-transaction Elements
- Installation, warranty, alterations, repairs, parts
- Reverse logistics programs
- Product tracing
- Handling customer claims and complaints
- Temporary replacement of products that require repair or replacement

the transaction occurs between individuals or entities face-to-face or electronically makes no difference. Customers must be satisfied!

During the actual sales transaction, several customer service elements are important. Organizations must determine the proper levels of inventory to stock in order to optimize product availability, while at the same time minimizing costs. The issue of inventory carrying costs will be examined in Chapter 4. Additionally, information about the customer's order, especially if the sale is electronic, must be available. Organizations spend significant amounts of time, money, and personnel developing Internet sites that provide real-time information about product availability, terms of sale, shipment options, and many other order-related pieces of information. When transactions occur electronically, especially over the Internet, there must be sufficient customer assistance to allow sales to be made; in essence, the electronic transaction must be as efficient and effective as a "person-to-person" transaction.

Figure 2.1 identifies some of the key elements of the transaction aspects of customer service. Some of the specific items listed will be examined in subsequent chapters of this text, such as order information and the order cycle (Chapter 3) and shipment options to customers (Chapter 5). Product substitution policies when products are out-of-stock (OOS) are an important part of the transaction. Also, if the seller has multiple locations and the item or items requested by the customer are available somewhere else, a "transshipment" might take place. Transshipments refer to moving products between locations, from where they are to where they should be. Obviously, this improves customer service but requires additional costs to the firm to get the items to the correct location.

Post-transaction Elements of Customer Service

Post-transaction Elements of Customer Service

Sometimes it seems, at least to customers, that once a transaction has been completed, the seller's job is done. Occasionally it seems that way when retailers, Internet sellers, or others tend to forget the customer once they have the buyer's money. However, a vital part of obtaining and maintaining customer satisfaction occurs after the sale has been made.

If the customer does not immediately take possession of the product at purchase, it is delivered to him or her at a later time using some form of transportation. In almost all cases, products arrive at the customer's location at the right time, but sometimes items do get lost or delayed in shipment. In those few instances, customers want to know where the product is in the system and some indication as to when it will arrive. The ability of firms to be able to trace products is an important after-sale service element. Even though only a few customers experience delayed or lost shipments, the ones that do want timely and accurate information about the status of their orders, and, if necessary, replacement products shipped to them expeditiously.

As shown in Figure 2.1, warranty programs are important post-transaction elements of customer service. Most products have some type of warranty, and for consumers the length of the warranty period can often determine if a sale is made at all. After purchase, some products malfunction or quit working entirely prior to the expiration of the warranty. In those instances, products must be returned to the seller or some other intermediary for processing for repair or replacement. The ability of a firm's reverse logistics system to process product returns in a timely and efficient fashion is important to satisfying the customer and optimizing the returns process from a cost and service perspective.

Perhaps one of the most important post-transaction elements of customer service relates to the handling of complaints. Customers want firms to exhibit empathy with them concerning the problem that has caused their complaint and be able to resolve that complaint in a single contact with the company. Many firms are well known for their ability to resolve complaints in the first contact, but too many organizations still take too long to resolve problems. Often, this inability to resolve complaints in the first contact results from having poorly trained customer service personnel or information systems that do not provide the necessary data for personnel to assist the customer. FedEx has a policy that it will respond to a customer's inquiry within 24 hours. Even if it has not solved the issue, it will get back to the customer and let him or her know that it is still working on it.

The Importance of Consistency

One of the most important concepts relating to supply chain management is the notion that customers require consistent service and quality. Intuitively and in practice, it is much easier to operate a business in an environment of certainty, rather than one of uncertainty. Plans and forecasts are more accurate when market conditions are more certain and less variable. In the delivery of customer service, certainty in the marketplace, certainty in being able to count on suppliers and vendors, certainty in knowing that products will be produced and delivered on time, and certainty in the fact that product quality standards will be met allow individual firms and supply chains to provide high-quality, consistent service levels to customers.

To illustrate, New Age Electronics, a subsidiary of SYNNEX Corporation, distributes and markets consumer electronics and gaming products and services to retailers, smaller independent stores, and online retail businesses in the United States. As a $1 billion in revenues fulfillment company to retailers such as Walmart, Best Buy, Conn's, and Brandsmart, the company must provide extremely reliable service to its customers. In fact, the company has stated that customer service is the whole reason for its existence.[10] Customers are

---

[10] See the company website, December 2017, https://www.synnexcorp.com/newageelectronics/.

"brick-and-mortar" stores and Internet businesses. Both types of businesses require products in stock when and where customers want them! As a result, New Age has developed information systems and supply chain partnerships and alliances that ensure on-time delivery of products to customers.

Irrespective of the speed at which the customer's order is processed and filled, if there is significant variability in when the customer actually receives the product, it is very difficult for it to plan accordingly. For example, if an organization places an order for a product that will be in the firm's advertisements for a weekend sale, if the product does not arrive on time, customers will experience a product stock-out. This is a "lose-lose" situation in that customers don't get the product they want and expect from the advertisement and the firm loses any revenues and profits from making the sale. Organizations can plan for consistency; it is much more difficult to plan when inconsistency exists. Firms need to know when products will be available, and consistency is, therefore, the most important customer service element!

Examples of consistency include having products available for customers to buy when and where they want them, delivering products on time and in the right quantities, providing information to customers that is accurate and timely over and over again, and essentially "doing what you say you will do" consistently, so that customers can "count on it"! The use of data analytics, which will be discussed later in this textbook, enables firms to more accurately identify and anticipate customer demand so that optimal supply chain strategies can be implemented.

Customer Service and Satisfaction and the SCOR Model of Supply Chain Management

In the previous chapter, the SCOR Model of supply chain management was introduced and discussed. In this chapter, some of the most important customer service and satisfaction dimensions of the SCOR Model are presented. Table 2.2 identifies some of relationships between customer service and satisfaction and the six components of the SCOR Model.

TABLE 2.2

Customer Service and Satisfaction and the SCOR Processes

Source: Based on the six components of the SCOR Model as presented in APICS Supply Chain Council, *Quick Reference Guide: Supply Chain Operations Reference (SCOR®) Model, Version 12.0* (2017).

PLAN—Demand/Supply Planning and Management
- Balance human and physical resources of the organization and supply chain with customer service requirements and establish/communicate customer satisfaction plans and strategies for the whole supply chain.
- Manage business rules, supply chain performance, data collection, inventory, capital assets, transportation, planning configuration, and regulatory requirements and compliance that have a direct influence on the delivery of various service components to customers.
- Align customer service and satisfaction strategies with the overall financial plan of the organization.

SOURCE—Sourcing Stocked, Make-to-Order, and Engineer-to-Order Product
- Schedule deliveries; receive, verify, and transfer product; and authorize supplier payments to optimize service levels.
- Identify and select supply sources that are capable of providing consistently high levels of customer service.
- Manage business rules, assess supplier performance, and maintain data on customer service and satisfaction attributes.
- Manage inventory, capital assets, incoming product, supplier network, import/export requirements, and supplier agreements that have a direct influence on the delivery of various service components to customers.

(Continued)

TABLE 2.2
(*Concluded*)

MAKE—Make-to-Stock, Make-to-Order, and Engineer-to-Order Production Execution
- Schedule production activities, issue product, produce and test, package, stage product, and release product to deliver so that customer service requirements are met.
- Manage rules, performance, data, in-process products (WIP), equipment and facilities, transportation, production network, and regulatory compliance for production that have a direct influence on the delivery of various service components to customers.

DELIVER—Order, Warehouse, Transportation, and Installation Management for Stocked, Make-to-Order, and Engineer-to-Order Product
- Carry out all order management steps from processing customer inquiries and quotes to routing shipments and selecting carriers.
- Optimize warehouse management from receiving and picking product to load and ship product.
- Receive and verify product at customer site and install, if necessary.
- Invoice customer accurately and in a timely fashion.
- Manage DELIVER business rules, performance, information, finished product inventories, capital assets, transportation, product life cycle, and import/export requirements that have a direct influence on the delivery of various service components to customers.

RETURN—Return of Raw Materials and Receipt of Returns of Finished Goods
- All Return Defective Product steps from source—identify product condition, disposition of product, request product return authorization, schedule product shipment, and return defective product—and deliver—authorized product return, schedule return receipts, receive product, and transfer effective product; this should be a transparent process, one that is understood by and visible to all customers.
- All Return Maintenance, Repair, and Overhaul product steps from source—identify product condition, disposition of product, request product return authorization, schedule product shipment, and return MRO product—and deliver—authorize product return, schedule return receipt, receive product, and transfer MRO product.
- All Return Excess Product steps from source—identify product condition, disposition of product, request product return authorization, schedule product shipment, and return excess product—and deliver—authorize product return, schedule return receipt, receive product, and transfer excess product; to be completed in a timely manner.
- Manage Return business rules, performance, data collection, return inventory, capital assets, transportation, network configuration, and regulatory requirements and compliance that have a direct influence on the delivery of various service components to customers.

ENABLE—Management of All Supply Chain Strategies and Tactics
- Manage supply chain business rules.
- Manage supply chain performance.
- Manage supply chain data and information.
- Manage supply chain human resources.
- Manage supply chain assets.
- Manage supply chain contracts.
- Manage supply chain network.
- Manage supply chain regulatory compliance.
- Manage supply chain risk.
- Manage supply chain procurement.
- Manage supply chain technology.

Every aspect of supply chain management has either a direct or indirect impact on the level of satisfaction experienced by customers. Whenever any enterprise in the supply chain "fails" in its respective tasks or activities, there is the potential of a customer service failure taking place. For example, if a supplier or vendor of raw materials, components, or parts fails to deliver those items on time to a manufacturer, it can delay the creation of the product, which in turn delays the shipment of that product to distributors, wholesalers, retailers, and, ultimately, the final customer. Thus, it is important to understand the implications that various aspects of supply chain management have on customer satisfaction. To aid in that understanding, metrics assist the supply chain executive.

Measures and Metrics

In a supply chain management environment, the old management adage "You can't manage what you don't measure!" is even more important.[11] When attempting to deliver acceptable levels of service to customers, companies and supply chains must have defined metrics in order to determine if service goals and objectives are being met. These metrics often relate to ROI, efficiency, effectiveness, costs, revenues, and competitive advantage. While an organization will capture literally thousands of pieces of information, there will be some items, referred to as key performance indicators (KPIs), that are essential to most effectively and efficiently manage the company–customer interface.

Key Performance Indicators (KPIs)

Firms measure scores of supply chain components, but there will always be a few that will be keys to the success or failure of the company. These are the key performance indicators, and generally there are less than 20 such measures utilized by an organization. Even within these fewer KPIs, there will be some measures that will be more important than others. While many attributes contribute to customer satisfaction, there is a smaller group of factors that are "deal breakers" when it comes to purchasing a product or service from a retailer, wholesaler, manufacturer, or supplier. Some of these attributes vary by company and industry, but there are several factors that are extremely important to customers irrespective of the product or service.

AMR Research, a firm acquired by Gartner, Inc., an information technology (IT) research and consultancy company, developed a pyramid hierarchy of KPIs.[12] A total of 17 KPIs were identified. At the top of the pyramid, and most important, were demand forecast accuracy (DFA), perfect order fulfillment, and supply chain management cost. These three factors are considered to be the major ways to assess the overall health of a firm's supply chain. In the middle of the pyramid are three additional KPIs, including total inventory, days payables outstanding, and days sales outstanding. These factors are related to the supply chain cash-to-cash cycle, the process that begins when a firm receives payment from customers and ultimately has to pay its suppliers. The third and lowest level of the pyramid includes the remainder of the 17 KPIs (e.g., supplier quality, raw material inventory, finished goods inventory, plant utilization)[13] and are not reported here inasmuch as these can vary depending on the particular industry, company, and customer base.

[11] For a discussion of this concept in the context of supply chain analytics, see Eric Johnson, "You Can't Manage What You Can't Measure," *White Paper*, GT Nexus, November 2016.
[12] "The Hierarchy of Metrics for Supply Chain Success," *Benchmarking Success*, May 25, 2017, https://benchmarkingsuccess.com/the-hierarchy-of-metrics-for-supply-chain-success/.
[13] Ibid.

The Perfect Order

The optimization of customer satisfaction through supply chain management has been referred to as the "perfect order." The definition of the perfect order is one that meets all of the following conditions:

- "At the right time (100% on-time delivery).
- In the right quantity (100% fill rate).
- In the right condition and packaging (100% quality related to fulfillment).
- With the right documentation (increasingly electronic)."[14]

Five Rights of Customers

The concept of the *perfect order* was first presented by business executive E. Grosvenor Plowman, who, when discussing the outputs of physical distribution of finished goods, identified the "five rights" of customers, which included supplying the *right product* at the *right place* at the *right time* in the *right condition* for the *right cost* to customers purchasing the product. In some ways, the rights of customers reflected the utility creation concept of economics, which includes form, time, place, and possession utilities. These utilities serve to satisfy the wants and/or needs of customers.[15] In developing a metric of the perfect order, organizations simply divide the number of perfect orders achieved by the total number of orders handled. The resulting percentage is the KPI for the perfect order. While 100% is the optimal performance level, most organizations achieve something less than that, with most reporting levels of 60 to 70%.[16]

For example, to calculate the perfect order percentage, each of the perfect order components is represented by percentages, which are then multiplied together to get the overall perfect order percentage. Unless each of the components is at 99% or higher, it would not be possible for the organization to achieve an overall 95% perfect order (e.g., 99% × 99% × 99% × 99% = 96%). In a study of member companies of APQC, it was found that top performers, in regards to achieving the perfect order, scored 95%, while median firms scored 90% and bottom performers were at 82%.[17] Achieving very high perfect order percentages is difficult, but if achieved can result in significant benefits to firms and their customers.

Also, as is the case with many supply chain metrics, there are many variations of the perfect order measure depending on the number and types of components included.[18] To illustrate, in the purchasing activity, five components are often included in the perfect order percentage calculation: order entry accuracy; warehouse pick accuracy; delivered on time; shipped without damage; and invoiced correctly.[19]

It becomes apparent that the more components included in the perfect order percentage calculation, the more difficult it becomes for an organization to achieve extremely high percentages. Hence, it is important that firms include only those components that are the most relevant to customers.

An important question with respect to the perfect order is: "How does a firm develop a strategy that will provide customers with a perfect order?" That is, "What are the key components in providing seamless, omnichannel customer service and satisfaction?"

---

[14] "Understanding the Perfect Order Metric," *Spend Matters Chief Procurement Officer*, August 5, 2015, http://spendmatters.com/cpo/undertanding-the-perfect-order-metric/.

[15] A discussion of economic utilities can be found in almost any textbook that examines the basic concepts or principles of marketing.

[16] Donald J. Bowersox, David J. Closs, and M. Bixby Cooper, *Supply Chain Logistics Management*, 4th ed. (New York: McGraw-Hill/Irwin, 2012), p. 382.

[17] "Metric of the Month: Perfect Order Performance," APQC, April 22, 2016, https://www.sdcexec.com/warehousing/article/12193325/metric-of-the-month-perfect-order-performance.

[18] See the website http://www.supplychainmetric.com/ for an overview of some common supply chain measurements used by organizations.

[19] See the website of Supply Chain Metric.com for an example of the perfect order metric, http://www.supplychainmetric.com/perfect.htm.

Three key components are required: *centralized order management*; *inventory visibility*; and *utilization of market intelligence to optimize order allocation.*[20]

In most instances, *centralized order management* reduces supply chain costs associated with the order cycle. The need for organizations to decentralize their operations in order to optimize customer service and satisfaction are no longer valid generalizations. With computer technology, both hardware and software, being so sophisticated (i.e., speed and accuracy), traditional methods of meeting customer needs have changed significantly. With IoT and an interconnected marketplace, data availability is almost instantaneous. Combined with the use of data analytics, companies can meet a variety of customer needs more easily.

Inventory visibility means that firms in a supply chain can know exactly where products are located, irrespective of where in the supply chain those products are being managed (stored, transported, or manufactured). Organizations within the supply chain must possess information systems that are transparent to all other firms, and, sometimes, even with the final customer. Individual firms in the supply chain must utilize a single, centralized order processing system and implement inventory management software that provides real-time and accurate information on the status of all stockkeeping units (SKUs).

Optimal order allocation can occur when firms in the supply chain use customer analytics to determine customer needs and requirements. Combined with criteria on which to evaluate customer orders for fulfillment purposes, the technology allows firms to set up and apply rules for fulfilling customer orders and therefore reduce overall supply chain costs and optimize customer service and satisfaction levels.[21]

Specific benefits arising from being able to implement perfect orders for customers include "increased inventory turns, reduced fulfillment costs, minimized labor costs, increased customer service productivity . . . and store associates and support centers that can better serve customers across all channels. Companies that achieve the perfect order deliver significant business value and ROI in the form of high customer satisfaction, better retention and more repeat purchases."[22]

Strategic Profit Model

As an overall measure of performance, the strategic profit model, developed by the DuPont Company,[23] demonstrates that return on net worth, that is, the return on shareholders' investment plus retained earnings, is a function of three factors management can control: net profit, asset turnover, and financial leverage. Figure 2.2 shows the strategic profit model and its major components.

Net profit margin is determined by dividing net profits by net sales, which yields a percentage. The number is calculated using data from the organization's income statement. It is an important, but not the only, performance measure that can be employed by firms.

Return on assets (ROA) is the organization's net profit divided by total assets, so it considers both income and balance statement considerations. Like net profit margin, return on assets is not the only measure that should be used by an organization because it exhibits significant variability across industries. However, it is useful in comparing how well firms are able to utilize their assets to effectively and efficiently compete in the marketplace.

[20] "Critical Components to Achieving the Perfect Order," *White Paper*, Oracle and NetSuite, 2017, pp. 1–9.
[21] For an interesting discussion of why some customers may be more important than others, see Robert J. Bowman, "Yes, Some Customers Are More Equal Than Others," *SupplyChainBrain*, December 4, 2017, http://www.supplychainbrain.com/think-tank/blogs/think-tank/blog/article/yes-some-customers-are-more-equal-than-others/.
[22] "Critical Components to Achieving the Perfect Order," p. 9.
[23] Treasurer's Department, *Executive Committee Control Charts* (Wilmington, DE: E. I. DuPont de Nemours and Company, 1959).

FIGURE 2.2
Strategic Profit
Model

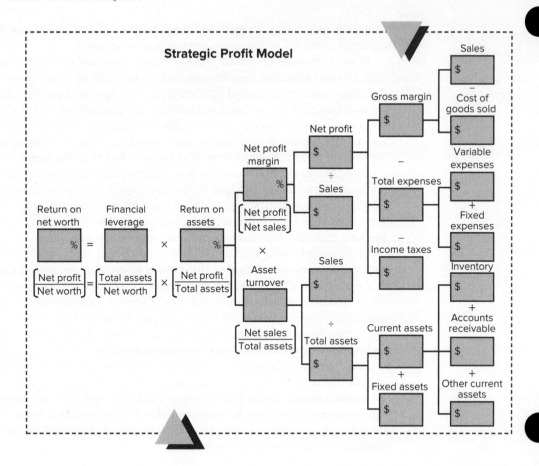

The variability across industries is often due to economic conditions (cost of capital, leasing options for physical assets) and an organization's ability and/or willingness to invest in physical assets.

Often, organizations will outsource various supply chain activities, thus shifting assets to various suppliers and vendors. This reduces assets, although it increases expenses—an illustration of a cost trade-off. A firm can improve its return on assets by increasing its profitability, such as through improved customer service, or by reducing its use of various assets (leasing rather than owning warehouses; eliminating a company-owned transportation fleet and contracting with an outside motor carrier for transport services).

Financial leverage is the organization's total assets divided by its net worth (what the owners have invested in the business). For a publicly held company, net worth would include common and preferred stock. Net worth or shareholders' equity equals the shareholders' investment in capital stock, plus retained earnings. It is a measure of how an organization employs outside financing. If an organization can borrow money at a lower rate of interest than what it can generate with the use of that money, it can be beneficial to utilize borrowed capital for expansion, improved information systems, customer service program improvements, and other supply chain initiatives. There is a caution to be noted, however. Too much borrowing can be a problem for an enterprise because it creates a liability that must be paid off over some period of time. Revenues from operations must be sufficient to pay principle and interest associated with such loans. Cash flow problems can result if revenues do not meet expectations, which can occur from the money not being used effectively, economic downturns, technological obsolescence of the firm's products, and many other reasons.

When the DuPont Company originally developed the strategic profit model, they identified an important financial truth. While an organization can be evaluated on many dimensions, the most important measure relates to the firm's performance relative to the return it is able to achieve on what its owners have invested in the organization. Financially, in a public company where shareholders own the organization, **return on net worth** (RONW) equals net profit divided by shareholders' equity.

To illustrate using a simple consumer example, suppose that a family purchases a new home for $200,000 and they borrow 90 percent of the purchase price, or $180,000. Their equity in the home is therefore $20,000. Assume also that the rate of interest for the home loan is 5%. If the family buys the home in an appreciating market (equivalent to a firm having increasing revenues), the market value of the home will increase. If the home increases in value by 10 percent during the first year (which would be equivalent to a modest sales increase for a business firm in a growing market), the new value of the home would be $220,000 [$200,000 + .10($200,000)]. If the family chose to sell their home after one year, the cost of simple interest for the one year would be $9,000 [.05($180,000)] based on the amount the family borrowed. The family would therefore net $11,000 after the sale of their home [$20,000 appreciation less $9,000 interest]. As a return on what they have invested in the house, the rate of return would be 55% [$11,000 ÷ $20,000] and not the 10% based on the total value of the home.

This is a simple illustration of how the use of borrowed capital can be beneficial to a family or a firm. Of course, there are costs to buy and sell a home that are not included in these computations, but the illustration is still valid. Variations in the computations can occur based on higher or lower rates of appreciation, different interest rates for borrowing money, or whether the buyer is able to secure a home loan with low or zero closing costs, but the fact still remains that the appreciation of the home is based not on just the owner's equity, but on the total value of the home.

Balanced Scorecard

One approach used by many companies is the Balanced Scorecard, which attempts to integrate performance measures and the firm's overall strategy.[24] The Balanced Scorecard framework was not designed specifically for the supply chain, but it most certainly can be applied to supply chain management. The approach includes consideration of both financial and nonfinancial issues. Specifically, the Balanced Scorecard framework consists of four components, only one of which is financial:

- *Financial performance*: Traditional measures such as ROI, profit margin, ROA, cost reduction, productivity levels, and asset utilization.
- *Internal business process*: Focuses on company metrics such as waste reduction, quality levels of products, order cycle time variability, and other time-based measures.
- *Customer service*: Measures that focus on customer requirements and satisfaction including number of customer contact points, order response time, customer satisfaction ratings, customer retention, new customer acquisition, and customer profitability.
- *Education and Learning*: Measures concerned with employees, systems, and procedures.[25]

---

[24] Robert S. Kaplan and David P. Norton, "The Balanced Scorecard—Measures That Drive Performance," *Harvard Business Review*, Vol. 70, No. 1 (1992), pp. 71–79.

[25] "The Balanced Scorecard Methodology for Supply Chain Performance Measurement," *Benchmarking Success*, September 16, 2015, https://www.benchmarkingsuccess.com/the-balanced-scorecard-methodology-for-supply-chain-performance-measurement/; also see Peter C. Brewer and Thomas W. Speh, "Using the Balanced Scorecard to Measure Supply Chain Performance," *Journal of Business Logistics*, Vol. 21, No. 1 (2000), p. 86.

Relating to the customer perspective component of the Balanced Scorecard, examples of metrics that could be used are satisfaction ratings from customer surveys, number and type of customer complaints received by the organization, overall market share or target market share achieved, product returns rate as a percentage of products sold, percentage of customers retained from one time period to the next, total number of new customers added since the last time period, consistency of the total order cycle time, percentage of damage-free shipments, percentage accuracy in filling orders, and many others.[26]

An example of a firm utilizing the Balanced Scorecard approach in supply chain management is Crane Army Ammunition Activity (CAAA), a munitions supplier to military warfighters. "CAAA uses the Logistics Modernization Program (LMP), an Enterprise Resource Planning (ERP) software program, to manage the Army's materiel, monitor and increase inventory accuracy, reduce cycle time of purchase orders, and improve overall business functions. . . . CAAA initiated a key initiative to establish effective performance-based metrics and created a balanced scorecard to measure supply chain efficiency."[27]

Developing Customer Satisfaction Strategies

Shaw Industries Optimizes Customer Satisfaction

One of the best ways of demonstrating the importance of developing optimal customer satisfaction is to show how various organizations have been able to deliver successful strategies to their customers. To illustrate, Shaw Industries, the world's largest carpet manufacturer, produces more than 600 million square yards of commercial and residential carpeting in more than 25,000 styles and colors.[28] In such a highly competitive industry and one that experiences cyclical ups and downs, it is important to provide optimal levels of service to its customers and to satisfy them to such an extent that they become repeat purchasers.

In an interview with the Manager of Logistical Systems and Forecasting at Shaw Industries, the executive stated that the company "wanted to become more demand driven by better linking the firm's demand process to its customers. The firm wanted customers to have more input into the firm's applications and process and be able to provide better and quicker feedback. This would enable Shaw to make sure customers did not get short-changed through back orders or that Shaw would not be carrying too much inventory." Shaw implemented systems improvements and hardware/software upgrades that resulted in reductions in obsolete inventory by 30 percent, improved margins by more than $1 million per year, and improved forecast accuracy of 19 percent. Customer satisfaction levels also improved, which led to increased business from key customers.[29]

NorthCape, an outdoor furniture manufacturer with more than 750 retail store customers, needed to have consistent and high levels of customer service combined with best-in-class manufacturing. To optimize all of the components necessary to achieve these goals, NorthCape partnered with LeSaint Logistics, a third-party provider. LeSaint has provided

---

[26] For examples of various customer-related satisfaction measures that could be used in a Balanced Scorecard framework, see Eric W. Noreen, Peter C. Brewer, and Ray H. Garrison, *Managerial Accounting for Managers* (Boston, MA: McGraw-Hill/Irwin, 2008), pp. 364–74.

[27] Casandra E. O'Neall and Scott S. Haraburda, "Balanced Scorecards for Supply Chain Management," *Defense Acquisition, Technology and Logistics*, Vol. 46, No. 4 (July–August 2017), p. 4.

[28] Jean V. Murphy, "Flooring, Carpet Maker Needed Better Feel for the Demand Stream," *Global Logistics & Supply Chain Strategies*, Vol. 11, No. 3 (March 2007), p. 10.

[29] Ibid., p. 12.

four services to NorthCape, including management of manufacturing and logistics, organizing inventory and assembly processes, establishing consistent measurements for all aspects of the operation, and placing a cap on fixed costs associated with company growth. What were the results?

- 50% reduction in backlog of past-due orders.
- 15% productivity improvement in outdoor cushion manufacturing.
- Improved customer service from tightly integrated manufacturing and distribution.
- Overhead eliminated by consolidating two small warehouses, while still expanding the business.[30]

Kone Corporation, a Finnish company that manufactures and installs elevators and other people-mover apparatus, has installed more than 1 million elevators worldwide. Those of you reading this example have likely been in one of Kone's elevators sometime in your life. The company is known for its quality systems and innovations that provide more value to people who make it easier for customers and the people who use Kone equipment.[31]

For example, high-rise buildings utilize elevators, and when an elevator has problems, it can be a monumental task to fix them. When you think of an elevator that moves people several hundred meters partially or completely up to the top of a multistory building, having it not working can be a significant inconvenience: Wait times for other elevators increase; cost to repair or replace elevator parts can be expensive; and the down time for the repair can be hours or days. A problem with elevators in high-rise buildings has always been that the elevator cables can get tangled and cease operating normally. Very tall buildings actually move or sway even though they are solidly constructed mostly of steel and concrete. That movement or swaying causes the cables to get tangled over time, and they then need to be replaced. However, when you think that the cable is not just one strand from the lowest level to the highest level, but actually multiple strands, the length of cable that must be replaced can be kilometers long! The time and cost to replace those cables are significant. What Kone has done through its research and development activities is to replace traditional steel cables with carbon fiber cables. While they cost more initially, they do not become tangled over time due to the movement or swaying of the buildings; therefore, they do not need repair or replacement. Customers utilizing Kone elevators experience less down time with the equipment, and people using the elevators are not inconvenienced by lengthy repairs.[32]

Benco Dental sells dental supplies and instruments to about 20,000 dentists. It is the largest independent dental supply company in the United States. As the firm's customer base grew, it found that it could not keep up with the documentation necessary to support each order. It was taking an average of more than 45 minutes to process each order, which made it very difficult for the firm to meet its standard of 96 percent fill rate in a timely fashion. Benco introduced a new software system that reduced the number of unique customer order documents from more than 100 to 32. The 45-minute processing time was reduced to 3 minutes, which resulted in a significant increase in customer satisfaction.[33]

---

[30] "Case Study: NorthCape," *LeSaint Logistics*, 2017, https://www.lesaint.com/blog/industries/durable -goods/3pl-increase-productivity/.

[31] "People Flow," *Kone's Magazine*, No. 16 (June 2016), http://www.kone.com/en/Images/magazine -kone-people-flow-issue-16_tcm17-26351.pdf.

[32] Interview with Kone Corporation executive in October 2017.

[33] Robert J. Bowman, "Growth Prompts Benco Dental to Scrap Old Document System," *Global Logistics & Supply Chain Strategies*, Vol. 11, No. 3 (March 2007), pp. 50–51.

Utilizing Marketing Research in Developing Customer Satisfaction Strategies and Programs

Customer Service and Supply Chain Competency

In an annual survey of supply chain executives across geographies and industries in North America, Europe, Asia, and Australia, conducted by PwC, a multinational firm providing quality in assurance, advisory, and tax services, the #1 key finding of its survey was "knowing what customers value is a real and persistent challenge for operations executives."[34] Factors of significance to customers often revolve around the following (customer satisfaction factors in *italics*): Product Reliability; *Fill Rate*; *Deliver Performance to Commit Date*; Product Design Quality; Product Conformance Quality; *Order Fulfillment Lead Time*; and *Perfect Order Fulfillment*.

Quality and service factors dominate SCM! Thus, it is vital that individual organizations and supply chains understand their customers and the service dimensions that are most important to them. Marketing research can be useful in providing this information.

In a research study of suppliers, CEOs, and CFOs of major companies, executives were asked why they had stopped doing business with some firms. Almost three-quarters of buyers had stopped doing business with vendors because of poor customer service. Interestingly, when the vendors were asked why they lost the business, four out of five indicated that it was because of price; that is, they believed that they were not the lowest-cost provider, and, thus, lost the business.[35] This example illustrates the disconnect that often exists in firms as they attempt to develop customer service and customer satisfaction strategies. Supply chain executives absolutely must have the right data so that the proper corporate actions can be taken if customers are not being satisfied and business is being lost. Even if customers are not reducing or eliminating their business with a company does not necessarily mean that customers are being satisfied. Only market research will provide the information that the company needs to make the right decisions!

Four Types of Data

When collecting data using marketing research techniques, it is vital to collect the best possible data available. The quality of the data directly impacts the quality of the results

---

Exhibit: Executives Talk about Customer Expectations

A TOYS "R" US EXECUTIVE STATED:
"The holiday season is our time to shine in the toy business because that's when customers' expectations of us are the highest. From September through the end of December, we roll up our sleeves and we're very hands-on and operational as we strive to ensure that customers can shop with us however, whenever, and where they want. In some ways, the volume during the holiday season makes the operational challenges very different for us than for other retailers.

"What we must deliver is a really smooth, integrated operation that allows us to compete on the dimensions our customers care about. Doing this requires planning and executing arm-in-arm across not only traditional operations functions, but also marketing and merchandising. And the need for coordination only increases with greater channel diversification."

A CITIBANK EXECUTIVE STATED:
"Citi touches clients nearly ten billion times a year. And when we acquire new clients, those clients are acquired through our Operations team. My instinct is that there's going to be a big pivot where operationally, we think about running our business by client journey and begin to organize ourselves against them. You can imagine that we may even align technology that way. So instead of having a technology infrastructure aligned to cards or the retail bank or the operational teams, we would have an organization aligned to how clients see the world."

Source: "Reimagining Operations," *PwC's 2015 Global Operations Survey*, October 2015, p. 5, http://operationssurvey.pwc.com /PwC-2015-Global-Operations-Survey.pdf.

---

[34] "Reimagining Operations," *PwC's 2015 Global Operations Survey*, October 2015, http://operationssurvey. pwc.com/PwC-2015-Global-Operations-Survey.pdf.
[35] Mitch MacDonald, "Exactly What Rock Have These Folks Been Under?," *CSCMP Supply Chain Comment*, Vol. 41 (July/August 2007), pp. 10–11.

and the ability of researchers to properly analyze and evaluate the data. Data that are collected can be of two basic types: metric and nonmetric. Nonmetric data includes nominal and ordinal data. Nominal data merely identifies something. Ordinal data identifies where an item would be in a ranking of attributes. For example, from a service or satisfaction perspective, knowing whether a customer was satisfied or dissatisfied with the firm's service levels would illustrate nominal data. Unfortunately, just knowing if customers are satisfied or not satisfied is not sufficient to help the supply chain executive make a decision to improve service. The nominal data merely identifies whether customers are satisfied or not.

Ordinal data ranks items from high to low and could be based on the perceived importance of an item. In the consumer sector, a basketball, football, or soccer poll that ranks colleges or universities would be an illustration. Knowing the rank order of an item is better than just having nominal data that merely identifies something into a strength or weakness. From a service perspective, the ranking could list customers who were most satisfied to those who were least satisfied. Again, the managerial value of such data is limited in terms of being able to respond with specific policies and/or programs to it.

Metric data is the best type of data that a firm can collect through marketing research and includes interval and ratio-scaled data. Interval data provides better information in that degrees or levels of an item can be identified. For example, asking customers how much they approve or disapprove of a new service policy would be an illustration. Typically, customers would be provided with a 5- to 7-point scale to use in responding with their degree of approval (a 5-point scale might consist of the following responses: strongly approve, moderately approve, neither approve nor disapprove, moderately disapprove, strongly disapprove). Using this type of data, organizations can get a sense of like-dislike, approval-disapproval, or agreement-disagreement, relating to some aspect of customer service or satisfaction.

Data collected in a ratio-scaled format is the best data of all. Many service elements can be measured using ratio-scaled data, for example, order cycle time and transit time (days, hours, minutes, and seconds), percentage of shipments arriving on time or those arriving late, and many others. Attributes such as time, monetary amounts, and individual or common occurrences as a percent of the total number of occurrences are illustrative. The major benefit of collecting metric rather than nonmetric data is that better data can always be grouped or categorized into lower forms of data, but the reverse is not true! Additionally, many of the more sophisticated data analysis techniques require that data be metric, and these methods of analysis cannot be used with nonmetric or "poorer" forms of data.

Whatever the form of data collected by the organization or supply chain, it is important that data be collected over time. Conditions and customers change, and it is vital that such changes are identified and responded to as necessary. Also, data must be current, so real-time collection of information is vital if firms or supply chains are going to be able to be agile and responsive to customers and environmental factors impacting the marketplace.

Product Stock-outs and Customer Service Implications

In an ideal world, products would always be available for customers. However, for both consumers buying at retail and business customers buying from various suppliers, vendors, and manufacturers, all too often (or at least so it seems) one or more products that are being purchased or ordered are not available at the specific time when they are being requested. When that occurs, we refer to it as a "product stock-out."

The causes of product stock-outs can be many things, such as unexpected production scheduling problems, delays in receiving shipments of products from international suppliers, unexpected increases in customer demand that depletes inventories faster than anticipated, product recalls for safety or health reasons, or products being damaged by transportation carriers, public warehouses, or other entities somewhere in the supply chain.

Impacts of Product Stock-outs

Whenever a customer experiences a product stock-out, there is a customer service failure. The results of that failure could result in customers doing nothing or, at the very worst, buying the product from someone else. A one-time stock-out typically does not result in significant customer response, unless the result of the stock-out is major or catastrophic (causes a plant shutdown, misses a very important new store opening, etc.). On the other hand, repeated stock-outs often result in firms losing customers. It is for that reason that consistently high levels of customer service must be maintained. In order to achieve that high level of consistency, many members of the supply chain must work cooperatively and collaboratively.

The lowering of customer service levels due to product stock-outs will typically impact revenues and profits negatively. For example, the likely sales loss from out-of-stocks for an average retail store is approximately 4 percent, which, in North America, translates into a cost of $130 billion.[36] Those out-of-stocks can result from several causes, including bad processes (poor training of employees, inadequate relationships with intermediaries or departments within the company), people problems (employee mistakes, insufficient number of people), data disconnect/systems (retailer does not measure the impact of stock-outs), supplier issues (late deliveries, wrong products shipped, vendor not able to fill orders), and theft (employee and customer theft).[37] However, actual consumer responses to stock-outs will vary internationally; thus, revenue and profit impacts will not be the same worldwide. Depending on the specific customer response to the product stock-out, the manufacturer will be the loser if another brand is selected, while the retailer will be the loser if the customer goes to a competitor's store to buy the item. Whatever the customer response, someone—either the manufacturer or the retailer—is a loser!

For example, with smartphones, approximately one-half of the stock-outs at retail stores occur because of poor ordering and replenishment/forecasting processes. And, as is the case for many specialty electronic items, customers who are not able to purchase the smartphone they want will buy it from a competitor. While customers may be brand loyal to Apple or Samsung, there are many stores that carry these brands. To minimize product stock-outs, many firms utilize collaborative planning, forecasting, and replenishment (CPFR) software.

Collaborative Planning, Forecasting, and Replenishment (CPFR)

CPFR was a process developed in 1997 by the Voluntary Interindustry Commerce Solutions Association (VICS) based on earlier efforts of Walmart and Warner Lambert. The process, implemented by hundreds of companies, is a "business practice that improves accuracy by combining the intelligence of multiple trading participants in the planning and fulfillment of customer demand."[38]

Table 2.3 identifies the major components and time frame for implementation of a CPFR process for a company like Motorola, a consumer electronics and telecommunications company. The process would be typical for most organizations. In most cases, implementation takes a significant period of time—many months—as it involves the integration of information systems and realignment of business strategies of many firms in the supply chain.

---

[36] Tom Ryan, "Retailers Suffer the High Cost of Overstocks and Out-of-Stocks," *Retail Wire*, May 15, 2015, http://www.retailwire.com/discussion/retailers-suffer-the-high-cost-of-overstocks-and-out-of-stocks/; also see Victoria Vessella, "How Stockouts Can Hurt Your Business (and How to Prevent Them)," *Repsly*, April 6, 2017, https://www.repsly.com/blog/consumer-goods/how-stockouts-can-hurt-your-business.

[37] Ryan, "Retailers Suffer the High Cost of Overstocks and Out-of-Stocks"; and Vessella, "How Stockouts Can Hurt Your Business."

[38] See the *SupplyChainDigest* website for an overview of the CPFR Model, http://www.scdigest.com/assets/reps/SCDigest_CPFR_Model.PDF; also see the *Global Language of Business* website, http://2016archive.gs1us.org/industries/apparel-general-merchandise/tools-and-resources/cpfr-resources.

TABLE 2.3
Components of CPFR (Motorola Example)

Source: Jerold P. Cederlund, Rajiv Kohli, Susan A. Sherer, and Yuliang Yao, "How Motorola Put CPFR into Action," *Supply Chain Management Review*, Vol. 11, No. 7 (October 2007), p. 30.

Components	Elements	Time Frame	Outcome
Collaboration	• Supplier develops a customer-focused organization • Build peer-to-peer relationships • Establish common goals and measures • Develop governance mechanisms with formal communication points	Long-term	Foundation for collaborative relationship
Planning	• Time-based decision making • Planning for events such as end of life, new product introduction, and promotions • Alignment of planning calendars • Focus on key execution items	Next five quarters	• Business goals and objectives • Major process changes • New product roadmaps • Broad promotion plans • Vision toward an end state
Forecasting	• Consider current run rates, more detailed promotions planning, competition among products, pricing to develop forecasts	Next 12 months with focus on immediate six-month horizon	• Material and capacity plans weekly for next 13 weeks and monthly for rest of year • Improved predictions of orders
Replenishment	• Measure execution performance • Record escalation and exception events • Monitor weekly run-rates and detailed promotional planning in very close detail • Plan in detail product ramp-up, end of life, and/or promotional inventory builds	Next 13 weeks with focus on the immediate four-week horizon	• Execution of the order forecast • More balanced inventory and sell through

As a result of Motorola's CPFR initiative, the company was able to reduce stock-out rates by two-thirds, reduce inventory by 30 percent, and improve customer evaluations of company performance on on-time delivery, ease of doing business, stock-outs, and order quality.[39] The initiative required 18 months and collaboration between Motorola and its major retail customers. Successful implementation requires "champions" or advocates from each participating organization maintaining their commitment for the process over the entire process adoption and implementation period.

In sum, because product stock-outs are a customer service failure, they should be kept to a minimum. Supply chain members must understand their customers and how they will respond to product stock-outs. By knowing how customers will behave when faced with a product being unavailable, firms can develop strategies that will minimize or eliminate

[39] Jerold P. Cederlund, Rajiv Kohli, Susan A. Sherer, and Yuliang Yao, "How Motorola Put CPFR into Action," *Supply Chain Management Review*, Vol. 11, No. 7 (October 2007), pp. 28–35.

stock-outs, or, alternatively, will shift customer purchases to other products that can satisfy the customer's desire for the item. As discussed earlier in this chapter, market research can be used to identify how customers respond to product stock-outs. Appropriate strategies can then be implemented to minimize stock-outs.

Cost–Service Trade-offs

An important aspect of providing customer service and satisfaction is to fully understand the cost issues related to providing acceptable levels of these items. Activity-based costing[40] and other financial accounting approaches can be useful in capturing the actual costs related to serving customers. By knowing the costs of serving customers, organizations can calculate customer profitability. Knowing customer profitability allows organizations to determine the appropriate levels of customer service to provide.

Typically, there is some trade-off between costs and service levels. Although there are exceptions, increasing service levels often results in increasing costs. Conversely, cost reductions often result in lower service levels. Computerization, information systems, implementation of better management, and other strategies can result in exceptions to this generalization.

Types of Cost–Service Trade-offs

Cost–service trade-offs can be of two types: within cost centers and between cost centers. If a trade-off only occurs within the transportation, warehousing, or inventory function, it is an example of a "within cost center trade-off." For example, a firm could substitute rail transportation for truck transportation. Rail rates are typically lower than truck rates, so the firm saves money. However, trains are slower and less consistent than trucks, so a service level decline would be expected using railroads rather than trucks. If we expand the concept to include multiple functions or processes at the same time, we would have an example of a "between cost center trade-off." If we take the same rail-truck illustration and add to it a consideration of inventory, we also get a between cost center trade-off. When a slower form of transportation is utilized, firms often have to have more inventory to cover customer demand over a longer period of time. This larger amount of inventory costs the firm money in terms of inventory carrying costs (a topic to be covered in a later chapter). The faster form of transportation may also allow the firm to utilize less warehousing because inventory levels will be lower. So, the decision to change from motor transport to rail impacts a number of supply chain activities.

Cost–Service Trade-off Analysis

The process of cost–service trade-off analysis is a fairly simple and straightforward analytical procedure for measuring variations in supply chain costs and customer service levels, on either a static or dynamic basis, for different supply chain configurations. The basic method involves three steps:

- Establishing distinct supply chain activity cost centers.
- Allocating costs to these centers.
- Analyzing cost and service variations from alternative volume projections and/or structural alternatives.

As already discussed in Chapter 1, the components of supply chain management are many and varied. Each one requires the expenditure of resources in order to implement its goals and objectives. It is important for an organization to know precisely, or at least as close as possible, the costs associated with these components and with implementing strategies associated with them. The most difficult part is making the process dynamic, that is, looking at various combinations of the elements and determining their impact on overall costs and customer service. The customer–product action matrix can be utilized to develop strategies in light of these trade-offs.

[40] Activity-based costing (ABC) differs from traditional cost accounting by tracing costs to products according to the activities performed on them.

Using a Customer–Product Action Matrix in Developing Service Strategies

"The customer/product action matrix is a tool that managers can use to better balance supply and demand constraints and identify opportunities. In that context, the matrix enables marketing and operations managers to develop tactical and strategic plans that incorporate both operations and marketing considerations to target enhanced customer service and prioritize product mix decisions."[41]

Prioritizing Customers and Products

Pareto's Law

The customer-product action matrix is based on the concept of profitability, although other ways of prioritizing customers and products are possible. Management must determine what factors should be used in prioritizing customers and products, recognizing that Pareto's Law applies. Pareto's Law, sometimes referred to as the "80/20 Rule," recognizes that relatively few customers or products contribute the most to sales and profits. Thus, organizations or supply chains should concentrate their efforts on satisfying fully the "few," without sacrificing the "many."

As shown in Table 2.4, customers and products can be prioritized or ordered into groups based on their profitability. Other factors could also be used, often in conjunction with profitability. For customers, factors such as sales revenues, future customer growth rate (or, alternatively, the potential for a customer to decline), needs of some customers to be offered a full or completed product line, ease in doing business with a customer, and customer loyalty might be relevant. For products, factors could include sales revenues, margins, stage of the product in the product life cycle, difficulty or ease in carrying out logistics activities, and potential for the product to become obsolete due to technology.

Implementing the Matrix

Once the priorities for customers and products have been determined, the next step is to develop and implement strategies focused on each customer-product group. Because some customers and products are more "valuable" than others, greater emphasis should be placed on them.

The organization with direct interface with the final customer, as well as those members of the supply chain that influence that interface, should determine the relevant service elements and standards that are important to customers. If the organization with direct

TABLE 2.4
Customer-Product Action Matrix

Source: Robert Sabath and Judith M. Whipple, "Integrating Marketing and Supply Chain Management to Improve Profitability," *CSCMP Explores*, Vol. 4 (Summer 2007), p. 8.

		Product Category			
		1	**2**	**3**	**4**
Customer Category	**A**	Perfection/ Never Miss	Regular/Priority Schedule	Reserve Capacity/ Inventory	Tough It Out/ Outsource
	B	As Promised	Regular Schedule	Schedule Capacity/ Inventory	Redirect/ Outsource
	C	If Available/If Scheduled	If Available	Only if Capacity or Inventory Is Available	Only if Transaction Is Profitable
	D	Respond to Transaction	If No Conflict	Only if Inventory Is Available/Cull Candidate	Cull

[41] Robert Sabath and Judith M. Whipple, "Integrating Marketing and Supply Chain Management to Improve Profitability," *CSCMP Explores*, Vol. 4 (Summer 2007), p. 3.

customer interface has conducted a comprehensive customer service audit that has identified those service factors that are important to customers, it can then develop strategies for achieving optimal customer satisfaction.

In Table 2.4, cells in the matrix that are in the upper left quadrant represent more important priorities. Cells in the lower right quadrant are of lower importance. Organizations should allocate resources to provide higher levels of consistent customer service to the higher priority cells. For example, customers that are the highest importance (Customer A) who order the products of the highest importance (Product 1) should receive the highest level of service: "perfection/never miss." These are usually key accounts purchasing some of the firm's "best" products. Walmart purchasing Pampers diapers would be an example of a key account ordering an important product from Procter & Gamble (P&G). Thus, P&G would attempt to implement policies and procedures that would optimize the service levels to Walmart.

No Customer–Product Combinations Receive Poor Service

Importance of Service Consistency

All customers require consistent service and organizations should strive to provide 100% consistency. However, delivering high levels of consistency over a shorter period of time requires more resources and costs more! Only the "best" customers should receive that level of service because of the higher costs associated with delivering it. Smaller, less important customers also deserve consistent service, but when delivered over a longer period of time, the costs to do so are lower. To illustrate, key accounts might consistently receive their orders within 24 hours, perhaps requiring the use of air freight or expedited motor carrier delivery. Less important customers might receive their orders in one week using standard trucking or rail service. In both instances, consistency could be 100%, but utilizing standard trucking or rail would cost considerably less.

In sum, all customers require and deserve consistent service. Customers can plan for consistency; it is more difficult to plan when faced with inconsistency. Longer order cycle times, so long as they are consistent, can be planned for! When order cycle times, whether short or long, are inconsistent, organizations have a much more difficult time planning and forecasts are typically more inaccurate.

Gap Analysis in Customer Satisfaction

In services marketing, practitioners often speak of service gaps. These gaps refer to the level of service or satisfaction achieved compared to the level of service or satisfaction required by customers. A positive gap means that the organization or supply chain delivers a higher level of service or satisfaction to the customer than he/she requires. A negative gap means that a lower level of service or satisfaction than is required is achieved.

A negative gap is the most troublesome to an organization or supply chain because it results in customer dissatisfaction. That is, when required service levels are not met, customers become dissatisfied. Over time, consistently underperforming relative to customer requirements (a negative gap) will often result in customers shifting business to competitors. "70% of customers facing an OOS situation for the first time in the store will decide to substitute the desired item with another similar one. The second time it happens in the same store, the probability is equal for the shopper to either substitute again, to not buy anything, or to go to another store. If this customer has to experience a third OOS in the same store, chances are 70% that they will go to another store and may not return for any more purchases in the future."[42]

---

[42] "The Out of Stock Problem and How to Approach It," *Streetspotr GmbH*, August 14, 2017, https://streetspotr.com/2017/08/14/out-of-stock/.

A positive gap will not result in customer dissatisfaction inasmuch as the organization or supply chain is exceeding customer requirements. However, overachieving in customer service or satisfaction usually costs more in terms of money, people, facilities, and equipment. As a result, the organization or supply chain is not being a good steward of its resources.

Supply Chain Customer Satisfaction Strategies—Some Examples

Developing the right strategies to optimize customer satisfaction, domestically or internationally, is not an easy task. It requires that employees in the various supply chain organizations have a customer focus. It requires having the right information, the correct software, and key performance indicators that identify to customers and firms whether customer-related goals and objectives are being met.

The Container Store, a firm that provides various types of storage solutions (racks, bins, boxes, shelving, etc.), builds a customer satisfaction culture in its business model. "First, it hires self-motivated, team-oriented people with a passion for customer service. Second, it provides 241 hours of formal training in the first year of employment, versus the industry average of 8 hours. Third, it employs a full-time sales trainer in each store and pays employees higher than industry average."[43] The result is less employee turnover, annual revenue growth rates above 20 percent, and being listed in *Fortune Magazine*'s 100 Best Companies to Work For.[44]

From an information perspective, data must be collected on a real-time basis; it must be accurate, timely, and relevant for decisions that must be made regarding customer satisfaction programs and strategies. Data standards are necessary so that uniform information is collected, thus aiding decision making.

In establishing data standards for easier and more accurate entry into IT systems, several issues should be examined:

- Investigate the data format and structure standards that pertain to your industry, and your customers' industries.
- Determine whether your customers are aware of existing standards, and if they are capable of using them.
- Recognize that customers in different industry sectors may require different data standards.
- Learn about the standards that pertain to your data-entry method.
- Educate IT personnel on the importance of conforming to existing standards.
- Insist that suppliers conform to these standards.
- Develop corporate policies to ensure compliance internally and among trading partners.
- Reevaluate your standards at regular intervals as new capabilities and technologies become available.[45]

Supply Chain Management Process Standards

One of the requirements prior to implementing customer satisfaction strategies is to determine the specific process standards that will be used to evaluate the strategies being pursued. The Council of Supply Chain Management Professionals (CSCMP) has published a series of *Supply Chain Management Process Standards*. Identified were suggested minimum process standards and typical best practices. Standards related to customer service and satisfaction are illustrated in Table 2.5.

---

43 Reported in Herb Kleinberger and Gina Paglucia Morrison, "Turning Shoppers into Advocates," *Executive Brief* (Somers, NY: IBM Global Services, 2006), p. 11. Original sources were "Top-Shelf Employees Keep Container Store on Track," *DSN Retailing*, March 8, 2004; and Kip Tindell, CEO, The Container Store at the VNU Fine Jewelry CEO Summit (February 21, 2006).
44 The Container Store ranked #49 on the 2017 *Fortune* list; see http://fortune.com/best-companies/the-container-store/.
45 Deborah Catalano Ruriani, "10 Tips: Step-by-Step Solutions," *Inbound Logistics*, Vol. 25, No. 12 (December 2005), p. 88.

TABLE 2.5

Selected Customer Satisfaction Process Performance Standards

Source: Adapted from Supply Chain Visions, *Supply Chain Management Process Standards: Manage Customer Service*, 2nd ed. (Lombard, IL: Council of Supply Chain Management Professionals, 2009), pp. 98–105.

	Suggested Minimum Process Standard	Typical Best Practice Process
Develop Customer Service Segmentation Prioritization (e.g., tiers)	• Favorable trading terms are primarily used to prevent customer defection. • Well-defined segments are targeted with varying service levels. • Customer segmentation is used to deliver a branded customer experience.	• Targeted service is based on individual customer preferences and requirements. • A process is in place to periodically (at least annually) review all service dimensions for all segments. • Information is used as a tool in negotiation to facilitate new ways of working together. • There is a formal segmentation strategy for customers, and to prioritize service resources and service levels for key (strategic) accounts. Customer service is organized to support this prioritization.
Define Customer Service Policies and Procedures	• First contact resolution is achieved for most requests. • Training is provided for customer-facing employees. • Customer self-service options include order inquiry, credit/financial inquiry, product inquiry, and account status. • The appropriate technology supports customer service processes.	• Multichannel options are part of a complete package offering. • A customer-centric culture is established across the entire enterprise. • Employees anticipate customer needs and are empowered to respond to customers' requests. • Customer service takes responsibility for full service to accounts.
Establish Service Levels for Customers	• Processes for establishing customer requirements focus on product and service reliability. • Performance metrics are set and measured.	• Service levels are based on customer specific expectations and agreements. • Key customer requirements are established jointly with the customer. • Provisions are in place for co-managed inventory programs and CPFR. • Service level benchmarks provide a gauge for improving the customer experience. • Customer relationship management (CRM) applications provide "lifetime value" data to determine a level of service for maximum ROI.

	Suggested Minimum Process Standard	Typical Best Practice Process
Plan and Manage Customer Service Workforce	• First-tier support is available 24x7 (may not be applicable to all industries). • There are written job descriptions and expectations. • Audits conducted on customer service activate the internal improvements identification process. • Customer service representative (CSR) performance is reviewed internally on a quarterly basis. • If managed by third party, customer service representative performance metrics are in place and report as part of contract requirements.	• Full support is available 24x7, with issues resolved within documented industry best standard time frames. • Dedicated operation resources are devoted to customer feedback analysis and reporting. • Customer satisfaction surveys are shared with CSR and improvement plans are developed as required. • CSR performance is reviewed daily, weekly, and monthly. • CSR KPIs are tied to the corporate goals and profit model. • If managed by a third party, CSR performance metrics are agreed to, in place, and visible on the website.
Receive Customer Request/Inquiries	• Informal software (e.g., Word, Excel, Access) or a CRM system provides customer tracking and input to CSRs, to keep the customer informed. • Logging of all customer inquiries takes place to ensure a correct response and that all inquiries are answered (closed). • The customer can receive support via call center. • CSRs have the necessary language skills to support selling geographies.	• CRM software provides customer input and keeps the customer informed. • A customer can receive support via call center or Internet (downloadable help and live chat) for order status. • Different levels of support are provided to customers based on customer profile or agreement. • Technology investments lead to efficiency and effectiveness in customer service. • FAQ knowledge base is available to customers online.
Respond to Customer Requests/Inquiries	• CSR has visibility into customer account and order information to support customer inquiries. • Employees are empowered to act on customer inquiries to improve brand image. • There is resolution of >80% of all inquiries during the initial call. • The process for resolving most common inquiries is defined and is part of the system knowledge base.	• CSR has visibility into customer account information and full access to order information, product information, and contract terms to support customer inquiries. • CSRs are empowered to handle most inquiries, with a maximum one level of escalation. • The system knowledge base is updated and catalogued, based on resolutions to customer inquiries, so that all CSRs have the information available.

(Continued)

TABLE 2.5
(*Concluded*)

	Suggested Minimum Process Standard	Typical Best Practice Process
Receive Customer Complaints	• A customer can receive tech support via call center. • Service parts orders are given priority. • The process for resolving the most common complains and technical inquiries is defined and is part of the system knowledge base.	• Different levels of aftermarket support are provided, including levels of service such as advanced replacement, 4-hour support, 24-hour support, etc. • A defined and documented process exists for the validation, approval, and recording of complaints and/or claims. • FAQ knowledge base is available online to customers.
Resolve Customer Complaints	• 80% of all technical issues are resolved during the initial call. • All technical issues are resolved within 4 hours, and with a maximum of one callback. • Formal processes are in place to close the loop on issues and increase customer satisfaction.	• All technical issues are resolved in a single phone call, with one transfer maximum. • There is a formal returns process for warranty and dead-on-arrival (DOA) deliveries. • The system knowledge base is updated and catalogued, based on resolutions to customer complaints; technical support updates the FAQ database.
Measure Customer Satisfaction/ Customer Complaint Handling and Resolution	• Audits are conducted on customer-by-customer basis to identify internal improvements. • The sources of customer service complaints are recorded to track trends. • Customer satisfaction is measured or otherwise determined. • Complaint handling performance is reviewed internally on a quarterly basis to a set of KPIs. • A periodic survey of product and service satisfaction takes place. • Information from product returns is used to reduce cost and recurrence.	• Regular in-depth interviews take place with key customers. • Customer scorecards measure KPIs as requested and at the frequency requested by the customer. • Ongoing, statistically reliable customer satisfaction surveys are conducted by a third party. • Sources of customer service complaints are tracked in a database to facilitate root cause analysis of problems, and to track trends by customer and market segment. • The elements of the perfect order are measured. • Process KPIs are tied to the corporate strategic profit model.

Customer Relationship Management (CRM)

Customer Relationship Management (CRM) Defined

Customer relationship management can be defined as "practices, strategies and technologies that companies use to manage and analyze customer interactions and data throughout the customer lifecycle, with the goal of improving business relationships with customers, assisting in customer retention and driving sales growth."[46] CRM is an approach to managing customer relationships and serving customers using various types of information systems technology.

[46] http://www.crmworks.asia/crm.

CRM can be applied to organizations of many sizes, from small firms to *Fortune* 500 companies. Eight essentials of CRM have been identified that can be typically found in "best practice" organizations. They include the following:[47]

Eight Essentials of CRM

- *Rapid time to value*—CRM systems can be installed and implemented in a relatively short period of time, often in a matter of weeks.
- *Point-and-click customization*—modifications to CRM systems can be made rapidly and are easy to use.
- *360-degree customer view*—all information systems encompassing the customer interface are integrated to provide optimal customer satisfaction.
- *Real-time visibility*—CRM metrics are available on a real-time basis.
- *No more "defective" data*—quality data is required to properly implement CRM and optimize customer satisfaction.
- *High adoption*—CRM systems are understood and utilized by most or all of the organization's functions and processes.
- *Extending your success*—the CRM system can be modified and adapted as the organization expands.
- *Broad community*—utilize the CRM system to interact with customer communities and build stronger relationships.

With the proper data availability, the firm and supply chain can utilize its CRM software to plan, implement, and control its customer satisfaction efforts.

The Garces Group Implements CRM

The Garces Group is a Philadelphia-based hospitality group with 14 restaurants across the East Coast of the United States. The company has presence on Facebook, Google, Instagram, OpenTable, Twitter, and Venga. The firm utilizes CRM software to allow its many locations to pool customer data from every location in real time. Using the CRM software, Garces identifies customers who have stopped coming, or are coming less often, to any of its locations and motivates them to return using promotions and advertising. Data from all of its social network platforms serves as input into the CRM software.[48]

The American Kennel Club (AKC) is an organization that registers purebred dog pedigrees. Maintaining and updating the records of all AKC-registered dogs and their owners is a monumental task, and AKC had to expend a great deal of effort to do so. The organization implemented a CRM system that provided an end-to-end registration solution that made it easy for it "to build, customize and deploy registration forms and flows, with screens for email verification, password reset and more. It also supports social login via a single API to manage Facebook and more than 25 other third-party identity providers."[49] As a result of the CRM implementation, AKC has saved 50 percent of its total costs associated with managing customer identities. It has also allowed customers a seamless registration experience that has helped acquire new customers given its ease of use. Additionally, "by knowing key pieces of information like what dog breeds a user likes or what dog shows they are interested in attending, AKC can reach them with relevant messages at the right time, increasing conversion rates and the value of each user."[50]

---

[47] Salesforce.com, "Eight CRM Essentials: An Executive Guide to the Eight Must-Have Elements of Every Successful CRM Initiative," *White Paper*, 2007 (12 pages), http://www.salesforce.com.
[48] Ibid.
[49] "American Kennel Club Drives Campaign Conversions with Identity-Driven Marketing," *Gigya Case Study*, 2017, https://2sep653x2vim4375oc23b3j9-wpengine.netdna-ssl.com/wp-content /uploads/2017/02/201702_Gigya_CS_American_Kennel_Club-WEB.pdf.
[50] Ibid.

Summary

"Doing it right the first time" is almost a given in today's society given the emphasis on the "perfect order." Mistakes almost always are costly, in terms of either loss of customer satisfaction, reduced sales and/or profits, or both! Certainly, competitors are always ready to jump at the chance of gaining an advantage when other companies make mistakes.

Organizations must develop optimal strategies as individual firms and as a group of partner firms within an integrated and coordinated supply chain. Each enterprise in the supply chain must recognize that customer satisfaction is paramount and that optimal service levels must be provided to customers before, during, and after the sale.

In order for organizations to properly plan, implement, and control customer satisfaction strategies, they must identify the key performance indicators (KPIs) that make a difference to customers. The optimization of customer satisfaction through supply chain management has been referred to as the "perfect order." The KPIs utilized by an organization should measure those aspects of the "perfect order" that get the *right product* at the *right place* at the *right time* in the *right condition* for the *right cost* to customers purchasing the product.

In developing customer satisfaction strategies, organizations within the supply chain utilize cost–service trade-offs to optimize customer service, while minimizing costs. The use of computers, information systems, and various management software and systems such as just-in-time (JIT); collaborative planning, forecasting, and replenishment (CPFR); customer relationship management (CRM); the marketing concept; and others can allow the organization individually, and the supply chain collectively, to satisfy customers. Marketing research can be used to identify areas of strength and weakness and the supply chain can then respond accordingly.

Suggested Readings

"Astute Customer Experience Maturity Framework," *White Paper*, Astute Solutions, 2017, http://crm.astutesolutions.com/rs/116-HUQ-234/images/CX-Maturity-Framework-eBook.pdf.

Bagram, Mohammad Majid Mehmood, and Shahzad Khan, "Attaining Customer Loyalty! The Role of Consumer Attitude and Consumer Behavior," *International Review of Management and Business Research*, Vol. 1, Issue 1 (December 2012), pp. 1–8.

Barwitz, Niklas, Boris Kors, and Sirus Ramezani, "Putting the Right Price on Customer Interactions," *McKinsey Quarterly*, No. 4 (November 2017), https://www.mckinsey.com/industries/healthcare-systems-and-services/our-insights/putting-the-right-price-on-customer-interactions/.

Bhagwat, Rajat, and Milind Kumar Sharma, "Performance Measurement of Supply Chain Management: A Balanced Scorecard Approach," *Computers & Industrial Engineering*, Vol. 53, No. 1 (August 2007), pp. 43–62.

Bowman, Robert J., "Yes, Some Customers Are More Equal Than Others," *SupplyChainBrain Blog*, December 4, 2017, http://www.supplychainbrain.com/think-tank/blogs/think-tank/blog/article/yes-some-customers-are-more-equal-than-others/.

Brown, Ryan, "Customer Satisfaction Begins and Ends with Your Supply Chain," *Material Handling & Logistics*, December 7, 2016, http://www.mhlnews.com/global-supply-chain/customer-satisfaction-begins-and-ends-your-supply-chain.

Christensen, Clayton M., Taddy Hall, Karen Dillon, and David S. Duncan, "Know Your Customers' 'Jobs to Be Done,'" *Harvard Business Review*, Vol. 94, No. 9 (September 2016), pp. 54–62.

"The CEO Guide to Customer Experience," *McKinsey Quarterly*, No. 3 (August 2016), pp. 30–39.

Douglas, Merrill, "Superstar Service: Supply Chain Strategies Win Satisfied Customers," *Inbound Logistics*, Vol. 31, No. 12 (December 2011), pp. 38–45.

"The Hierarchy of Metrics for Supply Chain Success," *Benchmarking Success Blog*, May 25, 2017, https://benchmarkingsuccess.com/the-hierarchy-of-metrics-for-supply-chain-success/.

"The High Cost of Poor Customer Service," *White Paper*, Purolator International, 2017, 16 pages.

Hochfekder, Barry, "The Growth of Demand-Driven Supply Chains," *Supply & Demand Chain Executive*, Vol. 18, Issue 5 (December 2017), pp. 6–10.

"How to Prepare for the Next Evolution of the Customer Journey," *White Paper*, Astute Solutions, 2017, http://crm.astutesolutions.com/Evolution-Customer-Journey-Whitepaper.html.

"If You Want to Improve Your Supply Chain . . . Think Maturity," *Benchmarking Success Blog*, August 16, 2017, https://www.benchmarkingsuccess.com/if-you-want-to-improve-your-supply-chain-think-maturity/.

Leggett, Kate, "How AI Will Transform Customer Service," *White Paper*, Forrester Research, June 16, 2017, https://www.forrester.com/report/How+AI+Will+Transform+Customer+Service/-/E-RES138044.

Minkara, Omer, and Sumair Dutta, "The Rising Financial Impact of Customer Service," *Aberdeen Group White Paper*, May 2013.

Parry, Tim, "New Digital Fulfillment Strategies Help Meet Customer Expectations," *MultiChannelMerchant Advertorial*, May 18, 2017, http://multichannelmerchant.com/research/new-digital-fulfillment-strategies-help-meet-customer-expectations/.

Shaw, Colin, "Customer Satisfaction Leads to Higher Stock Prices: New Evidence," *Beyond Philosophy Blog*, July 20, 2012, https://beyondphilosophy.com/customer-satisfaction-leads-higher-stock-prices-new-evidence.

Terry, Lisa, "Measuring Customer Service: The Up-and-Coming KPI," *Inbound Logistics*, Vol. 32, No. 12 (December 2012), pp. 34–42.

Wunderlin, Amy, "Retailers Leverage Brick-and-Mortar in an Amazon World," Supply & Demand Chain Executive, Vol. 19, No. 5 (December 2018), pp. 8–14.

Questions and Problems

LO 2-1 1. Are "customer service" and "customer satisfaction" the same, or are they different? Explain.

LO 2-2 2. What are the relationships between customer satisfaction and the marketing concept?

LO 2-2 3. Discuss the role of customer service during the pre-transaction, transaction, and post-transaction components of the company-customer exchange.

LO 2-3 4. Briefly discuss how the SCOR Model incorporates or considers customer service and satisfaction.

LO 2-3 5. What are key performance indicators (KPIs), and how are they used in supply chain management?

LO 2-3 6. What is a "perfect order," and what are some of the elements found in a perfect order?

LO 2-5 7. Generally, how are approaches such as the strategic profit model and the Balanced Scorecard used in supply chain measures and metrics?

LO 2-6 8. What is customer relationship management (CRM), and how is it used in developing customer satisfaction strategies?

Chapter

3

The Role of Information in Supply Chains

Objectives of This Chapter

LO 3-1   To describe the uses of information in supply chains.

LO 3-2   To describe tools used to capture and transmit data in supply chains.

LO 3-3   To describe tools used to support transactions, planning, and collaboration in supply chains.

LO 3-4   To describe the order management process.

Introduction

The digital world has made time and space obsolete. Consumers can shop online, at anytime, virtually anywhere in the world, and, in some cases, get what they ordered delivered to them within a few short hours. For this reason, information is the lifeline of a supply chain.

Every time a product is moved, stored, or acquired, the action must be recorded. The same is true of all assets used in supply chain operations, such as trucks, trains, pallets, and other equipment. This is needed not only for daily operations, but also for planning purposes. In daily operations, managers use information to decide how to fulfill orders, allocate assets, forecast sales, and plan warehouse operations. For example, a warehouse manager planning operations for the following day needs information about the orders to be delivered, inventory levels, readiness of warehouse equipment, labor availability, as well as current and forecasted customer orders. When planning, managers need information to decide how much inventory to keep in different locations, the level of service to offer various customers, and whether to use private or third-party logistics and transportation providers. Information is needed in every aspect of supply chain operations and planning. Accordingly, in this chapter we will first describe the different uses of information in supply chains and then look at different issues related to capturing, transmitting, and utilizing that information. We will describe the order management process, which is a key process in the operation of supply chains. Lastly, we'll look to see what role information will play in supply chains in the future.

The Uses of Information in Supply Chains

Supply chain managers need information for three basic purposes. The first is to know where the assets under the manager's control are. The second is to use information to manage daily operations. And the third is to make planning and strategic decisions regarding the management of the supply chain.

Maintain Asset Visibility

A supply chain manager controls assets belonging to firms in the supply chain, such as trucks, inventory, pallets, containers, and lift trucks. The manager needs to know where those assets are in order to maintain control and to make the best possible use of them. For example, vehicle routing software is used to optimize the utilization of trucks while maintaining a predetermined level of service to customers. In many cases, trucks may be rerouted to accommodate changes in the delivery schedule, weather conditions, accidents, or highway maintenance. Rerouting is only possible if the firm knows in real time the location of each truck. To this end, there are scores of firms that offer GPS tracking systems of trucks.

Asset visibility is also important to support safety and security. The same wireless technology available to track trucks is used to enhance the protection of drivers against possible crime. Another safety and security issue is visibility of inventory against theft or to counter product tampering. One of the most infamous cases involved Tylenol, a pain reliever, where bottles were criminally tampered with in 1982. The manufacturer was able to quickly trace the origin of the problem because all of the tampered bottles were traced to a single store in Chicago. This was only possible because the company had visibility of inventory assets in the supply chain.[1] Product tampering and contamination remains a recurring problem. For example, when an insecticide harmful to humans contaminated eggs sold in 15 EU countries, German buyers used an app to translate the eggs' serial number and determine where the eggs came from.[2]

Manage Daily Operations

Information is central to the daily operation of a supply chain. Walter Wriston, the former CEO of Citicorp, once wrote, "Information about money has become almost as important as money itself."[3] It could be said that in today's digital economy, information about products has become almost as important as the products themselves. Information sharing is critical both within individual firms and among firms in the supply chain. Within individual firms, information is needed to coordinate activities within and among functions. Firm functions refer to traditional organizational specializations such as marketing, logistics, manufacturing, or finance. For example, to decide the level of inventory to keep, managers must know the level of service promised to customers. Thus, information must be exchanged between the customer service and inventory management. Another example of information sharing among functions is when a customer's order is returned. Warehouse and inventory management need the information to put the product back in inventory, accounting needs to credit the customer's account, and customer service is tasked with

[1] Paul Shrivastava, Ian Mitroff, Danny Miller, and Anil Migliani, "Understanding Industrial Crises," *Journal of Management Studies*, Vol. 25, No. 4 (1988), pp. 285–303.

[2] Daniel Boffey and Kate Connolly, "Egg Contamination Scandal Widens as 15 EU States, Switzerland and Hong Kong Affected," *The Guardian*, August 11, 2017, https://www.theguardian.com/world/2017/aug/11/tainted-eggs-found-in-hong-kong-switzerland-and-15-eu-countries.

[3] Walter Wriston, *Bits, Bytes and Balance Sheets: The New Economic Rules of Engagement in a Wireless World* (Stanford, CA: Hoover Institution Press, 2007).

TABLE 3.1

Sample Information Typically Exchanged Among Functions of the Firm

Information Flow	Accounting/ Finance	Logistics	Manufacturing	Marketing/Sales	Procurement
Accounting/ Finance		Shipment/ Delivery Notifications	Production Forecasts	Sales Forecasts	Spend
Logistics	Customer Credit Releases		Production Schedules	Customer Service Requirements	Inbound Transportation Needs
Manufacturing	Capital Investment Approvals	Inventory Status		New Product Developments	Raw Materials Delivery Schedules
Marketing/Sales	Customer Credit Status	On-Time Delivery Reports	Available to Promise Information		Raw Materials Shortage Estimates
Procurement	Purchasing Budget	Emergency Resupply Requests	Raw Materials Need Estimates	Sales Forecast	

finding out the reasons for the return. Table 3.1 presents a sample of information typically exchanged among functions of the firm.

Exchanging information among firms in the supply chain is equally important, although it has been shown visibility decreases as one moves farther upstream to suppliers and suppliers' suppliers.[4] These information inefficiencies increase risk—and costs—and can be a catalyst for investigation and change. To be effective, managers need input from other supply chain firms to make operational decisions affecting the supply chain and their individual firm. For example, a customer's sales forecast can be very helpful in determining a firm's production schedule because the size and timing of the customer's demand becomes less uncertain. As a result, the production schedule more closely matches the demand.

The exchange of information in the supply chain must include everyone in the supply chain—from third-party service providers to brokers to transportation providers. For instance, a public warehouse needs sales information from its customers in order to plan warehouse operations. The public warehouse also provides inventory availability information to its customers and, upon request, to its customers' customers. Figure 3.1 provides a sample of information typically exchanged among firms in the supply chain.

Planning and Strategy

The management of supply chains goes beyond daily operations. Managers must also use information to plan future operations and make strategic decisions.

Supply chain planning refers to decision making related to future operations in the supply chain. The objective is to meet service and quality requirements with the lowest possible use of resources. For example, in order to ship products to customers, supply chain managers must anticipate the number of trailers required before actually needing them. This is

---

[4] Mary Collins Holcomb, Karl B. Manrodt, and Tommy Barnes, "26th Annual Trends in Logistics Study," Council of Supply Chain Management Professionals Annual Conference, Atlanta, GA, September 25, 2017. Also see David J. Closs, Thomas J. Goldsby, and Steven J. Clinton, "Information Technology Influences on World Class Logistics Capability," *International Journal of Physical Distribution*, Vol. 27, No. 1 (1997).

FIGURE 3.1
Sample Information Exchanged by Firms in Supply Chains

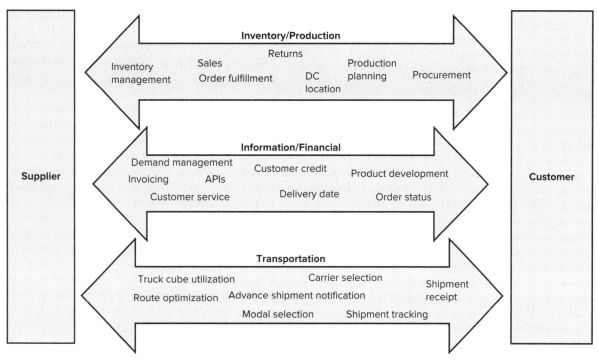

because time is needed to procure a sufficient number of trailers. The earlier the information is available, the more time can be allocated to finding the right trailers at a low cost.

Some of the key supply chain planning areas are listed below. In subsequent sections in this chapter, we will describe many of the tools available in supply chain planning.

- Demand planning
- Transportation
- Production
- Warehousing
- Inventory
- Collaborative planning

Supply chain strategy must fit within the overall corporate strategy. Corporate strategy refers to the use of resources to gain a competitive advantage. As proposed by Porter, there are three basic strategic choices: cost leadership, differentiation, and focus.[5] The first refers to using corporate resources to become a low-cost leader. In a differentiation strategy, firms seek to offer unique products and services to customers. Lastly, in a focus strategy, resources are concentrated on a narrow segment of the market.

Corporate strategy determines whether the supply chain organization will have a strategic or a supporting role. In the former case, the aim is to either provide differentiated services to customers or attain cost leadership.[6] The supply chain organization can play a key role in providing differentiated services to customers. These services may include just-in-time delivery and other forms of customer service.

[5] Michael E. Porter, *Competitive Advantage* (New York: The Free Press, 1985), pp. 11–15.
[6] Donald J. Bowersox and Patricia J. Daugherty, "Logistics Paradigms: The Impact of Information Technology," *Journal of Business Logistics*, Vol. 16, No. 1 (1995), pp. 65–80.

The supply chain organization may also support a low-cost leadership strategy. Walmart provides a good example. Through cost management, its supply chain organization has a strategic role in enabling the firm's low-price strategy.

Alternatively, the supply chain organization may have a supporting role when the focus of corporate strategy is to differentiate product on the basis of product design or branding, for instance. In this case, the supply chain organization provides cost and service management support.

Supply chain strategy is developed once the role of the supply chain organization in corporate strategy is decided. This involves three main issues. One is network design, where a decision is made regarding the number and size of nodes in the supply chain, particularly plant and warehouse sizes and locations. Network design decisions require a substantial amount of cost and customer service information. Some organizations, such as Limited Brands, an apparel, cosmetics, and housewares retailer, have designed their network to have two warehousing locations to support a national distribution effort. On the other hand, Cardinal Health, a distributor of pharmaceuticals, has more than 60 warehouses supporting its national distribution.

The second issue refers to the level of outsourcing in the supply chain. Should the firm own its supply chain assets, or should it outsource them to third-party service providers? What is the type of relationship, or strategic sourcing business model, that firms in the supply chain should maintain with each other?

A third issue in supply chain strategy is to decide which channels to use to bring products to market. A manufacturer or importer may select a direct-to-consumer channel, a wholesale-based channel, or a direct-to-retail channel. Often, combinations of channels are chosen. Today, many customers can be in a physical store while getting additional information from their mobile devices. Uniting all of these inputs and experiences into a coherent whole is the focus of the omnichannel, which will be discussed later.

The digital economy has made answering these three questions much more challenging. Recent research has shown that many firms are utilizing a "be all things to all people" approach to strategy.[7] Porter would refer to this strategy as being "stuck in the middle." This strategy places greater pressure on the supply chain, as it must be flexible, adaptive, effective, and efficient. For instance, think of all the ways Amazon can service its customers. In larger metropolitan markets, Amazon Prime Now can deliver products within two hours. Amazon Prime will deliver in two days, and normal shipments take longer. Each method serves different customer needs, and all at different price points. Each method is enabled by technology, making this approach more viable today than in years past.

These three issues will be examined in greater detail elsewhere in this book. For now, it is important to keep in mind that supply chain planning and strategy decisions require a great deal of information as input. In the next section we examine the tools available to obtain and manage such information.

Applying Information Technology to Supply Chain Management

We conclude from the previous section that the level of detail and volume of information needed to manage supply chains are quite significant. The information must be first captured and transmitted as data and then processed in support of supply chain transactions, planning, and collaboration. In this section of the chapter we will review the main tools available to manage the flow of information in supply chains.

[7] Joe Tillman, Karl B. Manrodt, and Donnie Williams, "DC Measures 2017," *WERCWatch*, Spring 2017, Warehouse Education Research Council, Chicago, IL.

Data Capture

Data capture is the process by which data enters an information system. This may be accomplished by manual or automated processes. In the former, a person types the data into a computer. Alternatively, in automated processes, data is captured electronically. In this case, data is captured with greater speed and accuracy. Automation is the only way to quickly capture large volumes of data. We describe below the two main forms of automated data capture: bar codes and radio frequency identification (RFID).

A *bar code* is simply a machine-readable alphanumeric code. It is made up of dark bars and spaces that represent ones and zeros. The ones and zeros are combined to represent numbers and letters. A code is needed to specify that each combination of ones and zeros corresponds to a single number or letter. One of these codes is the Universal Product Code (UPC) that is widely used in the packaged goods industry to identify products. Figure 3.2 shows a bar code and the number it represents using a UPC code.

Bar code technology is also available in two dimensions. While data in basic bar codes is only available in one dimension (horizontal), two-dimensional (2D) codes present data in a vertical dimension as well. Thus, 2D codes are able to either store more data than basic bar codes or enable faster scans. Two common types of 2D codes are Data Matrix and MaxiCode. Stacked bar codes hold more data than simple bar codes. MaxiCodes are designed to be read very quickly. They are used in the package delivery business where codes must be read quickly as each package passes by in a conveyor system. These two types are also displayed in Figure 3.2.

Applications of bar code technology are visible in everyday life. For instance, they are used by railroads to identify and track rail cars, by booksellers to identify titles, or by airlines, who use bar codes to track both boarding passes and passengers' luggage. However, bar codes are most widely used in consumer products.

Manufacturers and retailers of consumer products benefit from bar code adoption for several reasons. First, bar codes are a labor-saving technology. Consider, for example, a cashier at a supermarket who is able to quickly scan each item purchased by a customer. This is only possible because each item is identified with a bar code. In the past, cashiers would have had to read and then manually enter the price of each item purchased. Second, bar codes facilitate sales tracking, enabling both manufacturers and retailers to efficiently identify fast and slow movers. This data can then be used to improve store replenishment because items are shipped to locations where they are selling. The data can also be used to improve inventory control and serve as sales forecasting input.

FIGURE 3.2
Bar Codes and Two-Dimensional Codes

UPC bar code

Stacked bar code

Maxi code

Source: http://www.data-net.com/education/barcodes.html.

Another well-known bar code application is package tracking. Major package carriers, such as the U.S. Postal Service, FedEx, DHL, and UPS use bar codes to track their packages. This is done to plan operations and to provide customer service. When a carrier is able to track a package from origin to destination, it is able to better allocate resources. For example, if a carrier knows exactly how many packages must be picked up and delivered in a particular city, it also knows how much labor and transportation assets will be needed at that location. This improves planning efficiency and the utilization of resources. Moreover, whenever there is an unforeseen problem, such as a major snow storm, it is easier to amend plans because the location of each package is known. Package tracking is also a service to customers, who are able to use package location information in their own planning.

UPS serves as an illustration of how bar codes are used to track packages.[8] Each package receives a unique tracking identification number, which is represented as a bar code on the package. Whenever a package is picked up, is delivered, or moves through a UPS facility, it is scanned. The information is then relayed via cellular technology to UPS's mainframe repository in Mahwah, New Jersey. Once in the system, the package tracking information can be accessed either internally or by customers via e-mail, the Internet, and even cellular phone.

Radio Frequency Identification (RFID) technology is an advancement with respect to bar codes. Data is stored in a chip. Like bar codes, RFID chips also store alphanumeric data. However, contrary to bar codes, RFID chips can transmit the stored data via a radio frequency. Therefore, RFID chips do not require "line-of-sight" to be read, as do bar codes. This means that RFID chips are more efficient because data from RFID chips can be collected from a wider area.

RFID chips are also able to uniquely identify each unit of product, unlike a bar code that identifies all products with the same characteristics (i.e., a stockkeeping unit or sku). For example, in a supermarket, all boxes of a particular size, package, and brand of cereal made on the same day or same batch carry the same bar code. On the other hand, RFID chips are able to uniquely identify each individual box of cereal.

There are active and passive RFID chips. They differ because active chips are equipped with an antenna that enables them to be read from a longer distance. Active chips are also considerably more expensive. Most RFID chips in use are passive. The relatively lower cost of passive RFID chips makes them ideal to identify low-cost items in an environment where the chip can be read from a distance. For example, in order to improve product tracking in its distribution centers, Walmart was one of the first to mandate its most important suppliers identify pallets and cases with passive RFID chips. This was followed by the U.S. Department of Defense, Macy's, Target, and Bloomingdale's, just to mention a few.[9] Active chips are used to identify items either of higher value or that need to be read from a longer distance. For example, the location of lift trucks in a warehouse or yard can be tracked with active RFID chips.

There are many potential applications of RFID technology in supply chains. By tracking inventory more efficiently, firms are able to improve inventory replenishment in supply chain facilities and reduce shrinkage, that is, inventory reduction due to loss, theft, breakage, or deterioration. For example, the specialty retailer American Apparel implemented an RFID solution that led to increased sales and sales floor space, less shrinkage, and a 9 percent reduction in inventory levels over a two-year period.[10] Libraries across the globe

---

[8] "UPS Parcel Delivery Tracking Application," *Mobileinfo.com*, June 2001, http://www.mobileinfo.com.
[9] Anna Turri, Ronn Smith, and Steven Kopp, "Privacy and RFID Technology: A Review of Regulatory Efforts," *Journal of Consumer Affairs*, Vol. 51, No. 2 (Summer 2017), pp. 329–354.
[10] Xterprise, "American Apparel," 2014, https://www.ramprfid.com/wp-content/uploads/2014/07/American-Apparel-Case-Study.pdf.

are implementing RFID solutions for item identification, tracking, and automating many of their processes.[11] Advanced E-Textiles is developing a washable microelectronic RFID that is woven into the fabric. These tags can track the life cycle of a garment, and more easily identify counterfeit luxury items.[12]

In a supply chain environment, firms may implement RFID at different levels. These may range from major assets such as containers or trailers, to smaller units such as pallets, cases, and even individual items. The decision depends on a number of factors, including the goals of the application, cost, and privacy. For instance, if a firm's RFID application goal is to improve warehouse operations and store replenishment, such as in the American Apparel example above, then item-level implementation would be unnecessary. Tracking cases or pallets is sufficient to achieve the goals of the application because stores are replenished in pallet and case quantities. On the other hand, there are instances where the goal of the application is to track individual items, such as ensuring the authenticity of prescription medication.

The level of RFID implementation is also a function of cost. In general, the smaller the unit receiving RFID tags, the greater the cost of the implementation. There are two reasons for that. First, the smaller the unit, the more tags are needed. Tagging every individual unit requires more tags than tagging pallets, for instance. Over time, as the cost of tags continues to decrease, this reason may become less of a factor in RFID decisions. Second, there is also a substantial cost to keep the related information in databases. If every individual item receives a separate identification number, then each individual item is maintained as a separate line in a database, which boosts the size of the required database. Fewer lines are certainly needed if all items in a pallet are identified with the same tag.

In addition, in the case of RFID implementation at the individual item level, there are social concerns with the issue of privacy. Like any wireless technology, these devices can be read remotely, making them inherently insecure. Consumer privacy groups fear that RFID technology enables firms and the government to track the shopping habits of citizens without their consent.[13] These concerns may limit the use of RFID technology in stores but have a negligible impact on the tagging of cases and pallets elsewhere in the supply chain.

At the same time, significant obstacles to RFID implementation remain. First, the investment in RFID readers, supporting IT systems, and the chips themselves can be substantial. Second, the implementation is more complex when firms have to cope with legacy systems. Legacy systems are preexisting hardware or software that, while still functional, does not work well together with newer hardware or software being implemented. Third, significant issues remain with the technology itself. For instance, tag interference occurs when the chip's radio signal is not read because it cannot pass through metal or densely packed items. Uncertainty around the standards used by RFID components still needs to be addressed. Finally, as noted above, privacy may pose an additional obstacle to RFID implementation at the individual item level.[14]

[11] Yogesh K. Dwivedi, Kawaljeet K. Kapoor, Michael D. Williams, and Janet Williams, "RFID Systems in Libraries: An Empirical Examination of Factors Affecting System Use and User Satisfaction," *International Journal of Information Management*, Vol. 33, No. 2 (April 2013), pp. 367–377.

[12] Haniya Rae, "Stop Thief: These New RFID Tags Could Help Luxury Clothing Brands Guard Against Theft," *Forbes*, August 11, 2016, https://www.forbes.com/sites/haniyarae/2016/08/11/rfid-brands-theft/#cb61c3318de9.

[13] Zebra Technologies, "RFID and Your Privacy: Myths and Facts," *White Paper*, June 2013, https://www.zebra.com/content/dam/zebra/white-papers/en-us/rfid-your-privacy-en-us.pdf.

[14] Lynn Fish, "A Historic Perspective on RFID Implementation over the Past Decade with a Focus on Apparel Retailers: Are We at the 'Tipping Point'?," Proceedings for the Northeast Region Decision Sciences Institute (NEDSI), March 22, 2017, pp. 821–839.

Data Transmission

Once captured, data must be disseminated within the organization and the supply chain. In this process, both the transmitting and receiving parties must agree on how the data will be exchanged. We first describe two different forms of data transmission: Electronic Data Interchange (EDI) and EXtensible Markup Language (XML). We thereafter also look at an intermediated approach to data transmission, the Value Added Network (VAN).

Electronic Data Interchange (EDI), created in 1948, is a one-way communication standard designed to exchange structured computer-to-computer messages.[15] These messages are typically transaction-related documents such as purchase orders, invoices, order status inquiries, shipment information, and others. Each EDI document serves the same function as its paper-based equivalent but is transmitted electronically, usually via either a phone line or the Internet. EDI messages are structured because both parties must adhere to a standardized, predetermined format for each document. There are multiple standards available to be adopted by individual firms, industries, and regions of the world. Table 3.2 lists several documents typically used in supply chain information exchanges. These documents conform to the ANSI ASC X.12 standard, which is commonly used in the United States.

TABLE 3.2
Partial EDI Document List (ANSI ASC X.12 Standard)

	Order Series
810	Invoice
832	Price/SalesCatalog
850	Purchase Order
855	Purchase Order Acknowledgment
857	Shipment and Billing Notice
	Materials Handling Series
840	Request for Quotation
843	Response to Request for Quotation
845	Price Authorization Acknowledgment/Status
879	Price Information
	Warehousing Services Series
940	Warehouse Shipping Order
945	Warehouse Shipping Advice
947	Warehouse Inventory Adjustment Advice
990	Response to a Load Tender
	Financial Services Series
812	Credit/Debit Adjustment
820	Payment Order/Remittance Advice
829	Payment Cancellation Request
859	Freight Invoice

[15] Ben Ames, "IT Firm Rolls Out Platform to Expedite Data Exchange among Carriers, 3PLs, Shippers," *DC Velocity*, December 9, 2015, http://www.dcvelocity.com/articles/12051209-it-firm-rolls-out-platform -to-expedite-data-exchange-among-carriers-3pls-shippers/.

Manufacturing Series

846	Inventory Inquiry/Advice
867	Product Transfer and Resale Report
869	Order Status Inquiry
870	Order Status Report

Delivery Series

853	Routing and Carrier Instruction
856	Ship Notice/Manifest (ASN)
857	Shipment and Billing Notice
862	Shipping Schedule

Transportation Series

110	Air Freight Details and Invoice
204	Motor Carrier Load Tender
211	Motor Carrier Bill of Lading
300	Reservation (Booking Request) (Ocean)
310	Freight Receipt and Invoice (Ocean)
312	Arrival Notice (Ocean)
317	Delivery/Pickup Order
456	Railroad Equipment Inquiry or Advice
463	Rail Rate Reply
466	Rail Rate Request

ANSI is the American National Standards Institute. Founded in 1918, it is a nonprofit organization "overseeing the creation, promulgation and use of norms and guidelines that directly impact businesses."[16] It established the Accredited Standards Committee (now named X12) to develop EDI standards.[17]

In a typical but simplified transaction, a buyer sends a purchase order (EDI 850) to a seller and receives back an EDI 855, a purchase order acknowledgment. When the order is ready for shipment, the seller sends a motor carrier an EDI 204, motor carrier load tender, specifying shipment details such as scheduling, required equipment, and the commodity. The carrier responds with an EDI 990, a response to load tender, either accepting or rejecting the tender. When the order is picked up, the buyer sends an EDI 211, bill of lading, to the carrier. Prior to delivery, the seller sends the buyer an advanced shipping notice (EDI 856) informing the buyer of the delivery date and other details. After the order is delivered, the carrier sends the responsible party (e.g., the seller) a freight invoice (EDI 859), and the seller sends the buyer an EDI 810, an invoice. Both invoices may be paid electronically with an EDI 820, payment order/remittance advice.

EDI technology offers several advantages over paper-based document exchanges. EDI is less costly because minimal human interaction is required. This is mostly because the labor cost involved in preparing paper-based documents is avoided. The lack of human

---

[16] American National Standards Institute, "About ANSI," accessed January 9, 2018, https://www.ansi.org/about_ansi/introduction/history?menuid=1.

[17] American Standards Committee X12, "About X12," http://x12.org/x12org/about/asc-x12-about.cfm.

input also reduces the number of errors in documents because the data input into EDI documents is drawn directly from the firm's databases. Finally, because data moves faster than paper, EDI speeds up supply chain processes. Recent research has shown that firms should consider using EDI to improve relational and information flows between supply chain partners.[18]

On the other hand, the implementation of EDI can be challenging.[19] In addition to the initial setup cost of acquiring hardware, software, and the corresponding training expenses, EDI requires changes in business processes. This is because processes developed for paper-based transactions are often inadequate for EDI transactions. For example, payment of invoices can be processed much faster in an EDI environment because the order cycle time is shorter. In many cases, electronically transmitted invoices may arrive before the corresponding merchandise is received.

Moreover, data security is an issue in EDI implementation because sensitive data might be accessed by unauthorized parties. To minimize this possibility, EDI transactions are often encrypted. Finally, EDI implementation may alter the relationship between buyer and seller. In some cases, for instance, buyers may resist EDI implementation out of concern that automated transactions will reduce their control of the process. Despite these challenges, EDI technology is gaining worldwide acceptance.[20]

In many cases, EDI implementation is mandated by customers. For example, the Kroger Co., a retail grocery chain, considers EDI a key priority and mandates that its suppliers be able to send and receive certain EDI messages, including purchase orders and invoices. Kroger assists vendors in the implementation of EDI by providing information on its website. On the other hand, Kroger imposes a fine on vendors for each transaction executed manually.[21]

EXtensible Markup Language (XML) is an alternative technology to exchange data among firms in the supply chain. It is a simple and flexible syntax for exchanging data through the Internet. XML messages contain not only the data being transmitted but also "tags" located before and after the information. The role of the tags is to label each data point in the message. For example, part of an XML message (e.g., a purchase order) may read: <quantity>53</quantity>. In this case, the data point is 53 and the opening and closing tags indicate that 53 represents the quantity ordered. This is in contrast with an EDI message where there are no tags. In an EDI message the order quantity in known by the position of the number 53 in a standardized document.

XML is more flexible and less costly to implement than EDI. It is more flexible because partners do not have to conform to a rigid EDI standard. Documents can be customized for specific applications. XML is less costly to implement and use because it does not require customized mapping to each new customer or supplier.[22] Another advantage is that XML is human readable and thus enables people to look at the data without using software.

[18] T. Keah Choon, Vijay Kannan, Chin-Chun Hsu, and Keong Leong, "Supply Chain Information and Relational Alignments: Mediators of EDI on Firm Performance," *International Journal of Physical Distribution & Logistics Management*, Vol. 40, No. 5 (2010), pp. 377–394. Also see Cornelia Dröge and Richard Germain, "The Relationship of Electronic Data Interchange with Inventory and Financial Performance," *Journal of Business Logistics*, Vol. 21, No. 2 (2000), pp. 209–230.

[19] Margaret A. Emmelhainz, *Electronic Data Interchange: A Total Management Guide* (New York: Van Nostrand Reinhold, 1990), pp. 156–168.

[20] David J. Closs and Kefeng Xu, "Logistics Information Technology Practice in Manufacturing and Merchandising Firms," *International Journal of Physical Distribution and Logistics Management,* Vol. 30, No. 10 (2000), pp. 869–886.

[21] See "EDI Compliance Requirements," http://edi.kroger.com/edi/comp_001.htm.

[22] Remarkable, "EDI–Electronic Data Interchange–and XML Comparisons," http://www.remarkable .co.nz/ebusiness/edi.htm.

There are also disadvantages when selecting XML to exchange data in supply chains. Because tags are included in every message, XML files are larger than comparable files transmitted in EDI messages. This problem may be overcome by compressing files using a wide range of XML compressors.[23] Another disadvantage is the lack of one or two main XML standards; at this time there are dozens to choose from. And, as of now, EDI dominates the market, making newer market entries difficult.[24]

An intermediated approach to data transmission is the Value Added Network (VAN). Firms with the capability of transmitting EDI or XML messages benefit most by exchanging messages with multiple partners. As the number of partners grows, complexity also grows because different trading partners often use different standards. This is particularly true when partners belong to different industries and operate in different regions of the world. For example, a firm using the ANSI ASC X.12 standard may need to exchange messages with a European partner who uses the EDIFACT standard. This is the United Nations EDI standard used in Europe and other regions of the world.

This complexity means that firms must have the capability of exchanging messages in multiple standards, which is costly. VANs help to solve this problem by offering a translation service. This enables firms to transmit data in whatever standard they use and have the VAN translate that into the standard used by the recipient. Instead of sending the message directly to the receiver, the sender transmits a message to the VAN, which, after translating, resends the message to the receiver. VANs are also capable of translating EDI documents into XML documents and vice versa.

Most VANs provide additional services as well. One is a mailbox service whereby messages received by the VAN are stored for a customer in an electronic mailbox until the customer is ready to download them. This enables the customer to process incoming messages in batches, which is more efficient. Security services such as message encryption and firewalls ensure that messages are read only by the intended recipients. In broadcasting, the same message is distributed to a large number of recipients. Messages may also be audited through an automatic error detection service.

Transaction Support

Recall that we began this chapter with a description of the different uses of information in supply chains, namely to maintain asset visibility, manage daily operations, and make planning and strategy decisions. We subsequently explored different issues related to capturing and transmitting data in supply chains. In the former, we looked into two forms of data capture, bar codes and RFID. In the latter, we discussed EDI, XML, and VANs. We now turn to transaction support. Once data is captured and received, it must be organized to facilitate record keeping and to serve as input into the planning systems we discuss in future sections of this chapter.

Application Programming Interfaces (APIs) are a clearly defined means of communicating between various software programs. APIs happen in real time, without human intervention. When you check the weather on your phone, or order your favorite Starbucks from your phone, you are using APIs.

With APIs, transportation transactions such as requesting rates, dispatching a shipment, or tracking a shipment are automatically triggered and answered through the systems. This allows shippers, for instance, to spend more time on activities that can improve their business. Connectivity gaps inherent in EDI transmissions, as well as delays caused by batching EDI transmission, cause shippers to act on stale or inaccurate information. With

[23] Sherif Sakr, "Investigate State-of-the-Art XML Compression Techniques," IBM developerWorks, July 19, 2011, https://www.ibm.com/developerworks/library/x-datacompression/index.html.
[24] Steve Brewer, "Why Hasn't XML Replaced EDI?," *CovalentWorks*, May 21, 2013, https://blog.covalentworks.com/why-hasnt-xml-replaced-edi/.

cloud-based APIs, the data and information surrounding a shipment are reliable, up-to-date, and dynamic, providing supply chains the opportunity to maximize performance and implement proactive strategies.

One might compare EDIs and APIs by an analogy: EDIs are similar to buses, and APIs are like Uber. Information boards the bus, and it starts on its route. It makes a stop, and some passengers get off while others may board. In the same manner, information in an EDI message is routed through many stops and transformations, as information is pulled out.

In contrast, APIs are like Uber. Information from the API goes straight to where it needs to go, without transformation and with little need of processing. And with that speed comes greater flexibility and, most importantly, visibility. While sharing is possible, the network ensures that users specifically select this option with both cost and time dimensions immediately available as part of the decision-making process.[25]

Jett McCandless, cofounder of project44, an API transportation provider, notes another key advantage of APIs. Specifically, carriers can dynamically change rates—much like airlines, Uber, and hotels—instead of relying on static rate tables. For instance, if demand for freight movements to Miami increases, prices can be raised to reflect this increased demand.[26]

APIs are aggressively competing with EDIs in the marketplace. Given the dynamic nature of consumer demands and expectations, companies have to be able to respond to customer requests faster, an area where APIs excel. Regardless, both EDIs and APIs will coexist for some time, given the size and complexity of the market.[27]

Enterprise Resource Planning (ERP), as defined by Oracle, an ERP provider, refers to the systems and software packages used by organizations to manage day-to-day business activities, such as accounting, procurement, project management, and manufacturing.[28] ERPs emerged in the 1990s as an outgrowth of Materials Requirement Planning (MRP) and Manufacturing Resource Planning (MRP II) software that were initially used to schedule and manage manufacturing operations. ERP software evolved as improvements in computer capabilities enabled companies to add more functionality and promote their integration.[29]

Benefits from an ERP solution can be significant. Real-time information can improve business insight and assist in lower costs. Utilizing the same data enhances integration with other internal functional areas, as they are viewing the same standardized data. And this enhances collaboration with external customers and suppliers as data can be shared in a seamless manner. There is reduced risk, as data integrity and financial controls are in place.[30]

Figure 3.3 displays a typical ERP system. It shows how a central database is integrated with individual modules. These modules focus on business applications such as manufacturing, sales and delivery, finance, inventory and supply, service, human resource management, and reporting. The business application modules are connected to users inside the enterprise (management, sales force, administrators, etc.). Users will either input data in the system or use system output in the management of the enterprise. Finally, ERP systems can also be extended to include outside parties such as customers and suppliers.

[25] Karl B. Manrodt and Mary C. Holcomb, "Learn. Lift. Lead. The Road to Profitability Is a Web Service Connection," project44, Chicago, IL, http://manrodt.com/wp-content/uploads/2016/03/The-Road-to-Profitability-is-a-Web-Service-Connection-Freight-APIs.pdf.
[26] Ben Ames, "IT Firm Rolls Out Platform to Expedite Data Exchange among Carriers, 3PLs, Shippers," *DC Velocity*, December 9, 2015, http://www.dcvelocity.com/articles/12051209-it-firm-rolls-out-platform-to-expedite-data-exchange-among-carriers-3pls-shippers/.
[27] Ibid.
[28] "What Is ERP?," Oracle Corporation, https://www.oracle.com/applications/erp/what-is-erp.html.
[29] Robert F. Jacobs and F. C. (Ted) Weston Jr., "Enterprise Resource Planning—A Brief History," *Journal of Operations Management*, Vol. 24, No. 2 (2007), pp. 357–363.
[30] "What Is ERP?"

FIGURE 3.3
Typical ERP Solution

Source: Retrieved January 10, 2018, http://www.omni components.com/wp-content /uploads/2015/09/erpsoftware .jpg.

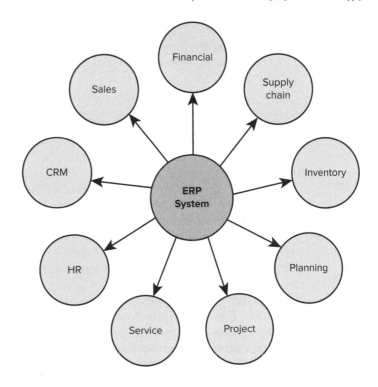

In addition to integrating information flows across business functions, ERP systems also serve as platforms for more advanced applications in supply chain management. These applications use data downloaded from ERP systems as input. Thus, firms may add customer relationship management (CRM) and supplier relationship management (SRM) software, which are designed to help manage relationships with customers and suppliers. Other "add-ons" include transportation management systems (TMSs), warehouse management systems (WMSs), and yard management systems (YMSs). These applications fill a significant role in the management of supply chains. TMS, WMS, and YMS will be described in greater detail in upcoming sections in this chapter.

Historically, the implementation of an ERP system was costly and complex.[31] The software itself was expensive and technically challenging to implement. Firms usually had to hire specialized consultants to assist with the implementation. The process required thousands of man-hours and could take more than a year to complete. Dedicated servers had to be purchased and maintained by the customer. Updating the system was difficult, especially if the system had been customized to meet the needs of the customer.

To keep costs down, and to expand the overall ERP market, providers began to offer their solution in the cloud. Cloud ERP solutions have several benefits. The solution is not on the customer's proprietary servers, making updates easier, as well as increasing connectivity both internally and externally. Research has found that cloud solutions offer scalability, reliability, and lower costs (both initial and ongoing costs).[32]

[31] Robert Plant and Leslie Willcocks, "Critical Success Factors in International ERP Implementations: A Case Research Approach," *Journal of Computer Information Systems,* Spring 2007, pp. 60–70.
[32] Mohamed Elmonem, Eman Nasr, and Mervat Geith, "Benefits and Challenges of Cloud ERP Systems: A Systematic Literature Review," *Future Computing and Informatics Journal*, Vol. 1, Issues 1–2 (2016), pp. 1–9.

There are several critical success factors that influence successful ERP implementations. Top management support is needed to break down barriers and resistance to change. This means a vision and objectives of the change have to be clearly communicated to the employees. Training of employees on the new system is also critical to long-term success.[33]

Planning Support

As discussed above, the main emphasis of ERP systems is to integrate data from different business functions and potentially with other participants in the supply chain. In this section we focus mostly on internal integration, while the focus of the subsequent section is on external integration.

While ERP systems have some planning capability, the main focus is on transactions among functions and not on planning. However, the data made available by ERP systems creates opportunities to improve the efficiency of supply chain operations. For example, warehouse operations are more efficient if managers receive timely demand and inventory replenishment information. When this happens, managers are able to anticipate the daily manpower required to operate the warehouse and have time to figure out the best way to use available equipment.

Thus, there are software tools available to assist managers plan efficient supply chain operations. These tools apply decision-making algorithms using data from ERP or other software systems as input. There are also software tools available at the strategic level. For instance, a network design tool enables firms to determine the optimal number, location, and size of facilities in the supply chain. In this section, we describe four of the supply chain planning tools available: inventory management, warehouse management systems (WMSs), transportation management systems (TMSs), and yard management systems (YMSs). The four supply chain planning tools and their main functionalities are summarized in Table 3.3.

Inventory management planning tools help companies decide on the optimal level of inventory to maintain. This decision is a significant challenge to supply chain managers. First, managers must balance the need to offer customers a competitive level of inventory availability with the cost of maintaining inventory. Second, this decision must be made at

TABLE 3.3
Supply Chain Planning Software Tools and Main Functionalities

Software Tool	Main Functionalities
Inventory Management	Single Location Inventory Optimization Multi-Echelon Inventory Decisions
Warehouse Management Systems (WMS)	Control Warehouse Operations Optimize Warehouse Utilization Improve Order Processing Visibility Optimize Labor Resources
Transportation Management Systems (TMS)	Carrier Bidding Transportation Planning and Execution Freight Audit and Payment
Yard Management Systems (YMS)	Improve Visibility of Containers and Trailers Optimize Asset and Driver Movements

[33] Ali Tarhini, Hussain Ammar, Takwa Tarhini, and Ra'ed Masa'deh, "Analysis of the Critical Success Factors for Enterprise Resource Planning Implementation from a Stakeholders' Perspective: A Systematic Review," *International Business Research*, Vol. 4, No. 4 (2015), pp. 25–40. Also see Dawn M. Russell and Anne M. Hoag, "People and Information in the Supply Chain: Social and Organizational Influences on Adoption," *International Journal of Physical Distribution & Logistics Management*, Vol. 34, No. 2 (2004), pp. 102–122.

every location where the company holds inventory, be it at plants, distribution centers, or stores. Third, managers must make a decision for every item in the firm's product line, which is especially complex because in recent years product lines have become more extensive. Product lines also change more often as products are added and deleted to meet the competitive challenges of the marketplace.

Inventory management decisions are made at two levels. One is the quantity of inventory needed at each location and the second is a multi-echelon decision where managers look at how inventory should be distributed throughout the supply chain. Multi-echelon inventory optimization (MEIO) decisions are only possible when there is inventory visibility. An inventory management planning tool takes advantage of the visibility of inventory in the supply chain to make MEIO decisions. This visibility is often made possible by the ERP and APS software suites we discussed previously.

The basic rule of MEIO is that inventory should be kept at the lowest-cost location given a customer service constraint. Depending on the situation, the inventory may be at a lower cost if held close to supply; in other cases, costs are minimized by being closer to the customer. Consider when new iPhones are released on the market. Inventory costs are minimized—and service levels maximized—by keeping them in a central location, shipping them out to the retail stores based on orders.

Stanley Black & Decker, a durable consumer products company, wanted to improve service levels for customers. In addition, it wanted to assure high inventory turns and achieve peak manufacturing performance. Its approach was to use MEIO, which was piloted at one facility and then rolled out across the rest of the supply chain. This process allowed it to learn at the one facility, test assumptions, and fine-tune its work. When the project was completed, it reduced inventory by 23 percent and increased service levels from 76 percent to be consistently above 90 percent.[34]

Warehouse management systems (WMSs) are software tools used mainly to control and optimize warehouse operations. Their functionality is comparable to an ERP system that focuses on the warehouse. At their core, WMSs have both transaction and planning capabilities. However, many WMS software suites also incorporate extended capabilities that overlap with other types of software tools such as ERP, inventory management, or transportation management systems.

The core capability of a WMS is designed to parallel key warehousing functions such as product receiving, putaway, packing, and shipment. For each function, the WMS controls and optimizes operations. For example, when picking, the WMS keeps track of the items to be picked, the orders they belong to, the location of each item, and the packing station where the orders will be prepared for shipping. In addition to these basic functions, the WMS controls several related activities. One is replenishment, whereby the pick area is restocked with product from other storage areas in the warehouse. Some of the others are inventory counting and value-added services such as light assembly or kitting. Kitting is the assembly of items from different origins into one package to be used for a single purpose. For example, a nurse may use a vaccine kit to immunize a patient. The kit contains all that is needed: syringe, needle, vaccine, cotton, and a bandage. In this case, the value-added service is to assemble all items in a ready-to-use package.

WMSs are designed not only to maintain control of operations, but also to optimize them. Optimization software embedded in WMSs determine, for instance, the sequence in which items should be picked, how items should be slotted (i.e., located in the warehouse), or how labor should be optimally allocated. Managers may select different goals for the optimization. The possibilities include improving warehouse throughput, maximizing usage

[34] Ann Grackin, "Thinking Anew: Transform Your Supply Chain Using Multi-Echelon Inventory Optimization," ChainLink Research, *White Paper*, 2018, http://www.clresearch.com/media/docs/original/ME-Inventory-Optimization.pdf.

FIGURE 3.4
A Typical WMS System

Source: Technology Scribes, https://www.technology scribes.com/inside-jda-ware house-management-system.

Warehouse management system (WMS) functionality

Warehouse design	Inventory tracking	Receiving
Putaway	Pick-and-pack	Shipping
Labor management	Yard and dock management	Reporting

Demand planning	Procurement & sourcing	Warehouse management	Order fulfillment	Transportation management	Logistics optimization

Supply chain management (SCM) applications

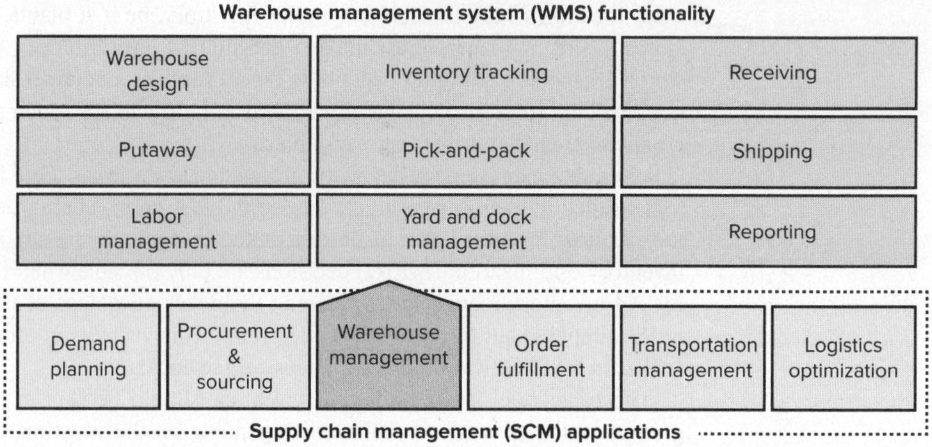

of warehouse capacity, minimizing cost, or meeting a customer service objective. Figure 3.4 shows a typical WMS system.

The main benefits of a WMS are better utilization of warehouse capacity, improved operational efficiency, better visibility of the order process, and better utilization of labor resources. On the other hand, WMS software is expensive to acquire and implement. In many cases, warehouse processes have to be redesigned to match the requirements of the WMS. As a result, WMS software systems are generally best suited to large warehousing operations.

All types of firms can benefit from the use of a WMS, be they manufacturers, retailers, wholesalers, or 3PLs. One 3PL, Atlanta Bonded Warehouse, started in the confectionery industry in 1948 and now operates contract food-grade, temperature-controlled services for a wide range of clientele. After an 18-month search, it implemented JDA's WMS to standardize its distribution operations across its 12 facilities, and improve customer service for its customers. Having the ability to track and trace food lot codes to support food safety requirements was critical, as the previous manual system was not very efficient. The WMS has allowed Atlanta Bonded Warehouse to onboard new clients faster, increase warehouse efficiency, and capture data to measure individual workers' performance. As Troy Snelson, General Manager of Public Warehouse Operations, noted, "JDA is critical to our business."[35]

Transportation management systems (TMSs) are software tools designed to manage transportation in the same way that WMS systems are designed to manage warehouses. Adoption of TMSs can be especially impactful because transportation is the largest cost in the supply chain. A unique feature of TMSs is that they have the task of integrating and sharing information among three different parties: shippers, customers, and third parties such as transportation and warehousing companies.[36]

Figure 3.5 shows a typical TMS. It depicts the three core functionalities and the internal and external links provided by TMSs. One key benefit of TMSs is that data flows seamlessly among functionalities, thus interlinking internal and external stakeholders of the system.

[35] "Atlanta Bonded Warehouse—Standardizing Warehouse Operations," *JDA White Paper*, 2017, https://jda.com/knowledge-center/collateral/atlanta-bonded-warehouse-case-study?ts=636516919946 233667&l=t.

[36] An infographic regarding the benefits of a TMS solution can be found at https://jda.com/-/media /jda/knowledge-center/infographics/infographic_a-holistic-approach-to-transportation-management -final.ashx.

FIGURE 3.5
A Typical TMS System

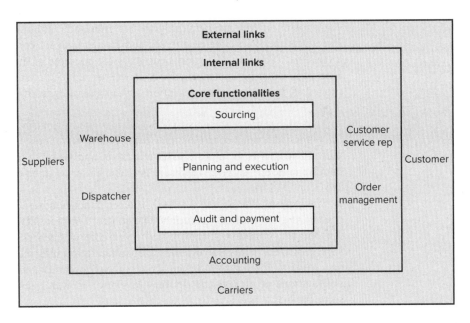

The first core functionality is carrier bidding. This enables the firm to automate the bidding of freight over specific lanes to pre-approved carriers. The bidding is often done over the Internet. This functionality also enables the firm to maintain records on carriers, carrier performance, and a freight rates database.

A second core functionality of TMSs is planning and execution. TMS plans and processes each shipment until it is received from a supplier or delivered to the customer. This includes processing order data to select transportation modes, optimizing load building, and determining shipment routing. Load building is the process of allocating cargo to a container or vehicle such that the resulting load is safe and compliant with regulations. It further balances efficiency of loading, weight distribution, and delivery sequence. The TMS also generates the appropriate documentation for each shipment and ensures that orders comply with all supplier or customer requirements such as pickup and delivery windows. This TMS functionality also enables shipment visibility throughout the delivery process and handles any order changes that might be requested by customers, such as altering the delivery date or adding a new item to the order.

Audit and payment is the third core functionality. The freight payment environment is very complex. The number of freight bills is generally large with different carriers and prices offered over many transportation lanes. In addition, freight billing and payment can take many forms: EDI, Internet, fax, or mail.

The audit functionality of a TMS keeps track of charges and discounts provided by carriers. It also checks for errors such as double billing to avoid overcharges. Once bills have been audited, the system authorizes and keeps track of payments.

One example of a TMS application is by Steelcase. This company, headquartered in Grand Rapids, Michigan, is the world's largest furniture manufacturer in the world, with 800 dealer locations throughout world. Prior to implementation finalized in 2017 it used a wide variety of planning software tools. Steelcase wanted to insource transportation planning to make better transportation decisions and better serve its customers. For instance, some customers wanted trucks loaded so that the office panels are unloaded first, followed by desks, and then chairs. Some buildings require elevator appointments to move the materials into the offices.[37] Steelcase uses SAP's

[37] "Steelcase, Nancy Hill, Presenting about Their TM Implementation with Novigo," https://www .youtube.com/watch?v=X5iyrUGisq0.

Transportation Management program for inbound, outbound, and interplant moves. The software allows Steelcase to see and know the exact cost of delivering an order to a customer. One of the biggest benefits it has received is increased visibility of where each of its shipments is at any time, as well as reduced costs, improved transportation processes, improved carrier selection, and global integration with the three other ERPs used by Steelcase.[38]

Yard management systems (YMSs) are designed primarily to manage containers and trailers in yards adjacent to manufacturing plants, warehouses, or other distribution facilities. Their goal is to improve asset utilization and visibility in order to reduce cost and improve customer service. YMSs are available either as stand-alone software or as part of WMS or TMS packages.

Similarly to WMSs and TMSs, the basic functionalities of YMSs are to automate control and to optimize execution. The control functionality of a YMS typically tracks the number, contents, location, and ownership of each container and trailer in the yard. It also keeps the corresponding documentation information about carriers, loads, and drivers. Finally, YMSs automate related communication tasks such as e-mail notifications of pickup and delivery to plant and warehouse managers, carriers, and shippers.

On the optimization side, YMSs assign trailers to drivers based on priority of movement, driver availability, and minimization of travel distance. Finally, YMSs also generate performance reports that serve as input to decision makers and to related systems such as WMS and TMS. For example, a YMS tracks the average time spent by a container or trailer in the yard or the average time spent on a warehouse dock.

Supply Chain Collaboration Support

Information technology tools are also needed to support supply chain collaboration. Some of these tools enable firms in the supply chain to collaborate in areas such as financial transactions, procurement, product design, or promotions. In each of these cases, data is exchanged among firms in the supply chain to improve operational efficiency and customer service. The data exchange is made possible by bar codes, EDI, and some of the other data capture and data transmission tools described earlier in the chapter. Two important areas of supply chain collaboration are coordinated inventory deployment and e-commerce, the buying and selling of products through electronic networks.

In coordinated inventory deployment, firms in the supply chain share demand, inventory, and promotional data to decide on the appropriate level of inventory to maintain throughout the supply chain. Vendor-managed inventory (VMI) is a form of supply chain collaboration whereby a supplier manages its customer's inventory using data supplied by the customer. It is important that the data is shared in a timely manner.[39] The level of inventory in the supply chain typically decreases because a single firm, the supplier, is able to coordinate inventory decisions for both firms. For instance, Ferrell Gas takes into account the location of all of its customers, as well as inventory, when scheduling deliveries, to maximize productivity and profits.[40]

[38] Ibid.; "Case Study: Steelcase," https://www.sap.com/about/customer-testimonials/finder.html?url_id=ctabutton-us-customer-finder&tag=solution:supply-chain/transportation-management.
[39] Andres Angulo, Heather Nachtmann, and Mathew A. Waller, "Supply Chain Information Sharing in a Vendor Managed Inventory Partnership," *Journal of Business Logistics*, Vol. 25, No. 1 (2004), pp. 101–120.
[40] Chris Jones, "A Different Approach to VMI," *DC Velocity*, August 12, 2013, http://blogs.dcvelocity.com/bestpractices/2013/08/a-different-approach-to-vmi.html.

Another form of coordinated inventory deployment is collaborative planning, forecasting, and replenishment (CPFR). CPFR works across organizational boundaries to develop a single forecast. In these cases their trading partners can use this forecast to effectively manage their supply chain activities, such as manufacturing, transportation, inventory, and labor utilization, to name a few. Inventory levels can be reduced, as well as the costs of transportation and manufacturing. For example, Sony (Canada) increased its in-stock levels from 87 percent to at least 95 percent while at the same time reducing overall supply chain inventory by 20 percent.

One of the first adopters of CPFR was Nabisco, which partnered with Wegman's, a grocery chain. Nabisco and Wegman's focused on improving the forecast of 22 Planter's peanut items. As a result, inventory levels decreased by 18 percent, while Nabisco's sales went up 31 percent and Wegman's dollar sales of nuts increased by 16 percent.[41] This points to the efficiencies of using information correctly: It is possible to increase sales, increase customer service, and reduce the cost of inventory.

Information technology tools are needed to enable e-commerce. E-commerce networks support either business to consumer (B2C) or business to business (B2B) settings. In a B2B setting, businesses exchange information through one or more computer networks, including the Internet. In a B2C setting, consumers may buy products from home using the Internet or use a kiosk in a store.

For instance, over the past several years personalized shopping assistants have increased on the Internet. Stitch Fix, Shop It To Me, Stylist, and M.M. LaFleur, to name a few, offer fashion consultants—and apps—to help select apparel choices for busy customers. Customers fill out a style profile and meet online with a stylist to determine preferences and the customer's budget. Items are selected and shipped to the customer, who keeps what he or she wants and sends the rest back.

Other B2C tools focus on apps developed by retailers and manufacturers, providing customers news about product updates, specials, or new arrivals. Almost everyone is getting in on the act. As of January 2017, over 2.2 million apps were available for download in Apple's iTunes App Store, with over 140 billion downloads worldwide! While shopping apps make up just over 1 percent of the available apps, they have one of the largest mobile audiences.[42]

What could possibly compare to Apple's iTunes App Store, or Google's Google Play? Businesses such as CDW and General Electric are developing their own enterprise app stores where employees can safely upload apps to communicate with vendors.[43]

Order Management

One of the key supply chain processes described in the SCOR Model is order management. It is important because orders are the triggers that set the supply chain in motion. The order management process starts with the initial contact between customer and supplier. It ends with the delivery of the order and subsequent after-sales service. While supply chain managers must manage both inbound and outbound orders, we focus on the customer, or outbound, side.

Steps in the Order Management Process

As indicated in Figure 3.6, the order management process might be separated into six steps: order generation, order receipt, order processing, order fulfillment, order shipment, and

[41] "Roadmap to CPFR: The Case Studies," Voluntary Interindustry Commerce Standards Association, 1999, pp. 33–44, https://www.scribd.com/document/41327891/04-1-4046-Nabisco-Wegmans-Pilot.
[42] "Number of Available Apps in the Apple App Store from July 2008 to January 2017," *Statista*, https://www.statista.com/statistics/263795/number-of-available-apps-in-the-apple-app-store/.
[43] Shane O'Neill, "The Enterprise App Store: 10 Must-Have Features," *CIO*, April 25, 2012, https://www.cio.com/article/2396723/mobile/the-enterprise-app-store--10-must-have-features.html.

FIGURE 3.6
The Order
Management Process

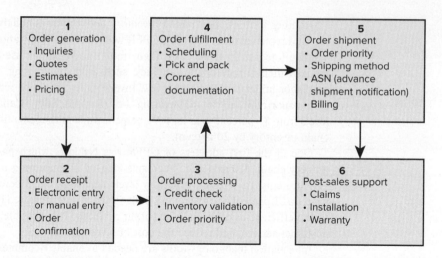

post-sales support. We first briefly describe each step. In the next section we discuss issues in the order management process.

Order generation encompasses the supply chain activities performed to obtain a customer order. These include responding to customer inquiries, preparing cost estimates, and pricing products. The second step is order receipt. An order may be received via a number of different methods, including EDI, which we covered earlier in this chapter. Alternatively, orders may be handed in by a salesperson, phoned in, or faxed. Usually the customer receives back an acknowledgment of the order, which may also be done via one of the methods listed above.

The order processing step is next. This refers to the preparation of an order to be filled. In this step, the customer's credit status is checked, as is the inventory availability of the ordered items. One additional preparatory activity is to prioritize orders to decide which ones will be filled first. This may be done according to a number of criteria. For example, orders may be filled on a first-come, first-served basis, by importance of customer; or to minimize production cost. In one such approach, customers are ranked by volume purchased. Orders are then allocated accordingly.[44]

The fourth step is order fulfillment, which starts by scheduling the picking of individual items and orders. The next activity is to produce a "pick list." The list triggers the warehouse activities of picking items, aggregating them by individual orders and customers, and then packing. The preparation of the related documentation for shipping occurs simultaneously. This step is described further in Chapter 6, *Warehouse Management*. Order shipment begins when deliveries are scheduled and the order is loaded in a vehicle for transportation to the customer's facility. Lastly, the customer also receives billing documentation, after the shipper receives a proof-of-delivery, or POD, that the order has been delivered. Chapter 5, *Transportation: Overview, Infrastructure, Measures, and Management*, covers additional information related to this step. The order management process does not end with the delivery of the product and the customer's payment. There is one more important step, post-sale support. This includes activities such as handling claims related to the order, for example, an unmatching weight or price. Post-sale support additionally includes warranty-related work, when an ordered product fails to match a performance requirement.

---

[44] For additional information on this approach, please see Walter Zinn, John T. Mentzer, and Keely L. Croxton, "Customer Based Measures of Inventory Availability," *Journal of Business Logistics*, Vol. 23, No. 2 (2002), pp. 19–44.

The Order Management Process

The role of a supply chain manager goes beyond understanding the steps in the order management process. The process needs to be actively managed to reduce cost and support customer service. An order is a key contact point between customer and supplier. It has been suggested that "every time an order is handled, the customer is handled. Every time an order sits unattended, the customer sits unattended."[45]

In order to reduce the cost of processing orders and managing the related level of customer service, managers need to first map the order process and then look for ways to reduce cost. Costs in the order management process often originate from one or more of the following causes:

- Gaps
- Bottlenecks
- Errors
- Duplication of activities

A process map is a visual representation of a process. In varying degrees of sophistication, it represents the path of the information throughout the supply chain, decisions and activities that occur at each point in the process, as well as the related timeline. If the process involves more than one function, as is the case with the order management process, the map should also represent the role of each function. Process maps may be paper-based or, as is often the case, be constructed with the help of specialized software.

There are many reasons for constructing a process map.[46] While they refer more generally to supply chain maps, some of the reasons also apply to mapping the order management process. First, mapping is crucial to redesign the order management process. It documents the current state of the process and provides a platform to examine potential improvements. Second, a process map facilitates a common understanding of the order management process. This is because the different people and functions involved in the order management process may develop different views of it. A process map promotes a common understanding because all involved base their views on the same information. Finally, a process map is an effective communication tool among all involved in the order management process.

Furthermore, to provide customer service, managers should work to reduce the time and uncertainty that it takes to move an order through the management process, especially the order cycle time. The order cycle time is the critical time period between a customer placing an order and its delivery. It is represented by steps 2 to 5 in Figure 3.6.

Customers value short order cycle times and low uncertainty about the time of delivery because this improves their ability to plan. Think, for instance, of a customer awaiting an express package. Knowing when the package will arrive is often as important as receiving it quickly. This is because the customer can make plans based on the arrival of the package. The customer could plan to be home to receive the package or to bring it on a trip and so on.

This same logic applies to business customers. The relevance of the order cycle time is straightforward: The longer the order cycle time, the longer customers must wait for ordered products. As a result, customers must either hold more inventory or anticipate their purchases. The earlier course of action results in a higher inventory carrying cost. A consequence of the latter course of action is that the customer works with a longer

[45] Benson P. Shapiro, V. Kasturi Rangan, and John J. Sviokla, "Staple Yourself to an Order," *Harvard Business Review*, July–August 1992, pp. 113–121.
[46] John T. Gardner and Martha C. Cooper, "Strategic Supply Chain Mapping Approaches," *Journal of Business Logistics*, Vol. 24, No. 2 (2003), pp. 37–64.

forecast horizon and thus a larger forecast error. Reducing order cycle time uncertainty is also an important factor in customer service. The greater the uncertainty about the time of delivery, the larger the investment in safety stock that the customer must make to ensure a smooth continuity to its operations.

The Future Role of Information

As we noted at the beginning of the chapter, the digital world has made time and space obsolete. Consumers can shop online, at any time, virtually anywhere in the world, and, in some cases, get what they ordered delivered to them within a few short hours. Amazon has even filed a patent for delivery trucks equipped with 3-D printers. When a customer orders a printable product, the order will begin printing as the truck drives to the final destination.[47] Where these and other technologies are headed—and the speed by which they will impact the market—are hard to determine. Two of the more impactful applications— blockchain and the Internet of Things (IoT)—are noted below.

Blockchain

More than at any other time in history do we care where products come from, and at the same time wish to have the ability to verify their pedigree. For instance, do you care where your coffee comes from? Do you care if it is Fair Trade? How do you know if the fish in your sandwich was certified by the Marine Stewardship Council? How do you know if the shoes on your feet really are from Nike? After all, one study estimates that counterfeit and pirated goods are worth nearly $500 billion each year.[48]

In part, labels, bar codes, and RFID tags have been used to verify where a product was produced, but these tags have limitations. Information about the product is not instantaneous or online. What is needed is a network available to everyone, and difficult or impossible to edit or alter.

Enter the world of blockchain. Suppose you want to buy a watch over the Internet. Usually there would be a middle person (or several!) involved in the transaction. A bank would record cash going from one account into another.

With blockchain, there are not middle persons. When the transaction is made, it is recorded on a ledger, or a block. These blocks are all joined together to form a chain, hence the name blockchain. Each of these blocks is shared across the network, making counterfeits or theft nearly impossible. It is assumed that consensus creates truth.

How would this apply to supply chains? It will differ by industry, but the impact could be significant. For instance, think about pharmaceuticals, where the chain of custody is critical and where ingredients for the medication may pass through several countries.[49] One study found the value of the counterfeit drug market to be around $200 billion.[50] In this case, a firm can create a block when the drug is made, another block when it passes quality assurance, and yet another when put in the DC. Other blocks would be added as the drug moves from the DC to a distributor, transportation provider, retailer, and finally to the hospital or patient. Information about the drug from its creation can be validated and verified by permissioned users.

---

[47] Brian Krassenstein, "Amazon Files Patent for Mobile 3D Printing Delivery Trucks," 3Dprint.com, February 25, 2015, https://3dprint.com/46934/amazon-3d-printing-patent/.

[48] "Global Trade in Fake Goods Worth Nearly Half a Trillion Dollars a Year—OECD & EUIPO," OECD, April 18, 2016, https://www.oecd.org/industry/global-trade-in-fake-goods-worth-nearly-half-a-trillion -dollars-a-year.htm.

[49] Alexandra Ossola, "The Fake Drug Industry Is Exploding, and We Can't Do Anything About It," *Newsweek*, September 17, 2015, accessed March 12, 2018, http://www.newsweek.com/2015/09/25 /fake-drug-industry-exploding-and-we-cant-do-anything-about-it-373088.html.

[50] "20 Shocking Counterfeit Drugs Statistics," HealthResearchFunding.org, https://healthresearchfunding .org/20-shocking-counterfeit-drugs-statistics/.

FIGURE 3.7
Types of Blockchains

Source: Timothy Leonard,
"Blockchain for Transportation:
Where the Future Starts,"
TMW Systems, Inc., *White
Paper*, 2017.

	Public	**Private**	**Consortium**
Structure	Decentralized	Centralized	Partially decentralized
Access	Open read/write	Permissioned	Permissioned
Speed	Slower (~10 minutes)	Faster (same as a transactional system)	Varies by the number of nodes
Consensus	Proof of work Proof of stake	Pre-approved	Pre-approved
Identity	Anonymous	Known identities	Known identities
Use cases	Cryptoeconomy	Reference data management	Secure data sharing
Examples	Bitcoin, ethereum, dash	MONAX, multichain	R3, EWF

There are three basic types or platforms for blockchains, as noted in Figure 3.7. Public blockchain is what we typically think of when it comes to blockchains. It is a decentralized network open to all; users read transactions, add themselves to the network, and transfer assets. Security is based on consensus; everyone has the same data, counterfeiting becomes incredibly difficult. Achieving this consensus can take time, ranging from 2 to 10 minutes.[51]

A private blockchain is centralized and users are preapproved, or permissioned, to be a member of the network. Because private blockchains are permissioned, speed to verify a block is much faster. Private blockchains are typical for internal functions within a firm.

A consortium blockchain is a hybrid of the previous two types. It is decentralized and permissioned. All of the rules and policies governing the blockchain are defined by the members.[52] For instance, Maersk is partnering with IBM to create a new company that "intends to help shippers, ports, customs offices, banks, and other stakeholders in global supply chains track freight as well as replace related paperwork with tamper-resistant digital records."[53] This will greatly increase efficiency and timeliness in transportation. IBM has also partnered with Walmart, Unilever, Nestle, and others in blockchains focused on supply chains and food safety.

Blockchains are not without limitations. One of the most mundane roadblocks is the current infrastructure between shippers and carriers. EDI has been around since before the 1950s, and getting everyone to change will be a daunting effort.

Another issue will be speed. In a public blockchain, security is based on consensus; everyone in the blockchain gets the same information. Achieving consensus takes time—and speed is needed for the digital supply chain to flourish.

Along with speed, there are few global standards. This situation of lacking standards is common in logistics and transportation. EDI formats vary, as do RFID standards.

Finally, blockchains are not an environmentally friendly solution. Blockchains require consensus; this means multitudes of computers are involved in this process. Bitcoin's blockchain is estimated to consume more energy than what 159 countries consume in a single year.[54]

---

[51] Timothy Leonard, "Blockchain for Transportation: Where the Future Starts," TMW Systems, Inc., *White Paper*, 2017.
[52] Ibid.
[53] Robert Hackett, "IBM and Maersk Are Creating a New Blockchain Company," *Fortune*, January 16, 2018, http://fortune.com/2018/01/16/ibm-blockchain-maersk-company/.
[54] Dom Galeon, "Mining Bitcoin Costs More Energy Than What 159 Countries Consume in a Year," *Futurism*, November 27, 2017, https://futurism.com/mining-bitcoin-costs-more-energy-159-countries-consume-year/.

Internet of Things (IoT)

Some of us started to learn about connectivity back in kindergarten, where we sang that the toe bone is connected to the foot bone, the foot bone is connected to the heel bone, and the heel bone is connected to the leg bone. In many ways, the sensors in our clothes are connected to our phone, and our phone is connected to our Mac or PC, which is connected to our garage door, oven, toaster, refrigerator, car, and dog, just to name a few. It is not just an Internet for people, but an Internet of Things (IoT) as well.

Conceptually, it is easy to understand the IoT. It allows our devices to connect to us, each other, and our applications over the Internet. Your clothes can tell us how effective your workout was and track the calories you burned. If you are on a diet, an app can recommend what you should eat today based on your workout, your diet, and what food you have in your smart refrigerator. Perhaps one day the refrigerator will send the car to the supermarket to pick up food you need for dinner—all without your prompting.

In fact, there are probably more things on the Internet than people. In 2016 it was estimated that there were anywhere from 6.4 billion devices (not including computers, phones, or tablets) to 17.4 billion devices (including everything).[55] World population? Less than 8 billion!

Information is critical to the effective and efficient operations of a supply chain, and for this reason the IoT could have dramatic impacts on how supply chain activities are completed. Internally, production efficiencies can increase and errors be reduced by using better technology. Prior to using RFID tags, Whirlpool used a manual process to track washing machines being made at the factory. Paper tags on the lid would fall off, resulting in lost and excess inventory. Now, using RFID tags, managers have real-time information about production and the location of the inventory. Items are assembled and painted based on real demand. Quality went up, and inventory levels went down.[56]

It is difficult to determine exactly when and how IoT (and blockchain) will impact logistics, transportation, and supply chain management. Both are merging technologies, still being tested in the field. Greater visibility of both can only benefit manufacturers, distributors, and retailers, especially as consumer's appetite for real-time visibility continues to grow. Both technologies play a critical role in the digital world that stands before us.

Summary

Recall that we began this chapter by referring to information as the lifeline of supply chains. This is because managers need information to support all activities and decisions in supply chain management. In particular, information is needed to maintain visibility of supply chain assets, to manage daily operations, and to support supply chain planning and strategy.

In addition to describing the uses of information in supply chains, there were three additional learning objectives for this chapter. First was to describe how information is used to capture and transmit data in supply chains. We reviewed tools available to support supply chain managers in each of those areas. Bar codes and radio frequency identification (RFID) are data capture tools. Supply chain managers may select Electronic Data Interchange (EDI), Extensible Markup Language (XML), and/or Value Added Networks (VANs) as data transmission tools.

[55] Amy Nordrum, "Popular Internet of Things Forecast of 50 Billion Devices by 2020 Is Outdated," *IEEE*, August 18, 2016, https://spectrum.ieee.org/tech-talk/telecom/internet/popular-internet-of-things -forecast-of-50-billion-devices-by-2020-is-outdated.
[56] Joe Mariani, Evan Quasney, and Michael Raynor, "Forging Links into Loops: The Internet of Things' Potential to Recast Supply Chain Management," *Deloitte Review*, Issue 17, July 27, 2015, https://www2 .deloitte.com/insights/us/en/deloitte-review/issue-17/internet-of-things-supply-chain-management.html.

In support of the second objective, understanding how information is used, we reviewed enterprise resource planning (ERP) as a software tool available to support transactions in supply chains. In the area of supply chain planning, there are tools available to support integrated operations, such as application programming interfaces (APIs), as well as tools to support specific functions. These tools support inventory management, warehouse management system (WMS), transportation management system (TMS), and yard management system (YMS). Information is also crucial to support supply chain collaboration in areas such as vendor-managed inventory (VMI); collaborative planning, forecasting, and replenishment (CPFR); and e-commerce.

The final objective of this chapter was to review the order management process, which is critical to both cost management and customer service. We discussed the steps in order management, the importance of process maps to manage the order management process, and the importance of the order cycle time and its related uncertainty.

In the next chapter, we will examine the role of inventory in the management of supply chains.

Suggested Readings

Ames, Ben, "IT Firm Rolls out Platform to Expedite Data Exchange among Carriers, 3PLs, Shippers," DC Velocity, December 9, 2015, available at http://www.dcvelocity.com/articles/12051209-it-firm-rolls-out-platform-to-expedite-data-exchange-among-carriers-3pls-shippers/.

Angulo, Andres, Heather Nachtmann, and Mathew A. Waller, "Supply Chain Information Sharing in a Vendor Managed Inventory Partnership," *Journal of Business Logistics*, Vol. 25, No. 1 (2004), pp. 101–120.

Grackin, Ann, "Thinking Anew—Transform Your Supply Chain Using Multi-Echelon Inventory Optimization" ChainLink Research whitepaper, 2018, http://www.clresearch.com/media/docs/original/ME-Inventory-Optimization.pdf.

Jacobs, Robert F., and F.C. 'Ted' Weston Jr., "Enterprise Resource Planning—A Brief History," *Journal of Operations Management*, Vol. 24, No. 2 (2007), pp. 357–363.

Jones, Chris, "A Different Approach to VMI," DC Velocity, August 12, 2013, http://blogs.dcvelocity.com/bestpractices/2013/08/a-different-approach-to-vmi.html.

Sanders, Nada, *Big Data Driven Supply Chain Management: A Framework for Implementing Analytics and Turning Information into Intelligence*, Pearson Education, 2014. (Upper Saddle River, NJ: /)

Tillman, Joe, Karl B. Manrodt, and Donnie Williams, "DC Measures 2017," WERCWatch, Spring 2017, Warehouse Education Research Council, Chicago, IL.

Questions and Problems

LO 3-1   1. Describe the role information plays in managing the supply chain. How important is it?

LO 3-2   2. What are the three basic reasons supply chain managers need information?

LO 3-3   3. Briefly describe any three tools used to support planning and collaboration in the supply chain. How would not having these tools impact supply chain performance?

LO 3-4   4. Briefly describe the order management process.

4

Sales Forecasting and Inventory Management

Objectives of This Chapter

LO 4-1   To describe methods used in sales forecasting.

LO 4-2   To describe measures of forecast error.

LO 4-3   To describe reasons for holding inventory.

LO 4-4   To show how to size inventory in support of a customer service policy. See: Inventory Management

LO 4-5   To review symptoms of poor inventory management. See: Symptoms of Poor Inventory Management

Introduction

In this chapter we describe two important issues in supply chain management: sales forecasting and inventory management. A sales forecast is an effort to estimate future sales to customers. It is a key input to supply chain management because it is the first step in planning supply chain operations. Supply chain managers are key participants in the firm's effort to forecast sales. They are also key users of sales forecasts. This is because supply chain managers are tasked with developing plans to ensure that enough assets are allocated to match sales. Some of these assets include labor, trucks, warehouse space, and production capacity. They further include inventory.

The second issue we take up is inventory management. The supply chain manager must decide on the level of inventory to be maintained for each individual item stocked by the company, as well as the size and frequency of inventory replenishments. The goal is to achieve minimum cost at a predetermined level of service. Note that the goal is not to reduce inventory investment as an end in itself, but rather to determine the proper level of inventory needed to minimize cost subject to a customer service policy.

We'll begin by describing methods available to forecast sales. We'll look into different approaches to measure forecast error. Next, we explain reasons why firms hold inventory. We distinguish between base and safety stock and use these concepts to look into how firms decide on the size of the inventory they need to maintain. In the final two sections of the chapter we review methods of inventory control and describe symptoms of poor inventory management.

Sales Forecasting

Sales forecasting is the process of gathering and analyzing information to estimate future sales. This can be done either by extending past sales data into the future or by harvesting the judgment of individuals. A common misconception about sales forecasting is that it needs to be perfect to be useful. A frequently asked question is: "Why bother to forecast if it is always wrong anyway?" While every forecast has some level of error, the bottom line is that firms are better off with the forecast than without it. Sales forecasts are needed to plan supply chain operations. It is better to plan with an estimated number than with no estimation at all.

Thus, there are important reasons to forecast sales: The level of production must reflect expected sales because failure to produce the right quantities of the right products results in either excess inventory or stock-outs. Expected sales are equally a key input to estimate transportation requirements, the amount of product expected to move through warehouses, and the level of inventory needed to support sales.

Sales forecast data is also shared among firms in the supply chain. This is because the supply chain operations of one firm in the supply chain are often dependent on the sales forecast provided by another firm in the supply chain. For instance, a supplier with access to its customer's sales forecast is able to adjust its own production schedule accordingly to reflect not only the expected sales to the customer but also the timing of those sales. In sum, it is not feasible to manage supply chains without a sales forecast.

Forecasting Methods

Forecasting methods may be divided into two basic categories: qualitative and quantitative forecasts. Qualitative forecasts are based on the judgment of one or more knowledgeable forecasters. They are generally used when historical sales data are scarce or judged useless. Quantitative forecasts are based on projections of historical sales data. They are best used whenever past sales are expected to be a good indicator of future sales.

Qualitative Forecasting Methods

While there are many qualitative forecasting methods available, we describe some that are commonly used. These include consensus panel, the Delphi method, and sales force estimates.

Consensus Panel

A consensus panel is formed by a group of experts who jointly decide on a sales forecast. Experts communicate with each other in the search for a consensus. One potential problem with this method is that the consensus may drift toward the experts with strongest personalities, who are not necessarily the ones with the best estimate. Alternatively, the experts may arrive at the estimate by averaging individual estimates. One classic example is Sport Obermeyer, a skiwear fashion firm that develops annual forecasts with a panel of six key managers that comprise its Buying Committee.[1] Because fashion changes yearly and the lead time from product design to the retail store is rather long, historical data is of little help. The Buying Committee meets for a day and attempts to develop consensus estimates. The forecast is arrived at by either adopting the consensus estimates or by a leading expert who decides on a final number after considering all the other experts' estimates.

---

[1] Janice H. Hammond and Ananth Raman, *HBS Case 9-695-022: Sport Obermeyer, Ltd.* (Boston, MA: HBS Publishing, 1994).

Delphi Method

The Delphi method is a variation of the consensus panel where experts work independently and anonymously to arrive at a consensus. This avoids the danger that the consensus is biased toward the experts with stronger personalities. A facilitator prepares a questionnaire and sends it to the experts. Each expert then answers the questions without consulting the other experts. After receiving all questionnaires, the facilitator prepares a summary report and sends it to the experts. After reading the summary report, experts have an opportunity to revise their answers. The revised answers typically begin to converge because all experts read the same summary report. This process is repeated until answers no longer converge, usually after a consensus is reached. This method works on a wide range of topics, for instance, making new policy recommendations on international ship emissions.[2]

Sales Force Estimate

Sales force estimates draw forecasts from the expert judgment of salespersons. The sales force is closest to customers and thus is in the best position to anticipate customer needs and detect changes in market trends. Sales force estimates can be particularly useful in situations where the accuracy of forecasts depends on landing a few large orders from customers. On the other hand, sales force estimates are subject to salesperson bias. Salespersons may have an incentive to under-forecast because the forecast may serve as a basis to establish sales quotas. Conversely, in a different situation, salespersons may have an incentive to over-forecast if they perceive that the higher estimate will generate more support for the products they sell. To counter this problem, it has been suggested that firms evaluate and compensate their sales force not only for meeting sales quotas, but also for providing accurate sales forecasts.[3]

Quantitative Forecasting Methods

Recall that quantitative forecasting methods are recommended whenever historical sales data is deemed a good indicator of future sales. We describe the following quantitative forecasting methods: moving average, exponential smoothing, exponential smoothing with trend correction, and exponential smoothing with seasonality index.

Moving Average

A moving average (MA) is a simple and easy-to-use forecasting method. It uses the average sales of a prespecified number of past periods as a forecast of the next period in the future. For example, if a firm wants to predict October sales using an MA of the past three months, then it needs actual sales data for July, August, and September. Assuming that sales for those three months were respectively 130, 170, and 120, the forecast for October will be the average of the three numbers, or 140.

More formally, the equation needed to compute the MA is:

$$F_{t+1} = \frac{A_t + A_{t-1} + A_{t-2} + \dots + A_{t-(n+1)}}{n}, \text{ where:}$$

F_{t+1} = Forecast for period t + 1

A_t = Actual sales in period t

n = Number of periods

[2] Michael Bloor, Helen Sampson, Susan Baker, and Katrin Dahlgren, "Useful but No Oracle: Reflections on the Use of a Delphi Group in a Multimethods Policy Research Study," *Qualitative Research*, Vol. 15, No. 1 (2015), pp. 57–70.

[3] Mark A. Moon and John T. Mentzer, "Improving Salesforce Forecasting," *Journal of Business Forecasting*, Vol. 18, No. 2 (1999), pp. 7–12.

TABLE 4.1
Sales Forecasting with the Moving Average Method

			Forecasts		
Year	Month	Actual Sales	MA (3)	MA (4)	MA (5)
2006	January	200			
2006	February	150			
2006	March	90			
2006	April	150	146.7		
2006	May	210	130.0	147.5	
2006	June	160	150.0	150.0	160.0
2006	July	110	173.3	152.5	152.0
2006	August	120	160.0	157.5	144.0
2006	September	160	130.0	150.0	150.0
2006	October	170	130.0	137.5	152.0
2006	November	180	150.0	140.0	144.0
2006	December	110	170.0	157.5	148.0
2007	January	90	153.3	155.0	148.0
2007	February	160	126.7	137.5	142.0
2007	March	210	120.0	135.0	142.0
2007	April	110	153.3	142.5	150.0
2007	May	150	160.0	142.5	136.0
2007	June	220	156.7	157.5	144.0
2007	July	130	160.0	172.5	170.0
2007	August	170	166.7	152.5	164.0
2007	September	120	173.3	167.5	156.0
2007	October		140.0	160.0	158.0

Table 4.1 shows a more complete example with forecasts for several months using three different moving average periods: 3, 4, and 5. Note how the moving average forecast reflects past changes in actual sales. Note also that monthly forecasts not only reflect the month that has been added since the previous forecast, but also the month that was dropped since the previous forecast. For example, the three-period moving average forecast for August 07 is higher than the equivalent forecast for July 07. The change reflects the dual facts that the August 07 forecast added the actual sales for July 07 and dropped the actual sales for April 07.

A key decision to make when forecasting with the MA method is to select the number of periods to use in the moving average. The larger the number of periods, the less the moving average reflects recent changes in sales. This is illustrated in Figure 4.1, which graphs a subset of the data in Table 4.1. Note how the five-period moving average (MA (5)) varies less than the three-period moving average (MA (3)). Note also how both moving averages vary less than actual sales. The optimum number of periods to select is the one that produces the smallest forecast error. Forecast errors will be discussed elsewhere in this chapter.

The moving average method has an important shortcoming. Without modification, it *does not consider either trend or seasonality in the data.* "Trend" means that average actual sales may be increasing or decreasing over time. "Seasonality" reflects predictable variations in demand due to an external factor. For example, sales for certain types of apparel are predictably higher during the "back-to-school" season, while skiwear sales are predictably lower in the summer.

FIGURE 4.1
Actual Sales History
and Moving Average
Forecasts

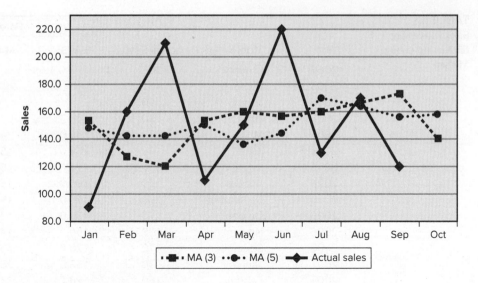

Exponential Smoothing

Exponential smoothing (ES) is a very popular forecasting method. It is easy to use and requires little data. In addition, through the use of a smoothing parameter described below, the ES method enables the forecaster to consider a longer sales history than the moving average method, which is limited to the number of periods included in the computation of the moving average.

On the other hand, the ES method is not recommended for long-term forecasts. It is best used to forecast one to three periods in the future. In addition, forecast errors may be large if the variability in the sales history is significant.

To forecast sales for a given period, all that is needed is the previous period's actual and forecasted sales, as well as the value of a smoothing parameter. An ES forecast is based on actual sales for the immediate past period plus a correction for the error in the previous forecast. The impact of the past forecast error is weighted by the smoothing parameter, which is represented by the Greek letter alpha (a). The smoothing parameter can take any value between zero and one. A value of zero means that the error in the previous forecast period is not considered in the next forecast. In other words, the forecast for the previous period is repeated for the following period. One the other hand, when $\alpha = 1$, the forecast for the following period is simply the actual sales in the previous period. More formally:

$$F_{t+1} = aA_t + (1 - a)F_t, \text{ where:}$$
$$F_{t+1} = \text{Forecast for period } t + 1$$
$$A_t = \text{Actual sales for period } t$$
$$a = \text{Smoothing parameter}$$

Table 4.2 displays sales forecasts with the Exponential Smoothing method using three different values for the smoothing parameter: .2, .5, and .8. The actual sales values displayed are the same ones used in Table 4.1. The forecast for October 07 with an alpha value of .2 was calculated as follows:

$$F_{t+1} = .2 \cdot 120 + (1 - .2) \cdot 158.6 = 150.9$$

Figure 4.2 graphs a subset of the data in Table 4.2, specifically the actual sales and forecasts since January 07 with .2 and .8 as values for the smoothing parameter. Note how the

TABLE 4.2
Sales Forecasting
with the Exponential
Smoothing Method

Year	Month	Actual Sales	Forecasts		
			$\alpha = .2$	$\alpha = .5$	$\alpha = .8$
2006	January	200	200.0	200.0	200.0
2006	February	150	200.0	200.0	200.0
2006	March	90	190.0	175.0	160.0
2006	April	150	170.0	140.0	110.0
2006	May	210	166.0	160.0	154.0
2006	June	160	174.8	188.0	201.2
2006	July	110	171.8	167.4	163.0
2006	August	120	159.5	140.9	122.4
2006	September	160	151.6	139.7	127.9
2006	October	170	153.3	155.8	158.3
2006	November	180	156.6	161.6	166.7
2006	December	110	161.3	168.3	175.3
2007	January	90	151.0	135.6	120.3
2007	February	160	138.8	120.5	102.2
2007	March	210	143.1	149.4	155.8
2007	April	110	156.4	176.5	196.6
2007	May	150	147.2	133.2	119.3
2007	June	220	147.7	148.6	149.4
2007	July	130	162.2	183.9	205.5
2007	August	170	155.7	146.1	136.4
2007	September	120	158.6	162.9	167.1
2007	October		150.9	139.3	127.7

FIGURE 4.2
Actual Sales History
and Exponential
Smoothing Forecasts

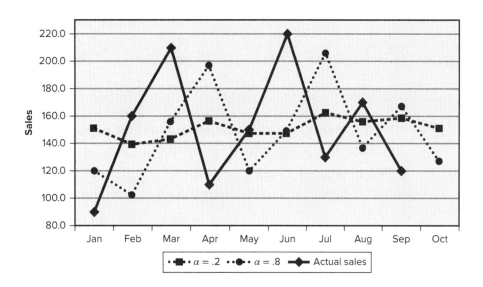

forecast values follow more closely the value of the previous period's actual sales whenever the value of α is high (.8).

The disparity in the forecasts obtained with the two different values for the smoothing parameter demonstrates the importance of selecting the right value for α. As was the case with selecting the right number of periods to forecast with a moving average, forecasters should select the value of α that leads to the smallest forecast error.

Exponential Smoothing with Trend Correction

We now focus on how to modify the ES method in order to incorporate trend in the data. The method is also known as *second-order exponential smoothing.* When sales trend up or down, the forecast needs to be correspondingly adjusted up or down. This is done by adding or subtracting a quantity known as trend value or T_t. The trend value is a function of the current period's trend, the past period's trend, and β, a trend smoothing parameter. The equation to compute the trend value is below:

$$T_{t+1} = \beta(F_{t+1} - F_t) + (1 - \beta)T_t, \text{ where:}$$

$$T_{t+1} = \text{Trend value for next period's forecast}$$
$$\beta = \text{Trend smoothing parameter.}$$

Note that the term $(F_{t+1} - F_t)$ represents the current trend. It is the forecast for the next period minus the forecast for the current period. The term T_t represents the previous trend. The trend value for the next period is determined as a balance between the two terms. Whenever β, the trend smoothing parameter, has a low value, the trend value for the next period relies more on the previous trend value. Conversely, a high β indicates that the trend value relies more on the current trend. The range of β is between 0 and 1. As is the case with the smoothing parameter α, forecasters should select the value of β that produces the smallest forecast error.

Once the trend value for the next period is computed, it is added or subtracted from the next period's initial forecast. The result is the trend-corrected forecast for the next period. Thus:

$$F_{t+1} = \alpha A_t + (1 - \alpha)F_t$$
$$T_{t+1} = \beta(F_{t+1} - F_t) + (1 - \beta)T_t$$
$$TF_{t+1} = F_{t+1} + T_{t+1}, \text{ where:}$$

$$TF_{t+1} = \text{Trend-corrected forecast for the next period.}$$

As an illustration, we will trend correct the ES forecast obtained previously with data from Table 4.2. Recall that the previously obtained forecast for the next period was:

$$F_{t+1} = .2 \cdot 120 + (1 - .2) \cdot 158.6 = 150.9$$

If we assume values of .4 and −5 for β and T_t respectively, the trend value is computed below. Note that the negative value for T_t means merely that sales are trending downward.

$$T_{t+1} = .4(150.9 - 158.6) + (1 - .4)(-5) = -6.1$$

And the trend-corrected forecast for the next period is:

$$TF_{t+1} = 150.9 - 6.1 = 144.8.$$

Exponential Smoothing with Seasonality Index

In addition to a trend component, sales data may also exhibit seasonality. One of the methods available to apply the ES method when there is seasonality in the data is to use a seasonality index.

When adjusted with a seasonality index, sales figures from different seasons become comparable. For example, if sales in the high season are typically 20 percent higher than average, than the seasonality index is 1.2. If the high season sales figure is divided by 1.2, the resulting seasonally adjusted figure becomes comparable to seasonally adjusted figures for different seasons.

The procedure for using a seasonality index to forecast sales is to first use the seasonality index to render sales figures comparable across seasons. The second step is to use the ES method to forecast sales. The forecaster may choose either the simple ES method or the trend-corrected ES method. In fact, this procedure also works with the moving average method. Finally, once the forecast with seasonally adjusted numbers is obtained, the seasonality index is used again to remove the seasonal adjustment from the forecast. The hypothetical example below illustrates the procedure.

We now focus on illustrating the computation of the seasonal indexes. Clearly, seasonality can occur in different periods. Fertilizer sales, for instance, tend to peak in the spring months, while back-to-school sales tend to peak in August and September. In this illustration, however, seasonality is weekly. Sales peak in the fourth week of every month. Therefore, we need to compute a seasonal index for every week of the month.

The computation of seasonal indexes requires historical sales data. The January to April actual sales data in Table 4.3, and presented graphically in Figure 4.3, serves this purpose. The first step is to compute average actual sales for every week. These are displayed in Table 4.4. Average sales for the first week of the month are 65.5. This number was obtained by averaging first week sales for the months of January to April. We next compute a grand average, which is the average for all 16 weeks from January to April. The seasonal index for the first week is the ratio of the first week average sales and the grand average. More specifically: 65.5/74.3 = .88.

TABLE 4.3
Actual and Deseasonalized Sales

	Week	Actual Sales	Deseasonalized Sales
Jan.	1	62	70.5
	2	68	80.0
	3	65	73.9
	4	100	71.9
Feb.	1	70	79.5
	2	63	74.1
	3	61	69.3
	4	105	75.5
Mar.	1	60	68.2
	2	62	72.9
	3	69	78.4
	4	98	70.5
Apr.	1	70	79.5
	2	60	70.6
	3	66	75.0
	4	110	79.1
May	1	65	73.9
	2	62	72.9
	3	67	76.1

FIGURE 4.3
Actual and
Deseasonalized Sales

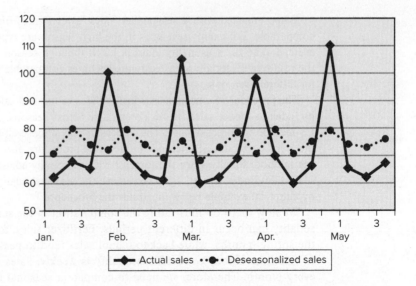

TABLE 4.4
Computation of
Seasonality Indexes

Week	Actual Sales Average	Seasonality Index
1	65.5	0.88
2	63.2	0.85
3	65.2	0.88
4	103.2	1.39
Grand Average	74.3	

The deseasonalized sales figures in Table 4.3 serve as the basis for the sales forecast. If we select a simple exponential smoothing method to forecast sales for the fourth week of May, we need to know the actual sales and the forecasted sales for the third week in May and the value of the smoothing parameter. Actual sales in the third week in May were 67. Let us assume that the values for the forecasted sales in the third week in May and the smoothing parameter are 64 and .5, respectively.

Because the forecast is made with deseasonalized data, we need to deseasonalize the values for the actual and forecasted sales in the third week in May. These are 76.1 and 72.7. Thus, the deseasonalized ES forecast for the fourth week in May is:

$$F_{t+1} = aA_t + (1 - a)F_t = (.5)76.1 + (1 - .5)72.7 = 74.4$$

To finalize the forecast, we need to restore the seasonality to account for the sales peak in the fourth week of the month. Thus, we multiply the seasonality index for the fourth week by the deseasonalized forecast obtained above: 74.4 · 1.39 = 103.4.

In the following section, we look at two methods firms use to avoid making forecasting errors by working more closely with suppliers and customers and building internal integration. Then, we'll discuss ways to measure forecasting error.

Integrating Qualitative and Quantitative Forecasts: S&OP and CPFR

Sales & Operations Planning (S&OP)

Sales & operations planning is an integrative process that encourages firms to integrate multiple functions in the organization to share information in order to develop more accurate forecasts so as to align resources to a single demand plan. S&OP focuses on three primary components: people, process, and technology. S&OP allows firms to share forecasts and plans in a collaborative environment, which are then shared with suppliers and customers.

The S&OP process has five critical steps that firms can follow. It utilizes both qualitative and quantitative data in order to develop a consensus plan for the firm.[4] Step 1 focuses on gathering data from sales and marketing to develop a baseline demand forecast, typically ranging from a 6- to 18-month planning horizon. Step 2 occurs simultaneously with Step 1, as the operations team gathers information regarding current inventory strategies and capacity, and develops an initial supply plan that is based on the current consensus plan developed by the marketing function. In Step 3, the formal S&OP team meets to develop the final operating plan for the next period. In these cross-functional meetings, representatives from marketing, operations, purchasing, logistics, and finance make key decisions regarding personnel involved and the meeting frequency needed to implement the final S&OP plan. Step 4 is when the S&OP team distributes and implements the plan, primarily through the operations and sales team, who carry the primary burden of meeting required production targets and adjusting the sales plans. The final step is to measure the results and effectiveness of the S&OP process.

Collaborative Planning, Forecasting, & Replenishment (CPFR)

Collaborative planning, forecasting, and replenishment (CPFR) is a cohesive bundle of business processes whereby supply chain trading partners share information, synchronized forecasts, risks, costs, and benefits with the intent of improving supply chain performance through joint planning and decision making.[5] CPFR was developed by practitioners in the mid-1990s through a pilot project conducted by Walmart, Warner Lambert, SAP, Manugistics, and Benchmarking Partners to enable retailers and manufacturers to jointly forecast demand and schedule production. CPFR allows the supply chain partners to share information and exchange complex decision support models and manufacturing/retailer strategies. CPFR is a similar process to S&OP; however, where S&OP primarily focuses on internal cross-functional demand forecasting alignment, CPFR seeks to integrate multiple firms across the supply chain into the demand planning process in order to synchronize inventory strategies up and down the supply chain. Certainly, advances in technology have made this approach possible; however, it must be stated that this approach to demand planning requires a high level of trust between supply chain partners, as significant amounts of data and information must be shared in order to be effective using CPFR.

The standard CPFR model has four primary activities that manufacturers and retailers engage in to improve their activities: (1) strategy and planning; (2) demand and supply management; (3) execution; and (4) analysis (see Figure 4.4).[6] The CPFR process is a closed-loop process that is built on the foundation of synchronized product data and electronic messaging standards. This allows point-of-sale data to be shared and distributed throughout the supply chain, thus enabling collaboration of the participants in order to meet demand. Many firms have benefited from increased information sharing and collaboration through the CPFR process. The nearby Exhibit demonstrates how Sony integrated consensus forecasting, S&OP, and CPFR to achieve greater results both internally and with its supply chain partners.

---

[4] J. Andrew Grimson and David F. Pyke, "Sales & Operations Planning: An Exploratory Study and Framework," *International Journal of Logistics Management*, Vol. 18, Issue 3 (2007), pp. 322–46.

[5] Robert L. Hollmann, Luis F. Scavarda, and Antonio M. T. Thome, "Collaborative Planning, Forecasting and Replenishment: A Literature Review," *International Journal of Productivity and Performance Management*, Vol. 64, Issue 7 (2015), pp. 971–93.

[6] *Collaborative Planning, Forecasting & Replenishment: An Overview*, VICS (Voluntary Interindustry Commerce Standards), 2004, https://www.gs1us.org/DesktopModules/Bring2mind/DMX/Download .aspx?Command=Core_Download&EntryId=492&language=en-US&PortalId=0&TabId=134.

FIGURE 4.4
CPFR Process Model

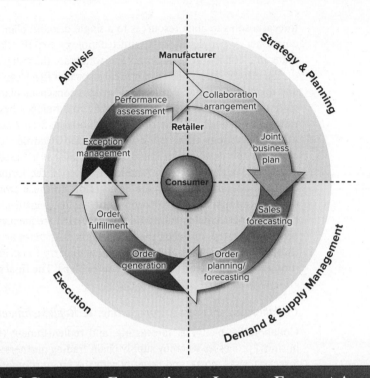

Exhibit: How Sony Used Consensus Forecasting to Improve Forecast Accuracy and Collaboration with Retail Partners

Coming out of the global financial crisis in 2008, Sony Electronics, the sales and distribution subsidiary of Japan's Sony Corporation, needed a strategy to survive and succeed in a new environment where a decade of upheaval was changing the rules of supply chain excellence. This strategy required a new focus on sharing information and collaborating with key retail partners in order to get more accurate forecasting projections.

Sony integrated its S&OP plan with its current collaborative planning, forecasting, and replenishment (CPFR) process in order to achieve results that go beyond the traditional, short-term benefits typically realized from each process on its own. After focusing on cost reduction strategies in order to reduce number of parts and material suppliers by 50 percent, targeting purchasing cost reductions of 20 percent in FY 2010, and divesting assets, it then realized the need to collaborate more effectively with its key retail partners. Here is how it achieved its goals:

- *Move from tactical and reactive to strategic and proactive:* Yuka Yu, VP of Supply Chain Operations at Sony, created a dedicated cross-functional team with representatives from sales, business planning, channel management, and supply chain groups to focus on improving planning and forecasting. This group created standardized metrics to provide more accuracy in the forecasting process, formalized the CPFR partnership, and gave added focus to discussions with retailers.

- *One plan, one number:* With collaboration established, deeper levels of analysis and partnership with retailers allowed greater levels of information sharing through consolidated forecasts. This consolidation allowed Sony and its partners to create a consensus demand plan, which provided a "one-number" plan needed for the S&OP. The benefits were immediate, as Sony shared the plan with factory suppliers, who used the consensus forecast to develop production and shipment schedules, which allowed for greater accuracy concerning product allocation in various sales channels.

- *Share and exploit data:* Sony then gained access to its retailers' store-level demand data in real time by utilizing an offshore team in India to analyze sales trends in the stores and have that information waiting for store managers' morning CPFR calls. This resulted in an increase of in-stock levels at stores by up to 18 percent with the same aggregate inventory levels, with forecast accuracy improved by up to 40 percent.

This success story earned Sony Electronics the recognition by Walmart Stores, Inc., as its 2009 Supplier of the Year, along with improved performance of financial growth versus the prior year, market-share gains, ability to provide new technology and innovative design, marketing collaborations, and support of Walmart's online business.

Source: Yumiko Kato, "Sony Electronics' S&OP Journey," *Supply Chain Quarterly*, Quarter 1 (2011).

Measuring Forecast Error

As noted earlier, every forecast contains a level of error. This does not make sales forecasting useless because firms are better off with a forecast than without it. With the forecast, firms can quantify an expectation of future sales and then use that information to plan supply chain operations.

There are three main purposes for measuring forecast error. The first is to assess the level of confidence managers should have in a particular forecast. The smaller the error, the greater the confidence in the forecast. Second, measuring forecast error is key to improving forecasts. For example, managers using the exponential smoothing method should select the value of the smoothing parameter that minimizes the forecast error. Finally, when forecasting sales for a large number of items, the forecast error works as a flag directing management to focus on the items with the largest forecast error.

Forecast errors are also impacted by two factors worth mentioning. The first is *time horizon*. The farther in the future is the period being forecasted, the larger is the error that should be expected. The second factor is *level of aggregation*. Forecast error is relatively larger when forecasting at a greater level of detail. Take, for instance, a forecast of automobile sales. If the forecast is done at a high level of aggregation, say a single forecast including sales of all makes, models, and colors of cars in the U.S. in the next 12 months, the error should be expected to be relatively small. Alternatively, a relatively large error should be expected if the forecast is for a particular make, model, and color of automobile for a specific town and week of the year.

In the remainder of this section, we describe three different measures of forecast error: mean absolute deviation (MAD), mean absolute percent error (MAPE), and mean square error (MSE).

Mean Absolute Deviation (MAD)

Probably the most intuitive approach to measure forecast error is to compare past forecasts with the corresponding past actual sales. More formally:

$$e_t = A_t - F_t, \text{ where:}$$
$$e_t = \text{Forecast error for period } t$$
$$A_t = \text{Actual sales for period } t$$
$$F_t = \text{Forecast for period } t$$

Except for one feature, the mean absolute deviation is simply a measure of the average error for all time periods considered. The feature is that the mean is computed using the absolute values of the errors. Absolute value signifies that the value of each error is considered without its sign, which may be positive or negative. This is to avoid a problem whereby two errors of opposing signs cancel each other. In other words, forecast errors might carry a negative sign in one period and a positive sign in the next. This would result in a small average error that would not be a true measure of the accuracy of the forecast.

The equation needed to compute the MAD is below. A computational illustration for all measures of forecast error described in this section is in Table 4.5.

$$\text{MAD} = \frac{\sum_{t=1}^{n} |e_t|}{n}$$

Mean Absolute Percent Error (MAPE)

The MAD measure of forecast error is a number: a mean quantity that represents the number of units that a forecast is off. While the MAD is an excellent number to measure the forecast accuracy for a specific product, it has a disadvantage: The MAD is not comparable across different products. In contrast, the mean absolute percent error is a percentage. Percentages are comparable across multiple products. Thus, with the MAPE, the accuracy of the forecast for one product may be compared to the accuracy of the forecast for other products.

$$MAPE = \frac{\sum_{t=1}^{n} \left| \frac{e_t}{A_t} \right| \cdot 100}{n}$$

Note the equation for the MAPE does not differ much from the equation for the MAD. It is the same basic concept of computing the mean value of the absolute error, except that in the MAPE case the error is represented as a percentage. That is why the error in each period is divided by actual sales for that period and then multiplied by 100.

Mean Squared Error (MSE)

The two previous measures, MAD and MAPE, are averages that treat all errors equally. In other words, one large error can have the same weight as several smaller ones. The purpose of computing the mean squared error is to have a measure that treats many small errors more favorably than a few large ones. The reason is that larger errors are more difficult to deal with when planning supply chain operations. The MSE attributes more weight to larger errors by squaring the error for each period. To understand how this works, consider the difference between the squares of the numbers 3 and 2. The difference between 3 and 2 is 1, while the difference between their squares is 5 ($3^2 - 2^2 = 5$).

$$MSE = \frac{\sum_{t=1}^{n} e_t^2}{n}$$

Table 4.5 illustrates the computation of the MAD, MAPE, and MSE. It is based on the data for the three-period moving average first presented in Table 4.1.

TABLE 4.5
Computation of Three Measures of Forecast Error: MAD, MAPE, and MSE

Year	Month	Actual Sales	MA (3) Forecast	Error	Absolute Error	Absolute Percent Error	Squared Error
2006	January	200					
2006	February	150					
2006	March	90					
2006	April	150	146.7	3.3	3.3	2.2	11.1
2006	May	210	130.0	80.0	80.0	38.1	6400.0
2006	June	160	150.0	10.0	10.0	6.3	100.0
2006	July	110	173.3	−63.3	63.3	57.6	4011.1
2006	August	120	160.0	−40.0	40.0	33.3	1600.0
2006	September	160	130.0	30.0	30.0	18.8	900.0
2006	October	170	130.0	40.0	40.0	23.5	1600.0
2006	November	180	150.0	30.0	30.0	16.7	900.0
2006	December	110	170.0	−60.0	60.0	54.5	3600.0
2007	January	90	153.3	−63.3	63.3	70.4	4011.1
2007	February	160	126.7	33.3	33.3	20.8	1111.1
2007	March	210	120.0	90.0	90.0	42.9	8100.0
2007	April	110	153.3	−43.3	43.3	39.4	1877.8
2007	May	150	160.0	−10.0	10.0	6.7	100.0
2007	June	220	156.7	63.3	63.3	28.8	4011.1

Year	Month	Actual Sales	MA (3) Forecast	Error	Absolute Error	Absolute Percent Error	Squared Error
2007	July	130	160.0	−30.0	30.0	23.1	900.0
2007	August	170	166.7	3.3	3.3	2.0	11.1
2007	September	120	173.3	−53.3	53.3	44.4	2844.4
					MAD = 41.5	MAPE = 29.4	MSE = 42088.9

For a sample calculation, let us select the month of July 2007. The forecast error is (−30), the difference between actual sales and the MA (3) forecast. The absolute error is the same value without the sign, or 30. The absolute percent error is the absolute error divided by actual sales and multiplied by 100, or 23.1. Finally, the squared error is 900. Thus, the MAD is the mean of the Absolute Error column (41.5), the MAPE is the mean of the Absolute Percent Error column (29.4), and the MSE is the mean of the Squared Error column (42088.9).

Inventory Management

One of the most important functions in business supply chain management is inventory management. The manager must make recommendations for the level of inventory to be maintained for each individual item stocked by the company, as well as the size and frequency of inventory replenishments. The goal of the recommendation is to achieve minimum cost at a predetermined level of service. Note that the goal is not to reduce inventory investment as an end in itself, but rather to determine the proper level of inventory needed to manage the supply chain and support the firm's customer service policy.

In this section of the chapter, we first review reasons why firms hold inventory. We then look into how firms decide on the size of the inventory needed and its corresponding replenishment policy. Next we introduce safety stock management extensions that enable managers to reduce safety stock without reducing the level of customer service. Finally, we review methods of inventory control.

Reasons to Hold Inventory

Maintaining inventory is costly. Firms incur the cost to hold inventory only if there is an associated benefit that is greater than the cost. There are several benefits that the firm may enjoy from holding inventory, as described below.

Firms may hold inventory to achieve *transportation economies of scale.* As we have seen in an earlier chapter, the tapering principle states that the larger the size of the shipment, the lower the transportation cost per unit. Thus, firms often consolidate shipments to save transportation cost, which results in higher inventory because inventory needs to accumulate before shipment.

A similar logic applies to *production economies of scale.* Because production in larger batch sizes reduces the production cost per unit, many firms invest in the additional inventory generated by a larger batch to reduce the unit cost of production. *Economies of scale in purchasing* are also a reason to hold inventory because firms are able to negotiate a lower price per unit purchased by increasing the purchased quantity.

In some cases, firms may hold inventory to prepare for *seasonality in demand.* Market demand may be seasonal, such as the back-to-school season for clothing and school supplies or the holiday season for electronics and toys. Firms often build up their inventory to prepare for the expected surge in demand.

Two other reasons to hold inventory are to prepare for *new product introductions* and to *maintain a source of supply.* In the former case, firms often accumulate inventory to support a marketing strategy of introducing a new product simultaneously in multiple markets. As an example, the publishers of Harry Potter books accumulate inventory in multiple warehouses across the country to support a national release date for a new Harry Potter book. In the latter case, firms often buy from small suppliers who provide specialized, difficult-to-find products. To maintain the source of supply, firms agree to buy a larger quantity than needed to enable the supplier to sell the product at a profit.

Finally, a key reason to hold inventory is to *support a customer service policy*. Maintaining inventory is how firms support services such as product availability and delivery time. This is achieved by investing in the quantity and location of inventory. Next, we will demonstrate how to translate a desired level of service into the inventory quantity needed to support it.

How Much and When to Order

Now that we have established that firms have good reasons to hold inventory, a key question becomes the inventory quantity that the firm should hold. In other words, if the firm wants to support a predetermined customer service policy, how much inventory should it keep? And a clearly related question is how often should the firm resupply its inventory? The two questions are related because the more inventory is held, the less frequently it needs to be replenished. In order to address these two questions, we review two competing methods that firms use to decide how much and how often to order. They are the economic order quantity (EOQ) and the lead time demand quantity (LTD).

The Economic Order Quantity

There is a cost trade-off that firms must consider when deciding how much inventory to order. The trade-off is between the cost of ordering and the inventory carrying cost. There are costs associated with issuing orders. These include the administrative cost to issue the order, the related transportation and warehousing costs, and the additional administrative cost to audit and pay the freight bill. Thus, the greater the number of orders issued by the firm, the greater the ordering cost.

The inventory carrying cost is the charge incurred by the firm to hold inventory. The components of the inventory carrying cost include the cost of the capital tied UP in inventory and related expenses such as storage, insurance, and taxes, as well as the risks of damage, shrinkage, relocation, and obsolescence.[7] The inventory carrying cost is a function of the level of inventory. The higher the level of inventory, the higher the cost.

The economic order quantity (EOQ) determines the order quantity that minimizes the joint cost of ordering and carrying inventory. For a constant level of annual demand, larger orders mean fewer orders, which reduces the ordering cost. On the hand, larger orders also mean more inventory, which increases the inventory carrying cost. The opposite is also true. Smaller orders result in a higher ordering cost and a lower inventory carrying cost. The EOQ equation is below:

$$\text{EOQ} = \sqrt{\frac{2OD}{IV}} \quad \text{where:}$$

O = Cost per order (dollars per order)
D = Annual demand (in units)
I = Annual inventory carrying cost percentage
V = Average cost or value of one unit of product

An example is helpful to illustrate the application of the EOQ. Let us assume that the cost of issuing an order (O) is $70.00, the annual demand (D) for a particular item is 7,200 units,

---

[7] Reginald Thomas Lee, "Target: Carrying Costs," *Industrial Engineer*, Vol. 45, Issue 8 (2013), pp. 38–42.

TABLE 4.6
EOQ Cost Trade-offs

Order Quantity	Number of Orders	Ordering Cost	Inventory Carrying Cost	Total Cost
50	144	$10,080	$ 625	$10,705
100	72	5,040	1,250	6,290
150	48	3,360	1,875	5,235
200	36	2,520	2,500	5,020
300	24	1,680	3,750	5,430
400	18	1,260	5,000	6,260
600	12	840	7,500	8,340
800	9	630	10,000	10,630

the carrying cost percentage is 25 percent per year, and the value of one unit (V) of the item in question is $100.00. Then:

$$EOQ = \sqrt{\frac{2 \cdot 70 \cdot 7200}{.25 \cdot 100}} = 200.80, or \cong 200 \text{ units.}$$

This result means that the firm should order product in quantities of 200 units at a time. Because the annual demand is 7,200 units per year, there will be 36 orders per year (7200/ 200 = 36). This is equivalent to one order every 10 days because (36 · 10 = 360 days per year). The decision of how much to order and when to order is hence 200 units every 10 days.

Table 4.6 illustrates the example above. It shows the number of orders, the total cost of ordering, and the total inventory carrying cost that correspond to varying order quantities. It also shows the total cost incurred. Note how ordering quantities different from 200 units will not lead to the lowest total cost of ordering and carrying inventory.

The EOQ relationships are represented graphically in Figure 4.5, which shows how the EOQ is the quantity that minimizes the joint cost of ordering and carrying inventory and that the EOQ is at the point where these two costs are equal.

The EOQ is based on a number of restrictive assumptions with important implications for its use in practice.[8] First, the EOQ assumes *no uncertainty*. The cost of a unit of product, the transportation cost per unit, the annual demand, and the replenishment lead time are assumed known and constant. In reality, these values are almost never constant. Thus, in

FIGURE 4.5
The Economic Order Quantity

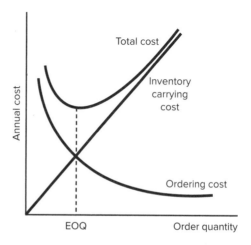

[8] Donald Erlenkotter, "Ford Whitman Harris's Economical Lot Size Model," *International Journal of Production Economics*, Vol. 155 (September 2014), pp. 12–15.

order to apply the EOQ, there are extensions that deal with the variability in the cost of a unit of product and the transportation cost per unit. These extensions are available in specialized publications.[9] The uncertainties of demand and replenishment lead time are addressed in the next section, where we discuss the use of safety stocks.

Second, the EOQ assumes *no interaction among different items*. Consider, for instance, two items consumed jointly, such as wheels and tires. A car manufacturer needs an equal number of these two items. Accordingly, the annual demand (D) for these two items is the same. However, because wheels and tires have a different acquisition cost, the value of a unit of product (V) entered in the EOQ equation is different. This results in a different EOQ for wheels and tires. The same is true for the inventory carrying cost percentage (I) and the cost per order (O). While the different EOQs reflect the difference in the cost to order and store wheels and tires, firms may perceive an administrative cost advantage to acquiring together products that are used together.

Third, the EOQ assumes *no limit in the availability of capital*. That is, the order quantity is determined without regard for the firm's ability to finance the recommended level of inventory. In many cases, firms may have to order less than the EOQ to accommodate a better alternate use of capital. Finally, the EOQ *does not explicitly consider the replenishment lead time*. While the supplier's lead time is known, it is not used to compute the EOQ. Below, we consider an alternate method to determine order quantity that explicitly considers the replenishment lead time.

Lead Time Demand Quantity (LTD)

Instead of ordering the EOQ, firms may elect to order just enough inventory to support operations until the next scheduled delivery. This is known as the lead time demand quantity (LTD). In contrast to the EOQ, which minimizes the joint cost of ordering and carrying inventory, the LTD minimizes the inventory carrying cost only because it recommends that the firm order the minimum amount of inventory needed. The LTD quantity is defined as the product of the daily demand in units and the replenishment lead time in days.

$$LTD = t \cdot d \quad \text{where:}$$
$$t = \text{replenishment lead time in days}$$
$$d = \text{daily demand in units}$$

Thus, if we assume that daily demand is 20 units and that inventory is resupplied every 10 days, the LTD quantity is 200 units.

$$LTD = 10 \cdot 20 = 200 \text{ units.}$$

There are two main reasons why firms adopt the LTD quantity. First, the LTD *minimizes the risk related to holding inventory*. That risk has increased in recent years because the rapid rate of technological innovation in many industries renders many products obsolete. By the same token, increased competition among firms accelerates the rate of new product introductions, which also renders many products obsolete. Thus, the lower the inventory level, the lower the risk of holding it.

The second reason is the *decline in the cost per order* (O). Advances in computer technology triggered a decline in the cost of processing information, which in turn leads to a significant reduction in the cost of an order. This helps explain the decreased usage of the EOQ because it makes the cost of an order relatively less important than the inventory carrying cost, thereby reducing the value of computing the trade-off between them.

---

[9] Robert Bartlay Fetter and Winston C. Dalleck, *Decision Models for Inventory Management* (Literary Licensing, LLC, 2012).

Sizing Inventory and the Impact of Uncertainty

Both methods introduced above assume out uncertainty. Demand is assumed known and constant, and so is the replenishment lead time. In practice, managers need to incorporate uncertainty into inventory management decisions because in reality demand does vary and suppliers can delivery early or late.

To manage uncertainty, we divide inventory into two complementary components: base stock and safety stock. *Base stock* is the inventory quantity needed to support daily operations. It does not consider uncertainty. The *safety stock* is an additional inventory quantity needed to protect the firm from uncertainty of demand and uncertainty of replenishment lead time. Thus, the average total inventory carried by the firms is:

$$INV = BS + SS \qquad \text{where:}$$

$$INV = \text{average total inventory}$$
$$BS = \text{base stock}$$
$$SS = \text{safety stock}$$

Base Stock

The inventory needed to support daily operations is known as base stock or cycle stock. It is usually referred to as an average. Base stock is high after a delivery is received and gradually declines as product is used. Base stock is zero immediately before the next replenishment delivery arrives. Thus, the average base stock is half the order quantity.

$$BS = OQ/2 \qquad \text{where:}$$

$$BS = \text{average base stock}$$
$$OQ = \text{order quantity (EOQ or LTD)}$$

The behavior of base stock is represented graphically in Figures 4.6 and 4.7, which illustrate order quantities of 400 and 200 units respectively. Compare the two figures and note how the average base stock is halved when the order quantity is halved as well. This highlights the importance of supplier relations to inventory managers. The lower the order quantity negotiated with suppliers, the lower the investment in base stock.

Safety Stock

Recall that the safety stock, sometimes also called *buffer stock*, is an inventory quantity maintained in addition to the base stock in order to protect the firm from the uncertainties of demand and replenishment lead time. In practice, demand and replenishment lead time are not constant. They vary. This means that inventory managers need to maintain safety stock in case demand is higher than expected and/or suppliers deliver late.

Figure 4.8 shows the integration of safety stock in the relationship between order quantity and base stock. Note how in one scenario a higher-than-expected level of demand forced

FIGURE 4.6
Relationship between Order Quantity and Base Stock with Order Quantity of 400

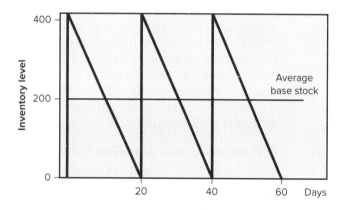

FIGURE 4.7
Relationship between Order Quantity and Base Stock with Order Quantity of 200

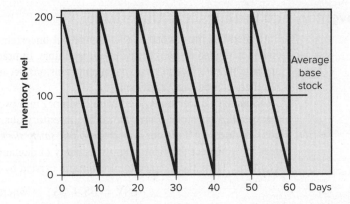

FIGURE 4.8
Relationship between Order Quantity, Base Stock, and Safety Stock

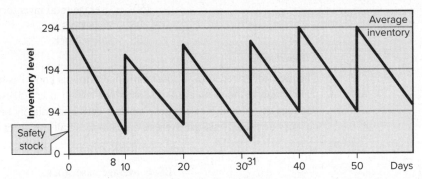

the firm to use some of the safety stock after day 8. In a second scenario, the safety stock became necessary when a replenishment arrived a day late, on day 31.

Safety stock is determined by:

$$SS = k \cdot s_c \qquad \text{where:}$$

SS = safety stock
k = safety factor
s_c = combined standard deviation of demand
and replenishment lead time

The safety factor represents the customer service level that the firm decides to maintain. The higher the service level, the higher the safety factor. The combined standard deviation of demand and replenishment lead time is a statistical measure that combines the two standard deviations into a single measure of uncertainty.

The quantification of the safety factor and the combined standard deviation of demand and replenishment lead time are discussed in the next two subsections. The first subsection focuses on demand and replenishment lead time uncertainties. The higher the uncertainty, the more safety stock is needed. The second subsection focuses on the choice of the measure of customer service to be used. In the determination of safety stock, customer service is construed more specifically as measures of inventory availability. We review two such measures, the *probability of no stock-out (PNS)* and the *fill rate (FR)*. The safety factor k is computed differently for the PNS and the FR. It is important to note that the choice of inventory availability measure results in significantly different recommendations for the size of the safety stock.

Demand and Supplier Lead Time Uncertainties

The uncertainties of demand and supplier lead time are quantified with the help of a statistical measure known as the *standard deviation*. This measure captures the variability in a series of observations. For instance, assume that the average daily demand is 20 units.

A large standard deviation means that in any particular day the demand could be much larger or much lower than 20. A small standard deviation indicates that daily demand observations tend not to depart much from 20. Thus, the larger the standard deviation, the more safety stock is needed to ensure that the firm has enough inventory to manage instances of high demand and/or delayed deliveries.[10]

An implication of the use of the standard deviation to quantify uncertainty is that two standard deviations are needed for each item in inventory, one to quantify the uncertainty of demand and the other to quantify the uncertainty of replenishment lead time. Presumably that means that there also must be two safety stocks, one for each type of uncertainty. This is costly and unnecessary. The two standard deviations can be combined into a single number, the *combined standard deviation of demand and replenishment lead time* (s_c), which is defined below.[11]

$$s_c = \sqrt{t \cdot s_d^2 + d^2 \cdot s_t^2} \qquad \text{where:}$$

$t =$ average replenishment lead time in days

$s_d =$ standard deviation of daily demand

$d =$ average daily demand

$s_t =$ standard deviation of replenishment lead time

As an illustration, assume that the average replenishment lead time is 10 days, the standard deviation of daily demand is 6 units, the average daily demand is 20 units, and the standard deviation of replenishment lead time is 5 days. The combined standard deviation of demand and replenishment lead time is:

$$s_c = \sqrt{10 \cdot 6^2 + 20^2 \cdot 5^2} = 101.78 \text{ units.}$$

Measures of Customer Service

Recall that the size of the safety stock depends on the combined standard deviation of demand and replenishment lead time (s_c) and on the value of the safety factor (k). The safety factor is a multiple of the number of standard deviations of demand and lead time that the firm decides to maintain to support a customer service policy.

There is a quantifiable relationship between values of k and levels of inventory availability that a firm decides to adopt. As noted earlier, the customer service level is defined as an inventory availability measure. For instance, a firm may decide to adopt a customer service policy of 95% availability. This percentage is interpreted differently if different measures of inventory availability are selected. Next, we examine two measure of inventory availability: probability of no stock-out (PNS) and the fill rate (FR).

Probability of No Stock-out (PNS) The PNS measures the percentage of lead times without a shortage. For instance, a 95% PNS availability policy means that there will be enough inventory to cover 100 percent of the demand in 95 percent of the lead times. Thus, if we assume a replenishment lead time of 10 days, we know that there are 36 lead times in a year ($360/10 = 36$). A 95% PNS availability policy requires that there is enough inventory to cover 100 percent of the demand in 34 out of the 36 lead times because $34/36 \cong .95$.

The actual determination of k depends on the distribution of demand in a lead time. If we assume that the distribution is normal, the value of k can be found in the normal distribution probability table in the chapter appendix. A 95% PNS availability policy

[10] For a review of statistical concepts such as the standard deviation and the normal distribution, consult a business statistics text such as Gerald Keller, *Statistics for Management and Economics*, Abbreviated 10th ed. (Boston, MA: Cengage Learning, 2016).

[11] Robert Bartlay Fetter and Winston C. Dalleck, *Decision Models for Inventory Management* (Literary Licensing, LLC, 2012).

corresponds to a k value of 1.65. Therefore, the size of the safety stock corresponding to a 95% PNS availability policy is:

$$SS = k \cdot s_c = 1.65 \cdot 101.78 = 168 \text{ units.}$$

The corresponding total inventory is given by:

$$INV = BS + SS = 200/2 + 168 = 268 \text{ units.}$$

Recall that earlier in the chapter we showed that the base stock (BS) equals half of the order quantity and that we used an order quantity (OQ) of 200 units as an example.

Fill Rate (FR)   While the PNS measures the frequency of inventory shortages, the fill rate (FR) measures the magnitude of shortages. More specifically, the FR is the expected percentage of units filled from stock in a lead time. For instance, a 95 % FR availability policy means that, on average, 95 percent of the demand in each lead time is satisfied with existing inventory. Thus, if we retain the assumption of 36 lead times in a year, the average demand filled from stock for the 36 lead times is 95 percent.

The computation of the FR is as follows:

$$f(k) = (1 - FR) \cdot s_c / OQ \qquad \text{where:}$$

$f(k)$ = a function of k that provides the area to the right of k in a normal distribution

FR = fill rate

s_c = combined standard deviation of demand and lead time

OQ = order quantity (EOQ or LTD)

The value of k is determined by checking it against the value of $f(k)$ in the normal loss distribution table available in the appendix. Therefore, the size of the safety stock corresponding to a 95% FR availability policy is:

$$f(k) = (1 - .95) \cdot 101.78/200 = .09825.$$

The corresponding value of k in the appendix is .92. Thus, the size of the safety stock is:

$$SS = k \cdot s_c = .92 \cdot 101.78 = 94.$$

The corresponding total inventory is given by:

$$INV = BS + SS = 200/2 + 94 = 194 \text{ units.}$$

It is important to note that the same nominal inventory availability policy of 95% almost always leads to very different corresponding values of safety stock. For instance, the required safety stock for a 95% PNS policy is 168 and for a 95% FR policy is 94. Except for the theoretical extreme of 100% service, the PNS will always require more safety stock for the same nominal level of inventory availability. This is because the PNS imposes an absolute limit in the number of lead times where a shortage can occur while the FR is an average where service failures at one point in time can be recovered from later on. This point is illustrated in Table 4.7, which compares the PNS and the FR for different nominal inventory availability levels.

TABLE 4.7
Comparing Safety Stocks under Two Different Measures of Inventory Availability

Nominal Inv. Avail. Level	PNS		FR		
	k	SS	$f(k)$	k	SS
85	1.04	106	.2948	.22	23
90	1.28	130	.1965	.51	52
95	1.65	168	.0982	.92	94
97.5	1.96	200	.0491	1.27	130
99.9	3.09	315	.0020	2.50	254

Exhibit: How John Deere Reduced Supply Chain Inventory

Deere & Company's Commercial & Consumer Equipment Division (C&CE) manufactures tractors, garden mowers, and ATVs. They are sold to U.S. consumers through a network of 2,500 dealers. Sales are seasonal; 65 percent of annual sales occur between March and July.

Surprisingly, most consumer purchases of C&CE products are made by impulse. In a typical scenario, a consumer walks into a dealership (usually a hardware store) looking to make a different purchase but ends up buying a tractor or mower after seeing it on display. To support impulse sales, dealers must maintain a significant level of inventory available. Thus, in the past Deere encouraged dealers to maintain as much inventory as possible by providing financing. However, even though the inventory was sold to dealers, it actually remained a Deere asset. This is because the inventory was financed and thus remained in Deere's books as accounts receivable.

With this policy, it is no surprise that the total level of inventory in the supply chain ballooned to 1.4 billion in 2001. Moreover, it was expected to reach about $2 billion by 2005. This represented a substantial share of the total sales revenue of $4 billion in its Worldwide C&CE division in 2005.

The excess inventory resulted in financial pressure, both internal and from Wall Street, to reduce inventory. Deere decided to reduce supply chain inventory by $1 billion in four years. The plan consisted of four major components. The first component was to introduce a sophisticated sales forecasting capability to help determine the amount of inventory that dealers should keep in order to adequately support sales.

The second component was to restructure production to introduce fast and flexible manufacturing. The goal was to add flexibility by producing in smaller lots. The flexibility translated into a greater ability to react to changes in demand. If a particular model sold more than forecasted, production could be adjusted upward and sales would not be hindered by a large inventory of a model with weaker-than-expected sales.

To change the production plan to increase production to match the sales season was the third component. This enabled Deere to avoid creating excess inventory by producing too much in the off-season. An important part of this component was to work with suppliers to ensure that their deliveries match the revised production plan. Finally, Deere worked to reduce delivery time to dealers from 10 to 5 days by adding DCs closer to key markets. This enabled dealers to carry less inventory. Deere inventory is slightly higher than it would be without the DCs, but overall supply chain inventory is lower.

As a result of the reduction in supply chain inventory, Deere's stock price went up from about $40 in 2001 to about $70 in 2005.

Sources: James A. Cook, "Running Inventory Like a Deere," *Supply Chain Quarterly*, Vol. 1, No. 3 (2007), pp. 46–50; David Maloney, "Billion Dollar Baby," *DC Velocity*, April 2006, pp. 43–46; and Lisa Harrington, "Inventory Velocity: All the Right Moves," *Inbound Logistics*, Vol. 25, No. 11 (2005), pp. 36–43.

Safety Stock Management Extensions

In the previous section we explored the relationship between inventory availability targets and the level of safety stock required to support them. In this section we suggest three extensions that enable an inventory manager to reduce the safety stock requirement while maintaining the same inventory availability target. The three extensions are sales forecasting, the portfolio effect, and form postponement. Each is discussed briefly. More formal presentations are available in other chapters because the implementation of each of these extensions goes beyond inventory management to affect the entire supply chain. For example, in addition to size safety stock, sales forecasts are used to plan transportation and warehousing requirements, schedule production, and plan procurement.

Sales Forecasting

We have demonstrated earlier how the size of the safety stock depends on the uncertainty of demand and how this uncertainty is quantified by the standard deviation of demand. Note that the value of the standard deviation of demand reflects *all* of the uncertainty of demand.

However, part of the demand uncertainty can be explained by a sales forecast. For example, if sales for a particular product are higher than average in a certain week, that might be explained by a change in pricing or by a promotion. The price change and the promotion could have been incorporated into the sales forecast, explaining at least partially the increase in demand.

Therefore, by using the error in the sales forecast instead of the standard deviation of demand as the basis to compute safety stock, firms can maintain the same level of inventory availability with less safety stock. This is because the size of the safety stock reflects only that part of demand uncertainty (the forecast error) not explained by the sales forecast.

To incorporate the sales forecast in the computation of the safety stock, the equation for the combined standard deviation is adjusted as follows:

$$s_c = \sqrt{t \cdot s_f^2 + d^2 \cdot s_t^2} \qquad \text{where:}$$

t = average replenishment lead time, in days

s_f = standard deviation of the sales forecast error

d = average daily demand

s_t = standard deviation of replenishment lead time

Unless the sales forecast error is unusually large and biased, the standard deviation of the sales forecast error is always a smaller number than the standard deviation of demand. This results in a smaller safety stock. In fact, research results suggest that, on average, using the sales forecast instead of the standard deviation of demand results in a 15 percent smaller safety stock for the same level of inventory availability.[12]

In addition, using the sales forecast to manage inventory requires that the order quantity (OQ) is changed in every lead time to reflect the sales forecast. This results in a variable OQ. However, the average base stock remains the same.

The Portfolio Effect

There is a relationship between the level of inventory needed to support a target level of inventory availability and the number of locations where the inventory is stored.[13] That relationship states that more inventory is needed as locations are added. The reverse is also true: As the number of locations decreases (inventory centralization), so does the inventory requirement.

The portfolio effect (PE) quantifies the percent decrease in safety stock that is achieved with inventory centralization. In the case of centralizing inventory from two to one locations, this is given by:

$$\text{PE} = \frac{\sqrt{M^2 + 1 + 2 \cdot M \cdot \rho_{12}}}{M + 1} \qquad \text{where:}$$

M = ratio of the standard deviation of sales between the 2 locations ($M > 1$)

ρ_{12} = sales correlation between the 2 locations

Therefore, the size of the PE depends on the relative sizes of sales in the two locations and on how correlated these sales are. The PE becomes smaller as the size differential between the two locations increases and becomes larger as the correlation approaches -1. These relationships are represented graphically in Figure 4.9.

---

[12] Walter Zinn and Howard Marmorstein, "Comparing Two Alternative Methods of Determining Safety Stock: The Demand and the Forecast Systems," *Journal of Business Logistics*, Vol. 11, No. 1 (1990).
[13] Gerald Oeser and Pietro Romano, "An Empirical Examination of the Assumptions of the Square Root Law for Inventory Centralization and Decentralization," *International Journal of Production Research*, Vol. 54, No. 8 (2016), pp. 2298–319.

FIGURE 4.9
Impact of Sales Correlation and Magnitude on the Portfolio Effect

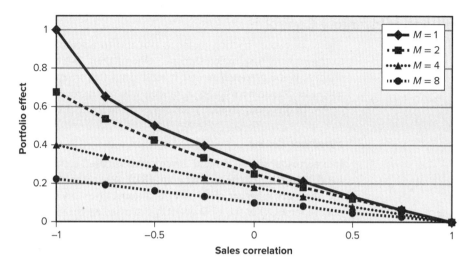

Form Postponement

The principle of form postponement has important implications for inventory management. It states that demand uncertainty can be managed by delaying a product's final form until the exact nature of the demand is known. For example, Benetton, the Italian clothing manufacturer, delays dyeing fabric until it receives a customer's order specifying the desired color of the items in the order. Benetton thus avoids dyeing fabrics in the wrong color. Had Benetton dyed fabric prior to receiving a customer order, it would have had to dye fabric in several colors to ensure that the right color would be available when ordered.

The greater the number of variations that a product is sold in, the greater the inventory requirement. Thus, the implication of form postponement to inventory management is that the firm does not have to maintain a separate inventory of each product variation. Instead, it keeps a smaller inventory of the common product (undyed fabrics) and only completes the product's final configuration after an order is received and the demand is therefore known.

There are four different types of form postponement: labeling, packaging, assembly, and manufacturing.[14] They are classified in terms of the stage in the configuration of the final product that is being postponed. Each is briefly described. In *labeling postponement*, a label is only affixed to a product once it is sold in one of many brands offered by the firm. For example, canned food is often sold by the same firm under different brands. By affixing the label after the product is sold, the firm is able to maintain a single inventory for all brands. In *packaging postponement*, the product is packaged after it is sold in a particular package size or type. Similarly, in *assembly postponement*, components are assembled in the product's final form after an order is received. The Benetton case described above is an example of assembly postponement. Finally, in *manufacturing postponement*, only a fraction of a product's components is shipped. Once close to the market, the product is then put together with the addition of locally sourced materials. Most manufacturers of soft drinks do this by transporting syrup to local markets, where syrup and carbon dioxide are added to manufacture the final product.

[14] Kanghwa Choi, Ram Narasimhan, and Soo Wook Kim, "Postponement Strategy for International Transfer of Products in a Global Supply Chain: A System Dynamics Examination," *Journal of Operations Management*, Vol. 30, Issue 3 (2012), pp. 167–79.

Methods of Inventory Control

There are two competing methods available to inventory managers to decide the timing to trigger inventory replenishments. One of them, which was assumed until now in this chapter, is the *perpetual review*. It establishes that inventory be checked after each transaction to determine whether a replenishment is needed. A second method is the *periodic review*. In this case, inventory reviews occur in fixed, predetermined, time intervals.

Perpetual Review

In a perpetual review method, inventory is checked continuously after each transaction to see if it has reached the reorder point (RP). Whenever the inventory level is at or below RP, the inventory manager must order additional inventory. The quantity ordered is Q, which may be the EOQ or the LTD quantity discussed earlier in the chapter. RP is determined by:

$$RP = d \cdot t + SS \qquad \text{where:}$$

$$d = \text{average daily demand}$$
$$t = \text{average replenishment lead time in days}$$
$$SS = \text{safety stock}$$

Thus, in the example described earlier in the chapter (under the heading *The Lead Time Demand Quantity (LTD)*), assuming that the order quantity is the LTD and the safety stock corresponds to a 95% FR availability policy, the reorder point is:

$$RP = 20 \cdot 10 + 94 = 294 \text{ units.}$$

This means that whenever the level of inventory reaches a quantity of 294 or below, the inventory manager should order a replenishment of 200, which is the LTD. In addition, any inventory already on order should be deducted for the current order.

Recall that in the earlier sections of this chapter we assumed a perpetual review method. Therefore, the average inventory in the perpetual review system remains the same as previously described:

$$INV = OQ/2 + SS$$

The perpetual system is very responsive to changes in demand and replenishment lead time, as the inventory level is being continuously checked. It is also a good way to keep the manager's attention on the items with the highest turn. On the other hand, the perpetual system requires continuous monitoring of the inventory. Finally, with the perpetual system it is difficult to combine orders. This is because each item reaches its reorder point at a different time.

Periodic Review

One alternative to the perpetual review is the periodic review method. In this case, inventory is checked at fixed preset intervals. The reorder point (RP) is computed differently in this case because the firm must hold additional inventory to also cover the review period. The decision rule is similar to the perpetual review method. After each review, the manager orders OQ (which may be the EOQ or LTD) whenever the inventory level is at or below RP. In the periodic review method, the RP is determined by:

$$RP = d \cdot (t + p/2) + SS \qquad \text{where:}$$

$$p = \text{the review period in days.}$$

Thus, if inventory is reviewed weekly (assuming the same data used in the perpetual review example):

$$RP = 20 \cdot (10 + 7/2) + 94 = 364 \text{ units.}$$

Note that the RP is higher in the periodic review system. This is because additional inventory is needed to cover the review period. The average inventory is consequently also higher in the periodic review method. It is determined by:

$$\text{INV} = \frac{\text{OQ}}{2} + \left(\frac{d \cdot p}{2}\right) + \text{SS}$$

Note also that the average inventory in the periodic review method differs only from the perpetual review method in that it includes the average inventory during the review period. When p equals zero (i.e., perpetual review), the two average inventory equations are the same.

The periodic review method has the clear disadvantage of requiring more inventory. On the other hand, it is recommended in situations when it is advantageous to order a large number of items simultaneously. This is often the case, for instance, in retail buying where the cost of ordering is greatly reduced by bundling orders for different items and where associates have limited time available to check inventory levels.

Symptoms of Poor Inventory Management

Symptoms may be viewed as "flags" that indicate potential opportunities to improve the management of inventories. Note that these symptoms do not necessarily point to a problem. They should be viewed as a starting point to review inventory management practices. Below is a list with some of the best-known symptoms.

- **High inventory levels and frequent stock-outs.** We have described in this chapter that there is a relationship between inventory investment and inventory availability. Higher inventory investment should result in fewer out-of-stocks. Therefore, simultaneously high inventory investment and out-of-stocks may be a symptom that the inventory on hand is not saleable and likely the result of poor inventory management practices.

- **Growing frequency of inventory transfers between units in the same firm.** This might be a symptom of poor inventory allocation. If inventory were allocated to the correct location in the first place, there would be less need for transfers. Some level of transfers is to be expected, but a growing number of occurrences is a symptom of poor inventory management.

- **Frequent sales to reduce inventory levels.** The two symptoms above often lead to special sales designed to reduce the level of inventory. Excessively frequent sales can be a symptom of poor inventory management and should trigger an examination of the causes of frequent inventory build-ups.

- **Time needed to find items.** Another symptom of poor inventory management is when items are known to be in inventory but cannot be located in a timely way. This may be the result of an inadequate information system.

- **Suppliers with long or unreliable delivery times** often prompt customers into maintaining excess inventory to cover for a potentially longer-than-expected lead time. This inventory appears as safety stock and may be reduced by improved supplier performance.

- **Purchases based on quantity discount.** When buyers are given an opportunity to earn a discount in the purchase price by buying a larger-than-needed quantity, excess inventory may result. While the quantity discount can be beneficial to the buyer, it must be evaluated in concert with the inventory carrying cost that it also generates.

- **Production planning based on batch sizes.** Production in large batches often results in a lower production cost per unit. Similarly to the quantity discount case, production batch size decisions must consider the impact on the inventory carrying cost. Failure to do so is a symptom of poor inventory management.

Summary

The goals of this chapter were to introduce the reader to the issues of sales forecasting and inventory management. We first described qualitative and quantitative forecast methods and examined how they are applied. We next described methods to measure forecast error.

Where is forecasting headed? With point-of-sale data, and the fast interchange of data, forecasting for some items becomes easier. Add to this 3-D printing, and other advances in technology, and sales forecasting may have to respond to shorter time periods.

We then focused on inventory management, beginning with reasons why firms hold inventory. We explored the difference between base and safety stocks. We also described two different methods (the probability of no stock-out and the fill rate) to set the level of safety stock that corresponds to a predetermined level of inventory availability. As a result, students should be able to compute the level of base and safety stock that satisfies the firm's requirements for inventory availability.

We introduced the reader to three safety stock management extensions: sales forecasting, portfolio effect, and form postponement. While these extensions have a broad impact in supply chains that exceeds their impact on inventory management, they nonetheless offer opportunities to reduce safety stock without reducing the level of inventory availability. Finally, we looked at two inventory control methods, the perpetual and the periodic reviews. These methods help managers decide on the appropriate timing to review the level of inventory and to order replenishments. Lastly, we reviewed symptoms of poor inventory management as potential indicators of opportunities to improve the management of inventories.

Suggested Readings

Boone, Christopher, C. Craighead, J. Hanna, and A. Nair, "Implementation of a System Approach for Enhanced Supply Chain Continuity and Resiliency: A Longitudinal Study," *Journal of Business Logistics*, Vol. 34, No. 3 (September 2013), pp. 222–35.

Cassidy, William, "What's On the Shelf? Shippers Are Approaching an Inflection Point That Could Require New Investments in Inventory Management Technology," *Journal of Commerce*, Vol. 18, No. 10 (May 15, 2017), pp. 2–73.

Cohen, Morris, "Inventory Management in the Age of Big Data," *Harvard Business Review Digital Articles*, June 24, 2015, pp. 2–4.

Goyal, Sandeep, B. Hardgrave, J. Aloysius, and N. DeHoratius, "The Effectiveness of RFID in Backroom and Sales Floor Inventory Management," *International Journal of Logistics Management* [serial online], Vol. 27, No. 3 (December 2016), pp. 795–815.

Lackes, Richard, P. Schlüter, and M. Siepermann, "The Impact of Contract Parameters on the Supply Chain Performance under Different Power Constellations," *International Journal of Production Research* [serial online], Vol. 54, No. 1 (January 2016), pp. 251–64.

Ludorf, Joseph, "How They Did It: Cipla's Journey to Driverless Forecasting," *Supply Chain Management Review* [serial online], Vol. 21, No. 6 (November 2017), pp. 30–34.

Ma, Y., N. Wang, A. Che, Y. Huang, and J. Xu, "The Bullwhip Effect on Product Orders and Inventory: A Perspective of Demand Forecasting Techniques," *International Journal of Production Research*, Vol. 51, No. 1 (January 2013), pp. 281–302.

McCrea, Bridget, "The Future of Retail Distribution," *Logistics Management*, Vol. 57, No. 2 (February 2018), pp. 52–55.

Mello, John, "Toward a More Rational Forecasting Process: Eliminating Sales-Forecasting Misbehaviors," *Foresight: The International Journal of Applied Forecasting*, Vol. 41 (Spring 2016), pp. 14–17.

Sillitoe, Ben, "Retailers Need New Insight on Demand Forecasting," *Computer Weekly*, July 25, 2017, pp. 26–29. Available from: Business Source Complete, Ipswich, MA.

Spithourakis, Georgios, F. Petropoulos, M. Babai, K. Nikolopoulos, and V. Assimakopoulos, "Improving the Performance of Popular Supply Chain Forecasting Techniques," *Supply Chain Forum: International Journal* [serial online], Vol. 12, No. 4 (December 2011), pp. 16–25.

**Questions
and Problems**

LO 4-1   1. What are some of the differences in qualitative and quantitative forecasts?
LO 4-2   2. What are some of the ways to measure forecast error?
LO 4-3   3. Managing inventory is a critical function in logistics and supply chain management. What are some of the reasons firms hold inventory?
LO 4-4   4. Define, compare, and contrast the perpetual review of inventory with the periodic review of inventory. When is it is best to use either?
LO 4-5   5. What are some of the more common symptoms of poor inventory management?

Appendix

Normal Distribution Table

Z	.00	.01	.02	.03	.04	.05	.06	.07	.08	.09
0.0	.0000	.0040	.0080	.0120	.0160	.0199	.0239	.0279	.0319	.0359
0.1	.0398	.0438	.0478	.0517	.0557	.0596	.0636	.0675	.0714	.0753
0.2	.0793	.0832	.0871	.0910	.0948	.0987	.1026	.1064	.1103	.1141
0.3	.1179	.1217	.1255	.1293	.1331	.1368	.1406	.1443	.1480	.1517
0.4	.1554	.1591	.1628	.1664	.1700	.1736	.1772	.1808	.1844	.1879
0.5	.1915	.1950	.1985	.2019	.2054	.2088	.2123	.2157	.2190	.2224
0.6	.2257	.2291	.2324	.2357	.2389	.2422	.2454	.2486	.2517	.2549
0.7	.2580	.2611	.2642	.2673	.2704	.2734	.2764	.2794	.2823	.2852
0.8	.2881	.2910	.2939	.2967	.2995	.3023	.3051	.3078	.3106	.3133
0.9	.3159	.3186	.3212	.3238	.3264	.3289	.3315	.3340	.3365	.3389
1.0	.3413	.3438	.3461	.3485	.3508	.3531	.3554	.3577	.3599	.3621
1.1	.3643	.3665	.3686	.3708	.3729	.3749	.3770	.3790	.3810	.3830
1.2	.3849	.3869	.3888	.3907	.3925	.3944	.3962	.3980	.3997	.4015
1.3	.4032	.4049	.4066	.4082	.4099	.4115	.4131	.4147	.4162	.4177
1.4	.4192	.4207	.4222	.4236	.4251	.4265	.4279	.4292	.4306	.4319
1.5	.4332	.4345	.4357	.4370	.4382	.4394	.4406	.4418	.4429	.4441
1.6	.4452	.4463	.4474	.4484	.4495	.4505	.4515	.4525	.4535	.4545
1.7	.4554	.4564	.4573	.4582	.4591	.4599	.4608	.4616	.4625	.4633
1.8	.4641	.4649	.4656	.4664	.4671	.4678	.4686	.4693	.4699	.4706
1.9	.4713	.4719	.4726	.4732	.4738	.4744	.4750	.4756	.4761	.4767
2.0	.4772	.4778	.4783	.4788	.4793	.4798	.4803	.4808	.4812	.4817
2.1	.4821	.4826	.4830	.4834	.4838	.4842	.4846	.4850	.4854	.4857
2.2	.4861	.4864	.4868	.4871	.4875	.4878	.4881	.4884	.4887	.4890
2.3	.4893	.4896	.4898	.4901	.4904	.4906	.4909	.4911	.4913	.4916
2.4	.4918	.4920	.4922	.4925	.4927	.4929	.4931	.4932	.4934	.4936
2.5	.4938	.4940	.4941	.4943	.4945	.4946	.4948	.4949	.4951	.4952
2.6	.4953	.4955	.4956	.4957	.4959	.4960	.4961	.4962	.4963	.4964
2.7	.4965	.4966	.4967	.4968	.4969	.4970	.4971	.4972	.4973	.4974
2.8	.4974	.4975	.4976	.4977	.4977	.4978	.4979	.4979	.4980	.4981
2.9	.4981	.4982	.4982	.4983	.4984	.4984	.4985	.4985	.4986	.4986
3.0	.4987	.4987	.4987	.4988	.4988	.4989	.4989	.4989	.4990	.4990

Partial Expectation Function—Normal Distribution

k	f(k)	k	f(k)	k	f(k)	k	f(k)
0.00	0.3989423	0.70	0.1428794	1.38	0.0383135	2.20	0.0048870
0.10	0.3509353	0.80	0.1202072	1.40	0.0366681	2.30	0.0036616
0.20	0.3068946	0.90	0.1004311	1.46	0.0320848	2.40	0.0027204
0.22	0.2985579	0.92	0.0968028	1.50	0.0293068	2.50	0.0020041
0.30	0.2667612	1.00	0.0833155	1.68	0.0191981	2.60	0.0014639
0.40	0.2304388	1.10	0.0686195	1.70	0.0182878	2.70	0.0010601
0.50	0.1977966	1.20	0.0561025	1.80	0.0142756	2.80	0.0007611
0.51	0.1947288	1.27	0.0485101	1.90	0.0110544	2.90	0.0005417
0.60	0.1686727	1.30	0.0455280	2.00	0.0084907	3.00	0.0003822

Exhibit: It's Not Always Smooth Sailing for Cargo Ships

A container ship had an engine room fire that forced it to make an emergency docking at Port Tampa Bay.

"The vessel had to be discharged immediately, and the shipping line scrambled to explore truck, rail, and any other transportation means to move their freight to its final destination. Ultimately, the carrier was left with 77 super-heavy loads that the rail lines rejected and trucks could not legally handle on the highways.

The shipping line then called Columbia Coastal Transport (CCT) to possibly assist with a barge to move the overweight containers. The logistics arm of CCT, working in tandem with the steamship line, was able to identify even more freight to add to the barge so that the carrier would benefit from improved efficiencies.

In total, the barge was able to move over 320 containers out of Port Tampa Bay. Cargo was successfully delivered to customers in New Orleans and Houston."

Source: "Columbia Coastal Transport Assists Major Shipping Line with Stranded Freight Due to Engine Fire," *Case Studies*, June 8, 2015, http://www.columbia-group.com/news/case-studies/.

The U.S. Postal Service provides both surface and air parcel post services to companies shipping small packages. The advantages of parcel post are its low cost and wide geographical coverage, both domestically and internationally. Disadvantages include specific size and weight limitations, variability in transit time (especially internationally), and higher loss and damage rates than other forms of shipment. The USPS also handles product returns, which has become a significant issue with Internet sales. More products that are purchased online are returned than would be the case for in-store purchases.

United Parcel Service (UPS) is a private business that, like the USPS, transports small packages using both air and ground transportation. It competes directly with the USPS and transports a majority of the small parcels shipped in the United States and throughout the world. The advantages of UPS include its low cost, wide geographic coverage internationally, and low variability in transit time. Its disadvantages include size and weight limitations (which are more restrictive than USPS) and inconvenience (UPS will provide scheduled pickups for larger shippers, but smaller shippers must deposit parcels at a UPS facility or "catch" the UPS driver when he/she makes a delivery in their area).

Characterized by high levels of customer service, the air express industry has significantly expanded since its inception in 1973. The FedEx Corporation, one of the most well-known examples of an air express company, illustrates how the concept of supplying rapid transit with very high consistency has paid off. In 2017, FedEx had worldwide revenues of US$60.3 billion, representing service to more than 220 countries. This represented millions of daily shipments of express, ground, and expedited packages; transported by more than 650 aircraft; and supported by 52,500 transport vehicles.[40]

Because some firms need to transport some products quickly, the air express industry is able to offer same day and overnight (or second day) delivery of small parcels to many locations throughout the world. In a few instances, shipments may have to arrive the same day, within hours, such as the transport and delivery of human organs, critical business documents, and some perishables (e.g., live animals, flowers, pharmaceuticals). "Companies of all sizes utilize time-critical transportation for ongoing, continuous, planned shipments every day, for a variety of reasons and broad range of products."[41]

Competition is fierce among the "giants" of the industry, including DHL, FedEx, and UPS. So long as there is a need to transport products quickly and with very high levels of service consistency, the air express companies will continue to provide a valuable service to many shippers.

[40] FedEx Co. website, 2018, http://s1.q4cdn.com/714383399/files/doc_downloads/statistical/2018/FedEx-Q2-FY18-Stat-Book.pdf.
[41] Partridge, "Time-Critical Transport: Devising a Master Plan."

Drones

Drones, or unmanned aerial systems (UASs), are classified in the category of unmanned aerial vehicles (UAVs) and, in the U.S., must be approved for use by the Federal Aviation Administration (FAA). Organizations such as Amazon, NASA, and UPS are expanding their drone fleets and testing them in various supply chain applications, especially in delivery of small packages. Drones have already been used to deliver medicines to remote locations, and they offer potentially significant application in disaster relief efforts when traditional infrastructure might not be accessible. When the FAA in August 2016 streamlined the process to legally operate drones for commercial purposes (Rule 107), more than 300,000 drones were registered in the first month after the new rules were implemented.[42]

There are a number of potential transportation and supply chain applications of drones, although their characteristics limit those applications. For example, drones are made of light composite materials, are battery powered, and have two to five rotors. They are controlled by remote control or GPS. Flight time varies, but typically ranges from 12–27 minutes, so their flying range only goes up to 7 kilometers or so.[43] Of course, with technological improvements in battery life, reducing weight of the drone, and enhanced guidance software, those parameters will likely expand.

Amazon was one of the first companies to successfully test drone technology in a supply chain setting. The test, called "Prime Air," occurred in Cambridge, UK, in December 2016. The test involved the following:

- "Customers place their orders online as usual.
- The package is prepped at the regional fulfillment center.
- Drones are then dispatched from the center with the package.
- Customers place QR codes on their property to indicate the drop-off point.
- The package is delivered at the customer's address within 30 minutes.
- The drone is operated by GPS and handles up to five pounds of cargo."[44]

The potential of drone deliveries in congested and/or confined urban areas is significant. While most consumers are familiar with two-day and same-day delivery, the fact is that the average delivery time for a traditional package is 4.1 days.[45] With drones, the average delivery time could be hours instead of days. However, many barriers will have to be overcome before drones become an everyday occurrence in the transportation industry. These issues include battery life, security of deliveries, varying regulations globally, external conditions (e.g., weather, time of day), safety, training of drone pilots, costs, and many others.[46]

Transportation Infrastructure

Often, we only talk about the transportation carriers and their customers. We sometimes ignore the fact that motor carriers must operate on highways, bridges, and tunnels; airplanes must utilize airports; trains have to traverse public rights-of-way, bridges, and tunnels; and

[42] Bertrand Moingeon, Lloyd Chisholm, and Elisabeth LeFranc, "The Day of the Drone—How Flying Robots Are Revolutionizing Business," *Forbes #Cutting Edge*, December 7, 2017, https://www.forbes.com/sites/hecparis/2017/12/07/the-day-of-the-drone-how-flying-robots-are-revolutionizing-business/#4fb56d6c93a0.

[43] Matt Steckowych, "Drones—A 'Buzz' Kill to Supply Chain Optimization," *Fronetics Blog*, May 16, 2017, https://www.fronetics.com/drones-buzz-kill-supply-chain-optimization/. Also see Jason McDowell, "Amazon Files Patent to Parachute Packages," *Inbound Logistics*, Vol. 37, No. 7 (July 2017), pp. 31–32.

[44] Steckowych, "Drones—A 'Buzz' Kill to Supply Chain Optimization."

[45] Paul Dittmann, "New Supply Chain Technology: Best Practices," *University of Tennessee White Paper*, April 2017, p. 13.

[46] Ibid., pp. 14–16.

ships dock in ports and navigate rivers, lakes, and other waterways. Without the proper infrastructure, freight does not move efficiently or effectively.

Domestic and International Dimensions

Certainly, growth in domestic and global trade has occurred and is now a significant portion of many businesses' annual revenues. Technology and transportation networks have helped facilitate this growth. At the same time, however, the transportation infrastructure has not and likely will not keep pace. Some examples will illustrate the problems.

"Congestion affects economic productivity in several ways. American businesses require more operators and equipment to deliver goods when shipping takes longer, more inventory when deliveries are unreliable, and more distribution centers to reach markets quickly when traffic is slow. . . . One estimate of urban congestion attributes 947,000 hours of vehicle delay to delivery trucks parked at curbside in dense urban areas where office buildings and stores lack off-street loading facilities. . . . Without operational improvement or additional capacity between now and 2035, recurring peak-period congestion is forecast to slow traffic on 20,000 miles of the National Highway System and create stop-and-go conditions on an additional 45,000 miles. . . . The top 10 highway-interchange bottlenecks cause an average of 1.5 million annual truck hours of delay each."[47]

Congestion impacts all transportation modes. When rail usage declined between 1960 and 2000, railroads reduced trackage by 50 percent. Intermodal movements used to be a relatively small part of rail traffic, but they are now a major source of revenue for railroads. Railroads are expanding roadways, equipment upgrades, and facilities in response to the increasing use of intermodal shipments, as well as increases in the use of traditional rail movements. However, those infrastructure improvements take time. "The Association of American Railroads reports that rail lines experiencing unstable flows and service breakdown conditions will increase from 108 miles today to almost 16,000 miles (30 percent of the network) in 2035 if current capacity is not increased."[48]

Water carriers experience congestion at ports when vessels arrive at the same time, or cranes and other equipment are not updated to meet the needs of larger ships. "Even when ports can berth and unload a ship quickly, the increasing size of container ships is moving congestion from ports to access roads and railroads. . . . On inland waterways, lock operations and aging infrastructure cause continuous bottlenecks." Approximately one-third of all commercial vessel passages through federal and state locks experience delays, which average about 90 minutes or more. Inland waterways are also susceptible to weather disruptions.[49]

Efforts to relieve congestion are taking place through programs such as congestion pricing and demand management. Cities such as London, Singapore, Rome, Oslo, and others limit traffic during certain periods of the day. They also charge tolls for entering the city at certain times and issue license plates to vehicles at varying costs for being able to drive into the city during business hours. User fees can reduce demand, and, hence, congestion, but such approaches are often not popular with commuters and trucking companies.

Constraints and Limitations

Historically, it has been easier to secure funds from governments for new transportation projects rather than monies for maintenance and repair of existing infrastructure. Coupled with increasing demands of customers for more products and services, infrastructure

---

[47] "Freight Management and Operation: Freight and Congestion," U.S. Department of Transportation, Federal Highway Administration, 2017, https://ops.fhwa.dot.gov/freight/freight_analysis/freight_story/congestion.htm.

[48] Ibid.

[49] Ibid.

investment has not been sufficient to properly maintain existing roads, rail lines, ports, and bridges. Various organizations give "grades" to the different types of infrastructure based on their condition. As of 2017, the American Society of Civil Engineers (ASCE) gave the following grades to the U.S. infrastructure: airports (D); ports (C+); highways (D); bridges (C+); rail (B); and inland waterways (D).[50] Similar situations exist in many industrialized nations throughout the world.

Because infrastructure improvements are usually funded by governments (federal, state, and local), there is a global problem because markets improve faster than infrastructure can be expanded and/or improved. Because both domestic and international trade have increased, outdated infrastructure is a problem that will not go away by itself.

In most countries, transportation projects are often administered by multiple agencies, committees, and commissions, which typically results in a lack of central coordination. In the U.S., there are 108 different federal surface transportation programs, which makes it very difficult to implement coordinated and cohesive transportation infrastructure programs.[51] Even when government transportation programs are more centralized, such as in China, infrastructure problems can still exist. Most of China's infrastructure is unbalanced, as it also is in Brazil and other countries;[52] that is, as you move inland from the coasts and/or away from major cities, the quality of transportation infrastructure declines significantly. In China, because their economy is growing so rapidly, the government is investing heavily in highways, seaports, airports, railroads, and waterways.[53] However, the pace of economic growth has exceeded the growth in infrastructure. In Russia, "poor road links and a population spread across nine time zones mean delivery times can be long by Western standards."[54] Many products are still shipped by rail because of infrastructure issues with motor transportation. For other former Soviet Union countries, infrastructure problems are often worse than in Russia.

The solutions to these infrastructure problems will have to be a collaborative effort of individual companies, industry groups, and government bodies. The economic costs associated with implementing comprehensive transportation infrastructure improvements will be enormous and will require the efforts of many constituencies.

At the same time, those who use the transportation infrastructure must be good stewards of the highways, waterways, bridges, tunnels, ports, and terminals that they use in order for the system to remain viable. The proper maintenance of equipment, optimizing routing and scheduling of shipments, and ensuring that load limits are not exceeded will help to maintain the infrastructure.

Measures and Metrics

The phrase "you can't manage what you don't measure" is widely accepted as true by supply chain executives. Whether such measurement occurs for the supply chain overall, or for a component of the supply chain such as transportation, is not the issue. Real-time, accurate data must be collected, analyzed, and used to develop strategies and tactics for all facets of supply chain management.

A survey of supply chain executives identified the fact that approximately three-quarters of all "best-in-class" organizations utilize cross-functional metrics and can access that data within a reasonable time so as to make optimal supply chain decisions. As an illustration

---

[50] "Infrastructure Report Card 2017," ASCE, 2017, https://www.infrastructurereportcard.org/.

[51] Peter Bradley, "It's a Long, Hard Road," *DC Velocity*, July 2008, http://www.dcvelocity.com/articles /20080701strategicinsight/.

[52] Paulo Fleury, "Brazil," *CSCMP Global Perspectives*, 2007, pp. 13–14.

[53] See Charles Guowen Wang, "China," *CSCMP Global Perspectives*, 2006, p. 30.

[54] Christopher Van Riet, "Supply Chain Evolution in a Crisis: Case Studies from Russia," *CSCMP's Supply Chain Quarterly*, Vol. 11, No. 1 (Quarter 1, 2017), p. 45.

of cross-functional metrics, in managing suppliers, the best-in-class firms measure in-transit shipment status, inbound supply chain data, international order/supplier event status, and supplier quality and manufacturing processes.[55]

Carrier and Shipper Metrics

Transportation plays a key role in the "source, deliver, and return" components of the SCOR Model of the supply chain. Products are moved into an organization (source) and out of the organization (delivery), and then items may be returned to the organization (return).

In the process standards and best-practice illustrations outlined in the CSCMP research study *Supply Chain Management Process Standards,* 2nd edition, Supply Chain Visions identified data that should be captured and evaluated by organizations. Some examples of good practice include the following:

- Managing strategic initiatives
  - Critical success factors are clearly defined with an actual-to-target gap analysis.
  - An embedded metrics hierarchy exists to associate functional metrics to top key performance indicators list.
  - Inter-enterprise metrics are tracked.
  - A balanced scorecard of customer, employee, operational, financial, and additional leading indicators is used to track performance and make informed decisions.
  - There is use of industry and cross-industry benchmarking for KPIs and metrics.[56]
- Appraise and develop suppliers
  - Supplier self-evaluations are based on total cost of acquisition and total service level.
  - There are balanced scorecards with weighting on critical performance measures.
  - Suppliers are measured on total cost of doing business.
  - Supplier metrics include outcome-based metrics for larger purchases or service contracts.[57]
- Service to customers
  - Customer scorecards measure KPIs as requested by the customer.
  - Ongoing, statistically reliable customer satisfaction/loyalty surveys are done.[58]
- Logistics networks
  - Logistics metrics include equipment efficiencies, building costs, and plans for ROI-based upgrades and changes.
  - Identifying customer profitability and product line profitability.
  - Triple bottom line metrics are integrated into accounting and reported to stakeholders.
  - Key account sales growth is measured.[59]
- Returns/reverse logistics
  - Metrics are captured for use in reducing the number of returns and increasing velocity in the returns process.
  - Having accurate tracking of product returns disposition.
  - A warranty analysis of defective components is developed with suppliers.
  - Mean time to repair or refurbish is measured.[60]

[55] Aberdeen Group, *The Supply Chain Executive's Strategic Agenda 2008*, January 2008, p. 14; and Bryan Ball, "Supplier Management: The Best-in-Class Approach to Drive Performance," *Aberdeen White Paper*, November 2016, http://v1.aberdeen.com/launch/report/knowledge_brief/14171-KB-procurement-purchasing-sourcing.asp.

[56] Supply Chain Visions, *Supply Chain Management Process Standards,* 2nd ed. (Lombard, IL: Council of Supply Chain Management Professionals, 2009), pp. 19–20.

[57] Ibid., pp. 63–64.

[58] Ibid., p. 72.

[59] Ibid., pp. 78–79.

[60] Ibid., pp. 95–98.

While firms typically utilize scores or even hundreds of various metrics, only a few (usually 10 or so) metrics are key. These metrics are referred to as key performance indicators (KPIs).

Key Performance Indicators (KPIs)

KPIs should allow for multi-year comparisons of performance and provide an accurate view of how the organization is doing in terms of its inbound and outbound transportation activities. They should be understandable, unambiguous, and easily measured. Examples of KPIs utilized by organizations include, but are not limited to, the following:[61]

- Labor productivity
- On-time pickup and delivery
- Revenue yield by specific units
- Fuel efficiency
- Maintenance costs
- Border delays
- Loading or unloading times
- Damages
- Freight cost per pallet shipped
- Outbound freight costs as a percentage of net sales
- Inbound freight costs as a percentage of purchases
- Transit time
- Claims as a percentage of freight cost
- Freight bill accuracy
- Shipment traceability
- Driver turnover
- Cost per mile or kilometer

The selection of specific KPIs for an organization will be dependent on what things are important to it and its customers. "One size does not fit all" when it comes to choosing which KPIs to use. The selection of KPIs should be part of an overall transportation management strategy.

Transportation Management Strategies

Transportation executives have many responsibilities. These include much more than just administering the movement of products. Specific functions of transportation management include:

- Being aware of transportation rates being negotiated by shippers in the marketplace.
- Selecting optimal transportation modes, intermodal combinations, and carriers within modes.

[61] Listings of various transportation KPIs were utilized in developing these examples, including the following sources: Adam Robinson, "9 KPIs to Track for Proper Freight Management," *Cerasis Blog*, May 4, 2016, http://cerasis.com/2016/05/04/freight-management-kpis/; Richard Simpson, "Transport Management KPIs—What Should You Look For?," *Walkers Transport Blog*, July 6, 2016, http://www.walkers-transport.co.uk/blog/transport-management-kpis-what-should-you-look-for; Mindy Long, "KPIs: Fleet Managers Watch Key Performance Indicators to Make Data-Driven Decisions, Improve Operations," *Transport Topics Blog*, October 11, 2017, http://www.walkers-transport.co.uk/blog/transport-management-kpis-what-should-you-look-for.

- Making shipment routing and tracking decisions.
- Identifying consolidation and breakbulk opportunities.
- Preparing a variety of transportation performance reports, such as loss and damage ratios, on-time performance, and costs versus budgets.
- Identifying KPIs for important elements of transportation.

Transportation or traffic management involves the administration of both inbound and outbound freight movements. Many times firms will be quoted product prices based on free-on-board (F.O.B.) destination. In other words, the price paid by the company for a product includes delivery to its location. However, the inbound transportation has not been obtained for free. The seller of the product has included the cost of transportation in its selling price. From a buyer's perspective, the seller may not be using the optimal transport mode and/or carrier, and thus the buyer may be paying additional costs of an inefficient system. What may be optimal or convenient for the seller may not necessarily be so for the buyer.

The carrier/shipper relationship is an important one; it directly affects the transportation executive's ability to manage successfully. In this section, we will look at shippers' and carriers' perspectives on transportation management. Specific issues that will be addressed include mode/carrier selection; core carrier concepts; outsourcing environmental, energy, and sustainability issues; last-mile delivery; and international transportation.

Mode and Carrier Selection

Economic and resource constraints mandate that organizations make the most efficient and productive mode/carrier choice decisions possible. Because of transportation's impact on customer satisfaction, time-in-transit, consistency of service, inventories, packaging, warehousing, and the environment, transportation decision makers must attempt to optimize the mode and carrier selection processes.[62]

Five separate and distinct decision stages occur: (1) problem recognition, (2) search, (3) choice/selection, (4) post-choice evaluation, and (5) feedback. For firms operating in the supply chain, transportation decisions should consider synergies (e.g., economies of scale, quantity/volume discounts) that might occur from joint mode and/or carrier selection by supply chain partners.

Problem recognition. The problem recognition stage of the mode/carrier choice process is triggered by a variety of factors, such as customer orders, dissatisfaction with an existing mode, and changes in the supply chain network. Typically, the most important factors are service related. In those instances where customers do not specify the mode and/or carrier, a search is undertaken for a feasible transportation alternative.

Search process. The supply chain or transportation executive scans a variety of information sources (past experience, carrier sales calls, company shipping records, advertising brochures, other supply chain members, and customers) as inputs into mode and carrier choices. The extent of the search process may be minimal if the decision maker uses only past experience as an information source. As additional information sources are examined, the time expended in the search process can be considerable. At the point where sufficient information has been obtained, a specific mode and/or carrier can be selected.

Choice/selection process. The task facing the supply chain or transportation executive at this stage is to choose a feasible alternative from among the several modes and carriers that are likely to be viable options. Using the information previously gathered, a determination

---

[62] For a discussion of mode and carrier selection in sourcing, see Sandra Beckwith, "10 Tips for Transportation Sourcing," *Inbound Logistics*, Vol. 37, No. 9 (September 2017), pp. 49–53.

is made regarding which option(s) can meet the organization's and supply chain's requirements. Generally, if a mode or carrier is within an acceptable price range, service-related factors become the major determinants in terms of who is selected. The mode or carrier that best satisfies the decision criteria is then selected and the shipment is routed via that option.

Post-choice evaluation. After a mode and carrier choice has been made, some evaluation procedure must be instituted to determine the performance of the mode/carrier that was selected after the movement has taken place. The post-choice evaluation process can range from being extremely detailed, to having none at all. For the most part, the degree of post-choice evaluation lies somewhere between these two extremes. It is rare that an organization does not at least respond to customer complaints about its carriers; this is one form of post-choice evaluation. Many firms use other techniques and metrics such as cost studies, audits, on-time pickup and delivery performance, and damage/claims reviews to evaluate transportation decisions. Some will statistically analyze the quality of a host of carrier service attributes. This has been referred to as *statistical process control.*

Feedback. An integral part of the mode/carrier choice is obtaining feedback. The feedback can be used as input at any point in the process. Feedback is invaluable because it occurs concurrently and independently of other performance measures. The mode/carrier choice decision is a universal process in that while the factors entering into the process may vary by geographic location or industry, the basic structure of the decision remains consistent regardless of these differences.

Mode and carrier selection is becoming much more important as shippers move toward the core carrier concept, reducing the number of carriers with whom they do business. By leveraging freight volumes to get bigger discounts and higher levels of service, shippers are able to reduce their transportation costs. At the same time, carriers benefit by having to deal with fewer shippers, each shipping larger volumes of product consistently, over longer periods of time. There is a potential downside or risk factor; that is, if fewer modes or carriers are used, service failures, although uncommon, can cause serious problems because there are no backups readily available.

Contracts

Shippers can obtain rates for each individual shipment they make, referred to as spot pricing, or obtain rates for a group or all shipments, referred to as contract pricing. The advantages of contracting are numerous. A good contract is the foundation of a successful strategic partnership or alliance between a shipper and a carrier. Contracts permit shippers to exercise greater control over their transportation. They help to assure predictability and guard against fluctuation in rates. In addition, contracting provides the shipper with service level guarantees and allows the shipper to use transportation to gain competitive advantage.

In most instances, contract prices will be lower than spot prices. One shipper saved over US$1.0 million using contract pricing.[63] Carrier-shipper contracts can prove valuable to both parties, but it is important that the contract include all of the relevant elements that apply to the shipping agreement. In soliciting carriers for possible contracting, a standard bid package or request for proposal (RFP) should be developed that includes the following components:

- *Commitment clause.* The shipper commits to a certain volume of freight and the carrier commits to providing the equipment necessary to move that volume.
- *Metrics clause.* The parties should establish how performance will be measured.

[63] Rick LaGore, "Transportation Contract versus Spot Pricing: Which Wins?," *Global Trade*, July 17, 2017, http://www.globaltrademag.com/global-logistics/transportation-contract-versus-spot-pricing-wins.

- *Pricing.* How much will the logistics service provider charge? Will charges be per-shipment, or will a flat fee be charged for the contract's duration?
- *Controlling law.* Which state's law will govern the contract if there is a dispute?
- *Description of services.* What services are to be performed by the various parties to the contract?
- *Tender of goods.* What constitutes delivery? What happens if the party receiving the goods refuses to accept the shipment?
- *Liability.* Who is responsible if goods are damaged during shipment?
- *Confidentiality.* A clause is needed to ensure that any information designated as "confidential" stays that way and is not shared with other shippers or providers.
- *Length.* How long will the relationship exist? What are the ramifications if one party wants to terminate the contract before it expires?[64]

The same components in the RFP should also form the basis of the contract that is ultimately negotiated between the shipper and carrier(s). Contracts are legal documents and, therefore, binding.

The exact format for each carrier-shipper contract will vary, depending on the mode/carrier involved, characteristics of the shipping firm, product(s) to be transported, level of competition, and other factors.[65] However, once the contract has been negotiated and entered into by all parties, the job is not finished! Post-contract evaluation is necessary to ensure that all parties are benefiting from the relationship. "Following a successful negotiation, record what went well and what can be improved. Use this historical analysis when you begin your next negotiation. Also, . . . consider opportunities where you may begin planning out long-term growth initiatives with your carrier."[66]

Private Carriage

A private carrier can be any transportation mode that moves products for a manufacturing or merchandising organization. The organization must own the equipment. The vast majority of private carriage involves truck transport. Private fleets primarily transport products owned by their organization or by other members of their supply chain. If excess capacity exists, as it does periodically, private fleets can haul products for other unrelated organizations. Prior to deregulation of the U.S. transportation industry during the 1980s, it was extremely difficult for private carriers to haul any products that were not owned by the organization, but the present regulatory environment has no such restrictions.

Private carriage is also a financial decision that organizations make. There are two major financial considerations that must be made in evaluating private carriage, including (1) a comparison of current cost and service data of the organization's for-hire carriers with that of a private operation and (2) the costs associated with implementing and controlling the private fleet.

A feasibility study should be undertaken whenever an organization is considering private carriage. This study should include an evaluation of the current transportation situation, along with corporate objectives regarding potential future market expansion. Objectives should include a statement outlining past, current, and desired service levels; identifying any issues that may impact supply chain partners; as well as a consideration of the general business environment, such as legal restrictions and economic trends.[67]

[64] Steven E. Salkin, "Breaking Up Is Hard to Do," *Logistics Management and Distribution Report*, Vol. 38, No. 4 (April 1999), p. 76.
[65] See Steven J. Trumper, "The Logistics Outsourcing Agreement—Strategies for Successful Contracting," *CSCMP Supply Chain Comment*, Vol. 39 (November/December 2005), pp. 14–15.
[66] "How to Negotiate Ocean Carrier Contracts," *Inbound Logistics*, Vol. 28, No. 11 (November 2008), p. 54.
[67] Private carriage has been a transportation option for many years, both before and after deregulation. For a brief discussion of the pros and cons of private carriage, see "Private Fleet vs. Dedicated: Which One Is Right for You?," *Ryder Special Report*, 2016, http://www.supplychainbrain.com/think-tank/research-analysis/whitepapers/single-article-page/article/private-fleet-vs-dedicated/.

The leasing of equipment and/or personnel (i.e., drivers) is an important consideration in private carriage and is the preferred strategy of firms such as Sherwin-Williams, the largest producer of paints and coatings in the U.S. The company leases from 350 to 450 trucks, depending on the level of sales activity.[68] It provides ease of entry and predictable cost and service levels. In contracting for the use of a full-service fleet, even inexperienced management can know the exact cost for transportation services, and can budget accordingly.

Other advantages of leasing include the ability to adjust vehicle resources for business cycles and seasonality through special lease agreements. Also, if the fleet is to be small, the organization will avoid investing significant amounts of capital in maintenance equipment and facilities. Another consideration is transportation obsolescence. New technology may render older vehicles obsolete, or the organization may outgrow its supply chain and transportation system.

Private fleet ownership may be preferable if capital is available and if it can be shown that vehicle investment will yield a favorable return. Other advantages might include the ability to buy needed equipment at a discount cost through reciprocity, the utilization of currently owned maintenance equipment and facilities, increased flexibility and freedom of utilization, and a potential to provide special customer services that a lessor would not allow.

Another form of leasing occurs when the shipper acquires both drivers and equipment from others or else leases its drivers and equipment to a for-hire carrier. Organizations can "single-source lease" and "trip lease." These options promise to expand the flexibility of shippers with private fleets and to provide additional opportunities to reduce operating costs. The two leasing options can be defined as follows:

Single-source leasing. An arrangement under which a private carrier acquires both drivers and equipment from a single source for at least 30 days.

Trip leasing. An arrangement under which a private carrier leases its drivers and equipment to a for-hire carrier for a period of fewer than 30 days.

There is a third alternative form of equipment acquisition that is particularly appealing from a cash flow viewpoint. An organization may be able to negotiate "third-party" equity loans from a financial institution that include a "guaranteed buy-back" from the dealer at the termination of the useful life of the equipment. This type of lease is fairly common in the acquisition of computer equipment. Under this approach, monthly payments cover interest on the entire purchase price but only an amount of principal equal to the difference between the purchase price and the guaranteed buy-back. This significantly reduces an organization's cash flow outlays and results in lower interest rates if the enterprise has established a high credit rating with its financial institutions. By using this technique, a national clothing retailer was able to save over $250,000 in interest charges on a three-year equity loan for 22 truck tractors. In addition, the company minimized its risk by obtaining buy-back guarantees from the selected dealer equal to 58 percent of the purchase price of each tractor.[69]

The future of private carriage can hold tremendous promise for those shippers able to take advantage of its benefits. For others, for-hire carriers offer the most opportunities for implementing transportation strategies within the supply chain.

Core Carrier Concept

When transportation carriers were viewed as "partners" by shippers, it was determined that long-term relationships had to be developed. Historically, unless the shipper utilized contract carriage, multiple common carriers were hired to move the firm's products.

[68] Dan Calabrese, "Painting a Picture of Private Fleet Profit," *Inbound Logistics*, Vol. 28, No. 8 (August 2008), p. 85.

[69] Material on third-party equity loans was obtained from Jay U. Sterling, Professor Emeritus, University of Alabama, and former director of distribution for The Limited Stores, Inc.

So, when carriers were viewed as partners, shippers made some important decisions. First, they decided that they would identify and develop "win-win" relationships with transportation carriers. Second, they consolidated shipments, both inbound and outbound, to fewer carriers, which would make it easier for them to develop the long-term relationships necessary in a partnership arrangement.

As a result of these two major decisions, shippers developed "carrier friendly" programs involving collaboration and coordination with just a few transportation companies. At the same time, because of events occurring in the marketplace, "carriers are now in a better position than ever to leverage their capacity to those shippers who best meet their service and profitability requirements. These new realities are encouraging shippers to refine their transportation management practices."[70]

Developing a carrier friendly program requires a new type of relationship between shippers and carriers. At a minimum, such relationships would include the following components:

- Understanding the carrier's ideal requirements and having the shipper's freight closely match those requirements.
  - Make freight easy to handle.
  - Reduce the cost of pickup.
  - Properly label and package products.
  - Match carriers with the locations that the shipper serves and the carriers service.
  - Provide carriers with flexible delivery schedules.
- Use technology to optimize cost and service aspects of the relationship.
  - Share capacity information with carriers.
  - Attempt to send orders directly to carriers from the shipper's order fulfillment system.
  - Minimize driver wait times by using technology to schedule appointments and being aware of delays.
  - Streamline border crossings by ensuring that all paperwork is complete and filed electronically whenever possible.[71]
  - Automate carrier communications.
  - Adopt incentive-based contracts that reward carriers for superior service performance and/or cost minimization.[72]

The implementation of a core carrier concept will often result in "win-win" for both the shipper and carrier. The shipper wins by having a reliable, cost-effective carrier transporting its freight. The carrier wins by having a long-term relationship with the shipper so that they can effectively plan their operations and invest in technology, equipment, facilities, and personnel, knowing that they will recoup their investment over the life of the relationship. Such relationships are often referred to as strategic partnerships or alliances.

Outsourcing: Third Parties (3PLs), Partnerships, and Strategic Alliances

Third Parties (3PLs)

The outsourcing of transportation has been a common practice for many years, although as firms attempt to improve various financial ratios such as return on assets (ROA) and asset turnover, utilizing fewer assets for servicing customers and maintaining sales revenues is an

---

[70] Beth Enslow and Dan Goodwill, "The New Transportation Best Practice: Creating a 'Carrier Collaboration' Program to Gain Control of Rates and Capacity," *CSCMP Supply Chain Comment*, Vol. 40 (January/February 2006), p. 16.
[71] Eric Johnson, "Global TMS Comes of Age," *American Shipper*, Vol. 58, No. 5 (May 2016), pp. 10–16.
[72] Enslow and Goodwill, "The New Transportation Best Practice," pp. 16–17.

attractive option. It has been estimated that the total third-party (3PL) market approximates $751 billion globally.[73] Outsourcing tends to be used more frequently by organizations located in Europe and Asia.[74]

There are many reasons why shippers would outsource transportation, including cost savings; revenue enhancing potential; transportation not being a core competency; internal problems associated with administering the transportation function; minimizing risk; availability of high-quality 3PLs; unfamiliarity with new markets, especially internationally; and logistics reengineering or redesign decisions.

Simplistically, the transportation outsourcing decision is a "make-or-buy" decision. Can a 3PL do the same job for less and provide the same, or perhaps better, customer service? With outsourcing long term expected to grow in the U.S. and internationally, many organizations have determined that 3PLs are viable transportation options within their supply chains.

The Use of 3PLs is Increasing

With the increasing emphasis on supply chain management, more companies are exploring the 3PL option. For some firms, dealing with one third-party firm who will handle all, or most, of their freight offers a number of advantages, including the management of information by the third party, freeing the company from day-to-day interactions with carriers, and having the third-party company oversee hundreds or even thousands of shipments. Activities such as freight payment and dedicated contract carriage have been administered by third parties for many years. However, additional transportation and logistics activities are being outsourced. In some instances, entire logistics operations are being outsourced to third parties.

Strategic Partnerships/Alliances

An effective logistics network requires a cooperative relationship between shippers and carriers. That cooperation must occur on both a strategic and an operational level. When such cooperation takes place, the shipper and carrier become part of a partnership or alliance. Companies that have implemented the concept include Black and Decker, GTE, IBM, Procter & Gamble, McKesson, Xerox, and 3M.

In too many instances, however, shippers and carriers do not act in concert because of differences in perceptions, practice, or philosophy. Sometimes the notion that "we never did it that way before" impedes cooperation and synergism. Such differences result in inefficiencies in the transportation system and conflicts between shippers and carriers.

In essence, a successful strategic partnership or alliance is more than just a set of plans, programs, and methods. Like the marketing concept, "partnershipping" is a philosophy that permeates an entire organization. It is a way of life that becomes part of the way a firm conducts its business.

Environment, Energy, and Sustainability

As prices for fossil fuels have increased and discussions have escalated regarding environmental issues such as global warming, pollution, and a growing waste stream, the energy-ecology aspects of transportation have become more important issues within transportation management. For example, rail transport in the U.S. has seen a resurgence due to the higher costs of energy coupled with the increasing level of customer service being provided by rail carriers. Some truck traffic has been shifting away from motor to rail, in part due to the fuel efficiency of rail versus motor. If fuel prices continue to remain high,

[73] "The State of Logistics Outsourcing: 2017 Third-Party Logistics Study," *Research Report*, Capgemini and Dr. C. John Langley, 2017, p. 12.
[74] Ibid.

or if supplies of petroleum become limited, firms will adjust their inbound and outbound shipping patterns.

Most organizations believe that succeeding long term in "green" initiatives occurs by coordinating and collaborating with suppliers, supply chain partners, and logistics service providers. In the short term, firms can implement energy-saving programs such as better routing and scheduling of vehicles, better driving methods that save fuel, and minimization of transportation equipment wait times.

UPS, one of the largest ancillary carriers in the world, was able to reduce its consumption of gasoline and reduce total vehicle emissions through a simple, yet innovative program of driver education. The company redesigned its delivery routes to eliminate as many left-hand turns as possible, which require more idle time as drivers are waiting for oncoming traffic to clear before turning. As a result, the company trimmed millions of miles off its deliveries and saved the cost of millions of gallons of gas. It also reduced truck emissions.[75]

Union Pacific Railroad has implemented a number of technologies that have resulted in improved environmental performance. Since 2000, Union Pacific has spent about US $7.5 billion to purchase more than 4,400 fuel-efficient locomotives. "Distributed power units (DPU) are locomotives that operate in the middle and/or end of trains rather than only having all locomotives at the front end. Distributed power technology carries fuel and safety benefits. . . . As a result, Union Pacific moves nearly two-thirds of its gross ton miles using the technology."[76]

Union Pacific also utilizes the Genset locomotive. "It is an engine that, by using multiple smaller diesel engines and generators instead of one large single engine, can achieve a better emissions profile than a conventional locomotive. . . . Compared to conventional diesel locomotives, Gensets reduce greenhouse gas emissions by as much as 37 percent, emissions of oxides of nitrogen by up to 80 percent, and emissions of particulate matter by 90 percent. Running fewer engines translates to burning less fuel and fewer emissions."[77]

Last-Mile Delivery

Whether transportation carriers move products short or long distances, the most difficult part of the process is delivering the shipment the "last mile." The importance of last-mile delivery to customers is important irrespective of whether the final customer is a business or a consumer; however, in the retail environment, last-mile delivery is absolutely crucial to achieving customer satisfaction. As an expression of "mass customization," a concept initially conceived in the 1970s, last-mile delivery in the retail sector requires transportation carriers to be extremely flexible and provide delivery of products at various times, perhaps even the same day as when the product was ordered!

In the supply chain, the final component of the transportation process is delivering the product to the customer—this can make or break a company. "One of the biggest tests of agility for the consumer products and retail industries currently is last-mile delivery and associated services (e.g., returns). . . . Next-day home deliveries, once the pride of Internet sellers, are now expected as a given. To differentiate anew, leaders have had to up their game with same-day or 'on-demand' services—from drone deliveries to advanced 'click and collect' options using nearby convenience stores, intelligent lockers in underground train networks, and even drop-offs to consumers' cars."[78]

---

[75] "No Left Turn," *Road & Track*, Vol. 60, No. 3 (November 2008), p. 40.
[76] See the "Technology" section of the Union Pacific website, 2018, https://www.up.com/aboutup/environment/technology/index.htm.
[77] Ibid.
[78] "Making the Last Mile Pay: Balancing Customer Expectations and Commercial Reality," *Capgemini White Paper*, 2016, p. 2.

Exhibit: Ways to Reduce Fuel Consumption in Motor Transportation

Beginning in 2006 and continuing in the years since, petroleum costs have exhibited dramatic increases, reaching almost US$150 per barrel in 2008. As a result of these significant increases, companies such as Ryder System, a truck leasing company, have initiated programs to reduce their fuel consumption. Ryder developed strategies to mitigate the rising fuel costs they were experiencing:

Practice #1: Train drivers in fuel-efficient driving techniques, including reducing truck speeds to 55 mph.

Practice #2: Improve tire maintenance by checking tire pressures, vehicle alignments, and tire rotation.

Practice #3: Update existing equipment or purchase new equipment with more fuel-efficient models, such as multi-fuel engines, fuel-efficient drive tires, auxiliary power units to reduce idling time, and tractors designed to reduce wind resistance.

Practice #4: Initiate ongoing preventive maintenance programs that adhere to strict schedules. Well-maintained vehicles are more fuel efficient.

Practice #5: Take advantage of new technologies such as onboard diagnostic systems, global positioning systems, route optimization software, and real-time fuel efficiency monitors.

Practice #6: Reduce unnecessary trips for trucks by closely monitoring inventory levels of products being ordered. Schedule product return pickups when deliveries are being made to the same location.

Practice #7: Optimize distribution networks by locating warehouses and distribution centers where transit distances can be minimized and customer service levels can be maintained.

Practice #8: Control routes, fuel consumption, and idle time with dedicated assets, drivers, and strategic route planning.

Practice #9: Better control transportation management practices by coordinating shipments to take advantage of consolidation programs. Develop coordination across all modes of transportation and not just a single mode.

Source: Adapted from "Ten Steps for Fuel Savings," *Outsourced Logistics*, July 16, 2008, http://www.outsourcedlogistics.com /operations_strategy/ten_steps_fuel_savings_0716, accessed July 28, 2008.

With today's mobile technology and the Internet of Things (IoT), complete visibility of product shipments is possible. Much of the paperwork that has traditionally accompanied products being transported can now be digitized. Optimal routing of shipments is possible with a good transportation management system (TMS) being in place and the use of GPSs in transport vehicles. Companies such as Amazon, Alibaba, and Walmart are examples of organizations that have mastered, better than most others, the nuances of last-mile delivery and are reaping the rewards of lower costs, greater revenues, and higher levels of customer satisfaction. The downsides of not having good visibility of freight shipments are many, including:

- "A factory might need to idle or ramp up a production line accordingly.
- A distribution operation might have to adjust staffing on its loading docks to account for both unproductive time and the need for personnel when a load does finally arrive.
- A retailer would have to work around the lack of inventory on store shelves."[79]

Amazon.com, which has revolutionized the omnichannel environment, keeps pushing the envelope in reducing the time between customer orders and delivery of the products. It can now deliver same day, and in some instances, within a few hours, after customers have placed their orders. And Amazon is going a step further. "Amazon, which is continually redefining last-mile service with new 'immediacy' solutions, is currently exploring 'predictive

[79] "Why Freight Visibility Is Important," *Descartes White Paper*, 2016, http://www.supplychainbrain .com/think-tank/research-analysis/whitepapers/single-article-page/article/why-freight-visibility-is -important/. Also see "Is Your Organization Prepared for TMS Implementation?," *Eyefreight White Paper*, 2015, https://eyefreight.com/our-customers/white-papers/.

Exhibit: Companies Are Recognized by U.S. Environmental Protection Agency's (EPA) SmartWay® Transport Partnership for 2017 Excellence Awards

©Dmitri Ma/Shutterstock

The U.S. EPA SmartWay® Transport Partnership annually recognizes carriers, shippers, and logistics companies that excel in environmental performance and efficiency. In 2017, 44 trucking companies, 11 shippers, and 4 multi-modal companies were selected for awards.

"Candidates in SmartWay's freight carrier category were evaluated based on their efficiency and environmental performance in moving products and merchandise . . . by demonstrating that they carry more goods per ton-mile, using less fuel and emitting fewer greenhouse gas and air pollutant emissions." Companies selected included firms such as Cliff Viessman, Inc.; Doug Andrus Distributing LLC; Eagle Transport; and Mesa Systems.

Shippers were selected based on their "effective collaboration, advanced technology and operational practices, a robust system to validate and report their SmartWay® data, and communications and public outreach efforts." Companies selected included Gap, HP, Johnson & Johnson, Lowe's Companies, The Home Depot, Kimberly-Clark, Kohl's Department Stores, McDonald's, and Whirlpool Corporation.

Logistics companies were evaluated similarly to shippers and awardees included Alliance Shippers, Knichel Logistics, and Union Pacific Distribution Services.

SmartWay® is a voluntary, market-driven partnership that aims to reduce emissions and foster the development of a clean and efficient freight supply chain.

Source: "SmartWay® 2017 Excellence Award Leadership Highlights," October 2017, https://www.epa.gov/sites/production /files/2017-10/documents/420f17018.pdf.

shopping' for example. This involves anticipating shoppers' needs in advance based on past purchases and other preference insights, with a view to holding merchandise close to customers—ready to delivery at very short notice."[80]

Organizations that are more successful in delivering products to customers over the last mile will reap the rewards of greater revenues, market share, and customer satisfaction. Even more important will be the attainment of competitive advantage by the leading-edge firms, which can be long term given the difficulties of implementing last-mile delivery programs.

International Transportation

Trade throughout the globe is increasing, especially in Asia. Over one-half of the total world container trade occurs in Asia.[81] Organizations operating internationally must be aware of the services, costs, and availability of transport modes within and between the countries where their products are distributed. As an example, air and water transportation are the major options available for international shipments, unless the countries happen to be contiguous. Within most countries, motor and rail shipments dominate. Management must consider many factors when it compares the various options.

Differences that exist between transportation modes can be due to taxes, subsidies, regulations, government ownership of carriers, geography, and other factors that vary by

[80] "Making the Last Mile Pay," p. 4. Also see Paul Simpson, "The Secrets behind Amazon's Success," Chartered Institute of Procurement and Supply (CIPS), January 2016, https://www.cips.org/supply -management/analysis/2016/february/the-secrets-behind-amazons-success/.
[81] "Container Port Traffic (TEU: 20 foot equivalent units)," *Containerisation International Yearbook*, The World Bank, 2016, https://data.worldbank.org/indicator/IS.SHP.GOOD.TU.

country or geographic region. For example, because of government ownership and/or subsidies of railroads in Europe, rail service benefits from newer or better-maintained equipment, track, and facilities that accompany the large budgets of governments. Japan and Europe utilize water carriage to a much larger degree than the U.S. or Canada due to the length and favorable characteristics of coastlines and inland waterways.

International Transportation Is More Expensive Than Domestic Transportation

Typically, international transportation costs represent a much higher percentage of merchandise value than is the case in domestic transportation. This is due to the longer distances involved, administrative requirements, and related paperwork that must accompany international shipments.

Intermodal transportation is much more common in international movements, and even though rehandling costs are higher than for single mode movements, cost savings and service improvements often result. For example, there are three basic forms of international intermodal distribution. They have been described as follows:

Landbridge

Landbridge, a service in which foreign cargo crosses a country enroute to another country. For example, European cargo enroute to Japan may be shipped by ocean to the U.S. East Coast, then moved by rail to the U.S. West Coast, and from there shipped by ocean to Japan.

Mini-landbridge

Mini-landbridge (also called mini-bridge), a special case of landbridge, where foreign cargo originates or terminates at a point within the U.S.

Micro-bridge

Micro-bridge, a service being provided by ports on the U.S. West Coast, in contrast with mini-bridge, provides door-to-door rather than port-to-port transportation. The big advantage of micro-bridge is that it provides a combined rate including rail and ocean transportation in a single tariff that is lower than the sum of the separate rates.[82]

A comparison of single-mode and intermodal movements between the Far East and the U.S. East Coast demonstrates the advantages of the latter. If we compare an all-water versus mini-landbridge (MLB) movement for comparable shipments, the costs are approximately the same. But MLB is significantly faster, thus offering the opportunity to reduce order-cycle times and improve customer service levels.

In making traffic and transportation decisions, the supply chain executive must know and understand the differences between the domestic and international marketplace. Modal availability, rates, regulatory restrictions, service levels, and other aspects of the transportation mix may vary significantly from one market to another.

Summary

In this chapter we examined the role of transportation in the supply chain. Transportation, together with warehousing, adds time and place utility to products. It also affects many other decision-making areas such as manufacturing, logistics, new product development, target market areas served, purchasing/procurement, facility location, and pricing.

The five basic modes of transportation—motor, rail, air, water, and pipeline—provide movement of products between where they are produced and where they are consumed. Each mode varies in its economic and service characteristics, and has a different cost structure based on product- and market-related factors. Supply chain executives must be aware of mode characteristics as well as various intermodal combinations, nonoperating third parties, and other options (e.g., piggyback, containers, freight forwarders, shippers' associations, brokers, UPS, FedEx, and USPS).

In recent years, transportation infrastructure issues, such as port and road congestion, and the degradation of bridges and highways over time, have sometimes limited the ability of the supply chain to maintain optimal levels of customer service. While these

[82] Definition of all three international distribution forms can be found at http://www.businessdictionary.com.

act as constraints to effective supply chain management, they do offer opportunities for leading-edge firms and for government-private sector cooperation.

Regulation and deregulation of the major modes of transportation have had significant impact on motor, rail, air, and water carriers. Some of the areas most affected by deregulation have been rates, market entry, use of shipper-carrier contracts, routing and scheduling decisions, mergers, service levels, and the use of transportation brokers.

We examined issues relating to carrier and shipper metrics and supply chain productivity and looked at some examples of the benefits that the use of key performance indicators (KPIs) and technology has brought to transportation management.

Finally, various transportation management strategies were discussed, including mode and carrier selection, use of core carriers, and transportation outsourcing. Issues relating to the environment, energy, and sustainability were discussed because these factors can have significant impact on transportation carriers and shippers. International supply chain issues were introduced in this chapter, and will be discussed in more detail in later chapters of this textbook.

Suggested Readings

Ames, Ben, "Today's TMS Deliver More Than Freight Savings," *DC Velocity*, Vol. 16, No. 9 (September 2018), pp. 49–50.

Bradley, Peter, "4 Steps to TMS Success," *DC Velocity*, Vol. 10, No. 3 (March 2012), pp. 48–49.

"Data Logging for Consumer Goods: Transporting High Class Guitars Safely," Bosch Case Study, 2017, https://cdn.sdcexec.com/files/base/acbm/sdce/document/2017/12/Case_Studies_Guitar_Nanny.pdf.

Heaney, Bob, "Intermodal Optimization—Enhancing Last Mile Visibility and Execution," *White Paper*, Aberdeen Group, January 2012.

Lacefield, Susan K., "It's All in the Delivery," *DC Velocity*, Vol. 9, No. 9 (September 2011), pp. 51–53.

McCrea, Bridget, "5 Trends Driving TMS Growth," *Logistics Management*, Vol. 51, No. 1 (January 2012), pp. 42–44.

McCue, Dan, "Casebook: Getting a Handle on Transportation Costs," *Inbound Logistics*, Vol. 31, No. 11 (November 2011), pp. 79–81.

O'Reilly, Joseph, "The Evolution of Third-Party Logistics," *Inbound Logistics*, July 2015, http://www.inboundlogistics.com/cms/article/the-evolution-of-third-party-logistics/.

O'Reilly, Joseph, "Managing Inbound Transportation: All on Board FOB," *Inbound Logistics*, Vol. 31, No. 12 (December 2011), pp. 77–79.

"Redefining Final Mile Delivery in the Age of the Customer," Eyefortransport and Convey *White Paper*, February 2017, http://go.getconvey.com/rs/200-AMW-516/images/EfTransport%20Convey%20Whitepaper%20FINAL.pdf.

Schulz, John D., "Tuesday Morning Shifts Modes," *Logistics Management*, Vol. 51, No. 2 (February 2012), pp. 24–27.

Solomon, Mark B., "Slow Steam Ahead," *DC Velocity*, March 5, 2012, http://www.dcvelocity.com.

"Special Supplement: Help Is on the Way!," *Inbound Logistics*, Vol. 31, No. 11 (November 2011), pp. 57–70.

"The State of Logistics Outsourcing: 2017 Third-Party Logistics Study," *Research Report*, Capgemini and Dr. C. John Langley, 2017.

Trunick, Perry A., "Improving Rail Infrastructure: On the Right Track," *Inbound Logistics*, Vol. 31, No. 10 (October 2011), pp. 41–47.

Vilacoba, Karl, "Factoring Freight into Complete Street Plans," *InTransition*, Vol. 27 (Fall 2017), pp. 12–15, 31.

Questions and Problems

LO 5-1   1. What is the role of transportation in the supply chain and supply chain management?

LO 5-2   2. Identify the five basic modes of transportation and briefly discuss the service and cost aspects of each mode. Also discuss other transportation options that would be classified as ancillary modes.

LO 5-3   3. Indicate how infrastructure acts as both a facilitator and inhibitor of transportation.

LO 5-4   4. What is meant by the "core carrier concept," and how does such a concept impact supply chain management?

LO 5-5   5. What is the role of transportation in the SCOR Model? What are some typical metrics that can be examined relating to transportation performance?

Appendixes

Appendix A: Legally Defined Forms of Transportation

In addition to classifying alternative forms of transportation on the basis of mode, carriers can be classified on the basis of the four legal forms: common, contract, exempt, and private carriers. The first three forms are for-hire carriers, and the last is owned by a shipper. For-hire carriers transport freight belonging to others and are subject to various federal, state, and local statutes and regulations. For the most part, private carriers transport their own goods and supplies in their own equipment and are exempt from most regulations, with the exception of those dealing with safety and taxation.

Deregulation has reshaped how logistics executives view the transport modes, particularly the legal forms of transportation. In principle, these legal designations no longer exist because of deregulation. For example, the distinction between common and contract motor carriers was eliminated by the Trucking Industry Regulatory Reform Act of 1994 (TIRRA). However, the terms are used within the industry and do provide some guidance with respect to transportation type.

Common Carriers

Common carriers offer their services to any shipper to transport products, at published rates, between designated points. In order to legally operate, they must be granted authority from the appropriate federal regulatory agency. With deregulation, common carriers have significant flexibility with respect to market entry, routing, and pricing. Common carriers must offer their services to the general public on a nondiscriminatory basis; that is, they must serve all shippers of the commodities that their equipment can feasibly carry. A significant problem facing common carriers is that the number of customers cannot be predicted with certainty in advance, and thus future demand is uncertain. The result has been that many common carriers have entered into contract carriage.

Contract Carriers

A *contract carrier* is a for-hire carrier that does not hold itself out to serve the general public; rather it serves a limited number of shippers under specific contractual arrangements. The contract between the shipper and the carrier requires that the carrier provide a specified transportation service at a specified cost. In most instances, contract rates are lower than common carrier rates because the carrier is transporting commodities it prefers to carry for cost and efficiency reasons. An advantage is that transport demand is known in advance.

Exempt Carriers

An *exempt carrier* is a for-hire carrier that transports certain products such as unprocessed agricultural and related products such as farm supplies, livestock, fish, poultry, and agricultural seeds. Carriers of newspapers are also given exempt status. The exempt status was originally established to allow farmers to transport their products using public roads; however, it has been extended to a wider range of products being transported by a variety of modes. In addition, local cartage firms operating in a municipality or a "commercial zone" surrounding a municipality are exempt.

Generally, exempt carrier rates are lower than common or contract carriage rates. However, because very few commodities are given exempt status, the exempt carrier is not a viable form of transport for most companies. In reality, however, because transportation deregulation has eliminated pricing regulations, almost all carriers can be considered exempt from pricing restrictions.

Private Carriers

A *private carrier* is generally not-for-hire and is not subject to federal economic regulation. With private carriage, the firm is primarily providing transportation for its own products. As a result, the company must own or lease the transport equipment and operate its own facilities. From a legal standpoint, the most important factor distinguishing private carriage from for-hire carriers is the restriction that the transportation activity must be incidental to the primary business of the firm.

Private carriage traditionally had advantages over other carriers because of the flexibility and economy it offered. The major advantages of private carriage have traditionally been cost- and service-related; however, with deregulation, common and contract carriage can often provide excellent service levels at reasonable costs.

Appendix B: Basic Transportation Management Concepts

Factors influencing transportation costs/pricing can be grouped into two major categories: *product-related* and *market-related*. These factors determine the basic pricing strategies of carriers: *cost-of-service* and *value-of-service*.

Product-Related Factors

Many factors related to a product's characteristics influence the cost and pricing of transportation. A company can use these factors to determine product classifications for ratemaking purposes. They can be grouped according to (1) density, (2) stowability, (3) ease or difficulty in handling, and (4) liability.

Density refers to a product's weight-to-volume ratio. Items such as steel, canned foods, building products, and paper goods have high weight-to-volume ratios; that is, they are relatively heavy given their size and, thus, have higher densities. On the other hand, electronic products, clothing, luggage, and toys have low weight-to-volume ratios and are relatively lightweight given their size. Generally, low-density products (those with low weight-to-volume ratios) tend to cost more to transport, on a per-pound (or kilo) basis, than high-density products.

Stowability is the degree to which a product can fill the available space in a transport vehicle. For example, grain, ore, and bulk petroleum have excellent stowability because they can completely fill the container (e.g., railcar, tank truck, pipeline) in which they are transported. Other items, such as automobiles, machinery, livestock, and people, do not have good stowability, or cube utilization. A product's stowability depends on factors such as size, shape, fragility, and other physical characteristics.

Related to stowability is the *ease or difficulty in handling* the product. Items that are not easily handled are usually more costly to transport. Products that are uniform in their physical characteristics (raw materials and items in cartons, cans, or drums), or products that can be manipulated with material-handling equipment, require less handling expense and are therefore less costly to transport.

Liability is an important concern for many products such as those with high value-to-weight ratios, those more easily damaged, and those subject to higher rates of theft or pilferage. In cases where the transportation carrier assumes greater liability (e.g., with computers, jewelry, and home entertainment products), a higher price will be charged to transport the product.

Other factors, which vary in importance depending on the product category, are the product's hazardous characteristics and the need for strong and rigid protective packaging. Such factors are particularly important in the chemical and plastics industries.

Market-Related Factors

In addition to product characteristics, important market-related factors also affect transportation costs/pricing. The most significant are (1) degree of intramode and intermode competition; (2) location of markets (i.e., the distance goods must be transported); (3) nature and extent of government regulation; (4) balance or imbalance of freight traffic in a market; (5) seasonality of product movements; and (6) whether the product is being transported domestically or internationally. Each of these factors, in combination, affects the costs and pricing of transportation and determines whether a transportation carrier will utilize a cost-of-service, value-of-service, or other type of pricing strategy.

Cost-of-Service versus Value-of-Service Pricing

Two methods are typically used to form the bases of establishing transportation pricing: cost-of-service and value-of-service. *Cost-of-service* pricing establishes transportation rates at levels that cover a carrier's fixed and variable costs, plus some profit margin. Naturally, this approach is appealing because it establishes the lower limit of rates. It has some inherent difficulties, however.

First, a carrier must be able to identify its fixed and variable costs. This involves both a recognition of the relevant cost components and an ability to measure those costs reasonably accurately. Many transportation carriers cannot measure those costs precisely, at least in terms of cause and effect. Second, this approach requires that fixed costs be allocated to each freight movement (shipment). As the number of shipments increases, however, the allocation of fixed costs gets spread over a larger number of movements, and thus the fixed cost-per-unit ratio becomes smaller. As the number of shipments decreases, the ratio becomes larger. In the end, the allocation process becomes somewhat arbitrary unless exact shipment volume is known or can be accurately forecast.

Transportation costs can vary within the cost-of-service pricing approach because of two major factors: distance and volume. As distance increases, rates generally increase, although not as quickly. In their simplest form, distance rates are the same for all origin-destination pairs. An example of such a uniform rate is the postal rate charged for a one-ounce, first-class letter. Another distance measure is built on the tapering principle. Rates increase with distance, but not proportionally, because terminal costs and other fixed costs remain the same regardless of distance. Due to the higher fixed costs of rail relative to motor transportation, railroad rates experience a greater tapering with distance.

The second factor concerns the volume of the shipment. Economies of scale are present with large-volume shipments. The rate structure can reflect the volume in a number of ways. Rates may be based on the quantity of product shipped. Shipments above a specified volume receive truckload (TL) or carload (CL) rates,[83] and those between these extremes receive less-than-full-vehicle-load rates. High volumes can also be used as justification for quoting a shipper special rates on particular commodities.

A second method of transportation pricing is *value-of-service*. This approach essentially charges what the market will bear and is based on market demand for transportation service and the competitive situation. In effect, this approach establishes the upper limit on rates. Rates are set that will maximize the difference between revenues received and the variable cost incurred for transporting a shipment.

---

[83] Smaller shipments transported by motor carriers are referred to as less-than-truckload (LTL). LTL can be defined as any quantity of freight weighing less than the amount required for the application of a truckload (TL) rate. Similarly, less-than-carload (LCL) rates would generally apply to rail shipments of less than one full rail car.

For example, assume that two manufacturers compete for business in the same target market area. Manufacturer A, which is located in the target market area, sells its product for $2.50 a unit and earns a contribution of 50 cents per unit. If Manufacturer B incurs the same costs, exclusive of transportation costs, but is located 500 miles from the market, 50 cents per unit represents the maximum that Manufacturer B can afford to pay for transportation to the target market. Also, if two forms of transportation available to Manufacturer B are equal in terms of performance characteristics, the higher-priced service would have to meet the lower rate to be competitive. In most instances, competition will determine the price level when it lies between the lower and upper limits.

F.O.B. Pricing

The pricing terms that are offered by sellers to buyers have significant impacts on logistics generally, and transportation specifically. For example, if a seller quotes a delivered price to the buyer's retail store location, the total price includes not only the cost of the product, but also the cost of moving the product to the retail store. This rather simple illustration highlights a number of important considerations for the buyer or consignee (the recipient of the product being distributed).

Why F.O.B. Terms Are Important
First, the buyer knows the final delivered price prior to the purchase. Second, the buyer does not have to manage the transportation activity involved in getting the product from the seller's location to the buyer's location. Third, and closely related to the second consideration, the buyer typically will not control the transportation decision, so it is possible that a mode and/or carrier could be selected by the seller that might be nonadvantageous to the buyer (i.e., due to poor service levels provided by the mode/carrier).

While it is easier from a management perspective to purchase products F.O.B. destination, the lack of control of the transportation function can potentially cause problems for the purchaser, such as the carrier selected by the shipper providing poor service in your area, or only making deliveries at certain times that may not correspond to when you would like to receive shipments. Buyers should always know the specifics regarding all shipments that include delivery to ensure that optimal decisions are being made on their behalf.

Delivered Pricing

In a delivered pricing system, buyers are given a price that includes delivery of the product(s). As mentioned in the F.O.B. pricing discussion previously, this form of pricing is, in essence, F.O.B. destination. The seller secures the transportation mode/carrier and delivers the product to the buyer. This option can be advantageous to one or both parties of the transaction, depending on which variation of delivered pricing is used by the seller.

For example, assume that two manufacturers compete for business in a market area. Manufacturer A is located in the market area, sells its product for $2.50 a unit, and earns a contribution of 50 cents per unit. If manufacturer B incurs the same costs exclusive of transportation costs but is located 400 miles from the market, 50 cents per unit represents the maximum that manufacturer B can afford to pay for transportation to the market. Also, if two forms of transportation available to manufacturer B are equal in terms of performance characteristics, the higher-priced service would have to meet the lower rate to be competitive.

Zone Pricing
Variations include zone pricing and basing point pricing. *Zone pricing* is a method that categorizes geographic areas into zones. Each zone will have a particular delivery cost associated with it. The closer the zone is to the seller, the lower the delivery cost; the farther away, the higher the delivery charge. Depending upon the buyer's location in a particular zone, some buyers will be paying more for delivery on a per-mile basis than will others.

Basing Point Pricing
In a *basing point pricing* system, the seller selects one or more locations that serve as points-of-origin. Depending on which origin is selected by the seller, the buyer will pay delivery costs from that point to its location. The seller will often use a manufacturing plant,

distribution center, port, free trade zone, etc. as a basing point. This method can be good or bad for the buyer depending on which basing point is selected. For example, a manufacturer may have a distribution center located in the same state as the buyer but uses the location of the corporate office located in another state as the basing point. The product may or may not actually originate at the basing point location.

Quantity Discounts

Cumulative versus Noncumulative Quantity Discounts

Quantity discounts can be cumulative or noncumulative. *Cumulative quantity discounts* provide price reductions to the buyer based on the amount of purchases over some prescribed period of time. *Noncumulative quantity discounts* are applied to each order and do not accumulate over a time period.

From a transportation perspective, buyers purchasing products under a cumulative quantity discount system can order smaller quantities, paying the higher transportation costs for smaller shipments, and still gain a cost advantage (i.e., the additional cost of transportation is less than the cost savings resulting from the quantity discount).

On the other hand, if a noncumulative quantity discount is applied, the buyer must purchase sufficient quantities in order to obtain TL or CL rates for larger shipments. While transportation costs on a per-item or per-pound basis will be less for larger shipments, there will be additional costs incurred by the buyer (warehousing costs, inventory carrying costs). These costs have to be considered when buyers are purchasing larger, but fewer, orders from sellers.

In today's business environment, companies must be very responsive to customer demand in the marketplace. The trend is for companies to purchase smaller quantities, more often, and to do so as quickly as possible, so it is more advantageous for the buyer to have a cumulative quantity discount applied.

Allowances

Sometimes, sellers will provide price reductions to buyers that perform some of the delivery function. For example, when using a delivered pricing system, the seller assumes all costs of delivery and adds those costs to the price of the product. If the buyer is willing to assume some of the delivery functions, the seller will often provide some allowances, or price reductions, to the buyer.

The most common allowances are provided for customer pickup of the product or unloading the carrier vehicle upon delivery at the customer's location. These services cost the seller money and if the buyer is willing to perform these functions, a price concession can be provided.

The important element of making the right decisions regarding whether or not to take advantage of allowances is to know the costs associated with each delivery function. The allowance should be equal to, or greater than, the costs to the buyer for assuming these responsibilities.

Pricing and Negotiation

During the last decade, shippers have tended to use fewer carriers and place greater emphasis on negotiated pricing. The goal of the negotiation process is to develop an agreement that is mutually beneficial, recognizes the needs of the parties involved, and motivates them to perform. Because most negotiation is based on cost-of-service pricing, it requires that carriers have fairly precise measures of their costs. Only when costs are known can carriers and shippers work together in an effort to reduce that carrier's cost base.

Categories of Rates

There are two types of charges assessed by carriers: *line-haul rates*, which are charged for the movement of goods between two points that are not in the same local pickup and delivery area, and *accessorial charges*, which cover all other payments made to carriers for transporting, handling, or servicing a shipment. Line-haul rates can be grouped into four types: (1) class rates, (2) exception rates, (3) commodity rates, and (4) miscellaneous rates.[84]

Class rates reduce the number of transportation rates required by grouping products into classes for pricing purposes. A product's specific classification is referred to as its class rating. A basic rate would be Class 100, with higher numbers representing more expensive rates and lower numbers less expensive rates. The charge to move a specific product classification between two locations is referred to as the rate. By identifying the class rating of a product, the rate per hundredweight (100 pounds) between any two points can be determined.

Exception rates, or exceptions to the classification, provide the shipper with rates lower than the published class rates. Exception rates were introduced in order to provide a special rate for a specific area, origin-destination, or commodity when competition or volume justified the lower rate. When an exception rate is published, the classification that normally applies is changed. Usually all services associated with the shipment are the same as the class rate when an exception rate is used.

Commodity rates apply when a large quantity of a product is shipped between two locations on a regular basis. These rates are published on a point-to-point basis.

Since economic deregulation of most transportation in the U.S., carriers have been discounting rates. In effect, the distinctions among the various types of rates have blurred as carriers actively market their services to shippers. The increasing use of negotiated rates, permitted under deregulation, has made this form of rate much more important.

Miscellaneous rates include other rates that apply in special circumstances. For example, contract rates are those negotiated between a shipper and carrier. They are then formalized through a written contractual agreement between the two parties. These types of rates are increasing in usage because of the growth of contract carriage. Freight-all-kinds (FAK) rates have developed in recent years and apply to shipments rather than products. They tend to be based on the costs of providing the transportation service; the products being shipped can be of any type. The carrier provides the shipper with a rate per shipment based on the weight of the products being shipped. FAK rates have become very popular with companies such as wholesalers and manufacturers shipping a variety of products to retail customers on a regular basis.

---

[84] It should be noted that while various rate categories exist, in the present deregulated environment in the U.S., where many rates are negotiated between carriers and shippers, such distinctions are more historic rather than actual.

Chapter 6

Warehouse Management

Objectives of This Chapter

LO 6-1   To show why warehousing is important in supply chain management.

LO 6-2   To identify the four major types of warehousing facilities.

LO 6-3   To examine the role of warehouse management systems (WMSs) in operating the warehouse.

LO 6-4   To examine environment, energy, and sustainability issues related to warehousing.

LO 6-5   To examine issues relating to warehouse facility development.

LO 6-6   To provide an overview of the importance of performance measures and metrics and to identify warehousing KPIs.

LO 6-7   To briefly overview international warehousing issues.

Introduction

Warehousing Is the Primary Link between Supply Chain Members and Customers

Warehousing is an integral part of the supply chain. It plays a vital role in providing a desired level of customer service at the lowest possible total cost. Warehousing is the primary link between producers and customers. Over the years, warehousing has developed from a relatively minor facet of a firm's supply chain system to one of its most important functions. We can define warehousing as the facility that stores products (raw materials, parts and components, goods-in-process, finished goods, and items processed through reverse logistics) at and between point-of-origin and point-of-consumption, and provides information to management on the status, condition, and disposition of items being stored. The term *distribution center* (DC) is also used, but the terms are not identical. *Warehouse* is the more generic term.

Warehouses store all products, typically for an extended period of time. Sorting products, shipping them out to customers, and replenishing stock are daily functions of warehousing. "Distribution centers can act as warehouses too, but warehouses can't double as a distribution center."[1] DCs hold minimum levels of inventories that are predominantly high-demand items. Warehouses handle most products in four cycles (receive, store, ship, and pick); DCs handle most products in two: receive and ship. Warehouses perform a

---

[1] APS Fulfillment, "What Are the Differences between Warehouses and Distribution Centers?," *Warehouse Fulfillment*, April 25, 2017, https://www.apsfulfillment.com/warehouse-fulfillment/what-are-the-differences-between-warehouses-and-distribution-centers/.

Exhibit: Where Was America's Alcohol Warehoused during Prohibition?

Many are familiar with the era of Prohibition (1920–1933) in the United States. It was a social experiment that failed. During the time when it was unlawful to distribute or sell alcoholic beverages in the U.S., alcohol was still being warehoused and sold from two small islands (French territories) located in the North Atlantic between New York City and Greenland—Saint Pierre and Miquelon. "Thanks to quirks of geography, history and law, the French archipelago served up much of the booze that Prohibition was supposed to keep Americans from drinking."

While liquor was being produced in Canada, it could not be legally sold in the U.S. Liquor was smuggled across the 3,987-mile U.S.-Canada border. As law enforcement cracked down on these illegal shipments, liquor entrepreneurs looked for other ways to get "booze" into the U.S. That's when Saint Pierre and Miquelon entered the business. At the time, a single fishing schooner could carry as many as 5,000 cases of liquor. Because both islands had been involved in fishing, there were plenty of boats to use for liquor shipments.

On the island of Saint Pierre, several warehouses were built to hold the liquor that came from Canada and other locations. Because the islands were French territories, there was no prohibition of alcohol there, so they served as gateways into the U.S. Fishing boats served as transporters of the liquor that was being stored in the warehouses located on the waterfront. The volume of liquor sent to America was immense. "Between 1911 and 1918, just 11,000 cases of alcohol in total were imported into St. Pierre and Miquelon. In the second year of Prohibition, 1922, the islands imported 123,600 cases of whiskey; the following year that more than tripled, to 435,700 cases, more than a 40-fold increase over the entire previous decade."

The alcohol trade made the islands rich, but alas, it all ended when Prohibition was repealed in 1933. The islands had to go back to cod fishing.

Source: Marc Wortman, "This Tiny French Archipelago Became America's Alcohol Warehouse during Prohibition," *Smithsonian.com*, January 17, 2018, https://www.smithsonianmag.com/history/tiny-french-archipelago-became-americas-illegal-warehouse-during-prohibition-180967868/.

minimum of value-added activity; DCs perform a high percentage of value-adding activities, such as transportation, cross-docking, order fulfillment, labeling, packaging, and final product assembly. Warehouses focus on minimizing the operating cost to meet shipping requirements; DCs focus on maximizing the profit impact of meeting customer delivery requirements.[2]

Nature and Importance of Warehousing in the Supply Chain

Warehouses and distribution centers are used for the storage of inventories throughout the supply chain. In simple terms, three basic types of inventory exist: (1) raw materials, components, and parts (physical supply); (2) finished goods (physical distribution); and (3) products and packaging undergoing reverse logistics processing. There may also be goods-in-process inventory, although in most firms, goods-in-process constitute only a small portion of a company's total investment in inventories.

Why Hold Inventories?

Why is it necessary to hold inventories in storage? In general, the warehousing of inventories is necessary for one or more of the following reasons:

- To achieve transportation economies of scale (larger quantities are cheaper to ship on a per unit basis when volumes are larger).
- To achieve production economies of scale (inventory is needed as inputs into production).
- To take advantage of quantity purchase discounts and forward buys (purchasing larger quantities provides cost savings).
- To maintain a source of supply (purchasing consistently from the same suppliers or vendors builds loyalty).

[2] Ibid.

- To support customer service policies (high customer service levels require more inventory or faster order fulfillment).
- To meet changing market conditions (seasonality, demand fluctuations, competition, and supply chain disruptions are difficult to forecast, so inventory is needed to maintain service levels to customers).
- To overcome the time and space differentials between producers and consumers (it takes time for products to move from one location to another, longer as the distances increase).
- To accomplish least total cost logistics commensurate with a desired level of customer service (warehousing costs have to be considered in light of other supply chain costs and competitive conditions).
- To support the just-in-time programs of suppliers, vendors, and/or customers (having products immediately available requires that products be on hand).

How Are Warehouses Used?

Warehouses can be used to support manufacturing, to mix products from multiple production facilities for shipment to a single customer, to break-bulk or subdivide a large shipment of products into many smaller shipments to satisfy the needs of many customers, to combine or consolidate smaller shipments of products into a higher-volume shipment, and to perform various value-added services such as product assembly, labeling, and product returns processing.

In supporting manufacturing operations, warehouses often function as inbound consolidation points for the receipt of materials shipments from suppliers. Firms order raw materials, parts, components, or supplies from various suppliers, who ship large (TL—truckload or CL—car/container load) quantities to a warehouse located in close proximity to the plant. Items are then transferred from the warehouse to the manufacturing plant(s). For example, Coca-Cola Parts (CCP) distributes installation and service parts in North America for Coca-Cola. "CCP manages the supply chain for over 30,000 vending, cooler, and fountain machine parts that it delivers to the field service providers who install and repair Coca-Cola equipment. It fills just under 900,000 orders annually—about 2.5 million lines—from a central distribution center in Dallas, Texas, that serves the United States and Canada."[3]

From a physical distribution or outbound perspective, warehouses can be used for product mixing, outbound consolidation, and/or break-bulk. Product mixing often involves multiple plant locations that ship products to a centralized warehouse. Each plant manufactures only a portion of the total product offering. Shipments are usually made in large quantities to the central warehouse, where customer orders for multiple products are combined or mixed for shipment.

When a warehouse is used for outbound consolidation, TL or CL shipments are made to a centralized location from a number of manufacturing plants. The warehouse then consolidates or combines products from the various plant locations into a single shipment to the customer.

Break-bulk warehouses are facilities that receive large shipments of product from a manufacturing plant. Several customer orders are combined into a single shipment from the plant to the break-bulk warehouse. When the warehouse receives the shipment, it is subdivided or broken down into smaller LTL (less than truckload) shipments, which are sent to customers in the geographical area served by the warehouse.

Transportation economies are possible for both the physical supply system and the physical distribution system. In the case of physical supply, small orders from a number of suppliers may be shipped to a consolidation warehouse near the source of supply; in this way the producer can achieve a truckload or carload shipment to the plant, which is

---

[3] Scott G. Hardesty, Donnie F. Williams Jr., Joseph Tillman, and Tina Ceaser, "On the Same Page," *CSCMP's Supply Chain Quarterly*, Vol. 11, No. 4 (Quarter 4, 2017), p. 40.

normally a considerable distance from the warehouse. The warehouse is located near the sources of supply so that the LTL rates apply only to a short haul, and the volume rate is used for the long haul from the warehouse to the plant.

Warehouses are used to achieve similar transportation savings in the physical distribution system. In the packaged goods industry, manufacturers often have multiple plant locations, with each plant manufacturing only a portion of the company's product line.[4]

Focused Factories

Usually, firms utilizing the focused factory concept maintain a number of warehouse locations from which mixed shipments of the entire product line can be made to customers. Shipments from plants to these field warehouses are frequently made by rail in full carload quantities or in full containers by truck. Orders from customers, composed of various items in the product line, are then reshipped by truck at truckload or LTL rates depending on the size of the customer order. The use of field warehouses results in lower transportation costs than direct shipments to customers. Savings are often significantly larger than the increased costs resulting from warehousing and the associated increase in inventory carrying costs.

Short production runs minimize the amount of inventory held throughout the supply chain by producing quantities near to current demand. But there are increased costs of setups and line changes associated with short production runs. Also, if a plant is operating near or at capacity, frequent line changes may leave the manufacturer unable to meet product demand. If so, the cost of lost sales (the lost contribution to profit on sales that cannot be made) could be substantial.

On the other hand, the production of large quantities of product for each line change results in a lower per-unit cost on a full-cost basis, as well as more units for a given plant capacity. However, long production runs lead to larger inventories and increased warehouse requirements. Consequently, production cost savings must be balanced with increased supply chain costs in order to achieve least total cost.

Warehousing is also necessary if a company is to take advantage of quantity purchase discounts on raw materials or other products. Not only is the per-unit price lower as a result of the discount, but if the company pays the freight, transportation costs will be less on a volume purchase because of transportation economies. Similar discounts and savings can accrue to manufacturers, retailers, or wholesalers. Once again, however, those savings must be weighed against the added costs that will be incurred as a result of larger inventories.

Holding inventories in warehouses may be necessary in order to maintain a source of supply. For example, the timing and quantity of purchases are important in retaining suppliers, especially during periods of shortages. It also may be necessary to hold an inventory of items that may be in short supply as the result of damage in transit, vendor stock-outs, or a labor strike against one of the company's suppliers.

Customer service policies, such as a 24-hour delivery standard, may require a number of field warehouses in order to minimize total costs while achieving the stated customer service standard. Changing market conditions may also make it necessary to warehouse products in the field, primarily because companies are unable to accurately predict consumer demand and the timing of retailer and wholesaler orders. By keeping some excess inventory in field warehouse locations, companies can respond more quickly to meet

---

[4] Such plants are often referred to as "focused factories." For a description of focused factories, see the classic article by Wickham Skinner, "The Focused Factory," *Harvard Business Review*, Vol. 52, No. 3 (May–June 1974), pp. 113–21. For a discussion of focused factories in the health care industry, see Robert A. Berenson, Suzanne F. Delbanco, Roslyn Murray, and Divvy K. Upadhyay, "Focused Factories—Specialty Service Expertise," *Urban Institute Research Report*, April 2016, https://www .urban.org/sites/default/files/02_focused_factories.pdf. An application of focused factories in German manufacturing can be found in Hendrik Brumme, Daniel Simonovich, Wickham Skinner, and Luk N. Van Wassenhove, "The Strategy-Focused Factory in Turbulent Times," *Production and Operations Management*, Vol. 24, No. 10 (October 2015), pp. 1513–23.

unexpected demand. In addition, excess inventory allows manufacturers to fill customer orders when shipments to restock the field warehouses arrive late.

The majority of firms utilize storage facilities in order to accomplish least total cost logistics at some prescribed level of customer service. The use of warehousing enables supply chain executives to select the transport modes and inventory levels that, when combined with communication and order processing systems and production alternatives, minimize total costs while providing a desired level of customer service.

Factors that influence storage policies include the type of industry; the firm's philosophy; capital availability; product characteristics, such as size, perishability, product lines, substitutability, and obsolescence rate; economic conditions; degree of competition; seasonality of demand; use of just-in-time (JIT) programs; technology; e-commerce;[5] and the production process being used.

Factors that will influence warehousing in the future include growth in e-commerce sales. Warehouse investments in WMSs and personnel will increase, mobility solutions will become necessary in warehouse operations, and the IoT and the need for data storage will become givens as society is becoming more interconnected.[6] Additionally, product life cycles will continue to shorten, requiring warehousing to be faster and more efficient. Customers will demand more "perfect orders." There will have to be a continuous flow of information between warehousing and vendors, suppliers, and customers; electronic tracking and control of products using RFID or other technologies will become commonplace; and there will be an increasing use of automation.

Types of Warehouses (Public, Private, Contract, Cross-Docking)

Direct Store Delivery

In general, firms have several warehousing alternatives. Some companies may market products directly to customers (called *direct store delivery*) and thereby eliminate warehousing in the field. Internet and mail-order catalog companies are examples of industries that primarily utilize warehousing only at a point-of-origin, such as at a sales headquarters or manufacturing plant. Organizations such as Amazon.com and eBay.com may or may not warehouse the products they sell. They may be the intermediary between another party and their customer, providing only the location where transactions can occur. In an omni-channel environment, however, even companies such as Amazon are investing in brick-and-mortar facilities in order to provide the high levels of service to their Amazon Prime customers and others. The majority of firms will store products at some intermediate point between plant(s) and customers, in facilities owned or leased by them.

When a firm decides to store products in the field, it typically faces multiple options: rent space short term, called *public warehousing*; lease space long term, called *contract warehousing*; or own space, called *private warehousing*. Firms must examine important customer service and financial considerations to choose between public, contract, and/or private warehousing.

Types of Public Warehouses

Public warehouses are facilities that are rented by a firm for a limited time, usually for 30-day periods. There are many types of public warehouses, although they can generally be classified into six major types: (1) general merchandise warehouses for manufactured goods, (2) refrigerated or cold storage warehouses, (3) bonded warehouses, (4) household

[5] See "How E-Commerce Is Changing Facility Planning and Design," *SupplyChainBrain,* March 29, 2017, http://www.supplychainbrain.com/featured-content/single-article/article/how-e-commerce-is-changing-facility-planning-and-design/; and Gary Wollenhaupt, "E-Commerce Reshaping Distribution Center Real Estate Strategies," *Supply & Demand Chain Executive,* Vol. 18, Issue 3 (June 2017), pp. 30–31.
[6] Christ Anton, "Trends in Warehouse Management, 2017 and Beyond," *Warehouse Management Blog,* December 22, 2016, http://blog.snapfulfil.com/trends-in-warehouse-management-2017-and-beyond.

goods and furniture warehouses, (5) special commodity warehouses, and (6) bulk storage warehouses. Each type provides users with a broad range of specialized services.

The *general merchandise warehouse* is probably the most common form. It is designed to be used by manufacturers, distributors, and customers for storing practically any kind of product. *Cold storage warehouses (refrigerated or frozen)* provide a temperature-controlled storage environment. Some general merchandise or special commodity warehouses are known as *bonded warehouses*. These warehouses undertake surety bonds from the government and place their premises under the custody of a government agent. Goods such as imported tobacco and alcoholic beverages are stored in this type of warehouse, although the government retains control of the goods until they are distributed to the marketplace. At that time, the importer must pay customs duties. The advantage of the bonded warehouse is that import duties and excise taxes need not be paid until the merchandise is sold.

Household goods warehouses are used for storage of personal property rather than merchandise. The property is typically stored for a period of time as a temporary layover option. *Special commodity warehouses* are used for raw materials and agricultural products such as grains, wool, and cotton. Ordinarily each of these warehouses handles one kind of product and offers special services particular to that product. *Bulk storage warehouses* provide tank storage of liquids and open or sheltered storage of dry products such as coal, sand, and chemicals.

The benefits that may be realized if a firm uses public warehousing rather than other forms of storage such as private warehousing include (1) conservation of capital; (2) the ability to increase warehouse space to cover peak requirements; (3) reduced risk; (4) economies of scale; (5) flexibility; (6) tax advantages; and (7) specific knowledge of costs.

Conservation of Capital

Public warehouses require *no capital investment* on the part of the user. The user avoids the investment in buildings, land, and materials-handling equipment, as well as the costs associated with starting up the operation and hiring and training personnel. However, the variable costs associated with public warehousing are typically higher than for other forms of warehousing.

Meet Peak Requirements

If an organization's operations are subject to seasonality, the public warehouse option allows the user to rent as much storage space as needed to *meet peak requirements*. A private warehouse, on the other hand, has a constraint on the maximum amount of product that can be stored and is likely to be underutilized during a portion of each year. Because many organizations experience variations in inventory levels due to business cycles or seasonality in demand or production, sales promotions, or other factors, public warehousing offers the advantage of allowing storage costs to vary directly with volume. With public warehousing, the user can switch to another facility in a short period of time, usually within 30 days. Thus, the public warehousing options poses less risk to the organization.

Economies of Scale

Public warehouses are able to achieve *economies of scale* that may not be possible for a small firm. Public warehouses handle the storage requirements of a number of clients at the same time, and that volume allows the employment of a full-time warehousing staff. In addition, building costs are nonlinear, and a firm pays a premium to build a small facility. Additional economies of scale can be provided by using more expensive, but more efficient, materials-handling equipment or automation (e.g., conveyors, robots), and by providing administrative and other expertise.

Public warehouses are often able to offer a number of specialized services more economically than other types of warehousing. These specialized services include the following:

- Broken-case handling, which is breaking down manufacturers' case quantities to enable orders for less-than-full-case quantities to be filled.
- Packaging of manufacturers' products for shipping.

- Consolidation of damaged product and product being recalled by the manufacturer for shipment to the manufacturer in carload or truckload quantities. In addition to the documentation and prepacking that may be necessary, the public warehouse frequently performs the rework of damaged products.
- Equipment maintenance and service.
- Stock spotting of product for manufacturers with limited or highly seasonal product lines. Stock spotting involves shipping a consolidated carload of inventory to a public warehouse just prior to a period of maximum seasonal sales.
- A break-bulk service whereby the manufacturer combines the orders of different customers located in a market and ships them at the carload or truckload rate to the public warehouse where the individual orders are separated and local delivery is provided.

Economies of scale result from the consolidation of small shipments with other companies using the same public warehouse. The public warehouse consolidates orders of specific customers from the products of a number of different manufacturers on a single shipment. This results in lower shipping costs, as well as reduced congestion at the customer's receiving dock. Also, customers who pick up their orders at the public warehouse are able to obtain the products of several manufacturers with one stop, if the manufacturers all use the same facility.

Flexibility   Another major advantage offered by public warehouses is *flexibility*. Owning or holding a long-term lease on a warehouse can become a burden if business conditions require changes in locations. Public warehouses require only a short-term contract, and thus short-term commitments. Short-term contracts available from public warehouses make it easy for firms to change field warehouse locations due to changes in the marketplace (e.g., population shifts, new product failures), the relative cost of various transport modes, volume of a product sold, or the company's financial position.

In addition, a firm that uses public warehouses does not have to hire or lay off employees as the business volume changes. A public warehouse provides the personnel required for extra services when they are necessary, without having to hire them on a full-time basis.

Public warehousing makes it possible for the manufacturer to experiment with a warehouse location to determine its contribution to the firm's supply chain, and to discontinue the operation with relative ease if cost savings or performance objectives are not realized.

Taxes   In most states a firm is at a definite advantage if it does not own property in the state because such ownership means that the firm is doing business in the state and is thus subject to various state *taxes*. These taxes can be substantial. Consequently, if the company does not currently own property in a state, it may be advantageous to use a public warehouse. In addition, certain states do not charge property taxes on inventories in public warehouses; this tax shelter applies to both regular warehouse inventories and storage-in-transit inventories. A free-port provision enacted in some states allows inventory to be held for up to one year, tax-free. Finally, the manufacturer pays no real estate tax. Of course, the public warehouse pays real estate tax and includes this cost in its warehouse rates, but the cost is smaller on a per-unit throughput basis because of the significantly larger volume of business possible.

Storage and Handling Costs   When a manufacturer uses a public warehouse, it *knows its exact storage and handling costs* because it receives a bill each month. The manufacturer can also forecast costs for different levels of activity because the costs are known in advance. Firms that operate their own facilities often find it very difficult to determine the fixed and variable costs based on variability in volumes. Activity-based costing may be used when operating private warehousing so that specific costs are known.

On the negative side, some public warehouse facilities find it difficult to effectively interface with some clients. The lack of standardization in contractual agreements makes communication regarding contractual obligations difficult. Many of these potential problems have been overcome with the advent of e-commerce, e-mail, electronic data interchange (EDI), IoT, and intranets.

Availability of Specialized Services

Specialized services may not always be available in a specific location. Many public warehouse facilities only provide local service and are of limited use to a firm that distributes regionally or nationally. Consequently, a manufacturer that wants to use public warehouses for national distribution may find it necessary to deal with several different operators and monitor several contractual agreements. Also, some public warehouses may not offer certain services unless a sufficient number of their clients require it. Sometimes, a public warehouse and a client(s) will cooperate to develop and financially support a new service(s).

Space Availability

Finally, *public warehousing space may not be available* when and where a firm wants it. Shortages of space do occur periodically in selected markets, and this can adversely affect the supply chain and marketing strategies of a firm. Unless an organization has developed a good relationship with a public warehouse in an area where a shortage exists, space may not be available, or else the price of that space may be very high.[7]

Private Warehousing

One of the most important warehousing decisions is whether public or private facilities should be used. In order to make the proper decision that includes cost and service perspectives, the supply chain executive must understand the advantages and disadvantages, as well as the financial implications, of each alternative. The appendix to this chapter illustrates the type of financial analysis that must be performed.

Many companies typically find it advantageous to use multiple forms of warehousing, such as private warehousing and/or contract warehousing. Private warehouses can be used to handle basic inventory levels required for least-cost distribution in markets where the volume justifies ownership. Public warehouses, a form of outsourcing, can be used in those areas where volume is not sufficient to justify ownership and/or to store peak requirements. Public warehouses typically charge on the basis of case or hundredweight stored or handled. Consequently, when the volume of activity is sufficiently large, public warehousing charges exceed the cost of a private facility, making ownership more attractive.

In private warehousing, the company that owns the goods typically exercises a *greater degree of control* over their storage, handling, and management. The firm has direct control of, and responsibility for, the product until the customer takes possession or delivery. This greater degree of control allows the firm to integrate the warehousing function more easily into the company's supply chain.

Flexibility as an Advantage

With this warehouse control comes a greater degree of *flexibility*—not flexibility to reduce or increase storage space quickly, but flexibility to design and operate the warehouse to fit the specific needs of customers and the characteristics of the firm's products. Organizations with highly specialized products requiring special handling and/or storage may not find other forms of warehousing feasible.

Cost

Private warehousing can be *less costly* over the long term. Operating costs can be 15 to 25 percent lower if the company achieves sufficient throughput or utilization (i.e., high inventory turnover). The generally accepted industry norm for the utilization rate of a private warehouse is 75 to 80 percent. If an organization cannot achieve at least 75 percent utilization, it would generally be more appropriate to use some other type of warehousing.

Human Resources

By employing private warehousing, an organization can make greater use of its present *human resources.* It can utilize the expertise of its technical specialists. In addition, the individuals working in the warehouse are company employees. Generally, there is greater

---

[7] For a discussion of various factors related to the use of pubic warehousing, including pros and cons, see Eric Dontigney, "Public Warehouse Advantages," *Bizfluent*, September 26, 2017, https://bizfluent.com/info-8539493-public-warehouse-advantages.html; and "The Disadvantages of Public Warehousing," *Warehousing Solutions*, January 12, 2017, https://www.apsfulfillment.com/warehousing-solutions/the-disadvantages-of-public-warehousing/.

care in handling and storage when the firm's own workforce operates the warehouse. On the other hand, some public warehouses allow their customers to use their own employees in the handling and storage of their products.[8]

Tax Benefits

An organization can also realize *tax benefits* when it owns its warehouses. Depreciation allowances on buildings and equipment can substantially reduce the cost of a structure or apparatus over its life.

There may also be certain *intangible benefits* associated with warehouse ownership. When a firm distributes its products through a private warehouse, it can give the customer a sense of permanence and continuity of business operations. The customer sees the company as a stable, dependable, and lasting supplier of products. This can provide an organization with potential marketing advantages.

Flexibility as a Disadvantage

A major drawback of private warehousing is the same as one of its main advantages: *flexibility*. A private warehouse may be too costly because of its fixed size and costs. Irrespective of the level of demand the firm experiences, the size of the private warehouse is restricted in the short term. A private facility cannot expand and contract to meet short-term increases or decreases in demand that might occur. When demand is low, the firm must still assume the fixed cost expenses, as well as the lower productivity associated with unused warehouse space. (This disadvantage can be minimized, however, if the firm is able to rent out part of its space; in essence, acting like a public warehouse.)

If a firm uses only private warehouses, it also loses flexibility in its strategic location options. Changes in market size, location, and preferences can be rapid and unpredictable. If an organization cannot adapt to these changes in its warehouse structure, it may lose a valuable business opportunity. Customer service and sales could also fall if a private warehouse cannot adapt to changes in the firm's product mix.

Investment

Because of the prohibitive costs involved, many organizations are simply unable to generate enough capital to build or buy their own warehouse. A private warehouse is a long-term, often risky *investment* that may be difficult to sell because of its customized design. Start-up is often a costly and time-consuming process due to the hiring and training of employees, as well as the purchase of materials-handling equipment, racks and shelves, and other items. And depending on the nature of the organization, return on investment may be greater if funds are channeled into other profit-generating opportunities.[9]

Cross-Docking

In addition to public and private warehousing, other options also exist, including *cross-docking*. Cross-docking is defined as a process that moves products quickly through a facility in order to minimize storage time.[10] Products are unloaded from transportation carriers and enter the facility for a very short time, usually less than 24 hours. Sortation and consolidation of products often occur during the time that items are being temporarily stored in the facility. The products are then reloaded onto transportation equipment for outbound distribution to customers. Because storage costs are a key element in overall warehousing costs, cross-docking reduces the need for warehouse space and limits storage costs. Additionally, cross-dock facilities are typically less costly to build and maintain than traditional warehouses. Technically, the product never enters the warehouse.

[8] For a discussion of some of the human resource issues in warehousing, see "Good to Great: How Yankee Candle Transformed Its Labor Management," *WERCSheet*, Vol. 38, No. 6 (July/August 2016), pp. 5–6; "Shift Your Thinking about Millennials," *WERCSheet*, Vol. 39, No. 6 (July/August 2016), p. 3; and "The Skilled Labor Drought," *WERCSheet*, Vol. 38, No. 2 (November/December 2015), pp. 4–5.
[9] For a discussion of the public versus private warehousing decision, see "Warehousing Ownership Considerations—Private versus Public/Contract," *White Paper*, REM Associates, http://www.remassoc.com/portals/0/remwpwoc.pdf.
[10] "How Is Cross Docking Beneficial?," *Darcy Logistics Blog* (May 4, 2016), http://www.darcylogistics.com/how-is-cross-docking-beneficial/.

FIGURE 6.1
How Cross-Docking Works

Source: Chris Doyle, "Cross Docking: Is It Right for Me?," *Warehousing Insights Blog*, Cisco-Eagle, December 5, 2007, http://www.cisco-eagle .com/blog/2007/12/05/brief -1-cross-docking-is-it-right -for-me/.

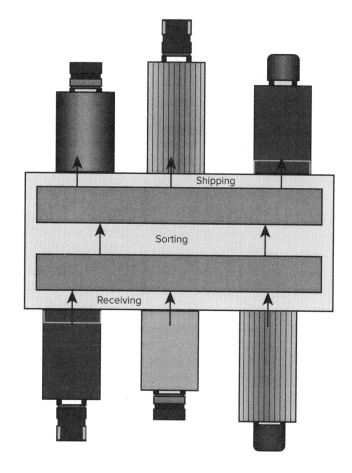

When Should Cross-Docking Be Considered?

Cross-docking is a good strategy when one or more of the following conditions exist:

- When products are prepicked to a customer order for a customer located nearby.
- Smaller LTL shipments.
- Products arriving from multiple plants being combined into single orders.
- Products being consolidated into larger TL quantities for delivery to large customers.[11]

Cross-docking has become an important option for many retailers, who can order in truckload (TL) quantities, then remix and ship items to individual store locations. For example, Laney & Duke, Hanes's third-party warehousing company in Jacksonville, Florida, tickets merchandise, places it on hangers, and boxes it up for individual Walmart stores to replace items sold. The trailer leaves Jacksonville for the Walmart distribution center where product is cross-docked to trucks for delivery to individual stores. At store locations, the boxes are opened and garments are ready to hang on display racks.

Cross-docking bypasses the storage activity by transferring items directly from the inbound receiving dock to the outbound or shipping dock (see Figure 6.1). A pure cross-docking operation would avoid put-away, storage, and order picking. Information transfer would become paramount due to the close coordination of shipments required.

[11] "2011 Cross-Docking Trends Report," eBook, Saddle Creek Corporation (2011); and "5 Absolutely Effective Ways to Maximize Cross-Docking Performance," *Abivin Blog* (June 8, 2017), https://www.abivin.com/single -post/5-Absolutely-Effective-Ways-to-Maximize-Cross-docking-Performance.

This activity has become very commonplace in warehousing because of its impact on costs and customer service. For example, more than 50 percent of companies utilize cross-docking to some extent.[12] Eliminating the transfer or put-away of products reduces costs and the time goods remain at the warehouse, thus improving customer service levels. Additional benefits can include reduced transportation costs, less warehouse space used, and more shipments to customers being consolidated.

Types of Cross-Docking Facilities

Three types of cross-docking facilities exist based on their level of complexity and the number of "touches" that products receive during the cross-dock process:

- *"Pure" cross-docking*—Receiving and shipping product immediately with a single touch as product is received and loaded outbound without being placed on the warehouse dock.
- *"Two-touch" approach*—Products are received and staged on the dock, then loaded outbound without being put into storage.
- *"Multiple-touch"*—Product is received and staged on the dock then reconfigured for shipment and loaded outbound directly from the warehouse dock.[13]

Contract Warehousing Defined

Contract warehousing is a partnership arrangement between the user and provider of the warehousing service. It has been defined as follows:

A contract warehouse handles the shipping, receiving and storage of goods on a contract basis. This type of warehouse usually requires a client to commit to services for a particular period of time. The length of time varies, often stated in years rather than months. The fee structure also varies based on transactions; it may be a fixed cost, cost-plus or a combination of both.[14]

The advantages of contract warehousing are several. First, there is no capital investment required as there would be in private warehousing. Firms do not have to have sufficient capital to build the warehouse, but they do enter into long-term contracts for storage space. Costs are lower than for public warehousing because storage space is contracted for a year or longer and the firm has access to the facility for a specified period of time. The contract protects the firm using the facility by fixing the costs for the contract period. The warehouse benefits because it has a client in its facility for an extended period of time, unlike public warehousing, which has tenants month-by-month. Additionally, the contract warehouse may provide additional services to its clients because they will be storing products for longer periods. The growth of contract warehousing has exceeded that of public warehousing in general, and will likely continue to be the dominant form of nonowned warehousing in the foreseeable future.[15]

Some examples of contract warehousing are the following:

- "A mid-sized pet food company had operated its own distribution center outside Boston, but decided to outsource DC operations to improve performance on inventory accuracy, code date tracking, food-grade compliant storage and other critical warehouse measures. 3PL Kane Is Able was chosen to operate the DC in Scranton, PA."[16]

---

[12] Ibid.

[13] "2011 Cross-Docking Trends Report."

[14] "What Is a Contract Warehouse and How Is It Beneficial?," *Commercial Warehousing Post*, December 22, 2014, https://www.commercialwarehousing.com/news/what-is-a-contract-warehouse -how-is-it-beneficial/.

[15] See "What Is Contract Warehousing," *Bonded Service Warehouse*, 2018, http://www.bondedservice .com/contract-warehousing/.

[16] "Pet Food Company Collaborates with KANE to Drive Distribution Efficiency," *SupplyChainBrain Case Study*, September 4, 2012, http://www.supplychainbrain.com/nc/think-tank/case-study-showcase /single-article/article/pet-food-company-collaborates-with-kane-to-drive-distribution-efficiency/.

- Sanofi, a global life science company, is using a Kuehne + Nagel temperature-controlled warehouse facility to store pharmaceuticals produced at its plant in Geel, Belgium.[17]

However, irrespective of the type of warehouse utilized, the operations of the warehouse must be managed. In today's sophisticated and complicated supply chains, various technologies are utilized to manage warehouse operations, especially warehouse management systems (WMSs).

Warehousing Management Strategies

Supply chain management principles are being applied to warehousing to enable firms to better respond to changing market conditions. There are many challenges facing the warehousing industry, including (1) more warehouse locations to meet the need for shorter lead times; (2) customers demanding more value-added services, including speed of the order cycle; (3) the need to effectively manage labor and control labor costs; (4) the desire to serve customers directly; and (5) the ability to keep up with the technology of e-commerce and omnichannel retailing.[18] These challenges have resulted in firms responding with the most appropriate warehousing management strategies, one of the most important being the adoption and implementation of a warehouse management system (WMS).

Warehouse Management Systems (WMSs)

A warehouse management system, or WMS, is defined as follows:

The systems used in effectively managing warehouse business processes and direct warehouse activities, including receiving, putaway, picking, shipping, and inventory cycle counts. Also includes support of radio-frequency communications, allowing real-time data transfer between the system and warehouse personnel. They also maximize space and minimize material handling by automating putaway processes.[19]

The benefits of implementing a WMS can be significant. The Topps Company is one of the largest sports card manufacturers in the industry. Perhaps best known for its famous 1952 Topps baseball set, which contained Mickey Mantle's rookie card, the firm needed a warehouse management system to meet both its current and future needs. Topps was using a paper-based system to ship 500 orders per day. The WMS allowed the firm to ship between 1,200 and 1,800 orders per day using the same number of personnel. The new WMS allowed Topps to integrate its e-commerce business with its Oracle ERP system.[20]

Selection of a WMS by a firm is vital if the organization operates in a just-in-time (JIT) environment.

Using Warehousing to Support JIT Operations

With many firms operating under just-in-time (JIT) conditions, it is important to maintain sufficient levels of inventory through rapid deployment to minimize or eliminate product or component stock-outs. This would be true for manufacturers that need components, parts, and raw materials to produce products, or retailers trying to have products available on

[17] "Sanofi Awards Logistics Contract to Kuehne + Nagel," *Kuehne + Nagel Media Release*, September 19, 2017, https://newsroom.kuehne-nagel.com/sanofi-awards-logistics-contract-to-kuehne--nagel/.
[18] See Stan Jaworski, "Top 4 Challenges of Warehousing Leaders in 2017," *DecisionPoint Systems*, August 23, 2017, http://blog.decisionpt.com/top-4-challenges-of-warehousing-leaders-in-2017; and "Tackling the Top 5 Challenges in Your Warehouse for 2017," *Zenventory*, February 2, 2017, https://www.zenventory.com/tackling-top-5-challenges-warehouse-2017/.
[19] Council of Supply Chain Management Professionals, "SCM Definitions (2013)," http://www.cscmp.org.
[20] "The Topps Company Scores Big with Snapfulfil's Flexible, Adaptable Cloud WMS," *Snapfulfil Case Study*, undated, https://www.snapfulfil.com/us/case-studies/The-Topps-Company/.

Technology: Five Benefits of a Warehouse Management System

©Prasit photo/Getty Images

Warehouse management systems (WMSs) have replaced manual methods for managing inventory and operations of the warehouse. There are several benefits to utilizing a WMS instead of traditional manual processes, including the following:

A WAREHOUSE MANAGEMENT SYSTEM SAVES SPACE

A WMS "enables accurate stocking, slotting and pulling of orders, giving companies the opportunity to gain higher-level insights into how much of each item is truly needed. Therefore, they can reduce overstock and minimize understock simultaneously to save space."

IT INCREASES CUSTOMER SATISFACTION AND SERVICE

A WMS improves customer service levels by reducing errors in the warehouse due to mispicks and incorrect shipments. Also, product damage rates are typically reduced.

THE WMS REDUCES WEAR ON EQUIPMENT

"A WMS can improve efficiency, reducing redundancies in picking routes and decreasing the per-equipment cost of shipping and managing inventory."

IT BOOSTS EFFICIENCY AND PRODUCTIVITY OF WORKERS

Because a WMS will specifically locate products in the warehouse and the most optimal routes to select them, employees "can pick more orders in less time, increasing overall profit margins and efficiency in order fulfillment."

THE SYSTEM REDUCES SECURITY VULNERABILITIES

WMSs keep very detailed and accurate records of inventory, and because the system requires users to have specific logins, it minimizes the likelihood of security breaches.

Source: Adapted from "5 Benefits of a Warehouse Management System," *Veridian Solutions Blog*, April 30, 2017, http://veridiansol .com/warehouse-management-system/.

their shelves to satisfy consumers wanting to buy sale items advertised in their local newspaper advertising insert. Trying to minimize inventory levels under a JIT program, while at the same time having sufficient inventories to avoid stock-outs, requires a coordinated supply chain.

Merchandise Warehouse Company (MWC) stores products for the food, grocery, pharmaceutical, and general commodity industries. The firm operates a 400,000-square-foot multi-temperature warehouse in Indianapolis, Indiana. With many of its customers operating JIT systems, MWC had to have a WMS that allowed it to process inventory accurately and quickly. The firm implemented the Datex WMS, resulting in fewer communications issues, elimination of redundancy in paperwork, and flexibility needed to meet customer requirements. Inventory availability improved from 98.6% to 99.9%.[21]

Generally, firms utilizing JIT systems must have all facets of their supply chain operating smoothly and efficiently. As part of the supply chain, warehouses need to be as efficient and effective as possible in order to optimize customer service and minimize costs. If individual firms cannot accomplish these dual objectives, outsourcing may be an option that needs to be explored.

[21] "Merchandise Warehouse Company Case Study," *Datex Corporation Case Study*, undated, https:// www.datexcorp.com/merchandise-warehouse-company-case-study/.

Outsourcing: Third Parties, Partnerships, and Strategic Alliances

There are many reasons to outsource warehousing to third parties, or 3PLs. Perhaps the major reason is financial. If a firm utilizes private warehousing, it will have a large amount of fixed assets in its financial balance sheet. This will impact the firm's asset turnover and return on assets ratios. The use of public warehousing can remove these assets from the balance sheet, but firms prefer to have more long-term control over their assets. As a result, the company can enter into contracts with various 3PLs, who carry the assets on their balance sheets, but who provide the storage service to their clients. Thus, the warehousing costs show up as variable expenses on a firm's income statement.

Also, 3PLs may perform the warehousing function better than the firm. When warehousing expertise is not a core competency of the firm, outsourcing to a 3PL should be considered. Sometimes, the cost structure of the 3PL is lower than that of the firm because of lower labor costs, higher productivity, economies of scale, and other reasons.

Outsourcing is not for everyone, however! For example, Urban Outfitters switched from utilizing a 3PL to building and operating its own DC. The $1+ billion company, which sells apparel, accessories, and home furnishings to customers in North America and Europe, built a 175,000-square-foot DC in Reno, Nevada, to service its customers in the Western U.S. Why would the company change from "outsourcing" to "doing it themselves"? Basically, the company "outgrew the 3PL relationship . . . the company expanded its stores and brands and needed to accelerate its supply chain. That was best done in-house."[22]

The company designed a facility that handled both cross-docked and traditionally stored products. The facility was specifically constructed to meet the needs of Urban Outfitters and its customers. It utilizes a high-speed conveyor and sortation system, a "pick-to-light" system, and a state-of-the-art WMS to process 100,000 items per day. Facility operating costs per unit have been reduced, and inventory turnover rates have increased.

Environment, Energy, and Sustainability

While environmental pollution, energy costs, and sustainability issues have always been considerations in implementing and maintaining a supply chain, they have become more important as energy prices have increased, concerns over pollution and global warming have arisen, and economic conditions become more uncertain. As a result, many organizations place more emphasis on environmental, energy, and sustainability aspects of warehousing.

How do we define "sustainability"? Deloitte Consulting defines it this way: "must reduce waste and promote recycling; minimize consumption of resources for products and services; emphasize the use of natural and organic materials; and reduce the net global footprint (i.e., zero net energy and zero net emissions buildings)."[23] A more general statement of sustainability from a warehouse or DC perspective would be a facility that would do no harm to the planet or to future generations.[24] Thus, companies must somehow blend sustainability issues with traditional financial issues such as return on investment (ROI), return on assets (ROA), and others.

Of course, one of the "tried and true" warehousing methods that can have a positive impact on the environment, energy usage, and sustainability is to just be as efficient and effective as possible. Utilizing as much of the cube space in a facility as possible results in less energy being consumed and fewer emissions (per unit or SKU). Locating facilities

---

[22] Bob Trebilcock, "Good Distribution Is Always in Fashion," *Modern Materials Handling*, Vol. 8, No. 1 (April 2008), p. 31; and "Urban Outfitters Reports Q3 Results," November 20, 2017, http://www.urbn .com/posts/FY18-Q3-Results.
[23] Peter Bradley, "Beyond Green," *DC Velocity*, Vol. 5, No. 8 (August 2007), p. 33.
[24] Ibid.

Exhibit: Nike's Sustainable Distribution Center

©Dmitri Ma/Shutterstock

Nike is a global company that ships more than 1 billion units of footwear, apparel, and equipment each year. Nike's European Logistics Campus, located in Belgium, was designed with sustainability in mind. The DC is powered by a combination of wind, solar, geothermal, hydroelectric, and biomass sources.

More than 95 percent of waste generated by the DC is recycled. Almost all inbound container shipments travel by water rather than road, which minimizes emissions and fuel utilization. The building is lighted by a combination of automated LED lighting and natural light from many windows.

"The facility was carefully designed to expand while supporting biodiversity. For example, sheep will help naturally maintain the landscaping, and on-site beehives will contribute to biodiversity through the pollination of flowers around the facility and in the local area."

Source: "The Supply Chain of the Future—Nike Unveils Advanced, Sustainable Distribution Center," *MHI Blog*, May 31, 2016, http://s354933259.onlinehome.us/mhi-blog/the-supply-chain-of-the-future-nike-unveils-advanced-sustainable-distribution-center/.

where transportation is optimized results in less fuel being consumed and fewer pollutants being emitted into the atmosphere. In essence, being as lean and efficient as possible is an excellent strategy to follow.[25]

There are, however, specific things that storage facilities can do that have direct impact on the environment, energy, and sustainability. In a study of warehouse initiatives on sustainability, a number of "green" strategies were identified. The most significant strategies included reducing the amount of waste sent to landfills, using recyclable materials and packaging, retrofitting buildings for energy efficiency, reducing the amount of packaging material used, using recyclable containers or pallets, and employing newer energy-efficient equipment.[26]

For example, specialty outdoor retailer REI opened a 393,000-square-foot distribution center in Arizona that utilizes solar panels on the rooftop and "a cooling system that maintains a relatively constant temperature from floor to ceiling while saving a million gallons of evaporated water per year, despite outside temperatures that can reach above 115 degrees Fahrenheit."[27]

Adidas, the multinational apparel company, has implemented a number of strategies for being "eco-friendly." As a consumer, "you may not have given much thought to the carbon footprint of the T-shirt or Armani suit you're wearing, but apparel makers are paying a great deal of attention to their garments' environmental impact these days."[28] Adidas "has established a far-reaching cradle-to-grave environmental program for its products. Its multifaceted initiative includes strategies to reduce the environmental impact of its merchandise from

[25] See "Embracing Lean Warehousing," Kenco eBook, 2017, https://info.kencogroup.com/embracing-lean-warehousing?hsCtaTracking=722fff3c-7ca1-401f-b408-696d525c5317%7C52d36cd5-0d0b-4bdb-9f8c-db1f8f89f28f; and Joel Holt, "How to Embrace Lean Warehousing Practices in 2018," *Kenco Supply Chain and Logistics*, February 6, 2018, https://blog.kencogroup.com/embrace-lean-warehousing.

[26] James A. Cooke, "Into the Green," *DC Velocity*, Vol. 7, No. 2 (February 2009), p. 40.

[27] Bob Trebilcock, "System Report: Sustainable Distribution at REI," *Modern Materials Handling*, December 14, 2016, http://www.mmh.com/article/systems_report_sustainable_distribution_at_rei.

[28] John R. Johnson, "Earning Its Stripes," *DC Velocity*, Vol. 6, No. 5 (May 2008), p. 49.

design and sourcing to production and packaging to end-of-life disposal and recycling."[29] As a result, the company implemented changes that essentially reengineered their supply chain, affecting manufacturing, transportation, and warehousing decisions worldwide.

Burt's Bees, a U.S. company that manufactures natural personal care products such as shampoo and lotions, needed to expand its warehousing facilities due to 25 to 30 percent annual sales growth. The company, founded in 1984, and dedicated to being environmentally friendly, "walks the talk" of sustainability. Every company employee, including the CEO, has yearly sustainability goals tied to their pay.[30]

When the company expanded into a larger storage facility, the new location was closer to the manufacturing plant (reducing transportation) and could be "retrofitted for energy efficiency and environmental sustainability."[31] For example, a conveyor system was installed that only ran when products had to be moved. The WMS that was installed improved the overall operating efficiency of the DC. Less exotic, but important, were the installation of low wattage fluorescent lights and walls painted white to reflect light and make the DC brighter. The results of the expansion were a 25+ percent increase in products shipped from the facility and a 2 to 3 percent reduction in electricity usage.[32]

Adidas, Nike, and Burt's Bees are only a few examples of companies that have determined that being "green" and sustainable is "not just good corporate citizenship, but also good business."

Warehouse Productivity

To obtain maximum logistics efficiency, each component of the supply chain must operate at optimal levels. This means that high levels of productivity must be achieved, especially in the warehousing area. Productivity gains in warehousing are important to organizations (in terms of reduced costs) and to customers (in terms of improved customer service).

Productivity has been defined in many ways, but most definitions include the elements of real outputs and real inputs, utilization, and warehouse performance.

Productivity *Productivity is the ratio of real output to real input.* An example would be the number of cases handled per labor-hour.

Utilization *Utilization is the ratio of capacity used to available capacity.* An example would be warehouse employee-hours worked versus employee-hours available.

Performance *Performance is the ratio of actual output to standard output (or standard hours earned to actual hours).* An example would be the number of cases picked per hour versus some standard rate.

Any working definition of productivity probably includes all three components because all are interrelated. The expression "you can't manage what you don't measure" is just as true in warehousing as it is elsewhere. Most organizations utilize a variety of measures to examine warehouse productivity, and these measures tend to evolve over time in terms of their sophistication.[33]

Additionally, performance data must be available and used as the basis for corrective action. It is not sufficient to merely identify problem areas. It is also vital that organizations take appropriate actions to improve poor performance whenever possible. Therefore, decision strategies should be created that will handle most problem areas before they develop further. This is the essence of contingency planning and proactive management.

[29] Ibid.
[30] Susan K. Lacefield, "Green Gear Takes Sting out of Burt's Bees' Expansion," *DC Velocity*, Vol. 6, No. 10 (October 2008), p. 32.
[31] Ibid., p. 33.
[32] Ibid., p. 34.
[33] A number of examples of productivity measurement approaches and systems are presented in Supply Chain Visions, *Supply Chain Management Process Standards*, 2nd ed. (Oak Brook, IL: CSCMP, 2009).

Exhibit: Radwell International's Automated Storage System Handles 22 Million SKUs

Radford International is a full-service supplier of new and used industrial parts and components. "Known as the 'AutoStore,' the automated storage and picking system enables workers to pick 9 or 10 products in the time it takes to select one product manually."

The Radwell facility "holds a lot of inventory because manufacturing machines—which are durable goods with long useful lives—need parts long after the original manufacturer has stopped providing replacements."

"The AutoStore houses parts in dense stacks of 16 bins that are arranged in a grid. There are nearly 50,000 bins in total, all containing a mix of small parts. . . . When parts are needed for orders, the robots deliver the bins to four picking stations. . . . The system is capable of delivering 140 bins an hour to each processing station."

Source: David Maloney, "22 Million SKUs? No Problem," *DC Velocity*, Vol. 15, No. 9 (September 2017), pp. 39–42.

There is no single "best" approach that a firm can pursue in warehouse productivity measurement. Management action is determined by a variety of factors, such as customer service levels (shipping performance, error rates, order cycle time), inventory accuracy (the quantity of each SKU is correct at all warehouse locations), space utilization (having the right inventory, square foot, or cube utilization of facilities), and labor productivity (throughput rates).[34] It is universally accepted, however, that problems should be pinpointed based on cause and effect. Once they are pinpointed, the organization can institute various controls and/or corrective actions to improve warehouse productivity.

Because warehousing is such a significant component of the logistics process in terms of its cost and service impacts, executives are acutely aware of the need to improve warehouse productivity. There are many ways in which productivity can be improved, some strategic and others more operational. A "top 10" list might look something like the following:

1. Use automation (including robotics, conveyors, automatic storage and retrieval systems, AS/RS).
2. Optimize labor productivity (because it is typically the largest cost in a warehouse).
3. Maximize vertical space (optimizes cube utilization of a facility).
4. Create organized workstations (optimal workstations maximize ergonomic benefits).
5. Analyze picking methodology (make the right order-picking choices).
6. Implement lean manufacturing (lowers costs and increases efficiency).
7. Take advantage of technology (IoT, WMS, blockchain).
8. Implement faster part and tool retrieval (AS/RS systems increase picking accuracy and provide better inventory control).
9. Evaluate storage equipment (improvement in storage density reduces cost and improves efficiency).
10. Focus on continuous improvement (continually look for ways to improve warehouse operations).[35]

All of the preceding programs can be implemented by most organizations. However, most will employ many or all of the methods in combination to improve warehouse productivity.

---

[34] *The Journey to Warehousing Excellence*, Monograph Series No. M0003 (Raleigh, NC: Tompkins Associates, undated), p. 22.

[35] Jennie Dannecker, "10 Ideas for More Efficient & Productive Warehouse Operations," *Cerasis*, March 5, 2015, http://cerasis.com/2015/03/05/warehouse-operations/. Also see Martin Murray, "Measures of Warehouse Productivity," *White Paper*, The Balance, November 18, 2016, https://www.thebalance.com/measures-of-warehouse-productivity-2221323; and Curt Barry, "10 Ways to Improve Warehouse Efficiency and Reduce Costs," *Multi Channel Merchant*, February 2, 2017, http://multichannelmerchant.com/blog/10-ways-improve-warehouse-efficiency-reduce-costs/.

Facility Development

One of the more important decisions facing supply chain executives is how to determine the size and number of warehouses to be utilized by the organization. In addition, where should those facilities be located? Finally, each warehouse must be laid out and designed properly in order to maximize efficiency and productivity. Examples of how to address some of these issues are presented in the appendix of this chapter.

Size and Number of Warehouses

Factors Affecting Warehouse Size

Two issues that must be addressed are the size and number of warehouse facilities. These are interrelated decisions in that they typically have an inverse relationship; *as the number of warehouses increases, the average size of each warehouse decreases.*

Many factors influence how large a warehouse should be, although it is first necessary to define how size is measured. Size is often defined in terms of square footage of floor space, and sometimes in cubic space of the entire facility. Public warehouses often use square footage dimensions in their advertising and promotional efforts. Unfortunately, square footage measures ignore the capability of modern warehouses to store merchandise vertically. Hence, the cubic space measure was developed. Cubic space refers to the amount of volume available within a facility. It is a much more realistic size estimate because it considers more of the available usable space in a warehouse.

While costs of construction can vary by geographical location, labor rates, materials costs, and other factors, it should be noted that warehouse facilities can vary in height. In calculating cubic space (length × width × height) in a facility, the higher or taller the building, the higher the cost to construct it. For example, for a general warehouse, if the building shell is completed, construction costs per square foot will be a little under $8 for 50,000 square feet of storage space, including 3,000 square feet for office space, which is about $380,000. If the building shell has to be constructed or if the facility is to be cooled or refrigerated, the cost can be much more. To illustrate, a 30,000-square-foot warehouse in Kansas City at a median cost index would require a capital outlay of just over $1.5 million.[36] Many factors impact the cost of building private warehouses or DCs, so these figures should be considered as examples only.

Exhibit: Amazon Rival JD.com Built the Equivalent of Monaco in Warehouse Space in Three Months

"JD.com Inc. added so much warehouse space in three months that the new construction could cover just about every inch of Monaco, a pace of expansion that rivals growth at Amazon.com Inc."

During the July to September period, the company added 2 million square meters of warehouse space. The result was that the Chinese company amassed a total of 405 warehouses encompassing 9 million square meters and became China's second-largest e-commerce service firm. On average, the firm added a warehouse to its network every one to two days!

JD.com operates its own logistics network, which is very costly. However, the firm believes it is crucial to competing against its major competitor, Alibaba Group Holding Ltd.

Source: See "Amazon Rival JD.com Built the Equivalent of Monaco in Warehouse Space in Three Months," *Laney & Duke Blog*, January 10, 2018, http://www.laneyduke.com/2018/01/10/amazon-rival-jd-com-built-equivalent-monaco-warehouse-space-three-months/.

---

[36] Nathan Smith, "How Much Does It Cost to Build Out Brand New Warehouse Space?," *Austin Tenant Advisors*, October 18, 2017, https://www.austintenantadvisors.com/blog/cost-to-build-out-brand-new-warehouse-space/; and "A Guide to Warehouse Construction Costs," Korte Company, August 23, 2016, https://www.korteco.com/construction-industry-articles/guide-warehouse-construction-costs.

Some of the most important factors affecting the size of a warehouse are:

1. Customer service levels.
2. Size of market(s) served.
3. Cost of land and buildings.
4. Number of products marketed.
5. Size of the product(s).
6. Materials-handling system used.
7. Throughput rate (i.e., inventory turnover rate).
8. Production lead times.
9. Economies of scale.
10. Stock layout.
11. Aisle requirements.
12. Office area in warehouse.
13. Types of racks and shelves used.
14. Level and pattern of demand.
15. Inclusion of reverse logistics processing in the facility.
16. Future needs for the facility to expand or contract.

Typically, as a company's service levels increase, it requires more warehousing space to provide storage for higher levels of inventory, UNLESS the throughput rate of products stored in the warehouse increases. An example of high throughput rates would be Amazon.com and Walmart.com facilities. As a warehouse serves more markets, additional storage space is normally required, unless cross-docking is used and/or throughput rates are increased.

When an organization has multiple products or product groupings, especially if they are diverse, larger warehouses will be required in order to maintain minimum inventory levels of each product. Generally, greater space requirements are necessary when products are large; low throughput rates exist; production lead times are long; manual materials-handling systems are used; the warehouse contains office, sales, or computer activities; or demand is erratic and unpredictable.

Warehouse Size and Materials-Handling Equipment

To illustrate, consider the relation of warehouse size to the type of materials-handling equipment used. The type of forklift truck a warehouse employs can significantly affect the amount of storage area necessary to store product. Because of different capabilities of lift trucks, a firm can justify the acquisition of more expensive units when they are able to bring about more effective utilization of space. The warehouse decision maker must examine the cost trade-offs involved for each of the variety of available systems and determine which alternative is most advantageous from a cost/service perspective (see Table 6.1 and Figure 6.2).

Demand also has an impact on warehouse size. Whenever demand fluctuates significantly or is unpredictable, inventory levels are higher because of safety stock requirements. The only exceptions to this are when the organization can manufacture or replenish products very quickly and meet stated customer service requirements.

Factors Influencing the Number of Warehouses

In deciding on the number of warehousing facilities, four factors are significant: cost of lost sales, inventory costs, warehousing costs, and transportation costs. Although *lost sales* are extremely important to a firm, they are the most difficult to calculate and predict, and they vary by company and industry. If the cost of lost sales is very high, a firm may wish to expand its number of warehouses. There are always cost/service trade-offs. Management must determine what level of customer service it desires and only *then* develop the optimal number of warehouses to service those customers.

Inventory costs increase with the number of facilities, due to the fact that organizations usually stock a minimum amount (safety stock) of all products at every location (although some companies have specific warehouses dedicated to a particular product or product grouping). This means that both slow and fast turnover items are stocked, and thus more

TABLE 6.1

Types of Forklifts (Forklift Classifications I–VII)

Source: "Forklift Classes I–VII: What's the Difference," *Blog*, Nitco, undated, https://www.nitco-lift.com/blog/types-of-forklifts/.

Class	Description	Ideal Uses	Benefits
Class I	Electric Motor Rider Trucks	Loading/unloading tractor-trailer; handling pallets	Electric means no emissions, minimal noise
Class II	Electric Motor Narrow Aisle Trucks	Operating in tight spaces, handling pallets, picking/storing inventory	Can be used to gain more storage space in same warehouse footprint
Class III	Electric Motor Hand Trucks or Hand/Rider Trucks	Unloading deliveries from tractor-trailers; short runs in smaller quantities	Rider and walk-behind ("walkie") options
Class IV	Internal Combustion Engine Trucks (Solid/Cushion Tires)	Moving pallets from the loading dock to storage, vice versa	Cushion tires great for low-clearance situations
Class V	Internal Combustion Engine Trucks (Pneumatic Tires)	Versatile; trucks in this class can handle single pallets to loaded 40-foot containers	Mostly for outdoor use, but also indoors in large warehouses
Class VI	Electric and Internal Combustion Engine Tractors	Commonly used for hauling or pulling loads rather than lifting; versatile	Example: airport "tugger" towing luggage carts
Class VII	Rough Terrain Forklift Trucks	Great for lumberyards/construction sites where crews need to lift building materials to high elevations	Some are equipped with telescoping mast to provide far greater reach

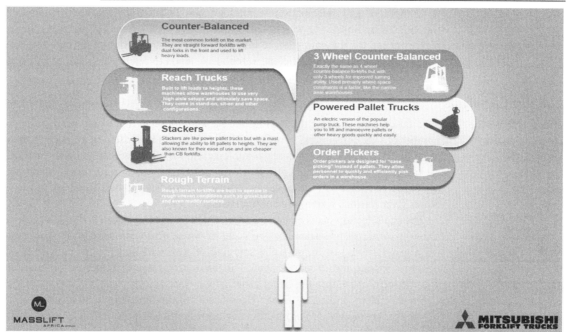

FIGURE 6.2

7 Different Types of Forklits

Source: Holly Caverni, "7 Different Types of Forklifts and What They Are Best for," *Blog*, Masslift Africa, April 4, 2017, http://www.mitsubishiforklifts.co.za/7-different-types-of-forklifts/.

total space is required. *Warehousing costs* also increase because more warehouses mean more space to be owned, leased, or rented. The costs tend to increase at a decreasing rate after a number of warehouses are brought online, particularly if the firm leases or rents space. Public and contract warehouses often offer quantity discounts when firms acquire space in multiple locations.

Transportation costs initially decline as the number of warehouses increases. But they eventually curve upward if too many facilities are employed due to the combination of inbound and outbound transportation costs. Firms must be concerned with the total delivered cost of their products and not just the cost of moving products to warehouse locations. In general, the use of fewer facilities means bulk shipments from the manufacturer or supplier. The shipments typically are rated on a truckload (TL) or carload/container (CL) basis, which provides a lower cost per hundredweight. When customer orders arrive, products are then shipped out of the warehouse on an LTL (less-than-truckload) basis but are rated higher. After the numbers of warehouses increase to a certain point, the firm may not be able to ship its products in such large quantities and may have to pay a higher rate to the transportation carrier. Local transportation costs for delivery of products from warehouses to customers may also increase because of minimum charges that apply to local cartage.

Other factors affecting the number of warehouses are the purchasing patterns of customers, the competitive environment, and the use of technology. If customers order small quantities on a frequent basis, an organization will sometimes need more warehouses located closer to the marketplace. This is what Amazon.com does since they are providing fast delivery to customers. An organization will usually also have more warehouses if the level of competition is high. When competitors offer rapid delivery to customers, a firm may be forced to match the service level unless it possesses some other differential advantage. If fast and efficient transportation and order communication are not available or are uncertain, then the only alternative might be additional storage facilities.

Computers and information technology can help minimize the firm's number of warehouses by improving warehouse layout and design, inventory control, shipping and receiving, and the dissemination of information. The substitution of information for inventories, coupled with more efficient warehouses, tends to reduce the number and/or size of warehouses needed to service customers.

Location Analysis

Where Is the Best Place to Locate a Warehouse?

Where would be the best place(s) to build a warehouse(s) that would service the greatest number of U.S. consumers? Vincennes, Indiana, would be closer, on average, to the majority of the U.S. population than any other location.[37] If a firm wished to locate facilities closest to its potential customers, using one or more warehouses in its supply chain network, a number of sites would be possible. Table 6.2 identifies the best locations in the United States given various warehouse configurations.

The site selection decision can be approached from both macro and micro perspectives. The *macro perspective* examines the issue of where to locate warehouses geographically (in a general area) to improve the sourcing of materials and the firm's market offering (improve service and/or reduce cost). The *micro perspective* examines factors that pinpoint specific locations within the larger geographic areas.

Market Positioned Warehouses

Production Positioned Warehouses

In his macro approach, Edgar Hoover identified three types of location strategies: (1) market positioned, (2) production positioned, and (3) intermediately positioned.[38] The

---

[37] "The 10 Best Warehouse Networks for 2015," Chicago Consulting, http://www.chicago-consulting .com/10BestTerritories.pdf.
[38] Edgar M. Hoover, *The Location of Economic Activity* (New York: McGraw-Hill, 1948), p. 11.

TABLE 6.2
Best Warehouse
Locations in the United
States (2015)

Source: "The 10 Best
Warehouse Networks for
2015," Chicago Consulting,
http://www.chicago-consulting
.com/10BestTerritories.pdf.

Number of Warehouses in the Network	Average Lead Time to Customers (Days)	Best Warehouse Locations		
One	2.31	Vincennes, IN		
Two	1.53	Ashland, KY	Porterville, CA	
Three	1.33	Boyertown, PA	Jackson, TN	Porterville, CA
Four	1.24	Lansdale, PA	Porterville, CA	Chicago, IL
		Meridian, MS		
Five	1.15	Brooklyn, NY	Porterville, CA	Chicago, IL
		Grand Prairie, TX	Statesboro, GA	
Six	1.11	Brooklyn, NY	Bell Gardens, CA	Chicago, IL
		Grand Prairie, TX	Statesboro, GA	Bonney Lake, WA
Seven	1.10	Brooklyn, NY	Bell Gardens, CA	Chicago, IL
		Grand Prairie, TX	Athens, GA	Bonney Lake, WA
		Palm Bay, FL		
Eight	1.07	Brooklyn, NY	Bell Gardens, CA	Chicago, IL
		Palestine, TX	Gainesville, GA	Bonney Lake, WA
		Palm Bay, FL	Aurora, CO	
Nine	1.04	Brooklyn, NY	Bell Gardens, CA	Chicago, IL
		Palestine, TX	Aiken, SC	Bonney Lake, WA
		Lakeland, FL	Denver, CO	San Juan, PR
Ten	1.04	Brooklyn, NY	Pasadena, CA	Chicago, IL
		Palestine, TX	Aiken, SC	Bonney Lake, WA
		Lakeland, FL	Denver, CO	Oakland, CA
		San Juan, PR		

market positioned strategy locates warehouses nearest to the final customer. *Production positioned* warehouses are located in close proximity to sources of supply or production facilities. The final location strategy places warehouses at a midpoint between the final customer and the producer. Customer service levels for the *intermediately positioned* warehouses are typically higher than for the production positioned facilities and lower than for market positioned facilities. A firm often follows this strategy if it must offer high customer service levels and if it has a varied product offering being produced at several plant locations.

Von Thunen's Model   Another macro approach includes the combined theories of a number of economic geographers. Many of these theories are based on distance and cost considerations. Von Thunen called for a strategy of facility location based on cost minimization.[39] Specifically, he argued, when locating points of agricultural production, transportation costs should be minimized to result in maximum profits for farmers. His model assumed that market price and production costs would be identical (or nearly so) for any point of production.

[39] See *Von Thunen's Isolated State*, trans. C. M. Warnenburg and ed. Peter Hall (Oxford, England: Pergamon Press, 1966).

Because farmer profits equal market price minus production costs and transportation costs, the optimal location would have to be the one that minimized transportation expenditures.

Weber's Model

Weber also developed a model of facility location based on cost minimization.[40] According to Weber, the optimal site was the location that minimized total transportation costs: the costs of transferring raw materials to the plant and finished goods to the market. Weber classified raw materials into two categories according to how they affected transportation costs: location and processing characteristics. Location referred to the geographical availability of the raw materials. For items with very wide availability, few constraints on facility locations would exist. Processing characteristics were concerned with whether the raw material increased, remained the same, or decreased in weight as it was processed. If it decreased, facilities would best be located near the raw material source because transportation costs of finished goods would be less with lower weights. Conversely, if processing resulted in heavier finished goods, facilities would be best located near final customers. If processing resulted in no change in weight, locating at raw material sources or markets for finished goods would be equivalent.

Hoover's Model

Other geographers included the factors of demand and profitability in the location decision. Hoover examined both cost and demand elements of location analysis. Once again, his approach stressed cost minimization in determining an optimal location. Additionally, Hoover identified that transportation rates and distance were not linearly related; that is, rates increased with distance but at a decreasing rate. The tapering of rates over greater distances supported the placement of warehouses at the end points of the channel of distribution rather that at some intermediate location. In that regard, Hoover did not fully agree with Weber's location choices.

Greenhut's Model

Greenhut expanded the work of his predecessors by including factors specific to the company (e.g., environment, security) and profitability elements in the location choice. According to Greenhut, the optimal facility location was the one that maximized profits.[41]

Center-of-Gravity Approach

An approach that is very simplistic locates facilities based on transportation costs. Termed the *center-of-gravity* approach, it locates a warehouse or distribution center at a point that minimizes transportation costs for products moving between a manufacturing plant and the market(s). This approach can be viewed rather simply. Envision two pieces of rope being tied together with a knot and stretched across a circular piece of board, with unequal weights attached to each end of the rope. Initially, the knot would be located in the center of the circle. Upon the release of weights, the rope would shift to the point where the weights would be in balance. Adding additional ropes with varying weights would result in the same shifting of the knot (assuming the knots were all in the same place). If the weights represented transportation costs, then the position where the knot would come to rest after releasing the weights would represent the center-of-gravity, or position where transportation costs would be minimized.[42]

The approach provides general answers to the warehouse location problem, but it must be modified to take into account such factors as geography, time, and customer service levels.

[40] See *Alfred Weber's Theory of the Location of Industries*, trans. Carl J. Friedrich (Chicago: University of Chicago Press, 1929).
[41] See Melvin L. Greenhut, *Plant Location in Theory and in Practice* (Chapel Hill, NC: University of North Carolina Press, 1956).
[42] For a similar discussion of the center-of-gravity approach, see Özgür Kabak, "Logistics Management Location Strategy," *PowerPoint Presentation*, June 20, 2012, http://web.itu.edu.tr/kabak/dersler/MHN521E/pdf/LM_w10_location_strategy.pdf.

Micro View of Location Analysis

From a micro perspective, more specific factors must be examined, such as the following:[43]

- Quality and variety of transportation carriers serving the site.
- Quality and quantity of available labor.
- Labor rates.
- Cost and quality of industrial land.
- Potential for expansion.
- Tax structure.
- Building codes.
- Nature of the community environment.
- Costs of construction.
- Cost and availability of utilities.
- Cost of money locally.
- Local government tax allowances.

Schmenner's Eight-Step Approach to Site Selection

Schmenner proposed an eight-step approach to a business location search that we can apply to the warehouse site selection decision (see Figure 6.3).[44] It has been used to select a site or location for a facility. The process includes the following steps:

1. After the firm has made the initial decision to establish a facility at a new location (not yet determined), it solicits input from those persons in the company affected by the decision.
2. Management designates a corporate team to examine potential sites and to collect information on selected attributes, such as land availability, labor requirements, transportation options, utilities, environmental factors, and products to be stored.
3. The firm establishes a separate engineering team to examine potential sites in terms of topography, geology, and facility design.
4. The corporate team develops a list of key criteria for the new location. Such criteria take into account the needs of all functional areas of the business.
5. Geographic regions are evaluated in view of the key criteria established; potential regional sites are identified.
6. Specific sites within acceptable regional areas are identified. Typically, 10 or fewer sites are selected for in-depth investigation.
7. The corporate team examines each prospective site, using the set of factors deemed to be important. The team makes frequent site visits and creates a ranking of potential locations.
8. A specific site is selected from the recommended locations. This decision is often made by the person most directly affected, normally the senior logistics or supply chain executive.

Each step in the process is interactive, progressing from the "general" to the "specific." It may be a highly formalized or a very informal process. The process can also be centralized at the corporate level, decentralized at the divisional or functional level, or some combination of each. What is important, however, is that even with the differences that exist among companies, most firms follow some type of logical process when making a location decision.

---

[43] See Hector Sunol, "Choosing a Warehouse Location: 7 Critical Criteria to Consider," Cyzerg Logistics Technology, January 3, 2017, http://articles.cyzerg.com/choosing-a-warehouse-location -7-critical-criteria-to-consider; and John Wisser, "Four Things to Consider When Choosing Warehouse Locations," *Supply Chain Digital,* August 14, 2014, http://www.supplychaindigital.com/warehousing /four-things-consider-when-choosing-warehouse-locations.

[44] Adapted from Roger W. Schmenner, *Making Business Location Decisions* (Englewood Cliffs, NJ: Prentice-Hall, 1982), pp. 16–21.

FIGURE 6.3
Approach to Site Selection

Source: Based on the site selection approach suggested by Roger W. Schmenner, *Making Business Location Decisions* (Englewood Cliffs, NJ: Prentice-Hall, 1982), pp. 11–15.

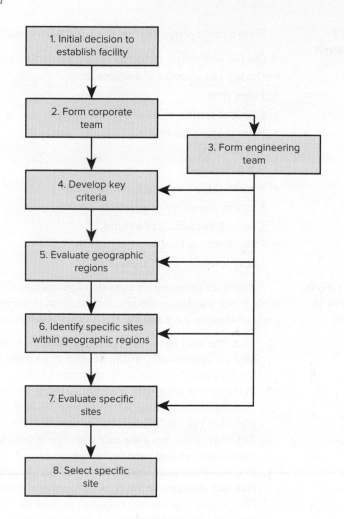

IKEA Utilizes a Simulation Model to Expand in North America

In some cases, firms use computer modeling approaches. When IKEA, the home furnishings retailer, sought to expand its presence in North America, the company set about to identify the best locations for establishing distribution centers that would meet current and future needs of the company. To get answers, IKEA used existing software from the vendor SLIM Technologies of Boston, Massachusetts, to develop a simulation model of its network. That network would include more than 100 vendor regions, up to 16 distribution centers, 50+ retail store locations, and almost 150 different product families.[45]

While simulations do not provide optimal supply chain strategies, they do allow firms to develop several scenarios that can then be evaluated and the "best" solution selected for implementation. In developing the simulation model, IKEA included a number of inputs, including:

- Distribution center capital investment costs
- Expansion options
- DC processes
- Operating capacities and costs
- Inventory turns and cost data

[45] "Building the Optimal Network," *WERCSheet*, December 2004, pp. 6–8.

- Forecasted merchandise sourcing over the next five years
- Policy and service constraints
- Freight rates[46]

After considering a number of potential solutions, IKEA determined that one option was superior to the rest. The firm would place slow-moving inventory items in a West Coast DC and an East Coast DC, while maintaining other inventory at other DC locations. IKEA would have two service regions that would be serviced from its DCs. As a result of the revised configuration, IKEA saved several million dollars per year. IKEA has since expanded throughout the United States and into Canada using a similar approach.[47] By 2017, IKEA had more than 400 stores being served by five regional DCs (with one more being built).[48]

Related to the location of facilities is the decision to design an optimal structure that maximizes efficiency and effectiveness. This is the warehouse layout and design decision.

Warehouse Layout and Design

Where should things be located in the organization's supply chain? More specifically, where should products be located within a warehouse? With an average warehouse containing thousands of SKUs, this is an important decision because it has a critical effect on system efficiency and productivity. A good warehouse layout can increase output, improve product flow, reduce costs, and improve service to customers.[49]

The optimal warehouse layout and design for an organization will vary by the type of products being stored, availability of financial resources, level and type of competition, and customer needs. Additionally, there are various cost trade-offs between labor, equipment, space, and information. For example, the purchase of more expensive, yet more efficient, materials-handling equipment can affect the optimal size of a warehouse facility. Installation of an automated conveyor system to reduce labor costs and raise productivity can affect the configuration of a warehouse. Also, "the reduced travel distances from using aisles or tunnels will improve picking efficiency up to 25%."[50]

Within a warehouse, randomized and dedicated storage are two general examples of how products can be located and arranged.[51]

Randomized Storage

Randomized storage. Randomized, or floating-slot, storage places items in the closest available slot, bin, or rack. Products are then retrieved on a first-in, first-out (FIFO) basis. This approach maximizes space utilization, although it requires longer travel times between order-picking locations. Randomized systems often employ a computerized automatic storage and retrieval system (AS/RS), which minimizes labor and handling costs.

Dedicated Storage

Dedicated storage. In dedicated or fixed-slot storage, products are stored in permanent locations within a warehouse. Three methods can be used to implement the dedicated storage approach, including storing items by (a) part number sequence, (b) usage rates, or (c) activity levels (e.g., grouping products into classes or families based on their level of activity or throughput rates).

[46] Ibid., p. 6.
[47] See Emily Atkins, "IKEA's E-commerce Expansion," *Materials Management & Distribution*, August 23, 2016, https://www.mmdonline.com/features/ikeas-e-commerce-expansion/.
[48] "IKEA Strengthens Distribution Network with Customer Fulfillment Centers in Baytown, TX and American Canyon, CA," *Business Wire*, November 7, 2017, https://www.businesswire.com/news /home/20171107005391/en/IKEA-Strengthens-Distribution-Network-Customer-Fulfillment-Centers.
[49] See "13 Tips for Your Ultimate Warehouse Design & Layout," *Formaspace*, September 6, 2017, https://formaspace.com/articles/material-handling/13-tips-for-ultimate-warehouse-design/.
[50] "Ideas for Improving Warehouse Performance (3)," *Supply Chain Update*, July 5, 2016, http://www .supplychainupdate.co.za/Article.aspx?ID=775.
[51] Ibid.

Compatibility

In terms of overall warehouse layout, products may be grouped according to their compatibility, complementarity, or popularity. *Compatibility* refers to how well products may be stored together. For example, pharmaceuticals cannot be stored with bagged agricultural chemicals in the U.S. because of federal regulations. And many years ago, before the development of newer paints, it was discovered that automobile tires and consumer appliances could not be stored together. Chemical vapors given off by the tires reacted with the pigments in the appliance paint, resulting in slight color changes. Appliances then had to be repainted or sold at a discount.

Complementarity

Complementarity refers to how often products are ordered together and therefore stored together. Computer disk drives, CD-ROMs, monitors; pens and pencils; and desks and chairs are examples of complementary products that are usually stored in close proximity to each other.

Popularity

Popularity relates to the fact that products have different inventory turnover rates or demand rates. Another term used for this turnover rate is *velocity*. Items that are in greatest demand should be stored closest to shipping/receiving docks. Slow-moving items should be stored elsewhere, at more remote locations within warehouses.

In addition to internal space layout, it is also important to analyze a warehouse's external configuration. Four aspects of external layout are critical: truck docks, rail requirements, external security measures, and physical features such as roof and windows.

In summation, once a decision has been made to utilize warehousing, a decision regarding whether to perform the storage function oneself or outsource it is necessary. Then determining the size and number of storage facilities becomes important, followed by where they should be located and what should be their layout and design. Such decisions are needed whether the firm and its supply chain are local, national, or global in scope.

Measures and Metrics

Management experts have stated that "you can't manage what you don't measure." Although all generalizations have exceptions, it is certain that efficient and effective warehouse and DC management cannot occur without the proper operating and performance measures and metrics. Often, the following scenario occurs:

> They can quote their facilities' order fulfillment rates off the top of their heads. They can recite line fill rates out to the hundredth of a percentage point. They can reel off stats for worker turnover, order cycle times, and distribution costs as a percentage of sales. But when it comes to gauging what really matters—how their customers view their performance—DC managers seem to rely more on guesswork than on the numbers.[52]

In order to efficiently and effectively manage a warehouse or DC, the supply chain executive must have measures and metrics for variables such as customers, operations, financials, capacity/quality, and employees.

Warehouse Efficiency and Effectiveness Metrics

Warehousing is an important part of most supply chains. It has been estimated that warehouse operations account for 30 to 50 percent of most companies' supply chain costs.[53] Thus, it is vital that these storage facilities operate at peak efficiency and effectiveness so that supply chain partners and customers achieve a "win-win" situation. This involves

---

[52] Karl Manrodt and Kate Vitasek, "Performance by the Numbers," *DC Velocity*, Vol. 5, No. 5 (May 2007), p. 52.

[53] Knut Alicke, Markus Leopoldseder, Deepak Mishra, and Wolf Axel Schulze, "What's in Your Warehouse?," *Supply Chain Europe*, Vol. 17, No. 2 (March/April 2008), p. 14.

Exhibit: A Food Manufacturer Uses SCOR to Improve Its Supply Chain Performance

The consumer products company was treating all customers the same, irrespective of size or ordering patterns. It had no consistent means of managing overall supply chain performance, with various divisions and groups utilizing measures that often were in conflict with each other. Processes were mostly informal and the company had functional silos. To address these problems, the company implemented the SCOR Model (see Chapter 1 for a discussion of this model).

As part of the process for implementing SCOR, the firm had to develop a scorecard to measure benefits and manage performance. The scorecard contained metrics definitions, benchmark data, and strategic competitive requirements. The measures included supply chain delivery reliability (perfect order fulfillment), supply chain responsiveness (order fulfillment cycle time), supply chain flexibility (upside flexibility), and supply chain asset management efficiency (total supply chain management cost, cash-to-cash cycle time, inventory days of supply). For each metric, the actual performance level was measured

and benchmark comparisons were made with other firms in the industry.

After developing a process map of the firm's supply chain, the company began to evaluate which components of the process could be improved. Two significant warehousing problems were identified: "Storage of commonly used, semi-finished materials and components was not planned or stocked in aggregate because each plant managed its own supply. Also product rejects were contributing to storage issues and problems with slow-moving and obsolete inventory" (p. 70).

As a result of the SCOR analysis, the firm implemented 11 projects aimed at improving its supply chain efficiency and effectiveness. One year after implementation, the company was able to measure notable improvements in almost every key metric that was being measured. Additionally, more than US$2.6 million in costs were eliminated.

Source: Peter L. Bolstorff, "From Chaos to Control," *CSCMP's Supply Chain Quarterly*, Vol. 2, No. 2 (Q2/2008), pp. 64–73.

breaking down the warehousing process into components and determining if any of them can be done better.

The Warehousing Education and Research Council (WERC) periodically conducts a study of warehouse metrics. As the marketplace changes, so do the metrics used to evaluate warehouse efficiency and effectiveness. Popular metrics that seem to remain important and are widely used by companies include average warehouse capacity used, order-picking accuracy, on-time shipments, percent of supplier orders received damage free, and order fill rate.[54]

In an era of "lean" manufacturing, "lean" supply chain management, and "lean" everything else, aspects of warehousing can typically be improved collectively, that is, a number of functions or processes can be improved rather than just one or a few. Organizations that have implemented successful lean programs report cost savings of 20 to 40 percent.[55]

Lean Warehousing

"Lean warehousing" can be viewed from either a strategic or tactical/operational perspective. With a strategic focus, supply chain executives would consider warehousing vis-à-vis overall supply chain strategy. "In strategic warehousing, we recognize the supply chain is an overall system, with many moving parts. Warehousing plays a key role in that system. . . . The second vantage point is . . . tactical lean warehousing. In this case, we focus inside the four walls of the warehouse and ask, 'How can lean principles and tools help us to run a more efficient warehouse?' Here we have made the assumption we need the warehouse and therefore want it to run as effectively and efficiently as possible."[56]

[54] Joe Tillman, Karl Manrodt, and Donnie Williams, "DC Measures 2017," *WERCwatch*, Spring 2017.
[55] Ibid.
[56] "Lean Warehousing—From Paradox to Operational Excellence," *Supply Chain Brief*, November 13, 2013, http://www.supplychainbrief.com/lean/six-sigma/warehousing/?open-article-id=2981974&article -title=lean-warehousing&blog-domain=leancor.com&blog-title=leancor.

In terms of "best practice," warehousing excellence can be achieved by developing optimal strategies in the following 11 areas:

1. Set up a vendor compliance program.
2. Electronically transmit advanced shipping notifications (ASN).
3. Utilize automatic data collections technology such as RFID or RF barcode.
4. Utilize hands-free selection such as wrist-mounted RF units, voice pick, pick- or put-to-light order fulfillment systems.
5. Utilize a WMS for preplanned picking waves.
6. Record every movement as a transaction to determine if unnecessary activities are occurring.
7. Minimize touches of the inventory.
8. Schedule shipments to arrive simultaneously.
9. Practice ongoing cycle count.
10. Use cross-docking given its cost savings and other benefits.
11. Implement dynamic slotting, which locates products based on demand.[57]

For each of the 11 areas, specific metrics can be developed and data collected to ensure that performance standards are being achieved. Typically, firms will measure a multitude of factors, but only a few will be key performance indicators (KPIs).

Key Performance Indicators (KPIs)

In a presentation to supply chain executives, the speaker stated that "warehouse operators, like most business executives, thirst for useful information even while they are drowning in data. Those responsible for creating the fire hydrants that spew data may not know which pieces of information truly are useful. As a result, valuable performance indicators can be buried like needles in a haystack."[58] Hence, there is a need for a few really important metrics, referred to as key performance indicators (KPIs) (see Table 6.3).[59]

Practically speaking, supply chain executives responsible for warehousing need to know the answers to four basic questions, each of which can be measured in many different ways: First, where is my stuff? Second, how much of my stuff remains in stock? Third, when will I get my order? And fourth, how much lead time do I need?[60]

TABLE 6.3

Source: "The Warehouse KPI's You Need to Know," Newcastle Systems, August 4, 2014, http://www.newcastlesys .com/blog/bid/352444 /warehouse-metrics-and -benchmarking-that-matter.

Warehouse Key Performance Indicators		
Internal KPIs	**Supplier KPIs**	**Customer KPIs**
• Perfect orders	• Inbound cost/order value	• Profitability
• On-time deliveries	• On-time deliveries	• Sales volume
• Inventory accuracy	• Lead time	• Growth potential
• Inventory carrying cost	• Fill rate	• Credit/payment history
• Inventory turns	• IT/technology resources	• Shared strategic vision
• Order cycle time	• Service flexibility	• Return rate
• Order entry accuracy	• Attitude	• Customer viability
• Workforce utilization	• Returns policy	• Order frequency
• Shipping accuracy	• Value-added services	• Loyalty
• Order fill rate	• VMI capabilities	• Cost to serve
• Customer satisfaction	• Ease of doing business	• Competitive pressure
	• Ethics/compliance	• Hassle to serve

---

[57] "11 Warehouse and Distribution Center Best Practices for Your Supply Chain," *Legacy Supply Chain Services*, undated, https://legacyscs.com/warehouse-and-distribution-center-11-best-practices/.
[58] Ken Ackerman, "Metrics and Visibility—What Is Really Worth Seeing?," *Warehousing Forum*, Vol. 22, No. 8 (July 2007), p. 1.
[59] "What Are the Top Warehouse Management KPIs Every Supply Chain Exec Should Measure?," Veridian, May 30, 2017, http://veridiansol.com/warehouse-management-kpis/.
[60] Ibid.

Warehouse executives are often asked which metrics they most often use. Table 6.3 identifies some examples of KPIs used in warehousing. The KPIs consider the warehouse, suppliers, and customers.

In order of frequency of use, the most popular measures are:

- Percentage of on-time shipments
- Percentage of shipments delivered on time
- Overtime as a percentage of total paid hours
- Percentage of inbound received on time
- Percentage of orders shipped complete
- Order cycle time (from order placement to order shipment)
- Fill rate, measured both by lines and by orders
- Inventory count accuracy
- Units handled per hour
- Order picking accuracy
- Percentage of storage capacity used
- Days of finished goods inventory on hand
- Annual workforce turnover[61]

When each of the above metrics is combined and a warehouse or DC does everything right, what you get is something called the "perfect order," defined as an order "that arrives complete, on time, free of damage, with the perfect documentation."[62] However, because no system or warehouse is "perfect," something less than the perfect order results most of the time. To illustrate, if a warehouse or DC has 93.57% on-time delivery, ships complete orders 93.30% of the time, has 98.35% of shipments damage free, and is accurate on invoicing the customer 98.27% of the time, the perfect order index (POI) score is only 84.46% [93.67 × 93.30 × 98.35 × 98.27 = 84.46].[63]

Interestingly, as seen from the listing of KPIs and the definition of a perfect order, "on time" is an important aspect of warehouse management. Complicating the calculation of the POI is the fact that on time means different things to different people and in different situations. For example, most of us would not be troubled with having to wait an extra five minutes to get a seat at our favorite restaurant. However, if we were to be involved in a life-threatening traffic accident, a five-minute wait would be unacceptable. In a survey of warehouse executives, individuals indicated six different ways that they defined on time: on or before appointment time; +15 minutes from the appointment time; +30 minutes from the appointment time; +1 hour from the appointment time; on the requested day; and on the agreed-upon day.[64] Therefore, depending on the particular definition used for on time, many different POI scores could be calculated, and each one could be right!

International Dimensions of Warehousing

Products must be stored at some point prior to their final consumption. Depending on the particular conditions in effect within each market area, products may be stored at different points within the channel of distribution.[65]

[61] Reported in Ken Ackerman, "What Are People Measuring?," *Warehousing Forum*, Vol. 22, No. 8 (July 2007), p. 3.
[62] Karl Manrodt and Kate Vitasek, "Getting Better All the Time," *DC Velocity*, Vol. 4, No. 5 (May 2006), p. 54.
[63] Ibid.
[64] Ibid., p. 55.
[65] Jared Mitchell, "What You Must Know about Global Warehousing," *PROFITguide.com*, December 5, 2014, http://www.profitguide.com/manage-grow/international-trade/what-you-must-know-about-global-warehousing-72123.

Examples of Warehousing throughout the World

For organizations located in Asia, warehouse sites may be selected in Bombay, Hong Kong, Kuala Lumpur, Manila, Melbourne, Shanghai, Singapore, and/or Tokyo. In South America, Buenos Aires, Bogota, Caracas, and/or Rio de Janeiro may be the locations of choice. Africa offers warehouse choices in Cairo, Cape Town, Kinshasa, Lagos, and/or Nairobi. In Europe, organizations such as Philips (electronics), Nestlé (food), and Perstorp (chemicals) must store a variety of products at factories and warehouses throughout Europe in order to provide market coverage to the EU. Optimal country locations for establishing warehouses and DCs include Germany, the Netherlands, and Poland.[66]

Warehousing Requirements Vary Globally

Due to differences in culture, technology, accepted practice, competition, etc., warehousing requirements will likely vary across geographic regions of the world. For example, in Japan, Europe, and elsewhere, the retail network is composed of a great number of small shops, each having little capacity for inventory storage. As a result, such shops order frequently from distributors, manufacturers, or other channel intermediaries. The burden of storage is carried by the manufacturer or other channel members rather than the retailer. In the U.S., because there are fewer retail stores and they are much larger, the storage function is more easily shifted away from the channel intermediaries directly to the retailer.

To illustrate, in Japan, multi-story facilities are more common than in other parts of the world. The cost and availability of land are the primary factors resulting in multi-story facilities. In Tokyo, land can sell for hundreds of dollars per square foot, if land is available at all. Construction costs are also higher, often three to four times higher than those in the U.S. The combination of these factors makes multi-story facilities a good choice in Japan.[67]

The type of transportation equipment available in an area can also impact warehouse decisions. Because of equipment variations and infrastructure (e.g., narrow roads, lack of alleys, local restrictions on deliveries) around the world, it is difficult to standardize warehouse design. In some parts of the world, loading and unloading occur straight from the ground, without the use of pallets.

When an international firm needs warehousing facilities in a foreign market, it may find an abundance of sophisticated, modern warehouses in some industrial nations. In Japan and Western Europe, organizations use high-cube automated warehousing. This is due primarily to higher land and labor costs that require warehouses to be built higher and automation be used to minimize labor.

Quality and Availability of Warehousing Vary Widely

On the other hand, in less-developed countries, storage facilities may be nonexistent or limited in availability or sophistication. In the latter instance, the product package or shipping container may have to serve the warehousing purpose.

In the U.S., many public warehouses provide services such as consolidation and break-bulk, customer billing, traffic management, packaging, import/export assistance, and product labeling. Public warehouses in many foreign markets may also provide services in addition to storage.

Like all supply chain–related activities, the warehousing and storage activity must be administered differently in each market. It is the responsibility of the supply chain executive to recognize how the storage activity differs and to adjust the organization's strategy accordingly. In Chapters 12 and 13, global issues impacting warehousing and the supply chain will be examined in more detail.

---

[66] "Customer Growth Strategies: Europe's Most Desirable Logistics Locations," ProLogis, October 2017, https://www.prologisgermany.de/sites/germany/files/documents/2017/10/prologis-research_europes-most-desirable-logistics-locations_0.pdf.

[67] See Kosuke Shimizu, "Foreign Companies Drive Japan's Distribution Center Boom," *Nikkei Asian Review*, February 6, 2017, https://asia.nikkei.com/Business/Trends/Foreign-companies-drive-Japan-s-distribution-center-boom; and Leonard Sahling and John M. Tofflemire, "Japan's Logistics Property Markets—Drive to Efficiency," *White Paper*, ProLogis Corporation, 2007.

Financial Dimensions of Warehousing

Financial control of warehousing is closely tied to supply chain productivity and corporate profitability. Before the various activities of warehousing can be properly integrated into a single unified system, management must be aware of the cost of each activity. This is where financial accounting and control techniques become important. "Due to increasing constraints, SCM has been moving from cost-oriented to demand- and value-oriented objectives."[68] As an important activity within SCM, warehousing has been impacted as well.

Activity-Based Costing

One approach, which has proven very successful in the financial control of warehousing activities, has been *activity-based costing* (ABC). Accurate and timely financial data allow warehouse executives to properly plan, administer, and control warehousing activities. Traditional costing systems, in place at many firms, often do not provide financial data in the proper form for use in making warehousing decisions. Frequently, it is difficult to identify how warehousing costs impact overall corporate profitability and how changes in costs in one area impact costs in another.

Many companies have implemented ABC in order to have better warehousing cost information. ABC is simply the tracing of overhead and direct costs to specific products, services, or customers. The tracing of costs follows a two-stage process. The first stage assigns resource costs based on the amount of each resource consumed in performing specific warehousing activities. The second stage assigns warehousing activity costs to the products, services, or customers consuming the activities based on actual consumption.

Companies are often at various levels of sophistication in terms of warehouse accounting and control. Warehouse costs can be measured in total (a macro approach), by warehouse function, and/or by warehouse activity. Examples of warehouse financial metrics are distribution costs as a percent of sales, distribution costs as a percent of cost of goods sold, distribution costs per unit shipped, inventory shrinkage as a percent of total inventory, days on hand—raw materials, days on hand—finished goods inventory, inventory days of supply, average days payable, and average days sales outstanding.[69]

This is what accounting and control are all about. Simply stated, it is having the right kind of financial data available when and where it is needed, and in a form that is usable by as many functional areas of the organization as possible. Ultimately, such data is essential to making the necessary cost–service trade-offs within the warehousing activity and between other supply chain functions.

In addition to having the right kinds of financial measures and controls, organizations need to remember that "most expensive" does not necessarily mean "best." To illustrate, Grayling Industries, a manufacturer of asbestos-abatement supplies with annual sales of $20 million, sells protective liners for intermediate bulk containers, bulk bags, totes, and disposal bags for hazardous materials. The company decided against purchasing a WMS and, instead, rented the necessary software.[70]

For just $500 per month, the firm was able to rent a software system that could

- Handle multiple tasks, such as informing suppliers of replenishment requirements, tracking inbound and outbound inventory, and integrating with ERP systems of its shippers.
- Be implemented without a long, costly implementation.
- Be affordable and easy for Grayling's supply chain partners, some of which were small, family-owned businesses.[71]

---

[68] "2017 Supply Chain Worldwide Survey," *White Paper*, Geodis, May 2017, p. 8, https://www.geodis.com/geodis-unveils-its-2017-supply-chain-worldwide-sur-@/en/view-2189-communique.html/1961.
[69] See "DC Measures 2017," pp. 10 and 12.
[70] Toby Gooley, "Little Cost, Big Benefits," *DC Velocity*, Vol. 6, No. 12 (December 2008), pp. 63–68.
[71] Ibid., pp. 65–66.

The new software was delivered via the Internet and thus was implemented quickly, in a matter of a few weeks. As a result, Grayling was able to successfully implement its JIT manufacturing operations and eliminate product slowdowns and shutdowns that had occurred in the past.

Nowhere are the financial issues more important than when a private warehouse is built.[72] Building a warehouse or DC is a major financial undertaking. "Typically, 80 percent of warehouse costs come from eight areas: concrete, steel, earthwork, site utilities, roofing, general conditions, fire protection, and design fees."[73] Also, there are the additional costs for equipment and racks, shelves, and storage containers. These costs vary greatly from one geographic area to another. They also vary according to size of the facility. For example, a "100,000-square-foot DC is 56 percent more expensive per square foot than a 600,000-square-foot building."[74]

Because of the costs associated with building and operating a warehouse/DC, it is important to maximize the cube utilization of the facility. In addition to designing the facility to provide optimal utilization, selecting the right equipment and materials inside the warehouse/DC is important as well. This topic will be the focus of the next chapter, Chapter 7—Materials Management and Handling in the Supply Chain.

Summary

In this chapter we discussed the importance of warehousing in the supply chain. Economies of scale, costs, and customer service are the most important considerations. The types of options available to firms include public (rented) warehousing, private (owned or leased) warehousing, and cross-docking. Each option has its advantages and disadvantages that must be understood in order to make optimal warehouse management decisions.

Optimal warehouse decisions are enhanced through the use of technologies such as warehouse management systems (WMSs) and just-in-time (JIT) programs. Other considerations in effectively managing a warehouse are environmental, energy, and sustainability issues. In some instances, outsourcing of warehousing to a third party may be the optimal solution.

Facility development is a large part of warehouse management. Decisions relating to the size and number of warehouses, location of facilities, and layout and design have significant impact on an organization's ability to satisfy its customers and make a profit. In order to successfully manage warehouse operations, it is necessary to develop various metrics to measure efficiency and effectiveness. Important in this effort is the identification of key performance indicators (KPIs) that indicate whether optimality is being achieved.

Supply chains operate globally, and we described international dimensions of warehousing. Due to differences in culture, technology, accepted practice, competition, and other factors, warehousing management will vary across geographic regions of the world. Chapters 12 and 13 will examine the global dimensions of the supply chain in more detail.

Finally, the financial dimensions of warehousing were discussed. Financial accounting and control techniques are important in managing warehouse operations within the supply chain. Companies are often at various levels of sophistication in terms of warehousing accounting and control, but it is vital that firms collect relevant financial data in order to determine the most appropriate warehousing strategies.

Within a warehouse, manual (nonautomated) or automated materials-handling equipment can be employed. Standard equipment can be categorized by the function it performs: storage and order picking, transportation and sorting, or shipping. Automated equipment includes items such as automated storage and retrieval systems (AS/RS), carousels, conveyors, handheld devices, drones, robots, and scanning systems. These items will be examined in Chapter 7.

[72] See "A Guide to Warehouse Construction Costs," *Guide*, Korte Company, August 23, 2016, https://www.korteco.com/construction-industry-articles/guide-warehouse-construction-costs.

[73] Philip C. LaBerge, "Building a Warehouse without Going Broke," *Inbound Logistics*, Vol. 26, No. 1 (January 2006), p. 102.

[74] Ibid.

Suggested Readings

Boyd, John, "The Right Site, at the Right Price," *DC Velocity*, Vol. 10, No. 1 (January 2012), pp. 77–80.

Bradley, Peter, "Red, White, and . . . Green," *DC Velocity*, Vol. 8, No. 3 (March 2010), pp. 31–34.

"The Connected Warehouse," *White Paper*, Tompkins Associates, undated, http://archive.tompkinsinc.com/wp-content/uploads/2017/06/The-Connected-Warehouse-White-Paper.pdf.

"Considering China's Warehousing Options," *White Paper*, C. H. Robinson, 2017.

"Considering China's Warehousing Options," *White Paper*, C. H. Robinson Worldwide, Inc., 2010, http://www.chrobinson.com.

Cooke, James A., "Carquest Revs Up Its Order Operations," *DC Velocity*, Vol. 10, No. 2 (February 2012), pp. 49–50.

"The Definitive List of Warehouse Metrics You Need to Start Tracking Today," *Blog*, Veridian, October 4, 2017, http://veridiansol.com/warehouse-metrics/.

"The Future Warehouse," Argon Consulting, 2019, https://www.thefuturewarehouse.com.

Gooley, Toby, "The BIG Rollout," *DC Velocity*, Vol. 10, No. 1 (January 2012), pp. 59–61.

Gresham, Tom, "Top 6 Factors for Selecting and Implementing a WMS," *Inbound Logistics*, Vol. 37, No. 9 (September 2017), pp. 106–109.

Hitch, John, "It's About Time: Welcome to the 'Now' Economy and Smart Warehouses," *Industry Week*, January 18, 2019, https://www.industryweek.com/technology-and-iiot/its about-time-welcome-now-economy-and-smart-warehouses.

Intrieri, Chuck, "Warehouse Cost Savings: 5 Key Areas of Focus and 13 Practical Objectives," *Supply Chain Brief Blog*, Cerasis, July 12, 2016, http://www.supplychainbrief.com/lean/six-sigma/warehousing/?open-article-id=5318744&article-title=warehouse-cost-savings--5-key-areas-of-focus-and-13-practical-objectives&blog-domain=cerasis.com&blog-title=cerasis.

Maloney, David, "On a Roll at Amway," *DC Velocity*, Vol. 10, No. 3 (March 2012), pp. 60–61.

MH&L Staff, "9 Ways to Transform Warehouses," *Material Handling & Logistics*, September 28, 2018, https://www.mhlnews.com/warehousing/9-ways-transform-warehouses.

O'Byrne, Rob, "Common Sense Warehouse Performance Metrics for Supply Chain Benchmarking," *Logistics Bureau*, July 19, 2017, http://www.logisticsbureau.com/common-sense-warehouse-performance-metrics-for-supply-chain-benchmarking/.

Pigorsch, Wendy D., Ron Cain, Ken Porter, Ruth Lund, and Chelle Stringer, "Shine a Light on Company Culture," *WERCSheet*, Vol. 37, No. 3 (May/June 2014), pp. 6–10.

"Robots in the Warehouse: A Supply Chain Game-Changer," *Tompkins Blog*, undated, https://www.tompkinsinc.com/en-us/Insight/Articles/robots-in-the-warehouse-a-supply-chain-game-changer.

Schofield, Jay, "The 15 Supply Chain Metrics That Make or Break Warehouse Efficiency," *Blog*, System ID, May 28, 2015, http://www.systemid.com/learn/warehouse-efficiency-metrics/.

Stringer, Chelle, Regina Clark, and Roxi Bahar Hewertson, "Pathway to Leadership," *WERCSheet*, Vol. 38, No. 2 (March/April 2015), pp. 6–9.

"13 Tips for Your Ultimate Warehouse Design and Layout," Formaspace, September 6, 2017, https://formaspace.com/articles/material-handling/13-tips-for-ultimate-warehouse-design/.

Questions and Problems

LO 6-1   1. Why is warehousing an important part of a typical supply chain?

LO 6-2   2. Briefly define the four major types of warehousing used in supply chains: public; private; contract; cross-dock.

LO 6-3   3. What is a "warehouse management system (WMS)," and how is it used to make a warehouse more efficient and effective?

Appendix[75]

Case Study–Public versus Private Warehousing

This case highlights the comparison of leased, private warehousing to public warehousing. It also illustrates how the treatment of certain costs can influence the results of the analysis.

Synopsis

The company's warehouse facilities have reached capacity in the mid-Atlantic region. Currently, the firm owns and operates two facilities in the area and utilizes approximately 150,000 square feet of outside public warehouse space. The most pressing need is for overflow storage, which is currently being handled by the public warehouse. Overflow requirements are expected to grow substantially in the next several years.

A variety of options are considered initially by the task force charged with recommending a solution to the space requirements problem. It is estimated that approximately 210,000 square feet of space will be required in the mid-Atlantic region. The alternatives have been reduced to the following: (1) use public warehousing or (2) lease 210,000 square feet at $2.75/square foot on a five-year lease with a five-year renewal option.

Financial Analysis

Alternative 1: Public Warehousing
A. Annual cost:

Handling charges, annual = $ 760,723
Storage charges, annual   =   413,231
Total   = $1,173,954

B. The public warehousing costs are based on a careful review of public operators in the area. The costs shown in the analysis above are based on the rates for the lowest cost quotation received from the vendors in the feasible set.

Alternative 2: Lease a New Facility
A. Costs are estimated on the basis of past experience and forecasted levels of expense in this specific market. Estimated yearly operating expenses–new facility: = $ 309.914
B. Investment in the new facility:
  1. Capitalized lease

   a. Annual lease payment = $ 577,500
   b. Present value of 10 annual payments of $577,500 = $3,547,600

[75] Source: Reprinted with permission from *The Financial Evaluation of Warehousing Options: An Examination and Appraisal of Contemporary Practices*, Thomas Speh and James A. Blomquist, © 1988, Warehousing Education and Research Council, 1100 Jorie Blvd., Oak Brook, IL 60523-4413; updated in 2009.

2. The lease is capitalized, i.e., the leased asset (building) is treated as a fixed asset, and the present value of future lease payments is treated as a debt. Capitalization of the lease is required for auditing purposes by the Financial Accounting Standards Board and is used in this type of analysis because future lease payments are as binding as if money had been borrowed by the firm to purchase the building. The net effect is to treat the lease as an asset. In this situation, the company considers their investment in the asset to be the present value of the future lease payments (as will be discussed in the commentary, not all financial analysts would agree with treating the lease in this fashion). The discount rate used to determine the present value of the lease payments is typically the firm's after-tax cost of capital, adjusted according to the risk of the project.

3. Other fixed assets required for the new facility:

Handling equipment	$ 170,800
Computer systems	26,740
Rack	252,000
Total	**$449,540**

4. Start-up costs-new facility:

Product movement	$ 10,500
5. Initial cash outlay	**$ 460,040**

Yearly Savings, Lease versus Public

Annual Public Warehouse Cost	=	$1,173,954
Annual Private Warehouse Cost	=	309,914
Annual Total Savings	=	**$ 864,040**

Private cost appears understated, but the annual lease cost is not reflected in the annual operating cost because the lease is capitalized and treated as an investment.

Ten-Year Cash Flows (000s)

Year	Initial Outlay	Capitalized Lease	Savings: Lease versus Public	Pre-Tax Net Cash In/Out Flow	Tax Depreciation*	Savings Less Depreciation	Taxes 39%	Savings Less Depreciation and Taxes	Depreciation	After-Tax Net Cash In/Out Flow
0	$460	$3,548	0	($4,008)	0					($4,008)
1	0	0	$ 864	864	$136	$ 728	$ 284	$ 444	$136	$ 580
2	0	0	864	864	109	755	294	461	109	570
3	0	0	864	864	71	793	309	484	71	555
4	0	0	864	864	50	814	317	497	50	547
5	0	0	864	864	45	819	319	500	45	545
6	0	0	864	864	25	839	327	512	25	537
7	0	0	864	864	22	842	328	514	22	536
8	0	0	864	864	3	861	336	525	3	528
9	0	0	864	864	0	864	337	527	0	527
10	0	0	864	864	0	864	337	527	0	527
Total	$460	$3,548	$8,640	$4,632	$461	$8,179	$3,190	$4,989	$461	$ 1,442

*Depreciation on rack, handling equipment, and computer hardware is factored in here to reflect the impact on cash flows as a result of the reduction of taxes.

For example:	Year 1
Savings	$ 864,040
Depreciation	– 135,839
Net Profit (before tax)	$ 728,201
Federal tax (39%)	– 283,998
Net Profit (after tax)	$ 444,203
Depreciation	+ 135,839
After tax cash flow	$ 580,042

Return on Investment
Internal Rate of Return (IRR)
A. Savings stream:

Year	Savings
0	($4,007,640)
1	580,042
2	569,222
3	554,768
4	546,741
5	544,587
6	536,774
7	535,654
8	528,146
9	527,065
10	527,065

B. IRR (after taxes) +6.13%

Net Present Value
A. Discount rate: 11% after taxes
B. NPV of the 10-year savings stream (discounted at 11%) = ($692,941)

Decision

Use Public Warehousing. IRR and NPV for the private facility do not meet company standards.

Discussion

It is interesting to note that the leased facility generates significant yearly operating savings, yet, the operating savings, as large as they are, do not generate a return on investment that exceeds the company's hurdle rate.

The cost elements included in the company's original analysis were all "hard dollars," and no incremental revenues were considered. The distribution function has its own capital "pool," but distribution projects must meet the hurdle rate that applies to all capital projects.

The lease capitalization in the case study provides an opportunity to review some fundamental financial concepts. As was described in the case, the lease is treated as an asset, and the present value of the future lease payments is shown as an asset on the balance sheet. The interesting point is that the company then treated the capitalized value of the lease as an *investment* in their cash flow analysis. That is, the capitalized lease is treated as a major cash outflow against which the cash savings will be compared to determine the rate of return.

Many managers would argue that the present value of the capitalized lease should not be treated as a lump sum cash outflow (i.e., as an investment). The present value of the annual lease payments is indeed a balance sheet item, but from a *cash flow perspective*, the annual lease payments should be treated as cash outflows in the years in which they are made. If the analysis of the leased space versus public warehousing alternative is recast to treat the lease payments as annual outflows, and the equipment outlay and start-up costs of $460,040 are treated as the initial investment, an entirely different decision would be reached. The data in the table below shows the revised analysis.

Ten-Year Cash Flow Analysis Using Annual Lease Payments ($000s)					
Year	Public Warehouse Annual Cost	Annual Cost of Leasing (Lease cost + Operating costs)	Initial Investment	Pretax Savings: Lease versus Public	After-Tax Savings (Savings, less taxes, plus depreciation)
0			$460		
1	$1,174	$888		$286	$228
2	1,174	888		286	217
3	1,174	888		286	202
4	1,174	888		286	194
5	1,174	888		286	192
6	1,174	888		286	184
7	1,174	888		286	183
8	1,174	888		286	176
9	1,174	888		286	175
10	1,174	888		286	175
Net present value of the cash savings of lease vs. public over years 1–10 (hurdle rate of .11 after taxes)					$1,624 998
Internal rate of return (lease vs. public, after taxes)					29.99%

Note that the net present value of the savings between leasing and public warehousing is $1.6 million compared to the negative net present value in the original analysis. The revised IRR is almost 30 percent compared to the original IRR of 6.13 percent. Clearly, this analysis would support a decision to lease the space.

This case study illustrates how the treatment of different costs affects the outcome of the financial analysis. In this instance, the way in which the lease payments are treated dramatically affects the final decision. The results suggest that all personnel involved in the warehousing analysis process must constantly challenge and carefully evaluate the way in which various cost elements are conceptualized and brought into the analysis process.

Chapter 7

Materials Management and Handling in the Supply Chain

Objectives of This Chapter

LO 7-1   To describe various types of nonautomated and automated materials handling systems.

LO 7-2   To examine the role of computerization and information technologies in materials management and handling.

LO 7-3   To examine the role of packaging in the supply chain.

LO 7-4   To examine the issues of cost, service, and sustainability from the perspective of materials management and handling.

Introduction

There are two primary goals associated with the handling and management of materials by individual firms or by multiple firms in the supply chain: (1) minimize cost and (2) optimize customer service. The importance of efficient and effective materials management across the supply chain is increasing. Material Handling Industry (MHI) defines materials handing as:

> The movement, protection, storage and control of materials and products throughout the process of their manufacture and distribution, consumption and disposal.

Thus, all aspects of supply chain management where items are stored, transported, or manufactured are included within materials management. From a logistics perspective, this would encompass both inbound and outbound logistics activities. The use of technology to manage material flows is widespread and includes the use of barcodes, RFID, satellite tracking systems, robotics, artificial intelligence, blockchain technology, and other software and systems solutions. These technologies combined with traditional materials handling and logistics equipment, systems, and approaches allow manufacturing and supply chains to operate at optimal levels of efficiency and effectiveness.[1]

Table 7.1 identifies some of the more significant events that have occurred in the development of materials management. Not only are physical products handled, but also information; both are assets that organizations must manage successfully. With the advent of Internet e-commerce in the late 1990s, and the use of the Web and improvements in computer and information hardware and software, materials handling developments have occurred with greater frequency. To illustrate, in July 1999, if you typed the words "materials handling" into a Web search engine, it yielded 200+ matches. By 2006, the same search returned almost 4 million hits![2] By 2018, the same Google search would result in 14.5 million hits.

TABLE 7.1
Historical Development of Materials Handling Management

Source: "Celebrate 60 Years of Materials Handling," *Modern Materials Handling*, Vol. 61, No. 5 (May 2006), pp. 35–46, http://www.mmh .com/index.asp?layout =articlePrint&articleID =CA6332658; and Adam Robinson, "The Evolution and History of Supply Chain Management," *Cerasis Infographic*, January 23, 2015, http://cerasis .com/2015/01/23/history -of-supply-chain-management/.

Date	Event	Significance
1887	A rudimentary hand truck is developed	First piece of equipment developed to assist workers in the movement of products.
1925	Use of pallets begins	Allows vertical stacking of products.
1926	Forklift trucks are first used	Greatly improves warehouse efficiency.
1946	First issue of *The Palletizer* was published by Norman Cahners, Director of the Materials Handling Laboratory; becomes *Modern Material Handling* later in the same year	The first magazine on materials handling equipment directed toward the industrial market.
1946	Grocery industry approves standard pallet sizes: 40"× 32" and 48" × 40"	Two standard sizes of pallets would be used in industry to achieve economies of scale.
1947	National Materials Handling Exposition held in Cleveland, Ohio	First conference on materials handling, which attracted 7,500 attendees and 110 exhibitors.
1949	Collapsible cardboard boxes are introduced	Streamlines packing and shipping by reducing costs up to 50 percent.
1950	Materials handling industry reaches $1 billion mark	Total materials handling equipment sales for 1950 = $1.175 billion.
1950s	Two-way radios are introduced into warehouse operations	Significant reductions in time and labor result from outfitting 2-way radios on forklift trucks.
1950s	Materials handling courses and laboratories begun at major U.S. universities	Wayne University establishes materials handling laboratory; Harvard offers summer program in materials handling; and Michigan State offers BS degree in Packaging Technology.
1952	Patent issued for barcoding	Allows products to be identified more easily
1953	First counterbalanced dock-levelers are introduced	Enables trucks of varying sizes to be able to load and unload cargo with optimal efficiency.

(Continued)

[1] MHI, "Definition of Material Handling and Logistics," 2018, http://www.mhi.org/about.
[2] "Celebrating 60 Years of Materials Handling—1990s," http://mmh.com/index.asp?layout =articlePrint&articlesID=CA6332660.

TABLE 7.1
(*Continued*)

Date	Event	Significance
1955	First AGVs introduced	Labor costs are reduced through the use of driverless tractor trains guided by wires strung from the ceiling or installed in the floor.
1955	Pallet loading equipment becomes mechanized	Companies introduce automatic or semiautomatic palletizing machines in their facilities.
1955–57	Warehouse computerization begins	B. F. Goodrich installs an "electronic brain" to track inventory (1955); Stanford University develops a computer program to find most efficient pallet patterns.
1956	Containerization begins in warehousing and transportation	Returnable shipping containers become more widely used by companies in a variety of industries; other containers such as drums and pods are also used.
1958	Cost-efficiency becomes major theme of material handling	Cost-cutting or lean operations become a focus of warehousing and materials handling.
1960–63	Automation becomes widespread in materials handling	First fully automated U.S. Post Office opens in Rhode Island; United Airlines opens mechanized air terminal in San Francisco; Sara Lee opens the first completely automatic food warehouse.
1963	Computer simulation is used to design conveyor layout	One of the earliest uses of computers to develop optimal warehouse layout.
1963–67	New materials are employed for unitization	Nonmetallic materials such as paper, nylon, and polypropylene are used for pallets, shrink wrap, and other materials handling items.
1966	Photocells read printed code patterns	Some sortation systems include photoelectric readers that scan early forms of bar codes.
1967	IBM develops the first computerized inventory management and forecasting system	Increases accuracy and minimizes time of inventory management.
1967–69	Robotics are employed in warehousing	Manufacturers utilize robotic arms for handling hazardous materials and cumbersome and other "difficult" products.
1970	Occupational Safety and Health Act (OSHA) is passed	The most significant and encompassing legislation impacting worker health and safety becomes law in the U.S.
1971–74	High-rise storage facilities are constructed	Storage density is maximized with rack heights reaching 100 feet; narrow-aisle forklift trucks, car-in-lane systems, and mobile racks make dense storage accessible.

Date	Event	Significance
1975	Warehouse Management System (WMS) is introduced at JCPenney warehouse in California	Software is developed and implemented to comprehensively manage all warehouse activities.
1975	Portable hand-held scanners debut	Productivity improvements result from the use of auto ID, high-speed scanners, higher density bar codes, standardized shipping codes, and in-plant printers.
1976–78	More pallet options are implemented in materials handling	Plastic pallets and slip sheets are introduced and become popular in the food industry.
1977	Warehousing Education and Research Council (WERC) is founded	Creation of first practitioner-centered organization dedicated to education and research in warehousing.
1979	Digital displays replace manual lists and computer punch cards	Digital displays allow picking without paperwork; early pick-to-light systems are implemented along with automated case picking.
1980	Patent for 3-D printing is issued	Ability to produce objects with small printers rather than through traditional manufacturing processes.
1983	National Wood Pallet Container Association develops computer program to design pallets	Wood pallet production reaches 300 million units.
1985–89	Computer hardware and software are used extensively in the warehouse	PC developments coupled with improved software allow warehouses to more efficiently and effectively manage operations.
1986	Just-in-time (JIT) and total quality management (TQM) are widely implemented	Warehouses become distribution centers; JIT leads to more frequent shipments, resulting in faster movement of products and delivery vehicles; and TQM leads to more emphasis on reduction of errors and improvements in customer service.
1993	OSHA expands regulations on worker safety	Companies focus on ergonomics with the implementation of tilters, balancers, turntables, pallet positioners, power-assisted dock levelers, and other items that reduce bending, reaching, and pushing.
1994–95	Compliance labeling becomes widespread	Sears, Walmart, and other retailers require suppliers to implement barcoding specifications.
1995	UPS constructs a leading-edge cross-docking facility	Emphasis is placed on increasing the flow through the warehouse using cross-docking and other methods of increasing the speed of materials handling operations.
1995	Forerunner of CPFR is launched by Walmart and Warner-Lambert	Software to manage the collaborative planning and replenishment of products within warehouses.

(Continued)

TABLE 7.1
(*Concluded*)

Date	Event	Significance
1999	E-commerce era begins	Internet usage expands and, with it, a new channel of distribution opens for many retailers and manufacturers.
2000	Reverse logistics emerges as a key aspect of supply chain management	Direct-to-consumer e-commerce places more emphasis on the handling of product returns.
2001	Outsourcing becomes a dominant paradigm for firms	Survey of U.S. manufacturers reveals that three-quarters of all firms use 3PLs for warehousing, transportation, and other services.
2001	Terrorist attacks in the U.S.	Terrorist attacks temporarily disrupt the supply chain and force firms to place more emphasis on risk assessment and contingency planning; traditional philosophies on inventory positioning are re-evaluated.
2002–04	Voice-directed picking systems are widely implemented	Use of "hands-free" systems increases accuracy and speed of picking products in warehouses.
2003	Walmart announces RFID requirements	Largest retailer in the world requires its largest suppliers to implement RFID tags on pallets and cartons.
2004	Lean warehousing debuts	Increasing focus on lowering costs while maintaining efficiency and effectiveness levels.
2010–20	Sustainability and environmental issues become more important	Rising energy prices coupled with fears of climate change cause consumers and the firms that supply them to place more emphasis on sustainability.

As an illustration of the importance of materials handling and management, on Cyber Monday 2016, Amazon reported 426 orders per second on that day. "That equates to over 36 million order transactions, an estimated 250 million picking lines at the distribution centers (DC), 40 million DC package loading scans . . . and 40 million outbound delivery truck scans."[3]

The items that materials management and handling move and store are financial assets. Therefore, it is important that organizations within the supply chain obtain adequate return on assets (ROA) and asset turnover rates. Materials management allows employees to optimally locate, process, and move items in warehouses, distribution centers, manufacturing operations, and retail stores. "Time spent searching for assets eats into productivity, and hence profitability. Workers lose the equivalent of one full 40-hour workweek per year if they spend only 10 minutes a day searching for and gathering needed items."[4]

The financial implications of lost time due to inefficiencies in materials handling can be significant. Utilizing the 10 minutes per day for employees to search for items, lost productive time would be 2,400 minutes per year (based on a 5-day workweek over 48 workweeks

[3] "The 2017 MHI Annual Industry Report, Next-Generation Supply Chains: Digital, On-Demand and Always-On," *MHI and Deloitte Report*, 2017, p. 14.
[4] "Increasing Profits and Productivity: Accurate Asset Tracking and Management with Bar Coding and RFID," *White Paper*, Zebra Technologies Corporation, 2007, p. 1.

per year). If worker wages and benefits equal US$20/hour, that equals $800 per employee. Multiplying the $800 by the number of employees would result in identifying the total lost-time costs for the workforce at a single facility. If multiple facilities are employed, the resulting number could be quite high.

This chapter integrates some of the key components that affect materials management and handling. Warehouse automation, selection and implementation of materials handling systems, packaging issues, digitalization, and information management are all vital issues in materials management within the supply chain.

Materials Handling Equipment

Materials Handling Expenditures Exceed $156 Billion Annually

The Material Handling Industry of America, an industry trade association for companies providing materials handling and logistics solutions for the supply chain, has estimated that the "consumption of material handling and logistics equipment and systems in America exceeds $156 billion per year."[5]

Materials handling equipment and systems often represent major capital outlays for an organization. Like the decisions related to the number, size, and location of warehouses, materials handling can affect many aspects of supply chain operations.

In the following sections, the various types of materials handling systems will be briefly examined. Examples of materials handling equipment include lift trucks; racks and shelving; totes, bins, and containers; dock equipment; packaging; including pallets; conveyors; cranes; automated storage; and automatic guided vehicles. Some of the basic systems will be introduced for the purpose of understanding how these systems can be used to handle, process, and collect information on products and materials used by firms throughout the supply chain.

Not all firms utilize automated systems for materials handling. Many small and medium-size companies have very effective systems that are basically manual, that is, nonautomated. However, firms of all sizes can implement automated systems. The combination of customer requirements and an organization's budgetary constraints will determine whether nonautomated, automated, or some combination of both will be employed in materials handling.[6]

Manual or Nonautomated Systems

Manual or nonautomated materials handling equipment has been the mainstay of the traditional warehouse or DC and will likely continue to be important even with the move toward more digitalization and automation. Generally speaking, manual systems do the best job when there is either very high or very low throughput of products in a warehouse. Manual systems provide a great deal of flexibility in order picking because they use the most flexible handling systems.

Equipment can be categorized according to the functions performed: (1) receiving, (2) storage, (3) order picking, (4) sortation, and (5) shipping/transportation.

Receiving can be performed either manually or via automation. Traditional manual processes typically use a lift truck to move or transfer pallets of incoming products to a location where individual items can be removed and placed into storage, or if the pallet is a single product, the lift truck can move it into its assigned storage location. Table 7.2 identifies some of the major types of lift trucks used for receiving, storage, and order picking.

---

[5] Material Handling Industry of America, 2018, http://www.mhia.org/about.
[6] For the pros and cons of automation and nonautomation, see Bob Trebilcock, "To Automate or Not to Automate," *Modern Materials Handling*, Vol. 66, No. 6 (June 2011), pp. 16–19.

TABLE 7.2
Seven Different Classes of Forklifts

Source: "Forklift Information," *Forklift Select*, 2018, https://www.forkliftselect.com/forklift-information/.

Class 1: Electric-Motor Rider Forklifts

These lifts are electric-motor rider trucks. Trucks in this class may have 3 or 4 wheels with cushion (solid) or pneumatic (air-filled) tires. This class includes both sit-down and stand-up types.

Class 2: Electric Narrow Aisle Forklifts

These lifts have electric motors and are used for narrow aisle or inventory stock/order-picking applications. They have solid tires. This class includes reach and deep (double) reach trucks as well as order-selector trucks, which are also known as "order pickers" or "cherry pickers." Other narrow aisle trucks include stand-up straddles, swing masts, sideloaders, and turret trucks.

Class 3: Electric Hand Pallet Jacks or Walkie/RiderJack Forklifts

Electric or hand-powered pallet jacks are primarily used for loading and unloading trailers and for short horizontal material handling. Low lift electric hand pallet jacks are also known as "walkies." They have solid tires. They use pallet forks or a platform to haul loads several inches off the ground.

Class 4: Internal Combustion Engine (ICE) Cushion Tire Forklifts

Traditional lifts powered by either liquid propane gas (LPG), compressed natural gas (CNG), or gasoline and used primarily indoors.

Class 5: Internal Combustion Engine (ICE) Pneumatic Tire Forklifts

Traditional lifts powered by either liquid propane gas (LPG), compressed natural gas (CNG), gasoline, or diesel fuel and used primarily outdoors.

Class 6: Electric and Internal Combustion Engine Tractor Forklifts

These lifts are sit-down riders or tow tractor forklifts and are supplied with electric or internal combustion engines. Solid or pneumatic tires.

Class 7: Rough Terrain Forklift Trucks

These lifts have pneumatic tires and are almost exclusively powered by diesel engines and used outdoors on rough terrain. Typical applications include agriculture, logging, and construction.

Pallet trucks or jacks are a basic type of unit load handler. They can handle loads of up to 10,000 pounds. The most common type of lift trucks are the *counterbalanced lift trucks*. They can be powered by liquid propane (LP), natural gas, hydrogen fuel cells,[7] diesel, or electric batteries. Units can have three or four wheels with pneumatic or cushion tires and have a capacity of up to 6,500 pounds or 2,955 kilograms. They have a lifting height of about 16 feet.[8] Narrow-aisle lift trucks include various varieties of reach trucks, turret trucks, and order pickers.

For operating in narrow aisle warehouses, *reach trucks* are useful for handling, storing, and retrieving pallets. *Reach trucks, turret trucks,* and *order pickers* are designed for operating in very narrow aisles (e.g., 8 feet or less in width) at heights of 25 feet or more. Rotating masts or forks allow the reach or turret lift trucks to stack pallets without turning. Load capacities of this equipment approximate two tons. The *order-picker lift truck* puts the equipment operator on an elevating platform along with the forks that hold the products. When the forks are raised, so is the operator. The operator then picks the items from the storage racks or shelves and places them onto a pallet or into totes.

[7] An overview of developments in hydrogen fuel cell technology for lift trucks can be found in "The Adoption of Hydrogen Fuel Cell-Powered Lift Trucks," Yale Materials Handling Corporation, 2017, http://www.yale.com/north-america/en-us/solutions-for-you/adoption-of-hydrogen-fuel-cell-powered-lift-trucks/.
[8] Lorie King Rogers, "Lift Truck Basics," *Modern Materials Handling*, August 2011, p. 40, http://www.mmh.com/article/equipment_101_lift_truck_basics.

Totes are simply plastic boxes in which items are placed and usually moved by conveyors or other automated equipment. They are ideal for automated or manual materials handling and picking systems, carousels, mini-loads, tote stackers, and automatic guided vehicles (AGVs). The majority of totes come in standard industry sizes, although specialized sizes are also available. Nonstandard totes are more expensive. The selection of a tote should be based on customer requirements and not system specifications. For example, a company committed to a specific automatic storage and retrieval system (AS/RS) and then investigated the acquisition of 17,000 totes for the system. Because the automated equipment could not handle the standard tote size, the company had to purchase custom-sized totes. The standard tote would have cost it $26.00 each; the custom tote cost $44.50, resulting in a total cost difference of $315,000.[9] The lesson learned is that system decisions should be made together, and not piecemeal.

In addition to lift trucks, *storage and order-picking* equipment includes racks, shelving, drawers, and bins. There are three general types of storage racks, including (1) low-density racks (single-deep rack, double-deep rack); (2) high-density rack (drive-in rack, drive-through rack); and (3) dynamic storage racks (gravity flow rack,[10] push-back rack). Figure 7.1 identifies the basic storage rack configurations. "At left is a single row of free standing pallet rack. Center is two rows of pallet rack setup back to back and tied together in the center. At right is a single row of pallet rack placed against a wall and tied to the wall using wall supports."[11] The major types of shelving, drawers, and bins include bin shelving systems, modular storage drawers, and cabinets.

FIGURE 7.1
Basic Storage Rack Configurations

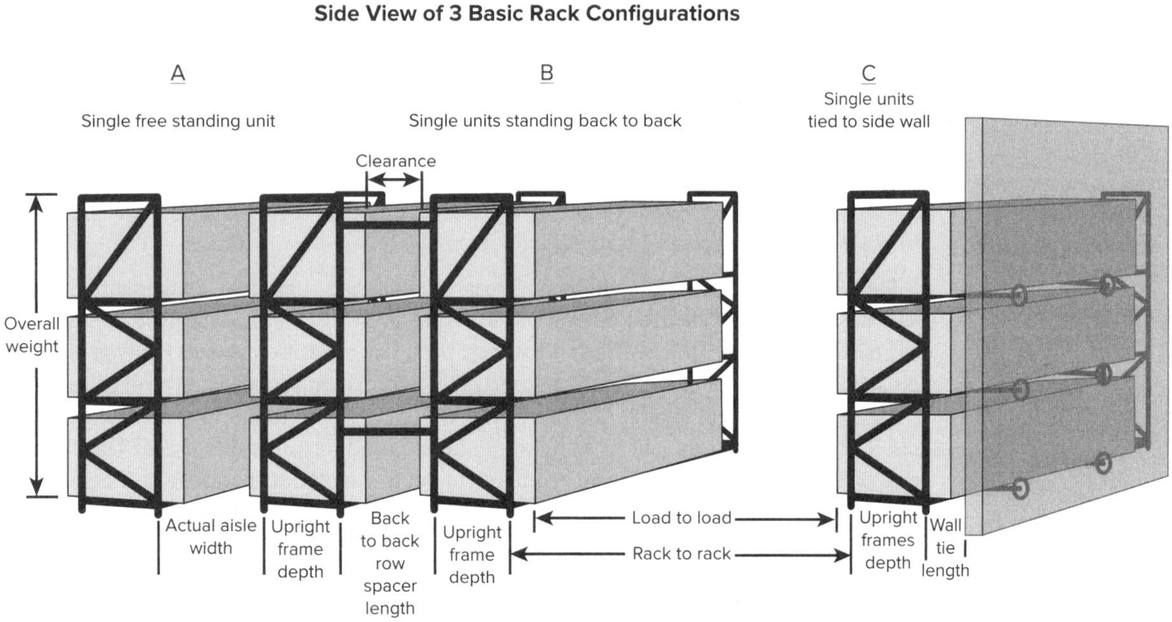

Source: "How to Guide to Pallet Racking Basics," *SJF Material Handling Tutorial*, 2018, https://www.sjf.com/pallet-racking.html.

[9] Clinton McDade, "Automated Warehouse Design: Selecting a Standard Tote First," *White Paper, Schaefer Systems International, Inc.*, 2007, 8 pages.

[10] "Gravity & Carton Flow Racks," Cisco-Eagle, 2018, http://www.cisco-eagle.com/catalog/category/147/gravity-carton-flow.

[11] "How to Guide to Pallet Racking Basics," *SJF Material Handling Tutorial*, 2018, https://www.sjf.com/pallet-racking.html.

TABLE 7.3
Manual Storage Guidelines in Materials Handling

Equipment	Types of Materials	Benefits	Other Considerations
Racking			
Conventional pallet rack	Pallet loads	Good storage density, good product security	Storage density can be increased further by sorting loads two deep
Drive-in racks	Pallet loads	Lift trucks can access loads, good storage density	Lift truck access is from one direction only
Drive-through racks	Pallet loads	Same as above	Lift truck access is from two directions
High-rise racks	Pallet loads	Very high storage density	Often used in AS/RS
Cantilever racks	Long loads or rolls	Designed to store difficult shapes	Each different SKU can be stored on a separate shelf
Pallet stacking frames	Odd-shaped or crushable parts	Allow otherwise unstackable loads to be stacked, saving floor space	Can be disassembled when not in use
Stacking racks	Odd-shaped or crushable parts	Same as above	Can be stacked when not in use
Gravity-flow racks	Unit loads	High-density storage, gravity moves loads	FIFO or LIFO flow of loads
Shelving	Small, loose loads and cases	Inexpensive	Can be combined with drawers for flexibility
Drawers	Small parts and tools	All parts are easily accessed, good security	Can be compartmentalized for many SKUs
Mobile racking or shelving	Pallet loads, loose materials, and cases	Can reduce required floor space by half	Come equipped with safety devices

Source: Originally published as "Storage Equipment for the Warehouse," *Modern Materials Handling 1988 Warehousing Guidebook*, Vol. 40, No. 4 (Spring 1985), p. 53; updated multiple times through 2018 in various forms that can be found at the *Modern Materials Handling* website: http://www.mmh.com.

Table 7.3 describes many different types of materials handling equipment. Storage racks normally store palletized or unitized loads. In most instances, some type of operator-controlled device places the load into the storage rack. The table also presents the type of materials stored, the benefits of the equipment, and other information about each type of equipment.

The storage rack configurations illustrated in Figure 7.1 are found in most storage facilities. They may be permanent or temporary and are used for product storage. They would be considered "standard" or "basic" components of any materials handling strategy. All of these storage racks are easily accessible by materials handling equipment such as lift trucks.

Gravity-flow storage racks are often used to store high-demand items. Products that are of uniform size and shape are well suited for this type of storage system. Items are loaded into the racks from the back, flow to the front of the racks because they are sloped forward, and then are picked from the front of the system by order-picking personnel.

For small parts, bin shelving systems are useful. Items are hand-picked, so the height of the system must be within the physical reach of employees. The full cube of each bin cannot typically be used, so some wasted space exists. Bin shelving systems are relatively inexpensive compared to other storage systems, but they have limited usefulness beyond small parts storage.

The modular storage drawers and cabinets are used for small parts. They are similar in function to bin shelving systems, but they require less physical space and allow items to be concentrated into areas that are easily accessed by employees. The drawers are pulled out and items are then picked. By design, modular storage drawers must be low to the floor, often less than five feet in height, to allow access by employees picking items from the drawers.

The previously described storage systems are classified as "fixed" systems because they are stationary. Others can be classified as "movable" because they are not in fixed positions. The bin shelving systems can be transformed from a fixed to a movable system. In the bin shelving mezzanine, wheels on the bottom of the bins follow tracks in the floors, allowing the bins to be moved and stacked together when not being accessed. This allows maximum utilization of space because full-width aisles are not needed between each bin.

Products are picked from the various storage systems using some order-picking approach. In a manual system, the personnel doing the order picking go to product location. In many cases, the order picker retrieves items from a flow-through gravity storage rack.

The order picker can use a large selection of powered and nonpowered equipment for *transporting and sorting* items located in the racks, shelves, and drawers. Examples of apparatus of this type include lift trucks, hand trucks, cranes, and carts. This equipment performs multiple functions in addition to transportation and sorting, such as order picking.

The manual sorting of items is a very labor-intensive part of materials handling. It involves separating and regrouping picked items into customer orders. In manual systems, personnel physically examine items and place them onto pallets or slip-sheets, or into containers for shipment to customers. This is a time-consuming process subject to human error. As a result, most firms attempt to minimize manual sorting whenever possible. To illustrate, Wet Seal, a specialty retailer of fashion apparel for younger women between 13 and 19 years of age, implemented automated sortation technology at its distribution center in California. As a result, the company was able to eliminate one work shift and reduce labor by 25 percent. Order processing time was reduced from four to five days to less than 24 hours, a significant improvement in customer service. Finally, shipment accuracy improved from 92 to 99.5 percent.[12]

Of particular concern in the materials handling process is "where should products be placed within the storage facility?" This is a *slotting* issue. Slotting impacts the activities of receiving, storage, and order picking. It has been estimated that these activities represent between 50 and 75 percent of the warehouse operating costs, so optimal slotting decisions are important.[13] "An ideal slot location and size minimizes the total cost of handling in the warehouse, specifically, labor cost (both picking and replenishment, including travel time); equipment cost (fixed and mobile); space cost; and the cost of 'shorts,' such as the cost of an out-of-stock pick."[14]

Effective product slotting will result in higher warehouse productivity, including reduced picking time, reduced travel time, and less aisle congestion.[15] Specific techniques that can be used include numbering of aisles so that "fast-moving items are located in the lower-numbered aisles with slow-moving product in the higher-numbered aisles."[16] This optimizes the time necessary to stock and pick items. Promotional, seasonal, or other fast-moving items can be placed on aisle ends to make them more easily accessible, reducing both stocking and picking tasks. Products that are often purchased in combination with other items can also be grouped together. Other ways of optimizing the location of products is to group

[12] Maida Napolitano, "Wet Seal's Slick Transformation," *Logistics Management*, Vol. 50, No. 3 (March 2012), p. 49.

[13] "Renewing Your Slotting Commitment," *WERC News & Notes for Distribution Professionals*, May 20, 2009, https://www.werc.org.

[14] Ibid. Also see Scott Stone, "Flow Storage and Inventory Slotting," Cisco-Eagle, October 26, 2017, http://www.cisco-eagle.com/blog/2017/10/26/whats-the-criteria-for-storing-inventory-in-carton-flow/.

[15] Nicole Pontius, "How Efficient Product Slotting Can Dramatically Boost Warehouse Productivity," Camcode, January 12, 2018, https://www.camcode.com/asset-tags/warehouse-product-slotting/.

[16] Ibid.

FIGURE 7.2
Warehouse Slotting: Before and After

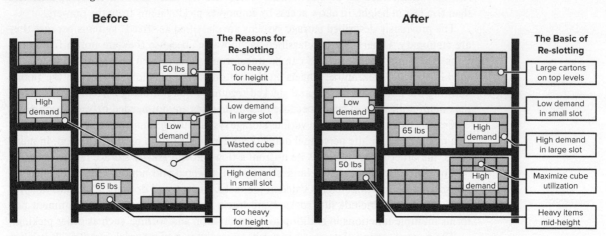

Source: Sara Pearson Specter, "Slotting Basics," *Modern Materials Handling*, Vol. 64, No. 2 (February 2009), pp. 24–26.

them based on similar characteristics, such as whether the items are stored as pallets, cases, or individual SKUs. Products that go to specific customers or customer type can also be slotted together to optimize material handling (see Figure 7.2).

Shipping of products to customers involves preparing items for shipment and loading them onto transportation carriers. The powered and nonpowered equipment previously discussed are used. Additionally, equipment such as pallets, palletizers, strapping machines, and stretch wrappers are important.

Automated Systems

Some facilities have attempted to automate the receiving activity because of the costs associated with manual processes. "In a typical DC, the cost of getting a case of product through the facility is somewhere around $1.05. Automating the front end of the DC could potentially offer a 15–30% cost reduction, reducing handling costs to approximately $0.75 per case."[17]

Automated storage and retrieval systems (AS/RSs), automatic guided vehicles (AGVs),[18] carousels, case-picking and item-picking equipment, conveyors (utilizing wheels, rollers, or belts), robots, and scanning systems have become commonplace in materials handling. As a result, many organizations have been able to achieve improvements in efficiency and productivity. (See Table 7.4 for a brief description of the major types of automated systems.)[19] "Where traditional automation systems were typically permanently installed and bolted to the warehouse floor, the use of mobile robots is building greater flexibility into supply chains."[20]

AS/RS systems are computer-controlled systems that store and pick items in warehouses or DCs. The systems are of two types: unit-load AS/RS (for handling pallets or pallet-sized containers) and mini-load AS/RS (for handling smaller items weighing less than 1,000 pounds in totes, trays, or cartons).[21] Figure 7.3 shows the unit-load and mini-load AS/RSs.

[17] "Industrial Packaging Brings It All Together," *Modern Materials Handling*, Vol. 61, No. 10 (October 2006), p. 74.

[18] For a discussion of AGVs, see Bob Trebilcock, "What Is an AGV?," *Modern Materials Handling*, Vol. 66, No. 6 (June 2011), pp. 22–28.

[19] For a summary of automation in general terms, see Bob Trebilcock, "The State of Automation," *Modern Materials Handling*, Vol. 65, No. 12 (December 2010), pp. 22–27.

[20] "The 2017 MHI Annual Industry Report," p. 26.

[21] Corinne Kator, "AS/RS Basics," *Modern Materials Handling*, Vol. 62, No. 8 (August 2007), pp. 50–52.

TABLE 7.4
Automated Storage Guidelines in Materials Handling

Equipment	Types of Materials	Benefits	Other Considerations
Unit Load AS/RS	Pallet loads, and a wide variety of sizes and shapes	Very high storage density, computer controlled	May offer tax advantages when rack-supported
Car-in-lane	Pallet loads, other unit loads	High storage density	Best used where there are large quantities of only a few SKUs
Mini-load AS/RS	Small parts	High storage density, computer controlled	For flexibility, can be installed in several different configurations
Horizontal carousels	Small parts	Easy access to parts, relatively inexpensive	Can be stacked on top of each other
Vertical carousels	Small parts and tools	High storage density	Can serve dual role as storage and delivery system in multi-floor facilities
Man-ride machines	Small parts	Very flexible	Can be used with high-rise shelving or modular drawers

Source: Originally published as "Storage Equipment for the Warehouse," *Modern Materials Handling 1988 Warehousing Guidebook*, Vol. 40, No. 4 (Spring 1985), p. 53; updated multiple times through 2018 in various forms that can be found at the *Modern Materials Handling* website: http://www.mmh.com.

FIGURE 7.3
Unit-Load and Mini-Load AS/RSs

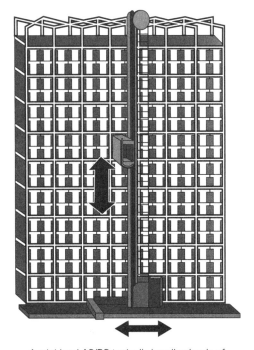

Unit-Load AS/RS

Mini-Load AS/RS

Unit-load AS/RSs automatically put away and retrieve heavy loads stored on pallets or in pallet-sized containers.

A mini-load AS/RS typically handles loads of 1,000 pounds or less in totes, trays, or cartons.

Source: Corinne Kator, "AS/RS Basics," *Modern Material Handling*, Vol. 62, No. 8 (August 2007), pp. 50–53.

Advantages and Disadvantages of Automated Systems

Automated systems can provide several benefits for materials management operations, including operating cost savings, improved service levels, and increased control through more and better information. In studies of users of AS/RSs, the great majority believe that they meet expectations for up time (time that system is operating), ROI, and space savings. For example, the average up time for an AS/RS is 97.34%.[22] However, automated systems are not without disadvantages.

Typical problems faced by firms choosing to automate materials handling operations include the high initial investment, routine maintenance and repair costs, lack of suitability for highly variable operations, and the required technical skill and retaining of employees.[23]

Regarding the cost of automated systems, there are several options available to companies to make the acquisition easier. Firms can purchase, rent, or lease equipment and software. Financing can be arranged from the equipment or software seller, or by using conventional financing through a bank. A general rule of thumb is that in low interest rate environments, if a purchase involves buildings or land, buy it; if the purchase involves equipment, lease it.[24]

Examples of Automated Storage and Order-Picking Equipment

Automated equipment can be grouped into the same categories used to discuss non-automated equipment: (1) receiving, (2) storage, (3) order picking, (4) sortation, and (5) shipping/transportation. Automation can begin immediately upon receipt of products at a warehouse or DC. For example, the German firm GmbH, which produces and sells sensors, controllers, and systems for industrial automation, moved into a new DC. In the DC, the firm utilized a shuttle-based automated storage and retrieval system (AS/RS). "Upon receipt, operators scan goods into the system and deposit them into single- or four-SKU cartons on trays. A shuttle then carries trays to available locations within the racking. For picking, trays are delivered to one of two destinations. Fast-movers, the top 250 products, are delivered as replenishment for the flow racks directly connected to the shuttle system. Slow-movers head to the goods-to-person workstations. Currently capable of handling 800 shipping cartons per hour, the system can be expanded across four additional aisles if demand increases."[25]

Blue Bell Creameries, one of America's "sweet" success stories, produces more than 50 ice cream flavors for supermarkets, convenience stores, and restaurants, primarily in the southeastern U.S. The Blue Bell brand is one of the top three selling brands in the country. Products are stored in a DC where the temperature is −20 degrees Fahrenheit or −29 degrees Centigrade. The Blue Bell AS/RS is nine levels high and includes more than 7,000 pallet storage locations. Approximately 100 pallets per hour are stored or otherwise processed per hour. The pallet storage system can handle pallets of varying sizes, from the 40" × 48" standard grocery pallets to the 36" × 40" Blue Bell pallets.[26]

With respect to the automation of *order picking*, the grocery, pharmaceutical, and cosmetic industries have long used various automated systems to process products. For example, labor costs in a typical grocery DC are incurred in the order-picking process, so

[22] "Do AS/RS Meet Expectations?," *Modern Materials Handling*, Vol. 62, No. 10 (October 2007), p. 3.
[23] Maxwell Ziegler, "Pros and Cons of AS/RS for Warehouse Automation," Conveyco, January 9, 2018, https://www.conveyco.com/pros-cons-asrs-warehouse-automation/.
[24] For an expanded discussion of each financing option, see "Material Handling Financing," Distribution Property Solutions, June 5, 2014, http://www.distributionpropertysolutions.com /material-handling-financing/; also see William Atkinson, "Cash Flow: Material Handling Equipment Financing Strategies," *Modern Handling Management*, Vol. 61, No. 4 (April 2006), pp. 20–23.
[25] Josh Bond, "Automated Storage: How to Grow Operations? . . . Make Them Smaller," *Modern Materials Handling*, January 19, 2018, pp. 17–18, http://www.mmh.com/article/automated_storage _how_to_grow_operations . . . make_them_smaller.
[26] Amanda Loudin, "Blue Bell Creameries Licks Its Storage Shortage," *Inbound Logistics*, Vol. 27, No. 10 (October 2007), pp. 77–79.

automation offers significant financial benefits.[27] In the cosmetics industry, Mary Kay, a large direct seller of makeup and skin care products, utilizes Lesley Cosmetics to distribute its products in Finland, Norway, and Sweden. The small warehouse stocks 600 items, and orders from Independent Beauty Consultants average 17 product lines. With the use of an automated picking system, the warehouse has been able to process 3,000 order lines every day. Picking times improved 200–300 percent. Picking errors were reduced from 1.5 percent to 0.87 percent. From a financial perspective, ROI for the system was one year.[28]

In automated systems, after items are picked from storage, conveyors quickly move the products away from the picking area and move them to the shipping and transportation area. Prior to reaching the shipping location, items must go through a *sortation* process, which prepares products for palletizing, packing, and shipping. "A key component of most modern sortation systems is a fixed-position bar code scanner. The scanner identifies each carton on the conveyor and sends that information to the sortation system controls. The controls have been pre-instructed about the destination of each product and can activate the sortation mechanism when the product arrives at its designated divert point."[29]

Sortation devices are usually classified by the speed of their operation: slow, medium, or high speed. Deflector arms or paddles are often used in slow-speed sorters. Products can also be pushed from the conveyor to the divert line. Medium-speed sortation uses pop-up sorters or belts to divert products. High-speed sorters use tilt trays and sliding shoe techniques to divert items to take-away conveyors.

A. H. Schreiber, women's and girls' swimwear manufacturer producing more than 14 million swimsuits each year under several brand names, had been utilizing manual materials handling systems in its DC. With more than 900,000 cartons shipped yearly, it was difficult for the company to continue providing optimal customer service levels. One of Schreiber's major customers was Target Stores, and in order to provide the necessary service to it, the firm was paying significant amounts of overtime to its employees. Schreiber invested in an automated labeling and sortation system. For its major customer, Target, the fulfillment process runs smoothly with the new system: "Orders received from the retailer are released from Schreiber's homegrown enterprise resource planning (ERP) system to the sortation system. The Schreiber system produces a separate pick ticket for each destination DC. Workers scan the cartons as they place them onto an accumulation conveyor, where the cartons are staged in zones ahead of the labeling section. The system spaces the cartons for optimum system speed and squares up the cartons to ensure proper label application."[30] After applying the label, cartons move to the sorter, where they are directed to one of eight outbound locations.

In the shipping/transportation arena, Valpak, a direct marketing company that ships more than 45 million coupons and promotions to consumers each month, utilizes automation and robotics for materials handling. In a facility in St. Petersburg, Florida, Valpak has installed an impressive array of automated equipment to handle the volume of coupons and mailings that occur each day. The nearly 500,000-square-foot DC employs the use of the following equipment: four-crane unit-load AS/RS (for storing 8,250 pallets); two-crane unit-load AS/RS (for buffer storage); 17-crane mini-load AS/RS (for 8,900 tray storage

[27] For a discussion on calculating the ROI from order fulfillment automation, see Doug Mefford, "Order Fulfillment Optimization: When to Make the Move from Paper Picking to Paperless," Honeywell Intelligrated, December 2017, https://www.intelligrated.com/white-papers/order-fulfillment-optimization.

[28] "High-Speed Order Picking of Cosmetics," *Kardez Remstar Case Study*, 2017, https://automatewarehousing.com/automated-storage-warehousing-distribution/distribution-solutions/high-speed-order-picking-of-cosmetics.

[29] Corinne Kator, "Sortation Basics," *Modern Materials Handling*, Vol. 63, No. 3 (March 2008), pp. 44–46.

[30] Peter Bradley, "Swimwear Maker Takes the Plunge," *DC Velocity*, June 2009, http://www.dcvelocity.com/articles/20090601equipmentapplications/.

locations); 14 AGVs (to transport printer materials); seven rail-guided automatic transfer vehicles (to move pallets); conveyor and sliding shoe sortation systems (transfer totes from mini-load AS/RS to collating area); and four robotic palletizers (for shipping and transport).[31] According to the company, "what used to be touched 10 to 12 times is now only touched once!"

When sufficient product (mailings containing coupons and promotions) is available, "they are retrieved from the mini-load system and sorted to . . . robotic palletizers. After palletizing, a cardboard cap is placed on the load. Then it's strapped in two directions, labeled, and stretch-wrapped. Ready for shipment, it's transferred by an AGV to the AS/RS."[32]

IKEA Utilizes an AS/RS

In totally automated systems, an AS/RS is supplied by conveyors, automated guided vehicles, or electrified monorail systems. IKEA, the international home furnishings company, utilizes an AS/RS in its 800,000-square-foot Savannah, Georgia, DC that serves the southeastern U.S. The facility can handle more than 1.3 million pallets per year. A majority of IKEA's volume into, and out of, the DC is full pallets; hence, a major advantage for having automated systems. The order turnaround time is now 24 hours instead of the 72 hours it took prior to implementing the AS/RS.[33]

Horizontal Carousel

Another form of AS/RS is the carousel. Carousels are mechanical devices that house and rotate items for order picking. The most frequently utilized carousel configurations are the horizontal and vertical systems. A *horizontal carousel* is a linked series of rotating bins of adjustable shelves driven on the top or bottom by a drive motor. Rotation takes place on an axis perpendicular to the floor at approximately 80 feet per minute. To illustrate, "a horizontal carousel is much like the carousel found in a dry cleaning shop. Instead of

Global: Greek Yogurt Producer Utilizes AS/RS and WMS to Achieve Efficiency and Growth

©leolintang/Shutterstock

Although the refrigerated warehouse of the company is only 33' high, which is the height of a typical conventional warehouse, the facility was able to increase storage capacity from 1,600 pallets to 4,100 pallet positions. Unlike the firm's three other plants in Greece, the New York location was not automated until the AS/RS and WMS were implemented.

The AS/RS consists of one storage/retrieval machine, racking, conveyors, and gravity-flow pick lanes. A WMS controls all product movements in the warehouse, including order picking. As a result of the facility update, there has been a 30%+ reduction in energy costs through reduced lighting needs, improved picking efficiency due to the WMS and automatic pick lane replenishment, and a reduction in product damage and need for shrink-wrapping.

Source: MHI, "Designing for Efficiency & Growth in 33' High Warehouse Using AS/RS & WMS," *Case Study*, undated, http://www.mhi.org/downloads/industrygroups/as-rs/casestudies/westfalia-asrs-yogurt.pdf.

[31] Bob Trebilcock, "Special Delivery," *Modern Materials Handling*, Vol. 64, No. 6 (June 2009), pp. 14–17.

[32] Bob Trebilcock, "Valpak's Automated DC Delivers," *Modern Materials Handling*, Vol. 64, No. 6 (June 2009), p. 19.

[33] Julia Ritchey, "IKEA Distribution Center in Savannah Filling Up Fast," *Savannah Now*, May 25, 2014, http://savannahnow.com/exchange/2014-05-24/ikea-distribution-center-savannah-filling-fast; also see Bob Trebilcock, "IKEA Thinks Global, Acts Local," *Modern Materials Handling*, Vol. 63, No. 2 (February 2008), pp. 22–26.

clothes hanging from the top rail, however, wire carriers are suspended from the rail. These carriers typically hold plastic bins full of small products."[34]

Vertical Carousel

A *vertical carousel* is a horizontal carousel turned on its end and enclosed in sheet metal. "Vertical carousels consist of shelves that rotate up and down inside a metal cabinet. These shelves often hold metal trays or plastic bins of small parts."[35] As with horizontal carousels, an order picker operates one or multiple carousels.

Carousel systems have been successfully implemented in a variety of organizations. Industrial Automation Supply (IAS), an electrical controls and automation components distributor, installed a vertical lift module (VLM) in its Portland, Maine, facility. "Prior to purchasing a VLM unit, workers had to walk around the warehouse area picking a single order at a time. This posed a challenge because much of the product that is stored and handled is received in the morning and often has to be shipped out to clients the same day. From the outset, IAS put a lot of thought into how they would optimize the shipping and receiving processes to make them as efficient as possible.

"The new VLM solution produced significant space savings, housing in 98 square feet more than 85% of its 1,500 products, which were previously stored on shelving. Operators report the unit has a very short learning curve and is user-friendly. Another major benefit is increased productivity and picking accuracy. Picking time has been cut in half, which has freed up time to work on other tasks. Using a put-to-light system has also enabled batch picking. Each time the VLM presents a tray, all parts required for multiple orders can be picked at a single time. They are also able to batch pick orders from a single picking location, further increasing throughput and worker efficiency as they no longer have to walk and search for needed items."[36]

The *transportation and shipping* activities are typically performed in combination with storage, order picking, and sorting. The three most-often-used pieces of transportation equipment are conveyors, automatic guided vehicle (AGV) systems, and operator-controlled trucks or tractors.

Many organizations utilize conveyors in their warehousing operations for order fulfillment and materials handling (e.g., receiving, picking, packing, and shipping). The majority of businesses that use some form of conveyors do so to move boxes and packages. The most common types of conveyors used for these tasks are pop-up wheel sorters, sliding shoe sorters, and tilt-tray/cross-belt sorters.[37] Pop-up wheel sorters "consist of wheels or rollers embedded in a belt conveyor which 'pop up' to lift or transfer items at an angle to another downstream conveyor." Sliding shoe sorters "consist of a 'shoe' that is attached to the conveyor surface that positively diverts items onto an aftersort conveyor. This type of sortation system is fed by a single stream of products merged from multiple areas of a building upstream." Tilt-tray and cross-belt sorters "consist of trays mounted to carts which run on a continuous-loop conveyor. These trays 'tilt' and transfer products into a chute when it has reached its sorting destination." Cross-belt sorters are similar but "consist of motorized belt conveyors mounted to carts running on a continuous loop."[38]

The major benefits of conveyors are efficient handling/flow, automation of processes, order fulfillment accuracy, reliability, speed, improved productivity, and reduced costs. Disadvantages include the cost of the system, lack of flexibility once they are installed, and system repairs and maintenance.

---

[34] Kator, "AS/RS Basics," p. 52.

[35] Ibid.

[36] Bond, "Automated Storage: How to Grow Operations?," pp. 5–7.

[37] Raymond Cocozza, "Pros and Cons of Popular Sortation Systems," April 3, 2017, https://www.conveyco.com/pros-cons-popular-sortation-systems/; also see "A Look at Features and Functions of Conveyor Systems," *White Paper*, Reed Research Group, January 2009.

[38] Cocozza, "Pros and Cons of Popular Sortation Systems."

Kroger Company Uses a Conveyor Sorting System to Handle 110,000 Cases per Day

For example, the Kroger Company, a national retail grocery chain in the U.S., has developed a conveyor system that handles over 110,000 cases per day, with a potential capacity of 160,000 cases.[39] What is really interesting about the Kroger automated system is that pallets of product entering the distribution center are only "touched" twice—the automated system performs all of the necessary actions to get the product initially received and put away, and, ultimately, picked, packed, and shipped to its various retail stores. The facility operates 7 days a week and 24 hours each day. The Kroger automated system includes the following components:

- Automatic pallet exchange and depalletizing machines.
- 10-crane unit load automated storage and retrieval system (AS/RS).
- 32-aisle mini-load AS/RS with nearly 400,000 tray positions for temporary storage of cartons.
- Transfer vehicles that deliver pallets from the system receiving area to a pallet exchange station and from the conveyor system to the put-away location.
- Custom designed palletizers and stretch wrap machines for preparing mixed pallets of product for individual stores.[40]

Kroger has realized significant efficiencies in its supply chain, including higher accuracy in orders processed, reduced product damage, and better cube utilization of transportation equipment.

Automatic Guided Vehicles (AGVs)

An automatic guided vehicle (AGV) system includes materials handling equipment that is driverless and moves through a facility over defined paths using floor guidance systems. "Navigation is achieved by following a path defined by buried inductive wires, surface mounted magnetic or optical strips; or alternatively by way of inertial or laser guidance."[41]

AGVs are often used in automated warehouse operations involving an AS/RS. The benefits of AGV systems include reduced labor costs, increased safety, increased accuracy and productivity, and the ease of adding additional AGVs as necessary. Disadvantages include high initial investment, not being suitable for nonrepetitive tasks, and decreased flexibility of operations.[42] While relatively few firms utilize AGVs, the market is expected to more than triple to US$4 billion by 2026.[43]

NASA, located at the Kennedy Space Center in Florida, implemented AGVs more than a decade ago to allow it to process 200 components per hour. Prior to the implementation of the AGVs, NASA was able to process less than half that amount of components. NASA replaced a conveyor system with the AGVs, which provided it with more floor coverage and higher reliability. The AGV system is integrated with the WMS and manages thousands of SKUs.[44]

Operator-controlled trucks or tractors can also play an important role in materials handling automation. Small tractors pull carts of parts, components, or completed products to

[39] Bob Trebilcock, "Kroger Changes the Game," *Modern Materials Handling*, Vol. 64, No. 5 (May 2009), p. 18.
[40] Ibid., pp. 17–18.
[41] MHI, "Automatic Guided Vehicle Systems (AGVS)," 2018, http://www.mhi.org/agvs.
[42] Chris Benevides, "The Advantages and Disadvantages of Automated Guided Vehicles (AGVs)," Conveyco, November 7, 2016, https://www.conveyco.com/advantages-disadvantages-automated-guided-vehicles-agvs/.
[43] "Global Automated Guided Vehicle (AGV) Market Is Estimated to Reach USD 3977.8 Million in 2026: Polaris Market Research," *EIN Newsdesk*, 2018, https://www.einnews.com/pr_news/431019784/global-automated-guided-vehicle-agv-market-is-estimated-to-reach-usd-3977-8-million-in-2026-polaris-market-research.
[44] Noël P. Bodenburg, "NASA's Workhorse: AGVs," *Modern Materials Handling*, Vol. 61, No. 13 (December 2006), p. 61.

and from various points in the warehouse of a manufacturing facility. Operator-controlled trucks, or *tuggers*, move parts and other items from storage to the manufacturing floor.

The robot is another type of equipment used in many phases of materials handling. Robots have been used in the manufacturing process for some time. However, advances in robotics technology have enabled robots to be used in a large number of materials handling applications.[45] It is likely that materials handling robots will have steady growth in many application areas. To illustrate, Amazon's acquisition of Kiva (now called Amazon Robotics), the company that first introduced robots into warehouses, demonstrated the significance of bringing the product to the DC worker rather than the worker going to the product-slotting location. These robots can move independently using sensors and cameras, rather than traveling on fixed paths as would AGVs. They travel at approximately 1 meter/second and can carry up to 1,300 pounds or 591 kilograms.[46] Sometimes referred to as "goods-to-person systems," these robotic carriers bring cases and totes of products to stations and then return the products to storage. "The pick and placement of items is directed and the operator works at a highly effective rate due to no travel, system direction, and the fast introduction and removal of goods and orders to process."[47]

Staples utilizes robotic materials handling equipment in its many fulfillment centers. The equipment can pick items with high or low throughput rates. The Staples facilities employ two types of automated guided vehicles in the AS/RS that bring items to a centralized pick and pack station. The result is a "win-win" situation for Staples inasmuch as the system requires less capital investment and increases facility productivity and picking accuracy.[48]

Kroger, as mentioned earlier, one of the largest grocery chains in the United States, opened a new 215,000-square-foot DC in Denver, Colorado. The new facility processes regular and organic milk in half-gallon and gallon containers. The facility has a fully automated, robotic production storage, handling, and order-processing system. "The system can store up to 36,000 crates and is able to pick 32,000 crates per day with 100% accuracy.

"The solution includes a warehouse management system (WMS), robotic gantries, software modules and an inter-platform communications system. Instead of installing a traditional in-floor mounted 'drag-chain' style conveyor, the system handles stacks or single plastic dairy cases on knee-high plastic belt conveyors. The cases and/or stacks are picked according to Kroger's specified sequence on one end of the facility and then palletized for truck loading onto delivery trucks at the other end of the facility, allowing for significant storage buffering in between."[49]

Warehouse Information Systems and Computer Technology

In the past two decades, the most significant advances in technology have occurred in the information transfer area. The movement and storage functions require computerization at the mechanical level, where machines and equipment are utilized. There is also an electronic level, which requires computer-to-computer interface and involves data transmission.

[45] For a discussion of robotics and the ROI of robotics, see "The ROI of Robotics: Financial and Operational Sense," Yale Materials Handling Corporation, 2017, http://www.yale.com/north-america/en-us/solutions-for-you/The-ROI-of-Robotics/.
[46] Tompkins International Staff, "Robots in the Warehouse: A Supply Chain Game-Changer," Tompkins International, November 28, 2017, https://www.tompkinsinc.com/en-us/Services/Tompkins-Robotics/robots-in-the-warehouse-a-supply-chain-game-changer.
[47] Mike Futch, "Rise of the Warehouse Robots," *Material Handling & Logistics*, October 18, 2017, p. 6, http://www.mhlnews.com/technology-automation/rise-warehouse-robots.
[48] Mike Duff, "Staples Rolls Out Robotic Fulfillment Solution," July 20, 2017, https://www.homeworldbusiness.com/staples-introduces-robotic-fulfillment-solution/.
[49] Bond, "Automated Storage: How to Grow Operations?," pp. 5–7.

An important question facing materials management executives specifically, and supply chain executives generally, is when, and if, newer technology will replace old. This is particularly true in the electronic commerce arena, where electronic data interchange (EDI) is being evaluated relative to use of the Internet, artificial intelligence (AI), and blockchains. Likely, these technologies will continue to be utilized by organizations, much like some firms use public versus private warehousing, or contract versus common carriers. The technologies move data between individuals, departments, organizations, and other members of the supply chain.

Whichever approach a firm uses, the objectives are the same: to provide better control and security of information flows and to allow the warehouse facility to maximize effectiveness and efficiency. The roles of information and computer technology in materials management are significant, and growing every day. The pace of technological change is quickening, and supply chain executives often find themselves saying something like the following:

> You've undoubtedly been through it before—you purchase a new piece of technology or software, mastered it, then six months down the road find that it has become virtually obsolete. After the investment in time, money and energy, it's time to start over again with the latest and greatest to keep . . . moving forward.[50]

Of course, "staying on top" of the latest technology isn't easy, but it has become a necessity for successful materials management.

The importance of information in materials management is significant. Accurate and timely information allows a firm to minimize inventories, improve routing and scheduling of transportation vehicles, and generally improve customer service levels. Warehouse management systems (WMSs) were introduced in the previous chapter (Chapter 6). We will discuss the use of WMSs in more detail in this chapter.

A typical warehouse management system (WMS) achieves these improvements in three ways: (1) by reducing direct labor, (2) by increasing materials handling equipment efficiency, and (3) by increasing warehouse space utilization. For example, Eaton Corporation installed a WMS and improved shipping productivity by 700 percent and consolidated 13 warehouses into one facility.[51]

This has brought about the rapid development of industrial networks—a hardware and software solution that interconnects computers, peripherals, programmable controllers, and other intelligent devices. In effect, the handling and storage equipment they control are linked together. Networks are communications systems that allow transmission of data between a number and variety of devices such as terminals, word processors, bar code readers, robots, conveyors, automatic guided vehicles, and AS/RS.

In the future, materials management will move toward more and more computer utilization and systems that manage information and facilitate communication internally and externally with supply chain partners.

Warehouse Management Systems (WMSs)

In controlling warehouse operations and material handling processes, warehouse management systems (WMSs) are utilized in all kinds of organizations, including government, commercial businesses, and nonprofits.[52] If the WMS is used in an automated facility, it is usually referred to as a warehouse control system (WCS). Sometimes, both are used in

---

[50] "Mastering Technology," *WERCsheet*, Vol. 22, No. 1 (January 1999), p. 14.

[51] "Eaton Corporation Reduces Cost per Line Item in Warehouse by 40% Using Robocom's Warehouse Management Solutions," Robocom, press release, August 12, 2009.

[52] For an overview of the major WMS providers and the respective software that they offer, see Tom Gresham, "Top 6 Factors for Selecting and Implementing a WMS," *Inbound Logistics*, September 2017, pp. 107–15, http://resources.inboundlogistics.com/digital/WMSGuide_digital_0917.pdf.

tandem; i.e., the WMS manages inventory and orders, while the WCS runs the automated equipment.[53] For our discussion, we will treat them as being the same because they both manage materials in a storage facility.

As part of what is referred to as supply chain execution software, which is a US$1.5+ billion industry, WMS accounts for more than one-half of the industry.[54] WMG usage is growing rapidly and is estimated to be at $3.1 billion in the next five years.[55] Very simply, a WMS keeps track of inventory in a warehouse or DC, and administers tasks such as receiving, putaway, storage, and order picking. Don's Cold Storage, a warehousing company located in Rogers, Arkansas, was faced with the typical challenges confronting warehouse operators, namely pressure to meet growing demand, smaller order sizes, shorter lead times, and higher accuracy. The firm utilized Datex Corporation to provide consulting, hardware, and WMS software. "The system offered by Datex is based on the use of Radio Frequency and handheld devices, allowing the capture and management of information and tasks in real-time. This increases Don's accuracy when it comes to allocating inventory to different orders. During the receiving process, the company is able to capture product temperature, lot IDs, expiration date, weight, volume, pallet inventory, accessorial charges, and any other information that their particular business process may require. An e-portal was also included in the solution allowing Don's clients access to their information in real time."[56]

Merchandise Warehouse Company (MWC), located in Indianapolis, Indiana, provides storage services for the food, grocery, pharmaceutical, and general commodity industries. "MWC provides a wide array of value-added services including blast freezing, tempering, inspection, labeling, temperature monitoring, kitting and assembly, import/export and packaging. MWC was seeking new warehouse software in order to resolve communication issues, eliminate redundancy in paperwork and provide the flexibility needed to meet customer requirements. In addition, there was a need for real time information, greater accuracy and optimization of labor resources."[57]

Exhibit: Warehouse Management System (WMS) at GUESS?

GUESS? manufactures jeans and distributes them worldwide. In the United States, GUESS? constructed a new warehouse in Louisville, Kentucky to service its U.S. customers. "At one point the company mixed all multi-channel inventory together. Today, the company segregates wholesale and retail (including direct-to-consumer) inventory to better support its company structure as two business sectors under separate P&Ls.

With wholesale and retail inventory physically separated, GUESS? can interface each of its host systems directly with the warehouse management solution. Because direct-to-consumer inventory is mixed with retail, consumers can purchase goods online and return them at a store. The flexibility helps GUESS? present a unified brand to its multi-channel customer base.

Source: "Warehouse Management Helps GUESS? Makeover Its Warehouse and Distribution System," *Manhattan Case Study,* 2013, http://www.manh.com/sites/default/files/sys/en/document/manh-guess-makesover-its-warehouse-and-distribution-system-case-study-en.pdf.

---

[53] For a discussion of a WCS, see Scott Stone, "WCS vs. WMS: Complementary Warehouse Software," Cisco-Eagle, March 16, 2014, http://www.cisco-eagle.com/blog/2014/03/16/wcs-vs-wms-complimentary-roles/.

[54] James A. Cooke, "The Race isn't Over . . .," *DC Velocity,* Vol. 6, No. 1 (January 2008), p. 54.

[55] Seapee Bajaj, "Warehouse Management Systems Market by Industry Verticle (Automotive, Electronics, Food & Beverage, Transportation & Logistics, Pharmaceutical & Others)—Global Opportunity Analysis and Industry Forecast, 2014–2022," *Allied Market Research,* December 2016, https://www.alliedmarketresearch.com/warehouse-management-system-market.

[56] "Don's Cold Storage Case Study," *Datex Case Study,* undated, https://www.datexcorp.com/wp-content/uploads/Dons_CaseStudy_Web.pdf.

[57] "Merchandise Warehouse Company Case Study," *Datex Case Study,* undated, https://www.datexcorp.com/wp-content/uploads/2016/06/datex-case-study-merchandise-warehouse.pdf.

The company used a combination approach to solving its challenges. Handheld mobile computers were acquired, along with the Datex FootPrint WMS. The WMS enabled MWC to customize operations, reporting, billing, and more to suit its varied customer needs. "Using the workflow-based warehouse management system, MWC now can automate processes specifically developed for each customer. This helps to ensure greater accuracy and labor productivity."[58]

Real-Time Location Systems

As we have discussed, materials management allows employees to optimally locate, process, and move items in warehouses, distribution centers, manufacturing operations, and retail stores. The expression "time is money" is very appropriate when it comes to making the supply chain "visible" and efficient. The use of bar codes, RFID, GPS, voice technology, and pick-to-light systems are just a few of the many examples of technologies that provide real-time location data.

Bar Coding and Radio Frequency Identification (RFID)

In controlling the movement, storage, and processing of materials, which we earlier stated were assets that organizations need to manage efficiently and effectively, it is necessary to be able to identify items quickly and accurately. Bar codes and RFID are two technologies that are utilized.

Bar codes were developed more than 40 years ago. "A cashier at a Marsh Supermarket in Ohio scanned a pack of gum and the Uniform Product Code (UPC) took its first step to becoming the standard for tracking merchandise at retail."[59] The present UPC includes 12 machine-readable digits that identify items and their manufacturer. The UPC is used to scan billions of items each day at facilities around the world.

As an example of bar code technology, Kitsap County, Washington, operates an automated system for keeping track of the location, condition, and age of 18,000 road and street signs. "Each sign is labeled with an 11-digit serial number that is printed in text and a bar code. The serial number uses a schema that uniquely identifies the sign and describes its location. Whenever there is action performed on the sign, such as new placement, removal for repair, application of new coating or other maintenance, the serial number and activity is recorded in the field and re-entered into the county's database application."[60] In sum, bar codes have many advantages for firms as they manage inventory throughout the supply chain.

Radio frequency identification (RFID) is a more recent development in real-time location systems, although, due to a multiplicity of factors, implementation has been slow and sporadic. The technology utilizes two major components: a microchip or integrated circuit and an antenna. Digital data encoded in an RFID tag or "smart label" is captured by a reader using radio waves. The RFID tags can be either active or passive. Active tags have a power source and can transmit signals. Passive RFID tags have no power source but can be read using incoming waves from an RFID reader. Simply, RFID is similar to bar code technology but uses radio waves to capture data from tags, rather than optically scanning the bar codes from a label on the product.[61]

At a manufacturing plant in Finland, Siemens Enterprise Communications Manufacturing has implemented RFID in its business telephones. The firm embeds an

[58] Ibid.
[59] George Anderson, "The Barcode Turns 40, What Comes Next?," *Retail Wire*, June 27, 2014, http://www.retailwire.com/discussion/the-barcode-turns-40-what-comes-next/.
[60] "Increasing Profits and Productivity: Accurate Asset Tracking and Management with Bar Coding and RFID," *White Paper*, Zebra Technologies Corporation, 2007, p. 3.
[61] Shain Armstrong, "RFID Basics: How RFID Tags Work," *RFID Insider*, November 24, 2011, https://blog .atlasrfidstore.com/rfid-tag-basics.

Technology: Dairy Queen Offers RFID in Addition to Ice Cream, Hamburgers, and Hot Dogs

©Prasit photo/Getty Images

In a breakthrough use of technology, Dairy Queen implemented a mobile rewards loyalty program using RFID to send coupons and offers to consumers' smartphones. Customers place an RFID tag on their smartphones and are given instructions on how to text a code to activate their loyalty rewards membership. The company then sends out weekly offers on desserts, hamburgers, hot dogs, and beverages.

Here's how the system works: The customer receives a standard text message from Dairy Queen that they can redeem at any Dairy Queen store in their area. Offers are redeemed electronically using existing in-store RFID terminals. An added benefit is that the system can be used at other retailers in addition to Dairy Queen if the consumer signs up for other loyalty programs.

Source: "Dairy Queen Launches RFID-Based Mobile Loyalty Program," *Mobile Marketer*, undated, https://www.mobilemarketer.com/ex/mobilemarketer/cms/news/commerce/3380.html; for company statistics see https://www.dairyqueen.com/us-en/Company/About-Us/.

RFID tag inside each telephone that contains a unique product identification number. The information is used for multiple purposes. First, the product is packed and labeled based on the RFID-embedded information. "Data from the tagged phones are read in the logistics center without having to unpack them from the outer boxes. Previously all products had to be identified manually. . . . It is possible to track customer deliveries and gain base data for evaluations and stock overviews. . . . In cases where several hundreds or thousands of phones need installations or updates, it is a major saving in time and resources when this can be done electronically."[62]

Another interesting example of the application of RFID technology is the Moscow Metro transportation system. The city has phased out its magnetic swipe payment cards for RFID-based tickets. The Moscow Metro carries more than eight million passengers each day.[63] Multiple suppliers will provide the 30 million tickets needed each month. Significant cost savings and accuracy are anticipated.

Lord & Taylor was having difficulty in keeping track of shoes on display in its Fifth Avenue store in New York. To monitor the inventory of shoes, workers had to physically handle each pair of shoes so that they could be scanned by their bar code readers. It took about six to eight hours for two to four people to scan every pair of shoes in the store's inventory. By utilizing passive RFID tags, the store was able to monitor its inventory in real time.[64] Labor costs were reduced by 75 percent and Lord & Taylor can now manage existing inventory in less time and with higher accuracy. The system has now been implemented in all of its 48 stores in the United States.

In the food and beverage industry, New Belgium Brewing, a craft beer produced in Colorado, introduced RFID so that it could track its beer kegs. The RFID system lets the brewer know which beer kegs are being filled most often and with what brand of beer. Additionally, it will allow the company to know other information such as where

[62] Editorial Staff, "Siemens Unit Tackles Embedded Item-Level RFID Tagging of Consumer Electronics," *Supply & Demand Chain Executive*, August 10, 2009, http://sdcexec.com, accessed August 12, 2009.
[63] John R. Johnson, "RFID Gets a Thumbs-up in Moscow," *DC Velocity*, Vol. 5, No. 3 (March 2007), p. 33.
[64] DC Velocity Staff, "RFID Helps Lord & Taylor Manage Retail Displays," *DC Velocity*, February 10, 2017, http://www.dcvelocity.com/articles/20170210-rfid-helps-lord--taylor-manage-retail-displays/.

the kegs are located, the length of time the keg spends at the distributor, and keg turn-over rates.[65]

Overall, the adoption and implementation of RFID has been slower than originally anticipated when the technology was introduced. Although some major international companies and organizations have implemented RFID—U.S. Department of Defense, Target Stores, Walmart—a majority of companies have yet to do so. Part of the reason for the slow pace has been the cost of tags and equipment. Over time, however, prices will decline and more firms will take advantage of this technology that allows them to track and trace their products.[66] The importance of being able to locate products in the supply chain is very important, so implementation of RFID and other technologies should only increase.

Global Positioning Systems (GPSs)

In the same way that global positioning systems (GPSs) in automobiles such as Garmin, Magellan, Motorola, and TomTom are able to locate destinations, give directions, and let people know where they are, so too does GPS assist supply chain organizations in locating and tracking products in their supply chains. Creating the transparent supply chain requires that the location of products be known, whenever and wherever they may be in the supply chain. The information must be real time and accurate. With such information, organizations can make optimal decisions regarding the movement and storage of products, and also provide up-to-the-minute information to customers, suppliers, and vendors.

One aspect of the use of GPS technology is the ability to reduce product theft from containers or transport vehicles. For example, automotive plants have used GPS to track containers at sea and locate inventory entering U.S. ports. "If, for instance, an automotive plant is waiting on a delivery of parts for production on a particular car, any holdup could cost them as much as several thousand dollars a minute. . . . The ability to quickly locate the container at the port that has the parts so they can be routed to the manufacturing plant quickly has a real benefit."[67]

For many mass merchandising companies such as Walmart, Target, and Tesco, use of GPS technology can provide better asset tracking that could reduce inventory costs and product stock-outs. Combining the use of mobile GPS tracking on smartphones and an automated TMS would mitigate some of the problems associated with last-mile delivery and delays in shipments from overseas. Container locations could be identified and bottle-necks could be addressed in real time.[68]

Order Picking and Selection

The speed and accuracy of the order cycle are dependent on the ability of companies to pick and select the proper items for manufacturing, assembly, and shipment. There are three general forms of order picking used in warehouses and DCs, including discrete, batch, and "pick and pass." The information used by the people picking items is usually generated by the WMS, if the system is automated.

[65] "Fluensee: New Belgium Brewing Uses Fluensee's RFID Solution for Accurate Beer Keg Data," *Packaging Digest*, May 18, 2009, http://www.packagingdigest.com, accessed June 2, 2009.
[66] See John R. Johnson, "Money Can't Buy Me . . . Efficiency," *DC Velocity*, Vol. 3, No. 5 (May 2005), pp. 57–58; and Jean V. Murphy, "On the Edge: Understanding the RFID Framework," *Global Logistics & Supply Chain Strategies*, February 1, 2005, http://www.supplychainbrain.com.
[67] Beth Stackpole, "GPS Technology Helps Thwart Product Theft," *TechTarget*, December 2012, http://searcherp.techtarget.com/feature/GPS-technology-steers-towards-the-manufacturing-supply-chain.
[68] Batool Alhenaki, "Using GIS/GPS to Optimize Supply Chain Management and Logistics at Walmart," *International Journal of Scientific & Engineering Research*, Vol. 7, Issue 6 (June 2016), pp. 745–48, https://www.ijser.org/researchpaper/Using-GIS-GPS-to-Optimize-Supply-Chain-Management-and-Logistics-at-Walmart.pdf.

Discrete picking is where items are picked one item at a time, until the entire order has been picked. While this approach optimizes cycle time for a single order, it increases average cycle times for all orders and requires employees to travel the greatest distances (because only one order is being selected). Batch picking is where multiple orders are picked at the same time, thus saving travel time and distance, and minimizing cycle time for multiple orders. "Pick and pass" is where employees are assigned specific areas or zones of the warehouse/DC. They pick items within their zone and pass the collection equipment on to another employee, who then picks additional items from another area or zone.[69]

However, in some instances, the products can come to the employee who needs to pick them. For example, Kiva robots move products in Amazon warehouses directly to the individual work stations, where they are picked by an employee for shipment to customers. "In case you haven't seen the Kiva robot, it's a square-shaped, yellow machine that runs on wheels. They're about 16 inches tall and weigh almost 320 pounds. They can run at a steady 5 mph and haul packages weighing up to 700 pounds." The Kiva robots have reduced operating expenses by 20 percent, which translates into US$22 million in cost savings for each fulfillment center.[70]

Approaches to Order Picking

The task of order picking can be grouped into four categories: discrete picking, batch picking, zone picking, and wave picking.

- *Discrete picking* is one means of selecting an order. One order picker takes a single order and fills it from start to finish.
- With *batch picking* the order picker takes a group of orders, perhaps a dozen. A batch list is prepared that contains the total quantity of each SKU found in the whole group. The order picker then collects the batch and takes it to a staging area, where it is separated into single orders.
- *Zone picking* assigns each order selector to a given zone of the warehouse. Under a zone picking plan, one order picker selects all parts of the order that are found in a given aisle and then passes the order to another picker, who selects all of the items in another aisle, and so on. Under this system, the order is almost always handled by more than one individual.
- *Wave picking* groups shipments by a given characteristic, such as common carrier. For example, all of the orders for UPS might be picked in a single wave. A second wave would pull all of the orders destined for parcel post, and still other waves would select shipments routed by other carriers.[71]

When picking items, employees will use various types of technologies, including voice and pick-to-light systems, as well as manual systems.[72]

Voice Technology

"Growing in popularity, voice technology frees the picker's hands and eyes. Voice commands direct the picker to the next location; once there, the picker verifies the location

[69] Allison Manning, "Order Picking Basics," *Modern Materials Handling*, Vol. 63, No. 10 (October 2008), pp. 38–41.

[70] Eugene Kim, "Amazon's $775 Million Deal for Robotics Company Kiva Is Starting to Look Really Smart," *Business Insider*, June 15, 2016, http://www.businessinsider.com/kiva-robots-save-money-for-amazon-2016-6.

[71] See Tom Singer, "Catching a Wave: Is Wave Picking Right for You?," *WERCSheet,* Vol. 29, No. 10 (November 2006), pp. 1–4; for a discussion of waveless picking, see Peter Bradley, "Go with the Flow," *DC Velocity*, Vol. 6, No. 9 (September 2008), pp. 75–80.

[72] For another approach to order picking that is not dependent on technology, see Dan Gilmore, "Bees, Order Picking and Self-Organizing Logistics Systems," *Supply Chain Digest*, July 6, 2007, http://www.scdigest.com/assets/FirstThoughts/07-07-06.php.

by reading a check digit and verifies the pick by telling the device when an item has been selected. Voice devices are available in multiple languages."[73]

Dunkin' Donuts is the largest coffee and baked goods retailer in the world, selling coffee, donuts, sandwiches, and other food products. In its Mid-Atlantic Distribution Center (MADC), the company installed voice technology to enhance the ordering process from franchisee owners. The company implemented "VoiceLogistics, a voice-directed handling application that delivered significant benefits in workforce utilization, and enabled Dunkin' Donuts MADC to manage its growth while maintaining extremely high service levels. . . . When a selector arrives at a pick location, he or she is directed to pick all units of the item needed for all of the stops; the VoiceLogistics software directs the selector to put the correct number of items in the appropriate pallet location corresponding to each stop."[74] Picking accuracy has been as high as 99.9 percent with picking time reduced from 21 hours to 9 or 10 hours.

Many of the newer technologies, including voice, can be implemented by smaller firms as well. In Canada, Longos Brothers Fruit markets, a family-owned grocery chain, installed voice and bar code scanning systems in its Canadian DC. The new systems have allowed the company to increase its handling productivity from 140 to 164 cases per hour.[75]

Generally, the use of voice technology is increasing, with many firms utilizing the technology to improve productivity and accuracy in materials handling. Typically, the payback period for the installation of such systems is relatively short, justifying the expense of the equipment and software to support it.

Pick-to-Light Systems

Pick-to-light systems originated in the 1980s and are utilized to increase the accuracy and speed of picking items in a warehouse/DC. Sometimes, "put-to-light" systems are used. "Put-to-Light systems are an effective automated sortation method to break larger quantities of product into individual customer orders, using light devices to direct operators to 'put' items. Sometimes the Put-to-Light approach is referred to as 'scan and sort.' Merchandise that is typically batch picked beforehand is brought to a put station. Operators scan bar codes on individual pieces of merchandise, then lights turn on at any individual customer orders requiring that product. . . . Put-to-Light is frequently combined with computer monitor/LCD Displays, RF, Voice and/or other technologies on carts to enhance the accuracy of batch picking processes. One of these complementary technologies guides operators to the right product locations in a warehouse. Then an RF scan is used to confirm the correct shelf location and/or product is selected, lights on the cart guide necessary 'puts' to totes. These automated carts are often referred to as mobile Put-to-Light stations."[76]

How does a pick-to-light system work? "In a typical pick-to-light system, the operator scans a barcode attached to either a shipping carton or a tote, which is a reusable container for holding items temporarily. Alphanumeric displays—typically, light-emitting diodes (LEDs)—illuminate to guide the operator to the right storage location and indicate the number of items to be picked. The operator places the items in the container and confirms the activity, usually by pressing a button near the display. Displays continue to light up in the operator's work zone, directing them to the next picking location."[77]

---

[73] Manning, "Order Picking Basics," p. 41.

[74] "Voice Logistics Helps Dunkin' Donuts Deliver," *Voxware Case Study*, undated, http://www.werc .org/assets/1/workflow_staging/Publications/593.PDF.

[75] Bob Trebilcock, "Using Voice and Bar Code Scanning at Longos," *Modern Materials Handling*, Vol. 64, No. 7 (July 2009), p. 31.

[76] "Put to Light," *MHI Blog*, 2018, http://www.mhi.org/solutions-community/solutions-guide/put-to-light.

[77] "Pick to Light," *TechTarget*, March 2017, http://www.earcherp.techtarget.com/definition/pick-to-light.

The potential benefits of pick-to-light systems are numerous, such as reduced manpower requirements, substantially reduced errors in order picking, and real-time order tracking. Sorting and picking productivity is often double that of manual picking, and reduces space requirements.[78]

Hair care products manufacturer Goody Products was one of the early adopters of pick-to-light systems. However, over time, its system became obsolete. The firm installed a new pick-to-light system because of the benefits that had been achieved from the old system. Amazingly, after an initial study, the old system was replaced by the new system in a weekend. "The system notifies Goody by e-mail when inventory at a particular location runs low and needs to be replenished. Every two hours, it reports on whether the DC is maintaining the necessary picking performance levels, and Goody now can get statistics on individuals' productivity."[79] Overall, the new system has resulted in improvements in productivity of 23 percent and order-picking accuracy from 98.94 to 99.35 percent.

Packaging

Packaging is an important materials management issue and closely tied to efficiency and effectiveness. The best package optimizes service, cost, convenience, and sustainability. Good packaging has positive impacts on firms in the supply chain and their customers. We will overview the functions of packaging, discuss use of pallets to move and store products, examine some of the trade-offs between packaging and other supply chain activities, and look at packaging sustainability issues.

Functions of Packaging

Packaging Serves Two Primary Functions within the Supply Chain: Marketing and Logistics

Packaging serves two primary functions within the supply chain: marketing and logistics. In its marketing function, the package provides customers with information about the product, such as directions for use, ingredients or components contained in the product, and identification of the product's manufacturer. It also promotes the product through the use of color, sizing, photographs, labels, and so forth. From a logistics perspective, the functions of packaging are to organize, protect, and identify products and materials. In performing these functions, the package takes up space and adds weight. Industrial users of packaging strive to gain the advantages packaging offers while minimizing the disadvantages, such as added space and weight. We are getting closer to that ideal in several types of packaging, including corrugated containers, foam-in-place packaging, stretch wrapping, and strapping. Technology has created packaging machines that can produce custom-sized packages, so all packages do not have to be the same size.[80] With issues of sustainability becoming more important, the amount of packaging used has decreased for many consumer and industrial products. The environmental and sustainability aspects of packaging are also important because of the issue of reverse logistics.[81]

For example, relating to sustainability, Procter & Gamble has developed a shipping container for its Alldays feminine liners marketed in Germany. Its innovative design has won a DuPont Award for Packaging Innovation. The innovation reduces packaging

---

[78] Ibid. For a case example, see *Lighting Up the Lean Supply Chain: Pick-to-Light in Manufacturing Applications* (Germantown, WI: Lightning Pick Technologies, February 2009), p. 6.

[79] Susan K. Lacefield, "In a Whole New Light," *DC Velocity*, Vol. 6, No. 5 (May 2008), p. 69.

[80] "3 Reasons Why Having Custom Boxes and a Custom Box Making Machine Can Benefit Your Company," *Packsize*, October 3, 2017, http://www.packsize.com/3-reasons-why-having-custom-boxes-and-a-custom-box-making-machine-can-benefit-your-company/.

[81] See Tom K, "The Importance of Packaging in Today's Supply Chain," *Lean Supply Solutions*, September 8, 2017, http://www.leansupplysolutions.com/blog/the-importance-of-packaging-in-todays-supply-chain/; and James R. Stock, *Development and Implementation of Reverse Logistics Programs* (Oak Brook, IL: Council of Logistics Management, 1998).

materials by 28 percent while enhancing retail appeal and store merchandising efficiency.[82] One problem continually facing retailers is how to place more products into a limited space. The number of products available for sale keeps increasing, but stores remain fixed in their size. The Alldays product was redesigned so that it would fit into smaller packages. Specifically, "the tray-and-hood case concept improves on store labor and consumer appeal on retail shelves because it's sleek, offers product visibility, and actually improves store performance. It also uses less printing ink for an 80 percent printing savings. The proprietary cases saves 1,500 tons of corrugated, 375 truck trips and $1.8 million a year in material costs. The case also speeds up the production line by 33 percent, while shaving 50 percent of restocking time for P&G's customers."[83]

The Many Functions of Packaging

Within the general functions of packaging, several specific functions are performed:

- *Containment* – Products must be contained before they can be moved from one place to another. If the package breaks open, the item can be damaged, or lost, or contribute to environmental pollution if it is a hazardous material.
- *Protection* – To protect the contents of the package from damage or loss.
- *Transportation* – All products must be moved at some point in their life cycle, and that movement can cause damage or degradation of the product.
- *Apportionment* – Translating the large output of manufacturing into smaller quantities of greater use to customers.
- *Convenience* – Allowing products to be used with little wasted effort by customers (e.g., blister packs, dispensers).
- *Identification* – The use of unambiguous, readily understood wording, symbols, or pictures.[84]

The package should be designed to provide the most efficient storage. Good packaging interfaces well with the organization's materials handling equipment and the equipment of supply chain partners, and allows efficient utilization of both storage space and transportation cube and weight constraints.

IKEA, the Swedish manufacturer of "flat pack" furniture, has used packaging as a competitive advantage for many years. With the vast majority of its products disassembled, items can be shipped in much smaller packages, improving cube utilization of warehouses and transportation equipment, and maximizing the number of products in the IKEA retail stores. The customer purchases good quality products, but must assemble them. The success of IKEA suggests that customers are more than willing to assume the assembly responsibility.[85]

Pallets

Products that are received, stored, and shipped from warehouses are often placed on pallets. It has been estimated that 2 billion pallets are in use every day in the U.S.[86] These pallets are typically made of wood, which are the most common. Plastic, metal, and corrugated

---

[82] Lauren R. Hartman, "Big Brands Make Sustainable Strides," *Packaging Digest*, July 1, 2009.

[83] Ibid.

[84] Admin, "Functions of Packaging," June 1, 2015, http://www.trendingpackaging.com/functions-of-packaging/.

[85] Daniel Hellström and Fredrik Nilsson, "Logistics-Driven Packaging Innovation: A Case Study at IKEA," *International Journal of Retail & Distribution Management*, Vol. 39, No. 9 (July 2011), pp. 638–57, https://www.researchgate.net/publication/235310208_Logistics-driven_packaging_innovation_a_case_study_at_IKEA.

[86] Rick LeBlanc, "The 2 Billion Pallet Man: U.S. Pallet Industry Statistics Presented at Western Pallet Association Annual Meeting," *Packaging Revolution*, February 24, 2015, https://packagingrevolution.net/the-2-billion-pallet-man/.

paperboard can also be used. They can be owned by a company, or they can be rented or leased from a third-party pallet provider such as CHEP or iGPS.[87] Pallets were first used in the early-1900s, but were not widely adopted until World War II. The standard U.S. pallet (48" × 40") was developed in 1976 by the Grocery Manufacturers Association (GMA).[88]

Typically, pallets can carry weights up to about 2,000 pounds or 1,000 kilograms. They vary significantly in size because of varying international standards. For example, the Europallet and the U.S. Military use 35" by 45.5" pallets. The International Organization for Standardization (ISO) has approved six different pallet sizes, with the 48" by 40" size being used in North America for grocery and other products. When items are being handled within a specific country or region, the varying pallet sizes are usually not a problem. However, the differing sizes internationally can cause problems in storage and transportation.[89]

All pallets can be recycled, so they are potentially environmentally friendly. Wood (the most common), corrugated, and plastic pallets have their sustainability pros and cons. The correct choice depends on whether or not the firm recycles and reuses the pallets. Some basic questions that supply chain firms should answer prior to making the pallet choice include:

1. How eco-friendly is the raw material?
2. How much energy is consumed in making the pallet?
3. How durable is the pallet?
4. How much does it weigh?
5. Can the pallet be repaired?
6. Can the pallet be recycled?
7. Are there eco-friendly options for disposal?[90]

Technology: Who Invented the Shipping Pallet?

©Prasit photo/Getty Images

Shipping pallets are a basic item used in many aspects of warehousing, manufacturing, transportation, and other supply chain activities. It almost seems like pallets have always been around, but was there a time when shipping pallets did not exist? Prior to November 7, 1939, when a patent was granted to George Raymond Sr. and Bill House for pallets, they did not exist commercially. Certainly, pallets have come a long way since then with billions of pallets being used throughout supply chains globally.

"According to Raymond, who is George senior's grandson . . . the complete history of the invention of the pallet has been lost over time. What he does know is that his grandfather and House were also issued a patent for the modern day lift truck on the same day . . . family and company lore have it that George senior and House developed the lift truck first and then put the pallet together. . . . What happened next? Raymond is quite certain. The supposition around Raymond is that George senior and House saw the pallet as the thing that would drive the adoption of the lift truck."

Source: Adapted from Bob Trebilcock, "Shipping Pallets: Who Invented the Pallet?," *Modern Materials Handling,* January 24, 2012, http://www.mmh.com.

---

[87] Corinne Kator, "Pallet Basics," *Modern Materials Handling*, Vol. 63, No. 5 (May 2008), pp. 28–30.
[88] "Reducing Operating Costs through Pallet Management," *White Paper*, IFCO Systems, undated, http://www.ifcosystems.com, accessed August 14, 2009.
[89] The International Organization for Standardization (ISO) sanctions six pallet sizes in its ISO Standard 6780. Three of the pallet shapes are square and three are rectangular.
[90] Susan K. Lacefield, "How Green Are Your Pallets?," *DC Velocity*, Vol. 6, No. 11 (November 2008), pp. 67–72.

Life cycle assessment can be a useful tool for evaluating these questions. Calculating the trade-offs in pallet and packaging decisions becomes important, if the firm wishes to have confidence in making the right decision.

Because the vast majority of pallets are wood and each pallet weighs approximately 50 pounds, if corrugated pallets could be substituted for the wood pallets, an estimated 400 billion pounds of weight would result, resulting in less weight being moved by transportation carriers. The reduction in carbon dioxide (CO_2) emissions would be in the millions of tons.[91] Prior to 2009, IKEA used almost exclusively wood pallets. The company now directs its suppliers to ship items on lightweight, recyclable corrugated card-board pallets. By not shipping more than 1.4 billion pounds of pallets, the weight savings has saved billions of dollars and resulted in a reduction in CO_2 emissions by more than 550,000 metric tons since 2012.[92]

Trade-offs in Packaging

An Example of Cost Savings through Packaging

Packaging trade-offs have frequently been ignored or downplayed in logistics decision making. However, like all logistics decisions, packaging impacts both costs and customer service levels. From a cost perspective, suppose a company uses a carton that is 12" × 12" × 8" instead of a carton that measures 12" × 12" × 16". Assume the smaller carton costs $0.30 less. The smaller box also requires less loose fill, which can save a half cubic foot of dun-nage costing $0.50. In this hypothetical example, that represents a savings of $0.80 per carton. Multiplied by hundreds, thousands, or millions of packages distributed during a year and the savings add up pretty quickly.[93]

If there is empty space in the package, it is possible that the package could be downsized or even modified in its dimensions to reduce packaging material. For example, if you have a carton that is (1) 8" length × 8" width × 10" height, (2) 16" length × 10" width × 4" height, or (3) 8" length × 5" width × 16" height, they all provide 640 cubic inches of stor-age space. However, option (1) requires 448 square inches of packaging material; option 2 requires 529 square inches; and option 3 requires 496 square inches. Clearly, just from a packaging use perspective, option 1 uses less packaging material. If excess space within the package can be eliminated, there will also be reductions in the use of packaging mate-rials. In sum, sometimes some very simple decisions can have significant results in terms of cost reductions and environmental benefits. Of course, product handling and storage issues might be affected by changes in package size, so other factors have to be taken into consideration when changing the dimensions of a package.

At the same time as costs are being reduced, service levels are being improved because customers are able to obtain more or the same amount of product in less space, enabling them to achieve cost savings through better space utilization in their facilities. The cus-tomer is also likely to realize fewer partial or split shipments from suppliers because more products can be placed on the transport vehicles making deliveries.

Some specific examples of cost savings and/or customer service improvements resulting from packaging modifications include:

- "A frozen-foods supplier saved $3 million and a baked-goods company saved $1 million on annual freight costs by redesigning their packaging to better fit standard pallets. Both were able to put more product on a pallet and more pallets in each truck, thus greatly reducing the number of truckloads required.

[91] Roger Ballentine and Adam Pener, "Sustainability and Pallets: Making Change for the Long Haul," *Greenbiz*, June 8, 2017, https://www.greenbiz.com/article/sustainability-and-pallets-making-change -long-haul.

[92] Ibid.

[93] See International Trade Centre, "33 Ways to Improve Your Packaging and Avoid Costly Waste," *Export Packaging Note No. 12*, UNCTAD/WTO (undated).

- A pharmaceuticals company reduced freight costs on one product line by 25 percent by reducing the amount of packaging used—without compromising product protection."[94]

Although cost and service issues are the most important factors to consider in packaging, there are also sustainability issues that should be considered as well.

Sustainable Packaging

Packaging is an important materials management concern, one that is closely tied to supply chain efficiency and effectiveness. The best package optimizes service, cost, convenience, and sustainability. Additionally, it provides a number of advantages to the manufacturing, logistics, and marketing components of the supply chain.

The most widely accepted definition of sustainable packaging was offered by the Sustainable Packaging Coalition:

"Sustainable packaging . . .

- Is beneficial, safe & healthy for individuals and communities throughout its life cycle
- Meets market criteria for performance and cost
- Is sourced, manufactured, transported, and recycled using renewable energy
- Optimizes the use of renewable or recycled source materials
- Is manufactured using clean production technologies and best practices
- Is made from materials healthy throughout the life cycle
- Is physically designed to optimize materials and energy
- Is effectively recovered and utilized in biological and/or industrial closed loop cycles"[95]

Packaging has become front-and-center in many organization's supply chain strategies due to global concerns over global warming, deforestation of rain forests, disposal of hazardous and nonhazardous materials, and other environmental factors. However, there are many myths associated with packaging and the environment that many people believe, but are just not true. These myths often drive consumer, business, and government behaviors, and may not result in positive environmental or sustainable benefits. For an example of major myths regarding packaging and the environment, see the nearby Exhibit.

The Benefits of Good Packaging

Packaging is becoming a more visible issue with the current environmental and sustainability concerns related to recycling and reuse of packaging. Investing in efficient and effective packaging can save organizations money in several ways, including:

- Lighter packaging may save transportation costs.
- Careful planning of packaging size/cube may allow better warehousing and transportation space utilization.
- More protective packaging may reduce damage and requirements for special handling.
- More environmentally conscious packaging may save disposal costs and improve the company's image.
- Use of returnable containers provides cost savings as well as environmental benefits through the reduction of waste products.[96]

An example of a good package that optimizes cost, improves service to consumers, and has a positive environmental impact was the ready-to-eat cereal containers introduced by

---

[94] Ibid., p. 20.

[95] See the Sustainable Packaging Coalition website, https://sustainablepackaging.org/wp-content/uploads/2017/09/Definition-of-Sustainable-Packaging.pdf.

[96] For a discussion of reusable containers, see Jane Gorick, "Automation and Reusability Core to Future Supply Chain Success, Says PSE," *Supply Chain Digital*, February 20, 2018, http://www.supplychaindigital.com/procurement/automation-and-reusability-core-future-supply-chain-success-says-pse.

Exhibit: 16 Myths Regarding Packaging and the Environment

1. Packaging is the major contributor to the solid waste problem.
2. We are running out of landfill space.
3. Recyclable materials are always better for the environment than the alternatives.
4. Plastics are not recyclable.
5. Recycling paper saves tropical rain forests.
6. Paper and glass are environmentally superior to plastics.
7. Reducing the amount of waste we generate is more important than reducing the energy we use.
8. Paper carrier bags are better from an environmental standpoint than plastic ones.
9. We throw away more packaging today than we did 20 years ago.
10. Packaging represents half the weight of the waste/garbage disposed of by the average household.
11. Packaging materials can be recycled indefinitely.
12. We need to make plastics degradable.
13. Packaging with a recycled-content costs less than that made from virgin materials.
14. The terms "recyclable" and "recycled content" are synonymous.
15. Refillable containers are environmentally better than one-trip ones.
16. Many products are over-packaged.

Source: International Trade Centre, "How Much Do You Know About Packaging and the Environment? 16 Questions to Which You Should Know the Answer," *Packdata Factsheet No. 18*, UNCTAD/WTO (undated).

Target Stores for its Archer Farms brand. The "new" container has a reclosable, "easy-pour" spout that is designed to maintain the freshness of the cereal. "Along with convenience, advantages . . . for the canister design include less waste through spillage, good shelf life and environmental implications, because the body is made with two plies of paperboard containing 55-percent recycled material with 50-percent post-consumer content and a high-barrier liner as the cereal-contact surface."[97] The implications for the cereal industry are significant inasmuch as over three billion cereals in boxes are purchased each year at a value of US$6 billion.

Walmart, the world's largest retailer, introduced a packaging scorecard in 2006 as part of its mission to reduce packaging. The scorecard developed by Walmart was to be used by the firm's suppliers to evaluate the sustainability of their packaging. The metrics of the scorecard and their relative weights are as follows: carbon dioxide per ton of production (15%); material value (15%); product-to-package ratio (15%); cube utilization (15%); transportation (10%); recycled content (10%); recovery value (10%); renewable energy (5%); and innovation (5%).[98] The scorecard was replaced by Walmart's Sustainability Index, which included priority KPIs relating to packaging and packaging materials. "For every product category, there are 15 or so priority questions and KPIs that we are asking for. They are different by category, because the issues are different. So it could be about raw materials. It could be about how the product is made or produced or grown, if it's in agriculture. It could be how it's shipped and distributed. It could be how it's packaged—it's a complete life-cycle approach."[99] And, most recently, Walmart introduced the Sustainable Packaging Playbook for suppliers. The playbook contains best practice examples of various sustainable packaging solutions that suppliers could implement.

[97] Bernie Abrams, "Cereal Swings in Canisters," *Packaging Digest*, July 1, 2008, http://www.packagingdigest.com.
[98] "Walmart Unveils Packaging Scorecard," *Modern Materials Handling*, Vol. 62, No. 1 (January 2007), p. 15.
[99] Anne Marie Mohan, "From Scorecard to Playbook: Walmart's Packaging Evolution," *Packaging World*, October 31, 2016, https://www.packworld.com/article/sustainability/corporate-social-responsibility/scorecard-playbook-walmarts-packaging.

McDonald's, the worldwide fast-food restaurant chain, announced that it had established a 100% sustainable packaging goal for 2025, which would mean that all customer packaging would come from renewable, recycled, or certified sources. "The company said that it was making the move in response to customer demand and its desire to help reduce waste and have a positive community impact."[100]

Do it Best Corporation, a member-owned cooperative hardware and lumber retailer, has utilized reusable plastic containers for many years. The firm ships a variety of products, including light bulbs, tape, batteries, and garden tools, to its customers using 40,000 plastic containers located throughout its supply chain. The reusable plastic containers are favored over conventional corrugated boxes because they offer benefits of strength, stackability, and consistent size.[101]

The environmental benefits of reusable containers can be significant. It has been estimated that in the produce sector, reusable plastic containers require 39 percent less energy to produce, generate 29 percent less greenhouse gas emissions, and produce 95 percent less total solid waste than standard corrugated containers.[102]

Factors Influencing Package Design

What is involved in designing an "optimal" package? The package should optimize service, cost, and customer convenience.[103] Good packaging begins with the design of the product, and it ends with the re-use or disposal of the package.[104] In a very practical sense, the factors governing good package design include (1) standardization, (2) pricing (cost), (3) product or package adaptability, (4) protective level, (5) handling ability, and (6) product packability. Today, sustainability is also an issue. The importance a firm places on each of the factors, as well as the cost/service trade-offs it makes, varies by company, by industry, by supply chain, and by geographic location.

For example, because of the difference in products (cost and physical characteristics), a food processor is more concerned than a computer manufacturer with having a package that minimizes shipping and storage costs. A computer manufacturer emphasizes the protective aspects of packaging because of the fragile, expensive nature of computer systems.

Another illustration would be a company that recently completed construction of a fully automated warehouse. Such a facility would be very concerned with handling ability, cube utilization, and the ability to convey information in such a way so that it could be "read" by the equipment.

Packaging and Logistics Cost Trade-offs

On the other hand, a company doing business in the European Union (EU) would be very concerned with environmental and sustainable aspects of packaging due to very strict environmental laws. The packaging decision is truly one that requires using a systems approach in order to understand the true "total cost" picture.

Packaging should be designed to provide the supply chain with optimal levels of service, efficiency, and effectiveness. Often, packaging is not a major management concern. However, for those firms in the supply chain that give packaging sufficient attention, there can be very significant and positive impacts.

---

[100] David Carrig, "McDonald's Sets Goal of Recycling, 100% Sustainable Packaging by 2025," *USA Today*, January 16, 2018, https://www.usatoday.com/story/money/business/2018/01/16/mcdonalds-environmental-goals-sustainable-packaging-recycling/1037214001/.

[101] Sara Person Specter, "Do it Best Relies on Reusables," *Modern Materials Handling*, Vol. 64, No. 4 (April 2009), p. 32.

[102] Peter Bradley, "Contained Optimism About the Future," *DC Velocity*, Vol. 7, No. 3 (March 2009), pp. 57–59.

[103] A reusable transport packaging calculator has been created by the Reusable Packaging Association (RPA) that can help a firm examine the potential cost savings of reusable packaging. See "Reusables 102—A Cost Comparison Model for Reusable Transport Packaging," http://reusables.org/wp-content/uploads/2016/06/Reusables-102.pdf.

[104] A classic article describing the design of an optimal package is John F. Spencer, "A Picture of Packaging in the Context of Physical Distribution," *Handling & Shipping*, Vol. 18, No. 10 (October 1977), p. 54.

Summary

In this chapter we discussed materials handling systems and equipment. Both nonautomated and automated equipment issues were examined, and examples were provided of some of the major types of equipment commonly utilized by supply chain organizations. Equipment can be categorized according to the functions performed: (1) receiving, (2) storage, (3) order picking, (4) sortation, and (5) shipping/transportation. Automated equipment includes items such as AS/RSs, carousels, conveyors, robots, and scanning systems.

Packaging decisions were examined in that they often have warehousing and materials handling implications. A number of cost and service aspects of packaging were examined. Sustainability concerns are also an issue to supply chain executives, specifically the reuse and recycling of packaging materials.

In the next chapter, we will examine the role of sourcing and procurement in the supply chain process. Because materials that are obtained in the procurement process are often stored in warehouses or DCs, our knowledge of warehousing and materials management will allow us to more fully understand procurement within the supply chain.

Suggested Readings

Benady, David, "Four Technology Trends Transforming Packaging," Raconteur Media Ltd., August 1, 2018, https://www.raconteur.net/sustainability/technology-transforming-packaging.

Bowman, Robert J., "Wireless Technology Comes to the Fore in the Supply Chain," *SupplyChainBrain*, Vol. 13, No. 5 (July 2009), pp. 80–84.

Bradley, Peter, "Behind Delivering 'Wow,'" *DC Velocity*, Vol. 9, No. 11 (November 2011), pp. 54–56.

Bradley, Peter, "Does Your Conveyor Need a Tune-up?," *DC Velocity*, Vol. 9, No. 7 (July 2011), pp. 75–77.

Bradley, Peter, "It's all in the Carts," *DC Velocity*, Vol. 9, No. 3 (March 2011), pp. 69–70.

Bradley, Peter, "Start at the End," *DC Velocity*, Vol. 9, No. 8 (August 2011), pp. 57–59.

"The Essential Guide to Choosing a Sortation System for Your DC," Conveyco, *White Paper*, 2017, https://www.conveyco.com.

"15 Myths about Warehouse Automation Debunked," *Viastore Systems eBook*, undated, http://www.mmh.com/wp_content/viastore_wp_15_myths_warehouse_automation_020916.pdf.

Futch, Mike, "Rise of the Warehouse Robots," *Material Handling & Logistics*, October 18, 2017, http://www.mhlnews.com/technology-automation/rise-warehouse-robots.

Garcia-Arca, Jesús, A. Trinidad González-Portela Garrido, and J. Carlos Prado-Prado, "Sustainable Packaging Logistics. The Link Between Sustainability and Competitiveness in Supply Chains," *Sustainability*, Vol. 9, No. 1098 (2017), file:///C:/Users/JAMES/Downloads/sustainability-09-01098-v2.pdf.

Maloney, David, "Picking and Packing: Raise a Glass!," *DC Velocity*, Vol. 10, No. 2 (February 2012), pp. 64–65.

Manci, Lew, "7 Technology Trends Shaping the Future of Material Handling," *CSCMP's Supply Chain Quarterly*, Vol. 8, No. 4 (2014), pp. 30–36.

McCrea, Bridget, "Warehouse Management Systems (WMS)/Inventory Management Technology: 6 Trends for the Modern Age," Logistics Management, March 1, 2018, https://www.logisticsmgmt.com/article/warehouse_management_wms_inventory_management_technology_6_trends_for_the_m.

Partridge, Amy Roach, "Behind the Buzz about Flexible Automation," *Inbound Logistics*, Vol. 32, No. 1 (January 2012), pp. 173–82.

Rogers, Lorie King, "Pallet Rack: Behind the Backbone," *Modern Materials Handling*, Vol. 66, No. 2 (February 2011), pp. 60–64.

Rogers, Lorie King, "Unitizing: Keeping It Together," *Modern Materials Handling*, Vol. 66, No. 7 (July 2011), pp. 32–35.

"Three Ideal Areas for Automation Investment in Retail Distribution Centers," TGW Systems, *White Paper*, September 26, 2017, http://www.supplychainbrain.com/think-tank/research-analysis/whitepapers/single-article-page/article/three-ideal-areas-for-automation-investment-in-retail-distribution-centers.

Rosengren, Cole, "EPA Previews What's Next for Sustainable Materials Management Program," Waste Dive, March 1, 2018, https://www.wastedive.com/news/epa-sustainable-materials-management-program-WARM/518157/.

Stratton, Felecia, "Automated Material Handling Equipment Market Lifts Growth Projections," Inbound Logistics, November 13, 2018, https://www.inboundlogistics.com/cms/article/automated-material-handling-equipment-market-lifts-growth-projections/.

Trebilcock, Bob, "The Container Store: Lift Trucks Contain the Chaos," *Modern Materials Handling*, Vol. 66, No. 8 (August 2011), pp. 21–26.

Visich, John K., Pedro M. Reyes, and Suhong Li, "Is RFID Dead? Definitely Not!," *DC Velocity*, Vol. 9, No. 7 (July 2011), pp. 71–73.

Weber, Austin, "Industry 4.0 Drives Conveyor Technology," Assembly Magazine, April 4, 2018, https://www.assemblymag.com/articles/94236-industry-40-drives-conveyor-technology.

Questions and Problems

LO 7-1 1. Identify the major advantages of automated materials handling systems versus manual or nonautomated systems.

LO 7-1 2. In what ways do materials handling systems impact the efficiency and effectiveness of the warehouse?

LO 7-2 3. Why is information so important in materials management? Explain how warehouse management systems (WMSs) and materials management are related.

LO 7-2 4. Bar coding and radio frequency identification (RFID) are technologies utilized in materials management. In what ways are these technologies used to improve performance in the supply chain?

LO 7-3 5. Packaging serves two basic functions within supply chain management. Identify these two functions of packaging and how they impact the supply chain.

LO 7-4 6. What are some of the issues related to sustainability and packaging? Briefly identify and explain the issues that you have identified.

Chapter 8

Sourcing and Procurement

Objectives of This Chapter

LO 8-1   To identify the importance of good sourcing and procurement in the management of an organization's supply chain.

LO 8-2   To discuss the role of spend management in sourcing strategies.

LO 8-3   To discuss the importance of human resource skills of the chief procurement officer and other employees.

LO 8-4   To evaluate various external issues that impact sourcing, including risk, government regulations, and environmental and sustainability issues.

LO 8-5   To overview supplier relationship management and its major components.

LO 8-6   To examine how e-sourcing is being used in supply chains.

LO 8-7   To identify how metrics and key performance indicators (KPIs) are being used by organizations to manage sourcing strategies.

Introduction

Supply chain management (SCM) is a complex and multifaceted process that attempts to optimize customer satisfaction, company profitability, and total supply chain efficiency. While many functions and processes are part of SCM, ultimate success begins with being able to optimize the sourcing activity. As noted in Chapter 1, after the planning activity occurs, the SCOR© Model begins with "Source," which includes sourcing stocked, make-to-order, and engineer-to-order products.[1] Specifically, the sourcing activity includes scheduling deliveries; receiving, verifying, and transferring products; authorizing supplier payments; identifying and selecting supply sources when not predetermined, as in the case of engineered-to-order products; managing business rules; assessing supplier performance; and managing inventory, capital assets, incoming product, supplier network, import/export requirements, and supplier agreements. Over 50 percent of an organization's revenue might be used to acquire the goods and services needed to conduct business.

In this chapter we will overview some of the major factors and issues impacting sourcing and procurement, examine the importance of developing and maintaining good supplier relationships, view the role of e-procurement in sourcing, and identify key metrics for measuring the performance of sourcing activities.

[1] APICS Supply Chain Council, *Quick Reference Guide: Supply Chain Operations Reference (SCOR®) Model, Version 12.0* (2017).

We will begin by defining *strategic sourcing*. This approach to procuring items is a set of processes utilized by firms for the purpose of obtaining cost savings, improving product quality, and gaining service level improvements.[2] Best-in-class organizations that are able to effectively and efficiently implement strategic sourcing are able to realize many significant benefits, including much higher procurement contract compliance than other companies, a higher rate of realized cost savings, and a higher rate of spend management reductions.[3]

To begin this discussion, we will examine the issue of "doing more with less," that is, utilizing fewer resources to obtain the same or better results than in the past. Sometimes this is referred to as "lean management."

Spend Management

Spend Management Defined

It seems that past, present, and future supply chain environments have all emphasized the need for organizations to "do more with less." Sourcing and procurement are no exception to this pervasive issue. Organizations attempt to operate as lean as possible, while, at the same time, maintaining or improving customer service.[4] Within procurement, supply chain executives are focused more and more on "driving dollars to the bottom line." Specifically, this means that sourcing executives need to increase asset utilization within their suppliers and improve transport efficiency, remain agile and competitive, increase asset/inventory utilization, and optimize efficiency and supply-demand.[5] *Spend analysis* is the term used to represent the various efforts of an organization to manage how much they "spend" on various activities to conduct business. In this context, we are talking about managing expenses in sourcing and procurement. In a highly competitive environment, it may only be through cost containment that profitability can be improved. Hence, the vast majority of procurement executives are concerned with identifying cost reductions, a crucial outcome of good spend management practices.[6]

Spend management is part of an organization's overall sourcing process. "When organizations begin implementing spend management, they typically start with some form of strategic sourcing, based on highly visible factors such as quantity purchased, number of suppliers, or widely varying price points. Eventually organizations run through low hanging fruit and realize that in order to manage their costs they must understand where they are spending their resources: what goods and services are they purchasing, how often, at what cost, and from which suppliers?"[7] The overall process of spend management is fairly straightforward. It involves collecting the necessary data to make spend decisions; combining data from multiple sources into a single dataset; normalizing or standardizing the data so that they are directly comparable; classifying the data into a specific structure to aid analysis; and reporting and analyzing the spend data in order to assist decision makers.[8] Many firms utilize the "cloud" to manage spend inasmuch as it generally saves them money to not have the software in-house.

[2] See Christopher J. Dwyer and Constantine G. Limberakis, "The State of Strategic Sourcing: Building a Context for the Next Decade," Venture Outsource, *White Paper*, Aberdeen Group, April 2011, p. 2.
[3] Ibid.
[4] For a discussion of lean outsourcing, see Eric Olsen, "Strategic Sourcing and Lean Manufacturing with Value Stream Roadmapping," Venture Outsource, undated, https://www.ventureoutsource.com/contract-manufacturing/benchmarks-best-practices/lean-outsourcing/lean-manufacturing-and-outsourcing.
[5] Bob Heaney, "Strategic Sourcing and Segmentation: Prescriptive Control Tower Approach," Aberdeen Group, April 2015, p. 3; also see Christopher J. Dwyer, *Spend Analysis: Transforming Data into Value*, Aberdeen Group, September 2009, p. 5.
[6] For a discussion of successful spend management practices, see "12 Ways to Measure Business Spend Management Success: 2018 Benchmark Report," Coupa Software, 2018, http://get.coupa.com/rs/950-OLU-185/images/2018-CoupaBenchmarkReport.pdf; also see Brian Umberhauer and Lance Younger, "Leadership: Driving Innovation and Delivering Impact—The Deloitte Global Chief Procurement Officer Survey 2018," Deloitte LLC, 2018, p. 2, https://www2.deloitte.com/uk/en/pages/operations/articles/cpo-survey.html.
[7] "Spend Analysis—It's What You Don't Know That Costs You (Part I)," Iasta, *White Paper*, 2010, p. 4.
[8] Ibid., p. 18.

To highlight the importance of managing procurement expenses, the situation at a fast-food company illustrates what can happen when organizations don't implement spend management successfully. The company was having difficulty getting its franchisees to adopt the latest procurement technology, primarily due to the cultural history of the organization. "They needed something that its decentralized employees would adopt organically and easily. (High employee turnover in that industry didn't help either.) The desired outcome was to 'increase the number of participating restaurants, increase the number of spend categories in the marketplace, decrease order cycle times, and ultimately, achieve significant cost savings."[9] As a result of implementing the new spend management initiative, the firm achieved a 28 percent growth in voluntary restaurant participation and a decrease in purchase order cycle times.

The factors driving organizations to focus on successfully implementing spend management include items such as the need to identify and forecast savings opportunities, need to identify and prioritize top spend categories, and need to improve negotiation leverage for supplier contracts with the express purpose of obtaining lower costs.

Chief Procurement Officers (CPOs) Comment on Spend Management

Additionally, chief procurement officers (CPOs) indicate the need for having high-quality spend information that is easily available when making decisions. "Digital procurement solutions are allowing for many more physical and digital inputs to the connected, driving decision making and improving efficiency, and ultimately producing results in the form of improved insights and strategies, leading to accelerated cost leadership; enhanced process excellence, leading to greater organizational efficiency and effectiveness; better assurance of supply and improved risk mitigation; and operational efficiency and greater collaboration."[10] Interestingly, most procurement executives confess that measuring savings is very difficult. Often, the sourcing savings from supply chain management efforts is underreported. One of the major causes of this underreporting is that only the most easily substantiated savings are captured, while the difficult-to-measure savings are not.[11] Some efforts have been undertaken to improve the quality of data in the supply chain. Initiatives such as the Global Data Synchronization Network (GDSN) have established standards for data collection and reporting by organizations and their suppliers.[12] As a result, there is more accuracy and consistency in data, allowing more efficiency within the supply chain.

Traditional purchasing and procurement activities have become strategic in scope; that is, because of its impact on so many aspects of SCM, best-in-class organizations have developed strategic sourcing strategies. "Strategic sourcing is the process of identifying, evaluating, negotiating, and implementing the optimal mix of goods and services that best support the objectives of the enterprise."[13] Many of the aspects of strategic sourcing will be examined in the remainder of this chapter.

Historically, in logistics management, the foundations of good spend management in procurement were established. The concept of "total cost analysis" was introduced, which allowed organizations to examine all of the costs associated with a decision, rather than just those costs that might be directly related to that decision. In some cases, the lowest-cost

[9] Taras Berezowsky, "A Tale of Two Case Studies: Centralizing and Getting Spend Under Management in Fast Food and CPG," Spend Matters Network, November 21, 2017, http://spendmatters.com/2017/11/21/tale-two-case-studies-centralizing-getting-spend-management-fast-food-cpg/.
[10] "The Future of Procurement in the Age of Digital Supply Networks," Deloitte Development LLC, 2017, https://www2.deloitte.com/content/dam/Deloitte/us/Documents/process-and-operations/us-cons-digital-procurement_V5.pdf.
[11] Editorial Staff, "The Challenge Is Quantifying Savings from Supply Management," *Supply Chain Digest,* January 5, 2010, pp. 1–2, http://www.scdigest.com/ASSETS/ON_TARGET/10-01-05-2.php?cid=3101.
[12] "Global Data Synchronization (GDS)," IBM Knowledge Center, May 27, 2016, https://www.ibm.com/support/knowledgecenter/en/SSWSR9_11.5.0/com.ibm.pim.ovr.doc/pim_con_gds.html.
[13] Dwyer and Limberakis, "State of Strategic Sourcing," p. 4.

Exhibit: Implementing a Lean Outsourcing Program

There are nine considerations organizations should consider when implementing lean outsourcing programs. They include the following:

1. **Know what your customers value**. A thorough understanding of the cost and service level requirements of customers is vital to ensuring that the optimal sourcing decisions are made.

2. **Trade physical proximity for digital proximity**. While geographical proximity is important in obtaining materials quickly, instant communications access with suppliers is even more important.

3. **Outsource to lean companies**. It is difficult to implement a lean outsourcing program if your suppliers and vendors are not themselves involved in lean operations.

4. **Avoid the quantity discount trap**. While small quantities are important in JIT operations, examine the cost savings associated with ordering larger quantities and make the optimal cost–service trade-off decisions.

5. **Involve your customers in outsourcing decisions**. Participative management can be very successful. Involving customers in outsourcing decisions gets their "buy-in" and improves supply chain transparency.

6. **Recognize risk**. "Lean companies identify risk in all forms of variability and work to reduce it."

7. **Increase outsourcing efficiency with lean processes**. Removing waste in existing processes allows organizations to better identify the costs and savings associated with lean outsourcing.

8. **Support your lean initiative with response management tools**. This allows organizations to "collaboratively assess action alternatives so participants can drive optimal decisions in real time."

9. **Measure the right stuff**. Five elements need to be measured, including "first-time through quality, dock-to-dock cycle time, build-to-schedule on-time delivery, overall equipment effectiveness, and total cost."

The above considerations are useful for all types of organizations, although specifically applicable to manufacturing operations.

Source: Eric Olsen, Mark Zetter, and Randy Littleson, "Lean Manufacturing and Outsourcing," *White Paper*, Venture Outsource, 2006, p. 5.

---

option in one particular area or function was not always the lowest-total-cost option. This is especially true in procurement.

Total Cost Sourcing

Total cost sourcing or procurement has been around for decades, but has become much more expansive and complex in recent years. "Early versions of total cost analysis simply added transportation costs to the material costs. Then, with globalization came the importance of total landed cost calculation, which included tariffs and duties as well. Moreover, dramatically different lead times between domestic and off-shore sources have made it necessary to consider such things as transit times and the resulting extra safety stocks required. These other factors become critical in making sourcing decisions, as they can impact a company's agility—the speed and reliability of product introductions, ability to ramp up and down with demand fluctuations, and the amount of markdowns and write-offs when it is time to retire the product."[14]

It should be noted, however, that just because a source of supply is closer and the distance from the firm is smaller, this does not mean there are not other issues that impact the decision. For example, if a manufacturer in the U.S. chooses to source materials from Latin America rather than Asia, transportation infrastructure can be a problem inasmuch as many Latin American countries have poor transportation infrastructure. It may also be more difficult to locate suppliers that can meet the service requirements of the manufacturer. Countries that offer the best opportunities for nearsourcing in Latin America include Mexico, Costa Rica, Honduras, and Brazil.[15]

---

[14] Bill McBeath, "Larger Cost Savings Come from Total Cost Sourcing—Part 1," *The Brief,* ChainLink Research, April 6, 2010, p. 1, http://www.clresearch.com/research/detail.cfm?guid=BA3372D9 -3048-79ED-9971-5B3CAA36FF37; also see Martin Putter, "How to Measure Procurement Savings?," *Capgemini Blog,* September 6, 2013, https://www.capgemini.com/consulting/2013/09/how-to-measure -procurement-savings/.

[15] James A. Cooke, "So Near and Yet so Far," *DC Velocity,* Vol. 9, No. 6 (June 2011), p. 41.

TABLE 8.1
Calculating the Total Cost of Ownership

Source: "Total Cost of Ownership (TCO)—3 Key Components of TCO," *Purchasing and Procurement Center*, 2017, https://www.purchasing-procurement-center.com/total-cost-of-ownership.html.

There are three key components to TCO calculations: (1) acquisition costs, (2) operating costs, and (3) personnel costs.

Acquisition Costs
Acquisition/physical hardware costs include the cost of equipment or property before taxes, but after commissions, discounts, purchasing incentives, and closing costs. Sometimes this will include one-time peripheral equipment or upgrades necessary to installation or utilization of the asset.

Operating Costs
Operating costs include subscriptions or services needed to put the item into business use. This includes utility costs, direct operator labor, and initial training costs.

Personnel Costs
Personnel overhead may include administrative staffing, support personnel to the equipment and facility housing the equipment, and operators. This may include ongoing training and troubleshooting labor for maintenance purposes.

It is difficult to generalize regarding which sourcing cost components are most important. They vary by industry, commodity/product, service levels, and other factors. However, for the majority of organizations, the cost elements that are typically most important include acquisition costs, operating costs, and personnel costs[16] (see Table 8.1).

Human Resource Issues in Sourcing and Procurement

Key Leadership Traits of Procurement Leaders

A key ingredient in successful procurement is the presence of skilled employees involved in the sourcing process. One of the most important sourcing positions would be the chief procurement officer (CPO). In a research study of CPOs by Deloitte, successful CPOs possess several important characteristics or traits, including the following:

- Collaborating internally and externally to deliver value.
- Acting as a role model for organizational values.
- Delivering results, including stopping ineffective activities.
- Shaping and influencing future successful strategies.
- Creating alignment across the organization to enable the best allocation of resources and return on investments.
- Pioneering change and inspiring others.
- Identifying talent and optimizing their current performance while developing their future capability.
- Investing in innovation that delivers competitive advantage.
- Disrupting the execution of business plans or projects to drive more value from resources and/or investments.
- Leading digital and analytical transformation.[17]

Of course, while the CPO is a key figure in any successful sourcing strategy, he or she must have highly qualified people working for him or her. And, while many of the procurement activities have become automated through the implementation of state-of-the-art technologies, people still make the difference!

[16] For further discussion of the elements of TCO, see John Chrzanowski, "12 Key Elements of Total Cost of Ownership," Supply Technologies, January 16, 2015, http://www.supplytechnologies.com/blog/12-key-elements-of-total-cost-of-ownership.
[17] Umberhauer and Younger, "The Deloitte Global Chief Procurement Officer Survey 2018," p. 19.

Managing Technology with People

For example, while technology allows organizations to conduct spend analysis, evaluate supplier performance, create domestic and international documentation, and perform other tasks related to contract awards, supplier management, and risk analysis, it still takes people to make many of the day-to-day, as well as long-term, sourcing decisions. To illustrate, people are needed to manage the technology associated with the following activities and processes:

- Business planning and strategy development (including spend analytics and research).
- Sourcing and operational buying.
- Supplier management (including performance, risk, relationship, and innovation).
- Requisition/ordering.
- Category management.
- Payment (including financing).
- Contracting.[18]

The technologies that are expected to impact sourcing in the near and long term include analytics, ERP upgrades, mobile and social media, cloud computing, robotics, artificial intelligence (AI), cybersecurity, 3-D printing, IoT, augmented reality, and cognitive computing.[19] These technologies will assist people in making sourcing and procurement decisions, but in only a few instances (such as day-to-day, repetitive purchasing and procurement decisions) will they replace people.[20]

In this new technology environment, training will be very important. As is the case in most employee training programs, training must be viewed as an investment, and not an expense. It is important to be able to measure the results of training programs in order to determine the effective ROI achieved. There are three common measurement methods used to assess the value of training, including "before and after" (e.g., individual employee improvements), cost savings achieved (e.g., actual cost savings are captured in a database), and/or performance appraisals (i.e., are people doing a better job?).[21]

Employee Training Programs

The best sourcing organizations tend to have ongoing continuing education programs for their employees. Such programs can include certifications, advanced degree programs, in-house training, and hiring of recent college graduates from logistics and supply chain programs. The best training programs typically have the following characteristics:

- Effective program management from a person who is a "champion" for employee training.
- Needs assessment based on specific organizational requirements.
- Alignment with other organizational objectives.
- Specific goals and metrics that are measurable.
- Leadership buy-in from the top down.
- Relevant training to ensure employee engagement.
- Some creative aspect that generates employee interest.
- Inclusion of marketing strategy as a component of the training program.
- Reinforcement of the training to overcome the "forgetting curve."[22]

---

[18] Ibid., p. 30.

[19] Ibid.

[20] For a discussion on the impact of automation on procurement, see "The Drive to an Automated World," *White Paper,* GEP, 2016, https://www.nextlevelpurchasing.com/resources/GEP%20-%20 The%20Drive%20to%20an%20Automated%20World.pdf.

[21] "Measuring the Impact of Procurement Training," *White Paper*, Next Level Purchasing, undated, https://www.nextlevelpurchasing.com/resources/procurement-training-impact.pdf.

[22] Shannon Kluczny, "9 Characteristics of Top Employee Training Programs," *BizLibrary*, May 16, 2017, https://www.bizlibrary.com/article/employee-training-9-characteristics-of-top-programs/.

Additionally, because many organizations are sourcing globally, the quality and cost of international workers are important issues. When many in the "baby boomer" generation were growing up as children, products labeled "Made in Japan" were viewed as cheap, inferior goods; novelty items or knick-knacks; not something long-lasting or durable. Over the years, as Japanese industry developed and became more quality oriented, perceptions changed, and most products from Japan are now viewed as high quality and good value for the money. The cheap, novelty products now come from underdeveloped countries where wages are low and workers are many. For those reasons, many products have been sourced from China, India, and other countries. However, as is the case in all aspects of supply chain management, things change!

Neo-Neon Holdings, a company that sells lamps and lighting fixtures to large retailers such as Home Depot, Target, and Walmart, initially manufactured its products in Taiwan, primarily because of cheap labor. As labor costs rose, the company moved its manufacturing facilities to China, where labor costs were much lower. However, with Chinese labor costs rising in recent years, the company is again moving its manufacturing facilities, this time to Vietnam. Labor costs are one-third of what the company pays in China.[23]

Such changes in location of manufacturers and suppliers are becoming more commonplace. When sources of supply change, so does supply chain decision making. Vendors that were optimal choices in the past can become less than optimal as their costs increase. Of course, transportation, storage, information, and other costs must also be assessed because they too will change. In sum, it makes global sourcing more complex, and, thus, more difficult.

Global Sourcing Issues (Risk, Regulations, Customer Service)

It has been estimated that U.S. corporations import nearly $2.3 trillion worth of products from more than 150 countries, and each product has to be sourced and procured.[24] That is not to say that sourcing must always involve vendors and suppliers located internationally. In some instances, local sources may be superior to those farther away. Major factors such as risk, government regulations, and customer service issues determine the optimal sourcing strategy for an organization to pursue. However, whether sourcing occurs locally, nationally, or globally, almost two-thirds of procurement executives have limited or no supply chain visibility.[25] This adds to the risk factor associated with sourcing.

Risk

Global Risk Management

As discussed earlier in this chapter, cost reduction is probably the most important issue facing procurement executives. However, supply chain disruption and risk mediation are very significant as well. Contingency planning, certainly not a new concept, has taken on new significance in the last decade as local and global economies have been beset by economic uncertainties, major climatic events (e.g., earthquakes, hurricanes, typhoons, tsunamis), terrorism, and political events that make certain parts of the world unstable.

To illustrate, when certain parts of China were decimated by earthquakes in 2009, many companies in Europe and North America found themselves without key parts and components for their manufacturing processes because their suppliers' plants, facilities, and distribution capabilities were destroyed or severely damaged. In 2011, the Japanese

---

[23] Dexter Roberts and Bob Chen, "As Wages Climb in China, Factories Move," *Bloomberg Businessweek*, May 17–May 23, 2010, pp. 11–12.

[24] "U.S. International Trade in Goods and Services (FT900)," U.S. Department of Commerce, 2018.

[25] Will Green, "Just 6% of CPOs Have Full Supply Chain Visibility," *Supply Management*, February 26, 2018, https://www.cips.org/en/supply-management/news/2018/february/just-6-of-cpos-have-full-supply -chain-visibility/.

Exhibit: The Logistics of the 2018 Pyeongchang Winter Olympics

The Winter Olympic games in Pyeongchang represented one of the most challenging logistical hurdles of any Olympics, as evidenced by the following statistics:

A total of 8,800 procurement contracts were issued; the process began three years before the start of the games.

Approximately 7,000 meals for the Olympic athletes and other personnel had to be served every day, which translated into 500,000 pounds of raw ingredients for meals being prepared by 180 chefs.

The Procurement Portal, established at the 2016 Summer Olympic Games in Rio, was used by suppliers to participate in the procurement process. An e-procurement system was also available, but only in the Korean language.

Sustainability issues were a priority, with both suppliers and the games themselves.

Commentary after the 2018 Winter Olympics suggested that the logistics activities associated with the games were successful.

Source: Team Thomas, "The Logistics of the Pyeongchang Olympics," *Thomas Publishing Company*, February 15, 2018, https://blog.thomasnet.com/olympics-logistics.

---

earthquake severely limited the automobile industry, with Honda and Toyota hampered in their production of automobiles, and the securing of parts and supplies for the production process set back overall. In 2016 alone, there were 315 recorded natural catastrophe events that resulted in economic losses of US$210 billion.[26]

From the perspective of economic risk, in 2010, Toyota Motors stopped selling several of their "best-selling" automobile models for a period of time because of brake and accelerator pedal problems. Costs not only to "fix" the problems, but also lost sales, amounted to the hundreds of millions of dollars (US). While not all supply chain interruptions are as serious, any quality or delivery problems can cause difficulties for manufacturers and retailers that are dependent on those suppliers that do not perform at levels expected or required of them.

In recent years, cybercrime and hacking issues have become much more important. Cyber-attacks on U.S. government agencies increased from 5,500 to more than 77,000 per year, a 1,300 percent increase from 2006 to 2015. In the private sector, perhaps the most significant cybercrime example was the hacking of Equifax that resulted in 145.5 million people having their tax IDs, e-mail addresses, driver's license information, Social Security numbers, dates of birth, and addresses compromised.[28] And U.S. consumers were not alone; almost 700,000 British consumers were victims of the Equifax hack.[29]

Over the past three decades, organizations have attempted to do business with fewer companies, preferring to give more volume to fewer suppliers in exchange for better prices, quality, and service. While the use of core carriers, core suppliers, etc., can result in significant benefits, the risk factor goes up when a firm places all of its eggs in one (or a few) basket(s). If a disruption occurs, and there are no other suppliers that can fill the gap, significant problems can arise because the organization has few or no options available to it in the short term.

---

[26] "Global Risk Management Survey: Executive Summary," Aon Risk Solutions, 2017, p. 32, http://www.aon.com/2017-global-risk-management-survey/pdfs/2017-Aon-Global-Risk-Management-Survey-Executive-Summary-062617.pdf.

[27] Ibid., p. 27.

[28] Alison DeNisco Rayome, "Turns Out the Equifax Hack Was Even Worse Than We Thought," *TechRepublic*, February 12, 2018, https://www.techrepublic.com/article/turns-out-the-equifax-hack-was-even-worse-than-we-thought/.

[29] Megan French, "Got an Equifax Letter Saying You Were Hacked? The Helpline's Struggling—Here's What to Do," *MSE News*, November 1, 2017, https://www.moneysavingexpert.com/news/protect/2017/11/got-an-equifax-letter-saying-you-were-hacked-the-helplines-struggling---heres-what-to-do.

Regulations

From a regulatory standpoint, countries often impose standards and quotas that might seem appropriate from a country perspective but are very inappropriate from an industry or individual firm perspective. For example, the U.S. has initiated regulations that will ultimately require all containers entering the country to be inspected, whether electronically or manually. Because there are insufficient personnel and equipment, if the regulations were ever to be enforced, substantial delays and costs would be incurred, which would greatly increase the costs of doing business and decrease the level of customer service provided (due to delays in processing the containers).

Many of the strategies and tactics being explored to deal with global terrorism will result in shipment delays, and thus reductions in customer service levels. Much like increased airport screening has lengthened the time it takes airline passengers to pass through security, any increase in due diligence at border crossings, additional checkpoints for product screenings, or similar measures to safeguard people and property will result in declines in customer service levels and, most likely, increased costs associated with these various protective measures.

Customer Service

With supply routes becoming longer, that is, suppliers located globally and shipping items longer distances, minimizing order cycle variability becomes more difficult. Combined with ERP systems, global trade management (GTM) technologies help organizations to source worldwide and yet still maintain consistent lead times and product quality. Technologies such as e-commerce, electronic data interchange (EDI), improved forecasting algorithms, Internet portals used for purchasing, electronic document transmittals, and many others assist organizations in managing inbound materials, components, and finished goods into the enterprise from distances near and far.

When organizations are trying to implement just-in-time programs, lean manufacturing, or similar management processes to reduce costs and improve service levels, it is vital that suppliers and vendors in the supply chain be interconnected or linked. In Chapter 15 we will examine the use of "cloud technology," where firms utilize web-based technologies from 3PLs and 4PLs. Visibility in the supply chain is important. The way to obtain this visibility when items are being sourced from great distances is to have "the right information at the right time at each link in the supply chain. In a global sourcing environment, this means having information from each of your partners—and having that information synchronized so that each data element has the same meaning for every participant in the supply chain."[30]

Environmental and Sustainability Issues

During 2016, a total of 17,255 articles on environmental and energy topics were published in only six publications.[31] Because of the increased consumer awareness of various "green" issues, such as the environment, sustainability, energy costs and availability, and many others, organizations have placed greater emphasis on ensuring that company decisions either cause no harm or provide benefits to employees, customers, and society at large. For example, General Motors now has 142 landfill-free facilities, the most in the industry, which minimizes waste in all facets of supply chain management.[32]

[30] "Can Just-in-Time and Global Sourcing Strategies Co-exist?," GT Nexus, *White Paper*, 2011, p. 5.
[31] The publications included *Daily Environmental Report, Energy and Climate Report, International Environment Reporter, Water Law & Policy Monitor*, and *Environmental Due Diligence Guide Report*. If trade and popular press articles were included, the number would be significantly larger. See "Our Bottom Line Is Impact," *Bloomberg Annual Impact Report*, 2016, p. 20, https://data.bloomberglp.com/company/sites/28/2017/04/17_0421_Impact-Book_Final.pdf.
[32] Jennifer Hermes, "GM Now Boasts 142 Landfill-Free Sites—More Than Other Automakers, Company Claims," *Environmental Leader*, February 28, 2018, https://www.environmentalleader.com/2018/02/176050/.

Companies worldwide have implemented supplier codes of conduct relative to the environment and sustainability, including Karl Fazer (Finland), 3M, Hewlett-Packard (HP), Home Depot, Kone Corporation, and Walmart. These efforts are directed at ensuring that the entire supply chain is "green," as opposed to just a portion of it.

For example, Pirelli, the international tire company, has instituted a "Green Sourcing" strategy with its suppliers. Its strategy was developed using a collaborate approach involving personnel from several functions within Pirelli, including Health, Safety and Environment (HSE); Purchasing; Quality; R&D; and Sustainability. To initiate the program, Pirelli held meetings with about 120 key suppliers to explain the program and receive feedback. In the first year of the program's implementation, CO_2 emissions were reduced by 65 million tons, an equivalent savings of more than 681 million euros.[33]

Net-Works, the result of a partnership between Interface and ZSL, works with communities in the developing world to turn waste fishing nets into economic opportunities. It has been estimated that by 2025, there will be one metric ton of plastic for every three metric tons of fish in the sea. Since 2012, Net-Works has been established in 36 communities in the Philippines and Cameroon, and 142 metric tons of waste fishing nets have been collected for recycling. More than 62,000 people have benefited from a healthier environment, and 1,500 families have been given access to finance through community banks.[34]

Green Sourcing

Green sourcing is the purchasing of products and services from vendors and suppliers that consider the environmental aspects of those products and services. Suppliers and vendors are in strategic positions to assist other organizations in implementing green initiatives. They do this in two ways: (1) they influence other organizations in the supply chain and (2) because of their position in the supply chain, they can more easily identify any environmental risks. However, as has been discussed elsewhere in this chapter and in other locations of this textbook, the lack of information and complexity of the tasks inhibit development of green sourcing strategies in many organizations.

Organizations initiate sustainable supply chain strategies for a variety of reasons. Perhaps the most important is to improve customer relations inasmuch as many final customers have become "green conscious" and have begun to recognize the significance of supply chain sustainability efforts. Additionally, because green initiatives also have financial implications, the financial ROI of sustainability programs is important.

Organizations that optimize forward logistics activities also are more "green" because they utilize fewer energy resources to implement their supply chain strategies. Overall, they are more efficient than organizations that place less emphasis on sustainability initiatives. Other factors that are sustainability drivers include corporate responsibility or stewardship, government compliance, decreased expenditures on fuel, improved public relations, decreased risk, and improved investor relations.[35]

Green sourcing can help companies improve their financial results, allowing them to meet their cost reduction goals while also boosting revenues. It can also contribute to a better public image and reputation with stakeholders.

---

[33] "The Power of Green Sourcing," Pirelli website, October 20, 2015, https://www.pirelli.com/global/en-ww/life/the-power-of-green-sourcing.

[34] "Taking Net-Works Global," Net-Works website, 2018, http://net-works.com/about-net-works/scaling-up/.

[35] For an overview of global sustainability initiatives, see McKinley Muir, "The State of Sustainable Supply Chains: Building Responsible and Resilient Supply Chains," Ernst & Young, *White Paper*, 2016, http://www.ey.com/Publication/vwLUAssets/EY-the-state-of-sustainable-supply-chains/$FILE/EY-building-responsible-and-resilient-supply-chains.pdf.

Exhibit: Green Procurement in Hong Kong

Criteria to consider in green procurement include the following:

- Minimal use of virgin material in the product (recycled paper rather than virgin paper)
- Replacement of disposables with reusables or recyclables (reusable cups rather than paper cups)
- Minimal environmental impact from the entire product or service cycle
- Minimal packaging or elimination of packaging (avoid individual product packaging for bulk purchases)
- Reduced energy/water consumption (use energy- or water-efficient equipment)

- Toxicity reduction or elimination (products without toxic substances)
- Durability and maintenance requirements (avoid items that are not durable or are difficult to repair)
- Waste disposal requirements (use products that can be easily recycled)

Source: "Green Procurement," Environmental Protection Department, Government of Hong Kong, June 3, 2016, http://www.epd.gov.hk/epd/english/how_help/green_procure/green_procure4.html?expand=1#a1.

Supplier Relationship Management

"Sourcing by identifying and locating suppliers is relatively simple, but it becomes more complex as the amount of unique raw materials, ingredients, parts, components, connectors, apparatus, products, equipment, suppliers, and services increases and the number of buyers involved in the decisions expands. In a global enterprise, it is possible for one purchasing decision to impact numerous business processes or departments including manufacturing, receiving, distribution, marketing, sales or customer support."[36] Thus, an organization's decisions relating to the selection and administration of suppliers and vendors are vital to the success of the sourcing process.

Suppliers can be local or long-distance. In recent years, firms have attempted to utilize suppliers as close to their locations as possible. In fact, 72 percent of industrial B2B companies prefer to source locally if possible. That preference is due to the perceived recognition that keeping their supply chain as close to home as possible will result in more flexibility, greater control, reduced supply chain costs, more revenue, environmental benefits, and betterment of the local community.[37]

As shown in the nearby Exhibit discussing the automotive supply chain, there may be good reasons to have suppliers and vendors remain "close" to your organization. Suppliers proximal to your organization will be able to supply parts and services more quickly and easily than suppliers who may be located hundreds or even thousands of miles away. As discussed elsewhere in this chapter and elsewhere in this textbook, issues such as the price of energy or fuel, terrorism, equipment shortages, employee strikes, and "acts of God" can have devastating effects on infrastructure, transportation equipment, facilities, and information systems.[38]

Total Value Perspective

A common perspective to take when evaluating suppliers in a sourcing situation is to consider the "total value perspective." Thus, the important question that needs to be addressed is "which supplier is likely to provide the highest total value to the firm?"

[36] Tim Duffie and Larry Koester, "Strategic Sourcing: Building a Foundation for Success—Understanding the Difference between Sourcing and Strategic Sourcing and its Impact," UPS Supply Chain Solutions, *White Paper*, 2005, p. 1; also see Clifford F. Lynch, *The Role of Outsourcing in the Retail Supply Chain* (Memphis, TN: CFL Publishing, 2007).

[37] Zachary Smith, "Top Six Benefits of Local Sourcing," *Thomas Publishing Company Blog*, December 12, 2017, https://blog.thomasnet.com/top-6-benefits-of-local-sourcing.

[38] For a discussion of various factors impacting global sourcing, see Chris Blood-Rojas, "9 Things You Need to Consider before You Globally Source Your Goods," *Trade Ready*, July 14, 2017, http://www.tradeready.ca/2017/fittskills-refresher/everything-you-need-to-consider-before-you-globally-source-goods/.

Exhibit: Supplier Relations in the Automobile Industry—Locating Suppliers Close to Home

The automobile industry is a tough environment due to high levels of competition, government regulations, environmental and energy issues, and large amounts of fixed costs, including medical and pension benefits for employees, manufacturing facilities, etc. "Relentless" and "brutal" are terms often used to describe the industry.

Partnerships and alliances are all the rage in the auto industry. However, not all relationships are "win-win." Manufacturers often require suppliers to meet certain requirements and to reduce prices as well. These are nonnegotiable requirements and not what should be the "norm" in partnerships and alliances.

"Perhaps the biggest supply chain innovation . . . is the supplier park. Usually associated with new assembly plants, these parks are located very near the plant and inhabited by a variety of suppliers that feed parts to the line as needed and on very short notice. . . . The SEAT-Volkswagen factor in Martoreli, Spain, is one of the highest production automotive plants in the world, turning out nearly 2,000 cars daily in seven different models. There are 35 suppliers in the park" (Murphy, pp. 62–63). Ford has developed a supplier park in the U.S. at its South Chicago, Illinois, site, where suppliers provide parts and components for its products. The results have been higher levels of customer service, fewer supply disruptions, and lower overall total costs of ownership.

General Motors has increased efficiency at its Arlington, Texas, assembly plant by locating suppliers close to home with a new supplier park. Such an approach usually results in reduced transportation costs, better communications, and continuous improvement activities. The expansion of the Arlington plant is part of GM's US$1 billion pledge to reinvest in U.S. operations.

Sources: Jackie Charniga, "New Park for GM Brings Supplier Jobs Back from Mexico," *Automotive News*, June 16, 2017, http://www.autonews.com/article/20170616/OEM10/170619764/new-park-for-gm-brings-supplier-jobs-back-from-mexico; also see Jean V. Murphy, "The Automotive Supply Chain: Where Only the Best and the Tough Survive," *Global Logistics & Supply Chain Strategies*, Vol. 8, No. 9 (September 2004), pp. 58–66.

Purchasing and Procurement

The acquisition of materials has long been an important aspect of sourcing and procurement. Rapidly changing supply environments, periods of abundance and shortages, price fluctuations, and lead time variability provide ongoing challenges to organizations wishing to optimize purchasing efforts.

Purchasing and Procurement are Different

The terms *purchasing* and *procurement* are often used interchangeably, although they do differ in scope. Purchasing generally refers to the actual buying of materials and those activities associated with the buying process. Procurement is broader in scope and includes purchasing, traffic, warehousing, and receiving inbound materials.

Purchasing and procurement will likely increase in importance in the future. Many factors will influence this trend, including, but not limited to, the following developments:

Reasons for the Rising Importance of Purchasing and Procurement

- Digital technology growth is impacting every aspect of supply chain management, including purchasing and procurement.
- Emergence of a global economy requires that organizations locate potential suppliers around the world or close to home that can provide low-cost, high-quality goods and services.
- It will become more difficult to manage complexities effectively in markets that are becoming more global; hence, purchasing and procurement will become more important in corporate success.
- Complying with country-specific regulations and rules remains a challenge for most firms involved in global purchasing and procurement.
- Providing transaction transparency and coordination is possible, but implementation remains elusive.

Exhibit: Digital Technologies in Purchasing and Procurement

Technology is an enabler. If an organization has good business and supply chain practices in place, technologies can help achieve successful results faster. If an organization has poor practices, all technology can do is assist in making them do poor things exponentially faster!

In Deloitte's examination of the technologies employed in procurement, a number of technologies were identified that have been, or could be, employed in procurement. The research identified mature technologies that have been employed for some time and emerging technologies, which were expected to impact procurement in the future.

Mature Technologies

Cognitive computing and artificial intelligence: Leverages pattern recognition software and iterative machine learning algorithms to rapidly categorize unstructured spend, cost, contract, and supplier data.

Intelligent content extraction: Uses optical character recognition (OCR) and learning algorithms to read unstructured documents.

Predictive and advanced analytics: Combines modeling, statistics, machine learning, and artificial intelligence with multiple third-party data sources to predict most likely scenarios for cost/price.

Virtualization: Transforms data into user-friendly, executive-friendly, visual formats.

Collaboration networks: Platforms provide buyers and suppliers with visibility into all elements of their joint value chains.

Crowdsourcing: Through the capture of large and diverse inputs and usually leveraging mobile technology, organizations can access new supply markets, draw on the crowd to develop and collaborate on new products and ideas, and access consumer and industry experts to monitor trends and events impacting supply chains and supplier performance.

3-D printing: Additive manufacturing, or 3-D printing technology, can quickly make a physical object from a digital model.

Robotics: Robotics process automation is software that recognizes and learns patterns and can perform rule-based tasks.

Emerging Technologies

Blockchain: This cryptologic data structure uses a trusted peer-to-peer network to create digital transaction ledgers that can verify and validate transactions.

Sensors and wearables: Devices detect, capture, and record physical data.

Cyber tracking: Real-time tracking of online or physical activity can be used to provide proactive monitoring of supplier behavior and performance.

Virtual reality and spatial analytics: Detect events or changes of status using video, location data, or pattern analysis, and conducting supplier visits or audits.

Source: "The Future of Procurement in the Age of Digital Supply Networks," *Deloitte Development LLC*, 2017, pp. 4–5, https://www2.deloitte.com/content/dam/Deloitte/us/Documents/process-and-operations/us-cons-digital-procurement_V5.pdf.

- "A configure-to-order supply chain model for technologies is characterized by short product life cycles and varied dynamic configurations, which results in longer-than-desired lead times and complexities for landing technologies."[39]

In Table 8.2, a comparison is made between the traditional and limited role of purchasing versus the innovative and expanded role of procurement. Procurement offers significant potential to organizations in their pursuit of supply chain excellence and optimizing customer service.

It is important that organizations develop what is known as a "procurement brand." The new procurement function has become an activity that can provide high amounts of value for their company. However, not all organizations obtain the value-added they want from their procurement function. If they do, there are a number of benefits:

- The effective use of procurement will fundamentally improve the bottom line and make supply chains less complicated.

---

[39] Michael Brown, "Five Tenets to Ease the Journey of Rising Procurement Relevance and Global Complexities," *Supply & Demand Chain Executive*, June 1, 2016, https://www.sdcexec.com/risk-compliance/article/12186630/five-tenets-to-ease-the-journey-of-rising-procurement-relevance-and-global-complexities.

Exhibit: Six Common Purchasing Mistakes

How many of these six mistakes have you made?

1. **Assuming that a small order doesn't warrant much time.** A purchase doesn't have to involve a large monetary expenditure to represent a big risk to the organization.

2. **Assuming that supplier offerings are equal except for price.** Most suppliers strive to differentiate their products or services.

3. **Failing to allow suppliers to suggest alternatives.** Suppliers may know a better or cheaper way to accomplish your goals.

4. **Failing to build stakeholder consensus in purchasing decisions.** If you give suppliers a voice in the purchasing decision, the likelihood of compliance is much higher.

5. **Failing to qualify a new supplier.** You should select a supplier because that supplier is the best fit for your organization.

6. **Agreeing to things that the organization can't support.** When purchasing agents focus solely on price, there may be temptation to do anything to achieve savings.

Source: Charles Dominick, "Do You Make These Purchasing Mistakes?," *PurchTips*, Edition #206, June 15, 2010, https://www.nextlevelpurchasing.com/resources/purchasing-mistakes.pdf.

TABLE 8.2
Purchasing vs. Procurement

Sources: Geofrey Crow, "Procurement vs. Purchasing: What's the Difference?," *TendersPage,* January 9, 2017, https://tenderspage.com/procurement-vs-purchasing/; Matt Lim, "What Is the Difference between Procurement and Purchasing?," *Procurify,* 2014, https://blog.procurify.com/2014/02/07/what-is-the-difference-between-procurement-and-purchasing/; and Scott A. Elliff and Robert Sabath, "Beyond Purchasing: Managing Procurement for Advantage," *Mercer Management Journal,* No. 4 (1995), p. 70.

	Purchasing	Procurement
Role	tactical	strategic
Scope	narrow	broad
Staff profile	clerical	professional
Culture	reactive	proactive
Buying process	bureaucratic	streamlined
Supplier relationships	adversarial, inflexible	cooperative, flexible
Performance criterion	unit price	total cost & quality

- A proper working relationship between procurement and the wider business will allow both sides to achieve optimal value for the business, by embracing departmental competitive advantages.
- A successful brand will help attract and retain top talent, which will then further promote the department in the eyes of the business.[40]

Supplier/Vendor Selection

Because there are usually numerous vendor possibilities for sourcing goods or services in the marketplace, it is important to make the right selection from the often lengthy list of potential suppliers. Some organizations spend considerable time and energy identifying and evaluating suppliers. Others, not so much time. Unfortunately, in the vendor selection process, "haste does make waste." For some organizations, you just can't be too careful when selecting a supplier.[41]

However, in the same way that there are lots of suppliers and vendors from which to select, there are numerous ways of selecting those suppliers and vendors. Typically, organizations utilize some combination of electronic and manual systems in the selection

---

[40] Alejandro Alvarez, "Comment: The Importance of Building a 'Procurement Brand,'" *Supply Chain Digital*, September 30, 2017, http://www.supplychaindigital.com/scm/comment-importance-building-procurement-brand.

[41] See Perry A. Trunick, "Ready for Action?," *Outsourced Logistics*, Vol. 1, No. 4 (September 2008), pp. 26–28.

process. Some differences might occur when selecting international vendors versus local vendors. A five-step approach to vendor selection would include the following steps:[42]

1. Analysis of the business requirements
2. Vendor search
3. Request for proposal (RFP) or request for quotation (RFQ)
4. Proposal evaluation
5. Vendor selection
6. Contract negotiation

While the steps of the vendor or supplier selection process remain constant, elements do change in importance. For example, when considering Millennials who are in purchasing or procurement positions, because they have experienced online accessibility 24/7/365 to the goods and services they have purchased as individual consumers, they transfer that experience to the vendor selection process. "Why Millennials' Amazon experience is shaping vendor selection in the arena of procurement is that they want the process involved to be as effective as what they've seen on Amazon. As Millennials take their places in leadership tiers, pressure from them for procurement entities to conform to these new standards will only increase."[43] Being able to compare vendor options in real time using various criteria such as price, product, shipping times, etc., and having buyer reviews of vendors available electronically, will be features that Millennials want to apply in their vendor selection process.

In the B2B sector, outsourcing manufacturing is quite common, but the process is complicated by the fact that there are thousands of contract manufacturers that are potential suppliers, and they are located worldwide. Supplier evaluation is vital when an organization is faced with so many options. While a list of potential supplier evaluative criteria may seem endless, there are certain key items that companies should consider when evaluating and selecting a supplier. These key items include the quality systems possessed by the supplier (e.g., ISO 9000 certification, benchmarking activities, root cause analysis processes), management control systems (e.g., disaster recovery plans, environmental controls, capacity planning), design technology capabilities (e.g., new product introduction process, design evaluation tools, product reliability programs), production technology (e.g., equipment sophistication, equipment reliability, manufacturing software), processes employed (e.g., statistical process control, preventative maintenance programs, defect tracking and remediation), human resources (e.g., cross-training, manufacturing operations training, employee hiring and selection), and materials management (e.g., EDI and/or bar code capabilities, material planning system employed, on-time deliveries).[44]

Contract Negotiation and Management

Historically, companies with multiple divisions or groups would separately negotiate with suppliers to obtain the best prices and service. Unfortunately, companies pursuing such a strategy would not obtain the maximum economies of scale that could come from combining multiple divisions or groups together. For example, until recently, LG Electronics, the

[42] James Bucki, "6 Step Vendor Selection Process," *The Balance*, December 3, 2017, https://www.thebalance.com/the-successful-vendor-selection-process-2533820.
[43] "Why Millennials' Amazon Experience Is Shaping Vendor Selection," Centerpoint LLC, September 28, 2017, https://centerpointgroup.com/millennials-amazon-experience-shaping-vendor-selection/.
[44] For an overview of many of the issues relating to B2B procurement, see Ron Keith, "The Top 10 Myths About Selecting a Contract Manufacturing Partner," *Industry Week*, June 10, 2013, http://www.industryweek.com/supplier-relationships/top-10-myths-about-selecting-contract-manufacturing-partner.

world's third largest handset maker and manufacturer of flat-panel television sets and other electronics, allowed each division of the company to negotiate separately with suppliers. And in some instances, multiple divisions would negotiate with the same supplier, but be unaware of what deals were being negotiated.

Procurement at LG Electronics

LG Electronics now centralizes all purchasing in its Office of Procurement Engineering in Seoul, South Korea. The company spends more than US$30 billion annually for materials. That effort, combined with other marketing and supply chain initiatives, enabled LG Electronics to achieve a ranking of "7" on *Bloomberg Businessweek*'s list of "2010 Innovators." In the previous year, LG was ranked 27.[45] In 2017, *Forbes* magazine rated LG 28th in the world, which contributed to *Bloomberg* rating South Korea the number-one most innovative country in the world.[46] Additionally, the Institute for Supply Management named the company the winner of its "Award for Leadership and Innovation in Procurement."

Developing the Optimal Sourcing Contract

Developing, implementing, and administering supplier/vendor contracts is an important element of sourcing. In many instances, particularly with small- to medium-sized enterprises (SMEs), sourcing contracts are not reviewed frequently enough, or are entered into without sufficient forethought. When markets are highly competitive, economic conditions are difficult, and/or organizations have multiple target markets and products, developing and maintaining excellent supplier relationships are essential. When contracting with suppliers and vendors, organizations should investigate every opportunity to optimize cost and service components of the sourcing relationship, including areas such as the following:

- **Make the most of flexibility**—include provisions that allow the contract to change or adapt to changing customer and/or market conditions.
- **Recognize the formality of contracts**—day-to-day management of vendors and suppliers is often done informally, but to fully protect the organization, formality must be maintained relating to contractual provisions.
- **Review and renegotiate when necessary**—contracts are not meant to last forever without changes taking place; periodically they need to be reviewed and mutually adjusted or modified.
- **Leverage the relationship**—develop "win-win" scenarios for the organization and the vendor/supplier, so that when contractual changes are made, both parties benefit.[47]

Some additional specifics related to what should be included in a firm's contract negotiation strategy include ranking the contract priorities along with alternatives, knowing the difference between what the firm needs versus what the firm wants, knowing the "bottom line" number so that the firm can eliminate contracts that are unattractive, defining time constraints and benchmarks, and assessing potential liabilities and risks, as well as identifying other miscellaneous issues (e.g., confidentiality, noncompete clauses, dispute resolution, changes in requirements).[48]

[45] Chris Petersen, "LG Electronics," *Supply Chain World*, August 23, 2016, http://www.scw-mag.com/sections/manufacturing-distribution/723-lg-electronics; and Michelle Jamrisko and Wei Lu, "The U.S. Drops out of the Top 10 in Innovation Ranking," *Bloomberg Technology*, January 23, 2018, https://www.bloomberg.com/news/articles/2018-01-22/south-korea-tops-global-innovation-ranking-again-as-u-s-falls.

[46] "The World's Most Innovative Companies," *Forbes*, 2017, https://www.forbes.com/innovative-companies/list/#tab:rank.

[47] For a discussion of these and other contract issues, see Julian S. Millstein and Tim Roughton, "Cost-Saving Strategies for Contracts," *CSCMP's Supply Chain Quarterly*, Vol. 3, No. 1 (2009), pp. 34–36.

[48] James Bucki, "6 Step Vendor Selection Process," *The Balance*, December 3, 2017, https://www.thebalance.com/the-successful-vendor-selection-process-2533820.

Strategic Partnerships and Alliances

In sourcing and procurement, strong supplier relationships are important to supply chain success. In a research study of B2B companies and their relationships to their suppliers, an overwhelming majority of organizations indicated that supplier integration and collaboration were strategic initiatives of their firms.[49] In the development of alliances and partnerships with suppliers, information systems that connect these organizations to the manufacturer, wholesaler/distributor, or retailer are vital. Information networks such as E2open, GXS, Elemica, and Ariba are examples. E2open handles over $500 billion of transactions annually over its supply network involving more than 215,000 users in more than 180 countries, which allows companies to manage and automate data interchanges with suppliers. In addition, a collaborative platform enables process-like order management, inventory management, and forecast collaboration, as well as near real-time shipment tracking. A rich set of key performance indicators (KPIs) and analytics provide decision support in each of these process areas, or users can create and publish their own customized reports and KPIs.[50]

Not all suppliers become strategic partners. The special relationship that can exist with other companies that have become allied or integrated with your organization can only be developed and fostered with a few suppliers. Long-term relationships that are "win-win" for both parties take time just like personal relationships. Some suggestions for fostering long-term strategic partnerships and alliances include the following: sit down regularly to review goals and objectives; identify and begin measuring KPIs early in the relationship; focus on what needs to be accomplished rather than how things should be done; make certain that the relationship is win-win for both parties; make a long-term commitment with the supplier; and review the relationship periodically using an outside objective party.[51]

As organizations have become lean in their processes, employees, and other aspects of their supply chains, one strategy that has become commonplace has been to reduce the number of suppliers with whom an organization does business. There are numerous advantages to utilizing fewer suppliers, such as economies of scale, lower rates because of higher volumes, development of a symbiotic relationship with just a few suppliers, service level improvements, and many others.

For example, best-in-class organizations are able to improve supplier visibility, track supplier performance, and reduce supplier risks. More than 80 percent of suppliers of best-in-class firms were able to deliver on time and fully meet production and delivery requirements, compared to 59 percent for all other companies.[52] Significantly, these top firms experienced much lower catastrophic failures from their suppliers than did other firms. For example, because best-in-class firms have better visibility into in-transit shipment status than all other firms, when the Hanjin, the international container cargo carrier owning 97 container ships, was having financial difficulties and eventually went bankrupt, these firms were impacted less severely because they were more aware of the impending crisis.[53] Because such catastrophic failures often result in large costs and/or extreme service-level reductions, having earlier knowledge of their happening is important.

[49] Jean V. Murphy, "Stronger Supplier Relationships Are Post-recession Priority," *Supply Chain Brain*, Vol. 14, No. 3 (May 2010), p. 52.

[50] E2open website, 2018, https://www.e2open.com/.

[51] Susan K. Lacefield, "Pay for Performance," *DC Velocity*, Vol. 8, No. 2 (February 2010), p. 43.

[52] See Bryan Ball, "Supplier Management: The Best-in-Class Approach to Drive Performance," Aberdeen Group, November 2016, http://v1.aberdeen.com/launch/report/knowledge_brief/14171-KB-procurment -purchasing-sourcing.asp.

[53] See Bryan Ball, "Supply Chain Visibility: Know Sooner, Act Now," Aberdeen Group, November 2016, http://v1.aberdeen.com/launch/report/knowledge_brief/14120-KB-visibility-GTM-CSCO.asp.

E-Sourcing

E-sourcing can be defined as "the use of web-based applications to execute the buyer and seller procurement processes. The aim of e-sourcing is to use online platforms to bring greater efficiencies and better communication."[54] In the last decade, many firms have initiated various e-sourcing strategies that have resulted in cost savings and service improvements. A global leader in sub-sea systems and provider of technologies and services to the oil and gas industry used cumbersome manual systems to solicit transportation bids from suppliers in the air, ocean, and land freight sectors. The firm utilized e-sourcing to automate its bid process. The use of e-sourcing allowed the firm to automate its sourcing process, improve efficiency, and generate a 20 percent cost savings across its entire annual global spend on logistics.[55]

A leading pharmacy benefits company that works with health plans, hospitals, and employers to manage health benefit programs for millions of patients implemented an e-sourcing solution to provide a platform for competitive bidding and automating the collection of drug pricing from suppliers. The result was an almost 50 percent cost savings across many of its sourced products.[56]

Forms of e-Sourcing

There are many types of e-sourcing, including buying/requisition to pay (RTP) applications, supplier catalogue sites, electronic marketplaces, reverse auctions, and many others. The more common forms of e-sourcing are the following:

- **Buying/RTP applications**. Website that allows buyers to obtain information, search for products, place orders, pay for purchases, initiate product returns, and track orders.
- **Supplier catalogue sites**. The modern equivalent to the hard-copy catalogue that used to be sent to customers via the mail. Allow customers to visibly see products, view product features, order products online, and set up market baskets of products for ordering at a later time.
- **Electronic marketplaces**. "Web portals which offer an online store for buyers and suppliers to conduct transactions."
- **Reverse auctions**. Similar to some consumer auctions on sites such as eBay, where real-time bidding occurs with subsequent bids lower until a sale is completed.
- **e-RFX**. "A suite of applications which support buyer analysis of supply markets and suppliers. Includes search tools, supplier rating and scoring systems, bid analysis tools, evaluation techniques. Designed to improving decision making by buyers."[57]

RTP applications, such as e-Payables, offer significant potential cost savings and service-level improvements to organizations that "do it well!" The e-Payables process includes invoice receipt, approval, validation, and settlement/payment of invoices. Each process step is often conducted electronically. Best-in-class firms are much more likely to have electronic payment requirements as part of their normal supplier relationships. They are also more likely to integrate payment solutions with accounts payable systems and to standardize payment processes.

---

[54] "What Is eSourcing?," *Nextenders*, July 26, 2013, http://www.nextenders.co.uk/what-is-esourcing/.

[55] "Global Market Leader in Subsea Systems Implements ProcurePort eSourcing to Help Exploration & Production Customers to Improve Their Returns," *ProcurePort Case Study*, undated, https://www.procureport.com/view-case-studies-leading-subsea-systems.html.

[56] "Leading Pharmacy Benefits Manager (PBM) Implements ProcurePort eSourcing to Efficiently Source Prescription Drugs," *ProcurePort Case Study*, undated, https://www.procureport.com/view-case-studies-leading-pharmacy.html.

[57] Alan Smart, "Exploring the Business Case for e-Procurement," *International Journal of Physical Distribution & Logistics Management*, Vol. 40, No. 3 (2010), p. 183.

e-Payables

e-Payable systems are often implemented when organizations have a need to reduce overall payment costs, need better cash management, or need to reduce the risk of payment fraud.[58] The financial and service aspects of e-Payable systems are evident when comparing the cost of processing payments in best-in-class firms versus average firms. When sourcing internationally, best-in-class organizations are much more likely to measure supplier performance over a period of time than are "average" firms.

Illustrative of the advantages that best-in-class firms have with respect to e-Payables include the following: invoice processing costs average US$3.63 vs. $8.69; invoice processing time is 3.8 days vs. 11.1 days; on-time payment rate is 91% vs. 89%; and an exception rate (percentage of invoices flagged for managerial review) is 21% vs. 37%.[59] Additionally, they are 1.3 times more likely to conduct surveys of their existing supplier base to identify and evaluate the level of their integration and collaboration in the supply chain.[60]

It doesn't take much analysis to see that if an organization has a large number of payments to make (and all firms do, irrespective of size), significant cost savings occur with the use of e-Payables; and that does not take into account the potential service improvements or the impact on the firm's cash-to-cash cycle.

Evaluating Suppliers with Metrics and Key Performance Indicators (KPIs)

Metrics are needed to answer questions such as these: "How are our sourcing activities performing?" "Where do we need to improve performance?" "Are our suppliers meeting cost and service expectations?" The management expression *you can't manage what you don't measure* is applicable to determining whether or not an organization's sourcing strategies and tactics are being implemented successfully. Each activity within supply chain management, including sourcing, can develop metrics and key performance indicators (KPIs) for measuring performance.

Best-in-class Firms Use Metrics and KPIs

The development of metrics for evaluating and managing purchasing and procurement is fairly straightforward. First, the process being measured must be mapped. This provides a complete view of the sourcing process, which is needed in order to identify key elements that need to be measured. Second, strategic sourcing objectives need to be established. Third, costs for each of the sourcing objectives need to be established based on the achievement of stated performance goals. Fourth, all of the metrics need to be merged into a common framework, such as the Balanced Scorecard,[61] which can then be evaluated as a whole.[62]

The issue of identifying actual costs associated with sourcing can't be stressed enough! Fully one-third of all organizations do not have sufficient visibility into timely and accurate spend data.[63] Knowing actual costs and having that data available to decision makers is referred to as "spend visibility" and can provide sourcing savings of up to 12 percent, a

---

[58] For an interesting discussion of fraud in procurement, see Jason Finnerty, "Five Key Indicators of Procurement Fraud CPOs and Purchasing Heads Should Heed," *Maistro*, January 5, 2017, https://www.maistro.com/blogs/five-key-indicators-procurement-fraud-cpos-purchasing-heads-heed/.

[59] Bryan Ball, "Accounts Payable without Borders," Aberdeen Group, February 2018, p. 6, http://v1.aberdeen.com/launch/report/knowledge_brief/17219-KB-Global-Accounts-Payable.asp.

[60] Nari Viswanathan, "B2B Integration and Collaboration: Trading Partner Enablement for Multi-enterprise Supply Chains," Aberdeen Group, *White Paper*, March 2010, p. 14.

[61] For a thorough discussion of the balanced scorecard approach, see Robert S. Kaplan and David P. Norton, "The Balanced Scorecard—Measures That Drive Performance," *Harvard Business Review*, Vol. 70, No. 1 (1992), pp. 71–79; also, for a discussion of the use of the balanced scorecard in benchmarking, see "State of Benchmarking 2009 Report," APQC, *White Paper*, December 2009.

[62] For a framework for the entire supply chain management process, see Terrance L. Pohlen, "Supply Chain Metrics: Linking Performance with Shareholder Value," *CSCMP Explores*, Vol. 2 (Spring/Summer 2005), pp. 1–15.

[63] See Christopher J. Dwyer, "Strategic Sourcing: The 2010 Guide to Driving Savings and Procurement Performance," *White Paper*, Aberdeen Group, March 2010, p. 6.

significant amount in industries with slim profit margins.[64] With good spend visibility, an organization can "identify its top suppliers, top categories, and top commodities and do a comparison of spending patterns against market prices . . . it can quickly identify real savings opportunities that can be tackled immediately."[65]

With respect to minimizing the total cost of ownership (TCO) relating to the sourcing of materials, it is important to develop and understand process standards of purchasing and procurement and to identify best practices so that optimal efficiencies can be obtained. There are several key standards and best practices that can guide organizations in developing their sourcing strategies. For example, with respect to creating collaboration with suppliers and vendors, minimum standards that should be achieved by an organization are as follows:

- "A formal supplier relationship management (SRM) program is in place with designated supplier managers who communicate regularly with their suppliers.
- A performance management program[66] has been developed with input from the suppliers.
- There is collaboration with tier 1 suppliers on short- and long-term item requirements and forecasts.
- Supplier ratings tied to service level agreements include availability, quality, and other criteria.
- The financial condition of key suppliers is monitored."[67]

Best Practice Standards for Collaboration

However, world class organizations do not just achieve minimum standards! They achieve "best practice" levels. Examples include the following relating to supplier/vendor collaboration:

- "Onsite supplier representatives are fully integrated into supply chain activities including strategic planning, communications meetings, and regular performance reviews.
- There is partnering with internal and external suppliers to increase replenishment speed and efficiency.
- Suppliers share equitably in the financial benefits created from joint operations improvement ideas.
- Supplier ratings are extended to include suppliers' collaborative ability, and the dollar value or competitive advantage delivered by jointly executed improvement plans.
- The supplier financial condition is monitored on a regular basis as a specific duty of procurement. Contingency plans are developed if the supplier is weakening."[68]

Additionally, best practice organizations also do more, including:

- "Suppliers share responsibility for balancing supply and demand through joint service agreements.
- A Collaborative Planning, Forecasting and Replenishment (CPFR®) model is used to enhance the integration of supply partners by supporting and assisting joint practices."[69]

---

[64] "Strategic Spend Visibility: Untapped Potential for Cost Reduction," *White Paper*, Sourcing Innovation, April 2010, p. 6.

[65] Ibid.

[66] For a discussion of supplier performance management programs and measures, see Wayne Morris, "How to Leverage Supplier Performance Management for Continuous Supply Chain Improvement," *Supply & Demand Chain Executive*, Vol. 11, No. 2 (May/June 2010), pp. 15 and 17.

[67] Supply Chain Visions, *Supply Chain Management Process Standards*, 2nd ed. (Lombard, IL: Council of Supply Chain Management Professionals, 2009), p. 47; also see Mike Ledyard, "Is Your Metrics Program Measuring Up?," *CSCMP Explores*, Vol. 1 (Spring/Summer 2004), pp. 1–8.

[68] Supply Chain Visions, *Supply Chain Management Process Standards*, p. 47.

[69] Ibid., pp. 47–48.

Relating to on-site supplier representatives, one of the earliest examples of this concept was Bose Corporation, a global audio equipment manufacturer, which developed JIT II during the 1990s. The program involved having a representative of major suppliers locate at Bose manufacturing facilities, thus fostering communication, coordination, and collaboration. The JIT II approach improved mutual understanding between Bose and its suppliers, reduced waste and redundancy through better communication and joint planning, improved supplier responsiveness because of their proximity by being in-house, and created a positive working environment.[70]

Those items that have a significant impact on costs, profits, and/or customer service should form the basis of an organization's measurement program and be the ingredients of a portfolio of KPIs used by the organization to most effectively and efficiently manage the procurement processes of the firm.

Five Procurement Metrics That Matter

Generally, there are a few basic metrics that are important to measure irrespective of the type of company or industry. The first is *cost savings*. Cost savings in procurement can occur from a lower cost for the item being procured, reductions in freight or warehousing costs, or greater efficiencies in the various aspects of purchasing and procurement. The second metric is *cost avoidance*. Sometimes costs can be reduced by simply avoiding them; for example, engaging in forward buying where the company buys items before it needs them but obtains them at a cheaper price than it would pay at some point in the future. Purchasing raw materials before price increases occur will avoid the added cost of buying those materials. A third metric is *procurement ROI*, which is a macro-measure of the total cost of procurement. A fourth metric is *spend under management*. Spend under management (SUM) is the total amount of spend that is influenced by procurement, "the percentage of overall spend that is categorized and actively managed by procurement through savings optimization." And metric five is *spend under contract*, which is "a measure of total spend that is covered by an active contract, in comparison to all potential contractible spend."[71]

In sum, KPIs are essential to being successful in sourcing and procurement. The key, however, is to determine just which metrics should be measured and monitored because all of them cannot be KPIs.[72]

Summary

Throughout this textbook, the SCOR Model has been utilized to examine the supply chain management (SCM) process. As noted, the first stage of the SCOR Model is "Source." While other activities and processes of SCM might be considered by some to be more important, without optimal sourcing and procurement, the rest of the SCM process cannot be optimized.

In order to make the most efficient and effective sourcing decisions, the supply chain executive must know the components of SCM and their costs. This is where spend management is important. As organizations implement "lean" management techniques—doing more with less—costs must be minimized in order to remain competitive and achieve acceptable profit margins for the firm's goods and services. Additionally, as has been recognized for decades, the human element of sourcing and procurement is key to achieving the optimal supply chain. Hiring, training, and compensating employees who work in the sourcing area ultimately determine the success or failure of sourcing strategies and tactics.

[70] See Lance Dixon and Anne Millen Porter, *JIT II: Evolution in Buying and Selling* (Newton, MA: Cahners, 1994).
[71] Jennifer Engel, "Starting from the Bottom: 5 Procurement Metrics That Can Make a Big Impact," *Strategic Sourceror*, September 12, 2017, http://www.strategicsourceror.com/2017/09/a-universal -truth-in-any-organization.html.
[72] See Kenneth B. Ackerman and Art VanBodegraven, "Building a Lasting Service Provider Relationship," *Warehousing Forum*, Vol. 25, No. 7 (June 2010), pp. 1–2.

At the same time, organizations face many "uncontrollable" environmental factors, such as various types of risk, government regulations, and others not under the control of the firm. Somehow, the firm must be able to manage the activities, functions, and processes they do control, so that any adverse impacts of the uncontrollable factors are minimized or eliminated. An area that is becoming more important globally is the notion of sustainability. Certainly, sourcing and procurement have multiple environmental and sustainability impacts. Thus, sourcing personnel must be aware of the energy and environmental aspects of their jobs and strive to minimize the energy and environmental "footprints" of what they do.

Within the sourcing and procurement area, many executives outsource various tasks to companies outside their own firms. Thus, sourcing executives must interface with a number of vendors and suppliers. With some they develop strategic partnerships and alliances. With others, more traditional relationships are maintained. Therefore, it is important to properly select vendors and suppliers: those who will most support the strategies and tactics of the firm. Long-term contracts are typically established with strategic partners, and supplier management becomes an ongoing and important task of the sourcing and procurement executive.

Not all sourcing relationships are face-to-face, however. More and more electronic commerce is being used, especially when procuring standard goods and services. E-sourcing is less expensive than traditional sourcing methods and is very useful when dealing with vendors and suppliers globally. E-sourcing allows organizations to identify and procure goods and services from vendors "24/7" because e-mails, purchase orders, and the like can be transmitted any time of the day or night, 24/7/365.

When sourcing and procurement strategies and programs are implemented, it is necessary to determine if the supplier/vendor relationships are meeting expectations of the organization and the organization's customers. Metrics and key performance indicators are used to measure and manage supplier/vendor relationships. It is important that firms develop their key indicators of success and measure them precisely in order to successfully manage their supply chain.

In addition to sourcing and procurement, manufacturing, marketing, and finance are important supply chain functions and processes. These topics will be examined in Chapter 9.

Suggested Readings

Burnson, Patrick, "Near-Shoring/Right-Shoring Strategies: Weighing the Risks of Global Sourcing," *Logistics Management*, Vol. 50, No. 8 (August 2011), pp. 62–64.

Chapman, Tamara, "Purchasing Managers: Minding Everyone's Business," *Inbound Logistics*, Vol. 32, No. 1 (January 2012), pp. 167–71.

Dominick, Charles, "Procurement Talent Management: Recruiting, Training & Retraining a Modern & Awesome Buying Team," Next Level Purchasing Association, undated, https://www.nextlevelpurchasing.com/resources/procurement-talent-management-nlpa.pdf.

Hao, Dani, "Is There a Difference Between Spend Management and Expense Management?" *Procurify Blog*, June 18, 2018, https://blog.procurify.com/2018/06/18/is-there-a-difference-between-spend-management-and-expense-management/.

Harrington, Lisa, "Digitalization and the Supply Chain: Where Are We and What's Next?," *DHL Research Brief*, 2018, http://dhl.lookbookhq.com/ao_thought-leadership_digital-physical-1/research-report_digitalization-and-the-supply-chain?utm_medium=Eloqua-LP&utm_campaign=AO-Digitalization-1&utm_source=Eloqua.

Jones, Keith, "Drive Improvement with these Top 10 Procurement Metrics," ProcureWare Blog, August 9, 2016, https://www.procureware.com/drive-improvement-top-procurement-metrics/.

Limberakis, Constantine G., "Spend Analysis: Lessons from the Best-in-Class," *Supply Chain Management Review*, Vol. 16, No. 2 (March/April 2012), pp. 10–19.

Monczka, Robert M., and Kenneth J. Peterson, "The Competitive Potential of Supply Management," *Supply Chain Management Review*, Vol. 16, No. 3 (May/June 2012), pp. 10–18.

O'Shaughnessy, Kim, "Top 5 eSourcing Tools & Procurement Software," *SelectHub Blog*, 2019, https://selecthub.com/eprocurement/top-5-esourcing-tools/.

Quirk, Elizabeth, "Procurement Talent Management Trends for the Year Ahead," *Solutions Review*, January 17, 2018, https://solutionsreview.com/talent-management/2018/01/17/procurement-talent-management-trends-year-ahead/.

Schiele, Holger, Philipp Horn, and Bart Vos, "Estimating Cost-Saving Potential from International Sourcing and Other Sourcing Levers," *International Journal of Physical Distribution & Logistics Management*, Vol. 41, No. 3 (2011), pp. 315–36.

Smart, Alan, "Exploring the Business Case for E-procurement," *International Journal of Physical Distribution & Logistics Management*, Vol. 40, No. 3 (2010), pp. 181–201.

Stanley, Will, "Metrics: KPI's for Sourcers," *SourceCon*, September 18, 2017, https://www.sourcecon.com/metrics-kpis-for-sourcers/.

Questions and Problems

LO 8-2   1. What is "spend management," and how does it allow firms to more efficiently and effectively source goods and services?

LO 8-3   2. What are some of the skills needed by a successful chief procurement officer (CPO)?

LO 8-3   3. People have always been considered vital ingredients in any successful enterprise or supply chain. Briefly discuss how employee training programs (i.e., onboarding) help to optimize employee participation.

LO 8-4   4. Briefly discuss how sourcing issues, such as risk, regulations, and customer service, influence global sourcing.

LO 8-4   5. What is "green sourcing," and what are some basic elements of a green sourcing initiative?

LO 8-5   6. Are "purchasing" and "procurement" the same or different? If different, identify some of the ways in which they differ.

LO 8-5   7. Outsourcing has become a common practice in supply chains. How can strategic partnerships and alliances help to optimize outsourcing strategies?

LO 8-6   8. What role does e-sourcing have in purchasing and procurement? What are the most common types of e-sourcing?

LO 8-7   9. How do metrics and key performance indicators (KPIs) assist firms in evaluating suppliers and helping to optimize the supply chain?

9

The Role of Manufacturing, Marketing, and Finance in Supply Chains

Objectives of This Chapter

LO 9-1   To describe how the manufacturing function interfaces with the supply chain.

LO 9-2   To describe how the marketing function interfaces with the supply chain.

LO 9-3   To describe how the finance function interfaces with the supply chain.

LO 9-4   To examine selected technologies utilized in various supply chain management strategies within manufacturing, marketing, and finance.

Introduction

Recall the statement in the first chapter that "supply chain management is an integrating function with primary responsibility for linking major business functions and processes within and across companies into a cohesive and high-performing business model." Some of the major business functions referred to above are manufacturing, marketing, and finance. In this chapter, we examine the role of these three key business functions in supply chains. While the management of each of the three functions is an important area of study on its own, it is important to recognize that decisions made in manufacturing, marketing, and finance also significantly impact the efficiency and effectiveness of supply chains. Three short examples illustrate each of these relationships.

Impacts of Manufacturing on the Supply Chain

First, manufacturing lot sizes impact inventory levels because large production lots will often generate more product than required by short-term demand and the excess will be converted into inventory. Second, marketing promotions can create peaks and valleys in demand that affect transportation, warehousing, and inventory carrying costs. Finally, financial cash flows are impacted by order cycle time. The shorter the cycle, the smaller the financial burden on firms in the supply chain because customers receive products and pay for them more quickly; thus, accounts receivable are smaller and the cash-to-cash cycle is shorter. Accordingly, in this chapter we identify key issues relating to each of these three business functions. We also describe how each function interacts with the supply chain.

The Role of Manufacturing in Supply Chains

To understand the role of manufacturing in supply chains, we first review three key manufacturing issues: make-to-stock vs. make-to-order; material requirements planning; and, finally, lean and agile manufacturing. We then follow with an examination of two different ways whereby manufacturing impacts the supply chain: order cycle time and output location. We conclude with a description of the role of manufacturing in supply chain management, focusing specifically on the SCOR Model.

Key Manufacturing Issues

Manufacturing is an important supply chain function. Before examining its interaction with the supply chain, it is important to understand three key manufacturing issues: make-to-stock and make-to-order; material requirements planning (MRP);[1] and lean and agile manufacturing.

Make-to-Stock and Make-to-Order

Make-to-Stock (MTS) versus Make-to-Order (MTO)

While there are numerous variations available, there are two basic manufacturing strategies that a firm may pursue. One is make-to-stock (MTS), and the other is make-to-order (MTO).[2] As the name implies, in an MTS strategy, sometimes referred to as "build-to-stock," products are manufactured in anticipation of demand. In other words, products are manufactured and then held in a finished goods inventory until demanded by customers. The decisions of which products to make, and in what amounts, are based principally on demand forecasts and economies of scale in the manufacturing process. Economy of scale is a relationship between the quantity manufactured and its associated cost. Typically, the greater the amount produced, the lower the cost per unit produced. A key issue in MTS is the accuracy of the forecast. If the forecast is incorrect, there will be either too few products produced or too many products produced, both of which are not optimal for supply chain efficiency and effectiveness.

In contrast, in an MTO strategy, products are manufactured after a customer places an order. In some cases, each order is manufactured separately. In other cases, to benefit from economies of scale, orders are accumulated and manufactured in larger quantities or batches. There are variants to the basic MTO strategy. One is assemble-to-order (ATO), where subassemblies are put together into a final product. Another variant is build-to-order (BTO). In this case products are built to customer specifications. This is also known as custom manufacturing. Regardless of the MTO variant, the key difference between MTS and MTO is that the latter is triggered by a customer order.

The automobile industry serves as an example of MTS.[3] Cars are assembled in plants with components and subassemblies received from suppliers. The decision of which cars to assemble is based on sales forecasts and not on customer orders. Once assembled, the cars are sent to dealers, where they stay in inventory until sold to a customer. It is important to note that the car manufacturer only knows that a customer wants to buy a specific car once that customer arrives on the car dealer's lot.

Dell Computer Utilizes Make-to-Order

Alternatively, for their online or telephone orders, Dell Computer[4] makes a product only after a customer order is received. Customers place orders by phone or via the Internet. These orders are then downloaded every hour in Dell's plants. With order information, Dell

---

[1] For a historical overview of the development of MRP, see Vincent A. Mabert, "The Early Road to Material Requirements Planning," *Journal of Operations Management*, Vol. 25 (2007), pp. 346–356.
[2] For a discussion of MTS and MTO approaches, see Aaron Continelli, "Build-to-Stock or Build-to-Order?," SME—Society of Manufacturing Engineers, March 1, 2017, http://advancedmanufacturing.org /bto-or-bts/.
[3] For examples of make-to-stock, see John Spacey, "5 Examples of Make to Stock," *Simplicable*, August 22, 2017, https://simplicable.com/new/make-to-stock.
[4] See the Dell Inc. website at http://www.dell.com/learn/us/en/uscorp1/corp-comm?~ck=mn.

TABLE 9.1
Comparing Make-to-Stock and Make-to-Order Strategies

Make-to-Stock (MTS)	Make-to-Order (MTO)
Production based on demand forecast	Production based on customer order
Requires finished goods inventory	Requires production flexibility
Typically shorter delivery time	Typically longer delivery time
Typically more stock-outs	Typically fewer stock-outs
Better if demand uncertainty is low	Better if set-up costs are low

is able to tell suppliers exactly which parts are needed. The parts are then delivered to the Dell plant, typically within 90 minutes from nearby supplier hubs. Once parts are received, computers are assembled and shipped to customers within 8 to 12 hours of receiving the order. The customer typically receives the computer a few days later. Note that in this case it was a customer order and not a sales forecast that triggered the process.

Differences in Make-to-Stock and Make-to-Order

Table 9.1 compares the MTS and MTO strategies. These strategies differ in four important points, in addition to the previously mentioned point that the MTS is based on sales forecasts and the MTO, on customer orders. First, the MTS requires an inventory of finished goods. If products are made to a forecast, they have to be stored somewhere until bought by a customer. This raises a common problem in supply chains: Who keeps the inventory (and assumes the inventory carrying costs)? Sometimes manufacturers hold the inventory, and other times they try to push it to dealers or retailers. On the other hand, while the MTO strategy does not require a finished goods inventory, it does require a flexible manufacturing system. This is because production has to shift from one product to another as orders come in. The more flexible the production process, the faster the manufacturer can shift from one product to another.

Second, products that are made-to-stock are typically available to customers when ordered. This is because the ordered item is likely already in finished goods inventory. In contrast, in an MTO strategy the delivery time is longer because the customer must wait until the ordered product is assembled or manufactured. Third, the MTS strategy typically generates stock-outs. A stock-out occurs when the product ordered by the customer is not in inventory and therefore unavailable to the customer. Stock-outs happen because MTS production is based on sales forecasts and these forecasts have errors, causing the firm to make the wrong product and to fail to make the right product. In an MTO strategy, products are made after the customer order is received, making stock-outs much less likely unless there are component parts shortages.

Finally, when demand uncertainty is low, forecast errors are also low. In this case an MTS strategy is better because it is unlikely that the wrong products will be produced. Conversely, when set-up costs are low, the producer is able to make frequent changes in the product being produced. This enables the producer to adjust to orders as they come in. Set-up costs are incurred when equipment, such as an individual machine or a production line, is made ready to start producing a different product. There is a cost associated with that because the equipment stops producing while being prepared. There are also set-up costs related to cleaning the equipment or employing specialized labor to make the shift. Low set-up costs favor the MTO strategy.

What Is Material Requirements Planning (MRP)?

Material Requirements Planning (MRP)

Material requirements planning (MRP) is a planning system designed to manage the flow of raw materials and components to the factory floor.[5] Specifically, MRP computes the quantity needed of each raw material or component required to support a production plan.

---

[5] Mabert, "Material Requirements Planning," pp. 346–356.

FIGURE 9.1
Key Building Blocks of MRP Systems

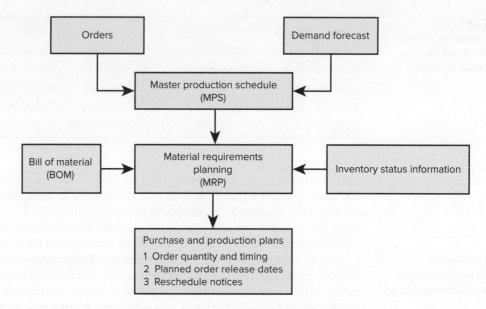

A second output of MRP systems is the timing when the raw materials or components will be needed and, therefore, should be ordered.

The logic of an MRP system is based on the key concept of *dependent demand*. It states that the demand for a raw material or a component depends on the demand for the product for which they are an input. Take, for instance, the demand for electric toothbrushes. A manufacturer of electric toothbrushes knows that each brush needs two batteries. Therefore, there is no need to estimate the demand for batteries once the demand for electric toothbrushes is forecasted. The demand for raw materials and components, batteries in this illustration, is computed using the concept of dependent demand. This is in contrast to *independent demand*, where the demand for each raw material or component is estimated separately, often as a function of past usage.

While earlier prototype installations existed, MRP systems were first popularized during the 1960s. Much of the pioneering working began with Dr. Joe Orlicky, who published the first comprehensive text outlining MRP systems.[6] The software was enhanced as time passed and the original MRP systems morphed into MRPII (to be discussed a bit later in this chapter). MRP installations gained popularity as computing power expanded. Figure 9.1 presents the main building blocks of an MRP system.

Master Production Schedule (MPS)

The operation of MRP systems begins with inputs from the customer order file and demand forecasts for the different products available for sale to customers. These inputs form the basis to determine what needs to be produced and when. This information is then joined with the availability of labor, materials, equipment, and capital to prepare a master production schedule (MPS). Thus, an MPS details the timing and volume of production of items to be manufactured in a specified period of time. If we extend the electric toothbrush illustration described above, an MPS would specify all the product variations (e.g., colors and/or hardness of bristles) to be produced in a period of time (e.g., a week).

Bill of Materials (BOM)

A second important building block of MRP systems is the bill of materials (BOM). The BOM is basically a listing of the raw materials and components needed to make one unit of product. For example, one electric toothbrush requires 1 set of bristles, 1 electric motor, 2 batteries, 1 plastic casing, 3 brand labels, and 4 screws. Inventory status information, both incoming and currently available, is the final key piece of information needed to run the MRP system.

[6] Joseph A. Orlicky, *Material Requirements Planning* (New York: McGraw-Hill, 1975).

Outputs of MRP

The outputs of MRP are to (1) compute and then release the quantities and related dates when raw materials and components will be needed to fulfill the master production schedule; (2) plan the dates when orders should be released to suppliers; and (3) when needed, issue rescheduling notices.

The MRP system first computes the raw materials and components needed to fulfill the MPS. This number is obtained by multiplying the number of units of each product to be produced in a given period (obtained in the MPS) by the amount of raw materials and components needed to make each unit of product (obtained in the BOM). This is called an *MRP explosion.* In our electric toothbrush illustration, if the MPS calls for producing 1,000 electric toothbrushes, then the MRP explosion indicates that 1,000 sets of bristles, 1,000 electric motors, 2,000 batteries, 1,000 plastic casings, 3,000 brand labels, and 4,000 screws would be needed. Those quantities are subsequently compared with the inventory on hand and the expected incoming supplies. The difference is what needs to be ordered from suppliers.

A reschedule notice is issued whenever there is a need to revise the MRP system due to an unanticipated event. For instance, a machine breakdown at a plant may force planners to revise the MPS. This, in turn, generates changes in orders to suppliers because raw materials and components are now needed at different times and quantities. Receiving a reschedule notice can be problematic to suppliers (and consequently to the supply chain) as it requires that suppliers reschedule their deliveries and possibly also alter their own production and purchasing schedules. Reschedule notices are typically issued to cancel, modify, or expedite orders. The instability they bring to MRP systems is often referred to as "nervousness."

Benefits of MRP Systems

Benefits of MRP Systems

Recall that the concept of dependent demand, whereby the requirements for each raw material or component are calculated on the basis of the demand for the finished product, is central to MRP systems. Consequently, in MRP systems there is no need to independently estimate the need for every raw material or component as a function of historical demand. The difference is especially advantageous to MRP systems when the demand for a raw material or component is lumpy. Demand is considered *lumpy* when its variability is quite high.[7] This makes it more challenging to estimate requirements using historical demand.

A second benefit of MRP systems is that it integrates information that would otherwise be handled separately. As shown in Figure 9.1, MRP systems integrate information from the order file, demand forecast, master production schedule, bill of materials, and inventory status. This enables the firm to coordinate action regarding how raw materials and components are acquired, stored, and utilized in production. For instance, by coordinating the information from different sources, MRP systems help firms manage *horizontal dependence,*[8] which indicates that all raw materials or components needed at a particular stage of the manufacturing process must be on hand for the process to be completed. For example, to make an electric toothbrush, all raw materials and components listed earlier must be available. If one item is missing, the toothbrush cannot be completed.

Finally, MRP systems are quick to adjust to changes generated either externally or internally to the firm. External changes include increases or decreases in the demand for finished products, or issues related to suppliers, who may fail to adhere to a previously

[7] To further explore the impact of lumpy demand on the production and distribution functions in supply chains, see Henry Canitz, "Simplify Supply Chain Forecasting: How Can a Demand Planner Improve the Accuracy of the Forecasts They Produce?," *Supply Chain Digest*, May 11, 2017, http://www.scdigest.com/experts/Logility_17-05-11.php?cid=12384.

[8] Gerry Poe, "Introduction to Manufacturing Inventory Requirement Planning Overview," APICS, June 22, 2016, https://www.scc-co.com/blog/introduction-to-manufacturing-inventory-requirements-planning-overview.

agreed delivery schedule. Internal changes arise from an unexpected lack of availability of labor or equipment. By inputting changes into MRP systems, firms may quickly understand the impact of the changes and make alternate supply and production plans.[9]

Weaknesses of MRP Systems

Weaknesses of MRP Systems

Conversely, MRP systems also have weaknesses that require managerial attention during implementation and operation. First, MRP systems do not account for lead time variability. They treat the lead time for each raw material or component as a constant. To cope with the inevitable variability present in real-life conditions, managers tend to overestimate lead times to prevent shortages. This results in increased investment in safety stock and warehouse space.[10]

Second, MRP systems are very dependent on data accuracy. Whenever a physical inventory count fails to match recorded levels, the MRP output is of limited value. This may happen if employees fail to record inventory movements in or out of a location. It may also happen if there are data inaccuracies in inbound inventory, such as wrong part numbers or inventory counts. A related data accuracy issue is the importance of updating the bill of materials whenever there are changes in product configuration. This is particularly important in firms whose marketing strategy emphasizes frequent new product introductions or changes to existing products. Failure to deal with these weaknesses often results in inflated values for order sizes, safety stocks, and lead times, as managers overinvest in inventory to prevent production stoppages.

MRP II: Manufacturing Resource Planning

MRP II

While MRP focuses on materials required for production, MRP II is a well-known extension that incorporates additional business functions, such as finance, marketing, and human resources, into manufacturing planning. Few firms will utilize MRP systems today and will have updated their systems to MRP II. The goal of MRP II is to help managers plan and execute complex manufacturing operations by integrating information from pertinent business functions. One additional important use of the capability to integrate information is that MRP II may also be used to develop budgets and to assist in firm-level decision making.[11] However, MRP II is more complex than MRP to implement and operate. It is typically implemented in phases and is considered more costly and complex than MRP.[12]

Lean and Agile Manufacturing

Lean production differs from traditional manufacturing approaches where products are manufactured in batches. In lean production, the production process runs as much as possible in a constant flow. The goal is to reduce production cost and improve quality through the elimination of waste. Waste appears either as excess inventory or excess capacity and is the result of variability in supply, processing time, or demand.[13] In contrast, the goal of

---

[9] Seyed-Mahmoud Aghazadeh, "MRP Contributes to a Company's Profitability," *Assembly Automation*, Vol. 23, No. 3 (2003), pp. 257–265.

[10] Edward A. Silver, David F. Pike, and Rein Peterson, *Inventory Management and Production Planning and Scheduling*, 3rd ed. (Hoboken, NJ: John Wiley & Sons, 1998).

[11] See Bob Turek, "Advantages and Disadvantages of MRP II," *Bizfluent*, September 26, 2017, https://bizfluent.com/info-8401517-advantages-disadvantages-mrp-ii.html; and Pritam Tamang, "MRP vs. MRP II: What's the Difference?," *Software Advice*, undated, https://www.softwareadvice.com/resources/mrp-vs-mrp-ii/.

[12] Turek, "Advantages & Disadvantages of MRP II."

[13] See Patange Vidyut Chandra, "12 Essential Lean Concepts and Tools," *Process Excellence Network*, June 25, 2013, https://www.processexcellencenetwork.com/lean-six-sigma-business-transformation/articles/12-essential-lean-concepts-and-tools; and Rachna Shah and Peter T. Ward, "Defining and Developing Measures of Lean Production," *Journal of Operations Management*, Vol. 25, No. 4 (2007), pp. 785–805.

TABLE 9.2
The Seven Wastes

Waste	Description
Overproduction	Producing more than required by demand. Creates excess inventory and makes it difficult to track errors.
Defects	Making defective parts generates scrap. Processing errors generate additional mistakes. Defects generate additional cost of rework and reinspection and tax capacity.
Unnecessary Motion	Motion that does not add value. Excessive job-related motion, such as bending, lifting, or stretching. Also excessive walking or time spent looking for items. May cause injury or time waste.
Unnecessary Inventory	Excess inventory, including work-in-process (WIP) inventory, is costly, requires warehouse space, and hinders the identification of problems.
Unnecessary Processing	Performing unnecessary steps in processes or using the wrong equipment.
Excess Transporting	Keep equipment and processes close together. Transporting products is costly, is time-consuming, and creates an opportunity to damage goods.
Excess Waiting	Time wasted when products are not moving or in process. Time wasted waiting for paperwork, materials, or equipment

agile manufacturing is to timely respond to changes in demand, including level, location, and product type. Agility relies heavily on manufacturing flexibility as a deliberate response to constantly changing markets.[14] In this section, we describe lean and agile manufacturing, as well as a hybrid approach known as "leagile" manufacturing.

Lean Manufacturing   *Lean Manufacturing*   Reduction of waste (known as *muda* in Japanese) is central to lean manufacturing. Waste is an activity that does not add value to the customer. In order to manage waste reduction, engineers at the Toyota Motor Company categorized waste according to their sources. These are known as the *seven wastes*: overproduction, defects, unnecessary motion, unnecessary inventory, unnecessary processing, excess transporting, and excess waiting.[15] Each is described in Table 9.2.

Lean manufacturing consists of a set of managerial practices that may be grouped into four broad categories: just-in-time (JIT); total quality management (TQM); total preventive maintenance (TPM); and human resource management (HRM).[16] JIT refers to improving product flow by reducing work-in-process inventory and minimizing delays. The associated management practices include lot size reduction, cycle time reduction, elimination of production bottlenecks, and reducion of changeover time. The latter refers to the time needed to switch the product being produced by a machine. It takes time to clean the machine and prepare it to produce a different product. Waste is reduced by decreasing the changeover time, during which machines are not producing.[17]

[14] For a discussion of both lean and agile manufacturing, see David Ingram, "The Similarities between Lean & Agile Manufacturing," *Chron.com*, undated, http://smallbusiness.chron.com/similarities-between-lean-agile-manufacturing-70619.html.

[15] Taiichi Ohno, *The Toyota Production System: Beyond Large-Scale Production* (Portland, OR: Productivity Press, 1988).

[16] See Mark Crawford, "5 Lean Principles Every Engineer Should Know," American Society of Mechanical Engineers, March 2016, https://www.asme.org/engineering-topics/articles/manufacturing-design/5-lean-principles-every-should-know; and Rachna Shah and Peter T. Ward, "Lean Manufacturing: Context, Practice Bundles, and Performance," *Journal of Operations Management*, Vol. 21, No. 2 (2003), pp. 129–149.

[17] For a definition of JIT and a brief history of the concept, see Rosemary Peavler, "Just-in-Time (JIT) Inventory Management," *The Balance*, September 9, 2016, https://www.thebalance.com/just-in-time-jit-inventory-management-393301.

The goal of TQM is to improve product and process quality by implementing quality and continuous improvement programs.[18] TPM practices aim at minimizing equipment breakdown time by implementing maintenance and safety programs. TPM is based on the foundation of 5S, which includes organization, tidiness, cleaning, standardization, and discipline.[19] Finally, HRM practices enable the operation of self-directed teams and flexible cross-functional workforces. A self-directed team is empowered with the responsibility of producing a product or service with minimal or no external supervision. In a flexible cross-functional workforce, workers are able to perform different jobs.[20]

Agile Manufacturing

Agile Manufacturing   While the focus of lean manufacturing is to reduce waste in processes that management *can control*, agile manufacturing focuses on helping management cope with factors it *cannot control*.[21] Specifically, agile manufacturing is a set of practices aimed at making manufacturing flexible and responsive to market changes such as variations in customer preference or changes in the business environment.[22]

Applications of Agile Manufacturing

Many companies have employed agile manufacturing, including 3M, Dell, Fitbit, Ford, GECMarconi Aerospace Company, Honda, John Deere, and United Colors of Benetton. For example, AstraZeneca, the international biopharmaceutical company, introduced an agile framework in the company beginning in late 2014 utilizing a team approach for implementation. The results of the initiative were faster time to value delivery, cost reductions, and improved quality.[23]

The importance of agile manufacturing has increased over time as the level of uncertainty faced by firms in the marketplace also increased. Several factors contributed to this. First is the fragmentation of markets. There is a proliferation of products available to consumers. For example, the number of product variations available in categories such as breakfast cereals, snack foods, personal care products, and insurance is substantial. This proliferation makes it harder for firms to predict the demand for each product variation offered. A second factor is related to product characteristics such as shorter product life cycles or the risk of obsolescence. Fashion products have short life cycles, and electronic products are often made obsolete by new technology within a very short time. Products with short life cycles are soon substituted and obsolescence cuts the demand for a product. Both contribute to a firm's uncertainty about the market because the rate of change is accelerating with the advent of the Internet and omnichannel retailing. A third factor is uncertainty related to the business environment, such as the onset of a recession, regulatory compliance, or other legislative actions. For any of these factors, firms with agile manufacturing capabilities are able to adapt faster to market changes.

[18] See Martin Murray (updated by Gary Marion), "Total Quality Management (TQM) and Quality Improvement," *The Balance*, December 5, 2017, https://www.thebalance.com/total-quality-management -tqm-2221200.

[19] For a more detailed discussion of 5S, see J. Venkatesh, "An Introduction to Total Preventive Maintenance (TPM)," *The Plant Maintenance Resource Center*, October 8, 2015, http://www.plant -maintenance.com/articles/tpm_intro.shtml.

[20] For a specific discussion of the impact of HRM on supply chain management, see Milena Gómez-Cedeño, José María Castán-Farrero, Laura Guitart Tarrés, and Jorge Matute-Vallejo, "Impact of Human Resources on Supply Chain Management and Performance," *Industrial Management & Data Systems*, Vol. 115, Issue 1 (February 2015), pp. 129–157; and Amit Kumar Marwah, Sheelam Jain, and Girish Thakar, "Implications of Human Resource Variables on Supply Chain Performance and Competitiveness," *International Journal of Engineering (IJE)*, Vol. 8, Issue 1 (2014), pp. 11–21.

[21] See Ingram, "The Similarities between Lean & Agile Manufacturing."

[22] Rajesh Krishnamurthy and Charlene A. Yauch, "Leagile Manufacturing: A Proposed Corporate Infrastructure," *International Journal of Operations and Production Management*, Vol. 27, No. 6 (2007), pp. 588–604.

[23] "Agile at AstraZeneca: Expediting Time-to-Value Delivery," Scaled Agile, Inc., Case Study, 2017, https://www.scaledagile.com/case-study/astrazeneca/.

Success in agile manufacturing requires firms to excel in six different areas: customer orientation; flexible manufacturing; human resource management; internal organization; supply chain collaboration; and information management. Customer orientation is key because the firm must offer customers the right products. The effort to adapt to changing market conditions will be wasted if the right product is not produced and marketed. With flexible manufacturing, the firm is able to quickly change the products made available to customers. For example, a John Deere manufacturing plant in Spain increased its manufacturing flexibility by reducing machine set-up times. This enabled John Deere to quickly accommodate changes in market demand by switching production more rapidly.[24]

An organization cannot be agile without appropriate human resource policies. This is because an organization cannot be quick and flexible without a workforce that is also quick and flexible. Thus, the workforce must be recruited, trained, and motivated accordingly. Another goal for the workforce is the ability to work in teams, as this is key to collaboration within both the firm and the supply chain. The structure of the internal organization is important because it must foster cooperation among the different functional areas so that the overall goal of agility is achieved. For example, to reduce the time needed to market products, companies need to develop the capacity to concurrently engineer products such that product design and manufacturing processes are developed simultaneously.[25]

With supply chain collaboration,[26] firms achieve manufacturing agility by engaging customers, suppliers, and sometimes competitors in product design and manufacturing. An early example of supply chain collaboration occurred with IBM, Motorola, and Apple, who collaborated in the development and manufacturing of a computer chip (the PowerPC) that competed with Intel.[27] Agile manufacturing also requires that firms manage information so that it is readily available whenever needed. This includes information about market changes, customer choices, product characteristics, manufacturing processes, as well as supplier inventories, lead times, and technical support.

Leagile Manufacturing

Leagile Manufacturing   Leagile manufacturing is a hybrid of lean and agile manufacturing. The concept is to apply lean principles in the segment of the manufacturing process where cost management is the primary goal and to foster agility in the segment of the manufacturing process where responsiveness to the market is the main goal.[28]

Consider, for instance, the Home Products Division of 3M Company in Spain. One of its products is "Scotch Brite," an abrasive fiber used in home cleaning.[29] The same basic fiber is the key component in a variety of cleaning products used to clean dishes, counter-tops, ovens, etc. The manufacturing process is comprised of two phases. The first is to manufacture the fiber. This phase is highly automated and designed to produce a large amount of fiber at low cost. The second phase stresses flexibility. In response to customer demand,

---

[24] See Daniel Vázquez-Bustelo and Lucía Avella, "Agile Manufacturing: Industrial Case Studies in Spain," *Technovation*, Vol. 26 (2006), p. 1152.

[25] Ibid., p. 1159.

[26] For a discussion of various types of manufacturing collaboration in a supply chain, see "Five Levels of Manufacturing Collaboration," *Infor Executive Brief*, December 5, 2013, http://ww1.prweb.com/prfiles/2013/12/05/11689158/Executive-Brief-Five-levels-of-manufacturing-collaboration-syteline-erp-software-godlan.pdf.

[27] See Brian Maskell, "The Age of Agile Manufacturing," *Supply Chain Management: An International Journal*, Vol. 6, Issue 1 (2001), pp. 9, 5–11.

[28] "What to Develop: A Lean Supply Chain, Agile or Leagile?," Oxford College of Procurement & Supply, May 1, 2017, https://www.oxfordcollegeofprocurementandsupply.com/what-to-develop-a-lean-supply-chain-agile-or-leagile/; and Thomas J. Goldsby, Stanley E. Griffis, and Anthony S. Roath, "Modeling Lean, Agile, and Leagile Supply Chain Strategies," *Journal of Business Logistics*, Vol. 27, No. 1 (2006), pp. 57–80.

[29] Vázquez-Bustelo and Avella, "Agile Manufacturing," pp. 1147–1161.

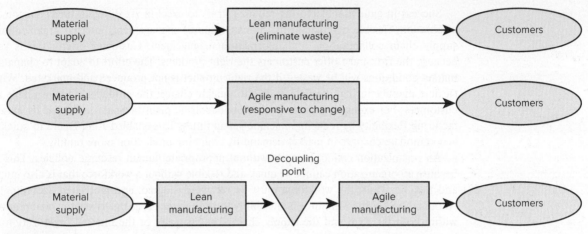

FIGURE 9.2
Lean, Agile, and Leagile Manufacturing

Source: Adapted from Rachel Mason-Jones, Ben Naylor, and Denis R. Towil, "Lean, Agile or Leagile? Matching Your Supply Chain to the Marketplace," *International Journal of Production Research*, Vol. 38, No. 17 (2000), pp. 4061–4070.

workers handle the readily available fiber to produce any of the different cleaning products sold under the "Scotch Brite" brand. Thus, by combining lean and agile manufacturing, 3M is able to simultaneously produce low-cost fiber and have the agility to be responsive to customer preference.

A key feature of leagile manufacturing systems is the *decoupling point.* This is the point where the manufacturing process converts from lean to agile. The decoupling point is often also the order entry point. This is the moment in time when a firm receives a customer order. With the order information in hand, the firm is able to produce the right product. In sum, decoupling points separate forecast-driven from customer-driven flows.[30] Figure 9.2 depicts the lean, agile, and leagile manufacturing processes.

Enterprise Resource Planning (ERP)

Enterprise Resource Planning (ERP)

ERP, while used extensively by manufacturers, is a software-based system that goes beyond MRP and MRP II and is implemented by firms of all types. While including all of the elements of those systems, ERP also incorporates core financials, customer relationship management (CRM), human resources, asset tracking, marketing automation, project management, and other aspects of supply chain management.[31] There are many options available to firms in their selection of an ERP software vendor.[32]

The significance of ERP is evident in the fact that a simple Google search using the term "ERP" results in 13.2 million "hits." As defined by Oracle, ERP contains "all the core processes needed to run a company. . . . At its most basic level, ERP integrates these processes into a single system and provides visibility, analytics, and efficiency across every aspect of

---

[30] Joakim Wikner and Eva Johansson, "Inventory Classification based on Decoupling Points," *Production & Manufacturing Research*, Vol. 3, Issue 1 (2015), pp. 218–235.

[31] Tamang, "MRP vs. MRP II."

[32] For an in-depth discussion of many of the most widely implemented ERP systems and the vendors that provide them, see Mary E. Schacklett, "Compare the Top ERP Systems and Decide Which Best Fits Your Business," *TechTarget*, September 2017, http://searcherp.techtarget.com/feature/See-the-top-ERP-systems-and-decide-which-best-fits-your-business?src=5724453&asrc=EM_ERU_92178891&utm_content=eru-rd2-rcpD&utm_medium=EM&utm_source=ERU&utm_campaign=20180315_ERU%20Transmission%20for%2003/15/2018%20(UserUniverse:%202541226).

a business."[33] A key feature of all ERP software is their ability to utilize a shared database, so that all activities associated with supply chain management can be accessed by all relevant corporate functions and processes. Additionally, the software allows employees to not have to maintain different spreadsheets or other databases; they can generate, merge, and summarize reports from other business units and functional areas. Finally, a common ERP feature is that "it includes a portal or dashboard to enable employees to quickly understand the business's performance on key metrics."[34]

Oracle Netsuite, an ERP vendor, has identified several benefits of ERP systems that provide business value to firms, including:[35]

- Assists employees to be more efficient by eliminating barriers between business units.
- Makes data available in real time, which helps the firm to be more proactive when circumstances require it.
- Helps to improve compliance with regulatory standards and reduce risk.
- Automates many business operations, including the cash-to-cash cycle, order-to-fulfillment, and procure-to-pay processes.
- Enhances customer service by providing one source for customer inquiries, including billing and tracking.

Some examples of organizations that have implemented ERP systems include Nissen Chemitec America, Nicolet Plastics, The Salvation Army, and many others.

Nissen Chemitec America is a plastic injection molding company that supplies parts to automobile manufacturers. The company relies on technology to manage its lean manufacturing initiatives. Nissen had an existing ERP system, but it was inadequate to do all of the things that the company needed it to do. For example, data was being transmitted via EDI that was modem-based. It was costing Nissen almost $3,600 monthly to transmit data and support customer requirements. In addition, there were between 30 and 40 EDI-related shipping errors per month. After installing the new ERP system, its monthly EDI cost dropped to $300, a 90 percent reduction, and shipping errors were almost completely eliminated. Data from the ERP system allows the company to set daily schedules, forecast demand, monitor what was occurring on the shop floor in real time, and more easily communicate with customers and suppliers. Specific ROI-related benefits of the ERP system have included reduction in maintenance costs by more than 70 percent, elimination of excess data entry requirements, and increased business from one of Nissen's largest customers.[36]

Nicolet Plastics manufactures complex component parts and provides expertise to its industrial and medical components customers. While the customer mix of the company is diverse, commonalities are that all of its customers require product consistency, don't want to overpay for products, and want the company to fill all of its orders. Some of the goals that Nicolet established for the new ERP system were to reduce order-to-delivery time of parts from 21 days to 7 days, reduce finished goods inventory, and be able to respond to changes in demand without sacrificing service levels. The new ERP system has allowed the company to add new customers based on the value the company delivers, rather than the price it charges. Additionally, Nicolet Plastics has improved inventory velocity from 2.3 times to 6.3 times, resulting in inventory turns going from 11 to 25, which reduces

[33] "What Is ERP?," Oracle, 2018, https://www.oracle.com/applications/erp/what-is-erp.html; and "What Is ERP?," SAP SE, 2018, https://www.sap.com/products/what-is-erp.html.
[34] "What Is ERP? Enterprise Resource Planning Systems Transform, Integrate and Scale Businesses," Oracle Netsuite, 2018, http://www.netsuite.com/portal/resource/articles/erp/what-is-erp.shtml.
[35] Ibid.
[36] "Leading Automotive Supplier Accelerates Lean Operations with EnterpriseIQ," IQMS Case Study, undated, https://www.iqms.com/files/case-studies/Nissen_Chemitec_America.pdf.

Exhibit: ERP in the Craft Beer Industry

The craft beer sector is growing rapidly in the United States and now accounts for almost one-quarter of all of the beer sold. One craft beer company, Catawba Brewing Company, with three locations in Asheville, Charlotte, and Morganton, North Carolina, manufactures nine flagship beers. The locations combine production facilities with tasting rooms.

Even though Catawba is a small brewery, it still can benefit from supply chain technology to run its operations, specifically enterprise resource planning (ERP). Ideally, an ERP software system should be employed as soon as possible, and best if done when the company first opens. Catawba began investigating ERP systems when it reached 5,000 barrels of craft beer.

To ensure the quality of the craft beer being produced and to be able to track the location of beer in the marketplace, an ERP system is invaluable. ERP software can include quality management aspects that will allow the company to ensure consistent production quality and taste. Because many craft beer companies experience rapid growth, an ERP system can assist in making certain that all of the necessary raw materials—hops, wheat, barley—are

purchased at the right times and in the right quantities. The software also allows the business to better know its costs so the proper cost–service trade-offs can be made. Over time, the ERP software can track the cost and production trends to determine if conditions are improving, staying the same, or getting worse. Inventory levels are known from the ERP software so that stock-outs can be minimized. As a result, customer service levels are improved as the craft beer drinkers find their favorite brew available when they go to the tasting rooms.

In sum, "thriving as a craft brewing company requires a repeatable—and scalable—recipe for success," which is an ERP system!

Sources: Company website at http://Catawbabrewing.com/about-us; and Pam Baker, "Why Craft Beer Makers Are Tapping into ERP for Brewery Software," *TechTarget*, March 2018, http://searcherp.techtarget.com/feature/Why-craft-beer-makers-are-tapping-into-ERP-for-brewery-software?src=5726254&asrc=EM_ERU_92447919&utm_content=eru-rd2-rcpD&utm_medium=EM&utm_source=ERU&utm_campaign=20180321_ERU%20Transmission%20for%2003/21/2018%20(UserUniverse:%202545788).

finished goods inventory from an average of $500,000 to $200,000. Lead time has been reduced by seven days from the 21 days originally, and, from a financial management perspective, has resulted in an improved working capital position that has allowed the firm to pay debt down.[37]

More than 31 million people in the United States receive assistance from the Salvation Army, best recognized for its red kettles outside retail stores during the Christmas and holiday period. The nonprofit organization was utilizing a manual, account-balancing process to monitor organizational performance by division. Through the implementation of ERP systems, the organization was able to create centralized reports and fund-specific accounting reports. It only required three months to upgrade its systems, resulting in improvements in productivity and enhanced reporting capabilities, and it was easier to use than the older manual system.[38]

A subsidiary of a global electronics conglomerate that manufactures and markets semiconductors, display, and storage devices with multiple locations in the United States implemented an ERP system to improve on-time delivery of its products to customers. The firm was utilizing a number of existing systems that were not necessarily integrated. Order cycle times were short given customer requirements and competition. The vendor, Infosys, introduced an ERP solution, combined with a transportation management system (TMS) and warehouse management system (WMS) to improve the company's business processes. Implementation of the new systems required 18 months and resulted in higher ROI for the company, provided higher visibility to supply chain management, improved demand

[37] "Nicolet Plastics' Quick Response Manufacturing Strategy," IQMS Case Study, undated, https://www.iqms.com/files/case-studies/quick-response-manufacturing.pdf.
[38] "The Salvation Army Improves Productivity and Expands Reporting Capabilities," Collins Computing Case Study, 2015, http://www.collinscomputing.com/pdf/TSA_Case_Study_2015.pdf?x76341.

Exhibit: Selecting and Implementing an ERP Solution

Choosing an ERP Vendor

1. How long has the vendor been in business?
2. Is the vendor an ERP specialist?
3. How many clients has the vendor worked with? If an active customer of the vendor in your industry is available, can it be contacted?
4. What experience do your ERP team members have?
5. Why would someone work with you rather than a competitor offering a similar system?

Implementation

1. How will the ERP system help your company make better decisions, save money, and increase revenues?
2. How long will it take to implement the ERP software?
3. What implementation tasks do we do, and what tasks does the vendor do?
4. What happens when, not if, problems occur during the implementation?

5. What is the communication plan for monitoring the progress of the implementation?

Post-Launch

1. What is the plan for training employees on the ERP system?
2. How long will it take for an employee to be fully trained?
3. Who at the vendor is the contact person(s)?
4. How are regular software updates provided and deployed?
5. Is the system scalable, that is, can new users or modules be added, and if so, what would be the cost and how long would it take?

Source: For an in-depth discussion of each of the checklist items, see "Questions to Ask When Purchasing an ERP System," Hitachi Solutions eBook (2017), https://1rzc5r2oh1d04afcje30z789-wpengine.netdna-ssl.com/wp-content/uploads/2017/04/erp-questions-to-ask-ebook.pdf .

planning and execution, and improved cash flows due to the systems being real time. More processes became automated, which increased efficiency and reduced costs, and, most important, customers experience higher levels of on-time delivery of products.[39]

The Impact of Manufacturing in Supply Chains

We now examine two different ways whereby manufacturing impacts the supply chain: order cycle time and output location. The first, order cycle time, was already discussed elsewhere in this book. Order cycle time refers to the time between ordering and receiving a product. The second, output location, refers to the separation between manufacturing location and the location of the demand. Each is discussed below.

Order Cycle Time

As described in Chapter 3, the order cycle time consists of several steps: order receipt, processing, fulfillment, and shipment. To fulfill an order, either there is inventory on hand or it must be acquired through procurement or manufacturing. Clearly then, the time required to manufacture an item may affect the order cycle time. Furthermore, the variability in the time needed to manufacture an item may also be an important factor in the order cycle time because the variability translates into order cycle time uncertainty, which, in turn, will likely require customers to maintain more safety stock.

The impact of manufacturing on the order cycle time also impinges on the manufacturing strategy adopted by the firm: make-to-stock or make-to-order. Both strategies were discussed earlier in the chapter. In the earlier case, the firm is able to rely on inventory to counter a long manufacturing time. That is, if the manufacturing time is long, the firm may produce more than required for immediate sales and build inventory that will be available to support a short order cycle time. On the other hand, if the firm employs a make-to-order strategy, the manufacturing time has a crucial impact on the order cycle time.

[39] "Oracle Implementation for a Global Electronics Conglomerate," Infosys Case Study, undated, https://www.infosys.com/industries/high-technology/case-studies/Pages/oracle-implementation-global.aspx.

Exhibit: How Rapid Manufacturing Using 3-D Technology Could Transform Supply Chains

To visualize the concept of 3-D printing, think of a fax machine that could print an object instead of a sheet of paper. 3-D printers inject materials in successive layers, thus building up products with each successive layer printed. This technology can be used to manufacture objects such as replacement parts, promotional materials, nuts and bolts, and material used in health care. One very interesting health care application of 3-D printing is the creation of custom-made prostheses for patients.

The effect of rapid manufacturing in a supply chain is potentially significant. First, the order cycle time could be reduced to almost zero because manufacturing occurs on demand. Second, inventory carrying costs are low because spares and other items would not have to be available in inventory, but could be produced when needed. An added benefit is that items would not have to be transported from a supplier or vendor, making 3-D printing environmentally friendly. Finally, customer service improves because 3-D printing machines can rapidly produce whichever part is needed by the customer.

While the potential for 3-D printing is great, there are some applications that have been developed now! In late 2014, a 3-D printer on the International Space Station printed a "faceplate" that included the names of organizations that collaborated on the 3-D concept. On future flights to Mars and beyond, 3-D printers would eliminate the need to carry some spare parts and other materials. They could be produced during the long space flight.

Sources: Matthias Heutger, "DHL: How 3D Printing Is Disrupting the Logistics Industry," *Supply Chain Digital*, June 25, 2017, http://www.supplychaindigital.com/logistics/dhl-how-3d-printing-disrupting-logistics-industry; Michael Gravier, "3D Printing: Customers Taking Charge of the Supply Chain," *Industry Week*, April 12, 2016, http://www.industryweek.com/supply-chain/3d-printing-customers-taking-charge-supply-chain; Phil Reeves, "How Rapid Manufacturing Could Transform Supply Chains," *Supply Chain Quarterly*, Vol. 2, No. 4 (2008), pp. 32–36; and "International Space Station's 3-D Printer," NASA, November 26, 2014, https://www.nasa.gov/content/international-space-station-s-3-d-printer.

Manufacturing flexibility was discussed previously as one of the requirements of agile manufacturing. Flexible manufacturing implies that firms are able to quickly change the product being manufactured, which means that the time between production runs for any particular product is reduced, thus shortening the order cycle time.

There are different approaches to manufacturing flexibility. One is to reduce set-up cost, which was described earlier in this chapter. A low set-up cost enables more frequent production changes. Another approach is to use specialized equipment, such as robots or 3-D printing (see Exhibit). Robots can be programmed to switch production in a short period of time. Finally, firms may also be flexible by assembling standardized or interchangeable parts in response to customer orders, as in the Dell example also described earlier.

Output Location

The location of manufacturing output is important to the design and operation of supply chains. For example, make-to-stock vs. make-to-order manufacturing strategies require supporting supply chains with different features. As discussed earlier in the chapter, a make-to-stock strategy typically requires more finished goods inventory, produces more stock-outs, and enables shorter delivery times.

Two additional manufacturing-related issues significantly impact the design and operation of supply chains and are discussed below. Both are related to the location of manufacturing output. The first is plant location. Manufacturing firms must decide to either centralize production in one or a few plants that are typically more distant from consumer markets, or decentralize production to locations near markets. For example, Nissan Motors, a car manufacturer, concentrates its U.S. manufacturing in five plants that produce automobiles (Mississippi and Tennessee), batteries, and engines.[40]

[40] Nissan Motors website, https://www.nissan-global.com/EN/COMPANY/PROFILE/EN_ESTABLISHMENT/NORTH_AMERICA/.

In contrast, the consumer packaged goods company Procter & Gamble maintains 25 U.S. manufacturing facilities.[41]

The reasons to centralize manufacturing or not are beyond the scope of this book. Nevertheless, the implications of this decision are noteworthy. Decentralized manufacturing is typically close to markets. Consequently supply chains tend to be longer on the inbound side. In contrast, centralized manufacturing facilities are typically farther from markets and thus require a longer outbound supply chain. In addition, this distance from markets adds pressure to the customer service policy. When customers require quick delivery, it becomes necessary to either move products at an accelerated pace or maintain inventory close to markets. In the Nissan case mentioned above, unsold cars are stocked near the market to ensure availability to demanding customers. In a nonmanufacturing example, Amazon.com must have warehouses/DCs located very close to customers if it is to provide delivery on the same day the customer orders.

The second manufacturing-related issue is single vs. multiple product line manufacturing facilities. When focusing on a single or limited number of product lines, manufacturing plants are often able to operate at a lower cost because people, processes, and equipment are targeted to a narrow set of tasks. Consequently, the firm enjoys the benefits of specialization as well as a lower overhead cost.[42] In contrast, a plant able to produce multiple product lines enjoys the benefit of greater flexibility to adjust production according to changing market conditions. Additionally, multiple product line manufacturing is less risky because the same product line may be produced in different plants. Production of a particular product line is thus less likely to be interrupted by catastrophic events such as strikes or natural disasters.

The decision to employ single or multiple product line plants carries implications to the design and operation of supply chains. By producing multiple product lines within the same plant, firms are able to mix shipments to customers. On the other hand, single line manufacturing plants are less flexible to combine deliveries to customers. Whenever a customer is unable to buy a full truckload quantity of a single line, products have to be combined from different plants to fill an order or be delivered in less-than-truckload quantities. To prevent such a costly arrangement, it is often advantageous to store products from different plants in a mixing warehouse. While this generates added warehousing and inventory carrying costs, it also generates transportation cost savings. It also improves customer service because customers are able to buy LTL quantities of each product line but receive product in TL quantities because different product lines can be combined in the same shipment.

The Role of Manufacturing within Supply Chain Process Management

Chapter 1 included a description of the Supply Chain Operations Reference Model (SCOR®), Version 12.0. SCOR is a process-based supply chain management framework used to describe the work, material, and information flows in the supply chain. It focuses on five business processes to link firms in a supply chain: Plan, Source, Make, Deliver, and Return. Of these, manufacturing, or "make" in SCOR terminology, is of interest in this section. Make is described as "the activities associated with the conversion of materials or creation of the content for services."[43]

---

[41] The Procter and Gamble Company website, http://www.pglocations.com/.

[42] The focused factory concept was originally published by Wickham Skinner, "The Focused Factory," *Harvard Business Review*, Vol. 6, No. 3 (May–June 1974), pp. 113–121; more recent updates of the concept can be found in Hendrik Brumme, Daniel Simonovich, Wickham Skinner, and Luk N. Van Wassenhove, "The Strategy-Focused Factory in Turbulent Times," *Production and Operations Management*, Vol. 24, Issue 10 (October 2015), pp. 1513–1523; and Luk Van Wassenhove, "How 'Focused Factories' Deal with Disruption," *Insead Operations*, November 9, 2015, https://knowledge.insead.edu/operations/how-focused-factories-deal-with-disruption-4357.

[43] APICS Supply Chain Council, *Quick Reference Guide: Supply Chain Operations Reference (SCOR®) Model*, Version 12.0 (2017). For further information on the SCOR Model and the APICS Supply Chain Council, see http://www.apics.org/apics-for-business/products-and-services/apics-scc-frameworks/scor.

Manufacturing and the SCOR Model

The SCOR model describes supply chains in three levels of detail. The first describes the five business processes listed above. The next two levels are known respectively as "configuration" and "element." A fourth level, implementation, is beyond the scope of this discussion of the SCOR Model. At the configuration level, the make process is separated into three configurations: make-to-stock, make-to-order, and engineer-to-order. These aspects were discussed earlier in this chapter. The third means that in addition to being built, products are designed to customer specifications. At the third level, element, each configuration is broken down into specific activities. For example, the activities corresponding to a make-to-order configuration include scheduling, issuing product, production and testing, packaging, staging for delivery, and release to delivery.

In addition to the three levels of detail used to describe the supply chain, the SCOR Model provides input to measure and benchmark the performance of supply chains. This is possible because processes at all levels are standardized. This makes it possible to apply standardized metrics, which serve as a basis to compare the performance of a supply chain over time, and also enables benchmarking across comparable supply chains.

In the next section, we will examine a second major function as it relates to supply chain management, and this is the role of marketing in supply chains.

The Role of Marketing in Supply Chains

The marketing function is deeply interrelated with supply chains. Marketing decisions affect the supply chain and vice-versa. For instance, one of the marketing decisions that a firm has to make is to determine the number of distributors authorized to carry a given product line. The more distributors there are, the more complex the resulting supply chain. Conversely, supply chain decisions also affect the marketing function. Take, for instance, the clear relationship between supply chain costs and pricing. The lower the costs, the greater the ability of firms in the supply chain to price their products competitively.

In this section of the chapter, we will look into selected marketing issues and their impact on the supply chain. Specifically, we will discuss consumer response to omnichannel distribution, product stock-outs, data analytics, and product returns.

Marketing and Supply Chain Interfaces

The Marketing Concept and Supply Chain Management

The core concept of marketing is the "marketing concept." This concept states that organizations should attempt to optimize customer satisfaction, integrate and coordinate the various activities and processes of marketing (sometimes referred to as the 4-Ps), and generate long-term profitability. The most significant link between marketing and the supply chain is customer service, which is a major component of customer satisfaction. Each firm in the supply chain provides logistics service to its customers. Such service is driven by marketing considerations. Customer service, given its importance to firms in the supply chain, was treated separately in Chapter 2. However, customer service is not the only important link between marketing and supply chain management. Within the supply chain, organizations must be efficient, that is, *do more with less*, and provide sales and marketing with the goods and services necessary in order to minimize costs and optimize profits.

In order for an organization or supply chain to be successful, any marketing effort must integrate the ideas of having the *right product*, at the *right price*, combined with the *right promotion*, and available in the *right place*—these are the 4-Ps of the marketing mix. SCM plays a critical role, particularly in support of getting the product to the right place at the right time.

Time and Place Utilities

Supply chain activities primarily occur in relationship to the "time" and "place" components of the marketing mix. Examples include on-time delivery of products to customers, manufacturers, wholesalers, distributors, and retailers; high order-fill rates so as to prevent or minimize product stock-outs; and consistent order cycle times that allow organizations to more effectively forecast and plan their activities.

From the perspective of utility creation—an important concept within economics and marketing—a product or service provides customer satisfaction only if it is available to the customer when and where it is needed, referred to as time and place utility. Achieving customer satisfaction requires integrated SCM involving all members of the supply chain. While the customer only sees the final result of the supply chain, raw materials producers, channel intermediaries, third parties, and others all contribute to excellent customer satisfaction, or, alternatively, to not achieving it!

Top management is quite concerned with the value-added of SCM because improvements in time and place utilities are ultimately reflected in profits. Both cost savings in SCM and a stronger marketing position due to an improved supply chain can result in improved bottom-line performance for an organization and its supply chain partners. The more that SCM contributes to the value of a product, the more important SCM becomes.

When SCM is combined with operational efficiencies and effectiveness from the adoption and implementation of various technologies and strategies, e.g., efficient consumer response (ECR), total quality management (TQM), just-in-time (JIT), quick response (QR), vendor management inventory (VMI), strategic partnerships and alliances, market segmentation,[44] and relationship marketing, then individual organizations, and the supply chains of which they are members, benefit.[45] Of course, customers are the ultimate beneficiaries of more effective and efficient supply chain management.

Let's look at some specific issues impacting both marketing and SCM, including the use of omnichannel distribution, product stock-outs, data analytics, and product returns (sometimes referred to as reverse logistics).

Omnichannel Distribution

Omnichannel Distribution Defined

Omnichannel distribution can be defined as "strategic customer care initiatives designed to deliver *seamless* customer experiences across multiple channels (e.g., phone, social media, web, mobile, and e-mail) and devices (in-store, laptop, and smartphone)."[46] Each of these possible channels may require a different or modified supply chain. Certainly, the "brick-and-mortar" stores of Walmart, Target Stores, and Apple are different than their websites, and each requires a slightly different supply chain structure and process. When done correctly, as these firms do, significant benefits result, including improved customer retention, higher average profit margin per customer, and greater customer lifetime value. Examples of results achieved by "best-in-class" organizations implementing effective and efficient omnichannel distribution are presented in Table 9.3.

The omnichannel approach is primarily utilized by retailers, although the concept can apply to all types of organizations. "The idea of the omnichannel shopper is now undeniable, made possible by massive and rapid adoption of 'smart' mobile technologies by consumers the world over. Most retailers find their operational models challenged as a result. . . . Omnichannel shopping breaks the traditional operational model. Now, consumers routinely investigate and select products in nonstore channels, even when they complete those purchases in the store. Consumers don't care about *channels*, but they do care about finding *solutions* to their lifestyle needs, and a retailer either satisfies a need or it doesn't."[47]

---

[44] For a specific examination of segmentation within supply chains, see "Supply Chain Segmentation Enabled: Why Focusing on Operations and Using New Technology Makes All the Difference," *White Paper*, GT Nexus, 2013, http://www.gtnexus.com.

[45] For an examination of SCM technology issues in Australian organizations, although applicable to all geographical regions, see "Project Noah: When It Comes to the Crunch," *White Paper*, GS1 Australia Limited, September 2013.

[46] Omer Minkara, "Omni-Channel Customer Care," Aberdeen Group, *White Paper*, October 2013, p. 1.

[47] Nikki Baird and Brian Kilcourse, "Omni-Channel Fulfillment and the Future of Retail Supply Chain: Benchmark Report," Retail Systems Research, *White Paper*, March 2011, p. 5.

TABLE 9.3
Top Performers in Omnichannel Distribution

Source: Omer Minkara, "Omni-Channel Customer Care," Aberdeen Group, *White Paper*, October 2013, p. 3.

Definition of Maturity Class	Mean Class Performance
Best-in-Class (Top 20%)	89% customer retention rate 9.5% average year-over-year improvement in annual company revenue 8.5% average year-over-year improvement in first contact resolution rates 7.5% average year-over-year improvement (decrease) in average cost per customer contact
All Others (Bottom 80%)	33% customer retention rate 3.4% average year-over-year improvement in annual company revenue 1.6% average year-over-year improvement in first contact resolution rates 0.2% average year-over-year improvement (decrease) in average cost per customer contact

Macy's Implements Omnichannel Distribution

As an illustration of how a major retailer has embraced the concept of omnichannel distribution, Macy's has planned a new direct-to-consumer fulfillment center in Oklahoma to support its omnichannel strategy. The cost of that new facility?—a cool $170 million, which includes the 1.3-million-square-foot building, materials handling equipment, and warehouse management system (WMS). The new facility will process orders from Macy's app, Macy's stores, and the macys.com website.[48]

From a supply chain perspective, fulfillment of customer orders in an omnichannel environment requires a number of approaches, including satisfying demand from all channels out of any of the firm's distribution centers and a channel-specific supply network that enables some inventory sharing across channels.[49] Either inventory can be procured centrally and allocated across all of the channels, or each channel can be responsible for maintaining its own inventory levels.

When leading-edge companies were asked about the potential use of technology in omnichannel distribution, more than 80 percent indicated that business analytics could be used to report cross-channel activity and geographic proximity of customers to retail stores. Additionally, more than three-quarters of those companies commented that distributed order management/customer order management technologies would add significant value to the fulfillment process.[50] Examples of omnichannel aspects that impact supply chain management include over 35% of customers expect to be able to contact the same person at a company irrespective of which channel they are using; 64% of customers expect to obtain assistance from every channel; 61% of customers have had difficulty in switching from one channel of a firm to another; within a few years, customers will expect "perfect order" percentages near 100%; 64% of marketers identified a lack of resources as the most significant barrier to achieving omnichannel retailing; 45% of in-store shoppers expect sales personnel to be knowledgeable about products the firm sells online; 50% of shoppers expect that they will be able to purchase online and pick up in-store; and 69% of consumers want in-store sales personnel to have mobile devices that can look up product information and check inventory levels.[51]

[48] "Macy's Invests $170 Million in New Omnichannel Fulfillment Center," *Apparel*, December 20, 2013, http://apparel.edgl.com/news/Macy-s-Invests-$170-Million-in-New-Omnichannel-Fulfillment-Center90201.
[49] "25 Amazing Omnichannel Statistics Every Marketer Should Know," *Relevate Auto*, April 13, 2017, http://www.relevateauto.com/25-amazing-omnichannel-statistics-every-marketer-should-know/; and Baird and Kilcourse, "Omni-Channel Fulfillment," p. 6.
[50] Baird and Kilcourse, "Omni-Channel Fulfillment," p. 20.
[51] "25 Amazing Omnichannel Statistics Every Marketer Should Know."

Data Analytics

Organizations have attempted to analyze and evaluate data since the dawn of market research. Collection of primary and secondary data to assist decision making and understand customers has been a priority of companies for decades. However, the sheer volume of data that are now available is so large that traditional methods of collection and analysis don't work as well, or fast enough, to make the rapid decisions that are required in today's marketplace. Fully 95 percent of C-level executives in companies believe that high quality data are integral in the development and implementation of their business strategies.[52]

The availability of enormous amounts of both structured and unstructured data is a major issue facing organizations as they try to better understand their customers, their markets, and their competitors. In a report published by IBM and MIT's *Sloan Management Review*, it was stated that "organizations that achieve a competitive advantage with analytics are over two times more likely to substantially outperform their industry peers."[53]

Data is everywhere in and outside of organizations. Companies have management information systems (MISs) that contain vast amounts of historical data on customer buying habits, invoices, market research studies, financial information, etc. That data could be examined, analyzed, and evaluated whenever an organization had to make a decision with respect to marketing and/or supply chain strategies. Often, the analyses would take considerable amounts of time, especially if in-depth and detailed results were needed. Today, however, organizations do not have the luxury of making decisions after days or weeks of analyses of the data in their MIS. Decisions often have to be made the same day, sometimes within hours, and the data may not be in the nice, structured formats found in an MIS. Much of the data needed by organizations would be considered unstructured, and often come from social media sources.

Data Rich, but Information Poor

Organizations typically are not held back because of a lack of data; they actually have too much data and are uncertain as to how to utilize it quickly and effectively to make business decisions.[54] This is often referred to as being "data rich, but information poor."

Data available to organizations can come from multiple sources, including the Internet of Things (IoT), social media (e.g., Facebook, Twitter, blogs), web data, manufacturing data, sales histories, RFID tags and bar codes, GPS, mobile apps, and many more. The dilemma is "how to use the data?" For example, if a company has a private fleet of delivery vehicles, it will likely collect data on vehicle movements, accidents, road conditions, delays, and traffic congestion. What would be some uses of that data?

There are traditional uses such as determining time-in-transit of shipments to customers and distances traveled by each vehicle, but are there any other nontraditional uses of the data being collected? In the same way that some organizations collect and sell data to clients, organizations have potential revenue streams from the variety of data they collect in normal day-to-day operations. For example, for the company operating its own fleet of delivery vehicles, insurance companies could assess the risk associated with different roads. Navigation data from various GPS equipment in vehicles could use tracking data to determine the quickest route between two locations at different times of day.[55] Of course, organizations could also utilize the data in a real-time fashion, such as making on-the-spot decisions about vehicle rerouting or rescheduling.

---

[52] "The 2018 Global Data Management Benchmark Report," Experian Information Solutions Report, 2018, https://media.bitpipe.com/io_14x/io_142148/item_1686758/2018-global-data-management-benchmark -report.pdf.

[53] Paul C. Zikopoulos, Dirk deRoos, Krishnan Parasuraman, Thomas Deutsch, David Corrigan, and James Giles, *Harness the Power of Big Data* (New York: McGraw-Hill, 2013), p. 3.

[54] Lisa Harrington and Toby Gooley, "Big Data Analytics in Supply Chain: Tackling the Tidal Wave," *DC Velocity*, January 16, 2018, http://www.dcvelocity.com/articles/20180116-big-data-analytics-in-supply -chain-tackling-the-tidal-wave/.

[55] "Big Data: Lessons from the Leaders," The Economist Intelligent Unit Limited, *White Paper*, 2012, p. 11.

Obstacles to Implementing Data Analytics

Supply chain decision makers are beginning to utilize data analytics in a variety of ways, including to increase supply chain visibility, evaluate risk, enhance demand planning capabilities, enhance S&OP planning, develop product and market segmentation strategies, support sustainability initiatives, and analyze data from social media to detect new market trends. Each of these ways has the potential of improving an organization's ROI and its understanding of customers. However, there are obstacles to implementing data analytics in SCM, and not all organizations will be able to implement such programs immediately. Common obstacles include difficulties in integrating big data with current information systems, understanding which data to collect and interpret, gathering and interpreting external unstructured data from social media sites, and updating older legacy systems found in many companies, including heavy reliance on spreadsheets.

In sum, the use of data analytics in marketing and SCM allows organizations to better know their customers, and by knowing their customers better, develop optimal strategies and tactics to serve them.[56]

Consumer Response to Product Stock-outs

A stock-out occurs when a customer attempts to buy an item and finds that it is unavailable. It is a customer service failure because it results from maintaining insufficient inventory to cover the demand. While stock-outs can also occur in business-to-business relationships, we focus here on stock-outs that occur in a retail environment.

Stock-outs Impact Manufacturers and Retailers Differently

The consumer's responses to stock-outs at retail affect members of the supply chain differently. For example, if the customer substitutes another product for the one he or she intended on buying, the retailer does not lose the sale, although it may lose margins if the substituted product has a lower margin than the one the customer wanted to buy. The manufacturer or producer of the original product being substituted for will lose the sale. If the customer goes to another store to make the purchase that he or she originally intended, the retailer loses the sale, but the manufacturer or producer of the item still makes the sale. To illustrate, a recent survey of consumers found that 73 percent of U.S. consumers would purchase from a different store than originally intended if they were unable to find an item they wanted in stock.[57]

The topic of product stock-outs was briefly mentioned in Chapter 2 and the example of smartphones was presented. It bears repeating here in that it illustrates the importance of having products in stock as much as possible. Motorola, one of the largest producers of mobile telephones, understands the importance of having each of its 120 models of phones in stock. One-half of the stock-outs of mobile phones at retail stores occur because of poor ordering and replenishment/forecasting processes.[58] And, as is the case for many specialty electronic items, customers who are not able to purchase the mobile phone they want will buy it from a competitor. Thus, Motorola faces the possibility of losing those customers for the life of the service contract.

If stock-outs do occur, the implications for retailers and manufacturers are generally as follows:

Implications of Product Stock-outs

- For retailers generally, brand switching in the short term will likely not adversely impact revenues significantly if the product stock-out is not repeated.

- Brand loyal customers will go to a different store approximately one-half the time to purchase the same product; therefore, for those shoppers, the stock-out cost is higher for the retailer than for the manufacturer.

---

[56] For some examples of how data analytics can be used to deliver better service to customers, see Trip Kucera and David White, "Towards Segments of One: Predictive Analytics for Marketing Delivers the Future of Offer Management, Today," *White Paper*, Aberdeen Group, April 2013.

[57] "The Supply Chain Impact Survey," Capgemini, *White Paper*, November 2013, p. 11.

[58] Thomas W. Gruen, Daniel S. Corsten, and Sundar Bharadwaj, *Retail Out-of-Stocks: A Worldwide Examination of Extent, Causes and Consumer Responses* (Washington, DC: Grocery Manufacturers of America, 2002), p. 40.

- If the item(s) that are out-of-stock are not needed immediately by the shopper, many will delay the purchase until a later trip to the same store.
- Brand switching results in direct loss of revenues and profits to manufacturers; thus, stock-out costs will be high in the short term.
- Brand loyal shoppers will wait to buy the product, buy a different size of the same product, or travel elsewhere to buy the product; thus, out-of-stock costs to manufacturers will be low in the short term.
- Overall, the cost of a stock-out is higher for manufacturers than retailers because most shoppers will engage in substitution behavior, often selecting another brand.

When retailers experience out-of-stocks in their stores, there are a multitude of options available to them, including, but not limited to, fulfilling orders from other stores or a distribution center, wholesaler, distributor, or manufacturer.[59] Other strategies that can help eliminate stock-outs, or help to minimize their potential adverse effects, include the following.

Strategies for Retailers

Retail Stock-out Strategies

- For products where shoppers exhibit significant brand loyalty, sufficient inventories should be maintained to cover variations in demand (higher safety stocks than normal will be required).
- Systems with manufacturers or food wholesalers should be developed to provide expedited delivery of certain products when stock-outs do occur.
- Because of the "hidden costs" of rain checks, product substitutions should be offered to customers experiencing stock-outs.
- Periodic surveys of customers should be conducted to determine their out-of-stock behavior for items in the major product categories carried by the retail store(s).
- Product availability of key items should be checked at least once each day, but preferably twice (prior to store opening/early in the day and mid-day), so that demand can be monitored more closely.

Strategies for Manufacturers

Manufacturer Stock-out Strategies

- Sufficient safety stocks should be maintained to minimize retailer stock-outs through the use of:
  1. EDI or Internet interface with retailers, wholesalers, and distribution centers.
  2. Frequent monitoring of stock levels in the store(s).
  3. Supplying retailers with multiple sizes and varieties of manufacturer's brand(s).

- Retail stores should be placed on scheduled delivery programs whenever possible.
- Direct store delivery should be made of some products, such as sale and other promotional items.
- Expedited transportation should be used when product stock-outs are expected to last more than one day.
- Cooperative efforts with retailers should be initiated for the purpose of conducting out-of-stock research at individual store location(s).

Use of Vendor Managed Inventory in Preventing Stock-outs

Of course, the best option is to eliminate the stock-out before it can occur. Good forecasting or the use of vendor managed inventory (VMI) would be useful in eliminating or minimizing product stock-outs. VMI could be especially helpful because the manufacturer could proactively monitor inventory levels of products and provide delivery of items that were going out-of-stock in the short term.

---

[59] For a discussion of various retail product stock-out options, see Baird and Kilcourse, "Omni-Channel Fulfillment," pp. 10–11.

Product Returns

A supply chain issue that has become more prominent in recent years is product returns. Consumers return products to retailers; retailers return products to manufacturers and distributors; manufacturers return items to vendors and suppliers. It is a normal part of doing business. According to the IHL Group, a retail analyst firm, the annual global cost of returns was close to US$600 billion, and the National Retail Federation estimated that product returns accounted for approximately 8 percent of total retail sales, or approximately US$265 billion annually.[60] With the rise of e-commerce, those numbers will likely increase because product return rates are higher in Internet sales than in brick-and-mortar stores.

For example, overall, the e-commerce return rate is about 18 to 25 percent, which is three times that of brick-and-mortar stores. Return rates can be even higher for certain products such as clothing and shoes.[61] However, some of those returns are controllable, as evidenced by approaches implemented by firms such as Lands' End. The firm makes certain that all sizes of clothing and shoes that it sells will fit a customer once it knows which size he or she wears. So, if a customer orders any shirt or blouse of a certain size, it makes no difference what style or design that item has, it will always fit. The same is true for shoes, which are notorious for having different widths and lengths, even when the shoe size says it's the same. Lands' End requires its shoe vendors to make certain that any size shoe they make for the company will fit the customer, irrespective of whether the shoe is a dress shoe, loafer, slipper, sandal, etc. That approach drastically reduces the number of returns due to the product not fitting.

Every person who has ever ordered items from the Internet, or purchased products in brick-and-mortar stores, for that matter, has probably returned a product for one reason or another. It can be a very frustrating experience for customers, especially during very busy holiday periods, such as Christmas, Mother's Day, Valentine's Day, and, of course, birthdays and anniversaries. This is becoming an increasingly significant issue for online retailers because consumers are ordering more and because they cannot use all of their five senses to evaluate the products they are purchasing. For that and other reasons, the majority of products returned to an online retailer are not defective. The Reverse Logistics Association estimated that in 2017, of the 400 million e-commerce product returns, 80 to 90 percent were not defective.[62]

To illustrate, of the one in seven cell phones that are returned by customers, more than one-half are not defective.[63] "Every year roughly 1.2 billion cell phones are sold throughout the world. . . . That means that 96 million phones—perfectly usable devices—are available for resale. That's a lot of money to be had on the secondary market—more than $15 billion annually."[64] Thus, it is important that organizations attempt to eliminate returns before they occur, and if they do, optimize their returns processing capabilities to maximize costs and maximize recovery value of the items that are returned.

---

[60] "Returns: The Dark Side of E-commerce," Swisslog, *White Paper*, August 2016, http://www.dcvelocity .com/files/pdfs/whitepapers/forte-returns_dark_side_of_ecommerce_wp.pdf; also see John Costanzo, "Is Your Business Ready for a Spike in Customer Returns?," *SupplyChainBrain*, September 9, 2013, http://www.supplychainbrain.com/content/index.php?id=7098&type=98&tx_ttnews[tt_news] =24120&cHash=da03e20e36.
[61] *DC Velocity* Staff, "Online Returns Activity Proves Adage That Bad Things Can Happen to Good Products," *DC Velocity White Paper*, January 24, 2018, http://www.dcvelocity.com/articles/20180124 -online-returns-activity-proves-adage-that-bad-things-can-happen-to-good-products/.
[62] Ibid.
[63] "Improving Sustainability with Better Reverse Logistics," *SupplyChainBrain*, March 18, 2011, http:// www.supplychainbrain.com/content/index.php?id=7098&type=98&tx_ttnews[tt_news]=10533&cHash =da03e20e36.
[64] Costanzo, "Is Your Business Ready for a Spike in Customer Returns?"

Returns consist of both products and packaging. By far, the most significant portion of returns, when measured by the value of items being returned, will be the products themselves. While packaging is an important component of reverse logistics, it represents only a small portion of the total value of the returned item. Thus, organizations place a larger emphasis on optimizing the recovery value of all products that are returned.

Controllable versus Uncontrollable Returns

When products are returned, the customer could be returning them for a variety of reasons. Generally, there are two types of returns: *controllable* and *uncontrollable*. Controllable returns are those that could have been avoided by an organization. For example, poor product quality due to manufacturing problems, damaged products from poor handling or transport, incorrect forecasts, shipping of the wrong product to customers, poorly written instructions accompanying products for their set-up and implementation, and others, are illustrations of why products might be returned by customers. Research has indicated that about two-thirds of the consumers who return online or telephone purchases do so because of seller error, such as delivering the wrong size or color of an item.[65]

Chargeback.com identified 10 common reasons for a product return. While some returns are "normal" and just a part of doing business, excessive amounts of product returns can have serious implications for customer satisfaction levels and company profitability. The most common return reasons include:[66]

- Incorrect product or size is ordered by customer.
- Product is no longer needed by the customer.
- Product did not match description on website or in the catalog (approximately 22% of returns are due to product appearance being different than what was seen on the company website).
- Product did not meet customer expectations (occurs in 47% of product returns).
- Company shipped the wrong product or size (57% returned due to retailer error).
- Customers are not familiar with the company website or confused by the process used for ordering or paying for the merchandise.
- Customers are unfamiliar with the product they are buying.
- Holiday purchases are returned after the holiday.
- Wardrobing, where customers buy an item for single time or limited use and then return the item; they never intended to keep the item.
- Fraudulent returns (which cost retailers an estimated US$16 billion each year).

Product Returns at Kellogg Company

In the grocery sector, it is estimated that approximately US$10 billion is lost each year due to product returns. Walmart and several other food companies and consumer packaged goods firms, such as Nestlé, Kroger, Unilever, and Dole, have partnered with IBM's blockchain platform to improve food supply chain visibility and traceability for the purpose of reducing the US$48 million food-borne illnesses that occur in the United States each year.[67] Additionally, the blockchain approach will help ensure that perishable items do not spoil before they can be sold in stores. Knowing exactly when and where those goods are in the supply chain can help to get them onto the supermarket shelves to be purchased by customers, rather than sitting around somewhere in a warehouse or distribution center.

---

[65] Voxware, "Repeat Business Threatened by Faulty Delivery and Returns Process, Survey Finds," *SupplyChainBrain*, January 21, 2013, http://www.supplychainbrain.com/content/index.php?id=7098&type =98&tx_ttnews[tt_news]=20290&cHash=da03e20e36.

[66] Cassi Matthews, "Top 10 Reasons for a Product Return," *Chargeback*, May 6, 2015, https://chargeback .com/top-10-reasons-for-a-product-return/.

[67] "How Blockchain Could Transform Food Safety," *CB Insights*, December 13, 2017, https://www.cbinsights .com/research/blockchain-grocery-supply-chain/.

All controllable returns can be nearly eliminated with better manufacturing, marketing, and/or logistics processes.[68] What cannot be eliminated are products being returned for uncontrollable reasons. Most notable of the causes of these types of returns is "buyer's remorse," where the buyers merely "change their mind" about purchasing the item.

Once products have been returned, the organization must attempt to recover as much value as possible from the items. Several disposition options are available.[69] For the packaging materials, reuse, refurbish, reclamation, recycling, and salvage are possibilities, each with its own recovery value. For products, returning them to the seller, reselling the items, selling them via an outlet store, salvage, donating items to charities, reconditioning the item, refurbishment, remanufacture, reclamation, recycling, and salvage are potential disposition strategies.[70]

ADT Security Systems Improves Its Product Returns Process

ADT Security Systems combined with Inmar Reverse Logistics to improve its product returns process. The company has approximately 7.2 million customers and responds to tens of thousands of alarm signals every day. A major problem facing ADT was its inability to quickly and efficiently return more than 800,000 defective parts each year back to its suppliers for credit, even though more than 30 percent of the returned parts were still under warranty. ADT sought assistance from Inmar, a reverse logistics service provider, to develop a solution that would both save money and improve customer service. "ADT technicians return all defective parts to the branches, which in turn ship them to Inmar at the same frequency. Inmar then verifies each item's warranty status, obtains return authorization and ships parts to the appropriate supplier. For their part, suppliers send replacement parts to an Inmar returns facility, which then redeploys them to the branches as requested. Inmar's real-time, interactive screening software oversees the process via the 3PL's Web portal."[71]

Customer-Friendly Returns Processes

Whatever process employed by organizations for handling product returns, it must be "customer-friendly." Research has shown that a large number of customers will not continue to shop at a brick-and-mortar store or online retailer that does not handle product returns well. In fact, about one-quarter of customers who have returned items to companies have limited their future shopping with those organizations where the returns process is either slow, inconvenient, difficult, and/or time-consuming.[72]

Customer-friendly returns management programs must be implemented, especially with respect to online returns. Online customers typically expect their returns to be processed within 48 hours.[73] So, how can the process be made more customer-friendly? Some possible approaches can include making the returns process as easy and convenient as possible by providing customers with shipping labels (either pre-paid or customer pay), sending e-mails to customers letting them know that their return has been received and when the credit is

---

[68] For a discussion of how organizations can reduce the number of controllable returns, see Cassi Matthews, "Top 10 Reasons for a Product Return."

[69] For a thorough discussion of various aspects of investment recovery, see Paul Wengert, *Investment Recovery Handbook* (Kansas City, MO: Investment Recovery Association, 2012); also see "The Product Return Effect," Midas Exchange, *White Paper*, February 13, 2017, http://www.midas-exchange.com /resources/thought-leadership/white-paper-the-product-return-effect/.

[70] For a discussion of the most common disposition options, see John Sell, "Returns in the Retail Supply Chain with a Specific Focus on e-Commerce," MD Logistics, *White Paper*, June 6, 2017, https:// www.mdlogistics.com/2017/06/white-paper-returns-in-the-retail-supply-chain-with-a-specific-focus-on -e-commerce/. For one of the earliest discussions on return disposition options, see Dale S. Rogers and Ronald S. Tibben-Lembke, *Going Backwards: Reverse Logistics Trends and Practices* (Reno, NV: Reverse Logistics Executive Council, 1999).

[71] "How to Improve ROI on Product Returns," *SupplyChainBrain*, December 15, 2011, http://www .supplychainbrain.com/content/index.php?id=7098&type=98&tx_ttnews[tt_news]=13241&cHash =da03e20e36.

[72] Siegfried Mortkowitz, Priyanka Asera, and Paddy Le Count, "Winning Omnichannel Supply Chain in Retail," Eyefortransport *Report*, 2017, https://www.eft.com/content/winning-omnichannel-supply-chain -retail; also see Voxware, "Repeat Business Threatened by Faulty Delivery and Returns Process."

[73] Costanzo, "Is Your Business Ready for a Spike in Customer Returns?"

likely to occur, allowing online returns to be made either online or at a brick-and-mortar store (if possible), and others.[74]

In a very interesting example of product returns, Rent the Runway, a fashion technology company that rents high- to mid-fashion designer clothing to customers, has a 100% product return rate. People rent various articles of clothing, from complete outfits to accessories, wear them, and then return them to the company. Items then must be dry cleaned before they can be rented again. Various rental plans are offered to customers, including an unlimited package where users can return pieces at any time. The rental concept has been so successful that Alibaba has invested in the company.[75]

In sum, product returns have become an important aspect of supply chain management and can be a competitive advantage for organizations that "do it right!"

In the next section, we follow up on the earlier discussions of the roles of manufacturing and marketing in supply chain management by examining the role of finance in supply chains.

The Role of Finance in Supply Chains

In Chapter 2, we saw how customer service issues interfaced with company financials such as the income statement and balance sheet. We examined the DuPont Model, or Strategic Profit Model, in terms of how supply chain activities could impact a firm's income statements via variable expenses, sales revenues, and other factors. In the balance sheet, factors such as inventories, assets, and other factors were affected by various supply chain activities. Additionally, we also saw how financial leverage, or the use of borrowed money, could be employed to impact firms through the financing of various assets needed to implement supply chain processes. In this section, we will examine how supply chains are financed and provide some examples of how various supply chain activities impact a firm's financial statements.

Supply Chain Financing Options

In a micro sense, financing in the supply chain involves a number of process areas where monies must be paid or received for services and materials. In Chapter 8, *Sourcing and Procurement*, issues such as e-sourcing were examined. The consideration of how and where firms in the supply chain pay and get paid are important. Contract negotiations in supplier/vendor selection must include terms of payment discussions. Technology such as e-payables software are often used to pay for materials and services that are procured. In later chapters of this textbook, where global commerce will be examined, supply chain financing often requires bank letters of credit and other forms of payment to be made between parties separated by great distances.

"The health of a global supply chain isn't just measured by revenues and profit. A more relevant indicator is how efficiently capital flows between buyers and suppliers. Slow moving capital, much like slow moving inventory, creates unnecessary costs and inefficiencies in a supply chain."[76] In sum, supply chain management must consider the financial aspects within and between each supply chain process activity.

On a macro level are issues relating to supply chain financing, which is defined as when some firm in the supply chain provides financing for part or all of the chain. Often, by creating financing from within the supply chain, the entire process of producing a product can

---

[74] For a discussion of various ways of making product returns more easy and convenient to customers, see Murphy, "Best Practices in Reverse Logistics Can Ease the Pain of Product Returns."

[75] Interview with Josh Builder, Chief Technology Officer of Rent the Runway, March 12, 2018; Jamie Grill-Goodman, "Rent the Runway: CTO Josh Builder on How Homegrown Retail Tech Drives Its Data-Driven Success," *Retail Info Systems*, March 5, 2018, https://risnews.com/rent-runway-cto-josh-builder -how-homegrown-retail-tech-drives-its-data-driven-success; and "Alibaba Invests in Rent the Runway," *E-Retailers*, March 12, 2018, https://internetretailing.com.au/alibaba-invests-rent-runway/.

[76] "Supply Chain Finance Fundamentals: What It Is, What It's Not and How It Works," PrimeReview *Report*, 2016, p. 2, https://primerevenue.com/what-is-supply-chain-finance/.

FIGURE 9.3
The Supply Chain
Finance Process

Source: "Supply Chain
Finance Fundamentals:
What It Is, What
It's Not and How it
Works," *PrimeReview
Report*, 2016, p. 7,
https://primerevenue
.com/what-is-supply
-chain-finance/.

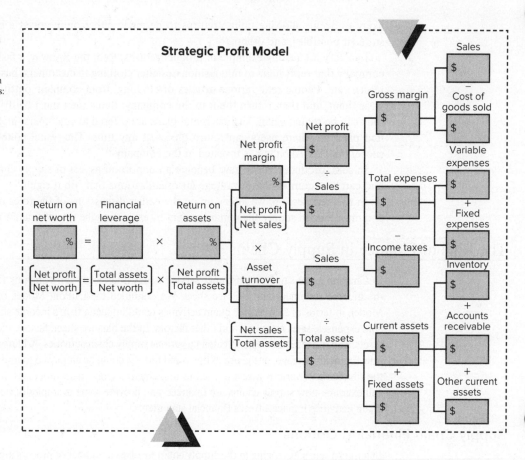

become more predictable and more profitable. To illustrate, with sole sourcing becoming more commonplace, if a company that utilizes a single supplier for components needed in its manufacturing process found that its major supplier, without warning, closed its doors because of severe cash flow problems, what would it do? If the firm was unaware of the financial problems of its sole supplier, it might be left without a source of supply for that component. It would take some time to replace that supplier, but in the meantime, there might be production slowdowns or shutdowns, which are very expensive, not to mention potentially severe customer service failures. If the manufacturer had better communications with the original supplier, it possibly could have been aware of the financial problems the supplier was experiencing, and might have been able to assist with helping the supplier arrange suitable financing. Hence, the importance of supply chain financing.

Supply Chain
Financing Defined

A very broad, but encompassing definition of supply chain finance (SCF) is as follows: "A broad term that encompasses a vast variety of financial solutions (finance) that provide support to the different commercial partners engaging in the different stages of the productive chain (supply chain) of a company, from the time the purchase order is issued until the corresponding invoice is paid."[77]

The supply chain financing process is illustrated in Figure 9.3.

---

[77] Elisabet Furió, "Supply Chain Finance: Solutions for Your Company's Working Capital," *BBVA Blog*, July 6, 2016, https://www.bbva.com/en/supply-chain-finance-solutions-for-your-companys-working-capital/; also see "Supply Chain Finance: Enhancing Working Capital Performance," PricewaterhouseCooper, *Working Capital Advisory*, 2014, https://www.pwc.co.uk/services/business-recovery/insights/supply-chain-finance-enhancing -working-capital-performance.html; "Supply Chain Finance," GTNexus, *Solution Overview*, 2017, http://www .gtnexus.com/solutions/supply-chain-finance; and Murray Stevenson, "How Does Supply Chain Finance Differ from Invoice Discounting and Factoring?," Woodsford TradeBridge, November 1, 2017, https:// woodsfordtradebridge.com/supply-chain-finance-invoice-discounting-factoring/.

In addition to the ways that organizations in the supply chain create and utilize financing to support their operations, another aspect of finance applicable to SCM is the financial dimension of various supply chain activities and the many cost trade-offs that are possible within and between supply chain activities and processes.

Financial Aspects of Supply Chain Activities

The chief financial officer (CFO) and the senior supply chain executive are two of the most important members of senior management. It is vital that they collaborate and coordinate their individual responsibilities and activities.[78] Specifically, the CFO can have a positive impact on supply chain management in several ways:

How the CFO Impacts Supply Chain Management

- Help to create consistency across the supply chain.
- Challenge rationale used for new supply chain investments.
- Use data analytics to support supply chain decisions.
- Effectively manage risk with a long-term approach to business decision making.[79]

Use of the Strategic Profit Model

One approach to examining the financial impacts of various supply chain activities is the strategic profit model. This model was previously introduced and discussed in Chapter 2. As seen in Figure 9.3, there are many elements of the profit and loss statement and balance sheet that can be impacted by SCM decisions. While the model could apply to supply chains overall, it has heretofore only been applied to individual companies.

The model is useful in that supply chain decisions can be tracked from a financial perspective through the examination of a decision's impacts on revenues, costs, and assets. To illustrate, let's look at a transportation example that seems fairly straightforward, but in reality, would be a very poor decision. Amazon.com is well known for its sophisticated "last-mile" delivery service to customers. The company can deliver products in two days, next day, or same day, sometimes within a four-hour time window; it all depends on what the customer wants. Amazon.com utilizes a number of transportation carriers such as the USPS, FedEx, and UPS, as well as its own drivers and vehicles to make deliveries. Such fast delivery carries some inherent risk. If a carrier fails to perform, there may not be sufficient time to use a backup carrier to make the delivery; thus, the product will be delivered late. In a very highly competitive marketplace, competitors such as Walmart, Alibaba, Target, and others are more than willing to step in when another competitor "fails." To provide for such an eventuality, Amazon.com might be willing to pay more for super-fast and super-efficient "last mile" delivery. The additional cost can offset the loss of customer goodwill arising from any service failure.

Another transportation example might be where a third-party logistics service provider has been delivering parts to an automotive plant on a just-in-time basis. Even if the company is using the core carrier concept, periodically the firm will issue an RFP (request for proposal) and solicit bids from other carriers for the service. Suppose a new, regional trucker who promises to provide the same service for 5 percent less submits a response to the RFP. If the automobile company selects the cheaper option, there could be significant cost savings. However, what happens if the new carrier is not able to perform up to the contract terms and their promised service levels? Missed scheduled deliveries could cause the plant to book expedited services at considerable extra cost. Inventory expense could increase as the plant, unsure of the vendor's ability to deliver on time, begins to stockpile parts to protect against product stock-outs. Within a short period of time, the "cheaper" carrier could result in significantly more costs!

---

[78] Nicole Lewis, "CFOs & Supply Chain Leaders: A Powerful Combination," *EBN Online*, November 26, 2013, http://ebnonline.com/author.asp?section_id=1059&doc_id=270004&amp.
[79] Ibid.

When one traces the implications of the decision to go with a new and different carrier, it becomes evident that a number of supply elements are impacted within the Strategic Profit Model (see Figure 9.3). Inventory management would be affected by transportation. "To a CFO, lean inventory means 'reduction in working capital tied up in inventory.' But to a logistics manager, it means 'greater need for expedited freight, complicated changes in transport mode, plus pressure for 100% accurate fulfillment. Typical impacts of lower inventory include: (1) higher freight costs because it precludes the use of cheaper, longer-transit modes, and may even require paying a premium for expedited freight; (2) stock-outs, which on the inbound side can cause plant or production line shut-downs due to lack of raw material or parts, and on the outbound side, can lead to empty shelves, missed sales or, at worst, the loss of a customer and the associated lifetime revenue; and (3) increased labor costs to rapidly process the inventory, monitor stock levels and arrange transport for urgent restocking."[80]

In Chapter 16, various financial aspects of supply chains will be discussed further. Issues such as the use of various metrics and the measurement of financial performance will be examined. Financial elements are important in all activities and processes of supply chain management.

Summary

Supply chain management (SCM) is an integrating function with primary responsibility for linking major business functions and processes within and across companies. Some of the major business functions that contribute to effective and efficient SCM are manufacturing, marketing, and finance.

Key manufacturing issues include make-to-stock (MTS) and make-to-order (MTO), material requirements planning (MRP), lean and agile manufacturing, and ERP. In an MTS strategy products are manufactured in anticipation of demand, while in an MTO strategy, products are manufactured after a customer places an order. Material requirements planning (MRP) systems are designed to manage the flow of raw materials and components to the factory floor. MRP computes the quantity needed of each raw material or component required to support a production plan and establishes the timetable for when raw materials or components will be needed and, therefore, should be ordered. Lean production differs from traditional manufacturing approaches where products are manufactured in batches. In lean production, the production process runs as much as possible in a constant flow. In contrast, the goal of agile manufacturing is to timely respond to changes in demand, including level, location, and product type. Agility relies heavily on manufacturing flexibility as a response to constantly changing markets. ERP also incorporates core financials, customer relationship management (CRM), human resources, asset tracking, marketing automation, project management, and other aspects of the supply chain to assist in the management of the process.

The marketing function is deeply interrelated with supply chains. Marketing decisions affect the supply chain and vice-versa. Organizations must be efficient, that is, do more with less, and provide sales and marketing with the goods and services necessary in order to minimize costs and optimize profits. In order for an organization or supply chain to be successful, any marketing effort must integrate the ideas of having the *right product*, at the *right price*, combined with the *right promotion*, and available in the *right place*—these are the 4Ps of the marketing mix. SCM plays a critical role, particularly in support of getting the product to the right place at the right time. Some specific issues impacting both marketing and SCM are omnichannel distribution, product stock-outs, data analytics, and product returns.

---

[80] "The Freight to Finance Translation Guide: A CFO Primer on Transportation's Impact on Financial Performance," PLS Logistics Services, *White Paper*, July 2012, http://info.pslogistics.com/freighttofinanceguide/.

When a firm—manufacturer, retailer, or supplier—supplies financing for part or the rest of the supply chain, that is an illustration of supply chain financing (SCF). SCF encompasses a variety of financial solutions that provide support to the different commercial partners engaging in the different stages of the productive chain (supply chain) of a company, from the time the purchase order is issued until the corresponding invoice is paid.

With this awareness of how various processes such as manufacturing, marketing, and finance relate to SCM, we will next examine in Chapter 10 how relationships with customers and suppliers can be managed effectively and efficiently.

Suggested Readings

"B2B Integration: Synchronizing Your Value Chain of Suppliers, Partners and Customers," IBM, *White Paper*, 2013.

Contributor, Shmula, "5 Important Characteristics of the Lean Supply Chain," Shmula Blog, September 19, 2018, https://www.shmula.com/5-important-characteristics -of-the-lean-supply-chain/27082/.

The Evolution of Decision Making: How Leading Organizations Are Adopting a Data-Driven Culture (Boston: Harvard Business Review Analytic Services, 2012).

Greve, Curtis, and Jerry Davis, *An Executive's Guide to Reverse Logistics* (Curtis Greve, 2012).

Gunnarsson, Martin, "Software Selection for Enterprise Resource Planning," IFS, *White Paper*, September 2015, https://www.bitpipe.com/data/demandEngage.action? resId=1444157440_981.

Jansson, Kade, "'Lean Thinking' and the 5 Principles of Lean Manufacturing," *KaiNexus Blog*, May 2, 2017, https://blog.kainexus.com/improvement-disciplines/lean-thinking -and-the-5-principles-of-lean-manufacturing.

Kirstein, Steven, Jeff Pike, and Bhaskar Banerjee, "Service Supply Chain Optimization Reduces Operational Costs, Increases Customer Loyalty and Generates Recurring Revenue," OnProcess Technology, *White Paper*, 2012.

Kucera, Trip, "Big Data for Marketing: Targeting Success," Aberdeen Group, *White Paper*, January 2013.

"Lean Logistics," *Creative Safety Supply Blog*, August 3, 2017, https://www.creeativesafety supply.com/articles/lean-logistics/.

McBeath, Bill, "Social Data Mining: Beyond Sentiment," *The Brief*, ChainLink Research, November 13, 2013, http://www.clresearch.com/research/detail.cfm?guid=2E19CCBA -3048-79ED-99FD-A6E692B69B1C.

Minkara, Omer, and Sumair Dutta, "The Rising Financial Impact of Customer Service," Aberdeen Group, *White Paper*, May 2013.

"The Missing Link: Technology Is Revolutionising Supply-Chain Finance," *The Economist*, October 12, 2017, https://www.economist.com/news/finance-and-economics /21730150-squeezed-suppliers-and-big-corporate-buyers-stand-benefit-technology.

Mortkowitz, Siegried, Priyanka Asera, and Paddy Le Count, "Winning Omnichannel Supply Chain in Retail," Eyefortransport *Report*, 2017, https://www.eft.com/content /winning-omnichannel-supply-chain-retail.

"The Out of Stock Problem and How to approach It," *Streetspotr Blog*, August 14, 2017, https://streetspotr.com/2017/08/14/out-of-stock/.

Rosenblum, Paula, and Steve Rowen, "The Great Leveler: eCommerce's Next Move," Retail Systems Research, *White Paper*, November 2013.

Stock, James R., *Development and Implementation of Reverse Logistics Programs* (Oak Brook, IL: Council of Logistics Management, 1998).

Tompkins International Staff, "The Future of Omnichannel Retail Supply Chain," Tompkins *Blog*, May 5, 2016, https://www.tompkinsinc.com/Insight/Tompkins-Blog /the-future-of-omnichannel-retail-supply-chain.

"The 2018 Global Data Management Benchmark Report," Experian Information Solutions *Report*, 2018, https://media.bitpipe.com/io_14x/io_142148/item_1686758/2018-global -data-management-benchmark-report.pdf.

"Top 9 Omni-Channel Logistics Challenges Businesses Face," *Legacy Supply Chain Services Blog*, undated, https://legacyscs.com/9-omni-channel-logistics-challenges/.

"We Know Where the Material Is, but . . . Where's the Payment?," *SupplyChainBrain*, March 14, 2018, http://www.supplychainbrain.com/featured-content/single-article/article /we-know-where-the-material-is-but-wheres-the-payment/.

Questions and Problems

LO 9-1   1. Define the terms "make-to-stock" and "make-to-order." What are the major advantages and disadvantages of each these approaches in manufacturing?

LO 9-4   2. Material requirements planning (MRP) is a process often utilized in manufacturing. Briefly describe what MRP is and define/explain the following elements or aspects of MRP:
   a. Master production schedule (MPS)
   b. Bill of materials (BOM)
   c. MRP explosion
   d. Reschedule notice

LO 9-1   3. What is "lean manufacturing" and how is it related to the managerial practices of just-in-time (JIT), total quality management (TQM), total preventive maintenance (TPM), and human resource management (HRM)?

LO 9-2   4. What are the most significant relationships between supply chain management and marketing, specifically the "marketing concept" and the "4Ps"?

5. Briefly discuss how "data analytics" can be applied in supply chain management to improve operations and customer satisfaction.

6. "Product stock-outs" and "product returns" are issues related to reverse logistics. How can more effective and efficient supply chain management impact each of these issues?

LO 9-3   7. Briefly discuss what supply chain financing is and how it impacts firms within the supply chain.

10

Managing Relationships with Customers and Suppliers

Objectives of This Chapter

LO 10-1   To define the spectrum of relationships that may exist between companies and their supply chain partners—the customers and supplier.

LO 10-2   To better understand and appreciate the impact relationships with customers and suppliers have on organizations.

LO 10-3   To examine why and when a company might want to adopt a more strategic approach for working with customers and suppliers.

LO 10-4   To develop an awareness of the factors that can help ensure successful relationships, as well as what elements should go into a contract.

Introduction

Chapter 8 briefly introduced the concept of supplier relationship management from the sourcing and procurement perspective. In this chapter we broaden the relationship discussion to include customers and dig deeper into the various types of trading partner relationships.

Managing relationships with customers and suppliers, or "trading partners," can range from being quite simple to very complex, and the universe of relationships is quite varied. For example, basic chemicals are "mainly sold within the chemical industry and to other industries before becoming a product for the general consumer."[1] This is in an industry with worldwide sales of £3.3 trillion in 2016, or just over $4 trillion.[2] In effect, one firm's output becomes a competitor's input; think about managing those relationships!

---

[1] "The Chemical Industry," Center for Industry Education Collaboration, September 13, 2016, http://essentialchemicalindustry.org/the-chemical-industry/the-chemical-industry.html.
[2] "Cefic Facts & Figures 2017," The European Chemical Industry Council, p. 5, http://fr.zone-secure.net/13451/451623/?startPage=14#page=5.

P&G, with annual sales close to $83 billion, has more than 70,000 suppliers.[3] Of that $83 billion, almost $10 billion is sold through Walmart.[4] Nike is supplied by approximately 580 factories in China, Vietnam, Indonesia, Thailand, Sri Lanka, and Malaysia, to name a few.[5]

And they are not alone—suppliers really matter.

- Even though they have thousands of suppliers, General Motors' top 400 suppliers account for 90 percent of spend.[6]
- McDonald's immediately ended a contract with a chicken provider after a video surfaced showing the unethical treatment of the animals.[7]
- Dell radically changed the way it worked with one of its 3PLs, GENCO, which assisted in returns. It saved millions just in the first two quarters of the contract, and, impressively, reduced scrap by 62 percent.[8]

Managing these complex relationships is critical to firm performance, and to firm success. The ability of a customer and supplier to work together and solve problems can positively impact a firm's financial performance. For instance, in a classic article, Dyer and Singh found that interfirm relationships can provide a competitive advantage in resource-specific assets, knowledge sharing, the use of complementary resources or capabilities, and effective governance.[9] In a followup study Dyer and Hatch found suppliers working with Toyota had reduced defects by 50 percent over a six-year period. These same suppliers reduced defects by only 26 percent to their largest U.S. customer (GM, Ford, or Chrysler). And these capabilities are relationship specific, meaning they cannot be easily transferred to other buyers.[10] Another study found that suppliers can have greater cost efficiencies and innovation when there is a transfer of knowledge from the buyer to the supplier.[11]

For our purposes, we will focus on relationships that are in the business-to-business category (P&G with Walmart, General Motors with 3PLs, etc.) versus business-to-consumer (Dollar Shave Club to its members). However, whatever the size of the business relationship, trading partners must always rely on three Cs of trading partner relationships: contracts, contacts, and collaboration.

[3] Matt Gunn, "How Supply Chain Transformation Saved P&G $1.2 Billion," GTNexus, http://www.gtnexus.com/resources/blog-posts/how-supply-chain-transformation-saved-pg-12-billion.

[4] PYMTS, "Is Walmart's Relationship with P&G In Trouble?," *PYMNTS.com*, June 17, 2016, https://www.pymnts.com/news/retail/2016/walmart-pg-trouble/.

[5] "Nike Inc.'s Comment on Supply Chain," *CSI Market.com*, 2017, https://csimarket.com/stocks/suppliers_glance.php?code=NKE.

[6] Mike Colias, "GM Takes Next Step to Strengthen Relationships with Suppliers," *Automotive News*, February 26, 2014, http://www.autonews.com/article/20140226/OEM10/140229907/gm-takes-next-step-to-strengthen-relationship-with-suppliers.

[7] "Tyson Foods Ends Contract with McDonald's Chicken Nuggets over Animal Abuse," CNN wire service, August 27, 2015, http://fox6now.com/2015/08/27/tyson-foods-ends-contract-with-supplier-for-mcdonalds-chicken-nuggets-over-alleged-animal-abuse/.

[8] Kate Vitasek, Mike Ledyard, and Karl Manrodt, *Vested Outsourcing: Five Rules That Will Transform Outsourcing*, 2nd ed. (Palgrave Macmillan, 2013), p. 196.

[9] Jeffrey Dyer and Harbir Singh, "The Relational View: Cooperative Strategy and Sources of Interorganizational Competitive Advantage," *Academy of Management Review*, Vol. 23, No. 4 (1998), pp. 660–679.

[10] Jeffrey Dyer and Nile Hatch, "Relation-Specific Capabilities and Barriers to Knowledge Transfers: Creating Advantage through Network Relationships," *Strategic Management Journal*, Vol. 27 (May 2006), pp. 709–719.

[11] David Preston, Daniel Chen, Morgan Swink, and Laura Mead, "Generating Supplier Benefits through Buyer-Enabled Knowledge Enrichment: A Social Capital Perspective," *Decision Sciences*, Vol. 48, No. 2 (2017), pp. 248–287.

The 3 Cs of Business Relationships

Contracts

Businesses use a variety of mechanisms as the basis of their formal or implied business relationship. The level of formality differs. Contracts are the most formal, sometimes being quite detailed as to what is expected from each party, perhaps even including a Statement of Work that describes in explicit detail the actions to be taken. Agreements, often called a Memorandum of Understandings (MOU) or Memorandum of Agreement (MOA), are typically less formal and may be as simple as confirming the desire to buy or sell products or services as needed. In some cases the agreement may be based on a "handshake" as opposed to a document with signatures. We will address the successful elements of a trading partner contract later in this chapter.

Contacts

Once the nature of the relationship is understood, the next step is to understand the contacts that you will work with to manage the relationship. Often there could be multiple contacts at different levels in each organization (functional, managerial, and executive) depending on the significance of the relationship. Individual contact responsibilities may vary, and could be clerical and transactional in nature or could be very strategic in nature including corporate executives. The nature of the interaction and frequency of interaction between contacts will differ considerably based on the role and level of the contact within the organization.

Collaboration

The final element is to define the level of collaboration. Some view it as working as a team to achieve a particular goal. Others view it as joint initiatives aimed at "delivering significant improvement over the long term."[12] For our purposes collaboration is a process where two or more people or organizations work together to realize shared goals.

Historically, "collaboration" has sometimes been viewed negatively when it was used to describe individuals who collaborated with enemy forces to help them overcome and occupy the local government or army, such as during WWII when the Nazis were working to overthrow Europe. While there may be instances where the same sort of negative collaboration applies in the supply chain, businesses today tend to view collaboration as a good thing and frame it as the definition suggests: working together to achieve the positive goal.

Unfortunately, many businesses seek collaborative relationships in name only, without a clearly defined goal or understanding of what it takes to truly collaborate. As we go forward, we will adopt the position that collaboration requires mutually defined and beneficial desired outcomes that explicitly define how success will be measured. Anything less is simple interaction and not real collaboration. Collaboration is a new way to compete as it allows everyone to benefit individually and collectively.[13] As Darwin noted over 160 years ago, "In the long history of humankind, those who learned to collaborate and improvise most effectively have prevailed."[14]

Regardless of the form of the relationship, one truth about it will always exist—the desire to achieve specific goals. For example, the Dell and GENCO relationship is very strategic in nature—cost per box was reduced by 32 percent, scrap was cut by 62 percent, and GENCO tripled its profit margins.[15] Dell's desired outcomes focused on reducing costs, while GENCO wanted to increase bottom-line profit. By collaborating with each other, and using specific measurable desired outcomes, they achieved their goals.

---

[12] Luis Benavides, Verda De Eskinazis, and Daniel Swan, "Six Steps to Successful Supply Chain Collaboration," *Supply Chain Quarterly*, Quarter 2, 2012, http://www.supplychainquarterly.com/topics /Strategy/20120622-six-steps-to-successful-supply-chain-collaboration/.

[13] Ensemble of Elan, June 9, 2017, https://ensembleofelan.com/2017/06/09/collaboration-is-the-new -competition/.

[14] Darwin Center for Biogeology, http://www.darwincenter.nl/Content/Downloads/def %20binnenwerkdarwin08•••.pdf.

[15] Robert Bowman, "Dell, GENCO Take the Plunge into Vested Outsourcing," *SupplyChainBrain*, December 20, 2013, http://www.supplychainbrain.com/content/nc/general-scm/business-strategy -alignment/single-article-page/article/dell-genco-take-the-plunge-into-vested-outsourcing/.

TABLE 10.1
Sourcing Business Models

Source: Kate Vitasek, Bonnie Keith, Jim Eckler, and Dawn Evans, "Unpacking Sourcing Business Models," University of Tennessee Center for Executive Education, *White Paper*, 2nd ed., 2015.

Sourcing Business Models	Sourcing Business Model Categories		
	Transaction Based	Outcome Based	Investment Based
Basic Provider Model	X		
Approved Provider Model	X		
Preferred Provider Model		X	
Performance-Based/Managed Services Model		X	
Vested Business Model		X	
Shared Service Model			X
Equity Partnerships (e.g., joint venture)			X

As we have seen above, typical goals from collaborative relationships include improved profitability, access to innovation and capabilities, lower cost structures, improved service levels, higher market share, or often a combination of these and perhaps other elements.

Types of Business Relationships

Supply Chain Partnerships Fall into One of Three Types

Recently, University of Tennessee researchers formalized a classification for managing business relationships. *Strategic Sourcing in the New Economy: Harnessing the Potential of Sourcing Business Models for Modern Procurement*[16] outlines three types of business relationship models. Each model as shown in Table 10.1 differs from a risk/reward perspective and should be evaluated in the context of the goals of the relationship.

As complexity and dependency increase, trading partners tend to migrate to more strategic relationships such as an approved provider or a preferred sourcing relationship. For the most complex high-risk/high-cost contracts, trading partners will tend to adopt outcome-based approaches.

In some cases, companies may fear they might not be able secure a business partner to achieve their objectives, and they may opt for an investment-based approach. Investment-based approaches can take the form of internal capability development or co-investment such as a joint venture. Under a joint venture, a company will often create an equity partnership or other legally binding business arrangement with a firm that gives the company access to the desired capabilities. Another common investment-based option is to centralize the service into a "shared services" group aimed at driving efficiencies.

Each of the types of relationships and implementation strategies is discussed in more detail in the following section.

Sourcing Implementation Strategies

Conventional Approaches

Transaction-Based

Conventional approaches to buyer-supplier relationships are transaction-based and keep trading partners at arm's length. In a transaction-based environment, procurement teams

[16] Bonnie Keith, Kate Vitasek, Karl B. Manrodt, and Jeanne Kling, *Strategic Sourcing in the New Economy: Harnessing the Potential of Sourcing Business Models for Modern Procurement* (New York, NY: Palgrave Macmillan, October 2015).

TABLE 10.2
Attributes of
Transaction-Based
Business Models

Sourcing Relationship	Focus	Interaction	Cooperation Level	Required Trust Level	Characterized by
Simple Transaction Provider	Cost and efficiency	Standard terms, fixed price	Low— Automated where possible	Medium— Single transaction	Abundant and easy to resource, no need for a relationship
Approved Provider	Economies of scale, ease of transactions	Blanket negotiated terms, pricing agreements	Medium— Based on pricing or specifications	Medium— Common terms and price agreement	Managed by category locally and across business sector, purchases bundled for economies of scale
Preferred Provider	Capability, capacity, and technology transactions	Contract, SOW, pricing agreement, possible gain–sharing SLAs	High—Set out in long-term service contract	High— Defined by contract, high spend zone	Integral supply across business units, delivering added value and capability, not so abundant, a pain to re-source

endeavor to limit relationship dependency in an effort to reduce the price of goods or services. Buyers strive to have uniformly available goods and services (e.g., commodities) that can be easily compared across various suppliers. A buyer's goal is often focused around the company's bottom line, which is typically reflected in terms of "price" paid. This procurement-focused approach works well for suppliers that provide general supplies, commodity goods, and general services. There is no intent to partner, only to achieve short-term goals related to pricing or delivery.

Three types of transaction-based business relationships have evolved over time as businesses wrestle with how to create relationships that are better suited for more complex business requirements. The three types are simple transaction providers, approved providers, and preferred providers.

Table 10.2 outlines typical characteristics of each of the transaction-based business models frequently used today.[17]

The economics for each of these types of relationships is very similar in that a buyer pays a supplier by the transaction. There is typically a predefined rate for each transaction, or unit of service. For example, a third-party logistics service provider would get paid monthly for the number of pallets stored, the number of units picked, and the number of orders shipped. A call center service provider would get paid a price per call or a price per minute.

Transaction-based business models are best suited when a buyer is seeking a commodity with standardized and stable specifications that are easily measured through a commonly

[17] Kate Vitasek, Bonnie Keith, Jim Eckler, and Dawn Evans, "Unpacking Sourcing Business Models," University of Tennessee Center for Executive Education, *White Paper*, 2nd ed., 2015. Also see Keith et al., *Strategic Sourcing in the New Economy*.

understood set of metrics. Payment can be triggered based on successful transactions completed.

The three types of transaction-based relationships can be described as follows.

Simple Transaction Based

A simple transaction relationship is one where there is very limited commitment between trading partners and is often used when there are abundant suppliers in the marketplace. Simple transaction-based relationships are typically best suited for commodity-type goods and services where there is little risk in impacting the business. Buyers often use competitive bidding tactics with a goal to achieve low prices.

Simple Transaction-Based Relationship

Simple transaction relationships are often triggered by a purchase order that signals that the buying company agrees to buy a set quantity of goods or tasks (or hours) outlined in the purchase order. The relationship is typically based on a review of performance against standard metrics (did the supplier work that many hours or provide the good or service in the quantities purchased?).

Approved Provider

Approved Provider Relationship

An approved provider relationship typically occurs when a buyer identifies a supplier that offers a unique differentiation from other transactional suppliers and provides a cost, efficiency, or other competitive advantage for the client company. The differentiation could come in the form of geographical location advantage, a cost or quality advantage, or a small disadvantaged business.

Typically, an approved provider is identified as a prequalified option in the pool of transactional suppliers and has fulfilled preconditions for specified service. Approved providers may or may not also have volume thresholds to be in an "approved" status.

An approved provider may or may not operate under a Master Services Agreement—an overarching contract with the buying company. Using a Master Services Agreement enables the buying companies to easily engage the approved supplier because it is already "under contract."

Approved suppliers typically also receive more management attention from buying companies. For example, they may be asked to register in a company's supplier diversity database. They may also be asked to participate in supplier summits or participate in formal supplier reviews.

Case Study – Simple Transaction Based

A hospitality company with several properties purchased a variety of low-cost basic food items such as salt, mustard and other condiments, snack items, and pasta.

The company believed there was a better way to manage these items and implemented a standard e-auction tool that was used by all properties to improve the efficiency of the procurement process and lower costs. Item requirements were entered into the online e-auction tool, the suppliers in the marketplace placed their bids, and the lowest-pricing supplier won the order. No negotiations were conducted, a purchase order was generated using standard terms and conditions, and the distribution program and the properties exerted limited effort to manage a multi-million-dollar spend, which allowed their purchasing resources to focus on higher-cost items.

Source: Kate Vitasek, Bonnie Keith, Jim Eckler, and Dawn Evans, "Unpacking Sourcing Business Models," University of Tennessee Center for Executive Education, *White Paper*, 2nd ed., 2015.

Case Study – Approved Provider

FinanceCo is a financial services firm that is heavily invested in information technology (IT) as part of its product offerings, requiring frequent refreshes in hardware. To support its core business the company has significant spend in the computer servers category. The category is critical to the organization, but there are many suppliers available in the market. Therefore, the company's sourcing strategy was to select multiple approved suppliers in order to simultaneously take advantage of best-in-class solutions and mitigate risk. The procurement and IT business functions within the organization worked closely together as part of the strategic sourcing initiative. This step in the sourcing process resulted in a market analysis, a needs assessment, and forecasts in annual spend. The two teams worked together to create requirements, build a specification, and identify a diversified supply structure.

After an initial qualification of solution providers and prior to the competitive bid (conducted as a Request for Proposal), the firm's engineers worked with the solution product engineers to benchmark the firm's current offerings and requirements, and complete an intense evaluation for qualification and proof-of-concept through lab analysis. This step in the process resulted in a ranked list of solution offerings, a shorter list of qualified suppliers, recommendations for improvement in the firm's product offerings, and specific requirements for the competitive bid. Along with those requirements, the firm issued an RFP with its annual spend forecast.

Following lengthy negotiations with solution providers, the firm selected two suppliers to support the category spend; one supplier supports mission-critical computer servers vital to the firm's own product offerings and a second supplier fills the need for noncritical business applications. Now sourcing happens from a master contract with approved providers operating from proven requirements. Providers are governed through a model that is flexible enough to support future product releases and ongoing procurement. The product-supplier decision was a balance of a total cost of ownership (TCO), which included base product cost and operating cost over the three-year life of the contract, and bottom-line savings.

Source: Kate Vitasek, Bonnie Keith, Jim Eckler, and Dawn Evans, "Unpacking Sourcing Business Models," University of Tennessee Center for Executive Education, *White Paper*, 2nd ed., 2015.

Preferred Provider

Preferred Provider Relationship

Buying companies often seek to do business with a preferred provider in an effort to streamline their buying process and build relationships with key suppliers. Buying companies often enter into longer term contracts with preferred providers using a Master Services Agreement that allows for the companies to do repeat business efficiently. It is common for preferred providers to work under a blanket PO with predefined rates for work where they simply have to "call off" work at short notice. For example, a labor-staffing firm may have a "rate card" that has the hourly rate established for various types of staffing needs. The buying company can easily request staffing support from the preferred provider using the predetermined blanket PO and rate card. Another example might be a facilities management firm having a pre-agreed rate of a certain price per square foot to manage a company's buildings. Often companies will work with a preferred provider under a supplier relationship management plan where both companies agree on improvement or other opportunities.

It is important to point out that a preferred provider is still engaged in a transactional business model, but the nature and efficiencies for how the companies work together go beyond a simple purchase order.

Outcome-Based

An outcome-based business model pays a supplier for the realization of a defined set of business outcomes, business results, or achievement of agreed-on key performance indicators. Outcome-based approaches are typically used when there is a service component to a business relationship (call center support services, facilities management and maintenance services, third-party contract logistics services), but they can be used for product suppliers as well.

Case Study – Preferred Provider

BankCo established a successful relationship with Standard Register to consolidate warehousing and inventory management of the bank's forms and marketing materials. The strength of this successful relationship was founded on a flawless execution during transfer of 17 tractor-trailers of materials into Standard Register's warehouse over a 10-day period, plus the supplier's commitment to reduce the client's baseline costs by 10%. Cost reductions were rapidly achieved through effective sourcing, reduced packaging, process savings, reduced shipping costs, increased inventory turns, on-demand print for selective forms, and storage cost reduction.

Standard Register soon approached its client to beta-test its new technology and process solution to manage commercial print bid and print production management. It collaborated with its client to implement integrated processes for competitive bids and print production management, in-sourcing a full-time manager into the client organization. Savings were in excess of 25% from previous experience, and the client experienced significant reduction in the previously manual work effort in print production management. For Standard Register, the client became a reputable reference and an enthusiastic spokesperson to its industry analysts.

Source: Kate Vitasek, Bonnie Keith, Jim Eckler, and Dawn Evans, "Unpacking Sourcing Business Models," University of Tennessee Center for Executive Education, *White Paper*, 2nd ed., 2015.

Outcome-Based Relationship

A good example of an outcome-based service business model is when an airline pays its outsourced ground crew for achieving a 20-minute turnaround time after the plane has been parked at the gate. In the simplest form, the service provider does not get paid if it does not deliver results. An outcome-based business model, as shown in Table 10.3, typically shifts some or all risk for achieving the outcome to the service provider.

Outcome-based models are used most widely in the aerospace and defense industries. In fact, the Wright Brothers' 1909 contract with the U.S. Army for an airplane contained specific desired outcome standards and tolerances based on airspeed, with incentives and penalties based on stated targets. In that contract, the airplane was to achieve a maximum speed of 40 mph with a minimum requirement of 36 mph. If the Wright Brothers could demonstrate this, the Army would pay $25,000.

For an incentive, the parties agreed that for every mph over the 40 mph target, the Army would pay an additional $2,500; for every mph under the target, the Army would deduct $2,500, down to the 36 mph minimum, below which point the contract was void.

TABLE 10.3
Attributes of Outcome-Based Business Models

Sourcing Relationship	Focus	Interaction	Cooperation Level	Required Trust Level	Characterized by
Outcome-Based/ Performance-Based Relationship	Outcomes or performance	SRM Governance, performance incentives, fees at risk	Integrated	Integrated	Longer-term relationship
Vested Outsourcing Relationship	Mutual gain, shared outcomes	Vested agreement, Vested governance framework, performance margin matching	Integrated— Cooperative, win-win	Integrated— Behave as single entity	Interdependent outcomes, aligned, mutual gain, managed performance, long-term relationship

The results: The final delivered speed was 42 mph, and the Brothers received an additional $5,000. This target statement becomes the measure of success, or metric, for that objective. In this example, the standard is 40 mph and the tolerance is a minimum of 36 mph with no maximums. Success against the desired outcomes is defined by the performance statement standards; the service provider is measured against those standards.[18]

Outcome-based business models have gained in popularity in the last few years as more companies outside of the aerospace industry have adopted the concepts and expanded the thinking to pure outsourced service deals. A well-structured, outcome-based agreement compensates a supplier's higher risk with a higher reward.

There are two types of outcome-based business models: a performance-based agreement and a Vested Outsourcing agreement. Table 10.3 outlines typical characteristics of each of the outcome-based relationship approaches.[19]

Performance-Based Agreements

The relationship between trading partners under a performance-based agreement is different than with a transactional relationship. Typically performance-based agreements begin to shift the thinking away from activities to outcomes; however, they often still pay a supplier using transaction-based pricing triggers. These contracts are often also called "pay for performance" because they often have an incentive or a penalty tied to specific service level agreements (SLAs) outlined in the contract.

Performance-Based Relationship

For example, a company outsourcing its customer order management to a call center service provider will likely still pay a cost per transaction (most often a cost per call or minute). However, they create incentives or penalties if the service provider does not hit a metric such as answering 80% of the calls within 20 seconds.

The term length of a performance-based relationship is typically longer in a performance-based agreement. It is not uncommon to see agreements spanning three to five years; however, the contract language may allow for termination at the client company's determination (termination for convenience) within 30, 60, or 90 days.

Performance-based agreements typically require a higher level of interface between trading partners in order to review performance against objectives and determine the reward or penalty options that are typically embedded in the contract. These reviews are periodically scheduled and generally include representatives from the supplier and the buying company contracting resources.

One of the criticisms of a performance-based relationship is the tendency for the buying company to solely make the reward determination. If this is not done properly and fairly, it can cause the buyer-supplier relationship to become more adversarial in nature.

Vested Outsourcing

Vested Outsourcing is a highly collaborative business model where both the client and service provider have an economic Vested interest in each other's success.

Vested Outsourcing

The term *Vested Outsourcing* was originally coined by University of Tennessee (UT) researchers to describe highly successful outcome-based agreements the researchers studied as part of a large research project funded by the U.S. Air Force. UT research revealed that the Vested Outsourcing agreements combined an outcome-based model with the Nobel

---

[18] Defense Acquisition University, Continuous Learning Center, Online Module CLL011, "Performance-Based Logistics," 2005. Also see Kate Vitasek, Jacqui Crawford, Jeanette Nyden, and Katherine Kawamoto, *The Vested Outsourcing Manual* (Palgrave MacMillan, July 2011).

[19] Vitasek et al., "Unpacking Sourcing Business Models." Also see Keith et al., *Strategic Sourcing in the New Economy*.

Case Study – Performance Based, U.S. Navy

The U.S. Navy was recognized by the Secretary of Defense for its "Performance-Based Logistics" contract with Raytheon for its H-60 FLIR program. The Navy set out to improve the performance of the H-60 FLIR system, which enables the Navy's H-60 helicopter to detect, track, classify, identify, and attack targets like fast-moving patrol boats or mine-laying craft. When first developed, the FLIR was expected to have at least 500 hours of operation before failure but in reality was averaging less than 100 hours. At one point, the Atlantic Fleet alone accounted for more than one-third of the 21 deployed H-60 helicopters that had FLIR system failures. This system, made up of three components, a turret unit (TU), electronic unit (EU), and a hand control unit (HCU), was experiencing only 41% TU availability, 17% EU availability, and 80% HCU availability.

The Navy and Raytheon implemented a 10-year, fixed-price agreement that was priced per flight hour and valued at $123 million. This fixed-price-by-flight-hour contract gave Raytheon incentive to improve reliability and help reduce the necessity for removal of these units from the aircraft. Originally cost savings were projected to be around $31 million but have now been estimated to exceed $42 million.

Raytheon also implemented an online Maintenance Management Information System that allowed for real-time data collection by NADEP Jacksonville; an online manual has eliminated the need to have printed copies made and distributed.

In the first three years of the contract, the H-60 FLIR components have experienced a 100% availability rate and achieved a 40% growth in system reliability improvement as well as a 65% improvement in repair response time.[20]

Source: Kate Vitasek, Bonnie Keith, Jim Eckler, and Dawn Evans, "Unpacking Sourcing Business Models," University of Tennessee Center for Executive Education, *White Paper*, 2nd ed., 2015.

Prize–winning concepts of behavioral economics[21] and the principles of shared value.[22] Using these concepts, companies enter into highly collaborative arrangements designed to create value for all parties involved above and beyond the conventional buy-sell economics of a transaction-based agreement.

The Vested Outsourcing business model is best used when a company has transformational, innovation, or competitive advantage objectives that it cannot achieve itself or by using conventional transaction-based approaches or performance-based approaches. These objectives are referred to as *desired outcomes*; it is these desired outcomes that form the basis of the agreement. A desired outcome is a measurable business objective that focuses on what will be accomplished as a result of the work performed. A desired outcome is not a task-oriented service-level agreement (SLA) that often is mentioned in a conventional statement of work or performance-based agreements; rather, it is a mutually agreed upon, objective, and measurable deliverable for which the service provider will be rewarded—even if some of the accountability is shared with the company that is outsourcing. A desired outcome is generally categorized as an improvement to cost, schedule, market share, revenue, customer service levels, or performance.

---

[20] Department of the Navy, Commander, Naval Supply Systems Command, Nominations for the Secretary of Defense Performance-Based Logistics Award, June 5, 2005.

[21] Behavioral economics is the study of the quantified impact of individual behavior or of the decision makers within an organization. The study of behavioral economics is evolving more broadly into the concept of relational economics, which proposes that economic value can be expanded through positive relationships with mutual advantage (win-win) thinking rather than adversarial relationships (win-lose or lose-lose).

[22] Shared value thinking involves entities working together to bring innovations that benefit the parties—with a conscious effort that the parties gain (or share) in the rewards. Two advocates are Harvard Business School's Michael Porter and Mark Kramer, who profiled their "big idea" in the January–February 2011 *Harvard Business Review Magazine*. The article states that shared value creation will drive the next wave of innovation and productivity growth in the global economy. Porter is renowned for his Five Forces model of competitive advantage. Due to his prominence, it is likely that his take on shared value, although focused on society, likely will cause practitioners to embrace shared value approaches.

Case Study — Vested Outsourcing

The secret sauce of McDonald's supply chain success is found within long-term Vested Outsourcing relationships based on the unwavering belief that everyone in the McDonald's "system" can and should win. The deep-seated culture for long-term, win-win relationships with suppliers dates back to McDonald's inception, when founder Ray Kroc established a precedent of trust and loyalty. Kroc believed that if the restaurant owner/operators and suppliers were successful, success would come to him as well.

Kroc's insistence on What's in It for We (WIIFWe) thinking has created the world's most powerful restaurant and supply chain. WIIFWe thinking is ingrained in the DNA of McDonald's, its suppliers, and its restaurant owner/operators. The results are staggering. Kroc's system has expanded to more than 100 countries and 33,000 restaurants serving more than 68 million customers a day, and the numbers grow more impressive every day. McDonald's has also set the standards in food quality, safety, and assured supply. Customers know they will get the same consistent food and service from Arkansas to Alaska and from Argentina to Azerbaijan.

And it all started with a vision and philosophy that "None of us is as good as all of us."

Kroc's ultimate desired outcome was profitable, individual stores serving consistent quality products. Finding suppliers who would be partners in the process was critical. Kroc was determined to work with suppliers that had the same long-term thinking. McDonald's "System First" philosophy stands the test of time. The unique supply chain model is based on an exceptional set of operating principles that create long-term wealth and competitive advantage for the entire system by mitigating costs, preventing safety issues, and producing quality and innovative products that delight customers in a uniquely McDonald's way. The result is increased customer value, better brand health, and stronger business performance.

The secret to making it work is the fact that McDonald's and its most strategic suppliers have a deep commitment to each other to continually deliver value for McDonald's system. Suppliers are confident the McDonald's business is not vulnerable to competitors' price-cutting and arbitrary change. And McDonald's is confident that its suppliers are delivering the best possible value and looking out after McDonald's interests to protect and grow the system.

Pete Richter, President, Global McDonald's Business Unit for Cargill and chair of the U.S. Supplier Advisory Council, explains how a long-term relationship founded on high degrees of trust has impacted how Cargill interacts with McDonald's. "The trust and confidence in the future means we shift a majority of our resources to driving innovation, quality, supply chain optimization, and investing in future growth initiatives. This takes trust on both sides of the table, but once you establish, it creates amazing leverage vs. the traditional arm's length RFP type approach."

Vested for Success

Together, McDonald's, its owner/operators, and their suppliers have created a system to be reckoned with—a system that continues to set records after 50 years. Many have credited McDonald's with transforming the food industry. But ask anyone at McDonald's and they will tell you they could not do it alone. The trust in the system inspires collaboration that is unparalleled in other supplier relationships that drive process and product innovations on a regular basis.

When you look back at McDonald's success, the results are simply staggering. In 2011, *Fortune Magazine* named McDonald's the No. 10 Most Admired Company in the World; No. 1 among all companies for Management Quality, "Global Competitiveness," and "Use of Corporate Assets"; and No. 2 among all companies for "Best Long-Term Investment."

The list of awards goes on and on.

Source: Kate Vitasek, Karl Manrodt, and Jeanne Kling, *Vested: How P&G, McDonald's, and Microsoft Are Redefining Winning in Business Relationships* (Palgrave-Macmillan, September 2012).

The Vested Outsourcing business model can be used for service or product suppliers. The case study below profiles how McDonald's has used a Vested approach for over 50 years to help it create and maintain a competitive advantage, consistently innovating in the industry.

Investment-Based Business Model

Investment-Based Model

Companies that struggle to meet complex business requirements using conventional transaction-based or outcome-based approaches typically invest to develop capabilities themselves. There are two primary types of investment-based business models: shared

TABLE 10.4
Attributes of
Investment-Based
Business Models

Sourcing Relationship	Focus	Interaction	Cooperation Level	Required Trust Level	Characterized by
Shared Services	Leveraging cost and investments	Cross-company services may include multi-company service	Integrated—Cooperative, win-win	Integrated, dictated by equity sharing	Formal charter, intercompany governance structure, interdependent outcomes, aligned goals and objectives, managed performance, win-win relationship
Equity Partner	Equity sharing	Joint venture Asset-based governance framework	Integrated—Cooperative, interrelated structure	Integrated, dictated by equity sharing	Legally bound, formal strategic partnerships, mergers and acquisitions, asset sharing/holding

services and equity partnerships such as a joint venture. Table 10.4 outlines the typical characteristics of both shared services and joint venture-type investment-based approaches.[23]

Shared Services

Shared Services

A "shared services" structure is the establishment of an internal organization to perform key functions on behalf of an organization. A key driver when developing a shared-services organization is to centralize and standardize operations that improve operational efficiencies. The results can be significant. APQC (American Productivity and Quality Center) research shows a direct correlation between low procurement cost and a centralized or shared-services procurement function. Specifically, companies with centralized and shared-services procurement functions have procurement costs almost one-third of those that have decentralized functions. Figure 10.1 shows the procurement cost performance of centralized, shared, and decentralized procurement structures.[24]

Shared-services organizations typically act like an outsourced service provider, performing services and then "charging" their internal customers on a per-transaction or headcount basis. Charges can be further reduced by using technology, such as Robotic Processing Automation (RPA).[25] This approach very much mirrors a conventional "preferred supplier" relationship.

---

[23] Vitasek et al., "Unpacking Sourcing Business Models." Also see Keith et al., *Strategic Sourcing in the New Economy.*

[24] Benchmarking statistics courtesy of APQC. To learn more about APQC, visit www.apqc.org. An interesting discussion on how to calculate the cost of processing a purchase order can be found at Kim Waterman, "How Much Does It Cost to Process a Purchase Order?," November 3, 2016, https://www.linkedin.com/pulse/how-much-does-cost-process-purchase-order-internally-kim-waterman/?articleId=7987006789269971974.

[25] Mary Lacity and Leslie Willcocks, "Paper 15/07 Robotic Process Automation: The Next Transformation Lever for Shared Services," *The Outsourcing Unit Working Research Paper Series*, https://s3.eu-central-1.amazonaws.com/fleming.events-webfiles/redactor/SmV3wRUSKoK1NHJ1ZF2ggoj5PvicU1V5NxPtZFiZ.pdf.

FIGURE 10.1
Cost of a Purchase
Order

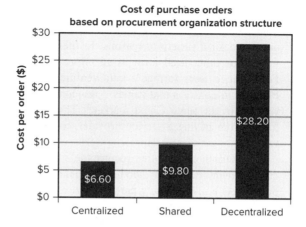

Case Study – Shared Services–Bell Canada/PSI

Bell Canada's distribution operations were operating at service levels of 10% to 15% below industry average and at a cost base of $100 million. Bell Canada (the largest telecom services company in Canada) decided to spin off the assets and the staff of the distribution business into a stand-alone, wholly owned subsidiary known as Progistix Solutions Inc. (PSI). The idea was that by creating a separate shared-services entity with its own P&L, PSI would be driven to operate more efficiently. PSI was chartered to provide a full range of order management and inventory management business processes for all of Bell's operating businesses, and a new CEO was brought in to turn around the business.

At its inception, PSI had an estimated revenue stream (benchmarked by Deloitte) of $55 million against its cost base of $100 million. Progistix had a mandate to achieve a financial breakeven state and to meet industry average service levels. The new CEO chose to judiciously blend new talent with experienced incumbent managers. This combination ensured that the valuable learnings embedded in the corporate history would not be lost and that best practices from outside could be introduced by new managers with direct experience in the new practices.

With the team in place, PSI put in place the basics of a business:

- Transactional services contracts were negotiated and executed between PSI and its client groups.

- A financial management system was built to support the business.

- Distinct HR policies and systems were built to manage the employee base of over 1,000, of which over 75% were unionized.

- A client management organization was assembled to better understand and meet client needs.

With its own P&L, the shared services group carefully reviewed where it needed to invest in business processes

and technology to meet its charter of becoming a profitable business unit and raising service levels to its Bell counterparts. PSI invested in three key areas:

- Replaced the aged technology infrastructure and outdated applications.

- Renegotiated the four collective agreements to align wage rates and work rules with the logistics services market.

- Commenced the long process of culture change from an entitlement-based telecom services company to a market-focused logistics services competitor.

Clearly the cultural change would be the most difficult. By moving noncore functions to an organization dedicated to enhance quality in their respective fields (shared services or outsourcing), these employees gain respect and self-confidence, enabling them to perform at much higher levels.

In addition to the attention to the key priorities above, the management team was driven through profit-sharing incentives to dramatically reduce costs in all parts of the organization. As a result of its efforts, PSI reduced its costs by $45 million, yielding a breakeven position in one year. In addition, systematic improvements raised service levels to industry standards, with over 95% of the orders processed during the day picked, packed, shipped, and delivered to customers by the end of the next day.

During the next two years, PSI was able to generate industry standard profits and grew the revenues by 15%. By the end of three years, PSI's shareholders at Bell Canada made a decision that they no longer needed to own PSI to benefit from its services. Bell Canada sold Progistix for $40 million to Canada Post Corporation, and it continues to provide services to Bell Canada–as well as many other customers.

Source: Kate Vitasek, Bonnie Keith, Jim Eckler, and Dawn Evans, "Unpacking Sourcing Business Models," University of Tennessee Center for Executive Education, *White Paper*, 2nd ed., 2015.

Equity Partnership

Equity Partnership

Some companies decide they do not have the internal capabilities, yet they do not want to outsource for a variety of reasons. In these cases, companies may opt to develop a joint venture or other legal form in an effort to acquire mission-critical goods and services. For instance, Sony formed a joint venture in China to more effectively make and market PlayStation consoles and games.[26] Renault-Nissan Alliance is working to produce electric vehicles in the same China market.[27] These equity partnerships can take different legal forms, from buying a service provider, to becoming a subsidiary, to equity-sharing joint ventures.

These partnerships often require the strategic interweaving of infrastructure and heavy co-investment. Equity partnerships, by default, bring costs "in house" and create a fixed cost burden. As a result, equity partnerships often conflict with the desires of many organizations to create more variable and flexible cost structures on their balance sheets.

Case Study – Equity Partner/Joint Venture—Samsung and Sony

The consumer electronics giants Samsung Electronics and Sony established a 50-50 joint venture in 2004 for the production of liquid crystal displays for flat-panel televisions. The companies formed a new company near Seoul, South Korea, S-LCD Corp., with an initial capital budget of nearly $2 billion.

The two tech giants—and fierce industry rivals—structured the venture so that stocks in S-LCD were held by South Korea's Samsung at 50 percent plus one share of stock and 50 percent minus one by Japan's Sony. "The two companies will invest evenly, but Samsung has the ultimate initiative," said a Sony spokeswoman.[28]

The upstart Samsung had begun construction of an LCD production facility in 2003 at a large projected capital expenditure over the next decade for what was then a relatively new technology and market, while Sony had no production base for large LCD panels. A joint collaboration was thus advantageous for both companies.

The deal was also controversial. Sony had pulled out of a Japanese-state-backed LCD-panel development group to close the deal with Samsung.

In 2006 *Bloomberg BusinessWeek* described the venture as a win-win: "They have pulled off one of the most interesting and fruitful collaborations in global high-tech

by jointly producing liquid-crystal display (LCD) panels. And it's an alliance that is reshaping the industry."[29]

The venture was instrumental in Sony's introduction of the hugely successful Bravia LCD-TV lineup. It also put Samsung's own LCD-TV business on the map, with the company emerging as a trend-setter in the LCD-panel industry, aided by Sony technology that helped ensure high-quality, sharp TV pictures.

"The Sony-Samsung alliance is certainly a win-win," said Lee Sang Wan, president of Samsung's LCD unit.[30]

The alliance had industrywide impact in the TV market for large-screen sets. It also changed the pecking order among LCD-TV makers.

In 2008 the companies strengthened the venture by committing another $2 billion to build a new facility to produce so-called eighth-generation panels.

In the intervening years, despite global economic and financial turmoil, currency fluctuations, heavy competition, and new entrants in the LCD and electronics market, and more recently the earthquake and tsunami in Japan, the S-LCD venture has survived.

The earthquake and faltering global demand in the LCD market did force S-LCD to reduce capital by $555 million in April 2011. There were even rumors that the joint venture

[26] "Sony Forms Joint Ventures in China for PlayStation," Reuters, May 26, 2014, https://www.nytimes.com/2014/05/27/business/international/sony-forms-joint-venture-in-china-for-playstation.html.

[27] Fred Lambert, "Nissan and Renault Announce a New Joint Venture to Produce Electric Vehicles in China," *electrek*, August 29, 2017, https://electrek.co/2017/08/29/nissan-renault-joint-venture-electric-vehicles-china/.

[28] Yoshiko Hara, "Samsung, Sony Complete LCD Joint Venture Deal," *EE Times-Asia*, March 8, 2004, https://www.eetimes.com/document.asp?doc_id=1148761.

[29] Moon Ihlwan, "Samsung and Sony's Win-Win LCD Venture," *Bloomberg BusinessWeek*, November 28, 2006, https://www.bloomberg.com/news/articles/2006-11-28/samsung-and-sonys-win-win-lcd-venturebusinessweek-business-news-stock-market-and-financial-advice.

[30] Ibid.

might be dropped due to losses in Sony's TV business, but Sony quashed that idea in August. "Televisions are a core business for Sony and it would be unthinkable for us to shrink that business," said Kazuo Hirai, Sony's executive deputy president. When asked about the Samsung partnership, Hirai asserted: "We are absolutely not thinking of abolishing the joint venture, and it's not something that would be easy to do."[31]

The venture is unusual and remarkable in terms of its scope and duration. Two fierce competitors put their rivalry aside to achieve the win-win in an emerging market.

Source: Kate Vitasek, Bonnie Keith, Jim Eckler, and Dawn Evans, "Unpacking Sourcing Business Models," University of Tennessee Center for Executive Education, *White Paper*, 2nd ed., 2015.

Reasons to Use More Strategic Approaches

Definition of Partnership

Partnerships Show a Desire to Work Together to Achieve a Goal

The *Merriam-Webster Dictionary* defines a partner as "one associated with another especially in an action" and a partnership as "the state of being a partner."[32]

The act of partnering or declaring that you want to be a partner brings a new dynamic to the relationship between business entities. As previously mentioned in the definition, partners work together to achieve a goal. That goal could be reduced cost, improved availability or customer satisfaction, or increased market share.

Whatever the reason, the effort put into partnering should be equal on both sides of the relationship, should lead to a common set of desired outcomes beneficial to both parties, and should not only be a win for each of the partners but create an improved relationship between them.

Research conducted by the International Association for Contract and Commercial Management (IACCM) shows that most companies operate under conventional transaction-based models that are constrained by a formal, legally oriented, risk-averse, and liability-based culture. The top three most negotiated contract terms were limitation of liability, indemnification, and pricing. Tim Cummins, IACCM's CEO, suggests that this is bad news, as it demonstrates a lack of progress as we move from a manufacturing to service-based economy.[33] There is growing awareness that transactional-based approaches do not always give each party the intended results, especially when the relationship is more strategic and complex in nature.[34]

Outcome-based approaches are gathering momentum as senior leaders see positive results from carefully crafted collaborative agreements. Outcome-based approaches—especially Vested Outsourcing—allow trading partners to structure highly collaborative and long-term relationships aimed at achieving mutually defined, desired outcomes and innovation that is often stifled in transaction-based relationships.

Partnership Success Factors

Trust Is a Key Factor in Relationships

Trust is widely recognized as a prerequisite to supply chain success; it is the one thing that has the potential to create unparalleled success or, if not evident in both parties, can destroy

---

[31] "Sony Rules Out Exiting TV Business or LCD Panel Venture," Reuters, August 4, 2011, https://www.reuters.com/article/us-sony/sony-rules-out-exiting-tv-business-or-lcd-panel-venture-idUSTRE7731TC20110804.

[32] Merriam-Webster Online, https://www.merriam-webster.com/dictionary/partner.

[33] Kate Vitasek, "Contract Terms Remain Stuck on Old-School Negotiating Tactics," *Forbes*, November 12, 2015, https://www.forbes.com/sites/katevitasek/2015/11/12/contract-terms-remain-stuck-on-old-school-negotiating-tactics/#7824db4c1f3e.

[34] Vitasek et al., *Vested Outsourcing*.

a relationship. The more strategic a relationship is to the business, the more there is a need for mutual trust, open communications, and balanced risk among partners.[35]

Highly successful companies recognize these values and use a trusting relationship to provide a foundation for collaboration, sharing of resources, and risk taking that help to ensure the highest level of profitability for themselves and their supplier partners, while delivering the utmost in customer satisfaction.

Suppliers who trust their customers to maintain a profitable long-term relationship will feel more compelled to make investments that can improve processes and reduce time to deliver and ultimately costs. Trust can spur the supplier to develop innovations for which it believes it will be rewarded by the customer. In an untrusting relationship, such innovations are generally kept secret in fear of the customer taking them to another supplier.

Customers who trust their suppliers will be less likely to shop around in order to shave a few percentage points off the costs, knowing that if costs can honestly be reduced, or processes be improved, their existing supplier will bring it to the table. Trusting organizations are open organizations that reward suppliers for their performance.

What happens when trust isn't present? According to a study by 3M of over 230 suppliers, half of the suppliers have held back from making a strategic recommendation to their customers. The reasons given were a lack of customer openness as well as a lack of an incentive to help the customer get better.[36]

Whether a firm is a customer or a supplier/service provider, it is essential that it understands the nature of its partner's business and what its objectives are.

Knowledge of a Partner's Business

Understanding a partner's business puts a company in a better position to create a winning relationship that can help both organizations succeed. The company can foresee how its organization's expertise can yield potential innovations that could improve market share, and help the customer bring them to market. For example, McDonald's suppliers have been widely known to provide innovations that have kept McDonald's at the cutting edge of the quick-serve restaurant business—both developing products (Chicken McNuggets) and patenting operations processes that provide McDonald's with a competitive advantage.[37]

Buying companies need to know enough about suppliers to be able to understand where suppliers have capabilities that can create a competitive advantage.

Likewise, suppliers need to know enough about their customer's business to help craft solutions and make investments in innovations that can help their customer with its goals.

Good Relationship Management Governance Framework

Partners must develop mechanisms to govern the relationship. A successful relationship management structure creates joint policies that emphasize the importance of building collaborative working relationships, attitudes, and behaviors. The parties monitor the agreement within the framework of a flexible governance structure that provides top-to-bottom insights into what is happening.

There are six key elements to a good relationship management governance framework.

1. Create a tiered management structure.
2. Establish formalized roles for service delivery, transformation, and commercial management.
3. Establish communication protocols.
4. Develop a communications cadence.

[35] Stephen M. Covey, *The Speed of Trust* (Free Press, 2008). For additional information, see Stanley E. Fawcett, Gregory M. Magnan, and Alvin J. Williams, "Supply Chain Trust Is within Your Grasp," *Supply Chain Management Review*, Vol. 8, No. 2 (March 2004), pp. 20–26.

[36] "Driving Growth and Innovation through Supplier Partnerships," 3M, February 2017, http://multimedia .3m.com/mws/media/1397989O/supplier-survey-whitepaper.pdf.

[37] Vitasek et al., *Vested*.

Daily Attended by peers from both parties	Operational management group	• Oversees day-to-day operations in each location • There will be several working management groups (for example, regional service delivery management groups or project-based transformation groups)
Monthly Attended by managers from both parties	Joint operations committee	• Provides direction regarding service delivery • Monitors progress of the outsourcing relationship and scope of work • Responsible for service quality across all locations • Sets continuous innovation and implementation priorities
Quarterly Attended by senior executives from both parties	Board of advisors	• Provides overall sponsorship, vision, and goals • Sets strategic direction and feedback regarding progress against desired outcomes and overall performance • Makes decisions related to escalated issues and grants approval of large transformation projects

FIGURE 10.2
Tiered Governance Structure

FIGURE 10.3
Traditional Bow Tie vs. Reverse Bow Tie

Source: Jeanette Nyden, "3 Elements for 21st Century Relationship Management," *SSON*, April 12, 2017, https://www.ssonetwork.com/sourcing-best-practices-sson/columns/3-elements-for-21st-century-relationship.

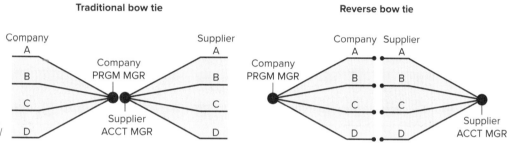

5. Establish a continuity of resources.
6. Establish performance management protocols.[38]

Each is discussed in more detail below.

Create a Tiered Management Structure

Once an initial agreement is signed, the focus changes to day-to-day operations and getting the work done. Too often, the parties put the "strategy" on the shelf in a vinyl binder and don't refer back to it until a new executive comes in and wants to create his or her own plan. This is often referred as "strategic drift." For this reason, governance structure should start by establishing an organizational structure that ensures vertical alignment between the executives and the employees in the organizations that are charted to get the work done, as noted in Figure 10.2.

Another goal is to develop multiple relationships between both firms at all levels, executive, management, and operational. Instead of having all communications flowing from one supplier to one buyer, the goal is to increase the flows between all levels, or reversing the bow tie (Figure 10.3).[39]

[38] Kate Vitasek, Gerald Stevens, and Katherine Kawamoto, "Unpacking Outsourcing Governance: How to Build a Sound Governance Structure to Drive Insight versus Oversight," 2011, http://www.vestedway.com/wp-content/uploads/2012/09/Governance.pdf.

[39] Kate Vitasek, "Adopt a 'Two-in-a-Box' Partner for Efficient Outsourcing Governance," *Vested*, http://www.vestedway.com/adopt-a-two-in-a-box-partner-for-efficient-outsourcing-governance/.

Establish Communications Protocols

A good contract will outline the communications protocols and expectations between the trading partners. As discussed above, more strategic relationships should strive to create peer-to-peer communication protocols to ensure that not only are day-to-day priorities executed efficiently but also that neither party loses sight of strategic goals.

Establish a Communications Cadence

Establishing a regular communications cadence is an important aspect of the governance structure. The formality and frequency of the communication cadence will vary based on how strategic the trading partner relationship is. Simple transaction-based relationships may simply rely on a purchase order while highly strategic Vested relationships should seek to establish a "rhythm of the business" to help the parties establish a formal mechanism for managing the business. The State of Tennessee outsourced all facility management and maintenance and required all respondents to propose a communications cadence for the proposal and the final contract.[40] The example in Figure 10.4 shows a communication cadence from the JLL proposal, showing the proposed governance structure and meeting frequency. In this, the executive layer meets quarterly, the operating committee meets daily/weekly/monthly, and the site teams meet more frequently.

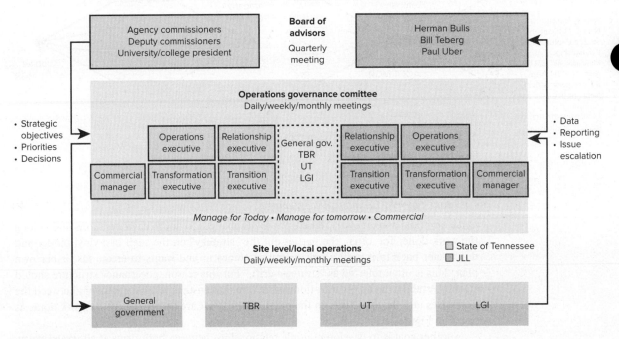

FIGURE 10.4
Governance Structure and Communications Cadence

Source: RFP #32110-17103 Technical Response from Jones Lang Lasalle.

[40] Contract between The State of Tennessee, Department of General Services, Central Procurement Office and Jones Lang Lasalle Americas, Inc., 2017, https://ren.edison.tn.gov/contracts/jamee11070052017-05-25-17.21.37.922SWC_458_Facilities_Management_Services_Contract-_Stamped.pdf.

Establish Continuity of Resources Protocols

The more strategic trading partner relationships, the more the need to spell out how the parties will deal with continuity of resources. A key reason to establish the protocols for how to manage the continuity of resources is to enable both parties to establish expectations for how key resources will be managed or changed out. For example, highly strategic outsourcing relationships often include Key Man Provisions that require the supplier to leave key personnel on an account for up to three years.[41] In addition, companies often outline the protocols for changing key resources in a strategic relationship.

Establish Formalized Roles for Service Delivery, Transformation, and Commercial Management

In general, many companies that outsource believe they have implemented a best practice when they deploy supplier relationship management (SRM) techniques. SRM is a practice for creating mechanisms to increase the efficiency and effectiveness in how a company works with its service providers to lower business costs. Some SRM efforts are designed to build deeper business relationships that foster improved collaboration and innovation. Yet, there is a significant difference between managing a supplier and managing a relationship. For these reasons, individual roles and responsibilities have to be considered and established after the tiered management structure has been put in place.

Establish Performance Management Protocols

For many companies, the most efficient way to oversee normal operations is through a well-designed scorecard. Scorecards play a key role in tracking performance against agreed-on metrics. Scorecards can be completed by the buyer or the suppliers, or both.

More strategic relationships often have joint scorecards that focus end-to-end desired outcomes and business needs. In strategic relationships it is critical to have an overall "business" scorecard because it is highly likely that the parties will need to work together to achieve the business goals. An integrated, business-focused scorecard can help the parties emphasize performance against the desired outcomes and business needs, not just performance against the service provider's tasks.

Knowledge of Special and Regulatory Requirements

In addition, to create a good relationship management framework, some governance structures require trading partners to understand and adhere to special requirements and regulatory protocols. Thus, a governance framework may need to include additional provisions that address specific market, local, regional, and national requirements. For instance, in supplier and supply chain relationships involving information technology and intellectual property, security concerns may necessitate special governance provisions outside the normal manufacturer-supplier relationship. Supply chain finance and transportation management are other areas that often require special handling under the governance framework.

More complex outcome-based relationships also require additional elements of governance. Outcome-based relationships are typically longer term in nature and, as such, require the trading partners to include provisions and protocols for managing change that strive for mutual accountability for desired outcomes and the creation of a culture that rewards innovation, agility, and continuous improvement.

Managing Innovation

The most strategic relationships often are used when there is a need to drive innovation that can lead to a competitive advantage between the trading partners. *The Vested Outsourcing Manual*[42] suggests that outcome-based relationships include mechanisms enabling trading

[41] If you look closely at Figure 10.4, you will see that JLL named its key personnel for this contract!
[42] Vitasek et al., *The Vested Outsourcing Manual*.

partners to drive transformation in a highly dynamic environment. Such mechanisms include:

- A documented change management plan to manage the dynamic nature of a more strategic and long-term business relationship.
- Process for driving overall transformation initiatives.
- Process for managing day-to-day continuous improvement efforts or business problems.
- A formal joint continuous improvement program.
- A defined process for updating and managing any changes to the agreement.
- A well-defined transition plan (optional).

Sometimes the best plan simply does not work out or is trumped by unexpected events. Companies should have a plan to bring to bear when assumptions change.

Exit Management

Contract Ending/Exit Management

Because nothing lasts forever, a valid question to ask is: What happens when the agreement ends?

If the agreement is properly structured and is achieving the desired outcomes while continually improving performance, renewal of the agreement or contract is likely. Most companies would like to envision a long-term productive relationship that spans decades—such as the famed Coca-Cola and McDonald's relationship that is in its 55th year.[43]

An exit management strategy can provide a template to handle future unknowns. The goal is to establish a fair plan and to keep the parties whole in the event of a separation when the separation is not a result of poor performance. This strategy should include the following elements:

- Adequate exit criteria are established, with equitable on and off ramps for both parties.
- Termination notice process is in place.
- There is a documented exit transition period.
- Exit transition plan is outlined or parties have agreed to the key elements in advance.
- Exit governance and reporting plan is documented.
- Exit transition manager and exit management team are identified (by roles)

Contracting Success Factors

Contracts Define the Basis of the Relationship

Regardless of the type of relationship or the formality, all business relationships should be based on some sound business elements.

A recent survey by the IACCM[44] shows that the biggest divide between trading partners today is in how they seek to allocate risk. A review of the top 10 negotiated terms reveals that most trading partners focus on intellectual property rights, liquidated damages, governing law, and payment terms. Notably missing is the lack of focus on goals and objectives of the partnership.

---

[43] "US: Coca-Cola Co Expands McDonald's Deal," *Just-Drinks.com*, http://www.just-drinks.com/news /coca-cola-co-expandsmcdonalds-deal_id97095.aspx.

[44] "2015 Top Terms in Negotiation—Most Negotiated Terms and Conditions," International Association for Contract & Commercial Management, 2015.

Exhibit: Top 10 Terms Used in Negotiations

1. Limitation of Liability
2. Indemnification
3. Price/Charge/Price Changes
4. Service Levels and Warranties
5. Payment
6. Intellectual Property
7. Warranty
8. Performance/Guarantees/Undertakings
9. Termination
10. Delivery/Acceptance

As the survey report illustrates, the negotiators are clear that this focus damages the value achieved from trading relationships; they are also clear about where effort in negotiations should be placed (scope and goals, change or amendment procedures, communications and reporting). But for as long as contracting remains a largely transactional activity dominated by a legal/financial axis, there is little likelihood of change. Executives should be demanding more from their contracts. They should be asking why so many relationships fail to deliver to their potential—and what role contracting and negotiation are playing in that failure.

Source: "2015 Top Terms in Negotiation—Most Negotiated Terms and Conditions," International Association for Contract & Commercial Management, 2015, https://www.forbes.com/sites/katevitasek/2015/11/12/contract-terms-remain-stuck-on-old-school-negotiating-tactics/#3d781d3d1f3e.

The Vested Outsourcing Manual,[45] written in collaboration with the IACCM, outlines 10 elements that should be included to create a successful strategic trading partner contract. These elements may be documented formally in a contract or become part of a more informal social contract that binds the company's cultures in how they work together.

Elements of a Successful Business Agreement

Element 1   Business Model

10 Elements of Successful Contracts

It is imperative that trading partners enter into the right type of business agreement to support their relationship. For example, many companies use a preferred provider business model when they should have used an outcome-based business model. Prior to establishing a formal agreement, trading partners should discuss the pros and cons of each of the various relationship models and determine which one is the best fit.

Element 2   Shared Vision Statement and Statement of Intent

Shared Vision Statement: A declaration of the shared vision of the relationship based on the desired outcomes, showing what has been documented and agreed to. It is frequently referenced in meetings and documents as a directional beacon for decisions. The shared vision is an affirmation of the What's in It for We (WIIFWe) approach to the relationship.

Statement of Intent: This is a formal document that outlines the overall intent of what the parties will include in the agreement. The document should outline the opportunity and the outcomes that are desired.

Element 3   Statement of Objectives/Workload Allocation

Work Scope: Trading partners should mutually define the work scope. Companies can use a Statement of Work (a very formal and detailed document that outlines in great detail the specifications of how the work should be performed), a Statement of Objectives (a less rigid document that specifies the buying company's desired outcomes in terms of high-level

---

[45] Kate Vitasek, "Time for a Change," *Logistics Times*, July 2011, p. 40. Also see Vitasek et al., *The Vested Outsourcing Manual.*

objective metrics with minimal prescriptive direction), or a Performance Work Statement (which is a detailed specification written by the suppliers). *The Vested Outsourcing Manual* suggests that highly strategic relationships use a Statement of Objective because it allows for more flexibility, which is needed in more strategic, longer-term relationships.

Workload Allocation: Trading partners should develop a formal management strategy that focuses on maximum integration (management and visibility) of end-to-end business process effectiveness when at all possible. A workload allocation strategy will show how trading partners work together to optimize the end-to-end process, versus internal process effectiveness. Workload allocation strategies should describe the level of transparency of each partner's involvement, showing clear roles and accountabilities for the overall processes/flow.

Element 4   Performance Metrics

Finalize Top Level Desired Outcomes: All trading partners' relationships should rely on performance metrics to measure the success. Metrics used should be clearly aligned to desired outcomes (ideally focused on achieving end customer requirements).

Metrics accountability should be aligned with the scope of trading partner's authority. More strategic relationships tend to have higher-level outcome-based metrics that measure the entire process level—across both partners—to best understand the performance across the entire process, while more tactical trading partner relationships tend to focus on transactional or activity level metrics that measure a specific task or focus area.

Element 5   Performance Management

Trading partners should determine which metrics reports they will use to manage the business, as well as determine the frequency of the reports. In some cases, performance reporting is as simple as an Excel spreadsheet, while in other cases reporting might be fully automated and integrated.

One example of a fully integrated reporting process for sharing sales data is Walmart. Walmart pioneered its Retail Link using a telephone line back in 1991, allowing retail partners access to sales data from every store going back for a period of at least two years. Partners can now access the data via an Internet portal, allowing them to track performance of their products in near real time.[46]

Element 6   Pricing Model

Contracts should spell out pricing or the pricing model that will be used to compensate a supplier. Well-structured contracts consider the balancing of risk versus simply shifting risk to a supplier. When possible, pricing models should also include development of a thoughtful plan to introduce improvements that can reduce total program risk where appropriate. This is very important in a highly strategic relationship that spans a longer-term relationship.

Partners should also regularly review their pricing models and the risk assigned to parties over the life of the agreement to ensure that compensation is appropriate to the level of effort and the risk. As the supplier gains more experience, the contract type can evolve into a more strategic form and the pricing model may need to shift from a transaction-based pricing model to a more strategic outcome-based pricing model.

Trading partners should also spell out the contract length. The contract length should be commensurate with the payback period for suppliers' investments. Longer-term contracts encourage suppliers to make long-term investments to improve product or process

---

[46] Charles Fishman, *The Wal-Mart Effect: How the World's Most Powerful Company Really Works— And How It's Transforming the American Economy* (Penguin Press, 2006).

efficiencies. Strategic contracts often typically have contract terms in excess of five years and can include automatic contract renewal if the supplier is meeting or exceeding business requirements.

We also recommend that buying companies also include some form of incentives in their pricing model, especially for more strategic supplier relationships. Incentives should be tightly aligned, promoting behaviors and outcomes that benefit both the buying company and supplier. Incentives can be immediate financial rewards or charges, or they can be intangible, such as an automatic extension of the contract length.

Element 7   Relationship Management Framework

As mentioned previously, all trading partner relationships should clearly spell out their relationship management framework. A good contract will clearly spell out all six of the relationship management components cited above.

Element 8   Transformation Management

Ramping up a supplier is important to ensure needed milestones are met. This is true if a supplier is providing a widget or is managing a critical outsourced service such as a distribution center. A good contract will outline any transition expectations as the supplier ramps up, including agreeing on project milestones, reviews, and escalation paths.

In addition, a contract should outline a formal change management process. For example, how will the companies handle bill of materials changes for a component supplier? Or how will the company share changes in sustainability policies to its janitorial supplier that may now prevent the supplier from using certain products? A formal change management procedure is important when a change impacts key elements of the agreement (that affect the price or related costs of the services or that impact the delivery of the services or the obligations of either party).

More strategic relationships may also include provisions for the parties to develop a continuous improvement process. Highly strategic relationships should outline a formal continuous improvement program (e.g., Six Sigma, Lean, etc.) that can effectively drive improvements against the top-level desired outcomes. The contract should also outline how the trading partners will manage innovations.

Element 9   Exit Management Plan

Successful contracts include adequate exit criteria and off ramps to cover probable contract end requirements. For simple transaction-based agreements, all that may be needed is a purchase order that outlines the terms. However more strategic relationships will need to spell out a detailed exit management plan. This is especially important for outsourced service providers that may take a significant amount of time to transition work to a new supplier. More strategic relationships also include provisions such as how the trading partners will manage more complex aspects of the relationships such as data rights, customer rights to asset ownership, or mutually created intellectual property.

Element 10   Special Concerns and External Regulations

Many trading partner relationships require the supplier to adhere to specific customer requirements or external regulations. For example, a 3PL will need to adhere to OSHA regulations. A good example of a specific customer requirement is when Microsoft outsourced its back office financial processes to Accenture, it required Accenture to use Microsoft systems.[47] Such requirements should be spelled out in the contract.

---

[47] Vitasek et al., *Vested*.

Perverse Incentives of Business Agreement

Business contracts and agreements are sometimes innocently structured with fundamental flaws in the business model that will ultimately impact the relationship. In other cases, a trading partner uses its power and negotiation tactics to shift risk to the weaker partner. In either case, a business agreement that is not structured well can result in "perverse incentives": direct negative behaviors or unconscious behaviors that drive unintended consequences.

Ailments Affecting Typical Relationships

The IACCM is convinced that current contracting practices are costing businesses at least 5 to 7 percent of their potential profit. It feels too much time is going into nonproductive effort at the expense of the things that would create a better framework for success.

The book *Vested Outsourcing: Five Rules That Will Transform Outsourcing*[48] identifies 10 of the most common flaws (referred to in the book as Ailments) that afflict and weaken business relationships. These Ailments stem from structural contract flaws or behavior or cultural issues that prevent strong and effective trading partner collaborations. These structural flaws and perverse incentives can and do lead to uncomfortable relationships and wasted opportunities for gains in efficiency that can affect all kinds of supply chain partner models, not just those thought of as outsourcing.

The 10 common Ailments are highlighted below.

1   Penny Wise and Pound Foolish

Buying organizations often focus too much on price versus lowest total costs or value. The danger in focusing on the cheapest offer is that it inevitably leads to trade-offs in quality and/or service. The thought of "stepping over a dollar to pick up a dime" comes to mind.

10 Flaws That Have a Negative Impact on Contracts

Often companies suffering from a "Penny Wise and Pound Foolish" mentality fall into a loop of using frequent bidding to pick the lowest-price provider, and then transitioning to the cheaper supplier without thinking through the costs involved in making the change. This can lead to a vicious cycle of bid and transition, bid and transition, bid and transition, and can increase transaction costs and overall total costs.

It can also stifle innovation and potentially cause harm to consumer confidence if the new supplier is not able to deliver on time or quality suffers.

2   The Outsourcing Paradox

The Outsourcing Paradox as described in the book applies to all types of supplier/customer relationships—not just outsourcing. It typically afflicts companies that work with partners that supply products or services that the customer considers itself to be fairly knowledgeable about. It begins when the "experts" at the buying company develop the "perfect" set of specifications for delivery of the product or service.

The result is an impressive statement of work document containing all the possible details on how the work is to be done. At last, the perfect system! However, this "perfect system" can actually sow the seeds of failure of the relationship. The reason: It's the company's perfect system, not one designed by the supplier whose team is supposed to be the experts at getting the job done.

Consider the real-world example of the Outsourcing Paradox at work in an unnamed third-party logistics provider that runs a warehouse of spare parts. The 3PL had approximately eight people servicing a facility that on average had less than 75 orders for spare parts per day. The reason for the excess headcount was that the company that is outsourcing

[48] Kate Vitasek, Todd Snelgrove, Dawn Evans, Wendy Tate, Bonnie Keith, and Sarah Holliman, "Unpacking Best Value," University of Tennessee, *White Paper*, 2013, p. 38. Also see Vitasek et al., *Vested Outsourcing*.

requires that staff size per the statement of work, so the 3PL staffed at that level to meet the contract requirements.

3 The Activity Trap

Traditionally, companies purchasing products and services have used a transaction-based model where the supplier or service provider is paid for every transaction—regardless of whether or not it is needed. Businesses are in business to make money; suppliers are no different. The more contracted work they perform, the more money they make.

In cases where the supplier is paid for each activity performed, there is simply no incentive for the supplier to reduce the number of non-value-added transactions because it would result in a reduction of revenue. Make sure your agreement is not based on pushing the cash register button every time a specified activity is performed, especially when that activity is not value-added.

In another real world 3PL warehousing example, the customer's products were sold to an unnamed "big box" retailer. Each day multiple orders came in from the various departments at each retail store and were picked and shipped as individual orders all destined for the same address. When a consultant suggested a better practice of consolidating shipments to reduce shipping charges, the 3PL said that the customer paid a transaction fee for each shipment and reducing the shipments would impact the 3PL's revenue.

4 The Junkyard Dog Factor

When the decision to shift from in-house to contracted manufacturing (buy vs. make) or logistics (warehousing, transportation, etc.) comes down, it usually means that jobs will be lost as the work and jobs transition to the contract manufacturer or service provider. This often results in employees hunkering down and staking their territorial claim to certain processes that "simply must" stay in house.

Even if the majority of the jobs are outsourced, many companies choose to keep their "best" employees on board to manage the new outsource provider. These employees are often the same ones who were asked to help write the statement of work (SOW). Is it any wonder then that SOWs become rigid documents that dictate conventional and less-than-optimal ways of performing the tasks being outsourced?

The same sort of ailment can be seen at times when the sourcing team at a company decides to issue an RFP in order to find an alternative source. In this case, the internal department using the product or services may try to create requirements that only the incumbent supplier can provide.

5 The Honeymoon Effect

At the beginning of any relationship, both parties go through a honeymoon stage. For example, suppliers will jump through hoops as they ramp up for their customers. Likewise, buying companies always feel the "grass is greener on the other side" when they ramp up a new supplier. Often the level of excitement wanes after the initial ramp-up of the relationship. But while the partner remains conscientious about meeting the company's expectations and service levels outlined in the contract, it never progresses beyond this point.

The Honeymoon Effect lingers on, even while performance levels for the services provided may be improving industrywide. The problem: While the honeymoon lasts, there's no inherent incentive to raise service levels (or decrease the price) beyond what's contained in the Service Level Agreements.

There is an opportunity in any relationship to use lessons learned to develop innovative new ways to deliver the desired outcomes in ways that can benefit both partners. Sadly these opportunities are frequently dismissed because there is no incentive to improve performance.

As the marriage moves toward the contract end date, the supplier may bring the innovations to the table in an attempt to secure a new agreement. This leads to the next ailment, "Sandbagging."

6   Sandbagging

Let's look at a typical contract manufacturing or logistics example of sandbagging. Many times during contract negotiation, someone on the company side, often a senior manager, will ask, "Just how much can I save?" Rather than establish the highest level of savings achievable as early as possible (which would be most beneficial to the buying company), the provider will sandbag and offer up the savings in smaller increments over time.

Why deliver everything up front when you know that your hard-nosed customer is just going to hammer you for more next quarter or next year? The providers know that total savings are made up of "low-hanging fruit" and long-term savings. They often hold back some improvements in an effort to manufacture future savings opportunities in case they don't perform well in a given quarter or year.

7   The Zero Sum Game

Companies that play this game believe, mistakenly, that if something is good for the trading partner, then it's automatically bad for them. Providers feel the same way from the other perspective.

Many organizations fail to understand that the sum of the parts, when combined effectively, can actually exceed the whole. This synergy was proven by John Nash's Nobel Prize-winning research, commonly referred to as "Game Theory." The theory's basic premise is that when individuals or organizations play a game together (or work together to solve a problem), the results are always better than if they had played against each other (i.e., worked separately).

In a properly structured relationship, both parties are aware of how working toward a common outcome can present opportunities for improvements that can benefit both parties. Perhaps an innovative new approach would be rewarded through pricing incentives or longer contract terms. Ultimately the innovation could grow the customer's business, creating more demand from the supplier partner.

8   Driving Blind Disease

The Driving Blind Disease afflicts companies that have not done their homework in preparing for the managing of contracted manufacturing and logistics services. Specifically, it relates to the lack of a formal governance process to monitor the performance of the relationship.

Research from the Aberdeen Group shows that one of the biggest challenges organizations face today is assuring through appropriate measures that negotiated savings are actually realized on the bottom line.

The subject of governance was covered earlier and includes elements of relationship management, transformation management, and exit management, including the reporting structures and metrics.

9   Measurement Minutiae

When companies try to measure everything, they usually succumb to the malady of Measurement Minutiae. What's remarkable is the scale of the minutiae that some organizations are able to create. Some organizations use spreadsheets with 50 to 100 metrics on them.

There are literally hundreds of measures listed from various sources that could be applied to supply chain operations. Many of these are simply a new word for the same metric. Some companies will seemingly toss a dart to decide which they will use, the "oh, that sounds good" strategy.

Measurement minutiae are often associated with companies that are suffering from the junkyard dog factor and with agreements that have fallen into the activity trap. Companies that find themselves micromanaging their trading partners either are bored or simply don't trust them.

10   The Power of Not Doing

The saddest of all Ailments is the one called the Power of Not Doing. This happens when a company falls into the trap of establishing measures for the sake of measures, without thinking through how those measures will be used to manage the business. This can happen when a company finds that some other firm is using a certain set of metrics and believes that "if it is good for them, it must be good for us." When dealing with trading partners, this ailment can cause much wasted time on the part of the partner collecting data—time that ultimately adds cost in the relationship.

We've all heard the old adage that "You can't manage what you don't measure." But neither should you attempt to measure things that you don't intend to manage. If you don't use your measures to make improvements, do not waste the effort to collect the data. If you do so, you should not expect positive results.

Looking back at the six common purchasing mistakes outlined in Chapter 8, it is clear that the mistakes commonly made in the purchasing function are closely related to the Ailments seen in many trading partner relationships.

Conflicts in Partnerships

During the course of business, a customer may be concerned that the trading partner's performance is not trending in the right direction in a specific area, or a supplier may believe that its customer has expectations beyond the scope of the expected outcomes. Issues between buyers and suppliers can be segmented into three categories: concerns, problems, and conflicts.

Conflicts between Trading Partners

Trading partners should talk about these terms at this stage of formulating the governance framework process because one party's issue is another party's problem. Who gets to decide if something is labeled an issue or a problem? In our experience, this is an easy exercise to undertake at this point. Discuss and decide the variance or tolerance level for performance indicators. From that discussion, you can decide at what point a variance triggers a problem-solving approach.

By documenting this thought process at the outset of the contract, partners can save countless hours exchanging e-mails as they try to understand how much attention to pay to a situation. They should also define the term *conflict*. The words *dispute* and *conflict* are often loaded with negative connotations. We suggest that firms reserve the term *conflict* for all unresolved problems. No party should tell the other party that they are having a conflict unless there is an intention to involve senior management.

In our opinion, a conflict is any circumstance that cannot be resolved by middle management. Conflicts, by their very nature, threaten the relationship and the agreement; for that reason, they require senior-level attention.

Resolving Conflicts

Once the partners have defined terms to use when differentiating issues that have little impact or little urgency from those that do, it is time to design a process for addressing issues, concerns, and problems. For example, routine daily conversations should resolve almost all issues. Issues usually are identified and addressed as a matter of course.

A high percentage of all issues will get resolved. A concern has more urgency. Therefore, concerns ought to be addressed at the QBRs. Place concerns on the agenda and set aside time to discuss them.

Problems are high impact and urgent. Parties must act immediately to solve problems using a predefined process. For example, the parties may decide that a problem requires three measures:

1. A middle manager at one company will notify the corresponding middle manager at the other company in writing about a problem.
2. The parties agree to convene a meeting within five business days.
3. The parties agree that each company will send someone with decision-making authority to that meeting.

If such a clear process is set forth in the agreement, implementing it, even in a time of high emotion, will be easy.

Exhibit: Relationship Issues—Impact and Resolution

Situation	Degree	Resolution
Issue:	Medium impact; low urgency	Resolved in routine conversations
Concern:	Medium impact; medium urgency	Resolved in QBR meetings
Problem:	High impact; high urgency	Escalate and call special meeting
Conflict:	Unresolved problem	Escalate to senior management or neutral third party
Breach of Contract:	Unresolved conflict	Third-party intervention, such as arbitration

Source: Kate Vitasek, Jacqui Crawford, Jeanette Nyden, and Katherine Kawamoto, *The Vested Outsourcing Manual* (Palgrave Macmillan, July 2011).

Summary

Today, virtually all businesses use the same transaction-based approach for procuring complex services (i.e., contract manufacturing and logistics outsourcing) as they do to buy more simple commodities and supplies. Unfortunately, many business professionals wrongly assume that a transaction-based sourcing business model is the only sourcing business model. For simple transactions with abundant supply and low complexity, a transaction-based sourcing business model is likely the most efficient model. But the real weakness of a transaction-based approach emerges when any complexity, variability, mutual dependency, or customized assets or processes are part of the transaction. Simply put, a transactional approach cannot produce perfect market-based price equilibrium in variable or multidimensional business agreements and instead increases transaction costs.

As companies strive to transform their operations through outsourcing or seek innovation from their suppliers, they will most certainly need to better understand their business environment and the various sourcing business models that are available. It is important that today's business leaders understand the fundamental differences of each type of sourcing business model and consciously strive to pick the right model for the right environment, ultimately picking the right approach to use for the right job.

As you embark on your journey to acquire products and services more effectively, the authors urge you to consider the fact that outsourcing is more than a make-or-buy decision— it is a continuum. As a sourcing, contracting, or outsourcing professional, it is your job to understand your business environment and use the right sourcing business model that will best accomplish your objectives. We also challenge companies that have created shared-services groups to explore the concept of Vested Outsourcing.

Agreements Must Be Flexible

10 Elements	Reason for Change	Frequency
Business Model	• When there is a significant change in the operating environment	At contract renewal (5+ years)
Shared Vision/ Statement of Intent	• When there is a significant change in the operating environment	At contract renewal (5+ years)
Exit Management Plan	• May be revised with new SOO	New SOO (5+ years)
Statement of Work, Workload Allocation	• When there is a significant change in the operating environment	Under continuous governance (yearly)
Relationship Management Framework	• When there is a change in the governance structure	Under continuous governance (yearly)
Transformation Management	• With improvements	Under continuous governance (yearly)
Top Level Desired Outcomes	• Change in the outcomes	Under continuous governance (yearly)
Pricing Model	• Improvement plans • Change in incentives • Revised assumptions • Margin matching	Under continuous governance (yearly)
Miscellaneous Terms	• With major contract revisions	Dependent on other changes, likely yearly
Performance Reporting Quality Plan Processes	• Change to the business rules • Change in processes • Change to operational measures	As required (weekly, monthly, yearly)

Suggested Readings	Vitasek, Kate, and Karl Manrodt, *The Vested Way: How a "What's in It for We" Mindset Revolutionizes Business Relationships* (Palgrave Macmillan, April 6, 2012).
	Vitasek, Kate, Karl B. Manrodt, Richard Wilding, and Tim Cummins, "Unpacking Oliver: Ten Lessons to Improve Collaborative Outsourcing," University of Tennessee, Center for Executive Education, Spring 2010.

Questions and Problems

LO 10-1 1. What are the 3 Cs of managing relationships with customers and suppliers?

LO 10-2 2. Describe how the terms "partner" and "partnership" apply to a supply chain relationship.

3. Discuss the three major types of business relationships.

4. Define the 10 Elements of a successful contract, and the 10 Ailments of traditional business relationships.

LO 10-3 5. What are the primary implementation strategies involved with the various partnering models?

6. Describe the advantages and disadvantages of partners, and recommend steps for conflict resolution.

7. What are the three key factors that must exist in order for a partnership to be successful?

LO 10-4 8. Describe metrics that can be used to measure success.

11

Supply Chain Process Integration

Objectives of this Chapter

LO 11-1 To define process integration and business process frameworks.

LO 11-2 To define and illustrate process mapping.

LO 11-3 To examine the strengths of leading supply chain process classification frameworks.

LO 11-4 To examine the future role of business process frameworks.

Introduction

In 2004, the Council of Logistics Management (CLM) changed its name to the Council of Supply Chain Management Professionals (CSCMP) to underscore and better understand the boundary-spanning discipline that had developed across functional silos, both within and across companies. The renaming ushered in some interesting dialogue and debate within the practitioner and academic communities.

At the center of this dialogue was discussion concerning the definition, scope, and conceptualization of supply chain management (SCM). While SCM definitions rightly consider SCM to be a cross-disciplinary concept, there is confusion regarding which organization within a business should "own" supply chain–related managerial decisions.

That confusion is widely evident. At many companies, departments are still operating within functional silos and managers are still performing the same logistics or purchasing activities as they were before the term "supply chain" was added to their job titles—even at companies that have reorganized functions into a single supply chain group. In fact, one author got into the habit of asking practitioners with a new title using "supply chain" what new responsibilities they had.[1] Moreover, there is still disagreement about which functions should fall under the umbrella of supply chain management. Managers at some companies, for instance, are expressing frustration that their "supply chain" organizations have been

---

[1] This was also confirmed by researchers looking at this. Out of 50 job descriptions using "supply chain," only one of those positions was a true supply chain management position. For more information, see Beth Davis-Sramek and Brian S. Fugate, "State of Logistics: A Visionary Perspective," *Journal of Business Logistics*, Vol. 28, No. 2 (2007), pp. 1–34.

defined as extending upstream from manufacturing/production to key vendors, while initiatives involving finished-goods distribution are largely marginalized. In essence, confusion has been created among the different players in the supply chain as to who is ultimately responsible for the efficient flow of goods and services.

To create order from chaos, many universities, industry professional organizations, and consulting firms have taken the first step in creating frameworks to better define supply chains, the processes needed to be successful, measures to monitor success, and practices that create success for companies. Generally, these models create a structure for organizing and standardizing processes used to manage the supply chain. They also provide a standard that facilitates communication among supply chain participants.

The emergence of several SCM frameworks undoubtedly has supported advances in supply chain management theory and practice. But we contend that it also has added to the confusion surrounding SCM because each framework has its own terms, processes, and metrics that often compete with those of other models. The frameworks are not broad enough in scope to capture the systematic, process-oriented, boundary-spanning, and strategic nature of SCM.

In this chapter, we will provide an overview of four SCM frameworks and provide a more in-depth examination of the two most popular.

Defining Supply Chain Process Integration

Earlier in this book, we noted there are a number of definitions being used for supply chain management. At the core of each definition is that supply chains integrate activities external and internal to organizations. Earlier we used the Council of Supply Chain Management Professionals' definition of supply chain management. "In essence, Supply Chain Management *integrates* supply and demand management within and across companies."[2] Mentzer and others define it as "the systemic, strategic coordination of the traditional business functions and the tactics across these business functions within a particular company and across businesses within the supply chain, for the purposes of improving the long term performance of the individual companies and the supply chain as a whole."[3] Another highly cited example is from Cooper, Lambert, and Pagh, who define supply chain management as "the *integration* of key business processes from end users through original suppliers that provides products, services, and information that add value for customers and other stakeholders."[4]

The striking commonality between most definitions is that supply chain management is an *integrating* function. That means supply chain management is primarily responsible for *linking and coordinating* major business functions and business processes within and across companies into a cohesive and high-performing business model. It includes all of the logistics management activities, as well as manufacturing operations and procurement, and it *drives* coordination of processes and activities within and across marketing, sales, product design, finance, and information technology.

This allows us to draw two important conclusions from the definitions. First, supply chain management is a strategy. Second, it modifies behaviors at the functional level in order to reach organizational goals. Therefore, an accurate and valuable supply chain management model will capture the strategic implications of supply chain management and how it drives functional behaviors within a company. In our view, an effective supply chain framework must support the CSCMP definition of supply chain management, which was fully defined in Chapter 1.

---

[2] Definition provided at Council of Supply Chain Management Professionals website, 2018, http://cscmp.org.

[3] John T. Mentzer, William DeWitt, James S. Keebler, Min Soonhong, Nancy W. Nix, Carlo D. Smith, and Zach G. Zacharia, "Defining Supply Chain Management," *Journal of Business Logistics*, Vol. 22, No. 2 (2001), pp. 1–25.

[4] Martha C. Cooper, Douglas M. Lambert, and James D. Pagh, "Supply Chain Management: More Than a New Name for Logistics," *The International Journal of Logistics Management*, Vol. 8, No. 1 (1997), pp. 1–14.

Looking at the respective definitions, we can then understand why integration is a key component to the definition of supply chain management. The sum of all processes that make up supply chain management must work in tandem in order to achieve the desired outcomes set by firms. When we think about supply chain process integration, we define it as seamless, coordinated processes that optimize informational and operational flows between departments and partners in the supply chain, which improves service capabilities while achieving lower total supply chain costs.

Methods to Define and Integrate Processes

Firms are made up of distinctive processes such as Finance, Information Technology, Marketing and Sales, Logistics, and Supply Chain that at times are not well integrated. To integrate and better align processes and/or the functional areas in a firm, companies can use two different methods—either a business process framework or process mapping. Both methods provide value for companies using them and can be used separately or together.

We discussed several different business process frameworks that firms use, including the SCOR Model, APQC's Process Classification Framework, and the Global Supply Chain Forum Process Model. For instance, the SCOR Model shown in Figure 11.1 divides business activities into six processes: Plan, Source, Make, Deliver, Return, and Enable. Business process frameworks attempt to link performance, practices, and processes to where in the organization the work is performed. Process mapping is different from business process frameworks and in many instances is used as part of the overall implementation of a business process framework. It identifies the flow of events in a process in addition to the inputs and outputs of each process step. First, we will look at process mapping and the value process mapping brings organizations. Next, we will examine business process frameworks (BPFs) and why firms choose to use BPFs as a way to help them better integrate functions.

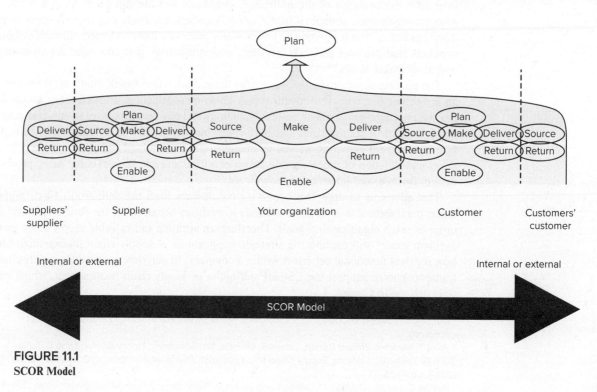

FIGURE 11.1
SCOR Model

Source: Peter Bolstorff, "SCOR 101, APICS Webinar Series," September 23, 2015, http://slideplayer.com/slide/7414109/.

Process Mapping

A process is a unique set of activities. Process mapping develops documentation around the activities being performed. Companies use process mapping as a tool to identify where the activities of a process are executed, who is responsible, and how other activities and processes interact with each other. It is also used to help a company identify bottlenecks in its workflows. Finally, mapping makes determining why a process is being executed visible, which can make it easier to identify activities within a process that are not adding value. The non-value-added activities should be targeted for modification or elimination.

Creating a Process Map

There are several types of approaches a company can use to create a process map. There are business scope diagrams, a geographic map, thread diagrams, value stream mapping, and finally workflow diagrams. Each of these techniques enables a company to model the overall process and activities in its firm.

Business scope diagrams set the scope of a project or an organization. A geographic map will display the material flows in geographic context and will highlight node intricacy or the convolutedness of the supply chain. Thread diagrams show how processes are interconnected and the complexity or redundancy of higher level processes. Value stream mapping, a technique used in lean manufacturing, analyzes and designs the flow of materials and information required to bring a product or service to a consumer. And finally, workflow diagrams bring together the lower-level processes to highlight information, people, and system interaction issues.

The use of a particular diagram is dependent on what is being displayed and is subjective to the firm's situation. Figure 11.2 provides an example of a workflow diagram from the SCOR Model. Figure 11.3 shows an example of a value stream map used by CHEP, a pallet provider, to help its customers reduce the costs associated with pallets.

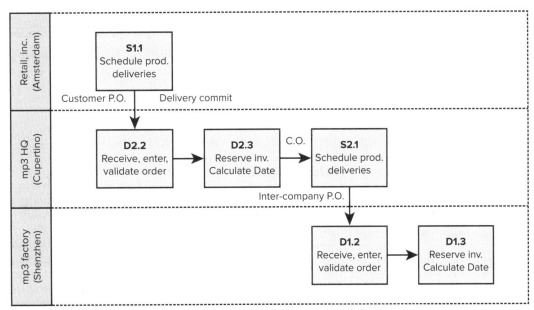

C.O. = Customer order, Inv. = Inventory, P.O. = Purchase order, Prod. = Product

FIGURE 11.2
Workflow Diagram Using SCOR Model Processes

Source: Supply-Chain Council, *SCOR Framework 2.1 Workshop* (PowerPoint slides), 2008.

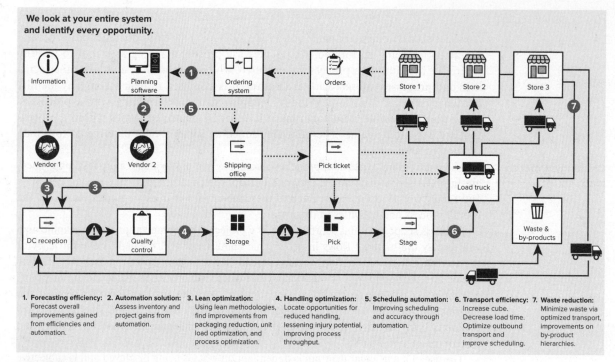

We look at your entire system and identify every opportunity.

1. **Forecasting efficiency:** Forecast overall improvements gained from efficiencies and automation.

2. **Automation solution:** Assess inventory and project gains from automation.

3. **Lean optimization:** Using lean methodologies, find improvements from packaging reduction, unit load optimization, and process optimization.

4. **Handling optimization:** Locate opportunities for reduced handling, lessening injury potential, improving process throughput.

5. **Scheduling automation:** Improving scheduling and accuracy through automation.

6. **Transport efficiency:** Increase cube. Decrease load time. Optimize outbound transport and improve scheduling.

7. **Waste reduction:** Minimize waste via optimized transport, improvements on by-product hierarchies.

FIGURE 11.3
Value STREAM MAP

Source: "Value Stream Mapping," CHEP, a Brambles Company, 2015, https://www.chep.com/us/en/consumer-goods/solutions/system-wide-solutions/value-stream-mapping.

Exhibit: Process Mapping in Action

When companies acquire other companies or outsource part of their business to a new service provider, opportunities abound to reduce costs, to eliminate redundancies in work procedures, and to establish a formal process for performing activities. Mapping a process makes it visible, illustrating how a process happens so it can be viewed, analyzed, and improved.

In 2007, Applebee's was acquired by IHOP Corporation, the parent to the International House of Pancakes restaurants. In an effort to align the companies' supply chains, the parent company (now known as DineEquity) created the Centralized Supply Chain Services, LLC (CSCS) in February 2009. CSCS became an independent company owned by its members, who are Applebee's, IHOP, and company restaurant operators.

In order to analyze the current situation and identify where to consolidate and streamline processes, CSCS used supply chain mapping. CSCS aligned its activities to achieve better execution, communication, and enhanced relationships—all of which help to make the process more productive than it was before. CSCS not only had to map component processes, but also had to map the supply chain itself.

The method used by CSCS was a five-step process to map its supply chain processes. The five steps were:

1. Form a cross-functional team.
2. Map the process.
3. Identify the delays and bottlenecks.
4. Identify and implement process changes.
5. Measure the results.

Supply chain mapping played an important role in helping CSCS deliver quantifiable benefits to the stakeholders in their cooperative's first two years. Most notable among those benefits is the improvement in the owners/operators' net positive financial impact. In addition, CSCS has documented tens of millions of dollars in actual net cost reductions through its cost impact reporting process. This process documents all savings, cost increases, and cost avoidances.

Because CSCS has developed documented processes that everyone understands, it has made rapid progress in the rationalization of the distribution network that serves the two brands. As of the beginning of 2011, it has reduced the network by consolidating or reducing the number of warehouses, distribution centers, and carriers used by 12.5 percent, with an additional 15 to 20 percent expected. CSCS is able to achieve financial benefits while increasing the synergy and economies of scale of the Applebee's and IHOP brands with every consolidation.

Most importantly, by having a collaborative process with established "rules of engagement," CSCS has established a firm foundation of mutual support and respect.

Source: Adapted from David Parsley, "Adding Value through Process Mapping," *CSCMP's Supply Chain Quarterly*, Vol. 5, No. 2 (Quarter 2/2011), pp. 42–50.

Business Process Frameworks

At the most basic level, BPFs provide a common language that can be easily adopted by an organization to facilitate communication between the different departments or functions such as IT, finance, marketing, distribution and transportation, and sales. It allows organizations to better understand their current state and define their future, or "To Be," state.

Business process frameworks are more comprehensive, when compared to process mapping, as they are typically implemented at a higher level within the firm. They are not predefined maps of your organization, a list of must-have metrics, or a must-have list of practices. A BPF enables an organization to quickly get on the same "process page" and drive consistency across performance initiatives. BPFs provide value to organizations in measurable ways and increase companies' fundamental ability to perform.[5]

Companies can create their own BPF that is very unique to their industry, operations, or customers. They may become a member of a forum, such as tmforum, a global association for communication and digital service providers and their suppliers. Or a company can use a generic approach, such as the SCOR Model or APQC's Process Classification Framework, and tailor the model to its particular environment. One such example of a company creating a BPF to improve its overall supply chain operations and performance is UPS. UPS developed a BPF to identify overlapping activities and eliminate non-value-added activities.

Exhibit: UPS Develops Its Business Process Framework

UPS is a household name to many in the United States and throughout the world. Few people have not sent or received a package that, in some way, has not been touched by UPS. With a company history of over 100 years, UPS has grown to deliver more than 14 million packages a day, supported by over 400,000 employees.

In order to deliver those 14 million packages, UPS has developed a system of processes, including a process framework, that helps it achieve its goals.

If UPS does not deliver as promised because of a breakdown in the processes that make it possible, UPS loses. In the early 1990s, this nearly became the case as forecasts and key performance indicators used by UPS were down and not very encouraging. As new competitors were coming onto the landscape in the small package delivery marketplace, UPS had to make a change to improve.

To better deliver to its customers and understand how to improve its overall business performance, UPS began to investigate its core processes. It took two years for the management team to create the "to-be" design of the new business process framework.

The "to-be" design of core processes consisted of four processes: package management, product management, customer relationship management (CRM), and customer information management (CIM).

Five support processes support the four core processes: business information analysis (BIA), shared services, finance and accounting, human resources, and IT. UPS used a simple question to determine whether it should be a core process or a support process: "What does the customer come to UPS for?"

For example, customers do not choose UPS for its billing process. They choose UPS for its package

(Continued)

[5] John Tesmer, Shaina Bielaz, and Travis Colton, *Using Process Frameworks and Reference Models to Get Real Work Done* (APQC, 2011), p. 76.

management process, but the billing process must still operate as efficiently and effectively as the package management process.

The cross-functional nature of several processes required adaptations. For instance, several functions require the use of billing such as sales, drivers, package management, and finance. The cross-functional billing process at UPS looks like this:

1. A shipping client provides electronic information about the package. (The sales group owns relationships with shipping clients.)

2. Drivers collect data while picking up and delivering packages. (Operations and technology own this.)

3. Information moves ahead of the package to the sender and the recipient. (Package management owns this.)

4. The actual billing processes occur. (Finance owns this.)

The old billing process required one process owner to coordinate with multiple functional owners. Under the new framework, the manager for the cross-functional process is responsible for both the results of the billing process and the continuous optimization of the process. When changes occur, the cross-functional manager must take great pains to ensure that changes within his or her process do not reduce the effectiveness of the other core processes.

For UPS, implementing a new cross-functional framework over the existing functional work was not done without effort. Ultimately, the required effort varied widely from

quickly adapting the product management process to taking almost 10 years to adapt the package management process.

Several factors impacted the speed of the adoption of the framework. The two primary factors were technical infrastructure and components. For instance, one set of functions within a process required moving large amounts of data (greater than 2 terabytes of data) in a relatively short amount of time. Because the technology did not exist in 1996, the process was reworked with the appropriate functional leaders and customers outside UPS to better understand which individual fields of data were needed first. As soon as the technology became available, the process once again was changed to use the new capabilities.

After 10 years of use, in true continuous improvement fashion, UPS started a strategic review of its operations in 2004. This led to the creation of the Strategy Roadmap, which communicates how the mission of the organization is related to the projects necessary for achieving its strategic imperatives.

While the UPS Framework is not a standard off-the-shelf framework, its framework of processes shows how companies, through introspection and teamwork, are able to develop a common language for a company to operate.

Source: John Tesmer, Shaina Bielaz, and Travis Colton, *Using Process Frameworks and Reference Models to Get Real Work Done* (APQC, 2011), pp. 119–129.

What Makes an Effective Framework?

Supply chain frameworks establish a common language for communicating ideas, concepts, and methodologies and for discussing and documenting supply chain activities. They build a structure for modeling supply chains and communicating with participants while supporting the communication and comparison of benchmarks and best practices.

They also create a process framework linked to performance measurement (metrics) that can communicate the relevance of the SCM strategy to everyone in the organization. Without such a framework, it is difficult to capture the strategic implications of SCM because decision makers cannot align or measure the effectiveness of actions and decisions relative to corporate strategy.

Elements of an Effective Framework

Thus, supply chain frameworks should contain certain essential attributes and functionality if they are to be effective as management tools. An effective SCM framework should have the elements in Table 11.1.

It is important to note that business process frameworks focus on the activities involved, not the persons or elements in the organization that perform the activity.

A key advantage of using a business process framework is to allow external organizations to benchmark themselves against each other. For this reason, several industry organizations have set out to develop business process frameworks that help companies compare their business processes and metrics to other companies. For instance, WERC (the Warehouse Education and Research Council) has developed benchmarks, process benchmarks, and standardized definitions for operating today's distribution centers. This chapter explores

TABLE 11.1
Elements of an Effective SCM Framework

Source: Chris Moberg, Abre Pienaar, Theodore Stank, and Kate Vitasek, "Time to Remodel," *CSCMP's Supply Chain Quarterly*, Vol. 2, No. 3 (3Q/2008), http://www .supplychainquarterly.com /topics/Strategy/scq200803 scmmodel/.

- Support a standard definition of SCM.
- Establish a common language that allows supply chain professionals to communicate.
- Provide standard definitions for key supply chain processes, allowing for the documentation of processes.
- Promote supply chain excellence by linking a common set of metrics to the framework, which allows the metrics to be measured in a standard manner that avoids ambiguity.
- Support continuous improvement by providing benchmarking data that is aligned to the framework, for the comparison of measured performance with best-practice performance targets.
- Provide an end-to-end supply chain model that can be applied to multiple industries.
- Provide a format that is easy to understand, implement, and practice as a supply chain modeling and improvement tool.
- Provide supply chain transparency by supporting global supply chain mapping through the description of the flows of materials and information.
- Facilitate a cross-functional/cross-enterprise view of the organization and its supply chain partners for process-focused measurement and continuous improvement in the end-to-end supply chain.
- Allow theories and practices to be presented to a facilitating or governing authority, which can share them with its membership using a common point of reference.
- Allow the development of training and education programs to further supply chain knowledge.
- Allow the supply chain profession to expand the awareness of the significance of supply chains to businesses and to the economy.

four such frameworks and goes in depth into two—the SCOR Model and APQC's Process Classification Framework (PCF). Both the SCOR Model and APQC's PCF take great strides to link processes, measures of performance, best practices, and the features associated with the execution of the business together.

Over the past four decades, several nonprofit professional organizations and academic institutions have created business process frameworks for companies to use to model their supply chains, link performance measures to processes, and provide best practices in achieving desired performance. In addition, consulting firms have created their own models to aid them in carrying out assignments and comparing best practices among clients. Table 11.2 identifies four of the most commonly used supply chain process frameworks.

While each of the frameworks is used in industry, it is important to point out there is no one "right" framework. For example, the SCOR Model is well suited to the electronics and consumer goods industries. APQC has taken the next step with its Process Classification Framework and created industry-specific models. Some of the industries the PCF covers are Aerospace and Defense, Automotive, Consumer Products, Pharmaceutical, and Telecommunications. The Supply Chain Consortium Framework has been particularly useful for Tompkins International's consulting firm, in helping it establish benchmarks for the retail industry.

In this chapter, we will discuss two of the most commonly used frameworks in the industry—the SCOR Model and APQC's Process Classification Framework.

Supply Chain Operations Reference (SCOR) Model

The SCOR Model Was First Developed in 1996

We have previously introduced the SCOR Model in early chapters, but will go into more depth here. The widely used SCOR Model, or Supply Chain Operations Reference Model, was developed by the Supply Chain Council to provide a standardized method for measuring supply chain performance and to create a common set of metrics that could be used for

TABLE 11.2
Popular Supply Chain Management Process Frameworks

The Supply Chain Council—Supply Chain Operations Reference (SCOR) Model

- Developed to provide a standardized method for measuring supply chain performance and sharing best practices.
- Released first edition of SCOR Model in 1996. It has been revised on 11 occasions and is currently in its 12th edition.
- Centered around five primary management processes—plan, source, make, deliver, and return.
- Provides a cross-industry standard application.
- Benchmarking services available to member companies only.
- Merged with ASCM in 2018.
- APICS changed its name to ASCM in 2018.

Supply Chain Management Institute—Global Supply Chain Forum Process Model

- Developed in the early 1990s by The Ohio State University's Supply Chain Management Institute.
- Suited for companies whose idea of SCM revolves around relationship management.
- Focuses on eight processes to be managed and integrated—customer relationship management, customer service management, demand management, order fulfillment, manufacturing flow management, supplier relationship management, product development and commercialization, and returns management.

American Productivity and Quality Center—APQC's Process Classification Framework

- Developed the Process Classification Framework in 1992.
- Created to be industry, company size, or geography agnostic.
- Benchmarking services available to member companies and nonmembers for a fee.
- Organized around 12 cross-organizational operating and management processes: develop vision and strategy; design and develop products and services; market and sell products and services; deliver products and services; manage customer service; develop and manage human capital; manage information technology; manage financial resources; acquire, construct, and manage property; manage environmental health and safety; manage external relationships; and manage knowledge, improvement, and change.

Supply Chain Consortium—Supply Chain Best Practices Framework

- Developed in 2004 by Tompkins International.
- Created to understand the practical implementation of characteristics common to "world class supply chains."
- Provides an integrated structure for defining, measuring, and improving supply chain processes.

benchmarking purposes.[6] The first version of the SCOR Model was released in 1996, the same year the Supply Chain Council was organized. The Supply Chain Council is a global nonprofit association whose goal is to help organizations make drastic and rapid improvements in their supply chain processes.

According to the Supply Chain Council, SCOR's goal is to enable users to "address, improve, and communicate supply-chain management practices within and between all interested parties."[7] The model is highly process-focused and enables users to build their individual scope to include the extended supply chain and bring in processes from a supplier's supplier to a customer's customer.

[6] CSCMP, "Supply Chain and Logistics Terms and Glossary," https://cscmp.org/CSCMP/Educate/SCM_Definitions_and_Glossary_of_Terms/CSCMP/Educate/SCM_Definitions_and_Glossary_of_Terms.aspx?hkey=60879588-f65f-4ab5-8c4b-6878815ef921.
[7] Supply Chain Council, "SCOR Model," http://www.apics.org/apics-for-business/frameworks/scor.

The SCOR Model provides a cross-industry standard application for modeling a company's supply chain processes, as shown in Figure 11.1. It is considered to be without boundary, as it is believed there are only two stopping points, the beginning of the chain and the end of the chain. A good example is how a raw material, such as a grain of sand, is turned into a finished product, such as a glass screen for an iPad, and finally sold to an end user. Another example is progression of sourcing cow's milk to manufacture of the ice cream to the delivery of an ice cream cone at McDonald's or Diary Queen to the consumer.

A key benefit of the SCOR Model is that it helps focus companies on improving the efficiency of internal processes. SCOR's assessment phase (phase two, involving the analysis and potential benchmarking of metrics) is very helpful in establishing the "as is" status of a company's supply chain and assists in developing the "to be" plan for supply chain users. It has been readily adopted by the information technology and consulting communities and is well suited for understanding the complexities of the electronics and consumer goods industries.

One of the criticisms of the SCOR Model is that it limits processes—focusing only on supply chain processes. Specifically, the SCOR model does not integrate cross-functional areas such as sales and marketing (demand generation), research and technology development, product development, and some elements of post-delivery customer support. This means that a company that wants to have a comprehensive view of all of its processes may have to use another process framework for other non-supply-chain-related processes. These areas are covered by other frameworks developed by APICS. As noted in Figure 11.4, APICS has developed one of the frameworks discussed in this text. PLCOR stands for the Product Life Cycle Operations Reference model and manages product innovation and portfolio management. Customer Chain Operations Reference model, or CCOR, manages the customer interaction process. DCOR, or Design Chain Operations Reference model, manages the product and service development process.[8]

A second criticism is that many companies find using the SCOR Model complex, and therefore it requires a significant amount of training to understand and build a custom SCOR Model. The SCOR framework model, revised in 2017, is nearly 1,100 pages long! The SCOR Model uses several different continuous-improvement processes, technologies, and techniques, as well as a vast taxonomy of terms, for teams to identify their supply chains. The various training programs offered by APICS for educators, industry professionals, and students introduces the SCOR Model taxonomy and walks them through implementing the SCOR Model in an example company. In addition, APICS provides certification for educators, industry professionals, and students on their knowledge of the model. Lastly, while the benchmarking data is very good and is aligned to the framework, the Supply Chain Council only provides quantitative benchmarks to its own members through its SCORmark benchmarking database.[9]

Components of the SCOR Model

The SCOR Model consists of five primary management processes, metrics aligned to measure the performance of those processes, and best practices. In the latest revision of the SCOR Model, the Supply Chain Council developed skills sets employees working in the supply chain profession should have based on their functional area within the organization.

Components of the SCOR Model

In this section we will take an in-depth look at each of the components of the most recent SCOR Model, Revision 12.0 (see Table 11.3).

---

[8] SCOR, "Supply Chain Operations Reference Model Revision 12.0," APICS, 2017, p. iii.

[9] APICS, "SCORmark," https://www.apics.org/apics-for-business/benchmarking/scormark-benchmarking.

FIGURE 11.4
APICS Frameworks

Source: SCOR, "Supply
Chain Operations Reference
Model Revision 12.0,"
APICS, 2017, p. iii.

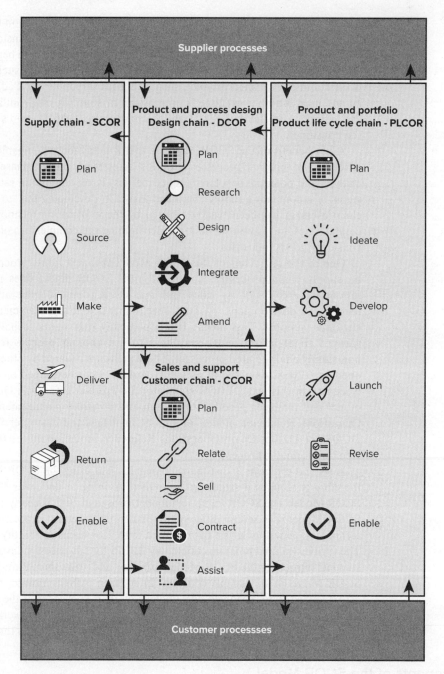

The Six SCOR Processes

**The Six SCOR Level 1
Processes**

A process is a distinctive activity performed to achieve a desired outcome. The SCOR
Model is based on six distinct high-level management processes: plan, source, make, deliver,
return, and enable.[10] These six categories are the top-level processes (or process types) and
are the Level 1 processes in the SCOR Model.

[10] SCOR, "Supply Chain Operations Reference Model Revision 12.0."

TABLE 11.3
Components of SCOR 12.0 Model

Source: SCOR, "Supply Chain Operations Reference Model Revision 12.0," APICS, 2017.

Components	High-Level Groups/Attributes	Description
Processes	• Plan • Source • Make • Deliver • Return • Enable	Standard descriptions of management processes and process relationships
Metrics	• Reliability • Responsiveness • Agility • Costs • Asset Management Efficiency	Standard metrics to describe process performance and define strategic goals
Practices	• Emerging • Best • Standard	Management practices that produce significantly better process performance
People	• Skill	Standards for describing skills required to perform tasks and manage processes specific to supply chain

Plan

The Plan processes are the distinct activities associated with developing plans to operate the supply chain. Plan processes determine the requirements and corrective actions needed to be successful in operating the supply chain and the other four high-level processes. These processes include the gathering of requirements and information on available resources, and balancing requirements and resources to determine planned capabilities. If there are gaps in demand or resources, then actions will be identified to correct these gaps.

Source

The Source processes are the distinct processes around ordering, delivery, receipt, and transfer of raw materials, subassemblies, products, and/or services. The Source process represents the release of purchase orders or scheduling deliveries, receiving, validating and storage of goods, and accepting the invoice from the supplier. Supplier identification, qualification, and contract negotiation processes are not part of the Source process elements. Sourcing engineer-to-order goods or services is the exception.

Make

The Make processes are the activities associated with all types of material conversions. These conversions include assembly, chemical processing, maintenance, repair, overhaul, recycling, refurbishment, remanufacturing, etc. Make processes are recognized by the fact that one or more item numbers go in and one or more different item numbers come out of this process. Note that the returning of items for recycling, refurbishment, remanufacturing, maintenance, repair, or overhaul is included in the Return processes.

Deliver

The Deliver processes are the activities generally associated with logistics; i.e., the creation, maintenance, and fulfillment of customer orders. The Deliver process represents the receipt, validation, and creation of customer orders; scheduling order delivery; pick, pack and shipment; and invoicing the customer. Unique to the SCOR Model's Deliver process is the D4 Deliver Retail. The D4 Deliver Retail process was created to provide a simplified view of the Source and Deliver processes, which are unique to a make-to-stock-only retail operation. The D4 Deliver Retail process is used to acquire, merchandise, and sell finished goods at a retail store direct to customer using a point-of-sale process.

Return

Return processes are the activities associated with the reverse flow of goods in the supply chain. The Return process represents the return of products for repair, recycling, refurbishment, remanufacturing, or scheduled maintenance. The Make processes detail the activities associated with the actual repair, recycling, refurbishment, remanufacturing, or scheduled maintenance activities.

Enable

Enable processes are the activities associated with establishing, maintaining, and monitoring assets, business rules, compliance, contracts, information, and relationships that are required to operate a supply chain. The Enable processes interact with processes in other functional areas such as Finance, Information Technology, and Human Resources, to name a few.

The Four SCOR Levels

The SCOR Model consists of four levels. Each level within the model allows companies to further refine the details of how their processes operate. Beginning at Level 1, which consists of Plan, Source, Make, Deliver, Return, and Enable processes as outlined above, a company will determine which Level 1 processes are used in its company, as denoted in Figure 11.5.

At Level 2, the main SCOR processes are broken down into "process categories," where each process type is developed and its application is specified at the task level. For instance, this level shows the organization's customized configuration of planning, enabling, and executing each process (as it applies to make-to-stock, make-to-order, or engineer-to-order products) in accordance with the model's standards.

At Level 3, the organization defines the Level 3 processes that are performed in a specific sequence in order to source materials, plan activities, make products, deliver goods, and handle product returns.[11]

Level 4 processes are generally specific to an industry, product, location, or technology. Here, companies may develop their own standard process descriptions of activities within the Level 3

FIGURE 11.5
SCOR Hierarchical Process Model

Source: SCOR, "Supply Chain Operations Reference Model Revision 12.0," APICS, 2017, p. vi.

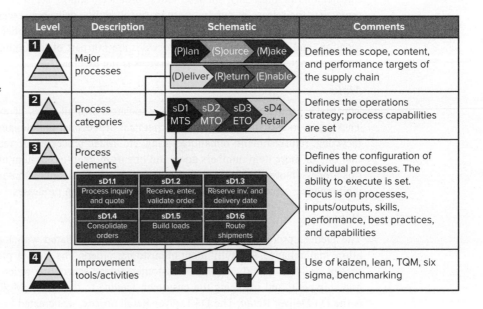

Level	Description	Schematic	Comments
1	Major processes	(P)lan (S)ource (M)ake (D)eliver (R)eturn (E)nable	Defines the scope, content, and performance targets of the supply chain
2	Process categories	sD1 MTS · sD2 MTO · sD3 ETO · sD4 Retail	Defines the operations strategy; process capabilities are set
3	Process elements	sD1.1 Process inquiry and quote · sD1.2 Receive, enter, validate order · sD1.3 Reserve inv. and delivery date · sD1.4 Consolidate orders · sD1.5 Build loads · sD1.6 Route shipments	Defines the configuration of individual processes. The ability to execute is set. Focus is on processes, inputs/outputs, skills, performance, best practices, and capabilities
4	Improvement tools/activities		Use of kaizen, lean, TQM, six sigma, benchmarking

[11] Ibid., p ix.

processes. Not every firm would use the same process to "receive, enter, and validate a customer order," but each company should have a defined process as to how that is accomplished.

While not defined in the SCOR Model, as these activities are thought to be company specific, Level 4, and possibly Level 5, further defines the process elements by creating a hierarchy or flow of tasks and activities within each element.

Table 11.4 shows the correlation between Level 1 and Level 2 SCOR processes.

TABLE 11.4
Level 1 and Level 2 SCOR Processes

Source: SCOR Model, "Supply Chain Operations Reference Model Revision 12.0," APICS, 2017, pp. 2.1.2–2.6.2.

Level 1 PLAN—The processes associated with determining requirements and corrective actions to achieve supply chain objectives. Level 2 processes include:
- sP1 Plan Supply Chain
- sP2 Plan Source
- sP3 Plan Make
- sP4 Plan Deliver
- sP5 Plan Return

Level 1 SOURCE—The processes associated with ordering, delivery, receipt, and transfer of raw material items, subassemblies, product, and/or services. Level 2 processes include:
- sS1 Source Stocked Product
- sS2 Source Make-to-Order Product
- sS3 Source Engineer-to-Order Product

Level 1 MAKE—The process of adding value to products through mixing, separating, forming, machining, and chemical processes. Level 2 processes include:
- sM1 Make-to-Stock
- sM2 Make-to-Order
- sM3 Engineer-to-Order

Level 1 DELIVER—The processes associated with performing customer-facing order management and order fulfillment activities. Level 2 processes include:
- sD1 Deliver Stocked Product
- sD2 Deliver Make-to-Order Product
- sD3 Deliver Engineer-to-Order Product
- sD4 Deliver Retail Product

Level 1 RETURN—The processes associated with moving material from a customer back through the supply chain to address defects in product, ordering, or manufacturing, or to perform upkeep activities. Level 2 processes include:
- sSR1 Source Return Defective Product
- sDR1 Deliver Return Defective Product
- sSR2 Source Return MRO Product
- sDR2 Deliver Return MRO Product
- sSR3 Source Return Excess Product
- sDR3 Deliver Return Excess Product

Level 1 ENABLE—The processes associated with coordinating supply chain processes with processes in other functional areas of the company such as finance, human resources, information technology, relationship building, and compliance and contract monitoring. Level 2 processes include:
- sE1 Manage Supply Chain Business Rules
- sE2 Manage Supply Chain Performance
- sE3 Manage Data and Information
- sE4 Manage Supply Chain Human Resources
- sE5 Manage Supply Chain Assets
- sE6 Manage Supply Chain Contacts
- sE7 Manage Supply Chain Network
- sE8 Manage Regulatory Compliance
- sE9 Manage Supply Chain Risk
- sE10 Manage Supply Chain Procurement
- sE11 Manage Supply Chain Technology

Performance Attributes in the SCOR Model

After clearly defining each process, one may ask how one knows the processes have been implemented correctly, or what metrics to use? SCOR continues by helping to define the metrics, processes, and process maturity of each process to measure performance.

One of the key features of the 12.0 SCOR Model is that it utilizes three distinct performance elements: performance attributes, metrics, and process/practice maturity. Performance attributes are a grouping of metrics used to describe a strategy. The attribute itself cannot be measured; instead, it is used to set strategic direction or an objective for the company. Metrics are used to measure the ability to achieve the strategic direction or objective. Process/practice maturity evaluates how well processes and practices execute best-practice process models as well as leading practices.[12]

Metrics are aligned to performance attributes. A performance attribute is a "grouping or categorization of metrics used to express a specific strategy. An attribute itself cannot be measured; it is used to set strategic direction."[13]

Table 11.5 provides the definition of the performance attributes in the SCOR Model and the key performance indicators for each performance attribute.

The hierarchical nature of the metrics allows users to diagnose performance problems and decide on future courses of action. Level 1 metrics are cross-functional in nature and

TABLE 11.5
Performance Attributes and Corresponding Level 1 Metrics

Source: SCOR Model, "Supply Chain Operations Reference Model Revision 12.0," APICS, 2017, pp. 1-2–1-3.

Reliability—The ability to perform tasks as expected. Reliability focuses on the predictability of the outcome of a process and is a customer-focused performance attribute.

Key Performance Indicator is:
RL.1.1 Perfect Order Fulfillment

Responsiveness—The speed at which tasks are performed. It is also the speed at which a supply chain provides products to the customer. This performance attribute is customer focused.

Key Performance Indicator is:
RS.1.1 Order Fulfillment Cycle Time

Agility—The ability to respond to external influences, the ability to respond to marketplace changes to gain or maintain competitive advantage. Flexibility and adaptability are included in this performance attribute. This is a customer-focused performance attribute.

Key Performance Indicators are:
AG.1.1 Upside Supply Chain Adaptability
AG.1.2 Downside Supply Chain Adaptability
AG.1.3 Overall Value at Risk

Costs—The cost of operating the supply chain processes. This includes labor costs, material costs, management costs, and transportation costs. This is an internal focused performance attribute.

Key Performance Indicators are:
CO.1.1 Total SC Management Cost
CO.1.2 Cost of Goods Sold (COGS)

Asset Management Efficiency—The ability to efficiently utilize assets. Asset management strategies in a supply chain include inventory reduction and insourcing vs. outsourcing.

Key Performance Indicators are:
AM.1.1 Cash-to-Cash Cycle Time
AM.1.2 Return on Fixed Assets
AM.1.3 Return on Working Capital

[12] Ibid., pp. 1–2.
[13] Ibid.

generally are meant to measure organizational performance that is tied at a high level to the organizational strategy. Because they are derived from the company's performance on lower-level metrics for individual processes, they facilitate root-cause analyses. For example, the Level 1 metric "perfect order fulfillment" is calculated from the cross-functional Level 2 metrics "percent of orders delivered in full," "delivery performance to customer commit date," "perfect condition," and "accurate documentation."

Performance Metrics in the SCOR Model

Metrics are a standard for measurement of process performance. Metrics are diagnostic and are divided into three levels in the SCOR Model. Because Level 1 metrics are cross-functional, they are typically referred to as key performance indicators (KPIs). They assess how well the company is achieving its strategic objectives as detailed by the performance attributes.

Level 2 metrics are process-level measures that serve as diagnostic metrics for Level 1. The Level 2 metrics help identify the root cause or causes of a performance gap for Level 1 metrics. The Reliability performance attribute's Level 1 metric is "perfect order fulfillment." Level 2 metrics for "perfect order fulfillment" are "percent of orders delivered in full," "delivery performance to customer commit date," "documentation accuracy," and "perfect condition."

Level 3 metrics are results measures that serve as diagnostic measures for Level 2 metrics. For example, the Level 2 metric "percent of orders delivered in full" has two Level 3 metrics to identify root causes for performance issues. The Level 3 metrics are delivery item accuracy and delivery quantity accuracy.

The SCOR Model provides a unique breakdown for each Level 1 and Level 2 metric. First, a definition of the metric is provided. Then a qualitative and quantitative relationship description is given (depending on the applicability) to show how Level 2 metrics are aligned to the Level 1 metrics. Next, a calculation is provided followed by where within the SCOR Model data to be used in the calculation can be found. Then a discussion is provided on common issues that may arise and further refining of the definition provided at the beginning. Finally, a hierarchical structure is given to show which Level 2 and Level 3 metrics align to Level 1 metrics.

Process/Practice Maturity in the SCOR Model

As we have heard over and over, practice makes perfect. APICS research suggests that there is a strong correlation between performance (as measured by the metrics noted above) and the effectiveness of supply chain processes. For instance, take the process of eating. As babies we couldn't feed ourselves, but as we got older, we learned how to use a spoon, then a fork and knife. Along the way we spilled food on ourselves, parents, family, and the floor, all to the delight of our pets.

Just like eating, what is interesting about supply chains is that not all processes have the same level of maturity, or capability. For this reason, the SCOR model defines five levels or stages of Maturity for processes, as noted in Table 11.6.

TABLE 11.6
Stages of Process Maturity

Source: SCOR Model, "Supply Chain Operations Reference Model Revision 12.0," APICS, 2017, pp. 1–4.

Stage	Description
1	**Initial:** little or no process structure.
2	**Managed:** basic functional capabilities with limited cross-functional alignment and integration.
3	**Defined:** some integration across supply chain functions, but limited integration with other functions.
4	**Quantitatively managed:** highly integrated supply chain processes across the enterprise, with selective integration with supply chain partners. General alignment to business strategy and goals.
5	**Optimized:** highly integrated supply chain processes across the enterprise and with supply chain partners.

TABLE 11.7
Example Best Practices in SCOR Model

Source: SCOR, "Supply Chain Operations Reference Model Revision 12.0," APICS, 2017.

Practice	Definition	Performance Metrics	Process(es)
Long-Term Supplier Agreement or Partnership	Communication framework of buyer and supplier relationship. May include sharing of know-how and involvement in early product development.	CO.2.1 Cost to Plan RS.2.1 Source Cycle Time AG.1.1 Upside Supply Chain Adaptability AM.2.2 Inventory Days of Supply	sP2 Plan Source sE6 Manage Supply Chain Contracts
Pull-Based Inventory Replenishment	Approach that utilizes customer demand to replace and optimize inventory while reducing total net landed cost	RL.1.1 Perfect Order Fulfillment AM.1.3 Return on Working Capital AM.2.4 Supply Chain Revenue AM.2.8 Inventory	sP1 Plan Supply Chain sP2 Plan Source sP3 Plan Make
Stocking Keeping Unit (SKU) Rationalization or Cost of Sales Analysis	Inventory reduction practice to determine which SKUs can be terminated using cost of sales analysis	AM.1.3 Return on Working Capital AM.2.4 Supply Chain Revenue AM.2.8 Inventory	sP1 Plan Supply Chain

What is a practice? "A practice is a unique way to configure a process or a set of processes."[14] What makes a process unique? It could be skill-based, a technology that is applied in the process, a unique sequence for completing the process, or a unique way of connecting processes between organizations.

The SCOR Model includes 175 practices that range from Demand Planning and Forecasting to Sales and Operations Planning to Supply Chain Risk Management to Workflow Automation. A majority of the practices in the SCOR Model are shown in a table format with the name of the practice in the top left-most column, followed by a definition and measure of success in the middle, and the processes, metrics, and skills the practice will have the greatest impact on. (See Table 11.7 for example best practices.)

The SCOR Model provides in-depth information on several of the practices, such as Supply Chain Risk Assessment. The in-depth information provides a full explanation of the practice, the SCOR processes impacted, tools and techniques to apply, the requirements needed to implement and sustain the practice, the impact it has on the SCOR Performance Attributes and Metrics, and any additional resources available on the practice.

Each of these practices has a certain amount of risk and provides rewards according to those risks. The SCOR Model has classified emerging, best, and standard practices by categories to help users of the SCOR Model to identify practices currently in use. There are 19 practice categories varying from Customer Support and Distribution Management to Transportation Management and Warehousing and 175 different practices a company can use. The SCOR Model provides detailed information on several of each type of practice by linking processes, people, and performance back to the practice.

Emerging Practices

Emerging practices are the riskiest practices to implement because they are unproven and not easily repeatable. Emerging practices may be the introduction of new technology, knowledge, or a fundamental change in the organization of processes. Emerging practices carry with them the highest level of rewards; however, the overall success of the project will

---

[14] Ibid., p. ix.

be low because they have not been proven in a wide variety of operations and industries. In 2017 APICS added 10 emerging practices to the SCOR model. These covered practices about blockchain, the Internet of Things, and the omnichannel, to mention a few.

Best Practices
Best practices, while having a proven track record of successes, carry a moderate amount of risk to implement because not all best practices will yield similar results for all industries and supply chains. In addition, best practices are current, repeatable, and structured—they have a track record of positive impacts on supply chain performance. The success of best practices is more dependent on how a company implements them (i.e., project management). Best practices provide a moderate level of rewards because of their proven track record.

Standard Practices
Standard practices are the default practices companies use to do business. While these practices get the job done, rarely do they provide the competitive advantage or any significant cost savings. As such, there is little risk or reward for implementing these practices.

People in the SCOR Model

People in the SCOR Model
One unique aspect to the SCOR Model was added in an earlier version of the SCOR Model, SCOR 10.0, released in 2011. The Supply Chain Council, as well as industry practitioners, felt that the skills of workers in the supply chain needed to be evaluated. Essentially, the People section of SCOR introduces standards for managing talent in the supply chain that is complementary to the other sections of SCOR—Processes, Performance, and Practices.

The SCOR Model has identified over 150 skills for supply chain employees. Aptitudes, experiences, training, and processes further define each skill. While a competency scale is provided in the SCOR Model, a minimum level of competency needed for each skill is left for individual companies to determine.

Each skill focuses on four areas—practices, experiences, training, and processes. Skill is simply defined as the ability to deliver predetermined results with the minimum amount of energy and time. Aptitude refers to the natural ability, acquired through either learning or developing, to perform a certain kind of work at a certain level. Accuracy and natural leadership are examples of aptitude. Experience is the gathering of knowledge or skills through active participation or observation. Cross-docking and hazardous material handling are examples of experiences. Training is the instruction needed to develop a skill or a type of behavior. CSCMP SCPro, SCOR-Professional, and APICS CPIM are examples of training. Training includes on-the-job training, and it is during on-the-job training that an individual gains experience.

Exhibit: SCOR Model in Action

Different results don't happen overnight. And they won't happen unless you change your processes, and the way you think about these processes.

This was the challenge facing GE Oil and Gas. As Lorenzo Romagnoli took over the reins of the materials management group, he faced several challenges. He inherited an organization that hadn't made an investment in training and professional development that was common across other GE areas.

GE Oil & Gas had several goals. It wanted to increase operational performance and customer satisfaction. It wanted to strengthen its talent pipeline of materials management professionals, and position materials management as a strategic enabler for the business.

To start, Romagnoli's team in Florence, Italy, selected APICS's Certified in Production and Inventory Management (CPIM) for selected professionals that could have the greatest impact on the organization. Employees sought out the training, and being selected was a badge of honor.

Results? As of 2012 the team had:

30% improvement in on-time delivery

30% increase in inventory turns

50% improvement in capacity utilization

30% reduction in slotting lead time

Source: Adapted from the case study "GE Oil & Gas Improves Customer Service and Enhances Operational Efficiency," APICS, 2013, https://www.apics.org/docs/default-source/case-studies/14-2240-ge_case_study_final-.pdf?sfvrsn=0.

APQC's Process Classification Framework

APQC, a member-based nonprofit organization (formerly known as the American Productivity & Quality Center), was founded in 1977 to help organizations improve productivity and quality by providing best practice research, metrics, and measures. The mission of APQC's Process Classification Framework (PCF) is to "establish an open, universal standard for a process framework, created by industry for industry." The framework was developed to be independent of industry, company size, or geography.[15]

The PCF Was Developed in 1992

The PCF was released in 1992, after an extensive review by over 80 companies, organizations, and practitioners. On the simplest level, the PCF is a list that is organized in a hierarchical structure. It is categorized by function, and the elements are business processes, which are both mutually exclusive and collectively exhaustive. This allows companies to use the PCF to broadly define and eliminate repetitive work processes. In addition, companies and organizations are able to use the PCF to support benchmarking and manage content and other important performance management activities.

Like the SCOR Model, the PCF is highly process focused. Some practitioners find the PCF easier to understand, apply, and use than the SCOR Model. Also, as an enterprise-wide framework, the PCF provides a better cross-functional view of the enterprise. See Figure 11.6 for the scope of coverage within an organization by the PCF.

While the PCF is a standard framework applicable to all industries, it also provides industry-specific versions of the PCF tailormade to industries such as Aerospace and Defense, Banking, Petroleum Downstream/Upstream, and Retail. Given the generic nature of the PCF, new companies can readily use it as a starting point for analyzing

FIGURE 11.6
APQC's Cross Industry Process Classification Framework

Source: "APQC Cross Industry Process Classification Framework version 7.1.0," APQC, 2016, https://www.apqc.org /knowledge-base/download /407328/K08204_PCF _Cross%20Industry_v710 _2.pdf.

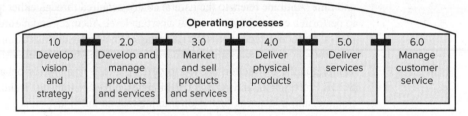

Operating processes

| 1.0 Develop vision and strategy | 2.0 Develop and manage products and services | 3.0 Market and sell products and services | 4.0 Deliver physical products | 5.0 Deliver services | 6.0 Manage customer service |

Management and support services

7.0 Develop and manage human capital

8.0 Manage information technology

9.0 Manage financial resources

10.0 Acquire, construct, and manage assets

11.0 Manage enterprise risk, compliance, remediation, and resiliency

12.0 Manage external relationships

13.0 Develop and manage business capabilities

---

[15] APQC, "APQC Process Classification Framework," http://www.apqc.org.

their supply chains. Organizations can begin with enterprisewide standard processes and measurement and later tailor them to meet specific needs through the APQC benchmarking gap analysis. A benchmarking gap analysis is a method to understand the distance between current performance (both quantitative and qualitative) and future desired performance of a company. The company will need to complete a list of actions it can take to close the gap between current performance and future desired performance. Because the PCF-derived benchmarking data is neutral in regard to industry, geography, and company size, the information can be further analyzed by these peer groups for relevant comparisons.

It is very useful for open-standards benchmarking participants that have modeled their processes under PCF to compare their performances with industry peers. Open-standards benchmarking is the process that APQC uses to collect data from member organizations. By providing data to their Open Standards Benchmarking Collaborative, companies are able to receive performance data for the processes and measures they provided data for.

Moreover, because organizational strategies can be mapped into the PCF's supply chain framework, both internally and externally integrated companies can use the framework in managing their supply chains. The model is well suited to organizations that realize the importance of strategic partnerships as well as collaboration within functions.

While the other industry-related frameworks rely more on the members of the creating organization for model development and enhancement, the PCF continues to develop based on input from both within and outside of APQC's membership. APQC acts as a neutral party, facilitating cross-industry working groups and practitioner forums as needed. The organization continuously collects inputs from working groups and through follow-ups; it then reviews, evaluates, and arbitrates suggestions and changes to the PCF and publishes revisions.

Components of the PCF

The PCF organizes operating and management processes into 13 enterprise-level categories, including process groups and over 1,000 processes and associated activities. Table 11.8 provides details on the components of the PCF. Built around the PCF, the APQC Open Standards Benchmarking Collaborative[SM] (OSBC) performance benchmarking program invites companies to participate in a performance survey that produces widely accepted performance metrics for their company, and comparative benchmark metrics for their industry. The OSBC database contains hundreds of supply chain–related measures and thousands of data points from over 7,000 organizations (across the globe). In addition to quantitative performance metrics, the OSBC links the PCF back to qualitative best practices through its knowledge management database.

In this section we will take an in-depth look at each of the components of the PCF.

The PCF Processes

In the context of the full enterprise, the PCF organizes its processes and activities into levels, similar to the SCOR Model. The levels themselves represent two separate functions within an organization: operational processes and management and support services processes. Whether the process is operational or support service, each level is made of five different groupings: Category, Process Group, Process, Activity, and Task.

Level 1, the Category, represents the highest level of processes in the enterprise such as Manage Customer Service, Supply Chain, Financial Organization, and Human Resources. Level 2, the Process Group, represents a group of processes such as Manage logistics and warehousing, Deliver service to customer, or Develop products and services.

TABLE 11.8
Components of Process Classification Framework

Source: "APQC Cross Industry Process Classification Framework version 7.1.0," APQC, 2016, https://www.apqc.org /knowledge-base/download /407328/K08204_PCF _Cross%20Industry_v710 _2.pdf.

Components	High-Level Groups/Attributes	Description
Processes	**Operating Processes:** • 1.0 Develop Visions and Strategy • 2.0 Develop and Manage Products and Services • 3.0 Market and Sell Products and Services • 4.0 Deliver Physical Products • 5.0 Deliver Services • 6.0 Manage Customer Service **Management and Support Services:** • 7.0 Develop and Manage Human Capital • 8.0 Manage Information Technology • 9.0 Manage Financial Resources • 10.0 Acquire, Construct, and Manage Assets • 11.0 Manage Enterprise Risk, Compliance, and Resiliency • 12.0 Manage External Relationships • 13.0 Develop and Manage Business Capabilities	Enterprise-level operating and management processes
Metrics	• Cost Effectiveness • Productivity • Process Efficiency • Cycle Time	Standard metrics to describe process performance linked to the Open Standards Benchmarking Collaborative[SM]
Best Practices	• Management Database	Extensive research on best practices from industry-leading companies

Level 3 is the Process level and focuses on the interrelated series of activities that turn inputs into results. Processes consume resources and require standards for repeatable performance. In addition, processes respond to control systems that direct the quality, rate, and cost of performance. Define logistics strategy, Plan and manage inbound material flow, and Operate warehousing are examples from the Manage logistics and warehousing process group.

Level 4 is the Activity level and indicates the specific events performed when executing a process or an individual activity from Level 3. Authorize and process returns, Perform reverse logistics, Perform salvage activities, and Manage repair/refurbishment and Return to customer/stock are examples of individual activities from the Manage returns/reverse logistics process. Finally, Level 5 is the Tasks, which further decomposes an activity at Level 4. Tasks are typically much more firm specific and generally vary widely across industries.

Operating Processes

The PCF Operating Processes

The six operating processes focus on the overall structure of the firm and operating functional silos such as marketing, customer services, supply chain, and product development. They are similar to SCOR's management. Overall, the six operating processes deal more with supply chain as a strategy and look to integrate the processes into a more normal enterprise structure

1.0 Develop Vision and Strategy. This Category looks at how the enterprise has structured itself. This is where the long-term vision is set, key performance indicators are selected, and the generic operating strategy is developed.

2.0 Develop and Manage Product and Services. This Category details the processes of research and design of new products and services and how to manage the existing portfolio.

3.0 Market and Sell Products and Services. This Category focuses on the creation and management of the marketing strategy and sales plans. In addition, understanding capabilities, customers, and markets is emphasized.

4.0 Deliver Physical Products. This Category focuses on the supply chain function of the firm from planning operations, to sourcing raw materials, manufacturing products, delivery of products and services, and the return flow of goods.

5.0 Deliver Services. This Category focuses on establishing service delivery governance, managing service delivery resources and the actual delivery of the service to the customer.

6.0 Manage Customer Service. This Category focuses on understanding customers, their wants and needs, and responding to their inquiries.

Management and Support Services Processes

The PCF Management and Support Services Processes

The Management and Support Services processes are considered the back office or behind-the-scenes processes that enable a firm to support and operate its core business. There are seven support processes from human resources and information technology to managing knowledge and relationships with external parties.

7.0 Develop and Manage Human Capital. This Category focuses on development, recruitment, and rewarding of employees.

8.0 Manage Information Technology. This Category details the processes around the management of information technology.

9.0 Manage Financial Resources. The Financial Resources processes focus on the accounting and financial strength of the enterprise. Budgeting, payroll, investment risk, taxes, international investments and funds, and accounts payable and expense reimbursements are included.

10.0 Acquire, Construct, and Manage Assets. This Category details the processes focused on the assets of the enterprise. The building and designing of new facilities, property maintenance, installation of equipment and tools, and the disposal of assets are the focus in this process group.

11.0 Manage Enterprise Risk, Compliance, and Resiliency. Enterprise risk, compliance, and resiliency processes focus on maintaining a healthy organization. Contingency plans, evaluations of risk (terrorism, natural disasters), regulatory compliance, and environmental health and safety are the areas of focus. Supply chain risk assessments would be included in this process category.

12.0 Manage External Relationships. External relationships processes emphasize the connections with external parties that have a stake in the overall performance of the enterprise and with the public in general. Stockholders, boards of directors, industry associations and memberships, and legal and ethical issues that may arise are the areas of focus.

13.0 Develop and Manage Business Capabilities. This Category details the processes needed to maintain competitiveness in the marketplace around a continuous improvement philosophy. Benchmarking, maintaining a process framework, disseminating information and knowledge between functional areas, measuring success in achieving organizational goals, and establishing a change management framework are the focus of this category.

The Open Standards Benchmarking Collaborative[SM]

Performance Metrics in the PCF

Much as the Supply Chain Council did with its SCOR Model, APQC developed standard measures for processes. APQC's metrics are tied to the PCF, making it easy to link a metric and the associated benchmark to a process. The database of benchmarking performance measures is called the Open Standards Benchmarking Collaborative, or OSBC for short.

APQC's OSBC assessments enable quantitative (standard metrics and key performance indicators) benchmarking in the categories of cost effectiveness, productivity, process efficiency, and cycle time. The best practice data subsequently derived is reported to all benchmarking participants. In addition, the research drives and reports qualitative best practices that are also tied to PCF processes and activities. Member-contributed and supported case studies are added to the management knowledge database on a monthly basis and sent to the APQC community at large through industry-related newsletters. This allows other members to access and understand best practices other companies are using.

To participate, firms must complete an in-depth assessment through the OSBC Survey. The survey is specific to the area of operation being benchmarked—and can include up to all seven areas APQC covers, such as Finance, IT, Product Development, Supply Chain Management, Human Capital Management, Sales and Marketing, and Innovation. Survey reports are free to APQC members who complete the survey. Nonmembers are able to take the survey and receive a report for a fee.

APQC will then send the report, which identifies the top, median, and bottom performance observations, plus sample size, for each measure that is completed in the OSBC survey. For example, if the components for On-time Delivery are completed, a copy of the survey results for that measure will be provided. In addition to the total sample results, APQC also provides peer group breakdowns by the firm's industry, revenue, and geographical region.

Once the survey is completed, an analyst from APQC will validate the firm's data. APQC then will prepare and send a report illustrating how the firm compares with top performers across region, industry, and firm size as well as all companies in the OSBC database. APQC updates its data frequently and its analysts normalize performance measures to ensure apples-to-apples comparisons.

The value of the OSBC comes from the attention that APQC gives each survey and resources available for companies to use on their own. This support from APQC enables a user-friendly model that does not require additional training or support from outside the company. In addition, other frameworks currently in use in the industry only make the information available to their members, whereas any company can use the information collected by APQC and is not required to become a member. However, a fee is charged for any information provided to nonmembers.

APQC and SCOR Standardized Common Metrics

One of the most positive things about APQC's benchmarking efforts is that APQC and the Supply Chain Council (now APICS) had worked together to standardize common metrics between the two organizations. This enables APQC to link the most common metrics to the SCOR Model. Additionally, APQC provides the actual benchmarking service for SCOR—known as SCORmark—for the Supply Chain Council members. This has created a new database of metrics that are unique to the SCOR Model definitions and are only available to Supply Chain Council members.

There are three major supply chain "hubs" in Asia: Singapore, Hong Kong, and Tokyo. Other locations are also developing rapidly, such as Shenzhen and Shanghai in China. Singapore ranks fifth on the World Bank's logistics performance index and handles one-half of the world's annual supply of crude oil and one-fifth of the world's transshipment cargo. Hundreds of ships enter Singapore's port every day.[52] Firms marketing products to many parts of Asia will find supply chain environments that are similar to those found in North America and the European Union (EU). While cultures and politics are different, transportation infrastructures are developed or developing, a variety of warehousing options exist, the use of automated systems is widespread, and customer service concepts are understood and accepted by logistics service providers.

In China, most supply chain activities are administered and/or controlled by the government. Despite some economic and distribution reforms by the government, the economy is still characterized by materials shortages, planned distribution, and a dual pricing system (planned prices and market prices).[53]

Organizations trying to penetrate the Chinese market will find great difficulties logistically. However, conditions are changing, more rapidly in recent years, for the better. Changes in distribution channels and infrastructures will continue to be very slow, requiring great patience both managerially and financially.[54] Involvement in countries like China will typically not show significant payback for several years, and firms will not be able to utilize the same financial criteria in evaluating Chinese supply chain efficiencies as in markets located in other parts of the world.

India, which has a population of more than 1 billion people, is also an important part of the Asian region. The country, while large in population, does not have commensurate supply chain infrastructure to adequately accommodate the needs of its many consumers and industries. Logistics costs as a percent of GDP are higher in India than in most other Asian countries. The logistics sector is largely fragmented and the use of 3PLs is relatively low.[55] Thus, there is more emphasis on the "future," rather than the "now" in India. However, there is no doubt that India will be a major player in the future of the Asian region and will require companies to develop supply chains to meet the diverse needs of the Indian population. Both India and China are the top-ranked country locations as listed on the 2017 A. T. Kearney Global Services Location Index.[56]

Other areas of Asia provide supply chain challenges to the global organization. The chaotic financial conditions that previously troubled the Asian region have abated, resulting in renewed growth and development in the region. Organizations are more cautious regarding

---

[52] Robert de Souza, Miti Garg, and Mark Goh, "Singapore," *CSCMP Global Perspectives* (Lombard, IL: Council of Supply Chain Management Professionals, 2010), p. 5.

[53] For an overview of China's logistics environment, see Charles Guowen Wang, "China," *CSCMP Global Perspectives* (Oak Brook, IL: Council of Supply Chain Management Professionals, 2006). Also see Gordon Milner and Alex Cao, "Outsourcing: China Overview," Thomson Reuters, *Practical Law*, October 1, 2017, https://uk.practicallaw.thomsonreuters.com/9-501-5775?transitionType =Default&contextData=(sc.Default)&firstPage=true&bhcp=1; and "Outsourcing 2017: China," *International Comparative Legal Guides*, January 8, 2017, https://iclg.com/practice-areas/outsourcing /outsourcing-2017/china.

[54] For a discussion of the Chinese market, see Dominic Lam, "Three Challenges of Chinese Logistics, and Three Steps to Overcome Them," WiseTech Global, *Viewpoints*, May 5, 2016, https://www .wisetechglobal.com/newsroom/blog/entryid/188/challenges-of-chinese-logistics; and Sameer Kumar and Kristoffer K. Kopitzke, "A Practitioner's Decision Model for the Total Cost of Outsourcing and Application to China, Mexico, and the United States," *Journal of Business Logistics*, Vol. 29, No. 2 (2008), pp. 107–139.

[55] See Janat Shah and D. N. Suresh, "India," *CSCMP Global Perspectives* (Lombard, IL: Council of Supply Chain Management Professionals, 2009); and Mukesh Singh, "Logistics in India 2017— Near Future Trends and Existing Challenges," *Internet & Mobile Wire*, July 11, 2017, https://www .wisetechglobal.com/newsroom/blog/entryid/188/challenges-of-chinese-logistics.

[56] Arjun Sethi and Johan Gott, "The Widening Impact of Automation," *2017 A. T. Kearney Global Services Location Index*, 2017, https://www.atkearney.com/digital-transformation/gsli/full-report.

the future market potential of Asian countries, but most companies are expanding production, marketing, and supply chain operations in the region.[57]

Markets in Japan, South Korea, Australia, and other Asian locations are sophisticated and provide a variety of supply chain services common to industrialized nations in North America and Western Europe. For example, Japan is the most densely populated and most land-constrained country in the world.[58] In the 1980s and 1990s, the country had efficient transportation and warehousing infrastructures, coupled with good information systems. However, newer facilities have not been built to replace older ones, the majority of warehouses are too small and designed primarily for storage rather than fast turnaround distribution facilities, and, recently, the trend has been for Japanese manufacturers to lease warehouse space rather than own it. Compounding the problem of obtaining warehouse space is the fact that two of the five highest rental rates are in Japan—Tokyo and Osaka.[59]

Although Japan is an archipelago comprised of more than 5,000 islands, the bulk of its population lives on the four major islands of Hokkaido, Honshu, Kyrushu, and Shikoku. Of these, the island of Honshu contains all the major cities and, therefore, most of the population of Japan.[60]

Some of the major characteristics of Japanese supply chains are the following:

Characteristics of Japanese Supply Chains

1. *Transportation modes.* Ninety percent of domestically transported tonnage goes by truck.
2. *Logistics heartland.* The main area for production in Japan is the triangle Tokyo-Nagoya-Osaka, in the island of Honshu, it being about 500 km from Tokyo to Osaka.
3. *Traffic congestion.* Traffic congestion on roads and highways is a critical problem in the triangle, especially in and around the major cities, where traffic speed averages less than 15 km/hr. For this reason, just-in-time systems require many small facilities, and/or substantial fleets of small vehicles, to meet customer requirements quickly and reliably.
4. *Distribution systems.* Distribution systems for different products are usually very different because of traditional differences in trade practices and channels of distribution.
5. *Distribution channels.* Nontraditional supply chains, especially nonstore channels, are booming, and often represent the best way to introduce new products into the Japanese market. These channels include the Internet, mail order, catalog sales, door-to-door sales, kiosks, and vending machines.
6. *Shared distribution.* Shared distribution is common, with competitors delivering to the same stores sharing delivery facilities and trucks.
7. *Palletization.* Large companies tend to use ISO standard pallet sizes; however, these are not mandatory, and a proliferation of different pallet sizes significantly complicates supply chain operations.

In other Asian regions, markets are also undergoing change, and these changes have significance for supply chain management. The establishment of high-tech centers in these areas allows all facets of supply chain management to benefit from the use of high-technology equipment, software, and systems. While the development of such areas is slow and somewhat limited, it does indicate that the Asian region is becoming an area that will potentially offer a number of opportunities for global organizations. As development occurs, supply chains will necessarily become more sophisticated as well.

[57] Ibid.
[58] Toshiyuki Kitamura, "Japan," *CSCMP Global* Perspectives (Lombard, IL: Council of Supply Chain Management Professionals, 2006).
[59] "Expansion Continues as New Top Growth Markets Emerge," *Prologis Report*, March 2016, https://www.prologis.com/logistics-industry-research/expansion-continues-new-top-growth-markets-emerge; and Leonard Sahling and John M. Tofflemire, "Japan's Logistics Property Markets—Drive to Efficiency," *White Paper*, Winter–Spring 2007, http://www.prologis.com.
[60] See Kitamura, "Japan."

European Union

Geographically, Europe is much smaller than North America, with the majority of the population living within *a five hundred mile radius*. Therefore, the pattern of transport and distribution is different in Europe to that of the United States.

Significant developments have occurred in western Europe with the creation of a single European market and the adoption of the euro currency throughout most of the European Union (EU). Referred to as "Europe 1992," the creation of a unified market comprised of over 300 million people in 27 countries has had dramatic impact on business and commerce, not only in Europe but also throughout the world.

Changes in the EU have had significant impacts on supply chains. Because the unification of Europe is an ongoing process, such changes will likely continue. Some of the major changes have taken place in the following areas: centralization of distribution centers; increasing number of partnerships and strategic alliances; use of outsourcing/third-parties; development of pan-European transportation networks; and restructuring of supply chain management.

Organizations in a variety of industries have been able to realize cost and service level improvements as a result of establishing pan-European supply chain strategies. Amazon launched its "pan-European Fulfillment by Amazon" program in 2016 that allowed sellers to use its European network of warehouses and delivery options. For small- and medium-sized enterprises (SMEs), being able to utilize Amazon's supply chain network will save them money and provide them with a much larger customer base.[61]

For SMEs, many of the fixed costs associated with shipping products to other countries, and which are independent of the amount of product being shipped, can make it difficult for them to reach customers in extended markets. Additionally, there are added costs of the personnel time needed to understand and properly implement various countries' policies and procedures with respect to customs regulations and compliance issues. For firms that can sell their products on eBay, the online auction site, the company has piloted a program whereby eBay helps the SMEs navigate the regulatory aspects of the countries from which they import or export. It was estimated that their volume of international sales could increase up to 80 percent.[62]

Pan-European transportation networks have increased because of transportation deregulation, more optimal routing and scheduling opportunities, and the development of pan-European services. Additionally, the channel tunnel, called the "Chunnel," has linked the UK with the rest of Europe and facilitated freight movement between England and France.

As a result of the unification of Europe and the addition of some Eastern European countries into the EU, the existing balance of local, regional, and long-distance transport movements has changed. Prior to the formation of the EU, the majority of transportation was local, within a 75-km radius. Since the formation of the EU, movements have tended to be more long distance.

The restructuring of supply chain management has occurred in a number of management areas such as the administration of logistics activities. The removal of customs procedures has resulted in greater efficiencies in transportation, packaging, and labeling. Technology improvements have been implemented throughout Europe instead of just within individual countries. More centralization of order processing, inventory control, warehousing, and computer technology has occurred with a unified Europe.

[61] Stuart Todd, "Amazon Expands European Logistics Role with Continent-wide 3PL Service," Informa PLC, May 3, 2016, https://www.lloydsloadinglist.com/freight-directory/news/Amazon-expands -European-logistics-role-with-continent-wide-3PL-service/66287.htm#.Wr14uS7wZhE.

[62] Bernard Hoekman and Selina Jackson, "Reinvigorating the Trade Policy Agenda: Think Supply Chain!," *Vox*, CEPR's Policy Portal, January 23, 2013, https://voxeu.org/article/reinvigorating-trade -policy-agenda-think-supply-chain.

Organizational changes to more centralized control of logistics have impacted organization charts and job scopes. Structures put into place since Europe 1992 have tended to be more broad-based, less cognizant of national boundaries, and located at some central location on the continent.

One of the most significant changes in the European Union (EU) was the Brexit vote of the United Kingdom. At some point in the near to medium term, the UK will be leaving the EU. The implications for supply chain management are potentially enormous because trading with the UK would no longer be under the EU, but likely under WTO rules and regulations. Some of the questions that will have to be addressed include the following:

- Will people be able to move freely between the UK and EU as they do now?
- Will different regulatory standards be imposed?
- Will trade barriers and/or tariffs impact revenues or profits of companies doing business with the UK?
- Will alternative Free Trade Agreements open new markets?[63]

While much uncertainty remains about a post-Brexit environment, some things are likely to occur, such as that foreign exchange rates will change; the VAT rate in the UK will change; ERP systems will have to undergo modifications to reflect that the UK is not part of the EU; and firms will enter into long-term contracts with greater hesitancy and may even shun contracts that cover too long a period of time.[64] A study by the Chartered Institute of Procurement & Supply (CIPS) identified several possible strategies being considered by businesses in the EU in dealing with the UK in a post-Brexit environment:

- Already mapping the potential costs of new tariffs.
- Strengthening relationships with existing European suppliers.
- Performing a risk analysis exercise.
- Looking for alternative suppliers outside of the EU.
- Looking for alternative suppliers inside the UK.
- Pre-emptively increasing costs.[65]

In sum, the competitive situation in Europe has intensified. Penalties for poor performance are greater for manufacturers, retailers, and logistics service providers. However, the rewards are great for organizations that can effectively implement optimal manufacturing, marketing, and logistics strategies in a unified European economy.

The Global Marketplace—Uncontrollable Elements

All forms of international market entry require awareness of the variables that can affect an organization's supply chains. Some of these factors can be controlled, while others, unhappily, cannot. However, these uncontrollable factors must still be addressed and dealt with in any global initiative. As a general indicator of the supply chain efficiency and quality of various countries, the World Bank has developed the *Logistics Performance Index* (LPI), which includes six items relating to logistics and the supply chain. They include efficiency of customs clearance; quality of transport-related infrastructure; ease of arranging

---

[63] "Supply Chain: Your Brexit Competitive Advantage," *PwC*, February 2017, https://www.pwc.com/gx/en/issues/assets/brexit-supply-chain-paper.pdf.

[64] Ibid., pp. 2–3.

[65] "Businesses Preparing to Sever Supply Chain Ties Between the UK and the EU to Avoid Brexit Tariffs," Chartered Institute of Procurement & Supply, May 15, 2017, https://www.cips.org/en/news/news/businesses-preparing-to-sever-supply-chain-ties-between-the-uk-and-the-eu-to-avoid-brexit-tariffs/.

competitively priced shipments; competence and quality of logistics services; ability to track and trace shipments; and the frequency with which shipments reach their destinations on time.[66] Each of these items would be considered uncontrollable by organizations marketing their goods and services in the global arena. They are factors that must be identified and dealt with in efficient and effective ways. Table 12.4 shows those countries where supply chain executives would find the most optimal business environments.

Anything that affects the organization's supply chain strategy, yet is not under the direct control of the supply chain executive, can be considered an uncontrollable element. The major uncontrollable elements of the environment include political and legal systems of the foreign markets; economic conditions; degree and type of competition; technology available or accessible; geography of the foreign market; and the social and cultural norms of the various target markets.

The uncontrollable environment is characterized by uncertainty and, in many instances, volatility. The supply chain executive must make decisions within this uncertain environment, including making cost–service trade-offs, determining and implementing customer service programs, and measuring cost components of various supply chain processes.

TABLE 12.4
The Logistics Performance Index—The "Top 20" Countries in 2016

Country	LPI Rank	LPI Score ▾	Customs	Infrastructure	International Shipments	Logistics Competence	Tracking & Tracing	Timeliness
Germany	1	4.23	4.12	4.44	3.86	4.28	4.27	4.45
Luxembourg	2	4.22	3.90	4.24	4.24	4.01	4.12	4.80
Sweden	3	4.20	3.92	4.27	4.00	4.25	4.38	4.45
Netherlands	4	4.19	4.12	4.29	3.94	4.22	4.17	4.41
Singapore	5	4.14	4.18	4.20	3.96	4.09	4.05	4.40
Belgium	6	4.11	3.83	4.05	4.05	4.07	4.22	4.43
Austria	7	4.10	3.79	4.08	3.85	4.18	4.36	4.37
United Kingdom	8	4.07	3.98	4.21	3.77	4.05	4.13	4.33
Hong Kong, China	9	4.07	3.94	4.10	4.05	4.00	4.03	4.29
United States	10	3.99	3.75	4.15	3.65	4.01	4.20	4.25
Switzerland	11	3.99	3.88	4.19	3.69	3.95	4.04	4.24
Japan	12	3.97	3.85	4.10	3.69	3.99	4.03	4.21
United Arab Emirates	13	3.94	3.84	4.07	3.89	3.82	3.91	4.13
Canada	14	3.93	3.95	4.14	3.56	3.90	4.10	4.01
Finland	15	3.92	4.01	4.01	3.51	3.88	4.04	4.14
France	16	3.90	3.71	4.01	3.64	3.82	4.02	4.25
Denmark	17	3.82	3.82	3.75	3.66	4.01	3.74	3.92
Ireland	18	3.79	3.47	3.77	3.83	3.79	3.98	3.94
Australia	19	3.79	3.54	3.82	3.63	3.87	3.87	4.04
South Africa	20	3.78	3.60	3.78	3.62	3.75	3.92	4.02

Source: World Bank, *Logistics Performance Index*, 2017, https://lpi.worldbank.org/international/global.

[66] World Bank, *Logistics Performance Index*, 2017, https://lpi.worldbank.org/international/global.

It is beyond the scope of this chapter to examine in detail each of the various uncontrollable factors impacting global supply chain management. Many international business textbooks address these elements.[67] It is sufficient to say that the uncontrollable elements affect the actions of the supply chain executive and must be considered in the planning, implementation, and control of the organization's global networks. In the following pages, a few of these uncontrollable factors will be presented so as to provide a brief glimpse at the multitude of issues that must be considered when making global supply chain decisions.

Economic

The economic-financial environment is likely to be the most important of all the external environments. In a global economy, economic activity goes on 24 hours a day, seven days a week, and 365 days per year (24/7/365). Information is transmitted by satellite and computer technologies without the constraints of national boundaries. Some of the areas where the economic-financial environment impacts supply chain management are the following:

- There may be difficulty in increasing prices, requiring that attention be paid to internal efficiency and, thus, the efficiency of supply chain expenditures.
- Slower or faster growth rates in some markets make it even more necessary that greater discipline be exercised by supply chain executives in planning and ensuring that maximum productivity be achieved for each dollar spent.
- High rates of interest during periods of inflation on short-term borrowing to meet cash flow requirements often result in greater attention to inefficiencies that may be caused by supply chain inefficiencies.
- Poor investment climates in some countries or world regions require strong profit performance, to both provide retained earnings for reinvestment and attract available investment monies.[68]
- Trading blocs are developed (see Table 12.5 for a list of the member countries in the major international trading blocs).[69]
- Foreign currency exchange rate fluctuations add complexity and uncertainty to decision making.
- Economic conditions (i.e., standards of living) in low-cost countries and/or emerging markets improve.
- Long-term pressures exerted on profits by inflation and recession often result in greater corporate emphasis on cost reduction and profits.

Inflation is particularly important to organizations generally, and supply chain management specifically. The specific impact of inflation on supply chain management will depend on five factors.

Type of Business. The type of business determines the proportion of assets to revenues employed in cash, receivables, inventories, and fixed assets. For example, some

---

[67] See Charles W. L. Hill and G. Tomas M. Hult, *International Business: Competing in the Global Marketplace*, 11th ed. (New York: McGraw-Hill Education, 2016); and Michael Czinkota, Likka A. Ronkainen, and Michael H. Moffett, *Fundamentals of International Business*, 3rd ed. (Bronxville, NY: Wessex Press, 2015).

[68] An interesting presentation of the various risks associated with global supply chain management, especially economic and political factors, can be found in the 2017 FM Global Resilience Index, which is online at https://www.fmglobal.com/resilienceindex and interactive and ranks 130 countries on supply chain resilience. Index is cited in Tom Wadlow, "Which Countries Are Most Resilient to Global Supply Chain Challenges," *Supply Chain Digital*, May 10, 2017, http://www.supplychaindigital.com/scm/which-countries-are-most-resilient-global-supply-chain-challenges.

[69] For a discussion of how trading blocs can impact global organizations, see Prateek Agarwal, "Trading Blocs," *Intelligent Economist*, December 20, 2017, https://www.intelligenteconomist.com/trading-blocs/.

TABLE 12.5
Major International Trading Blocs

Sources: Various Internet trading bloc websites.

Trading Bloc	Member Countries
Asia-Pacific Economic Cooperation (APEC)	Australia, Brunei, Canada, Chile, China, Chinese Taipei, Hong Kong, Indonesia, Japan, Malaysia, Mexico, New Zealand, Papua New Guinea, Peru, Philippines, Russia, Singapore, South Korea, Thailand, United States, Vietnam
Association of Southeast Asian Nations (ASEAN)	Brunei, Cambodia, Indonesia, Lao PDR, Malaysia, Myanmar, Philippines, Singapore, Thailand, Vietnam
European Union (EU)	Austria, Belgium, Bulgaria, Croatia, Cyprus, Czech Republic, Denmark, Estonia, Finland, France, Germany, Greece, Hungary, Ireland, Italy, Latvia, Lithuania, Luxembourg, Malta, Netherlands, Poland, Portugal, Romania, Slovakia, Slovenia, Spain, Sweden, United Kingdom (pre-Brexit)
Mercado Comun del Sur (MERCOSUR)	Argentina, Brazil, Paraguay, Uruguay, Venezuela
North American Free Trade Agreement (NAFTA)	Canada, Mexico, United States
Southern African Development Community (SADC)	Angola, Botswana, Democratic Republic of Congo, Lesotho, Madagascar, Malawi, Mauritius, Mozambique, Namibia, Seychelles, South Africa, Swaziland, Tanzania, Zambia, Zimbabwe
Union of South American Nations (UNASUR)	Argentina, Bolivia, Brazil, Chile, Columbia, Ecuador, Guyana, Paraguay, Peru, Suriname, Uruguay, Venezuela
World Trade Organization (WTO)	164 member countries

capital-intensive businesses, such as utilities, steel, chemical, and paper companies, require substantial investments in fixed assets in relation to revenues, whereas consumer product manufacturers and financial service companies have more modest fixed-asset requirements.

Inventory valuation methods and turnover rate. The selection of the last-in, first-out (LIFO) or first-in, first-out (FIFO) valuation method can be important in some organizations. The use of LIFO decreases the impact of inflation on the income statement, but it increases its impact on the balance sheet.

Age of business and assets. Business age is likely to have an important bearing on the age of the assets employed and the need for the reinvestment of funds. The earnings of new businesses and growth businesses in their early years are often only moderately affected by inflation because of the relatively recent vintage of much of their plant and equipment.

Composition of expenditures. It is axiomatic that inflation does not affect all types of expenditures in the same way. Energy, environmental, and labor costs for some organizations have increased at a rate that far outstrips the growth in the Consumer Price Index. Unit computational costs, on the other hand, have decreased because of technical advances in computer and information systems.

Capital structure of the organization. Capital structure is significant because organizations are hurt by inflation if their monetary assets exceed liabilities. Enterprises theoretically benefit from inflation if monetary liabilities exceed assets.

In general, economic resources act as constraints on enterprises. The availability and cost of economic resources during periods of inflation and recession restrict what the enterprise can and cannot do. For example, increased costs for logistics services can result in a firm curtailing its customer service activities or reducing expenditures elsewhere if budgets do not grow as quickly as costs. Higher interest rates increase the costs of carrying inventory, thus making it more expensive for an enterprise to provide the same level of customer service in terms of the amount of product in stock and available for sale.

The supply chain consulting company KPMG provides annual cost comparisons of a number of locations in Asia, Europe, and North America. These data organizations assist in determining, at least generally, the cost of implementing supply chain decisions in various parts of the world. For example, Mexico incurs lower costs generally than more developed countries. Of the established industrialized countries, Canada and the Netherlands have cost advantages over other countries in this category, while Germany and Japan have higher cost structures.[70] While other factors are also important in implementing supply chain strategies internationally, the cost aspects are significant components of supply chain decision making.

It should also be remembered that the economic environment influences, and is influenced by, other environmental components. Examples of the interrelationships include:

- A change in technology (such as the introduction of synthetic fuels) may alter the cost of a major raw material, or perhaps even bring about a change in the type of materials acquired.
- A change in the legal and regulatory environment (such as the election of a new government leader, or a change in monetary policy or tax laws) may alter the rate of inflation or the real cost of money.
- A demographic change (such as an increase in the number of retirement-age individuals) can influence the direction of federal spending.
- A social change (such as changes in attitudes toward the importance of the environment) may alter the manner in which environmental regulations impact product distribution, especially reverse logistics activities.

Competition

Organizations continue to face increasing competitive pressures from many sources. In the United States, manufacturers in certain industries have found themselves at a competitive disadvantage compared to their Asian and European counterparts. For example, the market for microwave ovens, a product invented in the U.S. in 1945 and introduced commercially to consumers in 1955, has been virtually taken over by Asian manufacturers. Similar trends have been evident in semiconductors, machine tools, apparel, industrial machinery, household appliances, and telephone equipment.

U.S. manufacturers have attempted to respond in several ways: manufacturing, research and development, marketing, and/or logistics. From a supply chain perspective, some of the responses have included:

- Increasing the number of cross-national partnerships, alliances, mergers, and/or acquisitions.
- Expansion of many previously domestic-based organizations into selected international markets.
- Development of global communications networks and information systems operating 24/7.
- Establishment of country and regional warehouses and distribution centers in various world markets.
- Identification and development of relationships with third-party service providers that offer transportation, storage, materials handling, and other services on a global basis.

[70] *Competitive Alternatives: KPMG's Guide to International Business Locations Costs* (March 2016), https://www.competitivealternatives.com/reports/compalt2016_report_vol1_en.pdf.

Nontraditional forms of competition are also occurring with greater frequency. For example, in the retail jewelry market, consumers are purchasing more jewelry from outlets such as the Internet, catalog showrooms, discount stores, and department and general merchandise stores, and less from traditional outlets, such as jewelry stores. With Internet sales, service levels become even more important because customers are not able to physically see and touch merchandise prior to purchase. Product returns are an important aspect of supply chain management because the percentage of returns is typically higher in Internet sales versus brick-and-mortar stores.[71]

Technology

In 1970, Alvin Toffler explored the changes resulting from advances in technology in his book *Future Shock* and foresaw acceleration in the rate of technological advancement. In the book *The Third Wave*, published in 1980, Toffler analyzed the shift from an agricultural economy to an industrial economy and finally to an information economy. *Powershift*, published in 1990, examined many issues, including how technology impacted the nature of power and wealth generation in many sectors of the world economy.[72] Toffler investigated the changes that were occurring in society and he observed that change was taking place at a more rapid pace. Certainly, almost three decades later, most supply chain executives would argue that technology has had a profound and significant impact on the world's business organizations. It should be noted that Toffler wrote his books prior to the Internet, or the concept of supply chain management being formalized, or the advent of sophisticated supply chain software and information systems.

The majority of organizations involved in international commerce utilize some form of technology in managing and administering their supply chains. The technology can be used to manage information, communicate with supply chain partners, operate warehouses and distribution centers, or conduct a myriad of other tasks related to the movement, storage, and management of goods and services in a global environment.

As an example, FloraHolland, a Dutch cooperative of flower growers with thousands of members and approximately 4,500 flower buyers, utilizes radio frequency identification (RFID) at its one-million-square-foot distribution center in Naaldwijk, Netherlands. In the flower business, a short order cycle is essential inasmuch as flowers have a limited shelf life. The firm employs RFID tags at strategic locations in its DC to track carts, or trolleys, as they travel between the receiving dock and storage areas. The system not only tracks their locations, but also how long it takes them to get from the dock to a climate-controlled storage area. FloraHolland has saved over US$200,000 per year just by not having to search for carts. And an additional benefit is that flowers can be processed more quickly, resulting in fresher flowers and higher prices for the flowers when they are sold.[73]

John Naisbitt, the futurist, in his book *Megatrends*, echoed the sentiments of Toffler when he identified his first transformation occurring in society: the megashift from an

---

[71] See Nick Winkler, "How to Reduce Ecommerce Return Rates & Predict What Customers Want," *Shopify Plus*, December 6, 2017, https://www.competitivealternatives.com/reports/compalt2016 _report_vol1_en.pdf; James R. Stock and Jay Prakash Mulki, "Product Returns Processing: An Examination of Practices of Manufacturers, Wholesalers/Distributors and Retailers," *Journal of Business Logistics*, Vol. 30, No. 1 (2009), pp. 33–62; and James Stock, Thomas Speh, and Herbert Shear, "Product Returns Processing: Impact on Profits and Competitive Advantage," *Sloan Management Review*, Vol. 48, No. 1 (Fall 2006), pp. 57–62.

[72] Alvin Toffler, *Future Shock* (New York: Random House, 1970); Alvin Toffler, *The Third Wave* (New York: William Morrow & Co., 1980); Alvin Toffler, *Powershift: Knowledge, Wealth, and Violence at the Edge of the 21st Century* (New York: Bantam Books, 1990).

[73] Bob Trebilcock, "RFID Blooms in Holland for FloraHolland," *Modern Materials Handling*, January 27, 2011, http://www.mmh.com/article/rfid_blooms_in_holland_for_floraholland/.

industrial to an information society.[74] Most certainly the advances in technology have been due, in large part, to developments in computers, data communications, and information systems. Examples include the use of computer graphics in warehouse layout and design, automated materials handling systems, robotics, transportation routing and scheduling models, global data transmission through the Internet, electronic data interchange (EDI), computer simulations of supply chains, data analytics, demand sensing, GPS, satellite communications, artificial intelligence (AI), blockchains, and the use of cloud technology. In sum, technological advancements have had significant impacts on all aspects of commerce, including supply chain management.

Advances in technology are not without their problems and concerns, however. New technology speeds up product obsolescence, making it more important that supply chain inefficiencies be minimized or eliminated. With products in demand for shorter periods of time, items cannot be "held up" on transportation equipment or in warehouses because the loss in sales can be significant.

As the speed of technology advancement accelerates, it becomes more likely that additional products will undergo "technological obsolescence." This is especially true in high-tech sectors such as computer hardware and software, consumer electronics, etc. It is important, therefore, that an organization engage in efforts to monitor the technology components of its environment. This is referred to as "technological forecasting" and should take place as a normal part of the enterprise's environmental scanning activities.

Geography

Different geographic areas have varying topographies that impact how products can be transported between locations. The distribution of population centers can vary significantly from one country to another. International transportation occurs primarily by air and ocean shipping, unless the countries are contiguous geographically. In those instances, motor, rail, and inland waterway transport can be utilized. The distances involved in crossing national borders can range from a few miles to many thousands of miles.

Indicative of the tremendous amount of freight that is transported internationally, Tables 12.6 through 12.9 present statistics regarding freight volumes, carriers, airports, and maritime ports located throughout the world.

TABLE 12.6
International Transportation by Air Freight Companies: The "Top 10" (2016)

Source: "Top 25 Cargo Airlines: FedEx Maintains Top Spot but ABC and Qatar on the Up," *Air Cargo News*, July 13, 2017, http://www.aircargonews.net/news/single-view/news/top-25-cargo-airlines-fedex-maintains-top-spot-but-abc-and-qatar-on-the-up.html.

Rank	Airline	Freight Tonne KM (FTK) Terms
1	Federal Express	15,712
2	Emirates	12,270
3	United Parcel Service	11,264
4	Cathay Pacific Airways	9,947
5	Qatar Airways	9,221
6	Korean Air	7,666
7	Lufthansa	7,384
8	Cargolux	6,878
9	Singapore Airlines	6,345
10	Air China	6,089

[74] John Naisbitt, *Megatrends: Ten New Directions Transforming Our Lives* (New York: Warner Books, 1982); see also John Naisbitt and Patricia Aburdene, *Megatrends 2000: Ten New Directions for the 1990's* (New York: William Morrow and Co., 1990).

TABLE 12.7
The "Top 10" Cargo Airports in the World (2016)

Source: David Harris, "Top 20 Cargo Airports for 2016,'" *Cargo Facts*, April 19, 2017, https://cargofacts.com/top-20-cargo-airports-for-2016/.

Rank	Airport	Cargo Tonnes Handled
1	Hong Kong, China	4,615,241
2	Memphis, United States	4,322,071
3	Shanghai, China	3,440,280
4	Incheon, Korea	2,714,341
5	Dubai, United Arab Emirates	2,592,454
6	Anchorage, United States	2,542,526
7	Louisville, United States	2,437,010
8	Tokyo, Japan	2,165,427
9	Paris, France	2,135,172
10	Frankfurt, Germany	2,113,594

TABLE 12.8
Major Ocean Carriers Involved in International Commerce (2017)

Source: Patrick Burnson, "Top 35 Ocean Carriers: Still a Puzzlement," *Logistics Management*, October 2, 2017, https://www.logisticsmgmt.com/article/top_35_ocean_carriers_still_a_puzzlement.

Rank	Ocean Carrier	Number of Vessels
1	APM-Maersk	655
2	Mediterranean Shipping Co.	508
3	CMA CGM Group	489
4	COSCO Shipping Co. Ltd.	325
5	Hapag-Lloyd	213
6	Evergreen Line	193
7	OOCL	101
8	Yang Ming Marine Transport Corp.	96
9	Hamburg Süd Group	103
10	MOL	78

TABLE 12.9
Lloyd's List of "Top 10" Container Ports: Rankings (2016)

Source: "Lloyd's List One Hundred Ports 2017," Informa PLC, 2018, https://maritimeintelligence.informa.com/content/top-100-success.

Rank	Port	2016 Annual Throughput (TEUs)
1	Shanghai, China	37,133,000
2	Singapore	30,903,600
3	Shenzhen, China	23,979,300
4	Ningbo-Zhoushan, China	21,560,000
5	Busan, South Korea	19,850,000
6	Hong Kong, China	19,813,000
7	Guangzhou, China	18,857,700
8	Qingdao, China	18,010,000
9	Dubai, UAE	14,772,000
10	Tianjin, China	14,490,000

Because countries vary in size, multiple countries may be traversed in a single product movement. Also, topography can vary significantly within and between countries, such as in western Europe and southern Africa. In certain instances, the shortest distance between two points may not be a straight line, especially when a possible transport route must go through mountainous terrain.

Finally, because markets can be geographically dispersed, or, in some cases, highly concentrated, supply chain networks are often different. Issues such as mode/carrier selection, warehouse location, and the amount of inventory to carry will necessarily be impacted by the geographical dispersion of an organization's target markets.

Social and Cultural

The social-cultural environment in which an organization operates is extremely important because the culture impacts how and why individuals, groups, and societies live and behave as they do. This impacts how people express themselves, the way they think, how they move, how they address and solve problems, how they relate to organizations for whom they work, how transportation systems function and are organized, as well as how economic and government systems are put together and function.

The task of understanding and scanning the social-cultural environment is difficult for the supply chain executive because of many factors, although the most important are the globalization of markets and the diversity of cultures in those markets.

The social-cultural environment of the global enterprise is comprised of several components: language, education, religion, values, technology, social organization, politics, infrastructure development, and regulatory systems. Each component singularly or in combination with the others can impact supply chain management.

For example, variations in language can cause difficulties in developing training manuals, written policies and procedures, and logistics strategies for moving products between and within different countries or regions. Accepted practices vary by region of the world with respect to how products are sold at retail (i.e., large mass merchandisers versus very small family-owned shops). Consumer perceptions of the family, religion, ethics, values, and education can impact how people view specific goods and services that are marketed, whether certain types of retail institutions are accepted, and what business practices are considered acceptable.[75]

Different social-cultural environments will usually require different strategies or tactics. Of particular interest to supply chain executives are the social and cultural trends that will impact decisions made on a daily basis. Some of these trends include:

1. The most valuable commodity to customers is time, rather than money. It is easier to make money than it is to "make time" for all of the activities in which people and companies want to engage. Additional money can be obtained, but everyone is limited to the same amount of time.

2. A continuing shift by industrialized societies to service economies will alter people's views of the world. The majority of persons in many countries, such as France, Germany, Sweden, the United Kingdom, and the United States, are now employed in the service and/or information sectors. This reflects a continuing trend toward higher levels of consumption of services and information.

3. The ability to obtain information almost instantaneously has already impacted diverse areas such as the structure of national and international commodities markets, outsourcing of labor, location for obtaining materials and components used in manufacturing, and individual views of world markets, governments, and products. Illustrative of this is the heavy reliance that many people in industrialized societies have on their smartphones.

---

[75] To illustrate, U.S. executives are prohibited by the Foreign Corrupt Practices Act of 1977 from paying bribes, but competitors may have no such limitations. In some parts of the world, bribes and "favors" are standard business practices.

Changes in the social-cultural environment must be constantly monitored by an organization. In addition to identifying trends that are occurring, it is important to understand their impact(s) on such corporate issues as profitability, product development strategies, distribution channels utilized, market segmentation policies, and promotion efforts.

Political and Legal

When operations are limited to a single country, supply chain executives only need to concern themselves with one set of laws and regulations, although they may be complex. Global operations must operate under many different legal systems, each with varying laws and regulations. Sometimes, there is an overlap between the political and competitive environments when foreign governments own or subsidize local competitors, methods of transport, or infrastructure.

Generally, political and legal issues can be grouped into four macro and six micro categories. From a macroeconomic perspective, there are *fiscal policies* (government budgets), *monetary policies* (supply of money), *exchange rates* (currency valuation), and *income policies* (wages and prices). From a micro perspective, there are *trade policies* (tariffs, quotas, restrictions), *foreign direct investment restrictions* (foreign ownership), *nationalization and privatization* (ownership of firms), *economic regulation* (transportation, energy, financial services), *competition policies* (antitrust regulations, cartel policies, monopoly pricing), and *subsidies* (grants, tax rebates).[76]

In the short run, organizations are impacted by many factors, including local laws and regulations, the political climate in foreign markets, levels of consumerism activity, judicial interpretation of antitrust laws, trade barriers, sustainability initiatives, and transportation regulations. Long term, organizations must be aware of trends and changes taking place in the environment. For example, in the United States, transportation carriers, especially motor, air, and rail carriers, had to be aware of what was happening in terms of deregulation during the late 1970s and early 1980s. Economic deregulation of transportation had significant impact on the logistics activities of companies and ultimately affected supply chain management. Such deregulation of transportation may or may not have taken place in some countries.

A particularly interesting example of how political issues can impact supply chain decisions is found in Brazil. Government tax policies can have a direct impact on supply chain decisions, sometimes influencing organizations to make what appears to be suboptimal decisions, but which, in reality, are beneficial to the organization. Manaus exemplifies how tax benefits can be more important than supply chain efficiencies. The city, located at the junction of the Amazon and Rio Negro rivers in the middle of the Amazon jungle, has only one road in and out. Brazil Route 174 cannot be used by heavy truck traffic, which would be the normal transport option of manufacturers located there. Complicating this scenario is the fact that the nearest consumer market is 1,500 miles away. However, tax incentives designed to promote manufacturing in underdeveloped areas are so attractive that dozens of multinational companies, such as Sony, Phillips, Nokia, Samsung, and Whirlpool, bring raw materials, parts, and supplies in for assembly and then ship out finished products for domestic consumption. Because the road system is so poor, manufacturers must utilize other transport modes, such as freighter aircraft, barges, and small ships, to move the goods into and out of the jungle. "It's hard to imagine that the benefits of manufacturing in Manaus outweigh the logistical drawbacks, but companies that manage to qualify for the full range of tax breaks can halve tax liabilities that would otherwise account for 45 percent of the goods' value."[77]

[76] Richard H. K. Vietor, *How Countries Compete: Strategy, Structure, and Government in the Global Economy* (Boston, MA: Harvard Business School Press, 2007), pp. 8–9.
[77] Toby Gooley, "The Rocky Road to Rio: What Shippers Need to Know About Doing Business in Brazil," *DC Velocity*, November 26, 2010, http://www.dcvelocity.com/print/article/20101126doing_business_in_brazil/.

Special-interest groups, industry associations, individual firms, governments and governmental agencies, and the judiciary can influence the political-legal environment. These entities can have indirect influence (such as interest groups lobbying for passage of a particular piece of legislation) or direct influence (such as the English Parliament or U.S. Congress introducing and passing specific supply chain–related legislation). Nowhere has this been more evident than in Europe, where environmental legislation has significantly impacted all facets of business, including supply chain management.[78]

Of importance to supply chain management is the impact on corporate strategy and operations of the political-legal environment. Typically, three questions must be addressed by logistics executives:

1. What specific corporate and/or supply chain strategies are affected by the political-legal environment?
2. What are the financial impacts (e.g., costs) of trends and changes occurring or anticipated in the political-legal environment?
3. What opportunities exist for the organization as a result of trends and changes in the political-legal environment?

Many facets of an organization's activities are affected by the political-legal environment, including the firm's marketing mix, international operations, merger and acquisition strategies, competitive responses, and personnel administration decisions. The specific impact(s) can be one or more of the following: (1) certain marketing and supply chain actions may be prohibited; (2) some actions may be mandatory or required; and/or (3) some actions may be limited in some way.

For example, much of the business-related legislation in the United States attempts to maintain competition, protect the rights of consumers, and preserve the environment. Various business activities may be mandated, such as listing product ingredients on the package; requiring that consumer goods firms have documented evidence to support product and service claims; utilizing government modes of transport within foreign markets for the distribution of products; and complying with host country regulations on exporting, joint ventures, and owned operations.

The political-legal environment can also impact the enterprise financially. Political risk comes from the many ways in which political forces in a country can negatively impact expected cash flows of an investment and undermine the assumptions on which the investment was made. To illustrate, a new political party in power or the new head of an old governing coalition can decide to change the fundamentals for operating and investing by altering the regulation of licensing, or by changing foreign equity restrictions, local participation requirements, or the basis of corporate taxation. Sometimes regulations can result in lost sales for a company. In a survey of U.S. supply chain professionals relating to their involvement in e-commerce, 24 percent of the companies surveyed indicated that they had faced regulatory penalties leading to delays and fines and 24 percent had experienced brand reputation damages due to recalls, legal actions, etc. Additionally, survey respondents indicated that the Consumer Product Safety Commission (CPSC) accounted for the largest percentage of delays for imports. Also, changing global trade regulations, primarily

---

[78] See Laura Thompson, "The Top 6 Government Regulations Impacting Your Supply Chain," *Inspirage*, February 4, 2015, http://www.inspirage.com/2015/02/top-6-government-regulations-impacting-supply-chain/; Cecilia Malmström, "Responsible Supply Chains: What's the EU Doing?," European Commission Speech, December 7, 2015, http://trade.ec.europa.eu/doclib/docs/2015/december/tradoc_154020.pdf; and Valeria Costantini, Francesco Crespi, Giovanni Marin, and Elena Paglialunga, "Eco-innovation, Sustainable Supply Chains and Environmental Performance in European Industries," Working Paper, March 14, 2016, http://www.isigrowth.eu/wp-content/uploads/2016/04/working_paper_2016_14.pdf.

a political rather than a business decision, was identified as one of the top concerns for shippers.[79]

As an example, the electronics industry is heavily regulated in Europe. The European Commission adopted WEEE practices that impact the amount of electrical and electronic equipment that could enter the European waste stream. Such waste is one of the fastest-growing waste streams in the EU. A number of restrictions and requirements were placed on manufacturers of these products relating to the collection, treatment, and recycling of these products so as to enhance resource efficiency and contribute to the circular economy.[80]

Additionally, the level of political corruption in a country or region can have an impact on supply chain operations. In some parts of the world, the paying of bribes is common. In fact, it has been reported that in almost 20 countries, bribes must be paid in more than one-quarter of all transactions. This necessarily increases the costs of doing business, including the costs of supply chain management. Table 12.10 identifies the countries where bribery occurs most frequently. Transparency International, the organization that develops the "global corruption barometer," identifies eight categories of bribery, but only five are included in Table 12.10.

Political-legal trends and events do not necessarily result in problems or increased costs to an enterprise. Opportunities may exist if management can recognize and respond to them. Because of increasing regulation of the environment, many third-party service

TABLE 12.10
Countries Reported to Be the Most Affected by Bribery

		Country/Territory
	Group 1: More than 50 percent	India, Liberia, Mexico, Vietnam, Yemen
	Group 2: Between 40 and 50 percent	Cambodia, Cameroon, Dominican Republic, Egypt, Moldova, Morocco, Myanmar, Nigeria, Pakistan, Sierra Leone, Sudan, Tajikistan, Thailand
% of respondents reporting that they had paid a bribe in the previous 12 months	**Group 3:** Between 30 and 40 percent	Albania, Azerbaijan, Colombia, Cote d'Ivoire, El Salvador, Gabon, Ghana, Guinea, Honduras, Indonesia, Kenya, Kyrgyz Republic, Mozambique, Nicaragua, Panama, Peru, Russia, Uganda, Ukraine, Venezuela
	Group 4: Between 20 and 30 percent	Armenia, Belarus, Benin, Bolivia, Bosnia & Herzegovina, Chile, China, Costa Rica, Ecuador, Guatemala, Hungary, Jamaica, Kazakhstan, Lebanon, Lithuania, Malaysia, Paraguay, Romania, Sao Tome and Principe, Serbia, Tanzania, Togo, Uruguay, Zimbabwe
	Group 5: Less than 5 percent	Australia, Botswana, Belgium, Cape Verde, Cyprus, France, Germany, Hong Kong, Japan, Jordan, Mauritius, Netherlands, Portugal, Slovenia, South Korea, Spain, Sweden, UK

Source: Coralie Pring, "People and Corruption: Citizens' Voices from Around the World," *Global Corruption Barometer* (Berlin, Germany: Transparency International, 2017), p. 8, https://www.transparency.org/whatwedo/publication/people_and_corruption_citizens_voices_from_around_the_world.

[79] "Benchmark Report Shows Need to Automate Global Trade Operations to Handle e-Commerce Growth," press release, February 10, 2017, https://www.amberroad.com/content/benchmark-report-shows-need-automate-global-trade-operations-handle-e-commerce-growth.
[80] "Waste Electrical & Electronic Equipment (WEEE)," European Commission, January 10, 2018, http://ec.europa.eu/environment/waste/weee/index_en.htm.

providers such as FedEx (GENCO) and Excel have emerged as major providers of reverse logistics service to manufacturers and retailers. Historically, international freight forwarders and others involved in global commerce have benefited from the complexity of international documentation, tariff and other trade restrictions, and customs requirements because they provide their expertise and experience to firms that do not have those skills in-house.[81]

It is beyond the scope of this chapter to examine in detail each of the various uncontrollable factors in the global marketplace. However, a number of international business textbooks and white papers address these elements.[82]

[81] For example, customs brokers can be used to facilitate export operations. See U.S. Customs and Border Protection, "Becoming a Customs Broker," January 11, 2018, https://www.cbp.gov/trade /programs-administration/customs-brokers/becoming-customs-broker.

[82] A particularly interesting examination of the uncontrollable environment and its impacts on supply chains is presented by Dow Jones and Company. The company offers clients a supplier and risk monitor that includes 400,000 articles on various global issues. Further information can be obtained at its website, http://www.dowjones.com.

Summary

More and more companies are expanding their operations into global markets. As organizations serve customers in various countries, they must establish supply chains to provide the goods and services that customers demand. While the components of a global supply chain may be the same as in a domestic system, the management and administration of the international network can be vastly different.

To be a global company, management must be able to coordinate a complex set of activities—marketing, production, financing, logistics, and procurement—so that least-total-cost supply chain management is realized. This allows organizations to achieve maximum market impact, optimize customer satisfaction, and develop sustainable competitive advantages over other firms.

In this chapter we examined some of the reasons organizations expand into global markets. Organizations that do so can enter those markets through exporting, licensing, joint ventures, or direct ownership. They may also choose to import goods and services globally. In addition, we looked at the importance of documentation, terms of trade, and the use of free trade zones.

The supply chain executive must administer the various supply chain components in a marketplace characterized by a number of uncontrollable elements—political and legal, economic, competitive, technological, geographical, and social and cultural. Each of these uncontrollable environments was briefly discussed.

With this chapter as background, we are now ready to examine how to manage supply chain activities in the global marketplace.

Suggested Readings

Blaeser, James, "International Transportation Management Benchmark Study—Winners See Strategic Value of Visibility," *American Shipper Benchmark Report*, November 2011.

Blaeser, James, and Renee Roe, "Export Operations & Compliance Benchmark Report: Going Global with Regulatory Reform," *American Shipper White Paper*, September 2011.

Burnson, Patrick, "2012 Customs & Regulations Update: Balancing Risk & Reward," *Logistics Management*, Vol. 51, No. 1 (January 2012), pp. 46–48.

Burnson, Patrick, "United Solar's Enlightened Partnership," *Logistics Management*, Vol. 50, No. 3 (March 2012), pp. 26–30.

Campanelli, Bryce, "A Deep Dive on America's Ports," Bipartisan Policy Center, July 27, 2017, https://bipartisanpolicy.org/blog/a-deep-dive-on-americas-ports/.

Cooke, James A., "Sharing Supply Chains for Mutual Gain," *DC Velocity*, Vol. 10, No. 3 (March 2012), pp. 56–59.

Gooley, Toby, "7 Steps to Speedier Border Crossing," *DC Velocity*, Vol. 9, No. 12 (December 2011), pp. 36–37.

Harrington, Lisa H., "Nearshoring Latin America: A Closer Look," *Inbound Logistics*, Vol. 32, No. 3 (March 2012), pp. 42–50.

"How to Create and Implement an Export Management and Compliance Program (EMCP)," Shipping Solutions, *White Paper*, undated, https://www.shippingsolutions.com/whitepaper-create-and-implement-emcp?hsCtaTracking=e8cec974-aeb1-463f-b46a-c33e82c87630%7C84d1b1e2-a759-44e0-aeec-72b928d8aeca.

"Incoterms," *International Trade Administration*, U.S. Department of Commerce, February 13, 2018, https://www.export.gov/article?id=Incoterms-Overview.

Kaye, Simon, "Using INCOTERMS to Simplify Global Sourcing," *Inbound Logistics*, Vol. 32, No. 1 (January 2012), pp. 193–196.

"Managing all Domestic and International Transport Together," *GT Nexus Perspective*, undated, https://www.gtnexus.com/resources/papers-and-reports/managing-domestic-international-transport-global-supply-chain.

Peterson, Beth, James Blaeser, and Geoff Whiting, "Global Trade Management Landscape—A Holistic View," *American Shipper Landscape Report*, March 2012.

Roy, Ewan, "What is Global Supply Chain Management?" *Trade Ready*, February 16, 2017, https://www.tradeready.ca/2017/topics/supply-chain-management/global-supply-chain-management/.

Sethi, Arjun, and Johan Gott, "The Widening Impact of Automation," *2017 A. T. Kearney Global Services Location Index*, 2017, https://www.atkearney.com/digital-transformation/gsli/full-report.

"2016 Global Trade Management Survey," Thomson Reuters and KPMG International *Report*, 2016, https://assets.kpmg.com/content/dam/kpmg/xx/pdf/2016/10/2016-global-trade-management-survey-from-thomson-reuters-and-kpmg-international.pdf.

Zakkour, Michael, "The New Retail: Born in China, Going Global," SupplyChainBrain, February 6, 2019, https://www.supplychainbrain.com/articles/29388-the-new-retail-born-in-china-going-global.

Questions and Problems

LO 12-1 1. What are some differences in domestic versus global supply chain management?

LO 12-1 2. Organizations that choose to enter the global marketplace have several strategies available to them, including (a) exporting, (b) licensing, (c) joint ventures, (d) direct ownership, and (e) importing. Briefly discuss each strategy, including advantages and disadvantages of each option.

LO 12-3 3. What is "nearshoring," and how does it differ from "offshoring"?

LO 12-3 4. Briefly discuss how organizations utilize free trade zones (FTZs) as part of a global supply chain network.

LO 12-4 5. Briefly identify the opportunities and challenges facing organizations seeking to manage supply chains in the following regions: (a) North America, (b) Asia, and (c) European Union.

LO 12-2 6. Considering the various uncontrollable environments that affect organizations, identify how each of the following might generally affect global supply chains: (a) economy, (b) competition, (c) technology, (d) geography, (e) social and cultural, and (f) political and legal.

Chapter

13

Managing Supply Chains in Global Markets

Objectives of This Chapter

LO 13-1   To understand that global supply chain management involves designing and operating domestic supply chains in countries where a firm operates.

LO 13-2   To clarify that supply chain concepts and principles apply universally, but the contexts within which they are applied vary from one country or region to another.

LO 13-3   To introduce the Global Supply Chain Assessment Model.

LO 13-4   To highlight important variables showing differences among countries and how they affect decisions in supply chain management.

Introduction

The Supply Chain Concepts and Principles We Studied Elsewhere in This Text Are Universally Valid

In an increasingly integrated world, supply chain managers have to operate globally. In a previous chapter we learned how supply chain managers should manage international supply chains covering multiple countries in a coordinated way. In this chapter we will examine a related global supply chain issue: how to operate domestic supply chains within individual countries of the world.

Multinational corporations, those with coordinated operations in multiple countries, must not only ship products between countries but also operate domestic supply chains within each country. These supply chains can vary substantially among different corporations and countries. Some corporations, like Honda Motor, for instance, operate a network of car manufacturing plants in several countries. These manufacturing plants supply each host country domestically as well as export to other countries. Thus, companies like Honda, in addition to engaging in international trade, need to operate supply chains within each country where they source, manufacture, distribute, or sell their products.

A basic notion of operating domestic supply chains in different countries is that the same supply chain concepts and principles we studied elsewhere in this text are universally valid, but that they must be applied differently because the environment differs from one country to another. As we shall see, these differences span a great many variables, though we will focus especially on the business environment and the logistics infrastructure. For example, firms in any country must decide whether or not to outsource transportation and generally consider the same variables before deciding. However, the decision might differ between, say, developed and developing countries. One reason might be that, in general, interest rates are lower in developed countries when compared to developing countries. Thus, firms in developing countries have an added incentive to outsource because assets cost more in a high-interest-rate environment. However, because the interest rate is not the only variable to consider in transportation outsourcing decisions, firms in developing countries might decide otherwise if another variable is deemed more important. For instance, a firm might decide not to outsource if there is low availability of trucks in a country and they want to have their own fleet to guarantee service. Hence, the variables one considers in outsourcing decisions are the same everywhere, but the outcome typically differs depending on the context within which the decision is made. Consequently, understanding context is crucial in global supply chain decision making.

Global Supply Chain Assessment Model

Clearly, it is important to appreciate the importance of context in global supply chain decision making. In this sense, context represents the relevant ways in which countries can differ from one another. To develop an understanding of context, we will look at general characteristics of countries, such as the economy and demographics. We will also look into the business environment and the logistics infrastructure and then make general observations to aid decision making. It is important to keep in mind that the number of variables that can describe a country is very large and that consequently we will focus on the most important ones. Thus, in order to learn about different countries systematically and to operate supply chains within them, we introduce in this chapter an assessment model. It is presented in Figure 13.1.

In Every Country There Are Significant Internal Differences

While in this chapter the discussion will be limited to countries, it is important to recognize that countries are heterogeneous entities. In nearly every country there are significant internal differences. These differences can appear with respect to any variable describing the country. For instance, countries can have major regional differences in income, education, or economic output. As a result, when a statistic is obtained for a country, the number is actually an average and might not describe every region of the country. Another important way that countries can differ internally is among industries. Within the same country some industries can be quite advanced and very competitive, while in others that is not the case. Supply chain managers must be aware of such differences and decide when country data applies to the region or industry that they are in or, alternatively, whether they have to seek more specific data. The Global Supply Chain Assessment Model can be successfully applied in either case.

To apply the model, there are four steps, or areas to examine: background, business environment, logistics infrastructure, and supply chain practices and issues. Background refers to general demographic and economic statistics aimed at shaping a general understanding of the country. Business environment refers to a number of issues descriptive of the setting within which businesses operate including inflation and interest rates, labor cost, government regulation, market competition, and others. The transportation, communication and information technology, and third-party services are described in the third step, logistics infrastructure. Finally, supply chain practices and issues is the step where the information in the three previous steps is distilled into specific actions that managers should consider undertaking to successfully establish and operate a supply chain in a particular country. Let us further explore each step.

FIGURE 13.1
Global Supply Chain Assessment

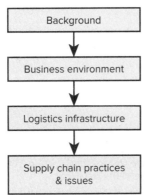

General Background

In the first step, background, we look at general demographic and economic information. These are often revealing about fundamental differences among countries. These differences typically put different requirements on the design and operation of supply chains. For example, some countries require more complex supply chains because they are very large geographically or because they have large populations. Note in Tables 13.1 and 13.3 that the United States and China are both geographically large countries and with large populations as well.[1] In contrast, Singapore and Ireland are much smaller in both dimensions.

These differences in area and population have important implications for the management of supply chains. One implication is the number of retail stores needed to achieve national distribution. Any corporation hoping to sell its products nationally will have to reach a subset of the 1.1 million retail establishments available in the United States according to the last U.S. Bureau of the Census.[2] In contrast, at the same time there were only 20,000 retail establishments in Singapore, clearly a much more manageable task to attain national distribution.[3] In other words, there are 55 retail stores in the U.S. for every retail store in Singapore.

Note also that countries differ in rates of population growth. Some grow at high rates, others more modestly, while a few actually face population declines. The population of India, for instance, grows at a rate that surpasses the population size of smaller countries. Note in Table 13.2 that India is estimated to add 15 million inhabitants in 2018 and that this is approximately three times the entire population of either Singapore or Ireland.

Rates of population growth are a good indicator of the growth of markets. It is more difficult to establish a supply chain and compete in countries where the population is stagnant or declining because market share must be wrestled away from existing competitors. In other words, current competitors must actually face a reduction in sales to enable the entrant company to sell more. Therefore, it is easier to compete in growing markets because every competitor is able to sell more.

It is also necessary to obtain important economic data. Table 13.4 shows gross domestic product (GDP) figures for several countries. GDP measures the yearly value of all the

TABLE 13.1
2017 Population (in millions)

China	1,379.3
India	1,281.9
USA	326.6
Brazil	207.3
Japan	126.4
Mexico	124.6
Germany	80.5
Italy	62.1
Hungary	9.8
Singapore	5.9
Ireland	5.0

TABLE 13.2
2018 Population Growth (in thousands)

China	65,655,130
India	14,998,230
USA	2,645,460
Brazil	1,513,290
Mexico	1,395,520
Italy	117,990
Singapore	108,824
Ireland	57,500
Hungary	−24,500
Germany	−128,800
Japan	−265,440

[1] CIA, *The World Fact Book*, 2018, https://www.cia.gov/library/publications/the-world-factbook/fields/2221.html.
[2] U.S. Census Bureau, *Statistical Abstracts of the United States*, 2012, p. 658, https://www2.census.gov /library/publications/2011/compendia/statab/131ed/2012-statab.pdf.
[3] Singapore Department of Statistics, *Retail Trade Report*, 2011, p. 2, https://www.singstat.gov.sg.

TABLE 13.3
Country Area (in square miles)

USA	3,794,100
China	3,705,407
Brazil	3,287,612
India	1,269,219
Mexico	758,449
Japan	145,913
Germany	137,846
Italy	116,348
Hungary	35,918
Ireland	27,132
Singapore	269

finished goods and services produced within a country's borders. It indicates the overall size of an economy. In addition, GDP growth from one year to another is a measure of economic performance. GDP statistics can be expressed eiether in absolute dollars or as an adjusted dollar figure. In the latter case, the GDP figure is adjusted to reflect the relative buying power of consumers in different countries. When this adjusted measure is adopted, it is said that the GDP statistic is adjusted for purchasing power parity (PPP).[4] The figures in Tables 13.4 and 13.5 are adjusted for PPP.

GDP statistics are helpful to compare the relative size of the economic output of countries. Countries with small economies have relatively small GDP figures. For instance, the value of all goods and services produced within the borders of the United States in 2016 was estimated to be US$18,624.48 billion, while the GDP of a medium-size economy such as Italy is under US$1,849.97 billion.[5]

While the GDP statistic measures the overall size of an economy, the GDP per capita is computed by dividing the GDP by the population size. It is a measure of the standard of living in a country. The data in Table 13.5 can also be interpreted as showing that the income of the average person living in, say, Singapore, exceeds that of other countries and is roughly double the income of the average person in Italy and four times the income of the average person in Mexico.

While the GDP per capita captures the average income, it fails to provide information about the distribution of income. Income distribution is important because it gives meaning to the GDP per capita statistic. When income in a country is reasonably evenly distributed, the GDP per capita statistic can be telling about the standard of living of the population. This is because a relatively large share of consumers belong to a middle class and have incomes not too far above or below the per capita GDP. In contrast, in countries where the income distribution is very uneven, the middle class is relatively small.

TABLE 13.4
2017 GDP (US dollars in billions)

China	$23,120
USA	19,970
India	9,447
Japan	5,405
Germany	4,150
Brazil	3,219
Italy	2,307
Mexico	1,758
Singapore	514
Ireland	345
Hungary	284

TABLE 13.5
2017 GDP per Capita (US dollars)

Ireland	$69,330
USA	59,532
Singapore	57,714
Germany	44,470
Japan	38,428
Italy	31,953
Hungary	14,225
Brazil	9,821
Mexico	8,910
China	8,827
India	1,942

[4] Werner Antweiler, *Purchasing Power Parity*, University of British Columbia, 2016, http://fx.sauder.ubc.ca/PPP.html.
[5] For updated information on global economic data, please refer to https://tradingeconomics.com.

TABLE 13.6
Gini Index

Brazil	49.7
Mexico	48.2
Singapore	47.3
China	46.5
USA	45.0
Japan	37.9
India	35.2
Italy	31.9
Ireland	31.3
Hungary	28.2
Germany	27.0

The Gini Index Measures the Distribution of Income

The GDP per capita statistic is thus less telling about the income of individual consumers. A minority of the population typically earns very large incomes while the majority has very small incomes.

Table 13.6 captures the distribution of incomes in different countries by reporting the Gini Index.[6] This index is a number between 0 and 100. Zero means that every person in the country has the same income. One hundred means that the entire country's income is earned by one individual. Thus, the higher the score in the Gini Index, the more uneven the distribution of income. Brazil and Mexico have the worst distribution of income among the countries listed (i.e., the biggest difference in income between wealthy and poor consumers), while in Hungary and Germany the difference is much smaller.

In sum, taken together, the GDP, the GDP per capita, and the Gini Index reflect the size of an economy, the purchasing power of its population, and the relative size of its middle class. Furthermore, GDP changes from one year to the next indicate the rate of growth of an economy. We will now review issues in the business environment of countries and how they affect supply chains. Together, understanding the general background and the business environment enables supply chain managers to assess the business and economic setting within which supply chains are developed and managed.

Business Environment

As noted earlier, in this section we review a number of issues descriptive of the environment within which businesses operate including inflation and interest rates, labor cost, government regulation, market competition, and others.

Inflation and Interest Rates

One of the key expressions of the business environment is the price inflation rate. Inflation is the rate at which the price of goods increases over time.[7] In countries where there is a high rate of inflation, managers must change the way they think about supply chain problems in at least two ways. First, rising prices increase the cost of raw materials and other supplies. As a result, supply chain managers must work on hedging strategies such as long-term supply contracts to guarantee a low price or buying products and holding them in inventory. Second, in an inflationary environment, holding certain assets, such as inventory, is a common policy used to protect against inflation because it is expected that the value of the asset will appreciate. This is a factor to be considered in outsourcing decisions, for instance. If, say, the warehousing function is outsourced to a third party, the price charged by the third party is likely to increase with inflation. On the other hand, if the firm does not outsource and elects to own the warehouse instead, the appreciation of the value of the building can become a hedge against inflation.

---

[6] CIA, *The World Fact Book*, 2018, https://www.cia.gov/library/publications/the-world-factbook/rankorder /2172rank.html.
[7] Available on the Internet at http://www.investopedia.com/terms/i/inflation.asp (2018).

TABLE 13.7 2013 Inflation Rates (% per year)		TABLE 13.8 2016 Interest Rates (% per year)	
Mexico	5.9	Brazil	13.8
India	3.8	India	6.3
Brazil	3.7	Mexico	6.3
Hungary	2.5	China	2.3
United States	2.1	Singapore	1.2
China	1.8	Hungary	0.9
Germany	1.6	United States	0.5
Italy	1.4	Japan	0.3
Ireland	1.3	Italy	0.25
Singapore	.9	Germany	0.25
Japan	.4	Ireland	.05

A High Interest Rate Cuts Demand and Increases the Cost of Owning Assets

Table 13.7 shows inflation rates for several countries. Note how they vary widely from one country to another. In addition to the variation in the rates themselves, the *perception* that managers have when judging the inflation rate to be high or low can also vary. When managers from different countries look at the inflation rate for the same country, they can have different perceptions about whether that rate is high or low. For example, the inflation rate in Brazil is 3.7%, while in the U.S. it is 2.1%. Thus, U.S. managers might judge the Brazilian inflation to be high because it is higher than in the U.S. However, Brazilian managers might look at the current inflation rate and compare it to historic inflation rates in Brazil, where at one point they reached stratospheric levels of over 1,000%. To them, the same 3.7% is low inflation.

Table 13.8 displays interest rates for several countries, measured as the central bank discount rate. Interest rates can also vary significantly among countries. When high, interest rates affect supply chains in at least two ways. First, they reduce the demand for products because consumer financing becomes expensive. Second, they increase the cost of owning assets such as inventory, transportation equipment, warehouses, or equipment used in information technology.

Note that two of the points made earlier lead to an interesting relationship between inflation and interest rates. First, supply chain managers sometimes own assets to hedge against inflation. Second, a high interest rate raises the cost of owning those same assets. The ability to use assets to hedge against inflation is limited by the real interest rate.

Interest Rate and Labor Cost

The interest rate also relates to labor cost. This relationship is equally interesting to supply chain managers and explains a difference in the behavior of firms in developed and underdeveloped countries. As a general rule, developed countries tend to have low interest rates and high labor cost. In developing countries the relationship tends to be reversed; Interest rates are high and labor costs low. When interest rate is low and labor cost is high, it is often more advantageous to replace assets instead of repairing them. In a developed country such as Germany, for instance, repairing trucks is likely expensive because of the high cost of labor, while replacing a truck is made easier by the low cost of financing one. In a developing country such as India or Brazil, the opposite might be true. Many firms prefer to repair a truck rather than replace it. For this reason, developing countries often have a labor force that is skilled at repairing things at affordable rates.

Government Regulation

Countries differ substantially in the efforts that their governments exert regulating business and the economy. To measure those differences and to offer guidance to the business world, the World Bank ranks countries every year on the ease of doing business there.[8] The rankings are obtained by tracking regulations affecting the operations of small and medium-size businesses operating in the biggest city of 190 different countries. The ranking measures the time and cost that it takes a business to perform the following 10 activities: starting a business, dealing with construction permits, getting electricity, registering property, getting credit, protecting investors, paying taxes, trading across borders, enforcing contracts, and resolving insolvency. The data for each activity is then combined into an index for each country. Countries are then ranked on the basis of that index. The results for a few of the 190 countries are shown in Table 13.9. To further understand how countries can differ in their approach to regulation, let us examine more specific information for three countries: China, Chile, and Japan.

In China, the government is a key player in nearly all significant business decisions. Despite the effort to liberalize the economy in the past decades, China's economy still maintains many features of a planned economy. The Chinese government controls the planning and operation of the logistics infrastructure and energy markets. It also controls access to markets by corporations and investors as well as the more common roles of government in taxation and market regulation. The liberalizing effort made by the Chinese government focused on the country's economic policies but left the administrative and political structures largely intact.[9]

Government Regulation Can Significantly Affect Supply Chain Operations

Key aspects of the country's logistics infrastructure are controlled by different departments and ministries in the central government. For example, highway, water, and port administrations are regulated by the Ministry of Communication. Railways are regulated by a dedicated organization, the Ministry of Railways. Virtually every aspect of the logistics infrastructure is regulated. The regulations issued have the force of law. Even industry associations, such as the China Association of Transportation and Communication and the China Federation of Logistics and Purchasing, are owned or controlled by the government.[10]

In contrast, the government of Chile chooses to have a much more limited role in regulating business and the economy. Its main goal is to maintain an environment of economic freedom that fosters foreign and domestic private initiative and promotes international trade. The logistics infrastructure is open to private foreign investment in ports and other infrastructure projects. In Chile, the entry of new competitors in the marketplace is only mildly regulated by the government, while in China the opposite is true. Still, as in all countries, some measure of economic regulation is needed. There are regulations affecting areas such as utilities, banking, securities, and pension funds.[11]

TABLE 13.9
Ease of Doing Business World Bank Ranking 2018

Singapore	2
United States	6
United Kingdom	7
Ireland	17
Germany	20
Japan	34
Russia	35
Mexico	49
China	78
India	100
Argentina	117
Brazil	125

[8] World Bank, *Doing Business 2017: Reforming to Create Jobs* (Washington, DC: World Bank Group, 2018).
[9] Charles G. Wang, "China," *Global Perspectives* (Council of Supply Chain Management Professionals, 2006), p. 7, available on the Internet at http://www.aplf.net/members/CFLP.aspx.
[10] Ibid.
[11] Available on the Internet at http://www.nationsencyclopedia.com/Americas/Chile.html (2018).

In Japan, government regulation is historically significant, but some aspects of it have been deregulated in recent years. Traditionally, small retailers or "mom-and-pop" stores were protected from competition from larger stores. As a result, Japan became a country with a very large number of small retail stores. To supply them, specialized institutions called "Ton'yas" are crucial. Ton'yas are a type of wholesale link in the supply chain. Their role is to provide logistics services like holding inventory, reducing lead times, consolidating transportation, and providing financing to their retail clients.

The transportation industry in Japan was also historically heavily regulated. Trucking companies had to follow rules regarding the routes they could take and regions they were allowed to operate in. Prices were subject to government regulations, and there were even rules to authorize consolidation of shipments. However, in recent years the government has removed most protection of small retailers and allowed trucking companies to compete more freely. These changes have enabled greater efficiency in the management of supply chains and contributed to the growth of the third-party logistics services industry in Japan.[12]

This brief comparison between China, Chile, and Japan shows how greatly the government's role in the economy can differ between countries, in terms of both owning assets and regulating the actions of private industry. Therefore, understanding the role of the government is crucial to operating supply chains. When operating in a foreign country, supply chain managers need to know which aspects of the supply chain are operated by the government and which are open to private investment. They also need to know the rules and regulations affecting operations.

Market Competition

The level of competition among firms in a country is another issue of interest to supply chain managers. In countries, or industries, where firms compete in free markets, decisions are more likely made with consumers and competitors in mind. Competitors enter and exit the market, and new products and services are offered to consumers as a competitive necessity. In contrast, there are countries and industries where monopolies (only one competitor) or oligopolies (a few competitors) have the market power to limit competition and, therefore, innovation and the entry of new competitors. In some cases competition is limited by legislation and in others by well-established competitors.

The same is true of suppliers and customers connected in the supply chain. If one or a few firms control the supply of a key material or component, it is more difficult for supply chain managers to negotiate prices and other issues in purchasing contracts. Thus, when operating in a particular country, or an industry within that country, supply chain managers need to consider the competitive structure already in place.

One interesting example of limits to competition imposed by governments is the retail liquor business in some states in the United States. In Virginia, consumers can buy certain types of liquor products only in government-owned stores.[13] This clearly impacts the supply chain for liquor products, as entry in the retail business is prohibited by the state. The state is also the only buyer, which restricts the ability of suppliers to negotiate prices and terms of sale.[14]

---

[12] Toshiyuki Kitamura, "Japan," *Global Perspectives* (Council of Supply Chain Management Professionals, 2006), p. 8.

[13] M.S., "America's Weirdest Government Monopoly," *The Economist*, September 6, 2010, http://www.economist.com/blogs/democracyinamerica/2010/09/liquor_virginia.

[14] Please note that the issue of the net public benefit of monopolies and oligopolies is the subject of intense debate among people with different political and economic viewpoints. Such a debate is beyond the scope of this book. However, our perspective is less controversial and focuses specifically on the consequences of monopolies and oligopolies to supply chain managers.

The Legal Environment

Supply chain design and operation are significantly impacted by the legal environment. Courts enforce issues such as labor laws, contracts, intellectual property rights, and international trade agreements. Courts in different countries vary greatly in the rigor of the enforcement, the time needed to decide cases, and the cost of lawsuits.

Labor legislation is a major issue in supply chain management. In some countries, such as Germany, for instance, labor unions play a major role in shaping legislation that courts must enforce.[15] Wages are often set by legally binding collective bargaining agreements. Legislation also concerns occupational safety and health and governs employee hiring and dismissal. German courts strictly enforce labor legislation. In Mexico, courts are equally tasked with enforcing labor legislation. Dismissed employees are entitled to compensation. They can also sue the former employer for reinstatement if the employee worked two or more years in the company and the dismissal is deemed to be without "just cause."[16]

The enforcement of contracts is equally crucial to supply chain managers. Some examples of situations when contracts are needed include renting plant and warehouse sites, financing a truck fleet, contracting third-party services, or signing purchasing agreements. Contract enforcement provides a stable environment for supply chain managers to make investments and plan operations. Conversely, the absence of adequate enforcement creates an environment of uncertainty whereby managers cannot be assured that, say, purchase price agreements or warehouse leases are adequately protected by law.

Countries vary greatly in the capacity of their legal systems to enforce contracts. This difference has been measured by legal experts using various methods. In one such method, researchers funded by the World Bank and Yale University used the time that it takes to collect a bounced check as a metric to estimate the contract enforcement proficiency of different countries. The data was collected from law firms in 109 different countries. It measured the time, in calendar days, from the day a complaint is filed, through trial, until the day the plaintiff collects. Table 13.10 presents results for selected countries.[17]

TABLE 13.10
Time Needed to Collect a Bounced Check (in days)

Country	Days
Singapore	47
United States	54
Japan	60
United Kingdom	101
India	106
Ireland	130
Germany	154
Russia	160
Brazil	180
China	180
Mexico	283
Argentina	300

Taxation

Tax policies affect supply chain decisions in major ways. Virtually every action is affected by taxation. Product shipments are taxed. Warehousing activities such as hiring labor, renting space, and equipment purchases are taxed. The selling of products from one firm in the supply chain to another is taxed as well. Broadly speaking, there are at least four dimensions of tax policy affecting supply chains. First, there is the general level of taxation. This affects everything: operating cost, profitability, and asset ownership. The second dimension is the complexity of the tax code and the related cost of compliance. The third dimension is the stability of tax policy. Whether taxes are high or low, a stable environment is an important factor for planning and decision making. Supply chain managers make

---

[15] Carl Marcus Wallenburg and Jan Simon Raue, "Germany," *Global Perspectives* (Council of Supply Chain Management Professionals, 2010), p. 19.

[16] Octavio Alberto Carranza Torres, "Mexico," *Global Perspectives* (Council of Supply Chain Management Professionals, 2007), p. 29.

[17] Simeon Djankow, Rafael La Porta, Florencio Lopez-de-Silanes, and Andrei Schleifer, "Courts," *Quarterly Journal of Economics*, May 2003, pp. 453–517.

TABLE 13.11
Taxation Level by
Country, 2018

	Corporate Income Tax (%)	Overall Taxation as % GDP
India	35	10.2
Brazil	34	34.9
Japan	30.86	34.3
Australia	30	33.2
Germany	30	43.8
Belgium	29	50.8
South Africa	28	26.9
United States	27	17.2
Chile	26	21.6
China	25	22.4
United Kingdom	20	38.4
Russia	20	17.3

Managers Must Be Aware of the Different Ways That Taxes Affect the Operation of Supply Chains

decisions on long-term investments such as warehousing networks, information technology systems, and so on. These investments have multi-year payback horizons, and changing taxation levels add uncertainty to the decision-making process.

The final dimension is tax distortion. Many countries enact tax incentive legislation (e.g., tax discounts or exemptions for certain regions, firms, or products) that creates different levels of taxation for corporations competing or operating in the same supply chain. Firms inattentive to tax incentives in countries they operate in find themselves at a competitive disadvantage.

Table 13.11 presents some basic tax data for corporations operating in selected countries. It shows income tax data[18] and overall taxation level as a percentage of GDP.[19] The data in the table illustrates how taxation levels differ among countries and how taxes usually are a significant cost factor in supply chains.

Let's review a few examples to illustrate the importance of tax policy in supply chain decision making. Brazil offers a noteworthy example of how tax policy can increase cost and distort supply chain decision making. First, the level of taxation affecting freight bills in that country is very high. In some cases it can be five times more than the cost of the freight itself.[20] Second, the tax regimen distorts decision making. One tax in particular, known as Tax on the Circulation of Goods and Services (ICMS), is a value-added tax charged over the movement of products. Firms are taxed every time a product moves between a supplier and a customer. Rates are different for in-state movements and out-of-state movements. The in-state rate is much higher. As a result, to save taxes, firms often require that products be supplied from out-of-state, even though the freight is more expensive and the delivery time longer. The tax is high enough that the outcome of supplying from out-of-state is a net saving.

In contrast, tax legislation in India generally favors in-state commerce. Goods are taxed whenever they move across state lines.[21] This creates an incentive to hold more inventory

[18] KPMG, 2018, http://www.kpmg.com/global/en/services/tax/tax-tools-and-resources/pages/corporate-tax-rates-table.aspx.
[19] CIA, *The World Fact Book*, 2018, https://www.cia.gov/library/publications/the-world-factbook/fields/2221.html.
[20] Centro de Estudos de Logística at Federal University of Rio de Janeiro, Brazil; Paulo Fleury, coordinator, "Brazil," *Global Perspectives* (Council of Supply Chain Management Professionals, 2007), p. 20.
[21] Janat Shah and D. N. Suresh, "India," *Global Perspectives* (Council of Supply Chain Management Professionals, 2009), p. 35.

by maintaining stocking points in multiple states. It might also increase delivery times as tax checkpoints in state border crossings slow transportation.

Supply chain decision making is also affected by tax incentives favoring the location of economic activity in certain regions or sites. This is a widespread practice. Governments often use such tax incentives as an economic development tool. To take advantage of a tax incentive, firms often select sites away from their markets and/or sources of raw materials. As a result, transportation costs tend to be higher and supply lines tend to be longer. In some cases, the quality of other inputs, such as labor or infrastructure, can be lower as well. For example, tax incentives have drawn numerous pharmaceutical manufacturing companies to Baddi, India.[22] These companies enjoy tax benefits that can extend for up to 10 years. Firms located in Baddi now produce more than 70 percent of pharmaceuticals sold in India.[23] In Mexico, the government maintains a special tax structure for companies known as "maquiladoras." These companies receive tax benefits to help foster the country's exports. Maquiladoras assemble products for export, typically with imported parts. While they were initially located in the northern part of the country, maquiladoras are now allowed to establish themselves anywhere in Mexico.[24]

The Labor Force

Firms often focus on cost when comparing the labor force in different countries. However, it is just as important to understand labor productivity and skill. Low-cost labor can sometimes appear inexpensive but actually be disadvantageous for its low output. The same is true for skill level. Supply chain jobs increasingly require a skilled workforce. In fact, one of the major concerns reported by companies today is the lack of availability of a skilled supply chain labor force.[25] On the other hand, there are instances when low cost can be the most important factor in evaluating a labor force. For example, the apparel industry traditionally sources its products in countries such as Vietnam and Bangladesh, where labor cost is low.

Thus, supply chain managers must consider multiple factors when evaluating the labor force in a particular country. We will focus on three factors: cost, productivity, and skill level. These factors vary substantially from one country to another. There are countries, such as Germany, where the cost of labor is high, while in others (e.g., the Philippines) the cost is much lower. On average, a German worker employed in manufacturing earns an hourly compensation more than 20 times higher than his Filipino counterpart.

That German worker is also likely to be more productive. Worker productivity is an important concept because it captures the idea that more expensive labor can be economically advantageous if it produces more output. More formally, labor productivity measures the amount of goods and services produced by one hour of labor.[26] As we discussed earlier in the chapter, the gross domestic product (GDP) is the measure of a country's production of goods and services. While beyond the scope of this text, it is worth noting that labor productivity is determined by variables such as tools and equipment availability, worker education, training and health, technology, and quality of infrastructure.

The dual concepts of labor cost and productivity are advanced further in Table 13.12, which shows how both labor cost and productivity vary significantly among countries.

[22] Ibid.

[23] Sushil Kumar and Sonia Vatta, "Hiring Trends in Pharmaceutical Industry—A Special Study of Baddi, Himachal Pradesh, India," *Indian Streams Research Journal*, Vol. 3, No. 1 (February 2013).

[24] Baker McKenzie, *Doing Business in Mexico*, 2017, pp. 22–25, https://www.bakermckenzie.com/-/media/files/insight/publications/doing-business-in-mexico/bk_mexico_dbi_2017.pdf.

[25] Lora Cecere, "Supply Chain Talent: The Missing Link in Your Future?," Supply Chain Shaman, reproduced in *Eye For Transport*, August 13, 2013, http://www.eft.com/general-supply-chain/supply-chain-talent-missing-link-your-future.

[26] http://www.investopedia.com/terms/l/labor-productivity.asp, 2018.

TABLE 13.12
Labor Cost and
Productivity, 2016

	Cost ($/hour)	Productivity (GDP/hour)
Norway	48.62	92.2
Germany	43.18	66.7
United States	39.03	68.9
Australia	38.19	56.3
France	37.72	67.2
Canada	30.08	53.3
Japan	26.46	44.9
South Korea	22.98	35.1
Argentina	11.24	n.a.
Portugal	10.96	34.6
Mexico	3.91	20.1
Philippines	2.06	n.a.

Labor cost is measured as the total hourly compensation earned in the manufacturing sector.[27] Consistent with the definition above, worker productivity is measured as the GDP output produced per hour of labor.[28]

The total hourly compensation received by workers can include benefits as well. This is important because in many countries benefits are a substantial share of the total compensation. For instance, workers in Brazil receive 13 monthly salaries per year instead of 12 because it is mandated by law that two salaries be paid in December. In fact, labor encumbrances paid in Brazil can amount to an additional 67 percent of the wages actually paid.[29]

Education, training, and local tradition are some of the key issues explaining differences in the skill level of labor forces. In many regions of the world, there is a concentration of workers with specialized skills, either handed down from one generation to another or as a result of labor migration. One example is the well-known quality of manufacturing labor in northern Mexico; another is apparel manufacturing in the Spanish region of Galicia. California attracts high-tech labor from around the world.

Worker skills are also developed by training and education. One remarkable example is Germany's apprenticeship system, whereby workers go through a dual program of training and education. They acquire work experience working for a company while also going through vocational education. Apprenticeships, which usually last about three years, train workers for a number of occupations, including supply chain–related jobs such as freight forwarding, transportation, and warehousing.[30] The training and education of supply chain managers typically require a college education that equips graduates to deal with the complexities of changes in the field of supply chain management as well as the relationships between supply chain–related decisions and other business functions of the firm, such as marketing, finance, and human resource management. Supply chain managers typically graduate from business or engineering colleges.

[27] *International Comparisons of Hourly Compensation Costs in Manufacturing*, Bureau of Labor Statistics, 2012, http://www.bls.gov/fls/ichcc.htm. https://www.conference-board.org/ilcprogram/.
[28] The Conference Board, *Total Economy Database™*, March 2018, https://www.conference-board.org/retrievefile.cfm?filename=TED_SummaryTables_Charts_may20171.pdf&type=subsite.
[29] "Labor Legislation," *Brazil Upstream Guide* (Deloitte, Touche, Tohmatsu Limited, 2010), p. 6.
[30] Carl Marcus Wallenburg and Jan Simon Raue, "Germany," *Global Perspectives* (Council of Supply Chain Management Professionals, 2010), p. 32.

One additional labor management issue worth mentioning is the issue of fair labor practices when sourcing products in low-skill, low-wage areas where the unemployment rate is typically high and workers are deemed overly dependent on employers for survival. There is a growing social concern with the issue. For example, Apple was suspected of violating labor regulations in China,[31] as was Zara in Istanbul.[32] Companies involved must deal with the resulting potential costs of bad publicity, large fines, and redesigning the supply chain.

The Logistics Infrastructure

Recall that in the Global Supply Chain Assessment Model the first step is to acquire some background about a country's key economic and demographic statistics. The second step is to learn about the country's business environment. In the third step we explore key issues in the logistics infrastructure. More specifically, we focus on transportation, communication and information technology, and third-party services.

Transportation

The Quality of the Transportation Infrastructure Reduces Supply Chain Cost and Contributes to Economic Efficiency and Consumer Welfare

The extension and quality of the transportation infrastructure are perhaps the most visible feature of a country's logistics and supply chain setting. A well-developed infrastructure opens access to markets in terms of both the ability to reach distant customers and the quality of service to all customers. For instance, good roads enable a higher frequency of delivery with fewer damaged goods. Trucks also move safely at higher speeds and break less often when roads are good, which enables firms to operate with fewer trucks. Thus, the quality of the transportation infrastructure reduces supply chain cost and contributes to economic efficiency and consumer welfare. In addition, by reducing supply chain cost, the transportation infrastructure enables firms to access a wider pool of suppliers in a cost-effective way.

The transportation infrastructure is also a key factor in economic development because it enables resources such as materials and labor to be mobile. For example, oil trapped in inaccessible fields does not contribute to development. Similarly, workers who cannot move to get to the best-paying jobs must settle for local alternatives. The importance of the transportation infrastructure explains why countries must invest significant resources in its development and maintenance. Because such investments are typically very costly, most countries rely on combinations of public and private investment.

The importance of the transportation infrastructure is highlighted further by the World Bank, which publishes an evaluation every two years of the state of logistics in 155 different countries.[33] The evaluation includes a ranking of the transportation infrastructure available in each country. Governments use it as a benchmark to compare their infrastructures to those of other countries. The ranking is based on a survey of third-party service providers operating either domestically or internationally from each country. It measures satisfaction with six items: roads, rail, ports, airports, warehousing and intermodal transfers, and information and communications technology. The results show a clear relationship between the transportation infrastructure and economic development. Developed countries such as Germany, the Netherlands, and the United States are ranked among the top five transportation infrastructures, while developing countries such as China, Brazil, and India are ranked 26, 46, and 56, respectively. Countries in earlier stages of development, in the sub-Saharan

---

[31] Yuan Yang, "Apple's iPhone X Assembled by Illegal Student Labour," *Financial Times*, November 21, 2017, https://www.ft.com/content/7cb56786-cda1-11e7-b781-794ce08b24dc.

[32] "Zara Clothes in Istanbul Tagged to Highlight Labor Dispute," November 3, 2017, https://apnews.com/e41d4976b67f4616be772b118a9cb947/Unpaid-Turkish-clothes-makers-tag-Zara-items-to-seek-help.

[33] Jean-François Arvis, Daniel Saslavsky, Lauri Ojala, Ben Shepherd, Christina Busch, Anasya Raj, and Tapio Naula, *Connecting to Compete 2016: Trade Logistics in the Global Economy* (International Bank for Reconstruction and Development, World Bank, 2016).

Exhibit: Low Tech and High Efficiency: How the Dabbawalas Deliver Meals in India

The *dabbawalas* are delivery men who perfected a system to bring more than 170,000 meals a day to customers in the city of Mumbai, India. The meals are picked up every morning in special lunchboxes in the customer's home by a *dabbawala*. The lunchboxes are then taken to the nearest train station, where meals are consolidated and sorted by delivery destination before being loaded in trains. At the delivery station, the meals are again consolidated and sorted by delivery building. The final delivery is then made before 12:30 pm, just in time for lunch. Using the reverse process, the empty lunchboxes are picked up by 3:30 pm and returned to the customer's home.

The consolidation and sorting process requires no technology or even paperwork and is entirely based on a color-coded system. The system also takes advantage of a remarkably reliable rail transport system. It works amazingly well. Only one in six million meals is reportedly misdelivered, which is better than the six sigma standard of one in a million.

Most of the 4,500 *dabbawalas* working in Mumbai are semi-literate. The system works because they are well trained, reliable, and work very well as a team. All

©Mike Abrahams/Alamy

dabbawalas are paid the same. Their reputation for efficiency and quality of service is well earned.

Sources: "The Cult of the Dabbawala," *The Economist*, July 10, 2008; and Janat Shah and D. N. Suresh, "India," *Global Perspectives* (Council of Supply Chain Management Professionals, 2009), p. 38.

region, for example, tend to rank at the bottom. In the remainder of this section, we will review the different modes of transportation in selected countries, including intermodal transportation.

Recall from our earlier chapter on transportation that there are five main modes of transportation: rail, motor carrier, water, air, and pipeline. Recall also that the transportation system in the United States is well balanced among modes. Consequently, supply chain managers operating in the U.S. can typically choose the mode that best fits their cost and service requirements. This balance among modes is not the norm in global environments. In most countries, supply chain managers have a narrower set of choices, and thus freight consequently funnels into the available modes. Table 13.13 illustrates this point for the two modes most commonly used in ground transportation: rail and motor carrier.[34] Note how in certain countries (e.g., Russia) freight tends to move primarily by rail, while in others, Japan and France, for example, road transportation is preferred.

Mode availability is one of the ways that transportation systems vary among countries. To operate in any one country, supply chain managers must understand the characteristics of its transportation system. Take, for instance, the Brazilian rail system. Historically undersized and inefficient, it is currently improving after a privatization process.[35] Still, most railways are concentrated in a few states and the network is poorly integrated because

[34] Table compiled from International Transport Forum, *Key Transportation Statistics*, OECD, 2013, http://www.internationaltransportforum.org/shorttermtrends/Output.aspx; and *Railway Goods Transported* (World Bank, Transportation, Water, and Information and Communications Technologies Department, Transport Division), http://data.worldbank.org/indicator/IS.RRS.GOOD.MT.K6.
[35] Centro de Estudos de Logística at Federal University of Rio de Janeiro, Brazil; Paulo Fleury, coordinator, "Brazil," *Global Perspectives* (Council of Supply Chain Management Professionals, 2007), p. 6.

TABLE 13.13
Domestic Freight
Movement by Rail and
Road, 2015

	Ton/Miles		Percentages	
	Rail	Road	Rail	Road
Russia	1,257,068	124,588	91.0	9.0
Australia	161,640	116,269	58.2	41.8
United States	1,535,290	1,908,688	44.6	55.4
China	1,531,991	2,711,854	36.1	63.9
Germany	66,121	271,250	19.6	80.4
United Kingdom	11,610	86,096	11.9	88.1
Korea	5,908	64,255	8.4	91.6
France	14,526	176,875	7.6	92.4
Japan	13,115	198,749	6.2	93.8
Turkey	6,426	118,978	5.1	94.9
Spain	4,637	89,769	4.9	95.1

there are four different gauge sizes. Thus, rail transportation in Brazil is available but represents a limited option for managers. Similarly, regional differences also exist in the Italian transportation system. In the more developed central and northern regions of the country, there is a significant issue with congestion, while in the south transportation services are less available and of lower quality.[36]

In addition to knowing the characteristics of individual modes of transportation, there are also opportunities to combine modes in a single shipment. The practice of using more than one mode in the same shipment is known as intermodal transportation. Its economic justification derives from the fact that each mode has different economic and market characteristics, which suit them best for different types of shipments. Intermodal transportation combines the best that two or more modes have to offer in such a way that the combined shipment is more effective than it would be if any single mode had been selected. Consider, for instance, the two most frequently used modes in domestic transportation, rail and motor carrier. Railways are more cost effective than motor carriers over long distances. On the other hand, motor carriers move faster and are capable of delivering shipments door-to-door. A rail/motor carrier intermodal shipment can both be cost-effective and deliver cargo door-to-door. The benefits of intermodal transportation render it an important option available to managers. In the United Kingdom and Germany, intermodal represented 30 percent and 39 percent, respectively, of all rail traffic in 2015.[37]

To be economically viable, intermodal shipments must be transferred from one mode to another in a cost-effective way. If mode transfers are expensive or slow, cost and service will be negatively affected. Cost-effective transfers require containerized cargo and suitable terminals. As in other aspects of the logistics and supply chain infrastructure, countries differ in the availability of terminals to transfer shipments. One of the most developed networks of terminals available to support intermodal transportation today is in Europe. Many countries in Europe have major facilities available that provide integrated logistics services. These include transportation terminals, warehousing facilities, and related services such as freight forwarding and banking. In addition, the available infrastructure attracts manufacturing. Depending on the

[36] Antonio Borghesi and Paola Signori, "Italy," *Global Perspectives* (Council of Supply Chain Management Professionals, 2006), p. 15.
[37] *Freight Transported in Containers—Statistics on Unitization*, 2018, http://ec.europa.eu/eurostat /statistics-explained/index.php/Freight_transported_in_containers_-_statistics_on_unitisation.

Exhibit: Spoiled Food: Why Proper Warehousing Matters

The importance of the warehousing function within the context of a supply chain is well known to managers. As we learned in earlier chapters, warehouses are used to reduce supply chain cost and improve customer service. When close to customers, warehouses can reduce delivery time. Firms also need warehouses to store products to be used or sold at a later date. Firms use warehouses to consolidate outbound shipments, break bulk inbound shipments, and provide a location to combine products of different origins into customer orders. For example, instead of making direct small shipments from plants to clients, a properly located warehouse enables firms to make a larger (i.e., cheaper) consolidated shipment to the warehouse, from where local deliveries are made. In this case, the supply chain is more efficient when the transportation savings are larger than the cost to operate the warehouse.

In a global context, especially in developing countries, the storage function of warehouses becomes especially important. Lack of warehousing space is a major reason why crops spoil. It is dreadful that, oftentimes, food is produced but not consumed because there is not enough space to properly store it. A case in point is the wheat crop in India. The wheat is vulnerable to attack by pests and likely to rot once the monsoon rains start. Lack of warehouse space also forces producers to sell their crops

©PhotosIndia.com LLC/Alamy

immediately after harvest, when the market price might not be best. As reported in *Bloomberg News*, 6 million metric tons of wheat were at risk in June 2012 for lack of warehousing space. The space shortage was caused by a previous increase in production not matched by an increase in storage space. The options to deal with the space shortage were to either sell the wheat at a loss or try to export it.

Source: *Bloomberg News*, http://www.bloomberg.com/news/2012-06-14/rain-pests-imperil-wheat-crop-in-india-as-warehouses-overflow.html, site accessed December 9, 2013.

combination of services offered, such complex industrial and logistics facilities can be known as logistics clusters, intermodal facilities, or freight villages.

The Bremen freight village in Germany offers an example of a complex industrial and intermodal facility in Europe.[38] Its intermodal terminals link rail and motor carriers, with easy nearby access to water and air transportation. It has dedicated space for warehousing and industrial facilities. More than 150 companies operate in the freight village, including third-party service providers. The operation of one of the service providers, BLG, serves as an illustration. It provides services to automaker Volkswagen. BLG receives and consolidates parts shipped from different locations by Volkswagen plants and its suppliers, and verifies and stores them. The cars and parts are then containerized and prepared for shipment overseas according to VW's export needs. The entire operation—receiving, warehousing, assembling, containerization, and preparation for export—is conducted within the Bremen freight village.[39]

Communication and Information Technology

Communication and information technology matter because firms can use them to improve utilization of their assets. The potential benefits of this are numerous. Information

[38] World Port Source, "Port of Bremen," 2018, http://www.worldportsource.com/ports/commerce/DEU_Port_of_Bremen_38.php.
[39] "BLG to Handle CKD Exports for VW Automotive Logistics," *Automotive Logistics*, September 15, 2010, http://www.automotivelogisticsmagazine.com/news/blg-to-handle-ckd-exports-for-vw.

Communication and Information Technology Enable a More Effective Use of Supply Chain Assets

technology is the basic enabler of warehouse automation. It also improves inventory control, as computers and technologies such as bar codes help identify and locate items. Information technology also enables firms to track shipments and make better routing decisions. For instance, in response to a newly received order, a truck might be rerouted from the field instead of having to first return to its base. Finally, information technology is key to processing orders quickly and with fewer errors, thus enabling reduced delivery times.

Countries, and regions within countries, differ in the quality of the communication and information technology available to firms. Wherever available, such an infrastructure enables the implementation of advanced technologies in supply chain management. For instance, radio frequency identification (RFID) technology uses wireless technology to track tags attached to almost any object. In addition to the object's location, the tags provide information about the object itself.

A leading supermarket chain in Brazil, Pão de Açucar, offers an illustration.[40] It introduced RFID technology to track shipments of fresh fish to its stores. The fresh fish are delivered in boxes from distribution centers to stores. The weight of fresh fish naturally varies, so prior to RFID implementation it was difficult to keep track of the exact weight of each box. Consequently, Pão de Açucar used an average weight for all boxes in its accounting system. This created discrepancies at the store level, where some stores had more inventory than accounted for and others less. The inventory inaccuracy resulted in lost sales, higher inventory carrying cost, and poor data for replenishment decisions. By attaching an RFID tag to each box, Pão de Açucar solved the problem because it now knows the correct weight of each box and the correct inventory in each store. It plans to expand the use of RFID chips to meat and produce shipments as well.

Communication and information technology can also play a major role in the development of supply chains in developing countries where the infrastructure might be lacking. In rural India, farmers typically lack information about markets for their products and sources of supply for agricultural inputs such as seeds and fertilizers. This information gap was in the past filled by intermediaries that often kept most of the farmer's profits. This supply chain was transformed by a private initiative that created a network of more than 10,000 kiosks providing computers and Internet access to farmers.[41] The kiosks, known as "eChoupal," are placed in villages and patronized by farmers in surrounding areas. Farmers pay a small fee to use the kiosks to research market prices, access government sites, buy agricultural inputs, and sell their products. The information helps shorten the supply chain and improves the profitability of farmers.

Third-Party Services

Third-party service is a broad term encompassing a range of services offered to companies in the supply chain by firms that are neither the buyer nor the seller in a transaction. A transportation company that is contracted to pick up auto parts from the manufacturer and deliver them to an auto parts retailer is an example of a third-party service provider.

The services offered by third parties range from traditional logistics-related services such as warehousing and transportation outsourcing to more sophisticated and

---

[40] Edson Perin, "Brazilian Supermarket Operator Improves Logistics, Inventory Accuracy," *RFID Journal*, October 13, 2013, http://www.rfidjournal.com/articles/view?11101.

[41] "'eChoupal' Supplies Farmers Up-to-Date Market Information and On-Line Sales Channels," *Handshake: IFC's Quarterly Journal of Public-Private Partnerships*, The World Bank, Issue 5 (April 2012), p. 61.

comprehensive services such as supply chain design and operation. In the latter case, the third-party service provider designs a supply chain for its client and then uses its own facilities, sometimes combined with the facilities of other third-party service providers, to operate the client's supply chain. Third parties can also provide ancillary services such as freight forwarding or transportation brokerage. For an overview of the range of services that a third-party service provider can offer, browse the DHL Worldwide website.[42]

The availability of a third-party service industry is a key component of a country's infrastructure. Its absence requires that firms themselves operate every component of the supply chain. If there are no transportation or warehousing services available, firms must acquire and operate their own. The lack of third-party services can pose a significant barrier to firms operating a supply chain. First, there is the significant investment required to acquire the necessary assets, such as warehouse space, transportation equipment, and so on. Second, third-party service providers are a source of local knowledge in markets where they operate. Finally, third-party service providers are specialists in the services that they provide and usually operate at a lower cost level than their clients would.

In countries or regions where a third-party service industry is unavailable or lacking in range or quality of service, supply chain managers have a limited set of options. The first, as mentioned above, is to insource and operate the supply chain with its own knowledge and resources. A second option is to either bring in one of its current service providers from another country to invest in the new market or develop a service provider by working with a local firm judged to have potential. Lastly, when available, firms might rely on strong regional wholesalers/distributors with the capability of reaching consumers in small cities and hard-to-reach consumers in major urban areas.

Supply Chain Practices and Issues

In the preceding sections of this chapter, we learned how a country's business environment and logistics infrastructure affect supply chains and their management. Let us now review a general set of practices and issues to help supply chain managers make decisions when operating in a specific country. These practices are not hard rules about decisions a manager should make in a specific country and industry. When applying the Global Supply Chain Assessment Model, managers need to arrive at their own set of practices based on what they learned from the previous three steps of the model.

To begin, it is important to restate the fundamental notion that *the supply chain concepts and principles studied elsewhere in this text are universally valid.* Firms operating in any country must manage cost and risk and strive for profitability. A few examples help illustrate this further. The principle of integrated logistics, whereby logistics cost is managed as a system rather than a collection of individual costs, is true everywhere. By the same token, the concepts we learned about working with suppliers to reduce supply chain cost and improve service are also universal. The supply chain processes we learned regarding source, make, delivery, and returns are valid in every country. However, although these concepts and principles are universal, the key point is that the contexts within which they are applied vary from one location, region, or country to another, and the supply chain manager must adapt them:

- **Learn as much as possible about the country where you are operating**. We have seen how the differences in the business environment and logistics infrastructure among

---

[42] DHL Worldwide, 2018, http://www.dhl.com/en.html.

countries are significant. These differences can significantly affect supply chain decisions.

- **Countries typically have significant internal differences**. General statements about countries can be inaccurate because countries are usually not homogeneous and have important differences among regions, industries, demographic variables, etc.

- **Beware of complexity**. As reviewed earlier in the chapter, many variables affect supply chain decision making in a country. They range from general issues such as population size, to economic issues such as interest rates and the specifics of the logistics infrastructure, such as the availability of rail service.

- **Involve locals**. There are limits to what anyone can learn in a reasonable period of time. Locals help complement knowledge gaps, can have expertise in key issues, and are connected to networks.

- **Merge local and outside ideas**. While local knowledge is important, good ideas can also be imported from other places in the region, country, or world where the company operates.

- **Involve third parties**. These can be beneficial in many ways. Third parties have local knowledge. They are also specialists in what they do, which can result in lower cost and better service. Finally, third parties usually employ their own assets, which lowers the risk and investment needed to operate a supply chain. On the other hand, local third parties might not be able to provide the required quality of service or might be already committed with competitors.

Summary

In this chapter we focused on how to manage domestic supply chains in different countries. As supply chains globalize, firms must not only design and manage supply chains connecting different countries, but also utilize supply chains that operate domestically within countries where the firm is active, sourcing, manufacturing, distributing, and selling its products. The fundamental idea about domestic supply chains in different countries is that the basic concepts and principles of supply chain management are universal, but the context within which they are applied varies among countries because countries differ from each other in important ways. To a supply chain manager, it is especially important to understand the specific business environment and logistics infrastructure.

It is not possible to learn everything about all countries and their differences! Thus, our approach in this chapter was to present and discuss a model that managers can use as a guide to learn about any country of interest. The Global Supply Chain Assessment Model consists of four steps of investigation into general background, business environment, logistics infrastructure, and specific supply chain practices and issues.

Background refers to a broad view of demographic and economic information that helps form a basic understanding of the country. We looked into some of the many variables that fit into this step, including population size and growth, economic output, and distribution of income. The business environment refers to the setting where supply chain managers operate, including interest rates, inflation, level of competition among firms, taxes, the regulatory environment, and so on. In the third step of the model, the supply chain manager examines the available logistics infrastructure, especially transportation, communication and information technology, and third-party services. In the final step of the model, the supply chain professional distills the insights gained in the previous three steps into specific practices suited to the situation at hand in the industry in which he or she is operating in the country or countries of interest.

Suggested Readings

Bals, Lydia, and W. Tate, "Sustainable Supply Chain Design in Social Businesses: Advancing the Theory of Supply Chain," *Journal of Business Logistics*, Vol. 39, No. 1 (2018), pp. 57–79.

Bookbinder, James, and Chris S. Tan, "Comparison of Asian and European Logistics Systems," *International Journal of Physical Distribution & Logistics Management*, Vol. 33, Issue 1 (2003), pp. 36–58.

Chiou, Jyh-Shen, Ley-Yu Wu, and Jason C. Hsu, "The Adoption of Form Postponement Strategy in a Global Logistics System: The Case of Taiwanese Information Technology Industry," *Journal of Business Logistics*, Vol. 23, No. 1 (2002), pp. 107–124.

Cooke, James, "From Bean to Cup: How Starbucks Transformed Its Supply Chain," *Supply Chain Quarterly* (Q4, 2010).

Cooke, James, "Sharing Supply Chains for Mutual Gain," *Supply Chain Quarterly* (Q2, 2011).

Malik, Yogesh, A. Niemeyer, and B. Ruwadi, "Building the Supply Chain of the Future," *McKinsey Quarterly*, Vol. 1 (March 2011), pp. 62–71.

Omar, Ayman, B. Davis-Sramek, M. Myers, and J. Mentzer, "A Global Analysis of Orientation, Coordination, and Flexibility in Supply Chains," *Journal of Business Logistics*, Vol. 33, No. 2 (June 2012), pp. 128–44.

Trent, Robert, "Five Supply Chain Trends," *Supply Chain Management Review*, Vol. 21, No. 2 (March 2018), pp. 20–24.

Vyas, Nick, "Four Compass Points for Global Supply Chain Management," *Supply Chain Management Review*, Vol. 19, No. 5 (September 2015), pp. 54–60.

Questions and Problems

LO 13-1   1. The chapter stated that supply chain concepts and principles are universal, but the design and operation of domestic supply chains in a specific context may differ from one country or region to another. What examples can you give of where this would apply?

LO 13-2   2. What are some of the factors that impact the operations of a supply chain? What factors can make operations more efficient? Which hinder operations?

LO 13-3   3. What is the Gini Index? Why would supply chain managers be interested in this index?

LO 13-4   4. Dabbawalas are a common sight in Mumbai. What makes them work in India? Are there reasons why this hasn't become more common in other countries? You should consider cultural and supply chain infrastructure when answering this question.

LO 13-3   5. Select a country of interest. How would you apply the Global Supply Chain Assessment Model to design and operate a supply chain in the country?

LO 13-3   6. Discuss the different ways interest rates affect the management of supply chains.

LO 13-3   7. How do priorities differ in the management of supply chains in industries where there is strong competition among firms from others where there is not?

LO 13-3   8. What are the four major ways that taxes affect the management of supply chains?

LO 13-3   9. What are the potential benefits and disadvantages of employing local third parties in the operation of supply chains?

14

Strategic Supply Chain Network Design

Objectives of This Chapter

LO 14-1 To examine the importance of supply chain networks to manufacturers, retailers, and other supply chain members.

LO 14-2 To describe the components of supply chain network design, synthesis, and optimization.

LO 14-3 To overview supply chain mapping or flowcharting.

LO 14-4 To examine some of the macro issues that impact supply chain design, such as strategy, technology, lean management, Six Sigma, organization structure, use of 3PLs, and reverse logistics.

LO 14-5 To identify some of the major uses of technology in supply chain management.

LO 14-6 To review the importance of enterprise resource planning (ERP) in supply chain networks.

LO 14-7 To discuss the importance of good data and information in supply chain network synthesis.

Introduction

One of the most basic, yet most important, considerations in supply chain management is the planning, implementation, and control of an efficient and effective supply chain network. In some ways, it is like the development of a good business plan. A poor business plan, implemented well, will result in poor outcomes. A good business plan, poorly implemented, will produce suboptimal outcomes, but at least the results will be positive. Obviously, to both develop and implement a business plan well is optimal. So too it is necessary to have an optimal supply chain network that will provide optimal benefits to customers and supply chain members alike.

Companies are being forced to optimize the design and implementation of their supply chain networks. While the use of the term "chain" in supply chain management implies a series of sequential links between organizations, the digitization of supply chains actually entails a more complex structure where linkages are both sequential, horizontal, and vertical; that is, relationships can go in any direction and occur in parallel. In a survey of supply chain professionals, 80 percent said that the digital supply chain will be the "norm" within five years. Firms are developing competitive strategies and redesigning their present supply chain networks to make them more efficient and effective.[1] As a result, approximately 40 percent of supply chain executives are in the process of redesigning their domestic supply chain network and about one-third anticipate modifying their international networks.[2]

Market Changes Requiring Supply Chain Optimization

Some of the structural and economic changes that are requiring companies to optimize their supply chain networks include:

- Rapid globalization.
- The "Amazon" factor that requires all firms to be faster and leaner.
- Variability in commodity prices
- Shifting global supply of materials and finished goods.
- Global availability of supply chain skills coupled with renewed focus on process standardization.
- Emphasis on the need to focus on more than one aspect of supply chain excellence to ensure some level of competitive advantage.
- Rising supply chain management costs.
- Growing complexity of global operations.
- Escalating customer demand for faster service.
- Significant development in technology, especially Internet of Things (IoT), blockchains, artificial intelligence (AI), driverless vehicles, drones, mobile technology, robotics, and automation.
- Increasing demand volatility.[3]

We have previously discussed several issues related to designing an optimal supply chain network and in this chapter and later will cover more. Topics such as the SCOR Model (Chapter 1); customer relationship management or CRM (Chapter 2); collaborative planning, forecasting, and replenishment, or CPFR (Chapter 3); enterprise resource planning, or ERP (Chapter 14); *Keiretsu* structures (Chapter 15); global sourcing (Chapter 12); partnerships and alliances (Chapters 5 and 8); communication/information systems (Chapter 3); and others are all related to the planning, implementation, and control of supply chains. The key to successful supply chain management is to have the right pieces to the supply chain puzzle, linked together, and operating at peak efficiency. Such are the objectives of network design.

What Is Supply Chain Network Design?

Network design is typically used when referring to the structure of telecommunications or information systems. However, supply chains also must be structured in such a way that the members and customers of the supply chain are both satisfied.

A typical network design plan includes activities such as planning, asset sourcing, operations, and performance monitoring. Each of these activities has both short-term and long-term perspectives. From an operations perspective, how should the supply chain operate day-to-day?[4] While there may be many different approaches used to design and manage a

---

[1] Merrill Douglas, "Digital Supply Chain: What's Your Reality?," *Inbound Logistics*, Vol. 38, No. 1 (January 2018), pp. 90–98.

[2] Kevin Permenter, "Cost and Complexity: Top Challenges of Today's Chief Supply Chain Officer," Aberdeen Group, *White Paper*, January 2012, p. 1.

[3] Ibid.

[4] For a discussion of network planning issues in the health care sector, see J. Paul Dittmann, "Best Practices for Managing Cost in the Healthcare Supply Chain," UPS, *White Paper*, 2015, https://www.ups.com/media/en/best-practices-managing-cost-part1.pdf.

Exhibit: Zara Designs Its Supply Chain to Deliver New Fashions in Two Weeks

The Spain-based apparel firm Zara, a division of Inditex, is one of the largest clothing retailers in the world. With more than 2,200 stores in 93 countries, its yearly revenues exceed US$17.2 billion. One of its competitive advantages is its well-designed and implemented supply chain.

Much like the U.S.-based retailer Limited Stores, Zara is able to bring new clothing designs to retail stores very quickly. Clothing designs can go through the entire development, manufacturing, and distribution processes and be in stores within two weeks, while its competitors take up to six months. Zara's supply chain is extremely efficient, utilizing RFID, demand sensing, and personal digital assistants (PDAs). Much of the manufacturing occurs in Spain, rather than being outsourced to low-cost countries in Asia. Employee wages are higher in Spain than in Asia, but the company saves money in transportation, warehousing, and inventory. Also, service levels tend to be higher, resulting in greater customer satisfaction. Zara utilizes just-in-time in its plants, which allows the company to minimize inventory levels and maintain excellent control over its processes. All warehousing is done in Spain, and European retail stores are able to receive merchandise within 24 hours after ordering. For retail stores in Asia and the United States, orders are received within 48 hours.

The company produces items in smaller quantities than most of its competitors. Thus, there is less of a chance of having apparel left over after a selling season that then has to be marked down to sell. Zara is able to charge more for its clothing than its competitors and has far fewer markdowns normally required to move out-of-season stock.

Sources: Kevin O'Marah, "Zara Uses Supply Chain to Win Again," *Logistics & Transportation*, March 9, 2016, https://www.forbes.com/sites/kevinomarah/2016/03/09/zara-uses-supply-chain-to-win-again/#47ac66ad1256; Kerry Capell, "Zara Thrives by Breaking all the Rules," *BusinessWeek*, October 20, 2008, p. 66; https://www.forbes.com/companies/zara/; and Zara website, http://www.inditex.com.

supply chain, no one can succeed unless all supply chain participants and the supply chain network operate as one seamless entity. Supply chain networks allow firms to take a big-picture perspective, giving participants a better understanding of the flow of material and information from start to finish, and ensure that the best value is being provided to the end customer.[5]

For example, Del Monte Foods, whose brands are found in eight out of ten households, realized that its outdated business processes and technologies were not able to support the firm's global supply chain. Its supply chain, which was mostly linear and sequential, could not respond to rapid changes that might occur in the marketplace. Symptoms of this core issue were evident at Del Monte: not meeting customer expectations, difficult to respond to customers quickly, inconsistent fill rates, high levels of inventory, low forecast accuracy, and performance volatility. After introducing a cloud-based software solution that linked all members of its supply chain and interfaced with its internal ERP system, Del Monte improved customer order fill rate to 99+ percent, reduced inventory levels by 27 percent, and was able to use scarce resources to invest in strategic projects with two-year paybacks.[6]

Steps in Designing the Optimal Supply Chain

Creating the optimal supply chain network involves three main steps. First, the supply chain must be designed, which involves determining where to place the various supply chain components and how to connect and coordinate them. Second, network synthesis is needed, that is, determining the makeup of each supply chain component: the performance

---

[5] See "What Is a Supply Chain Network?," *Logistics & Materials Handling Blog*, September 27, 2011, http://www.aalhysterforklifts.com.au/index.php/about/blog-post/what_is_a_supply_chain_network; and "Next-Generation Supply Chains: Digital, On-Demand and Always-On," *The 2017 MHI Annual Industry Report*, 2017, https://static1.squarespace.com/static/562164dae4b0099ac9c04b5c/t/595126ece4fcb533d1d7fe2d/1498490608835/Nextgen+-+MHI+2017+Industry+Report.pdf.

[6] "Unprecedented Collaboration from Shelf to Supplier: Del Monte's Journey to Demand Driven," *Del Monte Case Study*, One Network Enterprises, 2014, https://www.onenetwork.com/2011/09/del-monte-case-study/.

criteria to be used, information and communications systems to allow coordination and collaboration between supply chain members, the data requirements, and cost and service levels. Third, the supply chain design must be both reliable and consistent, and meet the requirements of customers and supply chain members. This step ensures that the supply chain requirements will be met by the network that has been designed.

Let's examine in detail how the supply chain network should be designed.

Designing a Supply Chain Network

The first step in developing the most optimal supply chain is to map or flowchart it. This representation will include all of the major components or elements of the supply chain and identify their position within the system. Process mapping, which is a cornerstone of reengineering activities, will often lead to a clearer understanding of the many relationships that exist in a supply chain. Understanding the elements and their relationships usually leads to improved decision making, increased flexibility, cost reductions, and identification of important interdependencies.[7]

The SCOR® Model that was introduced in Chapter 1 is an example of a supply chain map or flowchart. While it only includes a portion of the supply chain—Tiers 1 and 2 suppliers; a focal firm; and Tiers 1 and 2 customers—it does represent a supply chain process model. To complete the map or flowchart, one would add additional suppliers and customers. A complete supply chain map would most likely look like the PERT/CPM path models often discussed in operations management for organizations like Boeing and Lockheed.[8] The creation of an aircraft involves thousands of parts and components obtained and assembled from hundreds of suppliers or vendors. Such maps are extensive and complicated. Often, it can be sufficient to map or flowchart the key elements of the supply chain (Pareto principle), which is analogous to the critical path method (CPM) used in operations research for scheduling activities in the most efficient and effective manner.

Flowcharting or Mapping the Supply Chain

While a supply chain map or flowchart will be unique to a specific group of organizations, there are similarities between supply chains that allow a generic approach to be used and then modified for a particular supply chain. Considering the five stages of the SCOR® Model (introduced in Chapter 1), each can be represented in a flow chart where the five stages are repeated for each member of the supply chain. Because a supply chain involves so many different processes and functions, utilizing a cross-functional team in developing the process map would be optimal.

Developing a process map of a firm's supply chain network will provide the who, what, why, when, and where of the existing supply chain processes. This becomes the starting point for developing a more optimal supply chain network. For simple supply chain networks, manual methods can be used to develop the process maps. For more complex systems, modeling or simulation may be required. However, in each case, they will involve a series of steps or stages that are sequential but can occur simultaneously and involve varying lengths of time. These steps of flowcharting the supply chain network and a brief explanation of each one are presented below:

1. **Make the case/get buy-in**. Without the support of top management and the right people in the organization, supply chain mapping becomes just an exercise and not a strategic focus.

---

[7] Nick Schneider, "What Does Your Global Supply Chain Look Like from 30,000 Feet? Map It," *Supply Chain 24/7*, May 7, 2014, https://www.supplychain247.com/article/what_does_your_global_supply _chain_look_like_from_30000_feet_map_it.
[8] For a discussion of PERT/CPM, see any introductory operations management textbook.

2. **Identify team members**. Team members should possess certain qualities (e.g., vision, broad scope, boundary spanners, team players, multiple roles) that will assist them in taking an intercompany perspective.

3. **Determine mapping session format—live and/or electronic**. Frequent contact and communication among team members are essential.

4. **Node and link specification—icon selection, information depth, aggregation decisions, key business process integration information to display, key metrics to include**. Rather than trying to include everything in the supply chain map, only include those elements that are critical to the creation of an optimal system.

5. **Place and fill nodes and links—special attention to up- and downstream critical players**. Limit the number of entities to be included in the supply chain map because the initial map would be too complicated if every supply chain participant was included.

6. **Move and reposition nodes and links as needed. The map graphically shows who the players are and where the flows go**. The team will discuss the initial map and make decisions regarding how and where entities are best positioned.

7. **Disseminate/publish as-is map**. Send the map to key decision makers, customers, and other important members of the supply chain for their input.

8. **Look for redundancies, excessive interdependencies, consolidation possibilities, unexpected connections, loops, and other inefficiencies**. Look for ways to improve the initial as-is map after feedback has been received from key entities of the supply chain.

9. **Propose a new map and implement changes**. Develop the "final" supply chain map, which can now serve as the basis for strategic planning. Changes made from the as-is map should be implemented.

10. **Use dynamically with period or real-time updating—find the new gaps**. Because conditions and situations change, periodic updating of the supply chain map is needed.[9]

The Flexible Supply Chain

The last point should be emphasized. While a generic approach to supply chain network design may be generally appropriate, it should be noted that networks must be flexible to meet changing market conditions. Therefore, periodic review of the supply chain process map should be undertaken to ensure that it is up-to-date and meets the strategic and operational goals of the organization.

Some of the factors that require flexible supply chain networks include the following:

- **Stochastic demand**—demand is unpredictable. Demand changes occur more rapidly than adjustments made within the supply chain.
- **Longer supply chains**—the more steps or stages in the supply chain, the more likely it is that inventories must be accumulated to accommodate variable demand.
- **Differing capabilities of supply chain service providers**—no single 3PL can typically provide all of the services at the required service levels for a global supply chain.
- **Visibility**—given the lack of visibility both horizontally and vertically within the supply chain, it is difficult to develop synergies across supply chain components and enterprises.[10]

Being able to adapt to a changing environment is key to continued success as a business. With environmental changes occurring at a more rapid pace, organizations must be able to make the necessary adjustments in order to continue to serve their customers and other

[9] Martha C. Cooper and John T. Gardner, "Map Your Supply Chain," *CSCMP Explores*, Vol. 2 (Winter 2005), pp. 6–9.
[10] Tom DePew, "Supply Chain Optimization Is the Hardest Easy Thing You'll Ever Do," *SupplyChainBrain*, December 22, 2009, http://www.supplychainbrain.com/featured-content/single-article/article/supply-chain-optimization-is-the-hardest-easy-thing-youll-ever-do/.

Exhibit: Participants in the Supply Chain Mapping Process

Champion/Sponsor
Involves top management personnel supporting the mapping initiative.

Coordinator/Project Manager
A single person, typically a management individual, who is in charge of coordinating the mapping project.

Database Manager
Often an IT person who will manage the database or the database connection.

Data Providers
Individuals or departments who provide information for the mapping project.

Assembler/Compiler
The individual who gathers and presents the information collected in a centralized location and in a graphical representation of the supply chain.

Disseminator/Publisher
The person responsible for publishing and disseminating the supply chain map to relevant parties.

Users
Supply chain executives and others responsible for carrying out supply chain activities on a day-to-day basis.

Source: Martha C. Cooper and John T. Gardner, "Map Your Supply Chain," *CSCMP Explores*, Vol. 2 (Winter 2005), p. 7.

stakeholders. Being proactive regarding those changes will be important to long-term success of the enterprise and ensuring that the supply chain operates smoothly and efficiently.

Supply Chain Design for Services

Although supply chain design has been traditionally applied in a manufacturing sector, it also has application to services. In reality, even manufacturing operations perform services, such as after-sales services that support the physical product. Using an approach similar to the SCOR® Model, Infosys Technologies Limited has proposed a generic service supply chain network that includes the following components: planning (e.g., financial, budgeting, business planning, and forecasting), design (e.g., warranty policy, service campaign design, service product design, and service pricing), procure (e.g., vendor management, order management, inventory management, and logistics), provision (e.g., customer interfacing, service requests, and resource scheduling), deliver (e.g., service order, repair, invoice and claims, and service feedback), and dispose (e.g., parts return, refurbishing, and waste disposal).[11] Each of the components is enabled by operations and information technologies, human resources, and customer value management practices. While the framework is generic, it can be applied across a variety of organizations. Like all frameworks, however, good implementation is the key to success.

Others have also identified the basic steps or stages in supply chain network design. Tompkins International outlined a typical approach as including six components: project launch (performing a current "state-of-the-art" assessment); data collection, validation, and analysis; modeling of the network; scenario visioning and design; scenario analysis; and strategy formulation.[12] There are multiple ways of reaching a successful conclusion of a supply chain network design initiative, but whatever approach is taken, it must include consideration of the many factors that impact the supply chain, its members, and other stakeholders.[13]

A number of macro or strategic issues impact supply chain design, including, although not limited to, strategy, technology, lean management, Six Sigma, organization structure, use of 3PLs, sustainability, and reverse logistics.

[11] Nishant Vaid and G. Venugopal, "Infosys Service Supply Chain Framework: An Integrated Approach to Service Supply Chain Design," Infosys Technologies Limited, *White Paper*, June 2009.

[12] "What Is Supply Chain Network Design and Why Is It Important?," Tompkins International, *White Paper*, 2015, http://www.supplychain247.com/paper/what_is_supply_chain_network_design_why_is_it_important.

[13] For a discussion of many of the important factors to consider in supply chain network design, see "Supply Chain Network Design & Contributing Factors," *Management Study Guide*, 2018, https://www.managementstudyguide.com/supply-chain-network-design.htm.

Supply Chain Strategy

The supply chain flowchart or map must have a strategic, as well as operational, focus. The strategic focus should be in sync with the overall business plans of companies in the supply chain. More specifically, the supply chain plan should emulate the best practices of recognized supply chain leaders. For example, the supply chain strategy should be formally tested to ensure that it is feasible and do-able within the supply chain structure that has been developed in the mapping exercise. Data from key members of the supply chain need to be available on a real-time basis and with a very high degree of accuracy and relevance for proper decision making by supply chain executives. Additionally, processes should be in place that identify places in the supply chain network where increased flexibility and responsiveness could result in operational improvement.[14]

Some of the tools used in supply chain network design are presented in the nearby Exhibit. While not every tool is identified, the tools with the most impact on the supply chain, such as network planning and optimization, supply chain simulation, and inventory optimization, are presented. Many companies in the retail, automotive, hospitality, educational, and electronic sectors utilize such tools in their attempts to optimize their supply chains.[15]

Exhibit: Supply Chain Network Tools Classification

Category	Description	How Used
Network Planning and Optimization	Tools that help companies design optimal supply chain networks, managing trade-offs between cost (manufacturing, distribution, inventory) and service.	Traditionally, used occasionally (every few years) as a strategic way to reoptimize supply chains, often focused on distribution networks. Today, used to solve a much wider set of problems, spanning manufacturing and sourcing, and used by many on a continual, even tactical planning basis.
Supply Chain Simulation	Tools that enable companies to evaluate how different network designs and strategies "play out" based on some sequence of events. Frequently based on "Monte Carlo" analysis—a statistics technique for simulating a pattern of occurrences (such as unpredictable short-term demand).	Enables companies to get a better feel for how real-time variability can impact supply chain performance and risk. For example, simulation might allow analysis of inventory positions, their deployment and how they are affected by changes in downstream demand signals, and the reorder policies in place to respond to those signals. It can also show how the "optimal" solution may leave a company vulnerable to an unlikely but potential series of events or variability of supply or demand.
Inventory Optimization	Tools used to identify optimal inventory levels and policies for a range of inventories, especially for those with multiple "echelons" of inventory stocking points.	These are tactical applications used to optimize safety stock and related inventory policies used to meet customer service targets with the optimal levels of inventory at each level of the supply chain, based on forecast demand. Also useful for making postponement decisions and navigating push versus pull hybrid inventory strategies.

Source: "Network Planning and Optimization: Tools Continue to Gain Traction," *Supply Chain Digest*, Vol. 7, No. 1 (February 2007), p. 6.

[14] Supply Chain Visions, *Supply Chain Management Process Standards*, 2nd ed. (Lombard, IL: Council of Supply Chain Management Professionals, 2009), p. 13.
[15] For a brief discussion of network design and some examples, see "What Are Companies Looking For in Network Design Technologies?," *2017 Supply Chain Network Design Industry Report*, November 28, 2017, http://www.supplychainbrain.com/nc/technology/transportation-management/single-article-page/article/2017-supply-chain-network-design-industry-report/; and Shamus McGillicuddy, "Report Summary: Network Management Megatrends 2016," Enterprise Management Associates, 2016, https://www.riverbed.com/document/fpo/Riverbed-EMA-NetworkMgmtMegatrends-2016-RR-SUMMARY_CS1.pdf.

Use of Technology in Network Design

Many innovations in supply chain–related software have been developed in recent years. Some attempt to model the entire supply chain, such as software developed by SAP and Oracle. Others, such as CPFR, CRM, ERP, WMS, TMS, model portions of, or processes within, a supply chain. Some of these technologies have been discussed in earlier chapters of this book, but ERP in the context of lean management will be examined again in network design.

Oxford Industries Utilizes Technology in Supply Chain Design

When Oxford Industries, a traditional manufacturer of men's clothing, changed the focus of its business to become a firm specializing in apparel design and marketing, it required that the firm utilize additional technologies beyond its ERP system. Oxford faced similar challenges that many clothing manufacturers and retailers experience, such as short seasons; hard-to-predict variables of color, size, and style; and changing customer preferences. Outsourcing manufacturing to Asia and other parts of the globe added more complexity to its supply chain network.[16] The company had to invest in technologies such as demand planning[17] in order to more accurately forecast consumer demand for its products. Thus, the firm was able to provide its third-party manufacturers with more specific and accurate manufacturing requests, which resulted in fewer products having incorrect production amounts. Relatedly, more accurate forecasting also allowed Oxford to purchase the correct amount of raw materials from its suppliers. Both resulted in Oxford Industries having less waste because the products being produced more closely matched consumer demand. Profitability was also improved because fewer products had to be marked down at the end of a season if they did not sell. In essence, the company was utilizing technology to implement lean management principles.

Many factors impact the increasing use of technology within the supply chain, including the rising prices of oil and raw materials, sustainability issues, global competition, and even the technology itself. One area where technology is having a significant impact is in the area of product development and design.

Exhibit: Network Management Megatrends

In a study of North American IT professionals, Enterprise Management Associates identified several megatrends that were impacting network design and management. These megatrends were:

- Internet of Things (IoT) was pervasive (87% of companies were providing connectivity to devices or IoT).

- Use of the cloud was commonplace (70% of companies were using the cloud).

- Network analytics initiatives were under way in most firms (49% were using advanced analytics, with another 40% anticipating their use within one year).

- Companies were using too many tools to monitor and troubleshoot their networks (a majority of firms were utilizing between 4 and 10 networking tools).

- Outsourcing of network management functions was common (over 50% utilize a management services provider).

Source: Shamus McGillicuddy, "Report Summary: Network Management Megatrends 2016," Enterprise Management Associates, 2016, https://www.riverbed.com/document/fpo/Riverbed-EMA-NetworkMgmtMegatrends-2016-RR-SUMMARY_CS1.pdf.

---

[16] "Supply Chain Didn't Quite Fit after Apparel Company Changed Its Business Model," *Global Logistics & Supply Chain Strategies*, Vol. 13, No. 2 (March 2009), p. 30.

[17] For a discussion of the role of demand planning in supply chain management, including some examples of the benefits of demand planning, see Lora Cecere, "A Practitioner's Guide to Demand Planning," *Supply Chain 24/7*, July 23, 2014, https://www.supplychain247.com/article/a_practitioners_guide_to_demand_planning; and Bram Desmet, "A Five-Step Approach to Effective Demand Planning Implementation," *Arkieva*, June 16, 2016, https://blog.arkieva.com/effective-demand-planning-implementation/.

Technology: Electrolux Manages Outsourced Supply Chain through Planning Capabilities

©Prasit photo/Getty Images

Electrolux is a global company headquartered in Stockholm, Sweden, and is one of the world's largest home appliance manufacturers. Its products sell under a variety of brand names to consumer and professional markets, including Electrolux, AEG, Anova, Frigidaire, Westinghouse, and Zanussi. It had net sales of SEK 122 million in 2017 from customers located in more than 150 countries. Over the years, Electrolux has been viewed as an innovator, especially from a product and marketing perspective. In the 1960s, the company successfully marketed vacuums in the UK using the slogan "Nothing sucks like an Electrolux." The company's current slogan is "Thinking of you."

In 2003, the prices within the vacuum cleaner industry dropped, and this caused the Electronic Home Care Products division (EHCP) to look into alternate business models to maintain margins. ECHP North America shifted from a manufacturing model to a sourcing model of finished goods and components utilizing overseas suppliers. Even though the company reduced its costs, complexity increased. Unwelcomed side effects included higher inventory levels, increased percentage of obsolescence, and longer lead times. In addition, the company did not have a true demand planning or inventory planning approach in place. It was using Excel spreadsheets for forecasting and planning.

To remedy these difficulties, EHCP went with a third-party solution provider to provide improved forecast accuracy and higher levels of customer service.

Key benefits of the new systems included:

- Increase in forecast accuracy by 15 percent, which lowered days of supply by 20 percent, while simultaneously increasing customer service levels.

- Reduction and realignment of safety stock through better demand management, resulting in less lead time variability.

- Improvement in collaboration between supply chain stakeholders, both internal and external to the company.

- Better positioning of EHCP to respond to changing economic and competitive challenges.

Sources: Nari Viswanathan, "Strategic Supply Chain Planning," Aberdeen Group, *White Paper*, September 2010, pp. 17–18; and company website, http://www.electroluxgroup.com/en/electrolux -in-brief-492/.

| Product Development and Design | New product success has always been a "hit and miss" kind of process. Many new products fail for many reasons. If the new product does not reach its target markets efficiently and effectively, failure can also be the result. Certainly, if the product does not meet customer wants or needs, it likely will fail. And it is now being recognized that if supply chain considerations are not included in new product development and introduction, results can be suboptimal. In one study of supply chain executives, it was found that two-thirds of the time supply chain leaders were not involved in the new product planning process. "All of the best practices underpin the idea that innovation needs to be considered in a total business context," and that includes incorporating supply chain management into the new product development process.[18] |

Lean Management Principles

Lean supply chain management is based on the concept of lean manufacturing. Its foundations lie in the Toyota Production System (TPS) created by Toyota founder, Sakichi Toyoda, although the TPS likely has earlier roots in the teachings of W. Edwards Deming and the

---

[18] MH&L Staff, "Successful Product Innovation Requires Supply Chain Insight," *Material Handling & Logistics*, February 7, 2018, http://www.mhlnews.com/global-supply-chain/successful-product-innovation -requires-supply-chain-insight.

assembly-line practices of the Ford Motor Company.[19] Lean manufacturing means producing goods with less; it applies fewer resources without affecting the quantity or quality of the goods produced. Likewise, in the broader context of supply chain management, it means "doing more with less," that is, becoming more efficient (i.e., using fewer resources) and generating more (obtaining maximum output).

Benefits of Implementing Lean Management

It is argued that lean supply chains are stronger than conventional supply chains, and common logic would suggest that to be true.[20] As an example of the benefits of implementing lean principles in manufacturing, Kemet Corporation, an international manufacturer of capacitors, reduced logistics costs by 20 percent, reduced inventory by 11 percent, increased productivity from 1.1 million pieces per person to 3.4 million pieces per person, and reduced customer complaints from 0.49 part per million to 0.32 part per million.[21] North American Parts Operations (NAPO), a division of Toyota Motor Sales that procures and manages more than US$3 billion of automotive service parts and accessories for the many Toyota dealers and distributors located throughout the U.S., achieved similar success through its lean management activities. Toyota achieved the results by implementing several lean initiatives: (1) centralized warehouses or parts centers between suppliers and regional warehouses; (2) daily ordering throughout the supply chain; (3) reduction of lot sizes; and (4) daily ordering and delivery. Specific benefits included buffering of inbound flows and orders, consolidation of inbound deliveries, reduction in volume fluctuations resulting from inaccurate forecasts, and improved lead times and on-time deliveries.[22]

Many other companies in a variety of industries have applied lean principles to their supply chains, including REA Group (digital advertising company in Australia), SulAmérica (insurance company in Brazil), and the Hospital District of Helsinki and Uusimaa (group of public health care organizations).[23] In terms of doing more with less, these and other companies have reduced waste in key supply chain areas such as inventory, transportation, lead times, space, packaging, and process complexity.

Waste, or *muda* as the Japanese refer to it, is the enemy of lean management. In manufacturing, where lean principles originated, waste included overproduction, waiting, transporting, inappropriate processing, extra inventory, unnecessary motion, and product defects. The Toyota Production System has been extremely effective in eliminating waste, but it should be remembered that the TPS has been around for more than 50 years, allowing it to be developed and refined over a long period of time. The application of lean principles to supply chain management is still in its infancy, relatively speaking, and most companies are still developing their lean supply chain systems. And, importantly, applying lean principles beyond a single firm is much more difficult and complex than its application within one company. It has been estimated that up to 80 percent of supply chain waste comes from external processes and parties such as suppliers and vendors, rather than internal to the firm.

---

[19] Robert J. Bowman, "Born on the Assembly Line, Lean Principles Begin to Take Hold in the Supply Chain," *Global Logistics & Supply Chain Strategies*, Vol. 10, No. 5 (May 2006), p. 78.

[20] See Brian Bilsback and Dasha Maximov, "Why Lean Supply Chains Are Strongest," *Material Handling Management*, July 1, 2011, http://www.mhinews.com/facilities-management/lean-supply-chains-strongest-0701.

[21] Jim Moore and Bob Arndt, "Five Principles Guide Lean Success," *Distribution Business Management Journal*, Vol. 12 (2011), p. 58.

[22] Thornton Oxnard, Jennifer Hasegawa, and Michael Schad, "Leveraging Lean Principles in a Service Parts Supply Chain: The Toyota Story," *CSCMP Explores*, Vol. 3 (Summer 2006), p. 3.

[23] See Nigel Dalton, "How Lean Is Securing the Future of This Digital Advertiser," *Planet Lean*, February 20, 2018, http://planet-lean.com/how-lean-is-securing-the-future-of-this-digital-advertiser; Luciana Gomes, "Lean Management in a Brazilian Insurance Company," *Planet Lean*, February 6, 2018, http://planet-lean.com/lean-management-in-a-brazilian-insurance-company; and Markku Mäkijärvi and Jyrki Perttunen, "Lean Healthcare at a Large Hospital District in Finland," *Planet Lean*, August 9, 2016, http://planet-lean.com/lean-healthcare-at-a-large-hospital-district-in-finland.

However, just because it is more difficult and complex does not mean that lean management should not be implemented in a supply chain. The principles of lean management are applicable to all areas of a business and the supply chain because all waste is bad both for companies and customers. The Japanese lean principles of the "5S"—Sort (simplify), Set in Order (put things in their place), Shine (cleanliness), Standardization (uniformity), and Sustain (discipline)—which describe ways of organizing and standardizing processes in the workplace on a continuous basis, can be applied throughout the supply chain.[24]

Enterprise Resource Planning (ERP)

In the implementation of lean supply chain management, enterprise resource planning (ERP) is useful. Approximately 80 percent of organizations have implemented, or will implement, ERP software in the near term.[25] ERP systems are used to plan, control, and manage day-to-day transactions in running a business and to provide real-time access to information.

The ERP system is analogous to the central nervous system of the human body, in that it contains the basic data needed to plan, implement, and control the entire supply chain. Through the automation of various processes, ERP systems standardize and make more efficient processes such as accounting and finance, payroll, human resources, sales, customer resource management (CRM), purchasing, inventory, manufacturing, and distribution.[26]

ERP systems were evolutionary developments from material requirements planning (MRP I) and manufacturing resource planning (MRP II) systems originally developed in the 1970s and 1980s. While MRP systems were concerned almost exclusively with internal company operations, ERP is much broader and encompasses not only all major internal operations, but external linkages with suppliers, vendors, and customers as well.[27]

Early in the development of ERP, the systems were predicated on a "push" system. Today, ERP systems are "pull" based, that is, they focus on demand forecasting or demand sensing where the marketplace determines the requirements. Technology enables ERP and

---

Exhibit: Creating a Business Case for the Implementation of ERP Systems

When creating a business case for an ERP investment and the selection of the right ERP option, organizations should follow the following seven-step process:

1. *Describe the business challenge*—why is an ERP system needed?

2. *Assess the potential benefits of the ERP investment*—will the ERP system reduce costs and improve efficiency, provide better coordination, and improve decision making?

3. *Assess the potential costs of each ERP option*—what are the costs of acquisition, upgrades, training, implementation, and maintenance of the ERP system?

4. *Assess risks and issues that might arise during the implementation*—are there any operational, IT, or financial risks that may arise during implementation of the ERP system?

5. *Recommend the preferred solution*—if more than one ERP system is being considered, which one is best?

6. *Describe the implementation approach*—what are the credentials of the ERP seller and how well will the implementation be documented?

7. *Measure potential and actual ROI*—when considering time savings, cost savings, and increased revenues resulting from the ERP system implementation, calculate its ROI.

Source: "7 Steps to Building a Business Case for ERP," Sage Software, *White Paper*, 2011, p. 3.

---

[24] Chuck Intrieri, "What Is 5S? An Explanation of the Elements of 5S for a Lean Culture," *Cerasis*, September 30, 2013, http://cerasis.com/2013/09/30/what-is-5s/.

[25] "2016 Report on ERP Systems and Enterprise Software," Panorama Consulting Solutions, 2016, http://go.panorama-consulting.com/rs/panoramaconsulting/images/2016-ERP-Report.pdf.

[26] See "An ERP Guide to Driving Efficiency," Sage Software, *White Paper*, 2010, http://www .SageERPSolutions.com.

[27] See "What Is ERP—Enterprise Resource Planning?," https://www.sap.com/products/what-is-erp.html.

Exhibit: 5 Mistakes Firms Make When Implementing ERP

There are five common mistakes that firms make when adopting and implementing software solutions such as ERP. They are:

1. *Not involving senior management in the decision-making process*: Ideally, the team selecting the ERP system should include a senior executive with long-term vision; operations managers to confirm proper functionality; and IT personnel to ensure the best technology infrastructure.

2. *Skipping the planning phase because it is believed that it takes too much time*: The cornerstones of the evaluation process should include determining a budget, identifying and assigning an executive sponsor, identifying critical business issues and needs, and defining the criteria for selecting the right ERP provider.

3. *Considering a technology provider that does not understand your industry*: It is important to have an ERP provider that understands the business and has the functionality necessary.

4. *Assuming that you will do things exactly the same way you do them today*: You need an ERP provider that conforms to the business and not the other way around.

5. *Selecting a vendor that lacks a long-term vision*: Will the company's distribution software solution be able to grow with the organization and adapt to changes in the business?

Source: "5 Mistakes Distributors Make When Selecting an Enterprise Software Solution," Epicor Software, *White Paper*, 2011, pp. 2–8.

lean management to coexist in a synergistic fashion. The technology helps the organization to reduce inventories, eliminate waste, level the production schedule, and optimize supply chain processes.

The Aberdeen Group found that of the organizations that had implemented ERP, leaders or top performers were able to achieve customer service levels of 96 percent versus followers, who achieved 88 percent. Year-over-year productivity gains were 13 percent for leaders versus 1 percent for followers. Most importantly, profitability gains for leaders were 7.4 percent versus 2.1 percent for followers.[28] Such improvements provide top firms with competitive advantages over organizations that have not implemented ERP or those that have only done an adequate job in ERP implementation. In sum, the inclusion of lean management principles in supply chain network design is crucial to its success.

At the same time that supply chain firms develop lean processes and approaches, they often engage in Six Sigma programs to improve quality while they attempt to minimize costs.

Six Sigma

Six Sigma (6σ) is a methodology, initially developed by Motorola USA in the 1980s, for improving the quality of processes by eliminating errors. Originally applied only within manufacturing, the method has now been extended to many business processes, including supply chain management. The essence of Six Sigma is relatively simple: Errors should be minimized as much as possible. If you are aware of the concept of standard deviation in statistical analysis, Six Sigma is easy to understand conceptually. As many statistics students are aware, when you have a standard normal distribution, approximately 67 percent of all observations fall within one standard deviation about the mean. Two standard deviations would include 95 percent of all observations and three standard deviations would include 99 percent of the observations. Statistically speaking, that is where most market research stops. Unfortunately, from a quality perspective, a three sigma deviation would result in

[28] Bryan Ball, "ERP Integration for SMB Companies Preparing for the Future," Aberdeen Group, *White Paper*, February 2018, http://v1.aberdeen.com/launch/report/knowledge_brief/17237-KB-ERP-Integration -Collaboration.asp; and "ERP and Analytics: The Perfect Pairing for Business Execution," Aberdeen Group, August 9, 2017, http://aberdeen.com/research/16754/16754-RR-ERP-analytics-bi.aspx/content.aspx.

6,210 errors or defects per million. At Six Sigma, there would only be 3.4 errors or defects per million (99.99966%). Quite a difference!

"The fundamental objective of the Six Sigma methodology is the implementation of a measurement-based strategy that focuses on process improvement and variation reduction through the application of Six Sigma improvement projects. This is accomplished through the use of two Six Sigma sub-methodologies: DMAIC and DMADV."[29]

Six Sigma Sub-methodologies: DMAIC and DMADV

DMAIC refers to a methodology developed by Motorola and Toyota that is used for improving existing business processes and includes five phases:

1. *Define*: Map the project and understand your aims (includes defining customer requirements).
2. *Measure*: Gather the data to understand performance.
3. *Analyze*: Understand where the problems in the process are located (identifying what needs to be improved).
4. *Improve*: Work out how defects could be reduced.
5. *Control*: Plan out how you will implement your solutions (ensure that any deviations from target are corrected before they result in defects).[30]

The second methodology for Six Sigma, DMADV, is used for creating a new product, service, or process and includes the following five phases:

1. *Define*: Define the process and design goals that are consistent with customer demands and the firm's strategy.
2. *Measure*: Identify critical quality characteristics of the product, service, or process.
3. *Analyze*: Analyze the data.
4. *Design*: Optimize the design and test it.
5. *Verify*: Make certain that the design output meets the design input (verification) and the output performs satisfactorily (validation).[31]

Lean Six Sigma

A combination of Six Sigma and lean management has developed in recent years and is referred to as "Lean Six Sigma." Because both approaches attempt to make the supply chain more efficient and effective, they are somehow related. Table 14.1 compares the two approaches and presents the general rules followed when employing each approach. Essentially, Six Sigma focuses on planning and analysis, while lean management focuses on actions and activities (e.g., minimizing inventories, maximizing product flow).

The tools used by each method are also very different. For example, Six Sigma utilizes tools such as process mapping, statistical analysis and process controls, and experimental design. Lean management utilizes kaizen, production line balancing, value stream mapping, and standardized operations.[32] Of course, the outcomes of both approaches, individually or cooperatively, result in benefits to customers and members of the supply chain.[33]

[29] Kirsten Terry, "What Is Six Sigma?," *iSixSigma*, April 20, 2018, http://www.isixsigma.com/new-to-six-sigma/getting-started/what-six-sigma.
[30] Adam Henshall, "DMAIC: The Complete Guide to Lean Six Sigma in 5 Key Steps," *Process Street*, November 24, 2017, https://www.process.st/dmaic/.
[31] "DMAIC vs. DMADV," Purdue University, *Lean Six Sigma Online* (January 24, 2017), https://www.purdue.edu/leansixsigmaonline/blog/dmaic-vs-dmadv/; and Paul Hobcraft, "The Difference between DMAIC, DMADV, and Innovation Management," Hype Innovation *Blog* (April 10, 2017), https://blog.hypeinnovation.com/the-difference-between-dmaic-dmadv-and-innovation-management.
[32] Carl Wright, "Lean Manufacturing or Six Sigma—Which Method Is Best?," *isnare.com*, undated, https://www.isnare.com/?aid=173501&ca=Leadership.
[33] For a discussion of the relationships between Lean Six Sigma and the Malcolm Baldrige National Quality Award, see Brenda Lopez, "Strategic Planning and Lean Six Sigma," *LinkedIn Blog*, February 5, 2015, https://www.linkedin.com/pulse/malcolm-baldrige-strategic-planning-lean-six-sigma-lopez-m-a-b-s-/.

TABLE 14.1

Comparison of the Rules of Six Sigma and Lean Management

Source: The 10 rules of Six Sigma are from Rohit Ramaswamy, "Integrating Lean and Six Sigma Methodologies for Business Excellence," *White Paper*, STAT-A-MATRIX, 2007, p. 3; and the 10 rules of lean management are from Jeffry Liker, *The Toyota Way* (Boston, MA: McGraw-Hill, 2004).

Six Sigma	Lean Management
View performance from the position of the customer	Eliminate waste
Understand the process	Minimize inventory
Make decisions based on data and analysis	Maximize flow
Focus on the most important issues	Pull production from customer demand
Use statistical models	Meet customer requirements
Pay attention to variation	Do it right the first time
Use standard methodologies	Empower workers
Select projects for financial impact	Design for rapid changeover
Establish project governance structure	Partner with suppliers
Enlist senior management support	Create a culture of continuous improvement

Organizational Structures

In Chapter 15 we will discuss various aspects of firm and supply chain organizations. Organizational structures of individual companies and their respective supply chains are vital components of successful supply chain management. A report from the Council of Supply Chain Management Professionals (CSCMP) identified four coordination objectives that related to organizational structures, including the achievement of goal alignment within and among supply chain entities, the development of synergies, promotion of knowledge development, and management of interdependencies and information.[34]

Within companies in the supply chain, coordination can be achieved in many ways. While informal methods can be used, such as the use of social networks, more formal methods usually work best. Examples of formal methods include establishing corporate-level SCM-oriented councils to implement best practices, global supply teams to manage the suppliers, and customer account teams to provide a single point of contact.[35] Relatedly, it is expected that CEOs and other senior executives in organizations will take more active roles in SCM in the future, setting the strategic direction for the business, and then letting others execute the strategy. "Senior executive involvement, including hands-on attention from the CEO, is pivotal in managing the cross-functional trade-offs that underpin many supply chain decisions."[36]

Organizational structures facilitate the implementation of SCM within and across companies, but they do not guarantee success. As is the case in most instances, people will make the difference! In a study of chief supply chain executives, Gartner identified their top priorities as operations improvements, cost management, and profit improvement.[37] With these priorities, the two most significant indicators of a best-in-class supply chain organization are an ability of personnel to manage critical relationships through the end-to-end supply chain and the ability of personnel to view the supply chain holistically in terms of linked processes.[38] Likely, many organization structures can work for a company, but it is

---

[34] Morgan Swink, Judith Whipple, Joseph Roh, and Virpi Turkulainen, *Organizing Supply Chains in a Time of Change* (Lombard, IL: CSCMP, 2010), p. 20.

[35] Ibid., p. 25.

[36] Trish Gyorey, Matt Jochim, and Sabina Norton, "McKinsey Global Survey Results: The Challenges Ahead for Supply Chains," McKinsey & Company, *White Paper*, 2010, pp. 7 and 9.

[37] Viveca Woods, "A Four-Prong, Bimodal Approach for Chief Supply Chain Officers," Gartner, March 17, 2016, https://www.gartner.com/smarterwithgartner/a-four-prong-bimodal-approach-for-chief-supply-chain-officers/.

[38] Nari Viswanathan, "Strategic Supply Chain Planning: Three Key Priorities of the Chief Supply Chain Officer," Aberdeen Group, *White Paper*, September 2010, p. 16.

the combination of structure and people that will ultimately allow the supply chain to attain optimal efficiency and effectiveness.

Keiretsu Structures   When structuring or organizing a supply chain across multiple firms, the *keiretsu* structure, which will be discussed in Chapter 15, can be useful. Merriam-Webster defines *keiretsu* (literally, a system, series, grouping of enterprises, order of succession) as "a powerful alliance of Japanese businesses often linked by cross-shareholding."[39] A keiretsu can be horizontal or vertical. Whether the structure consists of a group of interrelated companies overseen by some committee or council representing firms in the supply chain (i.e., horizontal structure) or a large company supported by a number of smaller companies (i.e., vertical structure), these approaches can result in more optimal supply chains because of the integration, collaboration, and coordination that they foster. An important consideration in a keiretsu structure is that it facilitates the planning, implementation, and control of an efficient and effective supply chain.

Use of 3PLs

Because supply chains have become more complex with omnichannel marketing, global networks, and significant developments in the IT sector, organizations have become much more attentive towards trying to minimize the negatives and maximize the positives associated with complexity. One way of sharing the risk of this complexity with supply chain partners is the use 3PLs. Even before the development of supply chain management (SCM), firms utilized third-party service providers (3PLs) for various supply chain functions or processes. However, with the advent of SCM and the increasing complexity of the supply chain, the role of 3PLs has changed. Fewer 3PLs are being utilized, but their roles and responsibilities have greatly expanded. Typically, the 3PL will put more of its own investment into facilities, equipment, and personnel, and will provide more nontraditional services to its clients.

For example, a warehousing 3PL, because it is receiving more business from its clients, will often invest more heavily in automated equipment or advanced information systems in its facilities. Some 3PLs have implemented robotics, drones, driverless vehicles, pick-to-light systems, etc., in their warehouses. Such systems are not inexpensive, but justified given the expanded relationship with its partner firms in the supply chain. Also, some 3PLs have expanded their facilities to allow their clients to place more products into fewer facilities, thus reducing their warehousing costs. Finally, various state-of-the-art technologies have been employed, such as RFID and sophisticated WMS and TMS software linked to a client's ERP system.[40]

Since the end of the "Great Recession" that impacted companies worldwide until 2011 (or later for some areas and industries), many 3PLs have increased their investments in operations and people. As a result, supply chains have been strengthened as these important components of the supply chain have become more efficient and effective. 3PLs are now better able to respond to environmental disasters such as tsunamis, hurricanes, and earthquakes because they have embraced risk management principles. They are emphasizing sustainability initiatives, which have become more popular with both companies and customers. In sum, 3PLs have become even more the strategic partners so vitally needed in the supply chain.[41]

Reverse Logistics

Return goods handling, product disposal, remanufacturing, repackaging, reuse, recycling, and source reduction are elements of a larger process referred to as *reverse logistics*. Customers may return items to sellers for many reasons such as product defects, late

---

[39] "Keiretsu," *Merriam-Webster*, March 22, 2018, https://www.merriam-webster.com/dictionary/keiretsu.
[40] For examples, see "Overcoming Barriers to NextGen Supply Chain Innovation," *The 2018 MHI Annual Industry Report*, 2018, https://www.mhi.org/publications/report.
[41] For a discussion of how 3PLs have responded to various environmental events, see Toby Gooley, "A Tale of Two 3PL Studies," *DC Velocity*, Vol. 10, No. 2 (February 2012), pp. 55–58.

shipments, overages, shipping errors, trade-ins, warranties, or buyer's remorse. In the supply chain, items moving in reverse through the system are more troublesome to members of the network that handles them. Moving a product back through the supply chain may cost as much as five to nine times more than moving the same product forward in the supply chain from producer to consumer. Often, the returned goods cannot be transported, stored, sorted, or handled as easily as original goods, resulting in higher per-unit costs. If a member of the supply chain fails to process the returned items quickly and efficiently, customer satisfaction suffers and additional costs can be incurred. Thus, it is imperative that supply chains be designed to process product returns as efficiently and effectively as possible.

Interestingly, returned goods processing was not a part of the original SCOR Model, but was added during one of the model updates several years ago. The Supply Chain Council recognized the importance of returns in supply chain management. As an activity, program, or process, reverse logistics interfaces with many other functional areas and processes within an organization and with other supply chain partners. Decisions made in areas such as accounting/finance, manufacturing, marketing, packaging engineering, procurement, and sourcing impact product return rates and the processes used to "bring them back." Those decisions affect the ability of the supply chain to conserve resources, generate revenues from product disposition, and achieve green marketing and sustainability goals and objectives.[42]

In a research study of reverse logistics activities in the supply chain, it was found that when reverse logistics is being managed, it is almost always managed within single firms or between a few firms, but seldom managed across supply chains. Because good reverse logistics practices across the supply chain can result in cost reductions, customer value-added, and additional profits for firms, it is important that each member of the supply chain recognize its roles and responsibilities in bringing products back and dispositioning them in optimal ways.[43]

With the increasing interest by customers and firms in sustainability, reverse logistics activities have become more important. Sustainability is related to reverse logistics, but much broader in scope; it adds the dimension of environmental stewardship. Because of its broad scope, it must necessarily be multi-organizational, that is, involve multiple firms in the supply chain. What one organization does or does not do impacts others, so coordinated efforts are required across the supply chain if synergistic results are to be obtained.[44]

Omnichannel Networks

The concept of omnichannel supply chains has been included throughout this textbook, but the basics were covered in Chapter 9. In this discussion, we will examine the impact of omnichannel retailing on the supply chain, especially as it relates to network design.

In an omnichannel environment, customers place orders in person in a brick-and-mortar facility or online using their computer, smartphone, or tablet. Orders are fulfilled at the brick-and-mortar facility by the customer, while online orders are delivered to the customer

---

[42] For a thorough discussion of reverse logistics and the topics of green marketing and sustainability, see James R. Stock, *Development and Implementation of Reverse Logistics Programs* (Oak Brook, IL: Council of Logistics Management, 1998). For a discussion of reverse logistics from manufacturing, wholesaling, and retailing perspectives, see James Stock, Thomas Speh, and Herbert Shear, "Managing Product Returns for Competitive Advantage," *MIT Sloan Management Review*, Vol. 48, No. 1 (Fall 2006), pp. 57–62.

[43] Stock, *Development and Implementation*; Stock et al., "Managing Product Returns."

[44] Articles and reports that examine sustainability practices across the supply chain are Omar Keith Helferich, M. Douglas Voss, Zachary Williams, and Jim Moore, "DBMA Sustainability Longitudinal Study: Suggestions for Enhanced Supply-Chain Performance," *Distribution Business Management Journal*, Vol. 12 (2011), pp. 10–14; and Edwin Lopez, "What Is the Future of Sustainability in the Supply Chain?," *Supply Chain Dive*, November 13, 2017, https://www.supplychaindive.com/news/what-is-the-future-of-sustainability-in-the-supply-chain/510756/.

by USPS, DHL, FedEx, and/or UPS. They can also be picked up in the physical facility. What makes omnichannel different from multichannel is that the two systems are integrated rather than managed independently. For customers, the two systems must appear "seamless," that is, any and all order placement and fulfillment options are available to them.

VF Corporation, a branded apparel manufacturer, utilizes an omnichannel approach to service its customers. The firm has retail and wholesale channels in addition to an online channel that is direct-to-consumer. Whether customers are consumers or retailers, both groups expect that they will be able to order products when and where they want, and be able to change the channel from which they choose to order. Based on the "Amazon factor," customers are expecting short lead times and rapid delivery options.

As VF Corporation has grown over the years and its customer base has increased, it becomes more of a challenge to provide an exceptional omnichannel experience to its customers. So, the company has implemented a number of strategies, including the pooling of inventories where both channels draw from the same inventory pool, increased safety stock in order to meet the shorter lead times and rapid delivery requirements of customers, more optimal packaging approaches that reduce shipping weight but also are more environmentally friendly, and increased investment in hiring and training supply chain talent. As a result, VF Corporation has become more centralized in its supply chain network.[45]

Many observers believe that Amazon was the inventor of omnichannel. Certainly, with the offering of Amazon Prime in 2005, the free two-day shipping on qualified items forever changed e-commerce. As a result, other companies had to react to what Amazon was doing and began to offer similar programs. However, being first gave Amazon a competitive advantage that remains to this day. Amazon was able to be proactive, while its competition was mostly reactive. Omnichannel tears "down barriers between channels, synchronizing brand messages, and creating a seamless customer experience to better serve customers. . . . The success of mobile commerce and changing consumer behaviors have accelerated the evolution."[46]

In order to become proficient at implementing an omnichannel strategy, firms must address and answer a number of important questions:[47]

- Can an omnichannel strategy be profitable for my specific company or industry?
- Using the omnichannel approach, which customers should the company serve?
- Are bricks-and-mortar stores obsolete, or are they just another way of reaching selected market segments?
- What are some of the barriers or constraints related to implementing an omnichannel strategy?
- What changes are necessary in existing supply chains that will allow firms to sell successfully both online and in-store?

Because almost 90 percent of consumer goods firms believe that they can no longer rely solely on traditional sales channels to drive future growth, firms really have no choice but to adopt an omnichannel strategy.[48] Otherwise, they may be relegated to "also-rans" in the future.

[45] For a more in-depth case analysis of the VF Corporation, see David J. Closs, David J. Frayer, and Judith M. Whipple, "Omni-Channel Supply Chain Management: VF Corporation," *APICS Case Study*, 2017, https://www.apics.org/docs/default-source/scc-non-research/omni-channel-supply-chain-management—vf-corporation.pdf?sfvrsn=2.
[46] Randy Strang, "Omni-Channel Supply Chains Designed for a Retail World without Boundaries," *Supply Chain 24/7*, August 15, 2014, https://www.supplychain247.com/article/omni-channel_supply_chains_designed_for_a_retail_world_without_boundaries.
[47] For a discussion of these and other issues associated with an omnichannel strategy, see "Re-engineering the Supply Chain for the Omni-channel of Tomorrow," EYGM Limited, February 2015, http://www.ey.com/Publication/vwLUAssets/EY-re-engineering-the-supply-chain-for-the-omni-channel-of-tomorrow/$FILE/EY-re-engineering-the-supply-chain-for-the-omni-channel-of-tomorrow.pdf.
[48] Ibid., p. 4.

Network Synthesis

Network synthesis involves a variety of tasks, including the determination of the makeup of each supply chain component; performance criteria to be used; information and communications systems that allow coordination and collaboration between supply chain members; data requirements; and overall supply chain costs, service levels, and customer satisfaction objectives. In essence, these are aspects of managing the supply chain.

Data Requirements in Network Synthesis

Many of these elements of network synthesis have been discussed in earlier chapters of this textbook. However, two deserve special attention here: the identification of data requirements and supply chain costs. Because of the scope and complexity of supply chains, enormous amounts of data are necessary in order for members of the supply chain to make optimal decisions. To illustrate, in China, there are 274 million consumers who participate in online food delivery services, 106 million who use bike-sharing services, and 502 million who utilize online payments.[49] Worldwide, because of the high percentage of consumers who utilize the Internet, there are literally millions of Internet transactions that occur every day that have to be monitored and managed. Businesses are required to track, analyze, make decisions, and take actions based on the enormous quantity of data generated by their operations.[50] As will be discussed in Chapter 16, organizations in the supply chain will need to identify their key performance indicators (KPIs) and collect the necessary data to measure and monitor supply chain performance.

Some examples will help illustrate the importance of supply chain firms having the information about what is occurring within the supply chain. One of the world's largest aircraft manufacturers, with a large number of suppliers and vendors, was having difficulty keeping track of parts and components that were being inventoried at various points in its supply chain. With 16 manufacturing plants being served by these suppliers and vendors, it was critical to know specifically where items were located and when they would be delivered. The company utilized RFID tags to track products. The results were significant. Parts delivery errors were drastically reduced, and the time spent handling these items was reduced by 75 percent.[51]

A consumer electronics manufacturer introduced communications and information systems that allowed it to have quick access to data on inventory availability and production requirements. The firm had 19 different business units, so it was important for each unit to have access to accurate information on a timely basis. With implementation of the right systems, the firm could optimize inventories, reduce work-in-progress, and dramatically shorten the planning period for production and procurement.[52]

Supply Chain Management Costs

Measuring the performance of a supply chain usually involves three criteria: cost, cash, and customer service. "Total supply chain management cost is the sum of the costs associated with the process to Plan, Source, Deliver, and Return and is calculated as Sales – Profits – Cost to Serve (e.g., marketing, selling, administrative)."[53] Because supply chain costs will continue to be a major issue with senior supply chain executives, it is important for individual firms in the supply chain to be able to capture the true costs of performing

[49] As an illustration of the explosion in Internet users, there are 751 million Internet users with 96.3 percent of them accessing it through their cellphones. See Coco Feng and Sun Wenjing, "China Now Has 751 Million Internet Users, Equivalent to Entire Population of Europe," *Caixin Global Limited*, August 7, 2017, https://www.caixinglobal.com/2017-08-07/101127296.html.

[50] "Turning Decisions into Profit with Business Analytics & Optimization: The Platform Approach," Starview Technology, *White Paper*, undated, p. 2. Also see Bridget McCrea, "8 Steps to Supply Chain Visibility," *Logistics Management*, Vol. 50, No. 11 (November 2011), pp. 36–38.

[51] Karen Butner, "A Commanding View," *CSCMP's Supply Chain Quarterly*, Vol. 5, No. 3 (Quarter 3/2011), p. 30.

[52] Ibid., pp. 30–31.

[53] APQC Benchmarking Portal, undated, https://www.apqc.org/benchmarking-portal/glossary/term_description/10589/nojs.

various functions and processes, and make the necessary cost–service trade-offs required to optimize the supply chain.

There are many factors that impact supply chain costs, but the most important are time, transactions, mistakes, specialization, and management.[54] Each of these cost drivers impacts supply chain management because it requires usage of personnel, equipment, and materials. Thus, firms in the supply chain are constantly looking for ways to reduce these costs. And unlike trying to increase sales, supply chain cost reductions can improve profitability without increasing sales. For example, if net profit on sales is 5 percent, reductions in supply chain costs from 9 percent to 4 percent will double net profits.[55] If we examine "best-in-class" firms compared to industry averages, the best manufacturers have supply chain costs as a percentage of sales at 6.8 percent; average firms are at 10.3 percent. Similar results can be seen for distributors, industrial suppliers, and retailers.[56]

There are many things that companies can do to reduce supply chain costs, including better management of human resources; inventory management that minimizes excess inventories; use of warehouse IT solutions such as WMS, RFID, and automation; better management of transportation using TMS and other technologies; outsourcing to 3PLs that can provide services more cheaply or more efficiently than you can; and development of an overall supply chain strategy that results in synergies across multiple supply chain functions or processes.[57]

There will be a number of obstacles or constraints that can keep a firm or a supply chain from realizing all of the potential cost reductions that are possible, such as increasing product or service complexity, lack of performance metrics (to be discussed in Chapter 16), inability of firms to adapt quickly to changing company priorities or market conditions, and poor coordination of program management and/or production planning activities.[58]

Again, it is vitally important for organizations to have the necessary data and systems to allow them to make optimal supply chain decisions. Such data must be available on a real-time basis in order for the supply chain to be able to make the needed adjustments to changes in the marketplace that do and will continue to occur in the future.

Optimizing the Supply Chain Network

Supply chain executives must go from managing business processes within one organization to integrating business processes among multiple organizations. Supply chains must be reliable, be consistent, and meet the requirements of customers and supply chain members. At the same time, they must also be *agile*, that is, be responsive to changing market conditions and customer needs.[59] Therefore, optimizing the supply chain network determines how the

---

[54] Gary A. Smith, "Exploring Supply Chain Cost Drivers, Proven Methods for Making Your Process Better, Faster, and Cheaper," *APICS Magazine*, July/August 2016, http://www.apics.org/apics-for-individuals/apics-magazine-home/magazine-detail-page/2016/07/28/exploring-supply-chain-cost-drivers.

[55] Rob O'Byrne, "Reducing Supply Chain Costs," *Logistics Bureau*, April 9, 2016, http://www.logisticsbureau.com/reducing-supply-chain-costs/.

[56] Ibid.

[57] Christopher Moore, "6 Simple Strategies to Decrease Supply Chain Costs," *Business2Community*, January 17, 2017, https://www.business2community.com/product-management/6-simple-strategies-decrease-supply-chain-costs-01757662.

[58] David Snelson, "Six Ways to Achieve Sustainable Supply Chain Cost Reductions," Waer Systems, *White Paper*, January 2011, https://www3.technologyevaluation.com/research/white-paper/Six-Ways-to-Achieve-Sustainable-Supply-Chain-Cost-Reductions.html.

[59] For a discussion of various aspects of the agile organization, see Jonathan Webb, "How to Create an Agile Supply Chain," *Forbes*, December 26, 2017, https://www.forbes.com/sites/jwebb/2017/12/26/how-to-create-an-agile-supply-chain/#7301a71962f4; and Muhammad Sher, "The Agile Supply Chain Management: What Is It and Why Should You Care!," *Management Hubspot*, November 15, 2016, https://medium.com/supply-chain-hubspot/the-agile-supply-chain-management-what-is-it-and-why-should-you-care-966ad9829d19.

supply chain requirements will be met by the network that has been designed. Demand forecasting, identifying specific costs of each supply chain component, cost–service trade-off analysis, and other more tactical decisions of supply chain members are important aspects of network optimization.

Benefits of Supply Chain Network Optimization

When supply chain networks are optimized, customer satisfaction levels improve, costs are reduced, and risk is properly managed. Total supply chain network costs can be reduced by 10 percent or more.[60] Additional benefits occurring when supply chain networks are optimized include highlighting of excess costs or waste; improvement in supply chain productivity and flexibility; increase in product throughput; and reduced uncertainty.

When identifying supply chain costs and cost savings, the data should be available in the software systems, such as ERP, TMS, and WMS. Some of the general information, such as sales forecasts, corporate strategies, and key performance indicators (KPIs), would likely be found in the MIS of the firm.

A part of supply chain evaluation is having the ability to modify and change existing strategies and tactics. As we have previously discussed regarding market demand, forecasting is used to predict that demand, which in turn drives decisions made throughout the supply chain that respond to the demand. However, situations and environments are fluid, that is, in a constant state of flux or change. Therefore, it is important for firms and their supply chains to be able to reforecast. *Reforecasting* means taking a detailed resource and capacity plan and modifying it to reflect changes in demand or internal productivity levels and/or other business drivers.[61] As organizations and supply chains reforecast, they are able to make better decisions, for both themselves and their customers, creating more "win-win" situations. The ability to constantly update forecasts to make them more accurate and reflective of current conditions is vital to continuing supply chain success.

Some of the warning signs that may indicate that a supply chain redesign is necessary are identified in the nearby Exhibit.

Exhibit: Symptoms of Possible Supply Chain Network Design Problems

- Customer satisfaction levels overall are low.
- Manufacturing failure rates are high.
- Transportation is nonoptimal (variable lead times, slow or late deliveries).
- Supply chain productivity improvements are lacking.
- Supply chain disruptions occur too often.
- Financial performance measures, especially KPIs, are low.
- There are capacity problems in manufacturing and logistics.
- The firm is focused on objectives rather than strategies.
- Few people in the company frequently question "why do we do things this way?"

- Number of products and customers are growing faster than the budget.
- A consolidation of operations or collaboration with another company is imminent.
- A significant service failure with a major customer or customers has occurred.
- Senior management seems to be uncertain or tentative in their decision making.

Sources: Adapted from Keith Donnelly, Meghan Shehorn, and Debjit Banerjee, "Turn Your Supply Chain into a Competitive Weapon," *Bain Brief*, December 12, 2017, http://www.bain.com/publications/articles/turn-your-supply-chain-into-a-competitive-weapon.aspx; and Simon Bragg, Richard Stone, and Julian Van Geersdaele, "7 Signs Your Supply Chain Needs a Redesign," *CSCMP's Supply Chain Quarterly*, Vol. 5, No. 3 (Quarter 3/2011), pp. 46–52.

[60] "Optimize Our Supply Chain Network for Total Cost Savings," LLamasoft website, May 15, 2017, https://www.llamasoft.com/solutions/network-optimization/.

[61] See Dan Eyre, "5 Steps to Connected Supply Chain Planning," *Anaplan*, November 6, 2017, https://www.anaplan.com/blog/5-steps-to-smart-supply-chain-planning/; and "Managing Financial Performance: Integrated, Enterprise-Wide Performance and Risk Management," SAP AG, *White Paper*, 2011, http://www.findwhitepapers.com/content20535.

All supply chains will necessarily have to be redesigned occasionally because conditions are not constant; they change! Supply chain redesigns are time-consuming and costly because they impact so many firms, functions, and processes. Thus, firms often wait too long to redesign their supply chain if, when they were initially established, they worked reasonably well. However, waiting is typically not a good strategy because you are likely losing efficiency and effectiveness operating with a suboptimal supply chain network.

When putting together a team to design or redesign a supply chain network, it is optimal to include a number of participants that represent all of the supply chain functions or processes, as well as top management personnel who will be responsible for implementation of the network. Some of the major participants in this process would include top management and personnel from IT, material handling, logistics, customer service, sales and marketing, R&D, accounting, manufacturing, third parties, and customers. Each participant will bring his or her perspective into the network design process and will help to ensure that all important aspects of supply chain management are included.[62]

Summary

It is necessary to have an optimal supply chain network that will provide optimal benefits to customers and members of the supply chain. Both structural and economic changes are requiring companies to optimize their supply chain networks. Network design planning includes activities such as planning, asset sourcing, operations, and performance monitoring. Each of these activities has both short-term and long-term perspectives.

Optimal supply chain networks are developed in three main steps or stages. First is the design of the supply chain, which involves determining how to connect and coordinate supply chain components. Second, network synthesis determines the makeup of each supply chain component, the performance criteria to be used, information and communications systems used to allow coordination and collaboration between supply chain members, data requirements, and cost and service levels. Third, the supply chain must be reliable, be consistent, and meet the requirements of customers and supply chain members.

It is important to flowchart or map the supply chain network so that optimization can occur. A generic approach to supply chain network design may be appropriate, but networks must be flexible to meet changing market conditions. Additionally, because supply chains include activities and processes within and between firms, multiple individuals need to be included in the design and management of the supply chain network.

Many strategic issues impact supply chain network design, including, although not limited to, company strategies, technology, lean management, Six Sigma, organization structure, the use of 3PLs, and reverse logistics/sustainability issues. Especially important are ERP systems, which combine with lean management and other approaches to develop optimal supply chain networks. Ford, Toyota, Zara, Oxford Industries, Electrolux, and others are examples of companies that have utilized these strategic resources to successfully implement their respective supply chain networks.

Optimizing the supply chain network impacts how supply chain requirements will be met. Demand forecasting, identifying specific costs of each supply chain component, cost–service trade-off analysis, and other more tactical activities of supply chain members are important aspects of network optimization. Generally, when supply chain networks are optimized, customer satisfaction levels improve and costs are reduced.

[62] For a discussion of the engagement of colleagues in a supply chain design process, see Tuomo Pesonen and Timo Ala-Risku, "Supply Chain Transformation: The Complete Guide," *Relex Solutions*, 2018, pp. 11–14, https://www.relexsolutions.com/supply-chain-transformation/.

Suggested Readings

Balaji, L. N., and Sandeep Kumar, "How to Reduce Costs through Supply Chain Network Optimization," *Industry Week*, July 8, 2013, http://www.industryweek.com/planning -amp-forecasting/how-reduce-costs-through-supply-chain-network-optimization.

Betke, Ralf, and Stefan Lettig, "Rewiring Supply Chain Networks," Cognizant, *White Paper*, April 2015, https://www.cognizant.com/whitepapers/rewiring-supply-chain-networks -codex1129.pdf.

Bhat, Shreyas, "Four Ways to Optimize Your Supply Chain," *Inbound Logistics*, February 24, 2018, http://www.inboundlogistics.com/cms/article/four-ways-to-optimize-your-supply -chain/.

Bowman, Robert J., "Rethinking the Concept of Supply-Chain Optimization," *SupplyChainBrain*, Vol. 15, No. 5 (September/October 2011), pp. 48–50.

Burn, Elizabeth, Katya Fay, Mario Lazzaroni, Carl-Martin Lindahl, and Monica Murarka, "Designing a Winning Consumer Goods Organization," McKinsey & Company, *White Paper*, February 2012.

Byrnes, Jonathan L. S., "Join the Finance Revolution," *CSCMP's Supply Chain Quarterly*, Vol. 4, No. 4 (Quarter 4/2010), pp. 26–31, 54.

Cooke, James A., "From Bean to Cup: How Starbucks Transformed Its Supply Chain," *CSCMP's Supply Chain Quarterly*, Vol. 4, No. 4 (Quarter 4/2010), pp. 35–37, 55.

Cooke, James A., "Neways Invests for Success," *CSCMP's Supply Chain Quarterly*, Vol. 4, No. 3 (Quarter 3/2010), pp. 40–42.

Craig, Don, "What Is Supply Chain Network Optimization?," *Executive Insights Blog*, Transportation Insight, June 10, 2014, https://www.transportationinsight.com /blog/networks/2014/06/supply-chain-network-optimization/.

Forrest, Matt, "What is Supply Chain Network Design and How Does it Work?" *CARTO Blog*, November 9, 2017, https://carto.com/blog/what-is-supply-chain-network-design -how-does-it-work/.

Heaney, Bob, "Supply Chain Visibility Excellence: A Critical Strategy to Optimize Cost and Service," Aberdeen Group, *White Paper*, May 2013, https://www.gs1.org/docs/visibility /Supply_Chain_Visibility_Aberdeen_Report.pdf.

Henderson, James, "Manufacturers Falling Behind in Take-up of Digital Supply Chain Networks," *Supply Chain Digital*, November 21, 2017, http://www.supplychaindigital. com/technology/manufacturers-falling-behind-take-digital-supply-chain-networks.

Holcomb, Mary C., and James H. Foggin, "A Framework for Network Optimization," *CSCMP's Supply Chain Quarterly*, Vol. 1, No. 1 (Quarter 2/2007), pp. 72–77.

"The Internet of Things: How 'Process Robots' Are Transforming Supply Chains," One Network Enterprises, *White Paper*, undated, http://go.onenetwork.com/resources -download#whitepapers.

Juneja, Prachi, "Supply Chain Network and Technology," *Management Study Guide*, 2018, https://www.managementstudyguide.com/supply-chain-network.htm.

Jusko, Jill, "When Two Lean Cultures Meet—and Merge," *Industry Week*, April 20, 2018, http://www.industryweek.com/operations/when-two-lean-cultures-meet-and-merge.

"Lean Guiding Principles for the Supply Chain—Principle 1: People Involvement," Ryder System, *White Paper*, 2011.

"Lean Guiding Principles for the Supply Chain—Principle 2: Built-in Quality," Ryder System, *White Paper*, 2011.

Leedale, Bill, "ERP for Green Supply Chain Management in Manufacturing," Aberdeen Group, *White Paper*, January 4, 2012, http://www.findwhitepapers.com /content17028.

Lundin, Johan F., and Andreas Norrman, "The Misalignment Cycle: Is the Management of Your Supply Chain Aligned?," *International Journal of Physical Distribution & Logistics Management*, Vol. 40, No. 4 (2010), pp. 277–97.

Mandal, Nitesh, "5 Ways to Improve Your Supply Chain Network Design," *Damco Blog*, February 5, 2018, http://blog.damco.com/2018/02/05/5-ways-improve-supply-chain-network-design/.

Mussomeli, Adam, Doug Gish, and Stephen Laaper, "The Rise of the Digital Supply Network," Deloitte University Press, 2016, https://www2.deloitte.com/content/dam/insights/us/articles/3465_Digital-supply-network/DUP_Digital-supply-network.pdf.

O'Reilly, Joseph, "Distribution Network Optimization: Repairing Cracked Supply Chain Design," *Inbound Logistics*, Vol. 31, No. 7 (July 2011), pp. 191–93.

O'Reilly, Joseph, "Supply Chain Integration: Building Innovative Solutions," *Inbound Logistics*, Vol. 32, No. 1 (January 2012), pp. 88–124.

Pesonen, Tuomo, and Timo Ala-Risku, "Supply Chain Transformation: The Complete Guide," *Relex Solutions Research Report*, 2018, https://www.relexsolutions.com/supply-chain-transformation/.

"7 Reasons Why You Should Optimize Your Supply chain," *Industry Week*, August 1, 2016, http://www.industryweek.com/cloud-computing/7-reasons-why-you-should-optimize-your-supply-chain.

Robinson, Eric, "2018 Guide to Supply Chain Network Design," *Kenco Blog*, January 30, 2018, https://blog.kencogroup.com/guide-to-supply-chain-network-design.

Tompkins, James, "The Challenge of Strategic Alignment," *SupplyChainBrain*, February 6, 2019, https://www.supplychainbrain.com/articles/29391-the-challenge-of-strategic-alignment.

"Total Supply Chain Management Cost," APQC, *Glossary*, undated, https://www.apqc.org/benchmarking-portal/glossary/term_description/10589/nojs.

"What is Supply Chain Network Design and Why is it Important?" *Tompkins International*, 2015, https://www.supplychain247.com/paper/what_is_supply_chain_network_design_why_is_it_important.

Questions and Problems

LO 14-1 1. Briefly overview some of the major structural and economic changes that are occurring that require companies to optimize their supply chain networks.

LO 14-3 2. Why is flowcharting or mapping the supply chain important? What are some of the major steps or stages of flowcharting?

LO 14-2 3. Are supply chains for services the same as for physical goods? Identify some of the similarities and differences.

LO 14-5 4. Discuss how technology can be used in supply chain network design.

LO 14-4 5. What is "lean management," and how does it apply to supply chain management?

LO 14-6 6. What is "enterprise resource planning (ERP)"? How is ERP used to plan, implement, and control the supply chain?

LO 14-4 7. What is "Six Sigma," and how has it been applied to supply chain management? How is it similar and dissimilar to lean management?

LO 14-7 8. Why are accurate and timely data important in supply chain networks?

Chapter

15

Collaboration,
Cooperation, and
Integration in the
Supply Chain: Talent,
Organizational,
Technology,
and Strategy Issues

Objectives of This Chapter

LO 15-1   To identify how effective supply chain organization can impact a firm and its supply chain partners.

LO 15-2   To describe various approaches to organizing and managing a supply chain.

LO 15-3   To explore the factors that can influence the effectiveness of a supply chain organization.

LO 15-4   To examine various ways of achieving collaboration and coordination in a supply chain.

LO 15-5   To identify attributes that can be used to measure supply chain effectiveness.

LO 15-6   To overview hiring, onboarding, and compensating supply chain personnel.

Introduction

So far in this textbook, we have covered a number of supply chain management functions and processes, such as customer satisfaction, transportation, warehousing, information systems, and others. In this chapter, we examine elements of SCM that cut across each of those functions or processes—talent, organizational structure, technology, and strategy.

Quality, cost reduction, value-added, and customer satisfaction have become the mantras of top management. Embracing these concepts is only the first step, however. A supply chain organization must also be able to implement the strategies, plans, and programs that will deliver acceptable levels of quality, cost reduction, value, and satisfaction to customers. Supply chain management and the people that "do supply chain tasks" play vital roles in that process. "Traditionally, what separated an average company from a great company has been technology. We're in the middle of a transformation. Today, what separates an average company from a great company is talent."[1]

In today's highly competitive and global marketplace, adaptation, continuous improvement, creativity, employee autonomy, and unity of purpose are replacing optimum design, consistency of operation, command and control, and economies of scale. Teams have taken the place of corporate hierarchies. Creativity and innovation have replaced capital as the most important resources of an organization.[2]

In a study of almost 200 organizations from countries around the world, several barriers to instituting a high-quality supply chain strategy were identified. Three of the top barriers (two of which were related to employees and/or organizational issues) included company culture, lack of leadership by senior management, and poor visibility along the supply chain. Additional barriers included CEO lack of support, inadequate management skills, lack of clear goals, lack of IT systems, inertia/lack of urgency, lack of resources, lack of KPIs and tracking, fear of change, regulatory issues, and too many conflicting priorities.[3] Thus, the roles of people, systems, and processes are especially important in strategic supply chain management, and each will be explored in this chapter.

Supply chain executives have always had to face a multitude of issues, including economic uncertainty, inflation, product and energy shortages, environmentalism, regulatory constraints, global competition, and rising customer demands and expectations. Supply chain management has become increasingly complex, and, hence, more difficult to manage successfully.

Importance of an Efficient and Effective Supply Chain Organization

Tom Peters, the customer service guru and author of several books on excellent customer-focused organizations, has said that the problems and challenges that organizations face do not lie primarily in the area of strategic decision making, but in systems, structure, mission, people, corporate culture, and reward structure. "In a lean culture, every step in

---

[1] Wade Burgess, VP Talent Solutions, LinkedIn, found in Karl Manrodt, "Catch and Release: The Talent Challenge," *DC Velocity*, February 28, 2015, http://blogs.dcvelocity.com/talking_talent/.

[2] See Daniel Burrus, "Creativity and Innovation: Your Keys to a Successful Organization," Burrus Research, October 23, 2013, https://www.burrus.com/2013/10/creativity-and-innovation-your-keys-to-a-successful-organization/.

[3] Richard Wilding, Alan Waller, Silvia Rossi, Clive Geldard, Steve Mayhew, Roberto Cigolini, and Clare Metcalfe, "Supply Chain Strategy in the Board Room," *Research Report* (Cranfield, UK: Cranfield University and Solving Efeso, June 2010). Also see Nelly Oelze, "Sustainable Supply Chain Management Implementation—Enablers and Barriers in the Textile Industry," *Sustainability*, Vol. 9 (2017), p. 1435, for discussion of barriers that impact implementing sustainable supply chain management.

every process must add value for the customer. If it doesn't add value, you strive to eliminate it."[4] In essence, each process or element of the supply chain is an important strategic resource and a corporate asset. The ways they fit together and interact to create a synergistic system are critical to the success of the individual firm and supply chains to which they belong. Thus, many organizations have reengineered their supply chains, essentially re-creating their organizations and systems, rather than making minor changes.[5]

The challenge of developing the "right" organization can be likened to the challenge facing the military general who has prepared a superb campaign strategy and must now design the army that will execute that strategy. Without the correct assembly of different battle units and their support services, the campaign cannot proceed, let alone achieve victory. By design, we mean not only the selection of the right organization structure, but also the design of the support, planning, and control systems that deliver the strategy via the organizational structure and the people.

In the next section, we will examine the importance of talent in supply chain organizations.

Talent Issues in Supply Chain Management

When asked what constitutes a company's assets, a talent management firm responded: "It's basically two things: people and everything else. Up to 70% of an organization's spend today is on its people assets."[6] For example, labor is typically 50 to 70% of the warehousing operating budget.[7] The importance of having the right people involved in any aspect of business has been echoed for decades, but employee success does not come without extensive planning, implementation, and control. For firms that are multinational, the challenges can be even greater, as illustrated in the nearby Exhibit.

Annually, the Institute for Corporate Productivity (i4cp) conducts surveys of companies of various sizes, representing a broad spectrum of industries, to determine the most important talent issues facing organizations. While differences exist among small, medium, and large companies, several factors are considered important by high-performance organizations, including succession planning; leadership development; talent management; performance management; knowledge retention; engagement; innovation and creativity; workforce planning; managing/coping with change; and coaching.[8]

What this illustrates is that organizations tend to focus their talent efforts on growing their employee base and improving their ability to hire and retain a high-quality workforce. What this also illustrates is the continued need to manage the firms' talent. We refer to these management tasks as obtain, train, and retain.[9] In the following sections, these issues will be addressed.

---

[4] "Lean Guiding Principles for the Supply Chain—Principle 1: People Involvement," *White Paper* (Miami, FL: Ryder Supply Chain Solutions, 2011), p. 1. For an interesting early approach to the concept of lean management, see Frederick Winslow Taylor, *The Principles of Scientific Management* (Norwood, MA: Plimpton Press, 1911).

[5] For a basic discussion of reengineering, see the classic texts Michael Hammer and James Champy, *Reengineering the Corporation: A Manifesto for Business Revolution* (New York: Harper Business, 1993); and James Champy, *Reengineering Management: The Mandate for New Leadership* (New York: Harper Business, 1995).

[6] Taleo Corporation, "What Constitutes a Company's Assets?," *TalentTalk Newsletter*, March 2011, http://www.taleo.com.

[7] Peerless Research Group, "Labor Management Strategies in the Warehouse," Kane is able, *Research Report*, August 2014, https://www.logisticsmgmt.com/wp_content/kane_labormgmt_wp_091014.pdf.

[8] Eric Davis, "The Critical Human Capital Issues of 2011," *Report*, Institute for Corporate Productivity, 2011, p. 3.

[9] Karl Manrodt, "Catch and Release: The Talent Challenge," *DC Velocity*, February 28, 2015, http://blogs.dcvelocity.com/talking_talent/.

Exhibit: Work and the Social Enterprise

When does work end and life begin?

In global organizations today, the worker is always on. Company-provided cell phones and laptops mean beaches, bars, and bedrooms are the new mobile office for some employees. Availability is expected and, in some cases, demanded.

Projects today are no longer limited to a single site, even a single country. It is not uncommon for executives and consultants on global teams to work on a project spanning Europe, Asia, South America, and North America. Try a team conference call with five different time zones!

And teams are everywhere. Deloitte's Global Human Capital Trends reports have noted a movement toward a "network of teams" that aims toward greater agility and collaboration. These teams are not only internally focused,

but externally as well. In essence, firms are moving from a purely business enterprise to a social enterprise.

As defined by Deloitte, "A social enterprise is an organization whose mission combines revenue growth and profit making with the need to respect and support its environment stakeholder network. This includes listening to, investing in, and actively managing the trends that are shaping today's world. It is an organization that shoulders its responsibility to be a good citizen (both inside and outside the organization), serving as a role model for its peers and promoting a high degree of collaboration at every level of the organization."

Source: Deloitte, "The Rise of the Social Enterprise," *2018 Deloitte Global Human Capital Trends* (2018).

Hiring and Rewarding Personnel

Just hire someone. That would be great, if it were possible. Who is that someone? What skills does he or she need to have today? What is he or she expected to do in the future? How will he or she help build our brand, and our social enterprise?

Making recruiting even more difficult is the low birth rate in most developed countries, well below the replacement rate of 2.1.[10] What this means is that firms have to attract talent from other countries (who are also experiencing these same issues), tap into the older workforce, or replace talent with technology. Interestingly, "McKinsey & Co. finds that between 75 million and 375 million workers globally will have to switch occupational categories and learn new skills in just the next 12 years because of automation and the transition to AI and robotics."[11]

There is a significant need for skilled talent to help manage today's complex supply chains. Yet, many in the younger generation are not considering a career in the field for three basic reasons. First, there is an image gap, in that most people don't know what logistics, transportation, or supply chain management is about. Some parents think their sons or daughters will be driving a truck upon graduation! The industry hasn't shown the complex, technology-based nature of today's supply chains where firms' strategy becomes reality. Second, awareness of the discipline is not widespread. Few universities offer degrees, concentrations, or certificates in the field, although the number is growing. Fewer still are the high schools that touch on supply chain management as a career. Finally, defining supply chain positions can be difficult. It spans transportation, distribution, IT, and procurement, just to name a few. The complexity of the mosaic allows multiple entry points and paths, and can seem overwhelming to a novice looking for a defined career path.[12]

---

[10] Madhura Chakrabarti, "Bersin by Deloitte High-impact People Analytics Research," *Industry Study*, 2017, http://www.visier.com/wp-content/uploads/2018/03/Bersin-by-Deloitte-High-Impact-People -Analytics-Research-Report.pdf.

[11] Kevin Oakes, "A Robot Got Fired Right Before Christmas. Another Committed Suicide. When Will the Madness End?," *The i4cp Productivity Blog*, January 2, 2018, https://www.i4cp.com/productivity-blog /a-robot-got-fired-right-before-christmas-another-committed-suicide-when-will-the-madness-end.

[12] Andy Kaye, "The Top Three Barriers Facing the Next Generation of Supply Chain Professionals," *Supply Management*, October 31, 2013, https://www.cips.org/supply-management/opinion/2013 /october/the-top-three-barriers-facing-the-next-generation-of-supply-chain-professionals/.

Getting a new hire is just the start. Keeping that individual is another matter altogether. A "Talent Trends LinkedIn survey revealed that globally, 45 percent of professional employees were contacted by a recruiter in the previous year, and a full 75 percent said they were open to talking to recruiters."[13] Monster.com has reported that 30 percent of new hires leave their companies within their first two years of employment, and the Society for Human Resources Management reported that turnover could be as much as 50 percent in the first 18 months after hire.[14]

McKinsey & Company reported that while most companies recognize that employees are their biggest source of competitive advantage, "most of them are . . . unprepared for the challenge of finding, motivating, and retaining capable workers."[15] The study postulated that the acquisition of employees into an organization was a strategic decision, and not just a tactical one. To illustrate, Tesco, a UK retailer, utilizes a segmentation strategy to recruit and hire employees.

Going from "Good to Great"

Author Jim Collins, in his bestseller *Good to Great*, identified a number of factors that move companies from being good to being great. He had an interesting comment regarding using rewards to motivate people. "*It's not how you compensate your executives, it's which executives you have to compensate in the first place.* If you have the right executives on the bus, they will do everything within their power to build a great company, not because of what they will 'get' for it, but because they simply cannot imagine settling for anything less."[16]

Rewards and incentives can be strong motivators to those people who are "on the bus" (see nearby Exhibit). Some research has shown that performance-related pay is positively associated with job satisfaction, organizational commitment, and trust in management.[17] In fact, incentive programs can increase performance in firms from 25 to 44 percent.[18] However, incentive programs are dependent on the organization having accurate performance metrics and data for determining the level of incentives.

Use of Nonfinancial Rewards

While salary and benefits are important ways that companies can motivate people,[19] there are many nonfinancial rewards that can be used. In fact, salary and benefits are typically not the most important factors that motivate supply chain professionals. Other considerations include career opportunities, training and development, corporate culture, management recognition, relationships with co-workers, flexible work schedules, dress codes, workplace amenities, educational incentives, and company location.[20]

---

[13] Michael Leimbach, "Employees Are Investors, Not Assets," *Chief Learning Officer*, April 27, 2016, http://www.clomedia.com/2016/04/27/employees-are-investors-not-assets/.

[14] "What Is Onboarding Exactly," *PeopleAdmin Talent Management*, November 10, 2017, https://www.peopleadmin.com/2013/01/what-is-onboarding-exactly/. Also see "What Is Employee Onboarding?," *Panopto*, February 6, 2018, https://www.panopto.com/blog/what-is-employee-onboarding/.

[15] Matthew Guthridge, Asmus B. Komm, and Emily Lawson, "Making Talent a Strategic Priority," *The McKinsey Quarterly*, January 2008, http://www.mckinseyquarterly.com.

[16] Jim Collins, *Good to Great* (New York: HarperCollins Publishers, 2001), p. 50; also see Tamara Chapman, "Building an Effective Supply Chain Team," *Inbound Logistics*, Vol. 34, No. 12 (December 2014), pp. 59–64.

[17] See Chidiebere Ogbonnaya, Kevin Daniels, and Karina Nielsen, "Research: How Incentive Pay Affects Employee Engagement, Satisfaction, and Trust," *Harvard Business Review*, March 15, 2017, https://hbr.org/2017/03/research-how-incentive-pay-affects-employee-engagement-satisfaction-and-trust; Nicole Fallon, "Want to Boost Employee Productivity? Offer an Incentive," *Business News Daily*, October 21, 2015, https://www.businessnewsdaily.com/8506-employee-productivity-incentives.html; and IW Staff, "Checked Out: Workers Disengaged 26% of Time," *Industry Week*, May 3, 2018, http://www.industryweek.com/talent/checked-out-workers-disengaged-26-time.

[18] "3 Employee Incentives That Actually Improve Workplace Performance," *Justworks*, April 10, 2017, https://justworks.com/blog/employee-incentives-improve-workplace-performance.

[19] For a discussion of how various hiring perks are used in various countries around the world, see Jena McGregor, "The Right Perks," *BusinessWeek*, January 28, 2008, pp. 42–43.

[20] See Patrick Hull, "Motivation Mystery: How to Keep Employees Productive," *Forbes*, May 23, 2013, https://www.forbes.com/sites/patrickhull/2013/05/23/motivation-mystery-how-to-keep-employees-productive/#590bd1593b20; and Brian Neese, "7 Low-Cost Workplace Incentives to Boost Morale," *Alvernia University Online*, August 4, 2017, https://online.alvernia.edu/workplace-incentives/.

Exhibit: Salary Survey of Logistics Executives

Although logistics is a subset of supply chain management, it is interesting to note that salaries for logistics employees continue to go up. Likewise, it can be assumed that salaries for supply chain executives would also be increasing.

In their annual survey of logistics salaries, *DC Velocity* magazine found that 86% of respondents were satisfied with their careers in the logistics profession, and 90% would recommend the profession to a young person entering the job market. What logistics and supply chain managers like most about their jobs includes "no two days are ever the same"; "constant variables creating unique challenges"; and "flexibility." Of course, these employees are also paid well, with managers averaging US$85,528, directors averaging $125,875, and vice pres-

idents $125,875. However, salaries do vary by industry sector, with transportation services being the highest at US$147,621 and furniture and fixtures being the lowest at $63,333. There are also regional differences with the highest average salaries in the West at US$132,916 and the lowest in the South at $102,826. College graduates in logistics or supply chain management who have some type of industry certification (e.g., APICS, CSCMP, or other), average US$120,350 and if they have a Master's degree, $175,817. With all of the above, employee experience, supply and demand issues, etc., impact the averages.

Source: Diane Rand, "Logistics Careers are 'Driving Satisfaction,'" *DC Velocity*, Vol. 16, No. 3 (March 2018), pp. 38–39.

For example, ways of obtaining maximum people involvement could include communicating with employees frequently and in a courteous manner; encouraging employees through various activities and programs; providing the necessary tools and materials for employees to do their jobs; training and cross-training of employees; and providing recognition programs that involve nonfinancial rewards.

Important also in retaining high-quality employees is providing personnel with internal mobility, that is, "promotion from within." "Historical studies have uncovered significant relationships between internal mobility and corporate performance . . . the top 10 percent of companies with 'High Performance Work Systems' had four times the amount of sales per employee . . . these companies filled over 60 percent of jobs from within versus 35 percent for the bottom 10 percent."[21]

The hiring of supply chain executives is also very important. In the complex world of SCM, executives must be boundary-spanners; that is, they must have a broader set of skills than ever before because they are managing and coordinating a multiplicity of tasks and processes.[22] The most competitive and strategic organizations are leading the way with respect to establishing a senior supply chain officer position in their firms. For example, in the consumer packaged goods sector, "companies are less likely than ever before to differentiate themselves from their competition based on product alone."[23] Having a well-designed and managed supply chain is a key factor in new product introductions and sustainable competitive advantage.

Supply chain executives who are hired from the outside or promoted from within should possess three major core competencies: (1) strong verbal intelligence (e.g., good cognitive processing speed and an ability to communicate information to others); (2) high need for

[21] "Talent Mobility," *White Paper*, Taleo Research, 2011, p. 3; also see Adam Foroughi, "3 Reasons Promoting from Within Is Better for Growing Your Business," *Entrepreneur*, May 25, 2016, https://www.entrepreneur.com/article/274346.

[22] "Introducing the Chief Supply Chain Officer," *EY Provider Post*, undated, https://www.ey.com/us/en/industries/united-states-sectors/health-care/provider-post--introducing-the-chief-supply-chain-officer; and Merrill Douglas, "The Rise of the Supply Chain Executive," *Inbound Logistics*, Vol. 31, No. 10 (October 2011), pp. 49–54.

[23] Alexa Cheater, "All Across Business, Chief Supply Chain Officers Are on the Rise," *Kinaxis*, November 27, 2015, https://blog.kinaxis.com/2015/11/all-across-business-chief-supply-chain-officers-are-on-the-rise/.

achievement (e.g., more innovative); and (3) high adaptability to a workplace where job and environmental complexity vary.[24]

Characteristics of Supply Chain Leaders

In a study of the characteristics of supply chain leaders and how they might differ from other senior executives, some key findings were developed: (1) Senior supply chain executives are more strategic and innovative, and can act independently when necessary; (2) they are more "objective and task" focused, and more willing to challenge the status quo; (3) they are confident in driving forward progress even though many are interpersonally reserved; (4) while these senior supply chain executives are already good leaders, there are developmental areas where they could improve (e.g., use of more open and informal approaches to building better relationships with others; considering deadlines are flexible rather than rigid; being deliberate, but going along on their own pace); and (5) they have extensive cross-functional and global experience and a deep understanding of their organization.[25]

Workforce Performance Standards

In addition to the senior supply chain executive, it is vital that all employees in the area be evaluated. Organizations should establish workforce performance standards in order to effectively manage all supply chain employees. Of course, this assumes that appropriate metrics have been developed and implemented. Manual or automated performance systems can be utilized, but automated approaches are usually preferred given the size and complexity of most workforce decisions. Some of the general characteristics of a performance system include:

- Uniform performance standards for all tasks and subtasks—productivity, efficiency, etc.
- Cost expectations related to labor budget and profit margins.
- Mechanisms to indicate when performance standards are not being achieved.
- Provision of corrective actions to the supply chain executive for situations where underperformance occurs.[26]

Exhibit: Employee Skills Demanded by Employers for Supply Chain Management Jobs

While there may be variations within companies and/or industries, the following list represents the most desirable skill sets that potential employees in supply chain management should possess:

Technical Skills

- Supply chain tech management
- Business analytics insight
- Understanding of KPIs and benchmarking
- Ability to utilize mobile technology
- Ability to adapt to new supply chain technology innovations

Soft Skills

- Excellent communication skills
- Good problem-solving skills
- Friendly personality
- Cultural fit with organization
- Breadth and depth of analytical skills
- Education level (including certifications)

Source: "Five Key Tech Skills That Every Supply Chain Pro Needs," *Ajilon*, February 15, 2017, http://blog.ajilon.com/supply-chain-2/skills-supply-chain-pro-needs/; and "2017 Marketing Hiring Trends: An In-depth Report on Factors Shaping Demand for Marketing and Creative Talent," McKinsey Marketing Partners, *Report*, 2017, p. 19.

[24] R. Glenn Richey, Mert Tokman, and Anthony R. Wheeler, "Supply Chain Manager Selection Methodology: Empirical Test and Suggested Application," *Journal of Business Logistics*, Vol. 27, No. 2 (2006), pp. 163–190.
[25] Peter L. O'Brien and Marieke van der Drift, "Inside the Mind of the Chief Supply Chain Officer," Russell Reynolds Associates, October 23, 2017, http://www.russellreynolds.com/insights/thought-leadership/inside-the-mind-of-the-chief-supply-chain-officer.
[26] "Enhancing 'The Perfect Order' in Distribution and Logistics," *White Paper*, Kronos Inc., 2010; and Chris Brabic, "What Makes a Perfect Order?," *MPO—Customer Chain Control*, October 19, 2017, https://blog.mp-objects.com/what-makes-the-perfect-order.

The ultimate aim of workforce performance standards is to optimize human capital in the organization, but it is only one aspect of HR. Additionally, firms must manage employee development, train employees, and reward, recognize, and motivate employees.

In supply chain management, Six Sigma/lean, just-in-time, and many other strategies, programs, or processes, the key ingredient is always "people." For example, in supply chain management, people coordinate, collaborate, and assist in the integration of companies, teams, and processes. In lean management, it is the people that identify waste, eliminate its causes, and make the necessary improvements.[27] In just-in-time, it is the people who get the job done in a quick and efficient manner so that items arrive on time at their customer's location.

Onboarding

The training of employees, referred to as "onboarding," is a key ingredient of successful organizations. Employee training has been shown to improve individual performance, such as morale, company loyalty, efficiency, and effectiveness. Organizations with comprehensive training programs tend to provide higher customer service levels, retain employees for longer periods, and achieve greater overall profitability; those that do not tend to perform more poorly (see Exhibit).

In a recent study of onboarding practices of primarily U.S.-based companies, it was found that organizations do the following:

- 75% of companies have a formal onboarding program.
- 45% of companies begin onboarding prior to the new employee reporting to work.
- 33% of firms have an onboarding program for employees who change jobs or are promoted.
- 66% do exit interviews when an employee leaves the company.
- The most common onboarding metrics include employee turnover/retention (71%) and performance measures (63%).[28]

Exhibit: Reasons That Performance Objectives Are Not Met by Employees

- **They don't know what is expected of them.** If they don't know what is considered a job well done, they will be unlikely to meet expectations.
- **They don't know how.** Poor training is the main reason employees lack the know-how to perform their jobs.
- **They can't do the job.** This can result from poorly defined jobs or procedures/methods that do not accurately reflect the best way to do the job.
- **There are barriers beyond the employee's control.** This can be due to factors such as a lack of the proper equipment, the work environment not being established properly, or inventory or information not being available when needed.
- **They don't want to do the job.** In any company there are employees who simply don't want to do the job.

Source: Andrew Jensen, "Holding Employees Accountable for Performance," Sozo Firm Inc., April 2, 2018, https://www.andrewjensen.net/holding-employees-accountable-for-performance/.

---

[27] For illustrations of how people are involved in lean management, see "Lean Guiding Principles for the Supply Chain, Principle 1: People Involvement," *White Paper*, Ryder Supply Chain Solutions, September 15, 2011; and Chuck Intrieri, "9 Steps to Establish the Lean Supply Chain: A System of Interconnected & Interdependent Partners," *Cerasis*, May 6, 2015, http://cerasis.com/2015/05/06/lean-supply-chain/.

[28] "2017 Strategic Onboarding Survey: How to Activate New Employees," HR Daily Advisor, *Research Report*, August 8, 2017, https://www.silkroad.com/blog/new-2017-strategic-onboarding-report/. Also see Deepak Somaya and Ian O. Williamson, "Rethinking the 'War for Talent,'" *MIT Sloan Management Review*, Vol. 49, No. 4 (Summer 2008), p. 29.

Strategic Onboarding Occurring in Organizations

In best-practice organizations, employee training efforts include several key elements, including:

- Required competencies/skills are identified and documented for each position.
- Web-based training supports other training programs.
- Training extends beyond the organization to other members of the supply chain.
- Education and development are progressive, that is, they change along with the career development of the employee.
- Measures are in place to determine training effectiveness.
- Training outcomes are correlated with performance reviews.[29]

Best-in-class organizations tend to significantly outperform the average firm in several areas related to employee education and training. They are much more likely to train employees across multiple roles (i.e., cross-training), establish an executive who is specifically accountable for quality training, assign mentors or coaches for new employees, and provide a broad array of training materials for employees at all stages of their development.[30]

In many organizations, web-based training is being utilized to a large degree. Incorporating the Internet into education and training involves both stand-alone supply chain–related coursework and the integration of the technology into other, more traditional media.

Knowledge Management Defined

Related to training is the issue of retaining knowledge of employees who retire or leave a company. While most organizations collect formal or codified knowledge, such as documents, contracts, manuals, etc., few companies retain informal or uncodified knowledge. This kind of knowledge is referred to as "tacit knowledge" and "is what you know or believe from experience. It can be found in interactions with employees and customers. Tacit knowledge is hard to catalog, highly experiential, difficult to document, and ephemeral. It is also the basis for judgment and informed action."[31] Thus, it is important to capture the knowledge that people in the organization have and to not lose it if they leave the firm. A formal process to capture this knowledge is termed *knowledge management* and is defined as "a systematic effort to enable information and knowledge to grow, flow, and create value. The discipline is about creating and managing the processes to get the right knowledge to the right people at the right time and help people share and act on information in order to improve organizational performance."[32]

In sum, it is in the best interests of organizations to retain their workforce once they have been properly hired and trained, and if they do leave, retain their knowledge in some way so that new employees are able to assimilate that knowledge. Organizational and supply chain performance will be optimized when the right people are doing the right things in the right way.

Supply Chain Structures

To understand the way that various departments and groups within an organization interact and how organizations across the supply chain relate to one another, it is helpful to understand how business organizations have developed. A brief overview of this historical development will help understand current and future supply chain environments.

---

[29] Supply Chain Visions, *Supply Chain Management Process Standards*, 2nd ed. (Lombard, IL: Council of Supply Chain Management Professionals, 2009), pp. 106–107. For some interesting anecdotal examples of onboarding mistakes and some creative approaches taken by companies, see Dori Meinert, "Onboarding Mistakes to Avoid and Some Creative Ideas to Adopt," Society for Human Resource Management, June 1, 2016, https://www.shrm.org/hr-today/news/hr-magazine/0616/pages/onboarding-mistakes-to-avoid-and-some-creative-ideas-to-adopt.aspx.

[30] Bob Heaney, "Labor Management," *White Paper*, Aberdeen Group, March 2010, pp. 10–13.

[31] Carla O'Dell and Cindy Hubert, *The New Edge in Knowledge: How Knowledge Management Is Changing the Way We Do Business* (Hoboken, NJ: John Wiley & Sons, 2011), p. 3.

[32] Ibid., p. 2.

Historical Development of Business Structures

Around the time of the founding of the United States, companies tended to be "one-person" operations. This was also true in Europe and Asia, occurring much earlier in history. The companies were generally small and specialized, serving a localized region. One or a few people controlled the entire operation.

In the 19th century, as the industrial revolution was taking place in the U.S. and Europe, it became increasingly difficult for one or a few people to successfully manage all of an organization's operations. Companies were becoming too large for one person to manage. Therefore, they began to hire people who specialized in managing specific functions, such as manufacturing, sales, distribution, and accounting. It was believed that this created greater levels of efficiency and effectiveness.

Functional Specialization

By the beginning of 20th century, functional specialization was no longer sufficient for effective management, due primarily to increased corporate growth and product/service diversification. Large organizations created divisions or business units, organized vertically around similar product/service offerings. Employees became specialized in terms of both function and product. Governmental organizations, including the military infrastructure, also expanded tremendously.

In some organizations, functions that did not directly affect the organization's product or service offerings and that cut across divisional boundaries were left at a corporate level, supporting various divisions of the company. This was common for functions such as human resources, accounts payable, purchasing, and financial reporting. There was no reporting relationship between "line" divisional employees and "staff" or corporate employees.

By the 1950s, some large organizations such as Pillsbury Company realized that the division structure was not optimal. It did not provide linkages among line people in various division and corporate positions, so that the synergies of being part of a large organization were being lost. To combat this problem, many organizations began to implement other organizational forms.

4PL Defined

As the 21st century unfolds, there continue to be discussions about optimal organizational forms. With the continued development of supply chain management and the need to manage not only activities and processes within firms, but also between firms, there will be an increasing need to adapt organizational structures to match the ever-expanding needs of the supply chain and the customers they serve. Outsourcing will be an important element in effective supply chain management. To a greater extent, organizations will hire external companies (e.g., third parties) to perform various types of activities, including manufacturing, logistics, distribution, billing, sales, and marketing. In some instances, a 4PL might be used. "A 4PL sits on top of . . . networks and acts as the overarching entity. It identifies what nodes and networks should look like and who should manage them, then establishes the processes and governance for each supply chain node."[33]

According to the Council of Supply Chain Management Professionals (CSCMP), a 4PL company differs from a 3PL company in the following ways:[34]

- 4PL organization is often a separate entity established as a joint venture or long-term contract between a primary client and one or more partners;
- 4PL organization acts as a single interface between the client and multiple logistics service providers;

[33] Joseph O'Reilly, "4PLs Take Control," *Inbound Logistics*, Vol. 31, No. 1 (January 2011), p. 154; and "What Is the Difference between 3PL and 4PL?," ADLI Logistics, May 3, 2017, http://adlilogistics.com/blog/2017/03/03/difference-3pl-vs-4pl/.

[34] Kate Vitasek, "Supply Chain Management Definitions and Glossary," August 2013, https://cscmp.org.

Exhibit: Reasons Why You Might Need a 4PL

Carl Fowler, a Senior Director of Operations in Menlo Logistics' 4PL practice, has identified four reasons why organizations might want to utilize the services of a 4PL.

1. **Higher order-to-delivery cycle times, and order-to-cash cycles that are increasing in length.** Order-to-cash cycles affect other areas of the company and can be one big area where improvement can free up cash for important enterprise initiatives such as research and development.

2. **The need and demand for IT resources.** Lack of IT infrastructure to support an expanding global supply chain can inhibit growth. And in many companies, supply chain operations' IT investment is a low priority.

3. **Global growth, more inventory in more places, and a shifting revenue recognition point.** Companies often lack the ability to generate substantive supply chain performance improvement on their own. There's lack of leverage in the supply chain.

4. **Global expansion.** Companies wanting to get into markets they have not been in before need flexible, effective supply chain processes to be successful. If you struggle with your supply chain in the United States, you will really struggle when you try to go global.

Sources: Carl Fowler, Menlo Logistics, as cited in Joseph O'Reilly, "4PLs Take Control," *Inbound Logistics*, Vol. 31, No. 1 (January 15, 2011), http://www.inboundlogistics.com/cms/article/4pls-take-control/; and Jon Slangerup, "Why the Rise of the 4PL Is Good News for Your Business," *Supply & Demand Chain Executive*, October 16, 2017, https://www.sdcexec.com/warehousing/article/12374698/why-the-rise-of-the-4pl-is-good-news-for-your-business.

- All aspects (ideally) of the client's supply chain are managed by the 4PL organization; and
- It is possible for a major third-party logistics provider to form a 4PL organization within its existing structure.

Internally, organizations can also adapt their structures to better meet the needs of their customers, employees, and other stakeholders. For example, tasks and responsibilities can be distributed to many individuals (referred to as a "polyarchy" system) or to a single individual.[35] Whatever the structure chosen by the organization, it is imperative that the structure fosters agility, innovation, and market adaptation.

Agile organizations typically can be identified by five trademarks, including:[36]

- **Strategy:** co-creating value with, and for, all stakeholders.
- **Structure:** network of empowered teams that are highly engaged.
- **Process:** rapid decision and learning cycles.
- **People:** effective leaders that ignite passion in employees.
- **Technology:** technology is at the core of every aspect of the organization.

In an agile organization, coordination of the various supply chain activities can be achieved in several ways. The basic systems can be generally structured utilizing a combination of the following:

- Strategic versus operational
- Centralized versus decentralized

Strategic versus operational refers to the level at which supply chain activities are positioned within and across firms. Strategically, it is important to determine SCM's position in the corporate hierarchy relative to other activities, such as marketing, manufacturing, and

---

[35] For a discussion of polyarchy and other organization forms, see Teppo Felin and Thomas C. Powell, "Designing Organizations for Dynamic Capabilities," *California Management Review*, Vol. 58, No. 3 (2016), pp. 78–96.

[36] Wouter Aghina, Aaron De Smet, Gerald Lackey, Michael Lurie, and Monica Murarka, "The Five Trademarks of Agile Organizations," *McKinsey & Company Report*, January 2018, https://www.mckinsey.com/business-functions/organization/our-insights/the-five-trademarks-of-agile-organizations.

finance/accounting. Equally important, however, is the operational structure of the various supply chain activities under the senior supply chain executive.

Centralized management reflects a system in which supply chain activities are administered centrally. Centrally programming activities, such as order processing, traffic or inventory control, demand forecasting, and others, can result in significant cost savings due to synergies and economies of scale. On the other hand, decentralization of activities can be effective for some firms with diverse products or markets. With the use of technological advancements in computer and information systems, high levels of customer service can be delivered with either a centralized or decentralized network.

Matrix Management   Other organizational approaches are possible. A good example is the use of a matrix management structure (see Figure 15.1). Supply chain management is cross-functional and therefore requires a different organizational structure, not the "functional silo" approach.

Historically, some firms utilized a matrix management approach, including ABB Asea Brown Boveri Ltd. (European company specializing in electrical engineering and equipment), Caterpillar (earthmoving equipment), Dow Chemical (chemicals), and Royal Dutch/Shell Group (petroleum, gas, and chemicals). The matrix management approach requires the coordination of activities across unit lines in the organization. In the same way, managing a supply chain involves coordination of activities across many organizations. Thus, the complexities of coordination are difficult to master.

For example, when there are multiple reporting responsibilities, as is common in matrix organizations, problems may arise due to conflicts that result from people reporting to multiple managers who may have different goals and objectives.

It has been suggested by some individuals involved in supply chain management that a team structure might be more appropriate for managing the complexities of a supply chain. A team structure typically involves a small group of people with complementary skills, common goals, mutual accountability, and the resources and empowerment to achieve their goals. Thus, it is vital that significant coordination, collaboration, and cooperation be achieved within and between supply chain members.

A review of the multitude of organizational types found in supply chains reveals a variety of structural forms. Which form, however, is optimal for a specific supply chain? That is an

FIGURE 15.1
Matrix Organization Structure

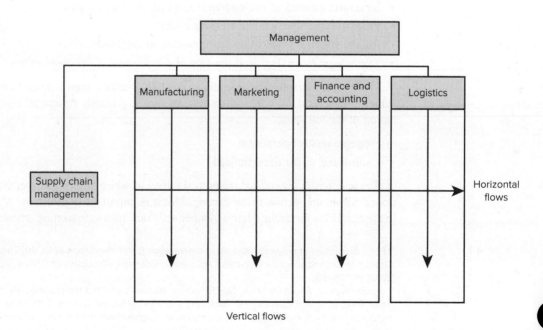

immensely difficult question to answer. Rather than examining organizational structures of several companies and speculating about "ideal" or "optimal" systems, we need to employ some empirical measures to correlate structure and efficiency/productivity. Obviously, the optimal system for a supply chain is one that maximizes its efficiency and effectiveness.

Keiretsu Structures

Keiretsu is a "Japanese term describing a group of affiliated corporations with broad power and reach."[37] Much like a supply chain, a keiretsu network provides financial, organizational, legal, and logistical support for its companies.[38] Add to those activities all of the activities included within supply chain management, and you have a supply chain.

Types of Keiretsus　　There are two types of keiretsus: horizontal and vertical. A horizontal keiretsu "consists of a group of interlocking companies, typically clustered about a lead manufacturer, a main bank, and a trading company, and overseen by a presidents' council consisting of the presidents of the major group companies. Horizontal collaboration in the supply chain is characterized by manufacturers sharing supply chain assets for mutual benefit. This can include sharing distribution centers, combining truckloads or collaborating on manufacturing. The important distinction is that horizontal collaboration is co-operation across rather than along supply chains (shipper + 3PL + retailer, for example) and can even be between direct competitors."[39]

By contrast, a vertical keiretsu consists of a large manufacturing company surrounded by numerous small and subservient suppliers and distributors that keep the operations running smoothly.[40] While these approaches usually are implemented separately and distinct from one another, it would appear that a combination of both would result in a realistic attempt to organize a supply chain.

For example, the use of a president's council could be advantageous in both types of keiretsus inasmuch as collaboration and coordination would likely be increased with such a group. Figure 15.2 illustrates what a typical vertical keiretsu looks like,[41] but with the

FIGURE 15.2
A Modified Vertical Keiretsu for Supply Chain Management Involving a Manufacturer

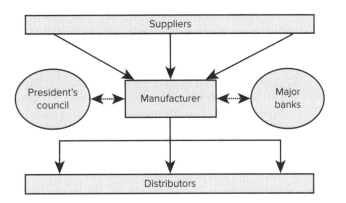

---

[37] "Keiretsu Definition," *Keiretsu Forum*, 2018, http://www.keiretsuforum.com/; and Matt Jancer, "How Eight Conglomerates Dominate Japanese Industry," *Smithsonian.com*, September 7, 2016, https://www.smithsonianmag.com/innovation/how-eight-conglomerates-dominate-japanese-industry-180960356/.

[38] Richard M. Steers and Luciara Nardon, *Managing in the Global Economy* (Armonk, NY: M. E. Sharpe, 2006), p. 185.

[39] McKinley Muir, "North American Horizontal Collaboration in the Supply Chain Report," eyefortransport, *White Paper*, 2011, p. 4. For a perspective on horizontal collaboration in Europe, see McKinley Muir, "European Supply Chain Horizontal Collaboration," eyefortransport, *White Paper*, December 2010. Both reports can be accessed at http://www.eft.com.

[40] Steers and Nardon, *Managing in the Global Economy*, pp. 185–186.

[41] Ibid., especially pp. 185–189.

addition of a president's council. Also, the figure represents only a portion of the supply chain. Much like the SCOR Model that only includes first- and second-tier suppliers, this illustration represents a portion, albeit large, of a typical supply chain where a manufacturer is the dominant member.

An important consideration in a keiretsu or any other supply chain structure is that the structure is only a facilitator to efficient and effective supply chain management. Organizations can have similar structures for organizing supply chain management but have much different levels of performance. Good structures facilitate the implementation of supply chain networks; they do not guarantee success. As with all business activities, success requires the right people, systems, and strategies.

Decision-Making Strategies in Organizing for SCM

As supply chain executives face new challenges in the decades ahead, it will become even more important that systems operate more efficiently and effectively. In the face of higher costs of operation and increasing pressures from customers for better service, organizations must change to meet the challenge. An understanding of the factors that make organizations effective and knowledge of how these factors interrelate are the first steps toward developing the optimal supply chain network.

Mission Statements

In general, mission statements provide the foundation or basis from which a company develops strategies, plans, and tactics. The mission statement defines the basic purpose of an organization and identifies the parameters under which it will operate.

As corporate mission statements serve to provide the starting point for developing corporate goals and objectives, so too will supply chain mission statements provide direction for developing supply chain strategies. When combined with a specific set of performance goals and measurement systems, the supply chain mission statement can help to eliminate organizational conflicts and provide direction to personnel.

The components of a corporate mission statement or a supply chain mission statement will be similar. They will vary in their specific content because the supply chain mission statement is only one element of a firm's total corporate mission, but they will both contain similar components. Typically, mission statements will focus on several key elements (see Table 15.1).

Components of a Supply Chain Mission Statement

Organizations need a clear statement of purpose in order to develop some optimal combination of supply chain activities that must be performed in the day-to-day operations of the enterprise. In sum, the mission statement is an important document to guide the planning, implementation, and control of an organization's supply chain activities.

TABLE 15.1
Components of a Supply Chain Mission Statement

Source: Adapted from Maha Muzumdar, "6 Strategies for Better Supply Chain Management in the Current Economy," *Oracle Supply Chain Management Blog*, July 12, 2017, originally authored by Stephen Slade in July 2010, https://blogs.oracle.com/scm/5-strategies-for-better-supply-chain-management-in-the-current-economy.

- Utilize a demand-driven planning and business operating model based on real-time demand.
- Build an adaptive and agile supply chain with rapid planning and integrated execution.
- Optimize product designs and management for supply, manufacturing, and sustainability, so as to speed up profitable innovation.
- Align supply chain and business goals by integrating sales and operations planning with corporate business planning.
- Include sustainability components into supply chain operations.
- Ensure a reliable and predictable supply of parts, components, work-in-process, and finished goods.

Factors Impacting the Effectiveness of a Supply Chain Organization

Many factors can influence the effectiveness of a supply chain organization. These factors are timeless in that they have historically determined how well an organization accomplishes its goals and objectives. There is no reason to believe that they would not also be relevant in today's supply chain environment. In general, the factors contributing to organizational effectiveness can be summarized as (1) organizational characteristics, (2) environmental characteristics, (3) employee characteristics, and (4) managerial policies and practices.[42]

Organizational Characteristics

Structure and technology are the major components of a firm's organizational characteristics. *Structure* refers to the relationships that exist between various functional areas—interfunctional (marketing, finance, operations, manufacturing, logistics) or intrafunctional (warehousing, traffic, purchasing, customer service). The relationships are most often represented by a company's organization chart. Examples of structural variables are decentralization, specialization, formalization, span of control, organization size, and work-unit size. *Technology* refers to how an organization transforms raw inputs into finished outputs.

Environmental Characteristics

The effectiveness of the organization is influenced by factors internal and external to the firm. Internal factors, which are basically controllable by the supply chain executive, are known as *organizational climate*.[43] Sometimes this is referred to as *corporate culture*.[44]

Organizational climate is related to organizational effectiveness. This is particularly evident when effectiveness is measured on an individual level (e.g., job attitudes, performance, satisfaction, involvement).

External factors, sometimes referred to as uncontrollable elements, include the political and legal, economic, cultural and social, and competitive environments.

Employee Characteristics

The keys to effective organizations are the employees who "fill the boxes" on the organization chart. The ability of individuals to carry out their respective job responsibilities ultimately determines the overall effectiveness of any organization.

All employees have varying outlooks, goals, needs, and abilities. These differences can cause people to behave differently, even when they are in the same work environment. These differences can have a direct bearing on two important organizational processes that impact organizational effectiveness: *organizational attachment*, or the extent to which employees identify with their employer; and *job performance*. Without attachment and performance, effectiveness becomes all but impossible to achieve.

Managerial Policies and Practices

Policies at the macro (entire company) level determine the overall goal structure of the organization. This would be the level where a firm's supply chain mission statement would be developed. Policies at the micro (department or unit) level influence the individual goals of the various corporate functions, such as warehousing, traffic, order processing, and customer service. Macro and micro policies in turn affect the procedures and practices of the organization. The planning, coordinating, and facilitating of goal-directed activities—which

---

[42] See Steers and Nardon, *Managing in the Global Economy*.

[43] "What Is Organizational Climate?," ERC, *HR Insights*, August 13, 2014, https://www.yourerc.com/blog/post/What-is-Organizational-Climate.aspx.

[44] For a discussion of the importance of culture on an organization, see Wendy D. Pigorsch, Ron Cain, Ken Porter, Ruth Lund, and Chelle Stringer, "Shine a Light on Company Culture," *WERCSheet*, May–June 2014, pp. 6–10.

determine organizational effectiveness—depend on the policies and practices adopted by the firm at the macro and micro levels.

An effective organization must also exhibit stability and continuity. It must find a unique offering that can be delivered to the market and stick with it to provide customer value. The use of technology can assist organizations in providing this value to customers through improved collaboration and coordination within the supply chain.

Collaboration and Integration through Technology

Certainly, all areas of business, including supply chain management, have been significantly impacted by technological developments. In fact, some of the greatest supply chain efficiencies have come from the implementation of technologies within various activities and processes of supply chain management. However, "two decades after EDI started to become popular, and more than 10 years after the explosion of web-based technologies, many companies still have limited connectivity to the majority of their trading partners."[45]

In the following paragraphs, some of the more recent technological innovations that have been applied within supply chain management are briefly discussed.

Information Systems

In the 1970s, information technology really began to explode in organizations. This gave them the ability to better monitor transaction-intensive activities such as demand forecasting, ordering, transportation, and the storage of goods and materials. The availability of more and better information, coupled with the development of sophisticated computer hardware and software, increased the ability of executives to manage material and information flows, optimize logistics systems, and more effectively measure performance levels. Systems such as materials requirements planning (MRP, MRP II), distribution resource planning (DRP, DRP II), and just-in-time (JIT, JIT II) developed rapidly during the 1970s and 1980s, allowing organizations to link many logistics and supply chain–related activities, from order processing to inventory management, ordering from the supplier, forecasting, and production scheduling.

E-commerce

Advances in electronic commerce (e.g., Internet, e-mail, cloud computing) enabled organizations to better manage their supply chains and were instrumental in allowing them to attain national and/or global market presence. In combination with an increased emphasis on customer satisfaction, quality, and lean manufacturing, plus growing recognition of the systems approach and total cost concept, and the realization that supply chain management could be used as a strategic competitive weapon, organizations were able to better develop fully integrated supply chains.

As the new millennium began, organizations increased their use of information technology to integrate their supply chains. Firms found that information systems could provide substantial benefits if implemented properly, including such benefits as the following:

Benefits of Implementing Information Technology in the Supply Chain

- Provided higher levels of overall efficiency and effectiveness than were possible with logistics management systems alone.

- Enabled companies to identify optimal inventory levels and inventory turnover rates, thus reducing needed warehouse space.

---

[45] See "The Growing Imperative for 100% Trading Partner Connectivity," *Supply Chain Executive Brief, Chief Supply Chain Officer Insights*, undated, p. 1; Luis Benavides, Verda De Eskinazis, and Daniel Swan, "Six Steps to Successful Supply Chain Collaboration," *CSCMP's Supply Chain Quarterly*, June 22, 2012, http://www.supplychainquarterly.com/topics/Strategy/20120622-six-steps-to-successful-supply-chain-collaboration/; and "The 7 Habits of Highly Effective Supply Chain Collaborators," *CSCMP's Supply Chain Quarterly*, April 6, 2018, http://www.supplychainquarterly.com/news/20180404-the-7-habits-of-highly-effective-supply-chain-collaborators/.

- Led to higher-quality products, enhanced productivity, more efficient use of manufacturing equipment, less space, and increased logistics flexibility.
- Provided economies of scale in sourcing and procurement through the formation of more long-term strategic alliances and partnerships with vendors and suppliers.
- Reduced time and improved consistency in the customer order cycle.
- Enhanced an organization's competitive position by providing sustainable advantages in cost control and customer satisfaction levels.[46]

However, it should be noted that many organizations have not yet developed systems that allow for better collaboration, visibility, and integration within their supply chains. In fact, for the majority of firms, collaboration initiatives involving the use of the newest information systems have occurred only within the last decade.[47]

Compared to the use of information systems prior to the development of supply chain management, information technologies and systems must be integrated across multiple firms that are members of the supply chain, as opposed to being integrated only within a single firm. Common databases, metrics, and other information-related items are needed by all organizations within the supply chain. When all firms in the supply chain have access to the same information and are aware of the goals and objectives of their supply chain partners, significant cost and service advantages are possible.

Three Technologies Impacting Supply Chain Management

Three of the most significant technologies that will impact supply chain management are mobile computing devices, analytics software, and social media.[48] The use of smartphones and tablet computers is increasing and allows supply chain executives to access data anywhere and anytime, thus allowing them maximum flexibility. Analytics software allows executives to analyze large amounts of data for the purposes of developing patterns and changes within the supply chain. Social media, such as Facebook, Twitter, and LinkedIn, allow people to more easily talk to one another, thus allowing for more collaboration and coordination.

While more and more organizations are recognizing the importance of implementing the newest information technologies into their business, they also know that such efforts can be very costly in terms of money, people, and time. In some instances, costs associated with supply chain information systems can be minimized through the use of 4PLs or cloud technology. The advantages of interconnected databases and information systems is especially evident in the use of cloud computing.

Cloud Technology

Some organizations have shifted to *cloud computing* in an attempt to become leaner and to improve service levels to customers. Instead of purchasing the hardware and software to operate and manage their supply chains, they are choosing to access the technologies they need through the Internet. In this way, the organization minimizes its assets while still being able to manage its supply chain. Basically, cloud computing is the IT equivalent of a third-party logistics service provider that manages physical distribution for a company.[49]

---

[46] Ram Narasimhan and Soo Wook Kim, "Information System Utilization Strategy for Supply Chain Integration," *Journal of Business Logistics*, Vol. 22, No. 2 (2001), p. 51.

[47] See Douglas M. Lambert and Matias G. Enz, "Co-creating Value: The Next Level of Customer-Supplier Relationships," *CSCMP's Supply Chain Quarterly*, Vol. 9, No. 3 (2015), pp. 22–28; and Sahir Anand and Nari Viswanathan, "State of Retail Supply Chain Collaboration, Visibility and Integration 2011," Aberdeen Group, *White Paper*, April 2011, p. 11.

[48] James A. Cooke, "Three Technologies That Will Change the Logistics Game," *DC Velocity Techwatch*, May 16, 2011, http://www.dcvelocity.com.

[49] See "WMS in the Cloud—Real-World Business Option, or Just Fluff?," *Special Report*, HighJump Software, 2010, p. 2, http://www.highjump.com; also see "The Cloud Supply Chain Data Network," *White Paper*, GT Nexus, 2010, http://www.gtnexus.com.

Cloud computing, which is similar to, yet an expanded version of, software-as-a-service (SaaS),[50] is an Internet service that can be accessed by a customer's own computer, rather than having the hardware and software at the customer's location. In essence, cloud computing is where someone else (i.e., vendor) hosts the software application and hardware infrastructure for you on demand. The vendor is the technology expert; the firm merely utilizes the technology of a third party.[51] Eliminating the need to install and run the application on the customer's own computer minimizes the customer's burden of software maintenance, ongoing operation, and support. This frequently takes the form of web-based tools or applications that users can access and use through a web browser as if it was a program installed locally on their own computer.[52] The National Institute of Standards and Technology (NIST) has defined cloud computing this way:

Cloud Computing Defined

"Cloud computing is a model for enabling convenient, on-demand network access to a shared pool of configurable computing resources (e.g., networks, servers, storage, applications, and services) that can be rapidly provisioned and released with minimal management effort or service provider interaction."[53]

The use of cloud computing is invaluable when firms are dealing with many suppliers or vendors because each organization can communicate through the "cloud" (see Figure 15.3). The cloud is also useful for sourcing various supply chain applications such as transportation planning, warehouse management systems, supply chain performance, and a number of other activities and processes. For example, the Department of Defense (DoD) utilizes cloud technology to manage a portion of its transportation network, including LTL, truckload,

FIGURE 15.3
Application of Cloud Technology by Best-in-Class Firms

Source: Nari Viswanathan, "Enabling Supply Chain Visibility and Collaboration in the Cloud," Aberdeen Group, *White Paper*, November 2010, p. 13. Also see Nick Castellina, "Cloud BPM: Platform for Continuous Improvement," Aberdeen Group, *Research Report*, January 2016, http://v1.aberdeen.com/launch/report/research_report/11772-RR-BPM-cloud-saas.asp.

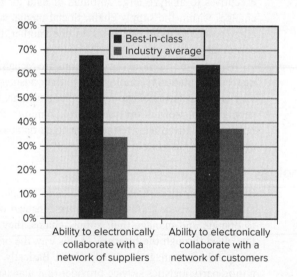

50 Amy Roach Partridge, "High Tech: The Rise of SaaS and the Cloud," *Inbound Logistics*, Vol. 31, No. 4 (April 2011), p. 44.
51 Ibid.
52 See Eric Knorr, "What Is Cloud Computing? Everything You Need to Know Now," *InfoWorld*, July 10, 2017, https://www.infoworld.com/article/2683784/cloud-computing/what-is-cloud-computing.html; and Anthony Clervi, "Cloud Computing Is Transforming Supply Chain Management," *Supply & Demand Chain Executive*, October 12, 2015, https://www.sdcexec.com/sourcing-procurement/article/12125647/cloud-computing-is-transforming-supply-chain-management.
53 Peter Mell and Timothy Grance, *The NIST Definition of Cloud Computing*, Special Publication 800-145 (U.S. Department of Commerce, National Institute of Standards and Technology, September 2011), https://nvlpubs.nist.gov/nistpubs/Legacy/SP/nistspecialpublication800-145.pdf.

Technology: Cloud Computing

©Prasit photo/Getty Images

Many experts believe that organizations, especially small- and medium-sized companies, will utilize cloud computing rather than invest in more expensive in-house hardware and software. Often referred to as software-as-a-service (SaaS), cloud computing is expected to significantly grow in usage in the future. Some of the applications of cloud computing in supply chain management include the following:

• Quality aspects of supply chain management can be managed in real time.

• Using cloud-based analytics, manufacturing cycle times can be managed more effectively.

• Equipment performance and maintenance can be managed proactively.

• Record keeping for compliance purposes can be accomplished in the cloud.

• Supply chain visibility can be enhanced as real-time tracking and tracings occur with cloud-based applications.

• Cloud computing allows for integration of various databases, applications, and systems using Application Programming Interfaces (APIs).

• Cloud-based WMS and ERP systems are less costly and just as effective as company-owned systems.

• Using an integrated cloud-based system allows organizations to reduce order cycle times.

• Cloud-based applications are integrating all aspects of new product development that improves the likelihood of new products being successful.

• Cloud computing allows for tracking perfect order performance metrics in complex manufacturing systems.

Source: Adapted from Louis Columbus, "10 Ways Cloud Computing Is Revolutionizing Supply Chain Management," *SelectHub*, December 15, 2017, https://selecthub.com/supply-chain-management/10-ways-cloud-computing-revolutionizing-supply-chain-management/.

and airfreight shipments to war fighters in the field. Nearly 100 government shippers and 5,000 destinations are assisted by the use of cloud technology.[54]

EBSCO, an information services company, manages thousands of e-journals, research databases, eBooks, and audiobooks. To improve efficiency and the quality of customer experiences with the company, EBSCO utilized cloud technology. Partnering with the Ariba Network (the cloud provider), EBSCO launched its Information MarketPlace, which allowed customers to shop, place orders, and pay for those orders in a secure environment. With the combination of EBSCO's information sources and the hundreds of thousands of companies that were part of the Ariba Network, EBSCO doubled the number of electronic orders. Customer satisfaction ratings improved, and customer retention rates increased dramatically.[55]

Social Networks

The success of a supply chain is dependent on the ability of its members to collaborate and coordinate their individual efforts. Social networks and related technologies can be used to enhance collaboration and coordination.

• Getting connected (integration)

• Making sure the data is correct (data management)

• Working together (process collaboration)

• Working together on the right things (network intelligence/performance management)[56]

[54] Partridge, "High Tech," p. 48.
[55] Editorial Staff, "Follow the Cloud for Leads," *Supply & Demand Chain Executive*, April 2011, p. 5.
[56] Trevor Miles, "Social Networks and Supply Chains: It's a Question of Maturity," *The 21st Century Supply Chain Blog*, January 6, 2011, http://blog.kinaxis.com/2011/01/social-networks-and-supply-chains-its-a-question-of-maturity/; Nari Viswanathan, "Enabling Supply Chain Visibility and Collaboration in the Cloud," Aberdeen Group, *White Paper*, 2010, pp. 15–17; and Shawn Casemore, "Social Media and the Coming Supply-Chain Revolution," *CFO.com*, February 29, 2012, http://www.cfo.com.

Social Networking

Social networking "refers to online places where users can create a profile and designate a network of people to see their posts and follow [sic] their activities."[57] Because supply chains involve multiple firms and a large number of individuals, collaboration is essential to successful supply chain management. This makes social networking an ideal means of enabling and enhancing collaboration among supply chain organizations. According to many supply chain executives and consultants, "the future of business commerce is about the networked enterprise. And it involves being connected, efficient and informed."[58] Many of the approaches to networking are found in cloud technology, thus helping firms reduce costs while increasing collaboration.

Uses of Social Networking in SCM

While the use of social networking is still in its infancy in terms of how many organizations have adopted the technology for use in supply chain management, some leading-edge firms such as Home Depot, Costco Wholesale, and Teva Pharmaceuticals have begun to use it as part of their business intelligence (BI) efforts to support operational, tactical, and strategic decision making.[59]

One important use of social networks is obtaining information. Online news sites, blogs, and other media channels provide a wealth of information, mostly free of cost. Additionally, various websites include postings of presentations by individuals that can be downloaded. These presentations can include simple overviews of new technologies, trends, or best practices, or they could include material that reveals business plans, financials, or other information about competitors. Common search engines such as Google and Bing can be used to access this information.[60]

It is interesting to note that companies spend significant amounts of resources acquiring and implementing various supply chain technologies. Some firms may spend millions of dollars on the "latest and greatest" improvements in technology. However, many organizations do not spend sufficient resources on other aspects of supply chain management that impact their efficiency and effectiveness. In the next section, we will examine the issue of measuring various aspects of the supply chain.

Measures and Metrics

Organizational performance can be measured against many criteria. Examples of the multitude of performance dimensions that are presently being measured by organizations include the following:

- Outbound freight costs
- Inventory accuracy
- Order fill rates
- Inventory turnover rates (finished goods, work-in-process, components, parts, etc.)
- On-time delivery
- Customer complaints (number and type)

[57] Carla O'Dell and Cindy Hubert, *The New Edge in Knowledge: How Knowledge Management Is Changing the Way We Do Business* (Hoboken, NJ: John Wiley & Sons, 2011), p. 3.
[58] Editorial Staff, "Business Gets Social," *Supply & Demand Chain Executive*, Sponsored Supplement, April 2011, p. 9.
[59] Shawn Casemore, "Social Media and the Coming Supply-Chain Revolution," *CFO.com*, February 29, 2012, http://www.cfo.com; Dragan Berak, "Role of Social Media in Supply Chain Management," *Chinavasion*, April 18, 2016, https://blog.chinavasion.com/39751/role-of-social-media-isocian-supply -chain-management/; and Kristy Smith, "Improving Supply Chain Management with Social Media," University of Waterloo, March 6, 2017, http://smbp.uwaterloo.ca/2017/03/improving-supply-chain -management-with-social-media/.
[60] Andrew K. Reese, "Make the Social Network Work for the Supply Chain," *Supply & Demand Chain Executive*, March 2011, pp. 41–43.

- Perfect order percentage
- Product out-of-stocks
- Returns and allowances
- Line item fill rates
- Inbound freight costs
- Back orders (number and type)
- Order cycle times
- Customer service and satisfaction levels
- Inventory carrying costs
- Logistics cost per unit vs. budget
- Reverse logistics costs (customer and product)

Examples of Metrics Used in SCM

From a labor perspective, APICS has identified five categories of metrics that could be used: reliability, responsiveness, agility, costs, and asset management efficiency.[61] In a survey of retailers, "best-in-class" organizations utilized four key metrics: established electronic communication with suppliers; perfect order rate; out-of-stock rate (year-over-year); and inbound logistics costs (year-over-year).[62] When compared to other organizations, the best-in-class firms had established electronic communication with almost 80% of suppliers, had a perfect order rate of 94%, decreased out-of-stocks by 21%, and decreased inbound logistics costs by almost 7%.[63]

Of course, it is not enough to merely identify dimensions or elements of organizational effectiveness, although this is a necessary first step. The next step is to prioritize these elements and develop specific measuring devices to evaluate their respective levels of effectiveness. It is vital that management identify the measures of organizational effectiveness it wishes to utilize, and prioritize them. It is impractical in most instances to employ every effectiveness measure in the evaluation process. Time and monetary constraints impede the collection and monitoring of all the data needed for such evaluation.

In addition, it is usually sufficient to examine only a portion of the available measures because patterns or trends are often exhibited very early in the evaluation process. The selection of particular organizational effectiveness measures must depend on a firm's particular characteristics and needs. Perhaps the most difficult process is developing the techniques or procedures needed to measure the effectiveness criteria. In this regard, there are a number of alternatives.

Cost-to-sales ratios are used extensively by businesses to evaluate organizational effectiveness. As with any measure used by a company, there are issues that must be addressed, especially with regard to which costs to include under each supply chain activity. All costs that are rightfully supply chain–related should be included when computing cost-effectiveness measures. If management has adopted and implemented the supply chain management concept, there is greater likelihood that all relevant costs will be included.

---

[61] For an explanation of each of these five performance attributes, see "Understand the Structure of SCOR," APICS, 2018, https://www.apics.org/apics-for-business/benchmarking/scormark-process/scor-metrics.

[62] See Abby Mayer, "Supply Chain Metrics That Matter: A Focus on Retail," *Supply Chain Insights*, August 15, 2012, http://supplychaininsights.com/wp-content/uploads/2012/08/Metrics_That_Matter-Focus_on_Retail-20AUG2012.pdf; Arlene Slivka, "Retail Suppliers: Why Supply Chain Metrics Are Critical to Retaining Your Business," January 26, 2018, http://www.weberlogistics.com/blog/california-logistics-blog/supply-chain-metrics; and Anand and Viswanathan, "State of Retail Supply Chain Collaboration, Visibility and Integration 2011," p. 5.

[63] Anand and Viswanathan, "State of Retail Supply Chain Collaboration, Visibility and Integration 2011," p. 8.

Metrics must be evaluated against *predetermined standards*. The standard may be generated internally; that is, developed within the organization so as to be compatible with corporate hurdle rates, return on investment percentages, cash-to-cash cycle, and other financial performance measures. In some instances, supply chain performance standards may be externally generated.

Performance measurement is critical for supply chain executives. Supply chain executives can be evaluated on a number of managerial and leadership dimensions, including line management ability, problem-solving skills, project management capabilities, and their level of strategic thinking. Additionally, as mentioned earlier in this chapter, executives can also be measured on the three major characteristics on which they were hired: (1) strong verbal intelligence, (2) high need for achievement, and (3) high adaptability.[64]

360 Degree Evaluation

Many organizations have used an approach known as a *360 degree evaluation* to assess various supply chain activities, including the supply chain executives who manage the process, logistics employees, and suppliers and vendors.[65] Decision making usually involves anonymous inputs from the boss, workers/peers, and subordinates. While the results generated are more qualitative than quantitative, the approach generates a clear picture of how the employee is perceived at all levels and identifies areas of ambiguity and conflict between participants. Once those problems are overcome, the person being evaluated becomes much more efficient and effective. When evaluating suppliers, the 360 degree evaluation is especially useful.[66]

One very interesting approach to measuring the performance of executives occurs at HCL Technologies, a high-tech outsourcing company in India. The CEO of the company is evaluated annually by all of the company's managers. The evaluations of the top 20 managers are published on the firm's intranet, where any employee can access them. "While many companies have '360-degree reviews' . . . HCL may be the only one in the world that broadcasts the results throughout the organization."[67]

If management is to measure organizational effectiveness, it must employ a variety of factors. In addition, the factors must be measurable, and standards of performance need to be established. Finally, management should compare the organization with others in its industry. It is likely that there is no single ideal organizational structure that every company should adopt. The most logical approach to organizing supply chain activities to maximize effectiveness is to understand the factors that contribute to organizational performance, and include them in the planning, implementation, and control of the organization.

In sum, measures and metrics are all about ensuring supply chain visibility. Supply chains become more transparent when firms are able to identify and measure key performance indicators (KPIs). And when organizations are measuring the right things, they are able to be more efficient and effective, resulting in greater profitability and higher levels of customer satisfaction. A more in-depth examination of measures and metrics will be presented in Chapter 16.

---

[64] R. Glenn Richey, Mert Tokman, and Anthony R. Wheeler, "Supply Chain Manager Selection Methodology: Empirical Test and Suggested Application," *Journal of Business Logistics*, Vol. 27, No. 2 (2006), pp. 163–190.

[65] For various applications of the 360 degree evaluation approach on supply chain activities, see "Using Predictive Analytics within Business Intelligence: A Primer," *Headline News*, May 3, 2007, http://www.supplychainbrain.com; and "Five Rules to Consider When Shopping for Supplier Performance Management Solutions," *Headline News*, July 27, 2010, http://www.supplychainbrain.com.

[66] Andrew Bartolini, "Best Practices in Supplier Management—A 360 Degree View," *CPO Rising*, March 28, 2018, http://cporising.com/2018/03/28/best-practices-in-supplier-management-a-360-degree-view/.

[67] Jena McGregor, "The Employee Is Always Right," *BusinessWeek*, November 19, 2007, p. 80.

Summary

In a classic onboarding article entitled "The Driving Force of Successful Organizations," Stanley Truskie, president of a management consulting company, asked: "What makes some organizations much more successful than their counterparts? Luck? More effective marketing strategies? Superior technology? Greater financial leverage? Perhaps all these, but beyond them, successful organizations possess two common properties, clarity and commitment, that provide the driving force to propel them to the forefront and help keep them there."[68]

It has been said that, "Where there is no vision, the people will perish."[69] Supply chain organizations with clear statements of purpose, specific and measurable objectives, strategies and plans for achieving those objectives, and a committed workforce undoubtedly achieve higher levels of efficiency and effectiveness.

In today's omnichannel environment, not only do companies compete with other companies, but supply chains compete with other supply chains. Strategic advantage comes from implementing excellent strategies at the firm level, and from interconnected, collaborative, and transparent supply chains that deliver consistently high levels of customer satisfaction.

Supply chains must, of necessity, become more cost-and-service-efficient. An understanding of the factors that affect a firm's organizational effectiveness, along with strategies to improve the factors that reveal weakness or deficiencies, can help create more efficient supply chain systems. Organizational changes form the basis for procedural modifications that can reduce costs and/or improve service to customers.

Of course, supply chain success is at least partially dependent on organizations having the right technologies in place, such as cloud computing, up-to-date information systems (software and hardware), and ability to utilize data analytics and business intelligence (BI) to evaluate the huge databases that comprise social networks, such as Facebook, Twitter, and Instagram.

In this chapter, we discussed the importance to a firm of an effective supply chain organization. Many firms have shown significant improvements in their cost/service mix as a result of organizational changes. The most important ingredient in successful management is integration of all of the supply chain activities under a single individual, department, group, or division.

Supply chain organizations are generally structured along the following lines: strategic versus operational, centralized versus decentralized, or some combination of these approaches. There is probably no single ideal organizational structure that allows all firms to be as efficient and effective as possible. At best, having the proper organizational structure is a facilitator to achieving optimal performance. However, there are important elements that comprise an effective organization. In general, the factors contributing to organizational effectiveness can be categorized as organizational characteristics, environmental characteristics, employee characteristics, and managerial policies and practices.

A number of approaches can be used to measure the effectiveness of supply chains. Each approach requires management to identify the elements that impact effectiveness, and then to evaluate their relative importance. Next, the elements must be measured and performance evaluated. Evaluation requires that standards of performance be established.

With this chapter and the preceding chapters as background, the concepts and principles already learned can be applied to establishing metrics and measuring the performance of supply chain activities, which is the subject of Chapter 16.

---

[68] Stanley Truskie, "The Driving Force of Successful Organizations," *Business Horizons*, Vol. 27, No. 4 (July/August 1984), p. 43.
[69] Proverbs 29:18, *The Bible,* King James Translation.

Suggested Readings

Apple, Rodney, "7 Creative Ways to Find Supply Chain Talent," *Supply Chain Management Review*, July 11, 2018, https://www.scmr.com/article/7_creative_ways_to_find_supply_chain_talent.

Barriere, Mike, Miriam Owens, and Sarah Pobereskin, "Linking Talent to Value," *McKinsey Quarterly*, April 2018, https://www.mckinsey.com/business-functions/organization/our-insights/linking-talent-to-value?cid=winningtalent-eml-alt-mkq-mck-oth-1804&hlkid=938c062c84a54bbfa3e77cce8f1f87a4&hctky=2271065&hdpid=b713dac9-a1c5-40c4-b544-2e2b3ffc1f3b.

Bhalla, Vikram, Jean-Michel Caye, Deborah Lovich, and Peter Tollman, "A CEO's Guide to Talent Management Today," *Boston Consulting Group*, April 10, 2018, https://www.bcg.com/publications/2018/ceo-guide-talent-management-today.aspx?utm_source=201805&utm_medium=Email&utm_campaign=201805_NoVal_EALERT_NONE_GLOBAL.

Blaeser, James, "Supply Chain Manager Benchmark Study—Role, Compensation and Career," American Shipper, *White Paper*, August 2011.

Bowman, Robert J., "For Supply-Chain Apps, the Forecast Calls for More Cloud," *SupplyChainBrain*, Vol. 15, No. 5 (September/October 2011), pp. 44–47.

Castellina, Nick, "Top Performers Know It's Time to Migrate to Cloud ERP: Here's Why and How," Aberdeen Group, *Report*, October 2016, http://v1.aberdeen.com/launch/report/research_report/14056-RR-Cloud-Migration-ERP.asp.

"Collaboration: Key to Transformative Contracting," *WERCSheet*, Vol. 41, No. 2, November/December 2018, pp. 1–3, 7.

Editorial Staff, "The Move to the 'Social Business,'" *Supply & Demand Chain Executive*, Sponsored Supplement, April 2011, pp. 12–14.

Elliott, Chris, "The Evolution of Supply Chain in the Cloud," *SupplyChainBrain*, February 6, 2019, https://www.supplychainbrain.com/articles/29387-the-evolution-of-supply-chain-in-the-cloud.

Goodman, Russell W., "CVN: Taking Collaboration to a Whole New Level," *SupplyChainBrain*, Vol. 15, No. 5 (September/October 2011), pp. 52–54.

Heaney, Bob, "Supply Chain Visibility Excellence: Fostering Security, Resiliency, and Efficiency," Aberdeen Group, *White Paper*, March 2011, http://www.aberdeen.com.

Herbert, Liz, and Jon Erickson, "The ROI of Cloud Apps," Forrester Research, *White Paper*, June 23, 2011, http://www.forrester.com.

"Logistics & Supply Chain Education Resources," *Inbound Logistics*, undated, http://www.inboundlogistics.com/cms/logistics-supply-chain-education/.

"Millennials and the Supply Talent Gap," HighJump Software *White Paper*, 2017, https://supplychainx.highjump.com/assets/documents/whitepapers/SupplyChainX-Millennials-Supply-Chain-Talent-Gap-WP.pdf.

Muro, Mark, Robert Maxim, and Jacob Whiton, "Automation and Artificial Intelligence: How Machines are Affecting People and Places," Metropolitan Policy Program at Brookings Report, January 2019.

Napolitano, Maida, "Workforce Metamorphosis," *Logistics Management*, Vol. 50, No. 8 (August 2011), pp. 66–68.

Natarajan, Shekar, "Spanning the Generational Divide: The Why, What, How of the Art of Building a Culture of Co-existence," *Supply & Demand Chain Executive*, October 11, 2011, http://www.sdcexec.com.

Nyden, Jeanette, and Kate Vitasek, "The Fine Art of Negotiation," *Supply & Demand Chain Executive*, Vol. 13, No. 1 (March 2012), pp. 8–16.

Samuga, Arun, "Making the Digital Pivot in Supply Chain Management," SupplyChainBrain *Blog*, February 14, 2019, https://www.supplychainbrain.com/articles/29386-making-the-digital-pivot-in-supply-chain-management.

Scott, Shay, Chad Autry, Michael Dittmann, and Theodore Stank, "The Top 10 Myths of Supply Chain Talent Development," *CSCMP's Supply Chain Quarterly*, Vol. 9, No. 3 (2015), pp. 30–34.

Smith, Dennis, "Cloud Computing Deployments Should Begin with Service Definition," Gartner, *Research Note*, July 28, 2016 (updated August 3, 2017), https://www.gartner.com/doc/reprints?id=1-3G2H8FE&ct=160826&st=sb.

Stevenson, Melissa, "Social Media Services Trends in Customer Care Outsourcing," *IDC Insight*, September 2011.

"Supply Chain Education: Aiming High," *Inbound Logistics*, February 15, 2017, http://www.inboundlogistics.com/cms/article/supply-chain-education-aiming-high/.

Supply Chain Quarterly Staff, "The 7 Habits of Highly Effective Supply Chain Collaborators," *CSCMP's Supply Chain Quarterly*, April 6, 2018, http://www.supplychainquarterly.com/news/20180404-the-7-habits-of-highly-effective-supply-chain-collaborators/.

"12 Diversity Practices of High-Performance Organizations," Institute for Corporate Productivity, undated, http://go.i4cp.com/12diversitypractices.

Questions and Problems

LO 15-6   1. Jim Collins, in his book *Good to Great*, states that "it's not how you compensate your executives, it's which executives you have to compensate in the first place." Do you agree or disagree with this statement? Support whichever position you take.

LO 15-6   2. What are some of the core competencies that chief supply executives should possess?

LO 15-3   3. The onboarding of employees is a key ingredient of successful organizations. What are some of the training efforts employed by best-practice organizations?

LO 15-2   4. What are "4PLs," and in what ways can they be utilized in supply chains?

LO 15-2   5. What is a keiretsu, and how can keiretsus be used in supply chain network design?

LO 15-4   6. What is meant by "cloud technology" or "cloud computing," and how can it be used to implement lean management principles in a supply chain?

LO 15-3   7. Social networks are extremely important to an increasing number of consumers. Can social networking be utilized in a supply chain? If so, how can it be done?

LO 15-5   8. Briefly overview why the use of measures and metrics is so important in supply chain network design.

16

Supply Chain Performance Measurement and Metrics

Objectives of This Chapter

LO 16-1 To discuss the importance of having measures or metrics of elements that impact supply chain efficiency and effectiveness.

LO 16-2 To identify those supply chain elements that should be measured.

LO 16-3 To identify the characteristics of high-quality data that are to be employed in supply chain performance measurement.

LO 16-4 To understand the concept of the "perfect order."

LO 16-5 To identify potential supply chain process and function metrics.

LO 16-6 To examine the use of benchmarking in supply chain performance measurement.

LO 16-7 To identify examples of key performance indicators (KPIs) utilized by organizations in successfully managing their supply chains.

LO 16-8 To examine the use of scorecards in reporting and evaluating supply chain performance metrics.

Introduction

It has been said by many management gurus that you can't manage what you don't measure. Therefore, it makes sense to measure those things that are most important to customers and members of the supply chain. Certainly, it would be ill advised to not be aware of customer needs, wants, and desires. At the same time, firms in the supply chain must be aware of their costs of doing business so that they can make an acceptable profit. The term often used to refer to obtaining the most important customer measures is "Voice of the Customer (VOC)," which can be defined as the process of capturing a customer's expectation, preferences, and aversions. At the same time, measures relative to the firm's operations are needed to ensure that the organization is operating at peak efficiency and effectiveness.

In their book *Fundamentals of Supply Chain Management: An Essential Guide for 21st Century Managers*, authors Ken Ackermann and Art Van Bodegraven state that "without good, relevant measurements you don't know whether you're winning or losing. You can't tell if you're gaining ground or falling behind. Actually, without metrics you don't even know if you're in the game."[1]

For organizations implementing the SCOR® Model, metrics are required to evaluate performance and establish diagnostics for all phases of the supply chain—plan, source, make, deliver, and return. The *Plan* process of SCOR, which includes processes that balance aggregate demand and supply, might use metrics such as planning costs, financing costs, and days of supply of inventory. The *Source* process includes processes that procure goods and service to meet planned or actual demand and would likely incorporate metrics such as material acquisition costs, source cycle time, and raw material days of supply. *Make*, which transforms products to a finished state, might utilize number of product defects, production cycle time, and product quality level. *Deliver*, the process that provides finished goods and services to meet demand, would often include metrics such as order fill rates, delivery lead times, and transportation delivery costs. *Return*, the processes associated with returned products, would utilize metrics such as product return rates, disposition costs per product, recovery value of products, and order cycle time for processing product returns.[2]

Importance of Metrics in the SCOR Model

It should be noted, however, that metrics are not merely numbers. Much like information is data that is useful, so too are metrics more than just numbers. Metrics should provide meaningful information with which supply chain executives can take action. "A good metric must be clearly defined, free of ambiguities and leaving no room for interpretation. If a metric doesn't mean exactly the same thing to every party in the supply chain, you're inviting all kinds of miscommunications."[3]

When organizations select metrics to assist them in achieving optimal supply chain efficiency and effectiveness, the measures selected must possess the following characteristics:

- "Objective—tied to the work being done;
- Results oriented—employees being measured should be involved in collecting performance numbers;
- Tied to root causes—why didn't we reach this goal? This shows where to focus efforts;
- Action-oriented—once causes are found, share them with all groups involved;
- Tied to corporate goals—your organization can't be the best at everything, so choose those goals that best align with your company's stated goals."[4]

What to Measure?

There are literally thousands of activities, processes, and outcomes that could be measured. Marketing mix components (e.g., product, price, promotion, distribution) are often measured by most companies, but others are specific to particular industries. "Healthcare firms need to track drug interactions, for example, while financial services companies must focus on fraud detection, and online firms study website metrics."[5] Certainly, the technology is available to capture, store, and analyze the volume of data available. Of course, organizations will not choose to ever measure "everything."

---

[1] Kenneth B. Ackerman and Art Van Bodegraven, *Fundamentals of Supply Chain Management: An Essential Guide for 21st Century Managers* (North Attleboro, MA: DC Velocity Books, 2007), p. 165.
[2] For a discussion of various metrics utilized in the SCOR® Model, see Chapter 5 in Michael Hugos, *Essentials of Supply Chain Management*, 4th ed. (Hoboken, NJ: John Wiley & Sons, 2018).
[3] Kate Vitasek and Joseph Tillman, "Back to School on Metrics," *DC Velocity*, September 15, 2010, http://www.dcvelocity.com/print/article/20100915back_to_school_on_metrics/.
[4] Tom Andel, "Mine Your Metrics for Meaning," *Material Handling & Logistics*, September 20, 2011, http://www.mhlnews.com/blog/mine-your-metrics-meaning.
[5] Tom Davenport, Jeanne Harris, and Angelia Herrin, "Analytics and the Bottom Line: How Organizations Build Success," *Key Learning Summary, Harvard Business Review*, September 23, 2010.

Data capture costs resources: people costs associated with collecting the data and technology costs associated with analyzing the data. In general, firms will attempt to measure a variety of cost and service elements associated with supply chain management. It is vital that the data that is captured be of the highest quality, inasmuch as poor data quality can result in many problems associated with decisions based on the data, including decreased revenues, increased costs, increased risk, and the risk of making the wrong decisions.

High-quality data exhibits certain characteristics that are important in supply chain decision making. These characteristics include:[6]

- *Uniqueness*: the data is only captured once and is not duplicated.
- *Accuracy*: data correctly represents whatever is being represented.
- *Consistency*: data in one data set is consistent with the same data in another data set.
- *Completeness*: data includes everything necessary to maximize its usability and appropriateness.
- *Timeliness*: this is the time between when data is required and when it is available.
- *Currency*: this reflects how up-to-date the data is.
- *Conformance*: data is formatted correctly and the same as other data representing similar items.
- *Integrity*: each data point is not duplicated, but is represented only once.

Dimensions of Data Quality

Perhaps the three most important data characteristics are accuracy, timeliness, and completeness (or level of detail).[7]

High-quality data measures should be obtained for every major functional and process component of the supply chain. For example, in the warehousing and transportation areas, the use of warehouse management systems (WMSs) and transportation management systems (TMSs) provides data on the important cost and service elements of these functions. The data can then be examined in light of performance standards established by the organization.[8] Key processes such as information flow, material flow, and financial flow should also be examined.

While the need for high-quality data is obvious, often there are operational challenges to actually having such data available to supply chain executives. Typically, quality data and related metrics are available to supply chain executives only one-quarter to one-third of the time.[9] Major obstacles to having high-quality data available include (1) globalization; (2) fast-changing markets; (3) quality and compliance; (4) bad data; and (5) lack of standards.[10] Thus, while data may be collected by organizations and made available in the firm's MIS, there is no guarantee that the data is "user friendly" and in forms that assist supply chain executives in making good decisions.

[6] Categories based on the discussion of data quality in David Loshin, "Monitoring Data Quality Performance Using Data Quality Metrics," Informatica, *White Paper*, November 2006, pp. 8–10, https://www.it.ojp.gov/documents/Informatica_Whitepaper_Monitoring_DQ_Using_Metrics.pdf.
[7] "Leveling the Playing Field: How Competitive Companies Use Data for Competitive Advantage," *The Economist*, report of the Economist Intelligence Unit (2010), p. 6.
[8] For a warehousing illustration, see Joe Tillman, Donnie Williams, and Karl Manrodt, "Infographic: Annual DC Metrics Survey," *DC Velocity*, Vol. 16, No. 5 (May 2018), pp. 42–43.
[9] "Business Analytics: Benchmarking the Analysis of Data to Gain Insight," Ventana, *Research Report*, March 2011, p. 6.
[10] See Andy Uhlenberg, "Key Issues in Supply Chain Management and How to Overcome Them," Liaison Technologies, September 18, 2017, https://www.liaison.com/blog/2017/09/18/key-issues-supply-chain-management-overcome/; and Robert Handfield, "Bad Data + Lack of Standards = Lousy Supply Chain Analytics," Supply Chain Resource Cooperative, February 14, 2017, https://scm.ncsu.edu/scm-articles/article/bad-data-lack-of-standards-lousy-supply-chain-analytics.

To illustrate, an examination of *Fortune* 1000 organizations found that high-quality data can have a significant impact on employee productivity. "Sales per employee, which is widely used in practice as a measure of productivity, is positively influenced by the usability of data. Usability of data involves presenting data more concisely and consistently across platforms such as corporate laptops and mobile devices, and allowing it to be more easily manipulated."[11] An increase of 10 percent in usability can improve sales per employee by more than 14 percent.

When good data is not available from the firm's own information systems, supply chain executives can go to extraordinary lengths to develop their own data in order to make better decisions. In some instances, managers, frustrated by the inaccuracy of some of the company's centrally distributed data, keep "shadow books" with their own information—primarily relating to spending levels and various cost data. Arla Foods, a Denmark-based dairy co-operative with US$10.3 billion in annual revenue in 2017, had such problems and the company initiated new and improved processes for collecting and reporting data. All divisions of the company now collect and report accounting data in the same way.[12]

Best-in-class organizations that have the ability to capture and access high-quality data have significant advantages over their competition. In a study of chief supply chain officers, best-in-class companies were able to find and access supply chain data necessary for decision making almost 80 percent of the time, while laggard firms could do so only 58 percent of the time.[13]

When organizations are developing systems for obtaining and maintaining high-quality data, there are several aspects of an organization's operations that should be considered:

- *Context*: the type of data and the purpose for which it was collected.
- *Storage*: where the data is to be collected or stored.
- *Data flow*: how the data enters the organization and is transmitted within the organization.
- *Workflow*: how work activities and workers use and interface with the data.
- *Stewardship*: identifying those individuals or departments responsible for managing the data.
- *Continuous monitoring*: regular validating of the data.[14]

Developing Systems for Obtaining and Maintaining High-Quality Data

In sum, high-quality data forms the basis for supply chain metrics and performance measures. Not having high-quality data can bring about a number of problems. For example, incorrect data can impact revenues. Without accurate data on customers, companies may not be able to achieve revenue goals because poor data quality can make it difficult to contact customers, respond to customer inquiries, and monitor customer purchasing habits. Data that may be suspect, that is, unreliable or incorrect, will often require organizations to check and recheck that data before making decisions, thus reducing efficiency and raising costs.[15] Having high-quality data results in several financial benefits (increased productivity

---

[11] Anitesh Barua, Deepa Mani, and Rajiv Mukherjee, "Measuring the Business Impacts of Effective Data," Chapter One of a Three-Part Study, University of Texas at Austin, 2011, p. 6.

[12] "Levelling the Playing Field: How Competitive Companies Use Data for Competitive Advantage," *The Economist* Intelligence Unit Ltd., January 2011, p. 6, http://digitalresearch.eiu.com/levellingtheplayingfield /report/section/critical-data-characteristics.

[13] Editorial Staff, "View from the CSCO's Office," *Supply & Demand Chain Executive*, September 2, 2010.

[14] See "Data Quality Strategy: A Step-by-Step Approach," Business Objects, *White Paper*, 2008, p. 5; and Lisa Morgan, "8 Ways to Ensure Data Quality," *Information Week News*, October 14, 2015, https:// www.informationweek.com/big-data/big-data-analytics/8-ways-to-ensure-data-quality/d/d-id/1322239.

[15] See "The Butterfly Effect: Everything You Need to Know About This Powerful Mental Model," *Farnum Street Media*, 2017, https://fs.blog/2017/08/the-butterfly-effect/; and Pragya Sugandha, "The 'Digital' Butterfly Effect in the Business World," *Happiest Minds*, May 29, 2017, https://www.happiestminds .com/blogs/the-digital-butterfly-effect-in-the-business-world/.

of employees, higher return on equity, higher return on invested capital, higher return on assets), customer benefits (expands the existing customer base, higher service/satisfaction levels), and operational impacts (better asset utilization, planning and forecast accuracy, on-time delivery of products).

Function and Process Metrics

Because supply chain management is a senior management position in most major organizations, it is important to develop metrics that are understandable to senior executives in the organization, such as the CEO, COO, and others. While there may be a large number of metrics or measures obtained by the company, senior management does not have the time or interest in looking at hundreds or thousands of individual metrics that are likely to be available in a complex supply chain network. For those executives, only a very few critical or key metrics are vitally important. We will discuss key performance indicators (KPIs) later in this chapter, but for now, we will identify four major metrics that are of most interest to senior management. Those metrics are (1) cash-to-cash cycle; (2) supply chain cost as a percentage of revenues; (3) perfect order percentage (which will be discussed later in a separate section); and (4) economic value-added (EVA).

Cash-to-Cash Cycle

Briefly, the *cash-to-cash cycle* is a measure of the time between when you get paid for an item that you sell and when you have to pay your suppliers and others for the item that you sold.[16] A classic example of this is the Dell Direct Model, where the company receives a credit card payment from the customer immediately for the particular computer he or she buys. Dell, however, does not pay its suppliers and vendors for the parts that went into the computer for several days or weeks. In essence, it can use the money paid by the customer for whatever it likes and it does not have to pay its suppliers until a later time. When you sell millions of computers each year, getting the cash quicker provides significant benefits to Dell in terms of lower inventory costs, lower obsolescence costs, and immediate use of the money paid by customers for the products they bought.

Supply Chain Cost

Supply chain cost is fairly straightforward. As a percentage of revenues or sales, it is merely a macro view of total supply chain costs compared to the company's revenues or sales. All companies want to know the costs for performing their major functions or processes. In fact, almost two-thirds of all companies utilize specific cost metrics when evaluating supply chain activities.[17] Of course, within that macro percentage, companies will also have to examine the many components that make up that overall percentage. *Perfect orders*, which will be discussed in the next section, is a measure of how well you do everything right, where the customer is completely satisfied and the company makes an acceptable profit on the sale.

Economic Value-Added

Economic value-added (EVA) is an estimate of a firm's profits. Simply, invested capital has to have a benefit greater than the cost of capital; thus, EVA is the profit earned by the firm less the cost of financing the firm's capital.[18] In a supply chain context, EVA reveals how supply chain performance affects the value of individual firms and multiple firms in a supply chain.

---

[16] See Abby Mayer, "Supply Chain Metrics That Matter: The Cash-to-Cash Cycle," *Supply Chain Insights*, November 26, 2012.

[17] See "Business Analytics: Benchmarking the Analysis of Data to Gain Insight," p. 6; and Marco Grossi, "10 Best Ways to Reduce Supply Chain Costs," *3PL Links*, September 26, 2016, https://3pllinks.com/10 -best-ways-reduce-supply-chain-costs/.

[18] "EVA—Economic Value Added," *ManagementMania.com*, May 18, 2016, https://managementmania.com /en/eva-economic-value-added.

Exhibit: Supply Chain Management Cost and Performance Metrics

STRATEGIC GOALS: SUPPLY CHAIN EFFICIENCY AND EFFECTIVENESS

Key Metrics:

Cost reduction

Inventory turns

Return on assets

Working capital

Time measurements (e.g., lead time, delivery time, transit time)

Performance Metrics:

Collaboration and communication between supply chain partners

Customer service levels

Balanced Scorecard

Technology applications

RFID, AIDC (automatic identification and data capture), and IoT Systems

Risk management

Cyber security

Global positioning systems (GPSs)

Supply chain visibility

Keeping up with supply chain trends

Source: Adapted from Chuck Intrieri, "3 Core Metrics & 10 Soft Metrics for Measuring Supply Chain Performance," *Cerasis*, April 25, 2016, https://cerasis.com/2016/04/25/measuring-supply-chain-performance/.

To illustrate the differences between macro versus micro metrics, GED Integrated Solutions, a manufacturer of window and door products, utilizes macro metrics to examine overall supplier performance levels on product quality, on-time delivery, and lead times. On a micro level, GED examines specific suppliers by company and location. As a result, the firm can evaluate overall supplier strategies as well as monitor individual suppliers' performance.[19]

While there are numerous metrics that can be employed by a company, there are some common metrics utilized by most organizations. These include the following, as illustrations:

- Perfect order measurement
- Cash-to-cash cycle time
- Customer order cycle time
- Order fill rate
- Supply chain cycle time
- Inventory days of supply
- Freight bill accuracy
- Freight cost per unit
- Inventory turnover
- Days sales outstanding
- Average payment period for production materials
- On-time shipping rate
- Gross margin return on investment (GMROI)
- Days of supply
- Inventory velocity[20]

Common Metrics Used by Organizations

Typically, a hierarchy of metrics is employed by an organization to manage its supply chain. Such an approach is consistent with the SCOR® Model that was introduced in Chapter 1.

[19] Jeff Kugler, "Intelligent Metrics Ensure Success," IFS North America, *White Paper*, 2009, p. 6.
[20] Team Tradecloud, "All 17 Key Metrics for Supply Chain Management That You Ever Need," *Tradecloud*, October 10, 2017, https://www.tradecloud1.com/blog/key-metrics-for-supply-chain-management.

Interestingly, only a minority of firms are satisfied with the state of their current efforts in developing and implementing supply chain metrics. Almost one-half of all companies indicated that they could improve their use of metrics and performance indicators. Curiously, very few firms said that they planned to upgrade their data collection systems and performance metrics in the short term, indicating that it was not a sufficiently high priority to take action.[21] Thus, there appear to be significant opportunities for further development of metric efforts within organizations of all types and sizes.[22]

The Perfect Order

The notion of a "perfect order" was initially discussed in Chapter 3. Simply, it is getting the right product to the right customer at the right time, and doing it, every time! Generally, organizations that can deliver perfect orders consistently have higher profit margins, earnings per share, and return on assets.

The Grocery Manufacturers Association (GMA) has defined the perfect order as "delivering the correct product, to the correct location, at the correct time, in the correct package, in the correct quantity, with the correct documentation, to the correct customer with a correct invoice."[23]

From the customer's perspective, anything less than perfection is unacceptable. Even with the implementation of Six Sigma programs by companies, some errors and problems still occur and those are considered failures in the eyes of customers. Long-term perfection is unachievable, however, because human and even mechanical systems make mistakes at some point. The objective of a perfect order approach is to attempt to eliminate all mistakes or errors except for the very few that occur from time to time.

Perfect Order Index   Forrester Research has suggested that a *perfect order index* be developed by companies, which would include five key metrics associated with delivering the perfect order to customers. "With the five key metrics, a perfect order index can be created by multiplying together the following metrics: (1) percentage of satisfied customers; (2) percentage of accurate orders captured; (3) percentage of orders fulfilled on time; (4) percentage of orders completed on the first attempt; and (5) percentage of invoices received within net time."[24] An acceptable "score" would depend on customer requirements and competition. A perfect score would be 1.0 ($1.0 \times 1.0 \times 1.0 \times 1.0 \times 1.0 = 1.0$). If a firm was to achieve a 95% level for each of the five components, the resulting perfect order index would be 77%; for a 90% score on each of the five elements, the perfect order index would be 59%; and so on.

Cost Metrics

It has been mentioned throughout this textbook that cost and service issues are the key elements of successful supply chain management. It is important to measure supply chain costs and the customer service and satisfaction outcomes of the supply chain. As a means

---

[21] "Business Analytics: Benchmarking the Analysis of Data to Gain Insight," p. 9.

[22] For a discussion of various supply chain metrics that measure operational excellence, see "How to Advance: Operational Excellence in your Business," *Improvement That Lasts*, October 12, 2017, https://www.eonsolutions.io/blog/how-to-measure-operational-excellence; Debra Hofman, "The Top 25 Supply Chains: Leadership in Action," *Supply Chain Management Review*, Vol. 15, No. 5 (September/October 2011), pp. 8–15; and Greg McMahon, "Operational Excellence Corner—These Things Called Metrics," PolymerOhio Manufacturing Solutions, 2015, https://ohmanufacturing.org/operational-excellence-corner-these-things-called-metrics/.

[23] Karen Butner, "The GMA 2010 Logistics Benchmark Report," Grocery Manufacturers Association and IBM Global Business Services, March 2010, https://www.gmaonline.org/downloads/research-and-reports/GMA_2010_Logistics_Benchmark_Report.pdf.

[24] See Courtney Bjorlin, "Perfect Order Management Requires End-to-End Process View," *Tech Target News*, March 25, 2009, https://searcherp.techtarget.com/news/1351795/Perfect-order-management-requires-end-to-end-process-view; and Ray Wang, "20 Steps to Delivering the Perfect Order," Forrester Research, *White Paper*, March 2, 2009, p. 8.

Exhibit: Santa Claus and the Perfect Order

On Christmas eve, or Christmas day, many people watch the movie *A Christmas Story*, about a little boy named Ralphie who goes to great lengths to get a Red Ryder BB gun for Christmas. But what if Santa doesn't deliver? For Ralphie, there is no room for error in the Red Ryder BB gun perfect order. His Christmas present has to be (1) delivered on Christmas morning, (2) a Red Ryder carbine action BB gun, (3) a 200 shot range model, (4) equipped with a compass, and (5) complete with a timepiece of some kind. If any of these elements were missing, Ralphie would not be a very happy customer. And if Santa missed any component of Ralphie's order, Santa would receive an "F" grade on his supplier scorecard.

Let's take a look at Ralphie's perfect order index. Santa has to deliver the BB gun on Christmas morning.

If there was some delay, irrespective of the reason, and Ralphie's order arrived after lunch on Christmas day, Santa would receive a zero for on-time delivery. Another thought on Ralphie's order: What if the BB gun Santa left for Ralphie didn't have "a thing that tells time"? Was it really *that* important to Ralphie? He just wanted a BB gun, right? Wrong! His preference was for the BB gun to have "a thing that tells time." It might not have been high on his priority list, and he might even think, "Okay, whatever—I'm still going to enjoy the gun." But he will not be truly happy. Even though Santa delivered the right product at the right time, damage free, the order was incomplete.

Source: Adapted from Kate Vitasek and Joseph Tillman, "Could Santa Screw up Christmas?," *APQC's Knowledge Base*, December 16, 2009, pp. 1–2, http://www.apqc.org.

of measuring costs, activity-based costing (ABC) is often used in examining the processes and activities occurring within the supply chain.

Deere and Company, a global manufacturer of agricultural equipment and related items, identifies and manages its "critical costs" utilizing a Cost Activity Worksheet. Its worksheet provides the company with the necessary information to effectively control costs in the supply chain. Some of the major cost categories utilized by Deere and Company include the following:

- **Direct Material**—purchased unit price; inbound freight and transportation; and customs, duties, foreign currency exchange.
- **Direct Labor**—direct labor; direct labor benefits and allowances.
- **Machine and Process Costs**—depreciation; maintenance; process costs (electricity, gas, water); process materials; production supplies.
- **Material Handling**—receiving; movement through manufacturing; storage; shipping.
- **Quality Costs**—audit/inspection; rework/repair; scrap and yield losses; warranty and returned goods.
- **Tooling Costs**—depreciation; maintenance; perishable tools and tool sets.
- **Facility Costs (buildings)**—receiving; manufacturing; shipping/warehousing.
- **Management Costs**—forecasting, order placement, expediting; data documentation/administration; inventory management; production control; supply management.
- **Engineering Overhead**—design engineering; materials engineering; process engineering; product research, development, and testing.
- **General and Administrative Costs**—corporate expenses; accounting, legal, HR; training; travel.
- **Selling and Distribution Costs**—packaging, freight, and transportation; market development (advertising, promotion); order processing; warranty, sales, and service support; distribution costs.[25]

[25] Worksheet adapted from Deere and Company and published in Jimmy Anklesaria, *Supply Chain Cost Management: The AIM & DRIVE® Process for Achieving Extraordinary Results* (New York: American Management Association, 2008), pp. 64–65.

While not all cost categories are included in the Deere and Company example, the list shows the considerable breadth and scope of cost information used by the company in managing its supply chain operations.

The U.S. Department of Defense utilizes cost metrics with respect to its primary mission of providing defense to the United States. It defines cost as "the price paid for the supply chain resources required to deliver a specific performance outcome."[26] The primary area of supply chain costs includes "the ratio of materiel obligations to supply management costs, where materiel obligations are the net materiel obligations for the purchase or repair of materiel that will be held in inventory or acquired from vendors for direct delivery to customers, and supply management costs associated with overhead, including personnel, receiving, storage, transportation payroll, personnel travel, operating materials and supplies, rent/communications/utilities, and other service contracts."[27]

Numerous cost metrics should be collected by an organization, with the most important ones being key performance indicators (KPIs). Some cost metrics are more macro or strategic in nature, while others are more micro or tactical. Common micro cost metrics can include costs per line, per order, per activity, and/or per shift; load factors, lines per order, and/or quantity per line; and freight costs per pound by mode and destination. Macro cost measures can include total supply chain management cost as a percentage of sales and total delivered costs. Other cost metrics that can be either tactical or strategic can include logistics costs as a percentage of sales; freight costs as a percentage of sales to customer; distribution costs as a percentage of sales; inventory shrink and obsolescence as a percentage of sales; labor productivity; over, short, and damage as a percentage of sales; and product returns as a percentage of sales.[28]

Service Metrics

The Malcolm Baldrige National Quality Award is awarded to organizations that demonstrate quality principles in all aspects of their strategies and operations. As part of the evaluation process, Baldrige examiners who evaluate firms that apply for the award provide quantitative scores of the various categories on which the award is based. In essence, the Malcolm Baldrige Award utilizes both qualitative and quantitative measures of each category.[29]

Malcolm Baldrige National Quality Award

To illustrate, scores can range from 0% to 100% for each category. The criteria are evaluated and assigned scores based on the level of quality achieved by the organization. A firm that has no systematic approach to quality management, that has little or no deployment of any systematic approach, and where organizational areas or work units operate independently would not score very well (0% or 5%). At the other extreme, firms that demonstrate an effective, systematic approach to quality management; who fully deploy the approach without significant weaknesses or gaps; and who have a systematic approach integrated with the firm's organizational needs would score very well (90%, 95%, or 100%). Each of these elements would require measures or metrics to evaluate them.

Examples of Service Metrics

Examples of service measures are numerous. We'll briefly examine three metrics as illustrations (these are considered important by most organizations). Order fill rate is one example. The fill rate is calculated by taking the total orders shipped and dividing that number by total orders, resulting in a percentage that could reach 100% if every order was always shipped correctly. Dock-to-stock cycle time is another example. It is calculated as total cycle time in hours to process all supplier receipts in a time period divided by the

[26] *Supply Chain Metrics Guide*, U.S. Department of Defense, March 3, 2016, p. D-1, https://www.acq.osd .mil/log/SCI/.policy_vault.html/Supply_Chain_Metrics_Guide_signed_3Mar2016.pdf.
[27] Ibid., p. 72.
[28] Mike Ledyard, "Is Your Metrics Program Measuring Up?," *CLM Explores*, Vol. 1 (Spring/Summer 2004), p. 4.
[29] For an overview of the Malcolm Baldrige National Quality Award, see http://www.baldrige.nist.gov.

total number of supplier receipts for the time period. A third example would be time to process a purchase order and would be measured simply by the time it takes to manually or electronically perform all of the steps associated with processing purchase orders.[30] In sum, there are many metrics that organizations can employ to measure customer service and satisfaction. The specific metrics utilized will vary by firm but will always include metrics related to the order cycle (defined as the time between when the customer places an order for an item and when it receives the exact item ordered), as well as metrics associated with various aspects of customer satisfaction.[31]

BNSF Logistics, a third-party logistics service provider, wholly owned by the Burlington Northern Santa Fe Railroad, identified additional service dimensions that it considers to be KPIs:

- Time taken to answer customer calls or fulfill quote requests
- Timeliness of EDI transactions, status updates, and reporting of data
- Number of customer visits and customer surveys undertaken
- Flexibility delivered by service providers
- Engagement level of the customer service personnel
- Performance in executing processes and other decisions
- Frequency and quality of supply chain inputs for decision making[32]

While service factors are important to both firms and customers, so too are costs important. Usually, organizations will employ a combination of cost and service factors in their company metrics.

Combination of Cost and Service Metrics

Because all decisions related to supply chain management are multifaceted, both cost and service components must be measured. Customers do not make purchase decisions based only on cost, or only on service. Customers want excellent service at a reasonable and acceptable cost. Thus, both are important, and metrics programs must include measures of both.

To illustrate how combinations of cost and service metrics can be used, consider two major components of logistics (which is a critical element of supply chain management): transportation and warehousing.

When evaluating the transportation aspects of supply chain management, consideration has to be given to the channels used to move products from producers to consumers. Approximately two-thirds of companies operate multiple channels when distributing products to customers. Each channel will have different cost and service aspects that must be measured. To illustrate, in the retail marketplace, 64% of products are shipped directly to consumers, 60% go through a traditional distribution center, 45% are distributed through a 3PL or e-fulfillment provider, 44% are shipped directly to stores, and 35% go through a free trade zone.[33] Each of these options will have different cost and service levels that must be measured.

[30] For a discussion of these and other supply chain metrics, processes, and standards, see Supply Chain Visions, *Supply Chain Management Process Standards*, 2nd ed. (Lombard, IL: Council of Supply Chain Management Professionals, 2009).

[31] For an examination of various service-related factors, see Ian Michiels, "Customer Analytics: Leveraging Customer Data to Fulfill the One-to-One Marketing Imperative," Aberdeen Group, *White Paper*, December 2009.

[32] Lisa Terry, "Measuring Customer Service: The Up-and-Coming KPI," *Inbound Logistics*, Vol. 32, No. 12 (December 2012), pp. 36 and 38.

[33] "Cost-to-Serve Modeling: Addressing the Logistics Challenge," *White Paper*, Aberdeen Group, February 2011, p. 2, http://www.aberdeen.com.

TABLE 16.1
The Most Commonly Used Warehousing Metrics

Sources: Joe Tillman, Donnie Williams, and Karl Manrodt, "Infographic: Annual DC Metrics Survey," *DC Velocity*, Vol. 16, No. 5 (May 2018), pp. 42–43; Karl Manrodt, Joseph Tillman, and Kate Vitasek, "Do You Hear What I Hear?," *DC Velocity*, Vol. 9, No. 4 (April 2011), pp. 44–46; and Karl Manrodt and Kate Vitasek, "DC Measures 2008," *Warehousing Education & Research Council Report*, pp. 1–18.

Metric	Rank in 2017	Rank in 2016	Rank in 2011	Rank in 2009	Rank in 2007
Average warehouse capacity used	1	2	2	7	4
Order picking accuracy	2	3	3	3	3
On-time shipments	3	1	1	1	1
Peak warehouse capacity used	4	7	4	*	7
Part-time workforce to total workforce	5	*	*	*	*
Overtime hours to total hours	6	*	*	*	*

* Item did not appear in the top 7 items.

In a study of warehousing metrics for WERC that has been done for a number of years, the "top 10" measures used have included both cost and service items. Table 16.1 identifies the most commonly used warehousing metrics for 2017 along with selected data from earlier years (some items become more or less important due to environmental changes such as technology improvements, changes in management philosophies, customer perspectives, etc.). It should be noted that there are changes in the metrics used from year to year, although the five most commonly used metrics in 2011 have consistently remained at the top of the list. For many companies, these become the key performance indicators (KPIs) for the warehousing activity. KPIs will be discussed specifically later in this chapter.

Benchmarking

Comparing the performance of one firm versus another is a process that has been occurring across companies and industries for many years. Evaluating one's performance against best-in-class firms identifies areas in need of improvement and can indicate where competitive advantage and disadvantage exist.

Metrics Suggested by the Supply Chain Consortium

The Supply Chain Consortium, which includes a variety of manufacturing, retailing, and wholesale distributor organizations, has conducted research into the key metrics and benchmarks utilized within supply chain management. The core benchmark areas examined by the Consortium each year include the following: financial; supply chain planning; sourcing; transportation; distribution; manufacturing; and technology.[34]

The American Productivity & Quality Center (APQC) developed a Process Classification Framework® (PCF) that has been used successfully by manufacturers, retailers, and service companies. "APQC's Process Classification Framework® (PCF) is a list of processes that organizations use to define work processes comprehensively and without redundancies. Beyond being just a list, the PCF serves as a tool to support benchmarking, manage content, and perform other important process management activities."[35] The PCF as developed by APQC and its member companies is an open standard to facilitate improvement through process management and benchmarking regardless of

[34] "Supply Chain Core Benchmarks: Understanding Key Metrics," *Core Benchmarks Report*, Supply Chain Consortium, January 25, 2011, p. 4.
[35] See "Cross Industry Process Classification Framework, Version 7.2.0," APQC, June 2018, p. 1, https://www.apqc.org/knowledge-base/download/426790/K08898_PCF_Cross%20Industry_v7.2.0_June_2018.pdf; and Supply Chain Visions, *CSCMP Suggested Minimum Supply Chain Benchmarking Standards*, eBook ed. (Lombard, IL: Council of Supply Chain Management Professionals, 2010), p. 4.

Exhibit: Selected Examples of Benchmark Metrics

Financial	Supply chain cost as % of revenue
	Financial inventory turns
	Days of purchases outstanding
Supply Chain Planning	Inventory turns
	On-time delivery to customer
	Outbound order fulfillment lead time
Sourcing	Supplier on-time delivery
	Lead time (days)
	In stock at stores
Transportation	On-time delivery
	On-time pickup
	Billing error rate
	Electronic status updates
Distribution	Storage utilization
	Order accuracy
	Order fill rate
	Perfect order completion
Manufacturing	Manufacturing cycle time
	Outgoing product quality
	Customer rejection rate on shipped products
Technology	% of inbound containers that are bar-coded
	% of outbound cartons that are bar-coded

Source: "Supply Chain Core Benchmarks: Understanding Key Metrics," *Core Benchmarks Report*, Supply Chain Consortium, January 25, 2011, pp. 5–7.

industry, size, or geography. The PCF organizes operating and management processes into 13 categories, including six operating processes (develop vision and strategy; develop and manage products and services; market and sell products and services; deliver physical products; deliver services; and manage customer service) and seven management and support services (develop and manage human capital; manage information technology; manage financial resources; acquire, construct, and manage assets; manage enterprise risk, compliance, remediation, and resiliency; manage external relationships; and develop and manage business capabilities).

APQC Metrics and the CSCMP Process Standards

The Council of Supply Chain Management Professionals (CSCMP), in conjunction with Supply Chain Visions, has used the APQC SCM process standards to develop "minimum acceptable" and "best practice" examples of supply chain benchmarks.[36] Within each category, process elements are presented by category, process group, process, and activity, with suggested minimum process standards and typical best-practice processes. With each process element, appropriate metrics can be established.

[36] Supply Chain Visions, *Supply Chain Management Process Standards*.

To illustrate, consider one of the items within the "deliver products and services" operating processes category, namely, the process "operate warehousing." The "pick, pack, and ship product for delivery" activity can be measured and compared with best practices. Examples of suggested minimum process standards for this activity would be "the warehouse picking document is generated based on slotting assignments; shift or individual productivity performance is measured; a record of weekly activity by major task and manning levels is displayed on warehouse shop floor; bar-coding is used to create effective put-away and picking"; and many others. Typical best-practices for this activity would include "items are packed to facilitate downstream activities (e.g., loading in unloading order); a record of daily activity and performance by major task and manning levels is displayed on the warehouse/shop floor; the ability to support a single order fulfillment process is irrespective of channel; pack travel path minimization is accomplished through order picking in travel path sequence, batch picking of the same SKUs for multiple orders, or wave pick sequencing to plan picks per zone in advance."[37]

To measure performance on the activity of "pick, pack, and ship product for delivery," the order fill rate could be the metric used. Best-in-class organizations achieve almost a 99% order fill rate, while the average firm achieves only 95%.[38]

APQC also utilizes benchmarks in its Open Standards Research surveys that it conducts periodically. Both macro and micro performance standards are examined. For example, if an organization was examining its logistics activities in light of whether or not the firm's organizational structure should be centralized or decentralized, it might utilize a metric such as total cost of logistics per $1,000 revenue, freight cost to operate outbound transportation per $1,000 of revenue, or other measures. Like the CSCMP and Supply Chain Visions process standards, best practices and normal practices could be identified, which could also be examined in light of whether the organization is centralized or decentralized logistically.

Whatever approach is used to examine the various processes and activities of supply chain management, organizations need to identify those items that are most important to the firm, the supply chain, and customers. These items are key performance indicators (KPIs).

Key Performance Indicators

While organizations may collect data to measure hundreds or even thousands of factors, a much smaller number of measures are key to successfully managing the majority of functions and processes of the supply chain. These measures are referred to as *key performance indicators* (KPIs) and assist supply chain executives in managing and evaluating supply chain performance. Some people have referred to KPIs as "metrics that matter," which is accurate because they are keys to planning, implementing, and controlling an optimal supply chain.

Four Components of Key Performance Indicators (KPIs)

"An individual KPI is constructed of four components: the business event to be measured; the starting benchmark; the targeted achievement; and a time frame."[39] KPIs must be well-defined, quantifiable, communicated to all personnel, important to achieving the company goals and objectives, and applicable to the business.[40]

The data that will be collected for each KPI will likely come from multiple sources (locations, information systems, departments, time frames) and will evolve over time because business conditions change over time and nothing ever really remains the same. KPIs will

[37] Ibid., pp. 86–87.
[38] Ibid., p. 9.
[39] "Using Supply Chain Performance Management Strategically," Ventana Research, *White Paper*, 2009, p. 6.
[40] Ted Jackson, "18 Key Performance Indicator (KPI) Examples Defined," *Clear Point Strategy*, August 3, 2017, https://www.clearpointstrategy.com/18-key-performance-indicators/.

also measure both efficiency and effectiveness, for without both, optimal customer satisfaction cannot be achieved.

Additionally, KPIs will vary depending on the level in the organization where the metric is being used. For the overall organization, financial metrics such as year-over-year sales growth, operating margin, days of inventory, return on assets, and revenue per employee are measures that can shed light on the firm's health or well-being.[41] For major functions or process areas, such as supply chain management, executives need macro KPIs such as profitability, supply chain costs, overall inventory levels, warehouse utilization rates, and so on.[42] These KPIs include the function and process activities of the organization's supply chain.

Cash-to-Cash Cycle (C2C)

An important KPI for many organizations is the cash-to-cash cycle (C2C). This KPI was introduced earlier in this chapter. The measure is comprised of three supply chain ratios: days of inventory (DOI); days of payables (DOP); and days of receivables (DOR). The calculation of the cash-to-cash cycle is straightforward:

$$\text{Cash-to-cash cycle} = \text{DOI} + \text{DOR} - \text{DOP}$$

"The shorter the cycle, or the lower the number, the better it is for the company's operations. In short, the smaller the number of C2C, the company can operate with less cash tied up in operations."[43]

At the operational level, such as in the warehouse or distribution center, or perhaps the transportation area, KPIs such as loss and damage rates, warehouse picking accuracy, vehicle on-time arrivals and departures, inventory shrinkage, and labor productivity levels will be employed.

With respect to employee performance metrics, KPIs can be developed using the Balanced Scorecard method (examined later in this chapter). The KPI can include aspects of how well the company is managing its employees, or how well the needs of supply chain partners are being satisfied.[44]

Sustainability KPIs

In recent years, more organizations are developing sustainability-related KPIs. Research studies have indicated that more than 2,500 different metrics on various aspects of supply chain sustainability have been reported.[45] Because of the increasing importance of issues such as reverse logistics, product returns, green marketing, environmentalism, and renewable energy, metrics specific to sustainability have become part of many corporate sustainability reports and annual reports of organizations around the world.

While there are numerous supply chain sustainability measures in use, there are a few items that are critical to most organizations, including:

- Supply chain waste from operations, packaging, expired products, or damaged goods
- Energy usage rates of equipment and facilities
- Load density (in transportation, high densities are better)
- Greenhouse gas emissions for the entire supply chain network[46]

[41] Abby Mayer, "Supply Chain Metrics That Matter: A Focus on Apparel," Supply Chain Insights LLC, *White Paper*, May 9, 2013.

[42] For an overview of various supply chain metrics that examine the relationship between a firm's financial ratios and performance in the financial markets, see Lora Cecere and Abby Mayer, "Launch of the Supply Chain Index: Which Supply Chain Metrics Matter to Financial Market Valuations?," Supply Chain Insights LLC, *White Paper*, June 11, 2013.

[43] Abby Mayer, "Supply Chain Metrics That Matter: The Cash-to-Cash Cycle," Supply Chain Insights LLC, *White Paper*, November 26, 2012, p. 5.

[44] Jeremy Hope, "How KPIs Can Help Motivate and Reward the Right Behavior," IBM Corporation, *White Paper*, 2010, p. 5.

[45] Cory Searcy and Payman Ahi, "Reporting Supply Chain Sustainability: A Myriad of Metrics," *The Guardian*, September 26, 2014, https://www.theguardian.com/sustainable-business/2014/sep/26/reporting-supply-chain-sustainability-metrics-gri-sustainability.

[46] Michael Wilson, "4 KPIs to Measure the Success of Your New Sustainability Strategy," *Afflink*, June 14, 2016, https://www.afflink.com/blog/4-kpis-to-measure-the-success-of-your-new-sustainability-strategy.

As discussed in the previous chapter, many firms are employing social media in their supply chain collaboration and coordination efforts. There are a number of reasons why social media can provide benefits to supply chain management, including:

- Organizations can utilize social media to sense and respond to supply and demand changes in the marketplace.
- Customers can be contacted more quickly and easily about shipping delays.
- Social media sites can provide leads to new supply chain partners.
- Social media increase supply chain transparency and visibility.
- Social media can be used to conduct market research on vendors, suppliers, customers, and others in the supply chain.
- Social media provide the opportunity to respond earlier to changes and/or disruptions in the marketplace.
- Relationships can be built through use of social media to contact customers and supply chain partners.
- Social media allow supply chain members to obtain feedback and information that allow process changes to occur.
- The social media platform is larger than traditional channels, making it easier to collaborate.
- Social media can be analyzed using big data analytics for demand sensing and other research.[47]

Social media metrics and KPIs must be established to determine the efficiency and effectiveness of the media. The CEO of a leading measurement and accountability research consultancy firm has identified a number of metrics that are important in measuring various social media and corporate website efforts. "Click-throughs, unique visitors, repeat visitors, number of friends, followers, comments, repeat comments, tweets and retweets . . . metrics will vary by goal, audience and vertical market."[48]

Such metrics as those above can also be applied to the media contacts between supply chain executives and professionals in other firms in the supply chain such as suppliers, vendors, distributors, and more. Determining which metrics are KPIs will depend on the goals of the organization. However, there must be some measure of how effective these contacts are between individuals and companies. Various descriptive statistics, social network analysis, and text analytics can be employed to evaluate these contacts.[49]

Adidas and FIFA have successfully employed social media in their supply chain. Spanning a relationship of over 50 years, Adidas launched its Twitter campaign (#allin), which allowed visitors to the site to follow the progress of the official World Cup soccer ball as it traveled around the world to various soccer match locations. As the World Cup began, Twitter visitors could become much more engaged in the tournament. Additionally, Adidas also utilized social media to foster direct communication between management and workers in the more than 1,000 independent factories around the world. "The system allows the workers to have anonymity, ensures transparency in tracking complaints. It also allows correction efforts to happen in real time."[50]

[47] "Using Social Media to Empower Your Supply Chain," *Inbound Logistics*, July 13, 2016, https://www.inboundlogistics.com/cms/article/using-social-media-to-empower-your-supply-chain/. Also see Raúl Rodriguez-Rodriguez and Ramona D. Leon, "Social Network Analysis and Supply Chain Management," *International Journal of Production Management and Engineering*, Vol. 4, No. 1 (2016), pp. 35–40.
[48] Katie Delahaye Paine and Mark Chaves, "Social Media Metrics: Listening, Understanding and Predicting the Impacts of Social Media on Your Business," *Conference Summary*, eMetrics Conference, San Jose, CA (May 2010), p. 3.
[49] For a discussion of these analysis tools, see ibid., p. 4.
[50] Elizabeth Hines, "An Example of Successful Social Media in Supply Chain Management," *Fronetics*, April 5, 2018, www.fronetics.com/example-successful-social-media-supply-chain-management/.

In sum, organizations must identify those metrics that are most meaningful to customers and the firm. Metrics also take time to develop and "test" to ensure that the right things are being measured. "Drafting of metrics is a task that needs to be approached with some degree of patience. Typically many measures will be reported and tracked before a key set will emerge. It is important to consider at first a large range of potential measures, and not to shortlist too many until an attempt is made to first trial them."[51] Once results are in, the organization can decide which of the metrics that have been developed are really important enough to be categorized as KPIs.

Scorecards

The use of scorecards to measure supply chain performance is a relatively recent phenomenon, but it's certainly not a new concept. College students are aware of grading schemes that determine their classroom performance. Athletes and fans of baseball, basketball, football, hockey, and soccer are aware of the use of scorecards in athletic events pitting one team against another. Scorecards are literally nothing more than devices used to evaluate the performance of operations and organizations within supply chains.

Basic Types of Scorecards

Scorecards can be used to monitor activities within a firm and organizations that are part of the supply chain. Their use is important because it has been estimated that only 63 percent of the financial performance promised by the strategies implemented within the supply chain is delivered.[52] Thus, scorecards are widely used. They can be of three different types: categorical, weighted point, or cost-based. "Categorical measurement systems require simple check-offs to items that describe . . . performance across different categories . . . a weighted point system includes a variety of performance categories, provides weights for each category. The third type—cost-based systems—is used least. It attempts to quantify the total cost of doing business with a supplier over time."[53] When weighting various metrics, while there are a number of software options available, people ultimately make the final decisions regarding setting the weights that are accurate for a particular activity, supplier, or process.[54] Perhaps the most widely known example of a scorecard is the *Balanced Scorecard* approach, which was introduced earlier in Chapter 2.

Balanced Scorecard Defined

As defined by the Balanced Scorecard Institute, it is "a performance management system that can be used in any size organization to align vision and mission with customer requirements and day-to-day work, manage and evaluate business strategy, monitor operation efficiency improvements, build organizational capacity, and communicate progress to all employees. The scorecard allows us to measure financial and customer results, operations, and organizational capacity."[55]

---

[51] John Mangan, Chandra Lalwani, and Tim Butcher, *Global Logistics and Supply Chain Management* (Hoboken, NJ: John Wiley & Sons, 2008), p. 193.

[52] Brett Knowles, "The Convergence of Scorecards, Dashboards and Business Intelligence," Actuate Corporation, *White Paper*, 2012, p. 2. Also see Seth Nagle, "Understanding the Difference: Scorecards vs. Dashboards," *RW3 Technologies*, February 2, 2018, https://www.rw3.com/understanding-the-difference-scorecards-vs-dashboards/.

[53] Robert J. Trent, "Creating the Ideal Supplier Scorecard," *Supply Chain Management Review*, Vol. 14, No. 2 (March/April 2010), p. 24. For additional discussion of scorecards, see Keith Peterson, "Five Steps to Launch a Supplier Scorecard," *Halo Business Intelligence*, undated, https://halobi.com/blog/five-steps-to-launch-a-supplier-scorecard/.

[54] For a discussion of various ways of developing and implementing scorecards for suppliers, see "Get Competitive with Supplier Metrics: Aligning Performance Improvement Drivers with Enterprise Objectives," Zycus, *White Paper*, 2011; and Jennifer Brusco, "Supply Chain Visibility and Supplier Scorecards: What You Need to Know," *TraceGains*, April 12, 2017, https://www.tracegains.com/blog/supply-chain-visibility-and-supplier-scorecards-what-you-need-to-know.

[55] Howard Rohm and Larry Halbach, "Developing and Using Balanced Scorecard Performance Systems," Balanced Scorecard Institute, *White Paper*, August 2005, p. 2; also see Ted Jackson, "What Is a Balanced Scorecard," *Clear Point Strategy*, February 26, 2018, https://www.clearpointstrategy.com/what-is-a-balanced-scorecard-definition/.

Exhibit: Benefits of Implementing a Balanced Scorecard Approach

In supply chain management, many factors go into making the supply chain efficient and effective. Managing the supply chain is enormously difficult. Measuring its performance is probably even more difficult!

The Balanced Scorecard (introduced in Chapter 2), offers supply chain firms many benefits relating to determining if the supply chain is being optimally managed. Some of the more important benefits of using Balanced Scorecards in supply chain management are the following:

- Establish a few strategic objectives;
- Reflect the primary focus of the strategic objectives through perspectives;

- Describe the cause-and-effect relationship of the strategic objectives;
- Formalize strategic priorities of each strategic objective;
- Communicate performance through strategic performance indicators;
- Provide one way to view the firm and how it's performing;
- Base everything management does on the strategic objectives.

Source: Adapted from Brett Knowles, "The Convergence of Scorecards, Dashboards and Business Intelligence," Actuate Corporation, *White Paper*, 2012, p. 4.

While scorecards are potentially very valuable in assisting supply chain executives in making decisions, they are not necessarily easy to implement. Adopting the Balanced Scorecard approach does not guarantee that the strategic objectives will be successfully implemented. Many organizations fail to execute what they claim to be their most important strategic objectives. It's not for lack of planning; it's when these strategies are implemented.

Moen, Inc., a manufacturer of plumbing products sold globally, has developed metrics in five major categories: service, cost, productivity, quality, and environmental health and safety. "Collected data are shared at several levels within Moen. Each month, the supply chain executive presents a high-level scorecard to the executive team, covering events needing attention at that level. He also shares measures with operations people—items they need to see daily, like fill rate to customer, percentage of phone calls answered appropriately, or parts per million defect rate for different manufacturing operations."[56] This is where the use of scorecards, such as the Balanced Scorecard, can be useful. While not necessarily easy to implement, the benefits are significant and outweigh any difficulties associated with using scorecards.

Jack Steele of ActiveStrategy, Inc., a consulting company specializing in assisting companies developing strategies, has identified a straightforward way of developing a scorecard-based performance system. He suggests that a company perform a SWOT (strengths, weaknesses, opportunities, and threats) analysis to identify the key components or inputs into the firm's strategic plan. Then, the firm identifies the causes or drivers of the outcomes the company expects from its various strategies in light of the components developed in the SWOT analysis. Then, the company should rank the most important or critical strategic objectives derived from the SWOT analysis and concentrate on those items highest ranked. Finally, the firm should identify measures (key performance indicators or KPIs) to determine if the firm is on course to achieving its objectives. "Targets or goals for each measure should also be determined and placed on the Scorecard to gauge performance of each measure."[57] Repetition of the process on a regular, consistent basis will ensure that progress is being made in identification of the key measures of the firm's strategies.

[56] Helen L. Richardson, "How Do You Know Your Supply Chain Works?," *Logistics Today*, Vol. 46, No. 6 (June 2005), p. 33.

[57] Jack Steele, "The Balanced Scorecard: Building a Balanced Scorecard Framework That Drives Strategy Execution & Business Results," ActiveStrategy, *White Paper*, 2007, pp. 3–4.

Steps or Stages in Scorecard Development

The process of building or developing a scorecard can be summarized in six steps or stages.[58] The first step is to assess the firm's foundations, core beliefs, market opportunities, competition, finances, goals, and understanding of customers. Second is the development of the overall company strategy or strategies. The third step is breaking down the overall business strategy into smaller elements, which we can refer to as objectives. Fourth, a strategic map of the overall strategy is created using the principles and concepts associated with process mapping. In step 5 performance measures are developed so that the firm can track its progress on achieving its objectives. And finally, in step 6, initiatives or tactics are identified that can be implemented to achieve the strategy or strategies. This would include making certain that sufficient resources are directed to each of the initiatives identified.

Summary

It should be remembered that having the correct measures and metrics of supply chain activities and processes is not sufficient in and of itself. The data must be made available to those supply chain executives and others with a "need to know." "Coursing through the electronic veins of organizations around the globe are critical pieces of information—whether they be about customers, products, inventories, or transactions. While the vast majority of enterprises spend months and even years determining which computer hardware, networking, and enterprise software solutions will help them grow their businesses, few pay attention to the data that will support their investments in these systems."[59] Thus, it is vital that the necessary information reach those individuals in the organization who require it to make supply chain decisions.

One of the first questions facing the supply chain executive is what to measure. While there are literally thousands of activities, processes, and outcomes that could be measured, certainly those most directly related to costs and service are the most important. Such data must be accurate, timely, and complete (i.e., detailed) if the organization is to fully optimize the efficiency and effectiveness of the supply chain.

Assuming that the organization is able to collect, manage, and maintain high-quality data of various performance metrics, firms must decide what data should be captured and what data is most important. Of most interest to senior management would be metrics such as the cash-to-cash cycle, supply chain cost as a percentage of revenues, perfect order percentage, and economic value-added. Within each of these categories of performance metrics the organization would identify key performance indicators (KPIs). Of the many performance metrics captured by a firm, less than 20 items would be considered KPIs.

Firms that optimize their key performance indicators, assuming of course that they are the most important and relevant to the business, consistently have higher profit margins, earnings per share, and return on assets. Often, when benchmarking supply chain performance metrics with other firms, areas of needed improvement, competitive advantage, and competitive disadvantage are identified. Thus, it is important to identify "best-in-class" performance when benchmarking other organizations' supply chain processes and activities.

In sum, organizations must identify those metrics that are most meaningful to customers and the firm. Once these and the KPIs have been identified, firms often develop scorecards to grade their performance. Scorecards are very valuable in assisting supply chain executives in making supply chain decisions. If everything goes right, then both the firm and its customers reap the benefits.

[58] Based on the discussion relating to building a Balanced Scorecard system as presented in Rohm and Halbach, "Developing and Using Balanced Scorecard Performance Systems," pp. 6–12.
[59] "Data Quality Strategy: A Step-by-Step Approach," p. 1.

Suggested Readings

"Assessing the True Value of Business Analytics: Creating a Disciplined Evaluation Framework," *White Paper*, Ventana Research, 2010, http://www.ventanaresearch.com.

Jan, William, "Enterprise GRC Management and the Impact of Global Reporting Standards," *White Paper*, Aberdeen Group, October 2011, http://www.aberdeen.com.

LaValle, Steve, Michael Hopkins, Eric Lesser, Rebecca Shockley, and Nina Kruschwitz, "Analytics: The New Path to Value," *Executive Report*, *MIT Sloan Management Review*, October 24, 2010, http://sloanreview.mit.edu/tnie.

"A Modern CFO's Guide to Finding the Right KPIs," *insightsoftware.com*, 2014 –2015, http://files.gohubble.com/ebooks/A_Modern_CFOs_Guide_to_Finding_the _Right_KPIs.pdf?_ga=1.56038573.70900221.1428755969.

Murray, Peter, Richard Howells, Rich Sherman, and Siddharth Taparia, "Driving Sustained Improvements with Supply Chain Metrics and Analytics," *White Paper*, SAP and Supply Chain Council, February 16, 2012, http://www.sap.com/scpm or http://www.supply-chain.org.

Perella, Maxine, "Better Data and Metrics: Next Steps in Powering a Circular Economy," *Sustainable Brands, News & Views*, June 27, 2018, http://www.sustainablebrands.com/news _and_views/new_metrics/maxine_perella/better_data_metrics_next_steps_powering_circular _economy?utm_source=newsletter&utm_medium=innovation&utm_campaign=jun27.

"The Perfect Order KPI: Is It the Best Metric Ever?," *Benchmarking Success*, January 8, 2018, https://www.benchmarkingsuccess.com/the-perfect-order-kpi-is-it-the-best-metric-ever/.

Rowe, Nathaniel, and Kevin Permenter, "Data Quality and the Supply Chain: The Benefits of MDM and Portals," *White Paper*, Aberdeen Group, October 2011, http://www.aberdeen.com.

Schrage, Michael, and David Kiron, "Leading with Next-Generation Key Performance Indicators," *MIT Sloan Management Review*, June 2018, Reprint No. 60180.

Stodder, David, "Strategies for Improving Big Data Quality for BI and Analytics," TDWI Report, January 24, 2019, https://www.em360tech.com/landing+page /Strategies+for+Improving+Big+Data+Quality+for+BI+and+Analytics.

"Three Checklists to Build a Successful Supply Chain Analytics Foundation," White Paper, Logility, 2018, https://www.logility.com/white-papers/three-checklists-to-build-a-successful -supply-chain-analytics-foundation/.

"Three Common Global Trade Compliance Deficiencies That Affect Your Bottom Line," Amber Road (2012).

"Three Key Measures You're Probably Not Tracking (But Should Be)," *Executive Brief*, Domo, 2011, http://www.domo.com.

"12 Ways to Measure Business Spend Management Success," Coupa Software, *Benchmark Report*, 2018, https://media.bitpipe.com/io_14x/io_143115/item_1719355/2018-Coup aBenchmarkReport.pdf.

"The Value of Metrics in Supply Chain Performance," *White Paper*, Kenco Group, undated, https://info.kencogroup.com/value-metrics-supply-chain.

Walsh, Ashley, "Improve Your Supply Chain Management with Social Media," Sourcing Industry Group, August 4, 2017, https://www.sig.org/improve-your-supply-chain -management-social-media.

Questions and Problems

LO 16-2   1. With literally thousands of activities, processes, and outcomes to measure in supply chain management, what items should be measured? Briefly identify several key categories of items that should be measured.

LO 16-3   2. Explain why "best-in-class" organizations have a competitive advantage if they are better able to capture and access high-quality data.

LO 16-2   3. Define the "cash-to-cash cycle" and explain why it is a major metric used in measuring supply chain performance.

LO 16-4   4. Identify specific metrics for measuring and monitoring perfect orders. Briefly explain how the "perfect order index" would be used in such monitoring.

LO 16-5   5. Which are more important: cost or service metrics? Provide support for your position.

LO 16-6   6. How can benchmarking be used in comparing the performance of various organizations or supply chains?

LO 16-7   7. More organizations are developing sustainability-related KPIs. Identify some metrics for measuring an organization's or supply chain's sustainability.

LO 16-8   8. How can scorecards be used in measuring supply chain performance?

Better Together:
A Solution to Level the Playing Field with Multinational Corporations (2016)

Steve Downey, Patrick Gibbons
GEODIS and Emerson Healthcare

Executive Summary

Summary of the Initiative

Through multiple innovative consolidation programs, Emerson and GEODIS (formerly OHL) have driven millions of dollars from Emerson's clients' supply chain costs, all while improving the experience for retailers. In the early stages of the relationship, GEODIS enabled Emerson Healthcare to achieve service levels of 99.97 percent in Inventory Accuracy and 99.97 percent in On-Time Shipping and exceed the required compliance rate with retailers and regulatory agencies while accommodating tremendous growth and change. While these numbers alone reflect operational excellence, the results are far more spectacular given all of the stakeholders involved. With the addition of an innovative multi-layered consolidation approach, GEODIS provided Emerson with a multifaceted solution when its clients and retailers demanded a less costly and more convenient model. GEODIS and Emerson worked together to develop a game-changing support structure to enable Emerson Healthcare to consolidate selling, ordering, and shipping for the benefit of its clients and retailers.

The Emerson Healthcare business model is logical, but most fail to understand the complexities behind the scenes that make it both possible and successful. With more than 75 clients serving multiple national and regional retailers, the data, visibility, and inventory must be incredibly precise and highly targeted. Emerson and GEODIS execute the consolidation across multiple orders from Emerson clients and GEODIS customers, shipping and payables, and service to retailers.

Innovation Statement

Emerson Healthcare is a very unique business model in which its sole purpose is to provide its small to mid-sized consumer brand clients with a supply chain competitive to those of large multinational brands. As pressure from both Emerson's clients and retailers have pushed it to further reduce costs, improve speed to market, and increase efficiencies, the implementation of a Freight Consolidation Services (FCS) program has brought Emerson's clients back into the competitive consumer marketplace, creating an innovative multi-layer consolidation program.

Impact Statement

With support from GEODIS, Emerson Healthcare's fulfillment costs declined by more than 20 percent, and one client saved over $2.8M within one year of entering the program. The enhanced freight consolidation program with added GEODIS customers is forecasted to save on average 14 percent in transportation costs by December 2016.

Applicability

Consumers are driving a more competitive retail environment; therefore, retailers are demanding far more from their suppliers than ever before. Those requirements will only increase, placing even tighter requirements on the supply chain. The Emerson/GEODIS consolidation programs offer innovative ways to take dollars out of the supply chain versus negotiating out nickels.

Emerson Healthcare and GEODIS Relationship

Founded in 1994, Emerson Group is a leading representative of small to mid-sized health, beauty, nutrition, and over-the-counter brands distributing to U.S. retail businesses. Originating as a sales management company, Emerson has evolved into the multifaceted company it is today. The evolution began when more and more opportunities for Emerson's clients were being missed or lost because retailers wanted to source product from large multinationals. For retailers, there was less risk involved with these large brands if a product failed and less cost associated with the purchase order cycle. Retailers also preferred larger, consolidated orders and shipments from a single vendor in order to receive and process more efficiently.

The Emerson Group reacted to the trend by implementing its own supply chain and distribution model to consolidate its clients and bring the efficiencies of one large company to all of the brands that it represented. It was at this time that Emerson clients were provided access to a holistic portfolio of solutions including sales, marketing, and logistics services through Emerson Group's business units: Emerson Consulting, Emerson Marketing, and Emerson Healthcare, respectively. The emulated structure of a standard consumer products company without ownership of any of the products was a game changer in the industry for both retailers and clients alike. Emerson's model afforded virtually any size consumer brands company the supply chain and resources equal to those of multinationals.

The strategic relationship between Emerson Healthcare, the logistics arm of the Emerson Group, and GEODIS is the foundation of the logistics infrastructure that enables this model to be successful. With this partnership, Emerson has grown and developed the brands of their 75+ clients while retailers such as Walmart, Target, CVS, Walgreens, and Dollar General have realized cost savings and efficiencies.

GEODIS navigated the complexities and requirements of all involved parties to deliver a comprehensive solution to support the Emerson Healthcare model of consolidated consumer brands. The first challenge for GEODIS was to select the optimal location for the Emerson warehouse. GEODIS began with an analysis of inbound and outbound transportation data to determine the ideal location of a single, national warehouse. The network optimization study identified Plainfield, Indiana, as the ideal site as its centralized location exhibited low transportation costs for both inbound shipments from vendors and outbound shipments to retail distribution centers across the United States.

After site selection, the next challenge was to successfully consolidate shipments to streamline and simplify the shipping process for Emerson's clients. GEODIS provided a transportation solution that combined the orders from all Emerson clients, yet gave visibility to each order and inventory within each shipment on the individual client level to allow Emerson to allocate costs out per client, for all modes, including TL, LTL, and parcel.

FIGURE 1

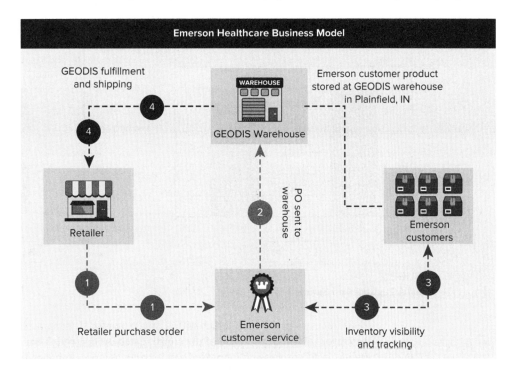

The final major component of this model was service to the retailers (Figure 1). Retailers order through Emerson's customer service team, usually via EDI, which is integrated with GEODIS's WMS. GEODIS then compares the order to the must-arrive-by date (MABD) and sailing schedules and picks and consolidates orders for the same retailer into one shipment. Clients have visibility at all times to their inventory and their orders only through GEODIS's web portals, WebSynapse and MercuryGate. Orders are optimized to ship TL, LTL, or parcel to the retailers based on volumes. Emerson invoices the retailers and collects the payment to be allocated to the client through a third-party accounting firm. Unlike a distributor model, clients of Emerson Healthcare maintain financial independence and ownership of their inventory. Emerson does not own the inventory at any point in the supply chain. Therefore, retailers have to understand that a new vendor number has to be created and accepted for a customer that does not take ownership of the brand or goods. It is a unique model in the industry that has implications to the retailers' liability insurance in how to insure products through the Emerson/retailer supply chain without ownership transfer. The logistics infrastructure managed by Emerson Healthcare and GEODIS is only feasible due to the support of Emerson Marketing and Emerson Consulting, which manage other facets of the business, including pricing, inventory levels, and desired service levels.

Dozens of Emerson clients are added to the model throughout the year, which means GEODIS must have the space, storage profile, and pick methodology to flex when new clients are brought on. GEODIS provides this support through one operation, one warehouse management system (WMS), and one transportation management system (TMS) to leverage scale. Each client involved in the Emerson model becomes part of this warehouse and consolidated business model. While complexities and variability of requirements drastically increase as more clients and retailers are integrated into the model, this also drives increased efficiencies and consolidation efforts for Emerson Healthcare's clients. Figure 2 outlines the savings one client realized utilizing the Emerson/GEODIS logistics model. In one year, it was able to cut almost $3M from its logistics spend, all while improving its service to retailers and increasing its revenue.

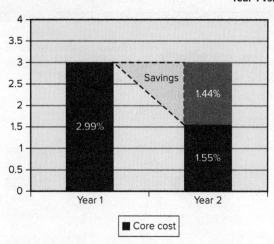
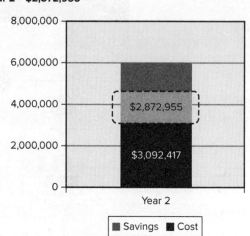

Year 1 vs. Year 2 = $2,872,955

FIGURE 2
Client A Logistics Cost Savings

As retailers prefer to interact with a single vendor, Emerson Healthcare in this case, they favor this model because of the consolidated orders, which equates to significant cost savings in PO processing, improved vendor maintenance, enhanced pricing control, better visibility, and faster service.

The Challenge

Although the Emerson Healthcare model continues to demonstrate many benefits for its clients, the market continues to rapidly evolve. Consumer expectations have had a significant impact on retailers, and these retailers are applying more pressure on suppliers to help meet these expectations. E-commerce has disrupted the traditional supply chain model in that retailers order smaller and more frequent shipments, with shorter lead times, resulting in higher transportation costs for suppliers. Retailers also expect to receive products shipped at the lowest cost in an ever-decreasing delivery window. Added to this, the constraints on traditional transportation modes are more challenging than ever. GEODIS identified the impact that this heightened consumer expectation and market change was having on retailers and suppliers and, thus, a creative solution involving freight consolidation services was required.

While GEODIS and Emerson have extensive experience in consolidating Emerson clients' shipments, expanding the program to include other GEODIS customers while maintaining the service and operational levels would prove to be challenging. With more stakeholders and associated requirements, this brought an additional layer of complexity to the Emerson model and Freight Consolidation program.

The Innovative Solution

With the shift in retailer and consumer demand, GEODIS and Emerson Healthcare were presented with another opportunity to collaborate on an innovative solution for Emerson's clients and other GEODIS customers. The process for this began by evaluating Emerson Healthcare's current distribution operation out of one of GEODIS's multi-customer distribution centers located in Plainfield, Indiana, to identify areas of optimization. When taking a larger look at GEODIS's Indianapolis campus, a dense cluster of GEODIS warehouses sharing space, labor, and other resources, GEODIS identified that several of its own customers were shipping multiple less-than-truckload (LTL) shipments per week to many of the same retailers. What emerged from this is a Freight Consolidation program in which

Emerson's already-consolidated brands are merged yet again with GEODIS's larger customer base, driving additional cost savings and faster transit times.

In order to build Emerson's LTL volumes up to a full truckload, GEODIS analyzed the outbound LTL volumes of several of its other customers in the Indianapolis campus and tailored the program to optimize the cost savings while maintaining, or increasing, the level of on-time performance and quality. While freight consolidation, often known as retailer consolidation, is not a new concept, the GEODIS model with Emerson Healthcare is a unique operation, as all shipment visibility and purchase orders must remain separated for each of Emerson's 75+ brands. This adds an additional layer of complexity to GEODIS's consolidation program. In the previous LTL model, Emerson Healthcare was capable of allocating transportation costs per client, a functionality that needed to remain the same in the freight consolidation model. In the new consolidation model, costs are now being shared not only across Emerson's client base, but across GEODIS's customer base as well.

As Emerson Healthcare's portfolio of customers grows, its outbound volumes will continue to increase, requiring GEODIS to be flexible with the new consolidation program. Because of the Freight Consolidation Services model, any GEODIS customer located within proximity to a GEODIS facility can benefit from the program, which provides Emerson with additional customization and flexibility during low- and high-volume times, as its volumes can be offset by a number of GEODIS customers to continue to keep its transportation costs low.

Results

Freight Consolidation Services alleviates the pressure that suppliers face today when shipping into retailers. FCS has proven to reduce costs and improve retail compliance among large retailers. FCS achieved a compliance rate 7 percent higher than one big box retailer's minimal requirement. GEODIS customers save on average 20 percent off LTL rates and realize over $300,000 in annual savings. As one of the anchor customers of GEODIS's FCS, Emerson Healthcare's metrics were, and continue to be, closely monitored and analyzed for sustainability efforts. Emerson is 4 percent above initial projected 2016 Q1 cost savings, and additional growth is forecasted. Maintaining operational excellence for Emerson Healthcare was the key metric during the initiation of the additional consolidation program. There was no change to the previous sailing schedule or modifications to existing MABD dates with the retailers. The program was seamlessly implemented without disturbing Emerson Healthcare operations.

Figure 3 illustrates how the addition of more customers into the FCS program results in greater savings for participants. GEODIS projects that average customer savings over a

FIGURE 3

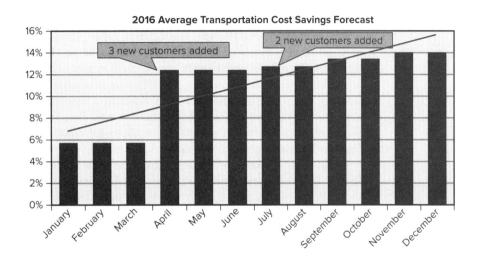

12-month period will increase by around 9 percent if five additional customers are added to the program. As one of the founding members of FCS, Emerson Healthcare stands to benefit from the addition of more program participants.

Next Steps

The strategic relationship between GEODIS and Emerson Group has proven to be mutually beneficial. GEODIS supported Emerson in its foray to compete with large multinationals. Consolidating orders and shipments from multiple brands, and among various GEODIS customers, benefits all of Emerson's customers and changed the industry. Emerson and GEODIS continue to challenge each other to innovate and continuously improve. Emerson Healthcare also wanted to maintain the model with individual client inventory ownership and visibility, yet expand into e-commerce shipping permitting orders of single units, or eaches. Emerson challenged GEODIS to support a front-end web platform and an e-fulfillment solution that worked in conjunction with its case inventory process. GEODIS executed with a unique each-level solution, interfaced to Emerson's shopHABA.com platform, and to other third-party e-commerce sites. Within the operation, GEODIS built out a system solution and an area within the warehouse to house each-level inventory that could be replenished from the case stock. Shipments for cases, pallets, and eaches are now all run out of the same facility. The clients have the same level of controlled visibility, and now have the flexibility to supply samples and eaches, through an e-commerce platform and case sales to retailers.

Because the each-level network is fully executed and successful, Emerson plans to integrate additional products and industries into its model. The program originated with health and beauty products, but Emerson realized the benefit it brings to retailers with all product categories. It has already expanded into general merchandise, and is adding capabilities around prescription pharmaceutical items, food, and much more.

The collaboration with Emerson was a foundational anchor for GEODIS's Freight Consolidation Services for the Midwest. GEODIS projects that customers in the FCS program will save 20 percent to 25 percent in LTL rates with more customers involved. As noted above, more customers = more volume = more consolidation opportunities = more customer savings. GEODIS also operates the program in other key strategic locations in the Northeast and on the West Coast.

Conclusion

Innovative solutions rarely succeed during the first iteration. Emerson provided GEODIS with the flexibility to test and learn as they journeyed toward a new business model. By starting with a few clients and growing up to dozens and dozens over many years, GEODIS was able to slowly build out the capabilities and expertise to support the consolidation functionality. For GEODIS, what started as an Emerson-only consolidation initiative grew to benefit more and more GEODIS customers. The key learning for GEODIS was to introduce and offer inbound freight management as part of the onboarding program. That allows Emerson clients to leverage GEODIS's transportation spend, not worry about coordinating freight pick-ups and dock time, gives them visibility from vendor order through shipment arrival, and reduces inbound freight costs. Because many Emerson clients also share common contract manufacturers, it allows for consolidated shipments from those facilities wherever possible.

A key learning for Emerson from the program was the handling of noncompliance fees. With the client relationship structure that Emerson has, any fees need to be traced to their source, be they product shortage due to inadequate inventory, missed arrival dates, damaged in transit, or the many other sources. Each one needs to be researched, triaged, and driven back to the appropriate client. Emerson has gone over three years without a fine from one of its large retailers, which is a tribute to how well it and GEODIS have executed.

The immediate economies of scale for Emerson clients were not a coincidence. Patrick Gibbons, Vice President of Operations and founding partner of Emerson Group, acknowledges that Emerson's relationship with GEODIS and the retailers was the key to success. One of the major complications that Emerson had to overcome was socializing and getting awareness out to the retailers about its business model. Innovations change the status quo, and Emerson, supported by GEODIS, did just that.

Council of Supply Chain Management Professionals

From Cradle to Cradle: Sustainable Sourcing for a Prosperous Planet (2016)

Keith (Vice President, Production Procurement); Charlene Mendoza, Oliver Campbell, Jennifer Allison, Scott O'Connell, Stephen Roberts, Alan Luecke, Rick Menchaca, and Janet Zhang

Executive Summary

Summary of the Initiative

In 2012, Dell announced our 2020 Legacy of Good Plan. This aggressive plan articulated four areas of aspirations and identified 12 goals. With Dell's supply chain optimized for efficiency, speed, and reliability, the intense focus of all key stakeholders (internal and external) is on standardized processes, cost control measures, and risk mitigation. However, we needed innovative, breakthrough thinking to achieve the end state illustrated by the lofty 2020 Legacy of Good goals.

Our challenge, outlined in this paper, was to create a framework that would enable innovative thinking and a platform for risk taking to achieve these goals. This framework was inspired by design consultancy IDEO's "Design Thinking" process and has been implemented across Dell's supply chain. There are three major elements of this framework: Design Thinking workshops, annual Innovation Olympics, and an annual Packaging Innovation Summit. Dell has created a governing body called the Supply Chain Sustainability Steering Committee, which helps prioritize projects and funnels ideas through the innovation framework. It is this governing body that is responsible for Dell reaching the 2020 Legacy of Good goals.

Innovation Statement

By applying the design thinking practices more typically used for product design toward the end-to-end applications across Dell's supply chain, we set out to enable a culture of innovation and create the opportunity to explore disruptive solutions in an organization whose success depends on reliability, efficiency, and cost competitiveness.

Impact Statement

The innovation framework implemented to help Dell reach the 2020 Legacy of Good goals has resulted in awards ranging from the 2015 Circular Economy Award at the World Economic Forum to the 2015 Sustainable Purchasing Leadership Council Award in Asia, the Green Electronic Council Catalyst Award, and the 2016 CES Innovation and Eco-Design Award. We are the first PC brand to employ in-mold rolled film and texture with complex geometry part design in an effort to reduce or, where possible, eliminate paint in our products. This project drove a cumulative $53.3 million savings in packaging costs and enabled a closed-loop recycling system that allowed Dell to use 11.7 million pounds of recycled-content plastics in new products.

Applicability

Dell's innovation framework is applicable to product design processes, which is a more traditional application of innovation practices. More importantly, it can also be used to identify and qualify more sustainable materials, as well as creating the new manufacturing processes necessary to integrate those materials into the affordable, high-quality, and sustainable products that customers' desire.

Our Challenge: Products, Materials, and Manufacturing Process

Environmental responsibility is about more than creating an eco-friendly product or initiative. It's about incorporating sustainability into every aspect of what we do, using our technology and expertise to innovate on behalf of our customers, our communities, and the planet. Sustainability is in Dell's DNA—and we've made very public, measurable commitments to progress in this area as part of our 2020 Legacy of Good Plan launched in 2012.

Dell's 2020 Legacy of Good Plan: Aspirations and Goals

Dell's aspirations and goals for 2020 reflect our approach of considering the environment at every stage of technology's life cycle—from design through manufacturing and use through end of life—and then measuring the impact to inform future efforts. Our 2020 Legacy of Good Plan includes four aspirations and 12 goals related to the environment.

Aspirations	Goals
• Reduce the environmental impact of our operations	• Reduce greenhouse gas emissions from our facilities and logistics operations by 50 percent • Reduce our water use in water-stressed regions by 20 percent • Ensure 90 percent of waste generated in Dell-operated buildings is diverted from landfills • Develop and maintain sustainability initiatives in 100 percent of Dell-operated buildings
• Drive social and environmental responsibility in the industry and our supply chain	• Demonstrate 100 percent transparency of key issues within our supply chain, working with suppliers to mitigate risks in those areas • Ensure 100 percent of product packaging is sourced from sustainable materials
• Enable customers to reduce the environmental impact of their IT infrastructure	• Reduce the energy intensity of our product portfolio by 80 percent • Use 50 million pounds of recycled-content plastic and other sustainable materials in our products • Ensure 100 percent of Dell packaging is either recyclable or compostable • Phase out environmentally sensitive materials as viable alternatives exist • Recover 2 billion pounds of used electronics
• Promote technology's role in addressing environmental challenges	• Identify and quantify the environmental benefits of Dell-developed solutions

Our Environmental Responsibility Meets Our Culture of Innovation

Our innate sense of responsibility as a corporate citizen is reinforced by the demands of our customers. Over the past two years, 22 percent of customer requests handled by our Corporate Social Responsibility Team have centered on the environment. Among other things, customers tell us they want to:

• Purchase IT products that are designed for the environment and for recycling and reuse.

• Reduce the amount of non-IT waste—specifically packaging, where they request recyclability, smaller packages, fewer packages, and more sustainable materials (for example, avoiding polystyrene foam).

• Obtain help with managing and disposing of IT assets responsibly at the end of the product life.

Governments, too, are responding to the clamor for more responsible stewardship of the environment. The number of climate change laws has increased dramatically over the past decade. Globally, 40 nations and more than 20 states, cities, and/or regions have adopted carbon taxes. In Europe, at least a score of countries levy landfill taxes, and the European Commission is planning to stiffen its already stringent waste reduction targets. Additionally, China is pursuing a circular economy strategy as part of the Chinese Communist Party's commitment to protect the environment.

The challenge Dell faced was not in convincing the supply chain about the importance of sustainability, but rather in determining how we could modify the existing culture to one that fosters innovation as a viable methodology to help us reach our goals.

Our Approach: Collaborate to Innovate

We've joined the efforts of internal teams, suppliers, and outside experts to drive a spirit of innovation and collaboration that keeps Dell—and, as we will see below, the entire IT industry—moving toward a more sustainable, future-focused supply chain.

Suppliers are indispensable partners in our battle to bring environmental responsibility into our products, our materials, and our manufacturing processes. Dell and our competitors operate in highly outsourced environments, where much of the innovation is sourced from suppliers and many activities are managed and executed by those suppliers. Moreover, we all use many of the same supplier partners. As a result, achieving better performance than our competitors becomes a battle to see who can manage the best ecosystems. The ecosystem with the most effective collaboration clearly wins. The leading ecosystem is the one that best aligns on top-down objectives, develops mutual goals, trusts the other ecosystem members' intentions, and has confidence in each partner's ability to execute.

Creating an Innovation Framework to Achieve a Legacy of Good

Dell's innovation approach is highly structured for effective, tangible results in the areas of product design, materials, and manufacturing processes. When we set the 2020 Legacy of Good goals in 2012, we reoriented our organization internally toward a future-focused supply chain. This was no simple feat in an industry such as ours, where competition is high and margins are often razor-thin. These competitive realities create pressure on the supply chain to drive out excess cost wherever possible. Critical to our ability to reach the 2020 goals was the creation of an innovation framework that would enable innovative thinking and a platform for risk taking to achieve these goals.

Dell's innovation framework was inspired by the design consultancy IDEO's (the inventor of disruptive innovations such as Apple's mouse and Steelcase's Leap chair) process called "Design Thinking." Design thinking offers a defined and efficient framework for individuals and teams to use valuable time and resources in pursuit of real-world solutions and has been implemented across Dell's supply chain. Nearly every Dell employee in the supply chain organization, as well as a number of our key suppliers, has attended this training. The framework consists of three major elements: Design Thinking workshops, Innovation Olympics (annual), and an annual Packaging Innovation Summit. There is an overall governance body, called the Supply Chain Sustainability Steering Committee, that helps prioritize projects and funnels ideas through the innovation framework. It is this governing body that is responsible for Dell reaching the goals in the 2020 Legacy of Good.

When tackling innovation, a critical first step consists of defining the challenge and framing the problem to be solved. Dell's 2020 Legacy of Good Plan became the primary framework to provide goals that are specific, relevant to daily work, and aligned with business priorities. Much of Dell's approach to sustainability-oriented supply chain innovation is inspired by design thinking.

Ideas are generated, prioritized, scoped, and approved for formal entry into the governed process in order to drive execution. Milestones are identified, steps are taken to develop relevant technology, the supply chain is enabled, support (and often funding) is provided to partners and innovators, goals are integrated into supplier metrics, and progress is rigorously tracked. The rigor defined here is another crucial aspect to this model. It provides the support and validation that the supply chain requires to mitigate risk and gain buy-in as processes, products, and/or materials are changed.

Our efforts to drive a more sustainable supply chain are governed by our Supply Chain Sustainability Steering Committee, co-led by our Supply Chain and our Environmental/

Exhibit 1: Joint Idea Creation with Suppliers Follows a Three-Step Process

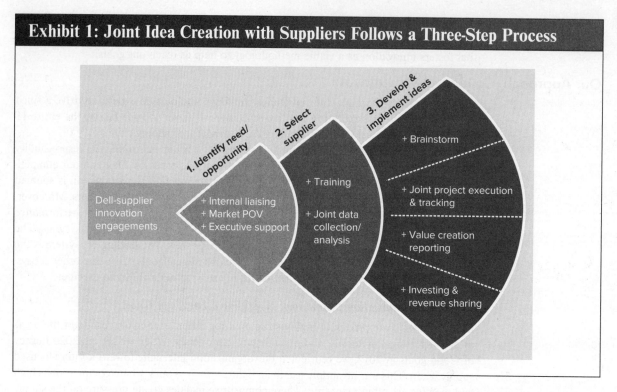

Regulatory Affairs teams. This committee, which meets monthly, ensures the company follows a holistic approach that brings together not only Supply Chain and Environmental/Regulatory Affairs, but also Industrial Design and Product Engineering. Many of the best supply chain sustainability ideas in Dell have come from the bottom up through annual competitions like the Global Operations Innovation Olympics and the Packaging Innovation Summit.

When sourcing innovation in our supply base, we follow the three-step process schematically represented in Exhibit 1.

A dedicated project management office is vital to keep the innovation-focused collaboration on track. The project office also ensures the proper integration of project goals into supplier metrics.

The tangible outputs of the different initiatives coordinated by the Supply Chain Sustainability Steering Committee are visible in three areas: product definition, use of materials, and manufacturing processes. Examples in each of these three areas are provided in the section "Our Results."

Extending Our Legacy of Good to the Entire IT Industry

Dell's investment in creating a culture of innovation along with a supporting framework to convert ideas into reality has resulted in many awards over the past 18 months. Among the recognitions are the 2015 Circular Economy Award at the World Economic Forum, the 2015 Sustainable Purchasing Leadership Council Award in Asia, the Green Electronic Council Catalyst Award, the 2016 CES Innovation and Eco-Design Award, and the 2015 EPA SMM Electronics Challenge Award.

As proud as we are of these awards, we are even prouder of how they allow us to influence our competitors' supply chains toward better environmental outcomes. For example, our recognized leadership in the use of closed-loop post-consumer recycled (PCR) plastics positioned us to convince our partners at EPEAT to include optional closed-loop PCR criteria in the revised 1680.1 standard. This revised standard will incentivize other manufacturers to increase their recycling rates of end-of-life IT plastics waste, which will be used to manufacture new IT equipment.

Likewise, when we encourage our suppliers to provide us with more carbon- and water-efficient solutions by requiring more than 100 of them to report their emissions to the Carbon Disclosure Project, the lower emissions and tens of millions of dollars in cost savings do not accrue to the sole benefit of Dell's supply chain. Because we share many of the same suppliers with our competitors, the lower environmental footprint we drive through this initiative extends to the entire industry—and benefits society at large.

Our Results: Sustainable Products, Materials, and Manufacturing

Many of Dell's sustainable supply chain problem statements come from the goals identified in the 2020 Legacy of Good. We feed these problem statements into Design Thinking workshops, our Innovation Olympics, or the Packaging Innovation Summits to find solutions. Many of these projects take several years to come to fruition.

Designing More Sustainable Products

An excellent example of how we have innovated in product design to reduce our environmental footprint is the reduction in emissions of volatile organic compounds (VOCs) from our product finishes. Following IDEO's thought-triggering process of asking questions like "how might we design products without VOC paint," Dell has reduced the relative VOC levels of the finishes on our products. Those launched over the past two years have decreased by 19 percent (notebooks) and 57 percent (desktops, all-in-ones, monitors) annually. On the one hand, we have designed our products to use less paint, by employing in-mold rolled (IMR) film and texture for surface. We were the first brand to use IMR with complex geometry part design (3D), and we are able to meet a variety of demanding industrial design (and customer) expectations such as soft touch and high gloss. On the other hand, where we continue to use paint, the solution we use is now more environment-friendly. For example, we are the first PC brand to use ultra-flat powder, which does not emit VOC. We are also using ultraviolet monocoat, which emits 60 percent less VOC than polyurethane monocoat, in addition to requiring less energy for solidification. Finally, we are also using waterborne paint solutions, whose VOC emissions are negligible.

Using More Sustainable Materials

As mentioned previously, a well-established staple of our approach is our annual Packaging Innovation Summit, now in its eighth edition. This summit gathers current and potentially new Dell suppliers of all sizes, from Fortune 500 corporations to start-ups, to identify new sustainable material solutions in an atmosphere of provocative discussion with an emphasis on creativity and innovation. Each summit focuses on specific packaging areas, with presentations centering on demonstrating the engineering fundamentals of each idea submitted—and, more specifically, on answering the questions of if it can work, how it can be applied to Dell's specified target area, how much it will cost, and how sustainable it is.

Beginning as far back as 2010, the packaging team asked the question, "What if the packaging material could be made from material that is easily renewable?" The question resulted in discovering bamboo as a new material resource. That began a renewable, sustainable trend that remains strong today. In 2014, 100 percent of the packaging for Dell tablet shipments worldwide and 92 percent of the packaging for laptop shipments were sourced from sustainable materials. Among the ways we increased the percentage of sustainable packaging material was by replacing petroleum-based foams with paper-pulp and wheat-straw cushioning, standardizing packaging configurations across models, and reengineering packaging to reduce the need for separate cushioning (e.g., our tablet packaging is now composed completely of cardboard). Additionally, the wheat-straw cushions are not only a more sustainable solution; they are less expensive, too.

In fact, in FY15 we used more than 1,000 tons of wheat straw, having introduced the new sustainable material in the second half of FY14. Even as we expanded the use of wheat

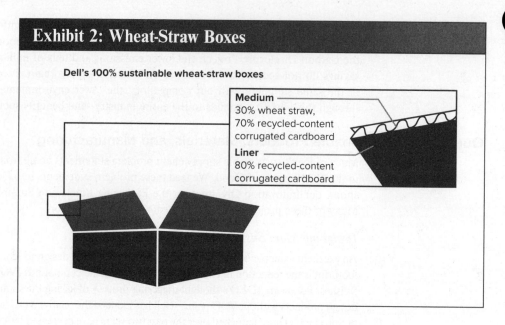

straw to the boxes and cushions for our laptops produced in China, the overall composition of our wheat-straw boxes remained the same: The boxes' liners were made from 80 percent recycled paper content and their medium (wavy, fluted paper between the liners) was made from approximately 30 percent wheat-based fiber and 70 percent recycled-content corrugated cardboard (see Exhibit 2). The molded pulp cushions inside the box are made from approximately 70 percent wheat straw and 30 percent recycled-content paper. It should be noted that by using wheat straw, we are taking what would otherwise be a waste product with negative economic value (as farmers typically burn it in their fields) and upcycling it into packaging for high-tech products. Additionally, the process to manufacture wheat-straw boxes uses 40 percent less energy and 90 percent less water than typical cardboard boxes. A key source of air pollution is averted, rural farmers obtain an additional source of income, we acquire a competitively priced material, and customers meet their own sustainability goals.

Finally, in 2014, we completed our testing of AirCarbon protective bags, which will initially be used to protect Dell Latitude shipments in the United States and Canada. AirCarbon is a carbon-negative material from our supplier Newlight Technologies. It is a plastic made not from oil but rather from industrial sources of carbon emissions, including dairy digesters and methane capture. Newlight uses a biocatalyst to process the gases in a reactor, where the carbon is then pulled out and rearranged into plastic polymers that can be used to make bags or other materials. The catalysts used with AirCarbon are nine times more efficient than other solutions, making it an economic—and carbon-negative—choice (see Exhibit 3).

Employing More Sustainable Manufacturing Processes

Use of recycled-content plastic and other sustainable materials   In 2014, Dell used 11.7 million pounds of recycled-content plastics to make Dell OptiPlex desktops and an assortment of display products. This number represented a 15 percent increase over the previous year.

The electronics industry has historically focused on using recycled-content plastics from clean, "open-loop" sources such as water bottles and used CD cases. Although open-loop sources account today for the majority of Dell's use, closed-loop recycled plastics—including

Exhibit 3: Recyclability and Compostability

The recyclability of Dell packaging

Packaging material	Recyclable	Compostable	Limited recyclability
Corrugated containers and boxes	●		
Wheat-straw boxes and molded cushions	●		
Bamboo cushions	●	●	
Mushroom cushions		●	
Molded paper-pulp cushions	●		
HDPE cushions			●
EPE cushions			●
Plastic bags (includes AirCarbon)			●

plastics derived from electronics recovered through Dell's take-back services—comprised 19 percent of our post-consumer recycled plastic use by volume in 2014, requiring us to reengineer our supply chain to accommodate it. As a result, in May 2014 the Dell OptiPlex™ 3030 All-in-One became the first mainstream desktop made with third-party-certified (by UL Environment), closed-loop recycled plastics. By the end of 2014, 16 Dell displays and three desktops were shipping globally with closed-loop recycled plastics.

By using a combination of traditional and closed-loop post-consumer recycled plastics instead of virgin plastic resin, Dell reduced greenhouse gas emissions by 8,100 metric tons of CO_2e—equivalent to taking more than 1,700 cars off the road for an entire year—and saved approximately $200,000. Achieving this required a major redesign of processes across Dell's engineering, industrial design, procurement, logistics, and marketing teams—as well as intensive coordination with our supply chain and recycling partners—to make sure that the plastics being used meet expectations for performance and aesthetics. This challenge will continue as we increase the use of such plastics in laptops, servers, and thin clients, which contain smaller parts and require plastics with different mechanical qualities.

As we expand the use of closed-loop recycled plastics, we are confronting the challenge of acquiring enough feedstock (see Exhibit 4). Today, much of these plastics comes from the recovery of old systems from U.S.-based customers who turn in their used products at Goodwill locations that participate in the Dell Reconnect take-back program. The plastics are separated and sorted. Then they are inspected, baled, and shipped to China, where Dell's partner Wistron Advanced Material (WAM) blends the plastics with virgin plastics to achieve structural integrity before molding them into new parts. Going forward, the challenge will be to collect a greater volume of closed-loop recycled plastics from more varied locations, particularly in regions that are nearer to where we manufacture our products.

Furthermore, we will continue to increase the amount of post-consumer recycled-content plastic from traditional sources (such as water bottles). Additionally, we will keep pursuing the sourcing and use of new types of recycled-content materials, such as recycled

Exhibit 4: Closed-Loop Recycling at Dell

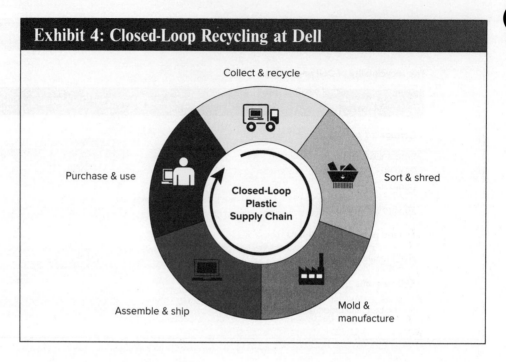

carbon fiber from the aerospace industry. Our plans are to introduce as much as 820,000 pounds of carbon fiber in our portfolio in 2016, up from 0 pounds in 2014 and 170,000 pounds in 2015. In addition to diverting nearly 500 tons of carbon fiber from landfills, we will have saved 3.1 million kilograms of CO2e compared to carbon fiber weave.

Used electronics recovery   E-waste is one of the fastest-growing waste streams globally. According to estimates from the StEP Initiative/United Nations University, the world's population discarded 75 million tons of electrical and electronic equipment in 2015, up from 65.1 million tons in 2012.

To address this issue, Dell is committed to the recovery and proper recycling of used electronics. We offer take-back programs for consumers in 78 countries, where we accept equipment of all brands. Our use of closed-loop recycled plastics, discussed earlier, creates an economically viable outlet for much of the equipment collected. This is particularly important, as local recyclers in many developing countries will only take back materials they can readily sell, leaving the rest to be incinerated or dumped.

Dell has worked hard to increase recovery of used electronics around the world. In China, we have expanded our consumer recycling collection program to 42 designated repair centers, allowing us to leverage existing Dell infrastructure and customers' awareness of service center locations. In India, we have launched a PC Exchange Program in 49 Dell stores across 12 cities. This trade-in program lets customers bring any brand of laptop, desktop, or monitor—in any condition—to a Dell store to receive credit for a new model. In 2014, we signed a five-year agreement with the United Nations Industrial Development Organization to cooperate in identifying and implementing a sustainable e-waste management model for developing countries. In this context, we have worked with Kenya to help set up an e-waste recycling hub and collection network, showing how a developing nation can move from an informal recycling culture to a safe, formal industry take-back program backed by legislation. We have also worked with Uganda to develop such legislation and presented an informal sector recycling model to India's Ministry of Environment and Forest.

Driving forward on our 3Cs strategy   Furthermore, we intensified our focus on executing against our 3Cs packaging strategy (cube, content, and curbside recyclability), saving a cumulative $53.3 million in costs and avoiding 31.3 million pounds of packaging. In this vein, in FY15 we began using Finite Element Analysis and Shock Response Spectrum to identify new opportunities to optimize our packaging configurations and use fewer materials. These tools enable us to more precisely determine where and how products need to be protected. Armed with this information, our engineers were able to develop new configurations of products within their boxes, reducing the amount of material needed for packaging while also decreasing the box size itself—letting us fit more boxes on each pallet. For example, we achieved a 27 percent increase in units per pallet for the Latitude E5550 laptop. And we achieved a 15 percent increase in units per ocean-going shipping container for the Inspiron 3441, adding 500 more units per container.

Conclusion

Dell's commitment to environmentally responsible operations is a fundamental part of our values, as we strive to become even more efficient in how we create and deliver technology solutions worldwide. It extends through our supply chain, where we work with our thousands of partners to find innovative ways to ensure consistent, transparent environmental stewardship. It ultimately provides customers with solutions that give them the power to do more while consuming less.

Our aspirations for 2020 and our achievements to date reflect our approach of considering the environment at every stage of technology's life cycle—from design through manufacturing, usage, and end of life—and then measuring the impact to inform future efforts. Our innovation framework is a critical enabler of our ongoing ability to maintain an efficient and cost-competitive sustainable supply chain.

Council of Supply Chain Management Professionals

How Johnson & Johnson Is Securing the Drug Supply (2016)

Michael Rose, Johnson & Johnson; Michael Sedlatschek, Johnson & Johnson; Robert Kennedy, DMLogic LLC; and Matthew Deep, DMLogic LLC

Executive Summary

Summary of the Initiative

The Johnson & Johnson Family of Companies (J&J) is at the forefront of the effort to ensure the integrity of the drug supply. Through their planning, investment, and commitment, J&J has built and implemented one of the first systems to comply with new federal and global regulations that will protect their drug supply for the patients who use their products, years ahead of the mandated schedule. In the future, every drug that passes through the entirety of the J&J supply chain will be serialized, and will be tracked at each point along the way.

The direction that J&J took, by retaining their legacy WMS and using the adaptive software tool, now positions them for DSCSA compliancy years ahead of schedule. And because the solution was designed in a way that minimized large-scale reinvestment, J&J can focus on their plans to move to their next WMS platform independent of the compliancy challenges.

Innovation Statement

Within the J&J distribution centers, their creative and innovative approach relied on the agility of an adaptive software platform making the design and development quicker to implement, much less expensive, and far less risky to their business than traditional alternatives. Their success positions them to initiate improvements beyond the requirements of the mandates. For these reasons, the J&J innovative approach is one from which supply chain companies across industries can benefit.

Impact Statement

J&J's decision to use the adaptive software brings compliancy to their operation with a total investment that amounted to 70 percent less than originally estimated. Further, their innovative solution has put an infrastructure in place that will require minimal changes as they continue their direction to eventually replace the legacy WMS.

Applicability

As the pharmaceutical industry moves toward serialization in compliance with the federal Drug Supply Chain Security Act, J&J's unique and innovative approach offers companies in any industry an alternative to expensive software development and customization. Utilizing an adaptive software approach, J&J developed a proven solution to bring their supply chain to compliancy offering a safer and more secure drug supply across the globe. That solution could translate to any industry in need of efficiency, safety, and compliancy.

Case Study

Drug manufacturers around the globe are preparing for one of the most vital and comprehensive challenges ever faced by the industry. The goal is total security of the world's drug supply, not just at the point of manufacturing but throughout the supply chain and the life cycle of these drugs. In concert with governmental agencies and regulatory bodies, this new challenge involves the pharmaceutical manufacturers as well as wholesalers, distributors, retailers, and suppliers. Additionally, this challenge will require the efforts of software, technology, and equipment suppliers. It will be pervasive, and it will require a major fundamental change in the way the pharmaceutical industry thinks about, manages, and moves inventory.

For years, the pharmaceutical industry has been dealing with issues of counterfeit and diverted drugs. Despite the considerable investment on the part of the manufacturers and the FDA, a number of counterfeit products continue to make it into the supply chain. These drugs pass through a complex system of distributors, brokers, and wholesalers making detection not only difficult but complicated.

The Johnson & Johnson Family of Companies (J&J) is at the forefront of the effort to ensure the integrity of the drug supply. Through their planning, investment, and commitment, J&J has built and implemented one of the first systems to comply with new federal and global regulations that will protect their drug supply for the patients who use their products, years ahead of the mandated schedule. In the future, every drug that passes through the entirety of the J&J supply chain will be serialized, and will be tracked at each point along the way. Within their distribution centers, their creative and innovative approach relied on the agility of an adaptive software platform making the design and development quicker to implement, much less expensive, and far less risky to their business than traditional alternatives. Their success positions them to initiate improvements beyond the requirements of the mandates. For these reasons, the J&J innovative approach is one from which supply chain companies across industries can benefit.

Evolving Mandates

In 2004 and 2005, Florida and California legislators enacted laws to require drug companies to secure their supply chains. The two states called for the serialization of any drugs entering the states to be captured and tracked. The law also called for a system of reporting on drugs as they moved from manufacturing all the way through to the pharmacy or physician. These two states, with their population size, held force in these efforts. California, for instance, fulfills 9 percent of the total prescriptions in the U.S.

Recognizing the burden the new laws required, first California and then Florida moved the deadlines for compliance to 2009. In those first years, pharmaceutical companies began investigating technologies for labeling and reading serial numbers, and some even went as far as to pilot new systems.

In 2013, the U.S. Congress passed the Drug Supply Chain Security Act (DSCSA). The DSCSA borrowed heavily from the California and Florida mandates, but moved compliancy to the federal level. The DSCSA superseded the state laws in both scope and timing, again pushing the dates for full serialization and compliancy into 2023, with milestones in between for phased tracking and recording.

At the same time California and Florida were developing mandates, similar initiatives were begun in South America, Asia, and the European Union. In addition to the U.S., there are now at least 40 countries that either have passed serialization compliancy laws or have those laws in the legislative process. Some of those countries include China, India, Germany, South Korea, Saudi Arabia, and Turkey. The compliance rules and timelines for each country are different, and they continue to change (for example, Brazil just postponed its deadlines). But the direction is clear: Securing the drug supply has become a global initiative.

Defining the Scope

After several early planning sessions, J&J quickly came to recognize the magnitude of what compliance meant. Major changes were needed to systems, processes, equipment, and packaging as well as the very culture that defined how inventory was managed. These changes would need to be undertaken by their manufacturing plants and distribution centers, and done in coordination with suppliers and customers.

Looking beyond the clear challenges of physically serializing their packages, they also delved into the scope of necessary changes they would need to make to their systems for track and trace, not just to the warehouse management system (WMS), but to the warehouse control systems (WCS). Further, J&J understood that they would need to build a serial number repository database for the exchange of serial information. Beyond these factors, an even greater step involved building the integration layer for reporting product serial numbers for their entire supply chain community.

Within the distribution centers, J&J investigated whether to build the solution onto their existing WMS, or whether to replace the legacy WMS with a new system. They decided on the former, but challenged the team to build the solution in a way that would be complementary to their eventual move to a new WMS platform. At the same time, J&J decided to move forward with barcoding technology for labeling with a vision to use RFID in the future.

In the U.S., J&J operates two distribution centers, one in New Jersey and one in Kentucky. Both facilities used the same WMS with an integrated WCS that manages the physical flow of containers. However, the operations were running on different versions of the WMS software. The J&J WMS system was first installed in 1996, but has had many upgrades and technology refreshes. The decision to retain the WMS necessitated a full technology upgrade to both the WMS and WCS, in order that both of the distribution centers would have these systems on exact versions so that the eventual solution would work with both. Recognizing the increased volume of data that serial number tracking would entail, J&J also decided to purchase a new suite of servers for the systems. With these decisions, the design process for how serialized data would be passed within the J&J systems took shape. J&J recognized that they would need to build a new integration layer to pass serial number information between systems. This included the ability to transmit serial numbers to and from SAP AII, but also to exchange information between the WCS and WMS.

J&J built a team of experienced resources to develop a new process design. Having no precedent for a serialization solution, the design team not only had to consider the standard process, but also had to anticipate exceptions and unanticipated events involving damaged goods, goods with labeling issues, inventory discrepancies, returns, and issues involving data transmission errors. This exercise underscored the reality that the solution would need to be even more comprehensive than originally defined.

Important to the entire initiative, J&J adopted a philosophy of using the serialization initiative to fulfill their compliancy requirements but, further, to bring incremental improvements to their operations and to their customers. This approach permeated every design decision undertaken.

J&J needed to determine the extent to which serial numbers would need to be tracked in the distribution operation. The key consideration was the approach of using a parent/child structure for tracking serial numbers. That is, when manufactured, the serial number of each sellable unit (the child), whether a case or an each, would be associated to the pallet (the parent) as depicted in the graphic below:

Single tier		**Child:** The individual package is the "child" package within the serialization hierarchy because it is the smallest of three tiers of serialization

Three tiers		**Parent:** The case is the "parent" tier of the hierarchy, with the "child" (individual package) serial numbers aggregated to the case

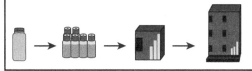

Four tiers		**Grandparent:** The pallet is the "grandparent" tier, with the "parent" (case) serial numbers aggregated to the pallet

In this manner, where pallet homogeneity was maintained, a "goalpost" approach of capturing numbers as they arrived and as they are shipped would be sufficient to provide an acceptable level of reliability. However, where that homogeneity was released, for example, when a case was pulled from a pallet for fulfillment, J&J determined that the child units would need to be positively tracked as they moved within the operation.

Given J&J's culture of strict standards for inventory accuracy and reliability as well as the recognition of exception processing, J&J determined to implement a solution that would provide maximum verification in the process.

Innovative Solution

J&J began the process of compliance long before the DSCSA was passed, driving their solution toward compliancy with the state mandates. Even though the new federal mandate moved the timeline for compliancy, at that point J&J determined that they would continue with their initiative. Considering the scope of the tasks this initiative required, their logical conclusion was that the solution would necessitate an equally enormous investment in time, people, and capital.

It is sometimes the case, however, that the best solution for the most complex of problems is the simplest one, and herein lies the genius and innovation of the J&J solution.

Once the decision was made to retain their legacy WMS, J&J investigated the cost of creating the serialization capabilities within the WMS. That investigation proved that not only was the investment going to be expensive, but it would take far too long and force J&J into a riskier position involving more pervasive disruptions to the operations. As an alternative, J&J looked to using adaptive software to solve these challenges.

The term *adaptive software* refers to a new body of software tools that essentially automate the process of building new code to extend and/or enhance the life of existing systems. Doing so empowers the user to customize and personalize their solutions, with minimal or no changes to source code. Adaptive software can be used to create new RF message streams, new screens, or reports. Because these tools have automated functions, much of any solution can be built through point-and-click selections to configure new features and create a decision path for an entire new process flow.

This unique and innovative approach yielded results and benefits beyond expectations. J&J already had an adaptive software tool in use with their WMS at one of their operations. The adaptive software platform that J&J uses is called STEPLogic. The platform is designed to enable users to create new functionality as an alternative, or as a replacement for existing WMS functionality.

The use of STEPLogic fit well with the multiple challenges faced by J&J in terms of mitigating risk and expense, while implementing a solution that met the rigors and timeline of the mandates. What this direction meant for J&J is that they could be flexible in applying "spot solutions" affecting their systems only where change was needed. This allowed them to avoid changing source code that would impact large modules of the system.

With their adaptive software tool in place, J&J gained tremendous agility both in how the system would track and trace serial numbers and in how those numbers would be transmitted between systems.

As the graphic below shows, J&J decided to use the tool to provide new functionality to the WMS, but also as the means to exchange information between SAP AII and the WMS, as well as the WMS and the WCS.

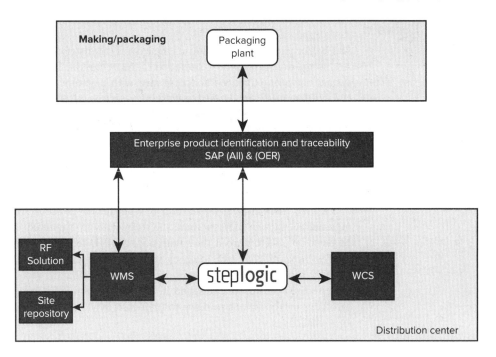

As an example of developing spot solutions, J&J designed their receiving operation solution to treat homogenous pallets differently than mixed or partial pallets. Relying on the integrity of the inferred parent/child relationship, J&J recognized that the existing WMS was perfectly suited to handle the receipt of full pallets in its current form. As a result, J&J needed to use STEPLogic only for partial pallet receipts, enabling the operation to capture case-level serial numbers. As such, J&J only needed to add a small new process flow for cases, avoiding a significant new investment in their WMS that would have been necessary without the adaptive software tool. The timing and expense saved by not altering the entire receiving module, and the minimal disruption this caused to the operation, proved highly beneficial to the project in terms of both the timeline and investment.

J&J's innovative use of the adaptive software tool provided similar spot solutions throughout the rest of the operation. With STEPLogic as the integration middleware, full cases that are picked using the existing WMS RF process move along a conveyor through an automated print and apply system. At that point, the WCS scans the serial number of the case for positive validation with the WMS.

Similarly, the existing WMS functionality is used when unit-level items are picked. These items are picked to an overpack container that subsequently moves to a packing operation. At packing, new screens developed using STEPLogic provide the staff with the ability to verify and record the individual bottle serial numbers and associate those serial numbers with the overpack container, and thus with the shipment.

Using their adaptive software system, J&J was able to implement the necessary changes to meet compliancy in their operations without having to change any core code of their WMS.

In both operations, J&J designed a scheme that provided full, positive identification and association of serial numbers with orders while avoiding the time-intensive means of doing so in the course of the pick operation. Therefore, the solution enabled J&J to maintain their current levels of productivity while complying with the mandates.

Moving Forward

J&J began piloting the solution in their two U.S. distribution centers in October of 2014. Additional drugs continue to be added to the operation. Since its original introduction, the system has been enhanced and upgraded with new functionality, further extending J&J's capabilities. Additionally, J&J is working with several of their larger customers to extend the tracking and tracing of serial numbers beyond the J&J walls. This progress puts J&J at the forefront of the industry for compliancy, as well as in front of the federal mandate for full unit-level traceability in 2023.

By their estimates, their decision to use the adaptive software brings compliancy to their operation with a total investment of only 30 percent of what it otherwise would have cost them.

Further, their innovative solution has put an infrastructure in place that will require minimal changes as they continue their direction to eventually replace the legacy WMS. J&J also intends to retrofit the solution with RFID technology in the near future.

The direction that J&J took, by retaining their legacy WMS and using the adaptive software tool, now positions them for DSCSA compliancy, years ahead of schedule. And because the solution was designed in a way that minimized large-scale reinvestment, J&J can focus on their plans to move to their next WMS platform independent of the compliancy challenges.

Council of Supply Chain Management Professionals

Global Telecom Giant Vodafone Gains 100 percent Transparency (2017)

Leveraging Big Data to Build a World-Class Purchasing Operation

Executive Summary

To keep up with the rapid change and to stay competitive in the digital age, telecommunications giant Vodafone realized that it had to transform and streamline its SCM operation to become world-class in terms of efficiency and agility. Vodafone was able to use Celonis Process Mining–a revolutionary big data analytics technology–to uncover hidden inefficiencies, and to automate and streamline supply chain processes. Vodafone was able to cut process costs by 11 percent (reducing the cost per purchase order from $3.22 to $2.85, a world class number), reduce time to market by 20 percent, and achieve 100 percent process transparency in less than six months.

The Challenge

With 470 million mobile customers and 14 million broadband customers, mobile operations in 26 countries, and fixed broadband operations in 17 countries, Vodafone is one of the world's largest telecommunications companies, providing a range of voice, messaging, data, and fixed communications. Operating in the market for over 30 years, Vodafone understands that its customers need a communications partner with solutions that scale and adapt as their businesses change beyond standard telephone operations.

To support the ever-changing needs of customers, Vodafone needed to transform its massive purchasing operations and adapt back-end processes, such as Purchase-to-Pay, to match changing business demands. Vodafone wanted to leverage the opportunities presented by the digital age, such as process automation and big data analytics, to get its operations to the next level. The gap between performance losses and determining the appropriate course of action to improve the situation was too wide to ensure the efficient operations desired.

What are the challenges with Big Data today?

Inefficiencies, bottlenecks, loss of time and money

Large number of SCM reports —they tell us that something goes wrong but not where and why

Getting to the root cause of problems takes far too long

However, driving this transformation is very challenging, with hundreds of thousands of transactions, which accumulate an enormous amount of data. Vodafone annually manages more than 800,000 purchase orders, 5 million invoices, and 40 million assets. The company lacked the necessary insights into how processes were executed and performing, especially compared to the desired "to-be" state.

Vodafone couldn't afford to waste any more time, as the company knew it needed to find a solution to not only bring transparency across operations, but provide actionable insights to help address the root causes of its process inefficiencies.

Que Process Mining

With the goal of creating the "perfect purchase order" and achieving business excellence, Vodafone selected Celonis for its revolutionary big data analytics technology: Celonis Process Mining. Process mining is an innovative technology that mines massive amounts of data to reconstruct what actually happens in companies' business processes, spots the inefficiencies, and suggests improvements automatically.

Process mining has been gaining a lot of traction in data science and artificial intelligence research, especially in the recent years. Partnering up with Celonis, Vodafone is at the forefront of adopting this exciting innovation, bringing this new concept to life at a true enterprise scale.

The idea behind process mining is simple: How can we use the tremendous amount of data accumulated in a large organization to understand human behavior, automatically reconstruct the way the organization works, and find ways to improve? Process mining achieves this by automatically reengineering a model for the organization out of the data. In Vodafone's case, it leverages the key systems used for supply chain execution such as SAP ERP, Ariba, and SAP SRM. The reengineered model then shows which cases are handled efficiently and where the organization needs to improve. Leveraging machine learning and artificial intelligence, the system can recommend improvement measures, which basically creates an X-ray and advisory machine for the day-to-day business.

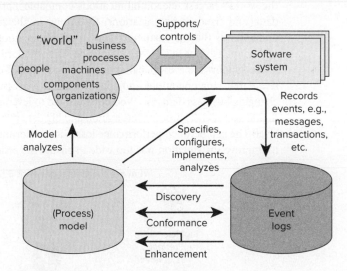

This business X-ray and advisory machine allowed Vodafone to easily build a bridge across the information gap between performance losses and determining the appropriate course of action, as the technology automatically learned how Vodafone's processes worked and was able to detect hidden vulnerabilities. Altogether, this helped Vodafone's big data analytics team to transform the entire organization and create the "perfect purchase order process."

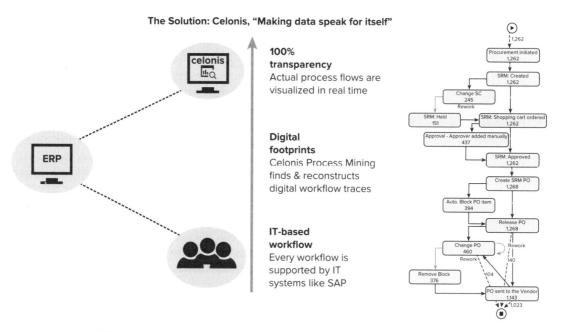

The "perfect purchase order" aimed to improve the procurement process and reduce the number of errors in the ordering process, to ensure "right-first-time ordering" for all customers. This can be challenging, given the size of the operation, variety of different suppliers, and quickly changing business needs in the adapting telecommunications market. Vodafone used Celonis Process Mining to "shine the light" and determine where inefficiencies and deviations were driving up costs or increasing delivery times—impossible without automation, given the company has more than 10 terabytes of data housed in various storage systems and applications, and also has data on SAP's HANA relational database management system.

The Findings Were Impactful

Celonis Process Mining discovered multiple variations and inefficiencies in the organization. For example, many of the orders with the longest throughput times were showing multiple deviations from the standard process, before the purchase order was even released to the supplier. Vodafone was able to see that the deviations could be attributed to three main causes:

1. Deviations due to low automation levels, when users need to manually insert values that could be automatically filled by the system if it had a solid set of rules on the backend.
2. Deviations due to incorrect data at the source (i.e., tax codes and payment terms).
3. Deviations that could be corrected by enhancing best practices within the buyers' community (i.e., streamlining material categories, bundling demand with desired suppliers, etc.).

When Celonis alerted Vodafone to low automated transactions, the technology highlighted where the company could improve by using robotic process automation. Because a high level of human interaction was still needed in these transactions, Celonis Process Mining was able to determine how robotic process automation could easily and automatically replicate the humans' role without error and at a faster speed, saving the company valuable time and money.

The Results

The initiative proved to be highly impactful to Vodafone's purchasing operation. Specifically, Vodafone was able to create 100 percent transparency, achieve a significant cost reduction, and improve time to market, helping Vodafone maintain its global-leader status in the highly competitive telecommunications market.

Full Process Transparency within Seconds

Prior to Celonis, running a root cause analysis every time something went wrong took around two days for each occasion to complete. With Celonis Process Mining, root cause analysis can easily be achieved in a matter of seconds, saving 48 hours per issue. That saves over a week's worth of valuable time employees were spending trying to figure out the problem with every four issues discovered. This helped Vodafone eliminate errors in procurement, as the company could see deviations from the standard process and intervene. Further, Vodafone was able to maximize catalog buying and speed up the release of a purchase order to a supplier. With achieving 100 percent transparency into its operations, Vodafone is now able to make all business decisions based on facts rather than assumptions.

Becoming World-Class by Reducing Operational Purchasing Costs by 11 percent

Through the "perfect purchase order initiative," 85 percent of purchase orders are now completed correctly the first time around without any mistakes, surpassing the organization's 80 percent goal in less than six months. With 85 percent of purchase orders completed correctly the first time around, Vodafone reduced the cost of each process order from $3.22 per PO to $2.85 per PO, surpassing the Hackett Group's world-class standard. This provided Vodafone with an 11 percent cost-savings improvement.

Reduced Time to Market by 20 percent

In a dynamic and competitive environment, time to market is critical in order to stay ahead of the competition. Through debottlenecking the purchasing operation, Vodafone was able to improve time to market by 20 percent, or two full weeks.

With the help of Celonis Process Mining, Vodafone created a world-class purchasing operation, improving customer satisfaction and saving the global leader valuable time and money.

Perfect PO—What success looks like...

85% of the purchase orders are created right first time (without any type of manual rework)

Target: 80%

+12%

Baseline	Apr'16	May'16	Jun'16	Jul'16	Aug'16	Sep'16
73%	76%	78%	79%	79%	80%	85%

Benefits:

Customer experience

Efficiency & effectiveness

Time to market

Powered by:

SCM Big Data Process Analytics Team

September 2016, Sainsbury's Acquires Argos

It's widely reported that one of the main attractions from Sainsbury's acquiring Argos was getting access to its retailers' online delivery network, to rival Amazon's fulfillment propositions.

Now that the network has been designed, Argos has taken Supply Chain Guru in-house so that the models can be changed to reflect new circumstances on the ground.

The team has taken a concept from the drawing board to operational reality and in doing so transformed the Argos supply chain to more ably deliver for its customers and to meet their strategic goals and future ambition.

Argos has now extended its hub-and-spoke distribution concept with a trial of a regional hub. The regional hub trial will provide the potential to hold a significantly higher number of products, potentially including third-party products, for same-day fulfilment.

The existing system enabled the introduction of same-day delivery service Fast Track, and is part of Argos's Transformation Plan to reinvent the company as a digital retail leader.

Same-Day Home Delivery, Fast Track Delivery

At Argos, Check and Reserve has been the shopping mission of choice for many customers since it was invented 15 years ago. For a while this was a differentiator. However, many retailers have now caught up. With the success of Check and Reserve, small-item delivery received less focus over this period.

This resulted in Argos having a home delivery offering that lagged behind, in an environment that was moving more customers online, and into home delivery. For small items delivery, they had an early, next-day cut-off, with a 13-hour (7 am to 8 pm) delivery window. This was not competitive or convenient.

Argos chose to build a disruptive proposition that would change the way people thought about home delivery for good. They wanted to innovate and, like Check and Reserve, build a unique proposition. Fast Track Nationwide Same-Day Home Delivery was born.

Fast Track is now the UK's leading home delivery proposition.

* 20,000 products available for same-day delivery.
* Four convenient delivery slots; 7 am–10 am, 10 am–1 pm, 2 pm–6 pm, 7 pm–10 pm.
* Three "in day" cut-offs for same day (5 am, 1 pm, 6 pm).
* Seven days a week—364 days a year.
* To 95 percent of UK households—Inverness to Isle of Wight; Holyhead to Great Yarmouth.

Customers were most excited that they could order up to 6 pm on a Sunday and still get their order delivered that evening!

To achieve this, Argos had to completely reengineer its operating model and systems infrastructure. This involved complementing our more traditional fulfillment model with a store-based fulfillment operation delivered by 3,300 drivers employed by Argos. This required collaboration and a huge effort across the entire Argos business and its supply chain partners.

Additionally, it was challenged to make sure that the operation had a lower cost to service; in other words it made sound business sense too.

Details of Execution

The ambition behind Fast Track meant the scale of change management would be larger than any other in Argos's five-year transformation plan.

The program was split into three core programs:

* **IT systems**
  * Changes to Voice Operations/Warehouse Management/Sterling OMS.
  * Introduction of Paragon Dynamic Routing Solution and EPOD systems.

- **Supply Operation and Systems**
  - Forecasting and replenishing home delivery across 163 hubs rather than one central site.
  - The ability to forecast and replenish a "Dark Hub" for North London to add additional capacity for the capital.

- **Operational Development—which included**
  - 25 teams including Store Operations/Home Delivery/Distribution/Marketing/Customer Experience/Contact Centre/Finance/Digital/Procurement/Supply/Brand Management/HR.

Additionally, Argos needed to recruit 3,300 customer fulfillment drivers, specially trained to deliver great customer service at the doorstep.

With this level of complexity, and moving at pace, there were times when systems didn't always behave as expected. Together Argos had to learn fast and fail fast. However, with a team of colleagues solely focused on the customer, delivering the final mile rarely failed, even in the pilot stages while trying to get the systems reconfigured. There were days when manifests could not be downloaded to the stores, and the teams still went out and delivered 90 percent+ without any routes or schedules.

At the same time, the pressure was on to let customers know about Fast Track. A powerful marketing and PR campaign was put in place. This meant the teams involved had to deliver in line with our demanding timelines, to get Fast Track launched in time for Christmas 2015.

> Fastest way to shop including same day delivery, 7 days a week for £3.95 and in store pick up in as little as 60 seconds.

Innovation

Argos was determined to set up, from scratch, the UK's leading same-day nationwide home-delivery proposition, aiming to genuinely surprise and delight customers and set new expectations—furthermore implementing this almost entirely within its own operation, giving it complete control of the performance, experience, and future development.

Argos wanted to bring its friendly store experience to the customers' door—through the faces of local store colleagues.

Many retailers and pure plays are chasing same-day delivery, often confined to urban areas using 3PLs, and early same-day cut-offs. Experience told Argos that the busiest order windows were early afternoon, so a midday cut-off was not good for many customers. Argos wanted as many customers as possible to experience same-day delivery even if they ordered in the afternoon, and regardless of whether they lived in Central London or Inverness.

> The modeling of North London showed a gap in our capacity to deliver the proposition. This resulted in the need to define and implement a technical and operational solution for a "Dark Hub." This was carried out in parallel to the main program and went from a property search to operational reality in 7 or 8 months and did not delay the timescales we were working to.

The technical challenge was immense and critical to the innovation too. Argos needed to offer slots in real time across various order channels (without common order taking services). The system had to be able to offer slots, book deliveries, and optimize routing in real time so that *it could cut off routes just one hour before departure.* And then it had to get these routes down to 163 fulfilment hubs and 900+ drivers so that they could load and depart in under 45 minutes.

Benefits

Fast Track Home Delivery is the leading delivery proposition across the UK. Not just for speed, but for convenience too. This has landed fantastically well with existing and new customers alike—the best way to demonstrate this is in their own words . . .!

Twitter Feedback from Satisfied Fast Track Customers

"The fact that Argos do same day delivery on a Sunday makes me so happy."

"Fantastic @Argos Online same day delivery. Lots of updates re delivery & txt when 15min away. Lottie is loving her freshly filled sand table."

"@Argos Online Love your same day delivery service. It's superb. Especially great for baby things. Very impressed."

"Big thanks to @Argos Online—only £3.95 for same day delivery, for something I urgently needed, that's amazing! @ArgosHelpers"

"Seriously impressed by same day delivery from Argos. It's blown my simple wee mind. #easily-impressed"

Argos's online delivery feedback metric has improved significantly, with calls per order to its contact center halved, with the exception of a 100 percent uplift in calls checking if the website offering same day is correct!

During the first two months of its introduction, Internet sales grew by 13 percent, and represented 55 percent of total Argos sales—up from 50 percent the year before.

The new business model relies on the strengths of the Argos hub-and-spoke network and stock accuracy to enable local same-day home delivery and covers 95 percent of UK population.

Council of Supply Chain Management Professionals

One Size Doesn't Fit All: How to Optimize Product Distribution for a Niche Market within a High-Velocity Logistics Environment (2017)

Supply Chain Product Distribution—Case Study

About the Company

Whirlpool Corporation is the world's leading global manufacturer and marketer of home appliances with $21 billion in annual sales, 93,000 workers, and 70 manufacturing and technology research centers throughout the world. Focusing on consumer needs fuels its growth and keeps it relevant in homes around the world. It exists to create purposeful innovation that helps keep homes running smoothly so personal and family lives can flourish. Consumers enjoy Whirlpool Corporation's innovative products marketed under Whirlpool, KitchenAid, Maytag, Consul, Brastemp, Amana, Bauknecht, Jenn-Air, Indesit, and other major brand names in nearly every country throughout the world.

Challenge

One of Whirlpool Corporation's strengths is its portfolio of exceptional brands to meet the needs of a diverse range of customers. This allows the company to leverage the overall volume in operational business processes, such as product distribution, to maximize value and minimize cost. However, there are niche markets that Whirlpool serves that may not reap the same benefits because of their lower volume. In these cases, one size doesn't fit all. An enhanced distribution strategy is needed to provide a superior level of service comparable to the higher-volume segments. The scope of this particular initiative was focused within the United States and the regional distribution centers supporting the U.S. market.

Approach

Customer first. A cross-functional team was formed to investigate and gain a better understanding of these particular customer expectations. The expectations were then compared against our current distribution strategy to identify the areas to work that would create more value for this unique customer segment and eliminate any current pain points. During this investigation phase, the team identified three niche customer expectations that were being sub-optimized with the high-velocity distribution strategy. The niche customer expectations were not very different from the mass customers, but there were shortfalls in the current strategy that constrained the logistics process from delivering the same or a higher level of service as the mass customers.

1. The majority of customers in this niche market have a different purchasing style than the mass segments. They are not shopping for replacement appliances, but instead are interested in buying a full suite of matching appliances. The high-velocity distribution model dictated that models not meeting a certain sales threshold would not be stocked at the regional distribution centers. This low-velocity product would only deploy when an order was placed. As a result, there could be a significant difference between delivery dates for each individual appliance within the suite order because the appliances are manufactured and deployed from different factories across the country with varying transportation lead times to the regional distribution centers. In some cases, this was enough of a deterrent for the customer to reconsider buying the suite at all from this particular brand.

2. A customer's choice in appliance platform can vary by region. For example, in the cooking category, fuel type (gas vs. electric) varies by region. In the high-velocity distribution strategy, some of these regionally preferred appliances would be held back at the factory distribution center because their historical sales did not meet the distribution thresholds compared to higher-volume SKUs. Customers not willing to wait the longer lead time may then be convinced to choose a competitive brand alternative by a sales associate.

3. The niche market customer isn't any different from the mass market customer in that they do not want to wait a long period of time for their appliances to arrive. However, the high-velocity distribution strategy dictated that lower-volume SKUs were not deployed or if deployed would reside in a mixing center until there was an actual order before being transported to their final distribution center. This transportation path created more lead time between when the customer placed an order and finally received the appliance.

Based on these three niche customer expectations, the team identified possible countermeasures to trial. The trials would allow the team to test their hypotheses and validate if these countermeasures would address the specific unfulfilled needs. See Table 1 for detailed problem/countermeasure information.

It is important to note that the inventory management organization also recognized the value in understanding the inventory patterns and trends of this unique business. As a result, a separate inventory management segment was created for the niche market. This allowed the niche market to have stocking logic parameters based on the SKUs within that business instead of being compared to the mass business volume. This change has created a framework for continued future success by managing the inventory parameters for the niche market separately.

Results

The countermeasures were put in place on a temporary basis (12-week trial) to evaluate their ability to address the issue. Any countermeasure that was deemed to be effective and sustainable would become a permanent solution and an enhancement to the distribution strategy for this niche market. At first glance, the countermeasures may appear to be adding more SKU complexity, inventory, and cost to the distribution network with very little chance of a large payback because it's a lower-volume business. However, on the contrary, it was discovered that the investment cost was very minimal and there was significant improvement in product availability, while lead time and lead time variation were

TABLE 1
**Distribution
Strategy Problem/
Countermeasure Chart**

Customer expectations (related to the lower-volume niche customer)	Problem (shortfall of high-velocity distribution strategy to niche market)	Countermeasure
1. A customer ordering a suite of appliances expects all the appliances to be delivered within the same week, if not all in the same day.	Individual product availability lead time within the suite varied significantly in some cases because the distribution stocking logic was determined by individual SKU historical sales. As a result, a customer could have significantly different delivery dates for each appliance.	Used suite sale history versus individual appliance sales to apply stocking logic for product distribution to minimize lead time variation among the appliances within the suite. This new synergy allowed the customer to have similar if not identical delivery dates for each appliance within the suite.
2. Customers residing in different regions of the country can have very different preferences in appliance platforms but still expect preferred appliances to be available within the same timeframe as a standard model.	Regional preferences are not considered in the distribution stocking plan for the regional distribution centers unless they meet a certain sales threshold within that region compared to the overall volume. Lower-volume product was held back at the factory distribution center until an actual order was placed, which added lead time from customer order to delivery.	Used sales history as well as competitive flooring data at main trade customers to strategically deploy and stock preferred appliances by region.
3. Niche customers expect their appliance to be available within the same timeframe as the mass customer. They expect to be provided the same level of service or higher and do not want to give more notice because their order is considered nonstandard.	In order to optimize truck loads, lower-volume SKUs are often sent to mixing centers as an intermediary step before going to their final destination. This transportation path created more lead time between order placement and delivery.	Used weekly sales data to create a distribution path that bypassed the mixing center and went directly to the final regional distribution center. Trucks were optimized by leveraging the volume of specific higher sales product within the same route to fill the truck without the risk of the lower-volume product being jeopardized because the higher-volume product consumed all the truck capacity.

reduced. Availability increased by 10 percent within Special Suites, 20 percent within Regional customization, and 40 percent within the direct-ship activities. Overall availability for niche customers surpassed mass customers by 1 percent. This was a significant achievement considering niche availability was historically 10 percent lower than mass availability. Lead time was reduced by 25 percent with the direct ship initiative, and overall lead time variation within Special Suites was reduced by up to 80 percent when considering extreme cases of customer orders with variable delivery dates. The trial results are also displayed in Graphs 1 through 4.

In addition, these improvements are having long-reaching effects throughout the organization. Market managers have reported increases in trade customer confidence, which has resulted in increased sales.

Internally, the logistics and inventory management organizations are considering similar approaches to other business segments within Whirlpool.

GRAPH 1
Percent Improvements in Availability*

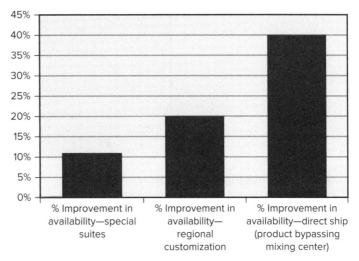

*Compared to pretrial averages

GRAPH 2
Percent Difference of Niche Business Availability Compared to Mass Availability

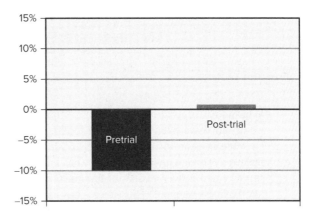

GRAPH 3
Pretrial Delivery Date Variation—Special Suites
(same scale used in both Graph 3 and Graph 4)

Graph is a representation of actual customer orders with significant delivery date variation.

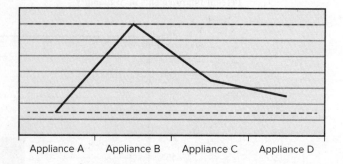

GRAPH 4
Post-trial Delivery Date Variation—Special Suites
(same scale used in both Graph 3 and Graph 4)

Up to 80% variation reduction in delivery dates when considering customers' orders represented in Graph 3.

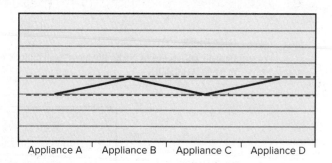

Conclusion

Whirlpool Corporation's continuous improvement mindset revealed an opportunity that would not have been identified if looking only at high-level metrics. One size didn't fit all when it came to the product distribution needs of a niche segment of the company's business. The enhancements that were made to the distribution strategy have helped the supply chain deliver a superior level of service and create great momentum for this particular business segment. This success has caused other Whirlpool business segments to take notice. Feedback from individuals in the field is also an important indicator of genuine progress. This is a quote from a market manager within the niche market: "I just wanted to send a note to let you know that I really appreciate your efforts . . . Not having to follow up on availability issues . . . has freed up so much of my time that I've been able to focus on more important things . . . like selling more appliances . . ."

The TransCelerate Comparator Network: Transforming the Supply Chain for Clinical Comparator Medicines (2017)

Nishchal Chudasama
Nish Chudasama is a Group Leader for Clinical Supply Chain Operations at
Bristol-Myers Squibb.

Jason LaRoche
Jason LaRoche is an Associate Director of the R&D Operations Innovation
department at Janssen.

Terry Walsh
Terry Walsh is the Head of Global Packaging, Labeling, Distribution, &
Comparators at GlaxoSmithKline.

The procurement of comparator medicines for use in clinical trials poses a formidable challenge for supply chain professionals within biopharmaceutical research and development. This case study describes the synthesis and evolution of the TransCelerate Comparator Network, a biopharmaceutical industry forum that facilitates the procurement of comparator medicines and exchange of information between participating member companies. The goal of this network is to enable member companies to conduct clinical trials more efficiently and with enhanced integrity.

In March 2016 Dalvir Gill, CEO of TransCelerate, was getting ready to type a congratulatory e-mail to the Comparator Network Team. Dalvir had a deep sense of satisfaction at how the Comparator Network, one of the five initial projects, had evolved since TransCelerate's inception in 2012 and surpassed the $100 million milestone in comparator spend across member organizations.

TransCelerate

In September 2012, 10 leading biopharmaceutical companies announced that they had formed a nonprofit organization to accelerate the development of new medicines. Abbott, AstraZeneca, Boehringer Ingelheim, Bristol-Myers Squibb, Eli Lilly, GlaxoSmithKline,

Johnson & Johnson, Pfizer, Roche, and Sanofi launched TransCelerate BioPharma Inc. (TransCelerate), the largest-ever initiative of its kind, to identify and solve common drug development challenges with the end goals of improving the quality of clinical studies and bringing new medicines to patients faster.

TransCelerate evolved from relationships fostered via the Hever Group, a forum for executive R&D leadership to discuss relevant issues facing the industry and solutions for addressing common challenges. In the words of the acting CEO of TransCelerate Garry Neil, MD, "There is widespread alignment among the heads of R&D at major pharmaceutical companies that there is a critical need to substantially increase the number of innovative new medicines, while eliminating inefficiencies that drive up R&D costs."

The mission at TransCelerate is to work together across the global biopharmaceutical research and development community and share research and solutions that simplify and accelerate the delivery of exciting new medicines for patients. TransCelerate membership is available to biopharmaceutical research and development organizations that engage in innovative discovery, development, and manufacturing of new medicines. TransCelerate has three membership tiers, based on an organization's global research and development spend, which allows companies of all sizes to consider membership.

In the words of Janet Woodcock, MD, director of the U.S. Food and Drug Administration's (FDA) Center for Drug Evaluation & Research, "We applaud the companies in TransCelerate BioPharma for joining forces to address a series of longstanding challenges in new drug development. This collaborative approach in the pre-competitive arena, utilizing the collective experience and resources of 10 leading biopharmaceutical companies and others to follow, has the promise to lead to new paradigms and cost savings in drug development, all of which would strengthen the industry and its ability to develop innovative and much-needed therapies for patients."

Members of TransCelerate identified clinical study execution as the organization's area of focus. Five initial projects were selected by the group for funding and development, including

✓ Development of a shared user interface for investigator site portals.
✓ Mutual recognition of study site qualification and training.
✓ Development of a risk-based site-monitoring approach and standards.
✓ Development of clinical data standards.
✓ Establishment of a comparator drug supply model.

In December 2012, TransCelerate appointed Dr. Dalvir Gill, PhD, as their chief executive officer to lead the newly created entity.

The Comparator Network

One of the five initial projects selected by TransCelerate member companies under clinical study execution was the establishment of a comparator drug supply model.

What Are Comparator Medicines?

Comparator medicines are marketed commercial drug products used in clinical trials to provide a direct comparison against an investigational medicinal product (IMP) or another commercial drug product. They may also be used in conjunction with the IMP or as a standard of care.

The purpose of conducting a clinical trial is to demonstrate the safety and efficacy (effectiveness) of an IMP in treating the target medical condition by comparing it to the existing standard of care (comparator medicine) or a placebo (substance with no active therapeutic effect). Depending on the study design, a clinical trial consists of one or more arms (treatment groups), i.e., an IMP arm, a comparator arm, a placebo arm (refer to Attachment A for details regarding the "Phases of a Clinical Trial").

Clinical trials usually involve randomly assigning patients to treatment groups and giving one group the IMP, another group the comparator, another group the placebo, as dictated by the study design. The goal is to ensure that the patients and often the doctors do not know which group is receiving the IMP, the comparator, or the placebo. This approach is followed to prevent any bias as regards the patient's response to the treatment.

When a comparator medicine is used in a clinical study, the IMP is being benchmarked against a commercial drug product that is already being used to treat patients. The rationale is that if an approved medicine is already available on the market, the regulatory bodies (FDA (U.S.), MHRA (UK), etc.) require an innovator (biopharma company) to prove that their IMP is equal to or better than the available treatment options. Depending on the goal of the study, the innovator's focus is to prove that its candidate (IMP) is just as good or better than the comparator medicine by way of superior efficacy or reduced risk (e.g., lesser side effects) or an alternate mechanism of action.

Given the importance of comparator medicines in the development of new therapies, historically, some biopharmaceutical companies have seen a competitive advantage in trying to prevent other companies from buying their products, the rationale being that if another company could not obtain their commercial drug product for use as a comparator, then that other company would be unable to develop a competing drug. This philosophy is flawed on two counts: First, if a company could prevent the development of new therapies, that strategy only hurts patients. There are many patients for whom the current therapies do not work, and those patients are desperately waiting in the hope that the next new therapy will be the one that works for them. Second, everyone in the industry has found a way of getting the medicine, if not directly from the manufacturer, then by using alternate channels. Biopharmaceutical innovator companies began to seek out ways of buying comparator medicines from "under the radar" of the manufacturing companies. In response, a new class of specialty-sourcing wholesalers arose in the market to provide their services in securing drug confidentiality on behalf of their clients. These intermediaries in the comparator supply chain seek out the supply of drugs globally and slowly accumulate quantities so as not to capture the attention of the manufacturing companies that closely monitor their global inventory. These specialty wholesalers became very adept and successful at this practice.

The selection and use of comparator medicines in clinical trials is thus challenging for biopharma companies in terms of both cost as well as availability of the comparator medicine.

The Traditional Supply Chain for Comparator Medicines

Under the traditional supply chain for comparator medicines, biopharma innovators approach the specialty comparator wholesalers with their demand for a specific comparator medicine, providing information like drug product name, presentation (bottles, blisters, vials, prefilled syringes, etc.), market, duration of the study, quantity needed, and desired expiry date.

A typical request for a comparator drug to a specialty wholesaler may read as follows:

Product Name: Warfarin Tablets

Strength: 5 MG

Presentation: 30 Count Bottle

Market: European Medicines Agency (EMA) Country

Quantity: 2,000 bottles per quarter from Q1 2016 to Q2 2017

Desired Expiry: 18 months from the time of purchase

Once a request is received, the wholesaler gleans its supply network and determines the feasibility of fulfilling the demand. If the wholesaler is in a position to fulfil the demand, the innovator (buyer) initiates a formal purchase and the wholesaler sells the comparator medicine by typically adding a markup to its acquisition cost.

The wholesaler's supply network consists of biopharmaceutical manufacturers. Depending on the comparator medicine that the wholesaler is seeking, on a case-by-case basis, the manufacturer may either not require the wholesaler to share the clinical study data (for the study that the comparator medicine will be used for) or may ask for detailed study data.

The value proposition offered by these specialty wholesalers is that they provide a buffer between the innovator organization and the manufacturing organization. Additionally, they have the infrastructure to facilitate the sale of comparator drugs.

Challenges Encountered under the Traditional Operating Model

Though the traditional operating model is an established norm within the biopharmaceutical industry, it has its limitations.

By buying drug product through a comparator wholesaler, the innovator is not securing it directly from the manufacturer and thus assuming supply chain integrity risk, particularly the introduction of counterfeit product, which is a significant risk within the biopharma industry. The introduction of counterfeit product not only compromises patient safety but also jeopardizes the results of the clinical study.

Another risk that the innovator assumes under this operating model is the risk of supply chain continuity. What this means is that the availability of the desired drug product during a time period does not guarantee availability in future periods; i.e., because the wholesaler was able to secure the desired product during the current time period does not guarantee assured supplies in the future. As a result, innovators may buy larger-than-needed quantities of comparator drug product when it is readily available and run the risk of expiry, if the medicines are not used in a timely manner, or obsolescence, in case a clinical study is discontinued ahead of schedule. The innovator is thus balancing supply chain continuity risk versus the risk of expiry or obsolescence.

Besides securing drug product, another important aspect of comparator sourcing is getting access to key documentation at the product level—e.g., Material Safety Data Sheet (MSDS), Equivalency Data, and Allowable Temperature Excursion Data—or at the batch level—e.g., Certificate of Analysis (COA). These documents are either not readily available or not possible to secure under the traditional model.

The TransCelerate Comparator Network

As described earlier, one of the five initial areas of opportunity (projects) identified by TransCelerate member companies was the establishment of a comparator drug supply model. The Comparator Network was initiated with an aim to leverage the opportunities for collaboration between member companies in the area of comparator drug supply.

The Comparator Network is open to all TransCelerate Member Companies, although not all member companies participate in the network. A Clinical Trial Supply Network Agreement was drafted and had to be signed by a member company as a prerequisite to joining the network. An operating model was developed within the confines of this agreement.

The process flow for the TransCelerate Comparator Network is as follows (refer to Attachment B for an overview of the operating model):

» All participating member companies enroll with each other as a "Customer" or "Vendor" to "Buy" or "Sell" drug product in each desired market.

» A buying member reaches out to a selling member and provides its forecast for a particular drug product in a particular market using the TransCelerate online portal.

» The selling member reviews the forecast with its supply chain planning team and confirms its ability to supply product during the requested time period.

  » On a case-by-case basis, the selling company is mostly able to fulfill the buying company's request for a desired shelf life, i.e., expiry date.

» Once a confirmation is received, the buying company issues a purchase order to the selling company.

» The selling company delivers the requested drug product to the buying company at a designated location within the requested market.

» Additionally, the buying company can request related documentation for the drug product being purchased, like batch–specific Certificate of Analysis, Allowable Temperature Excursion Data, and so on.

» An online portal has been developed to register and facilitate these transactions.

» All transactions remain confidential between the buying and selling companies, with a neutral TransCelerate representative available to facilitate the transaction.

This operating model marks a paradigm shift in the manner in which comparator medicines have been traditionally secured by the participating companies. It infinitely simplifies the process of securing comparator medicines by creating a direct relationship between the buying and selling companies and fosters a shared commitment to a more efficient supply chain. As of the end of 2016 there were 10 participating member companies in the Comparator Network.

Benefits Arising from this Transformative Approach

The TransCelerate Comparator Network marks a transformative shift in the manner in which biopharmaceutical companies have historically secured comparator medicines to conduct clinical studies. It has led to the creation of a collaborative environment that provides member companies access to clinical medicines, documentation, and data that facilitate their ability to conduct clinical studies more efficiently and with enhanced integrity. The key benefits arising from participating on the Comparator Network are described below.

Supply integrity leading to enhanced patient safety: The Comparator Network enables participating member companies to buy drug product directly from the manufacturer, which significantly reduces the risk of introducing counterfeit product into the supply chain. This ability to purchase medicines directly from a "known source," i.e., the manufacturer, enhances Patient Safety and reduces the risk of potentially jeopardizing the clinical study.

Transparency in sharing forecasts leading to assured supply: The sharing of forecasts between the buying and selling companies is mutually beneficial to both parties as the buyer now has access to assured supply and the seller has a reduced risk of potential outages in smaller markets (e.g., in some cases, clinical demand in the UK could equate to approximately 6 months of commercial demand) where the buyer would otherwise buy product "under the radar."

Flexibility to schedule periodic purchases and a corresponding reduction in obsolescence risk: Because under the comparator network operating model buying companies share their forecasts with selling companies and have access to assured supply, it enables them to schedule periodic purchases of smaller quantities of comparator medicines with desirable expiry dates. Unlike the traditional model, by adopting this approach the buying companies avoid stockpiling of large quantities of expensive comparator medicines. As a result they are able to significantly reduce the risk of medicines expiring or inventory becoming obsolete in case a clinical study is discontinued ahead of schedule.

Market access: The Comparator Network provides access to drug product in the United States and the European Union, as well as other markets, if the buying and selling companies are able to arrive at a collaborative agreement.

Access to documentation: In the biopharmaceutical research environment, access to documentation is probably as valuable as access to assured supplies of comparator medicines. The data provided by this documentation is a key enabler in planning and conducting clinical studies. Additionally some of these documents facilitate the movement of comparator medicines across borders, from a customs standpoint. The Comparator Network enables the buying company to access documentation like Material Safety Data Sheets, the Certificate of Analysis, and in select cases certain equivalency data, which facilitates their ability to conduct the clinical study.

Access to Stability Data: Stability Data is developed by biopharmaceutical companies to support manufacturing and logistics, as well as determine shelf life. This data demonstrates that the medicine is retaining its quality attributes over time. Allowable Temperature Excursion Data is derived from Stability Data. From a logistics standpoint, Allowable Temperature Excursion Data is key to evaluating "whether a medicine can be used or discarded," in cases where a product has undergone a temperature excursion either in-transit or during handling at the clinic. Access to Allowable Temperature Excursion Data is a key benefit to buying companies as it enables them to make usage decisions regarding the comparator medicine, in cases where the product has encountered temperature excursions that are outside the prescribed ship and store temperature conditions printed on the product label.

Savings: By buying directly from the manufacturer generally at wholesale pricing or equivalent, the innovator can source comparator medicines less expensively than it would when sourcing through alternate channels. This is, however, just one of the multiple dimensions across which the innovator can incur savings by participating on this network. The ability to schedule purchases in smaller quantities with desirable expiry dates reduces both the inventory carrying costs and the associated risks. Additionally, by having access to allowable temperature excursion data, the innovator can rescue product that encountered temperature excursions, which would have otherwise been discarded for lack of stability data.

The above listed are the explicit benefits of participating in the Comparator Network. There is also the added benefit of being part of the comparator network community that provides representatives from participating member companies an environment to foster relationships with industry colleagues from other organizations. These relationships not only provide new avenues for those member companies to seek input on issues relating to the business environment, but on an ongoing basis have been instrumental in facilitating the collaborative resolution of issues relating to ongoing clinical studies, which was not imaginable in the past.

TransCelerate Comparator Network: Moving Forward

Member companies participating within the TransCelerate Comparator Network have been successfully buying and selling product from each other since 2014 (refer to Attachment C for details regarding transactions, spend, and documents exchanged). In the initial years a Comparator Network lead role was created to provide leadership and orchestrate the activities during the "project phase" of this initiative. The network is administered by a core committee, where each participating member company nominates a representative. The core committee meets on a periodic basis to review ongoing challenges and future opportunities. One of the areas of opportunity that is steadily gathering traction within the network is the sale of placebo by biopharmaceutical manufacturers to innovators, an area in which innovators have to invest significant resources to develop placebo under the current scenario.

Phases of a Clinical Trial

Discovery	Preclinical	Phase 1	Phase 2	Phase 3	Approval	Consumer
The drug discovery process begins in the research lab where compounds and novel proteins are generated and tested for activity that could make them useful against a medical condition.	Viable candidates are tested in experimental models. These experiments test not only for activity, but also safety, toxicology, and pharmacology.	In Phase 1 the drug is tested primarily for safety. Small groups of patients are tested with increasing doses to determine the Maximum Tolerable Dose (MTD).	In Phase 2 increasing doses are used with more patients than in Phase 1. The efficacy and potential side effects of the treatment are determined at this stage.	Phase 3 is the critical phase during which the optimal dose is tested in a patient population large enough to provide statistically significant data. The number of patients may range from several hundred to thousands. Depending on the nature cf the treatment and the medical condition, the time span of this phase can vary considerably.	If a drug is successful in Phase 3, the government regulatory agency (FDA (US), EMA (EU), MHRA (UK)) may approve it to be used in the clinic.	Even after approval a company must submit periodic reports to regulatory agencies, including any cases of adverse reactions and appropriate quality control records. Some regulatory agencies may also require post-market trials (Phase 4) to evaluate the long-term effects of the drug.

Note: The process of identifying, developing, and testing new medicines is referred to as the drug pipeline. A typical investigational medicine requires 5 to 16 years of work and can cost anywhere from ~$500 million to over $2 billion depending on the therapy and the developing firm. The comparator spend on a typical clinical trial can run into millions of dollars.

Attachment A

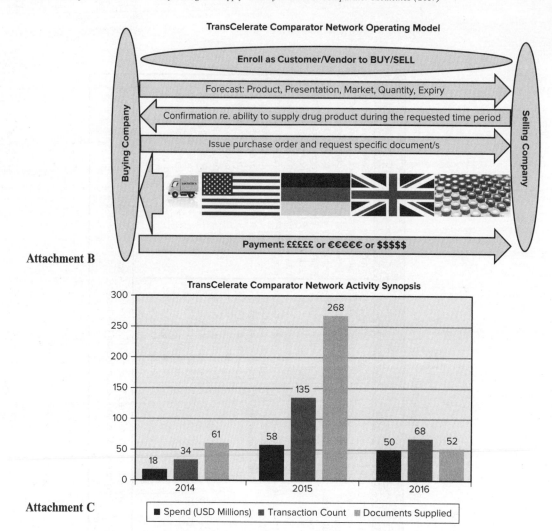

Attachment B

Attachment C

In 2016, the TransCelerate Comparator Network was transitioned from a "project phase" to a "realization phase." Based on the network's strong performance, TransCelerate leadership had the confidence that this initiative could function in a self-sustaining manner on an ongoing basis.

With a strong track record in place, other TransCelerate member companies continue to show keen interest in this initiative; as a result the membership is expected to grow in the future. The progress made by the TransCelerate Comparator Network has surely contributed toward the founding goal of TransCelerate, i.e., collaborating across the biopharmaceutical industry to address longstanding challenges in new drug development to ultimately bring innovative and much-needed therapies to patients.

Index